Second Edition

Writing by Choice

Eric Henderson

With Contributions from Danielle Forster,
Chris Higgins, And Susan Huntley

OXFORD

UNIVERSITY PRESS

OXFORD
UNIVERSITY PRESS

8 Sampson Mews, Suite 204, Don Mills, Ontario M3C 0H5
www.oupcanada.com

Oxford University Press is a department of the University of Oxford.
It furthers the University's objective of excellence in research, scholarship,
and education by publishing worldwide in

Oxford   New York
Auckland   Cape Town   Dar es Salaam   Hong Kong   Karachi
Kuala Lumpur   Madrid   Melbourne   Mexico City   Nairobi
New Delhi   Shanghai   Taipei   Toronto

With offices in
Argentina   Austria   Brazil   Chile   Czech Republic   France   Greece
Guatemala   Hungary   Italy   Japan   Poland   Portugal   Singapore
South Korea   Switzerland   Thailand   Turkey   Ukraine   Vietnam

Oxford is a trade mark of Oxford University Press
in the UK and in certain other countries

Published in Canada
by Oxford University Press

Library and Archives Canada Cataloguing in Publication

Henderson, Eric
Writing by choice / Eric Henderson.—2nd ed.

Includes index.
ISBN 978-0-19-543186-5

1. Academic writing—Textbooks.   2. Report writing—Textbooks.
3. English language—Rhetoric—Textbooks.   I. Title.
PE1408.H39 2011   808'.042   C2010-906159-4

Cover image: Lasse Kristensen/Veer

The book is printed on permanent acid-free paper ∞.
Printed and bound in Canada.

1 2 3 4 — 14 13 12 11

Contents

Chapter 10 Sentence Essentials 313

Chapter 11 Punctuation, Pronouns, Modifiers, and Parallelism 343

Chapter 12 Achieving Clarity and Depth in Your Writing 401

From the Publisher

Among so many texts available on writing and composition, one book stands apart. Oxford University Press is proud to introduce the definitive choice for today's students: *Writing by Choice*. Developed not just to teach the basics of writing but to empower students to write well, the new, second edition of this acclaimed text continues to emphasize choice by encouraging students to make appropriate choices in their writing, and by giving them the tools and the knowledge to do so. While retaining a focus on the three most common types of student essays—expository, argumentative, and literary—the second edition includes new and expanded coverage of rhetorical analyses and response forms. The text once again illustrates key principles through sample professional and student essays, a host of individual and group exercises, and new pedagogical features designed to guide students through the intricacies of grammar, style, and documentation.

Writing by Choice remains the first choice for engaging students in a detailed, holistic, and widely applicable approach to developing their writing skills and thinking critically about how—and why—they write.

Highlights of the Second Edition

A **new chapter structure** makes the text easier to navigate.

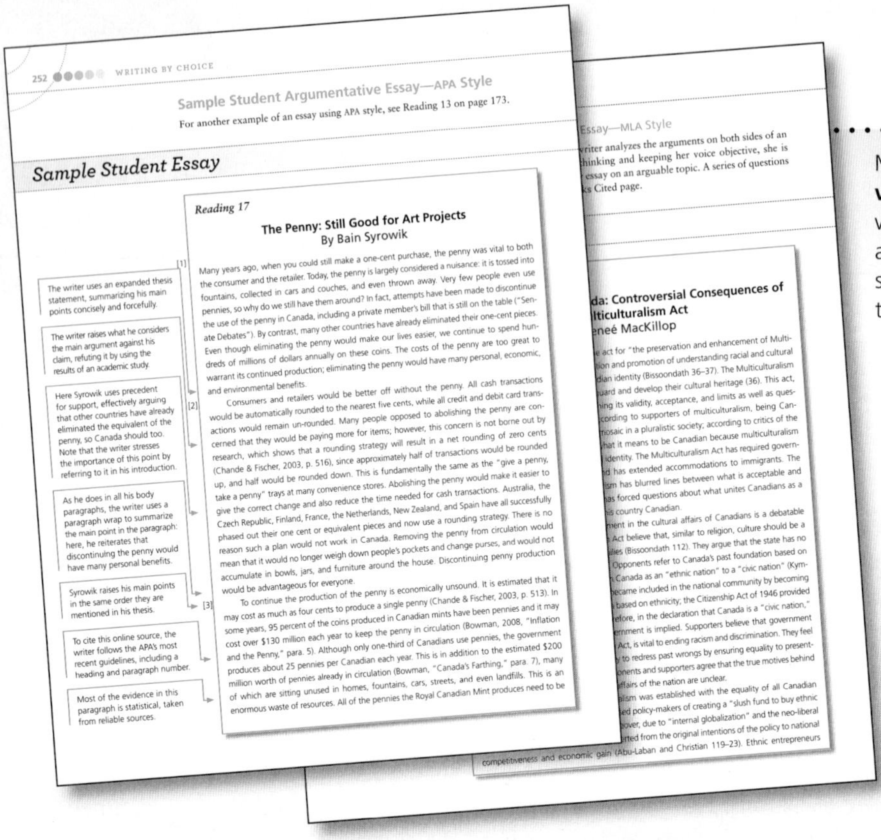

More examples of **student writing** provide readers with a peer-focused approach to honing their skills and developing technique.

Professional essays—almost all of them new—have been selected for currency and readability.

Readings now have **paragraph numbers**, making them more accessible and encouraging student to refer to specific text in their analyses.

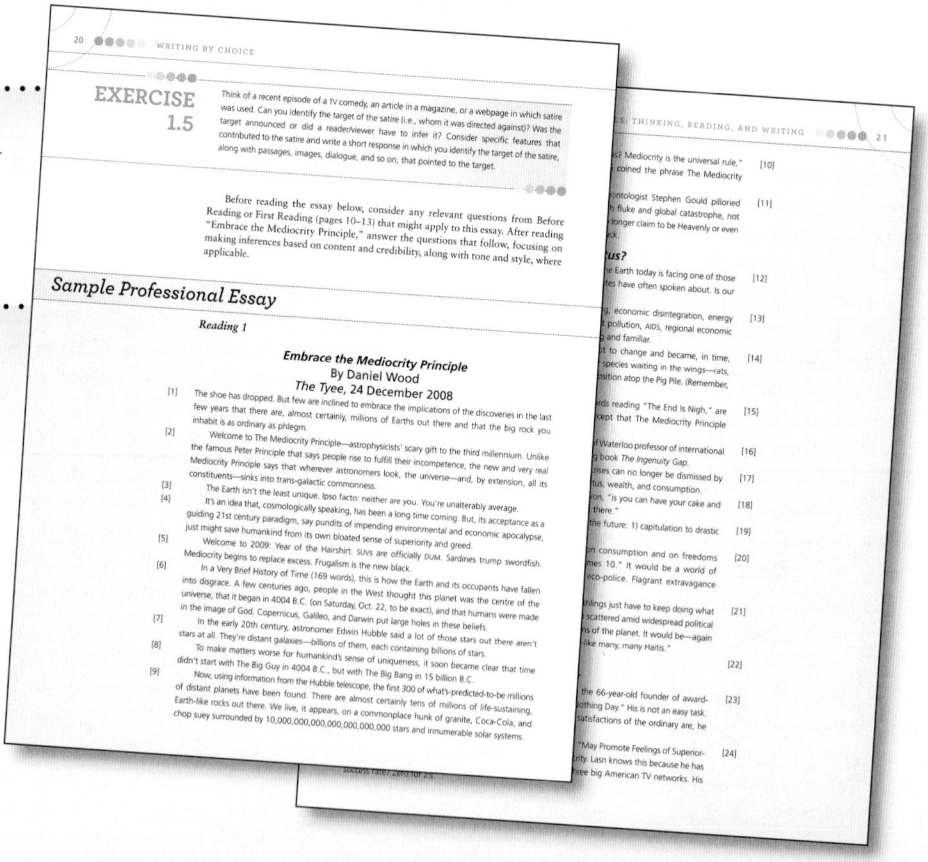

---

252 ●○○○ WRITING BY CHOICE

Sample Student Argumentative Essay—APA Style

For another example of an essay using APA style, see Reading 13 on page 173.

Sample Student Essay

Reading 17

The Penny: Still Good for Art Projects
By Bain Syrowik

Many years ago, when you could still make a one-cent purchase, the penny was vital to both the consumer and the retailer. Today, the penny is largely considered a nuisance: it is tossed into fountains, collected in cars and couches, and even thrown away. Very few people even use pennies, so why do we still have them around? In fact, attempts have been made to discontinue the use of the penny in Canada, including a private member's bill that is still on the table ("Senate Debates"). By contrast, many other countries have already eliminated their one-cent pieces. Even though eliminating the penny would make our lives easier, we continue to spend hundreds of millions of dollars annually on these coins. The costs of the penny are too great to warrant its continued production; eliminating the penny would have many personal, economic, and environmental benefits.

Consumers and retailers would be better off without the penny. All cash transactions would be automatically rounded to the nearest five cents, while all credit and debit card transactions would remain un-rounded. Many people opposed to abolishing the penny are concerned that they would be paying more for items; however, this concern is not borne out by research, which shows that a rounding strategy will result in a net rounding of zero cents (Chande & Fischer, 2003, p. 516), since approximately half of transactions would be rounded up, and half would be rounded down. This is fundamentally the same as the "give a penny, take a penny" trays at many convenience stores. Abolishing the penny would make it easier to give the correct change and also reduce the time needed for cash transactions. Australia, the Czech Republic, Finland, France, the Netherlands, and Spain have all successfully phased out their one cent or equivalent pieces and now use a rounding strategy. There is no reason such a plan would not work in Canada. Removing the penny from circulation would mean that it would no longer weigh down people's pockets and change purses, and would not accumulate in bowls, jars, and furniture around the house. Discontinuing penny production would be advantageous for everyone.

To continue the production of the penny is economically unsound. It is estimated that it may cost as much as four cents to produce a single penny (Chande & Fischer, 2003, p. 513). In some years, 95 percent of the coins produced in Canadian mints have been pennies and it may cost over $130 million each year to keep the penny in circulation (Bowman, 2008, "Inflation and the Penny," para. 5). Although only one-third of Canadians use pennies, the government produces about 25 pennies per Canadian each year. This is in addition to the estimated $200 million worth of pennies already in circulation (Bowman, "Canada's Farthing," para. 7), many of which are sitting unused in homes, fountains, cars, streets, and even landfills. This is an enormous waste of resources. All of the pennies the Royal Canadian Mint produces need to be

(margin annotations:)

The writer uses an expanded thesis statement, summarizing his main points concisely and forcefully.

The writer raises what he considers the main argument against his claim, refuting it by using the results of an academic study.

Here Syrowik uses precedent for support, effectively arguing that other countries have already eliminated the equivalent of the penny, so Canada should too. Note that the writer stresses the importance of this point by referring to it in his introduction.

As he does in all his body paragraphs, the writer uses a paragraph wrap to summarize the main point in the paragraph: here, he reiterates that discontinuing the penny would have many personal benefits.

Syrowik raises his main points in the same order they are mentioned in his thesis.

To cite this online source, the writer follows the APA's most recent guidelines, including a heading and paragraph number.

Most of the evidence in this paragraph is statistical, taken from reliable sources.

Essay—MLA Style

writer analyzes the arguments on both sides of an thinking and keeping her voice objective, she is essay on an arguable topic. A series of questions s Cited page.

da: Controversial Consequences of ulticulturalism Act
neé MacKillop

act for "the preservation and enhancement of Multi-
ion and promotion of understanding racial and cultural
dian identity (Bissoondath 36–37). The Multiculturalism
uard and develop their cultural heritage (36). This act,
ning its validity, acceptance, and limits as well as ques-
ccording to supporters of multiculturalism, being Can-
osaic in a pluralistic society, according to critics of the
that it means to be Canadian because multiculturalism
identity. The Multiculturalism Act has required govern-
and has extended accommodations to immigrants. The
m has blurred lines between what is acceptable and
as forced questions about what unites Canadians as a
is country Canadian.

ment in the cultural affairs of Canadians is a debatable
Act believe that, similar to religion, culture should be a
ilies (Bissoondath 112). They argue that the state has no
Opponents refer to Canada's past foundation based on
Canada as an "ethnic nation" to a "civic nation" (Kym-
became included in the national community by becoming
based on ethnicity, the declaration that Canada is a "civic nation."
efore, in the declaration that Canada is a "civic nation."
rnment is implied. Supporters believe that government
Act, is vital to ending racism and discrimination. They feel
to redress past wrongs by ensuring equality to present-
onents and supporters agree that the true motives behind
airs of the nation are unclear.

ism was established with the equality of all Canadian
ed policy-makers of creating a "slush fund to buy ethnic
over, due to "internal globalization" and the neo-liberal
ted from the original intentions of the policy to national
competitiveness and economic gain (Abu-Laban and Christian 119–23). Ethnic entrepreneurs

---

20 ●○○○ WRITING BY CHOICE

EXERCISE 1.5

Think of a recent episode of a TV comedy, an article in a magazine, or a webpage in which satire was used. Can you identify the target of the satire (i.e., whom it was directed against)? Was the target announced or did a reader/viewer have to infer it? Consider specific features that contributed to the satire and write a short response in which you identify the target of the satire, along with passages, images, dialogue, and so on, that pointed to the target.

Before reading the essay below, consider any relevant questions from Before Reading or First Reading (pages 10–13) that might apply to this essay. After reading "Embrace the Mediocrity Principle," answer the questions that follow, focusing on making inferences based on content and credibility, along with tone and style, where applicable.

Sample Professional Essay

Reading 1

Embrace the Mediocrity Principle
By Daniel Wood
The Tyee, 24 December 2008

[1] The shoe has dropped. But few are inclined to embrace the implications of the discoveries in the last few years that there are, almost certainly, millions of Earths out there and that the big rock you inhabit is as ordinary as phlegm.

[2] Welcome to The Mediocrity Principle—astrophysicists' scary gift to the third millennium. Unlike the famous Peter Principle that says people rise to fulfill their incompetence, the new and very real Mediocrity Principle says that wherever astronomers look, the universe—and, by extension, all its constituents—sinks into trans-galactic commonness.

[3] The Earth isn't the least unique. Ipso facto: neither are you. You're unalterably average.

[4] It's an idea that, cosmologically speaking, has been a long time coming. But, its acceptance as a guiding 21st century paradigm, say pundits of impending environmental and economic apocalypse, just might save humankind from its own bloated sense of superiority and greed.

[5] Welcome to 2009: Year of the Hairshirt. SUVs are officially too DUM. Sardines trump swordfish. Mediocrity begins to replace excess. Frugalism is the new black.

[6] In a Very Brief History of Time (169 words), this is how the Earth and its occupants have fallen into disgrace. A few centuries ago, people in the West thought this planet was the centre of the universe, that it began in 4004 B.C. (on Saturday, Oct. 22, to be exact), and that humans were made in the image of God. Copernicus, Galileo, and Darwin put large holes in these beliefs.

[7] In the early 20th century, astronomer Edwin Hubble said a lot of those stars out there aren't stars at all. They're distant galaxies—billions of them, each containing billions of stars.

[8] To make matters worse for humankind's sense of uniqueness, it soon became clear that time didn't start with The Big Guy in 4004 B.C., but with The Big Bang in 15 billion B.C.

[9] Now, using information from the Hubble telescope, the first 300 of what's-predicted-to-be millions of distant planets have been found. There are almost certainly tens of millions of life-sustaining, Earth-like rocks out there. We live, it appears, on a commonplace hunk of granite, Coca-Cola, and chop suey surrounded by 10,000,000,000,000,000,000,000 stars and innumerable solar systems.

6: THINKING, READING, AND WRITING ●○○○ 21

? Mediocrity is the universal rule,"   [10]
coined the phrase The Mediocrity

ontologist Stephen Gould pilloried   [11]
fluke and global catastrophe, not
longer claim to be Heavenly or even

us?
Earth today is facing one of those   [12]
es have often spoken about. Is our

g, economic disintegration, energy   [13]
pollution, AIDS, regional economic
and familiar.

to change and became, in time,   [14]
species waiting in the wings—rats,
sition atop the Pig Pile. (Remember,

ds reading "The End Is Nigh," are   [15]
cept that The Mediocrity Principle

f Waterloo professor of international   [16]
y book The Ingenuity Gap.

ses can no longer be dismissed by   [17]
us, wealth, and consumption.

on, "is you can have your cake and   [18]
there."

future: 1) capitulation to drastic   [19]

n consumption and on freedoms   [20]
es 10." It would be a world of
co-police. Flagrant extravagance

things just have to keep doing what   [21]
scattered amid widespread political
ns of the planet. We'd be—again
like many, many Haitis."

[22]

66-year-old founder of award-   [23]
oming Day." His is not an easy task.
atisfactions of the ordinary are, he

"May Promote Feelings of Superior-   [24]
ority. Lasn knows this because he has
ree big American TV networks. His

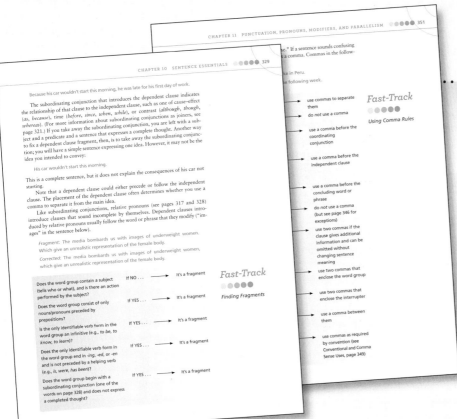

New feature called '**Fast-Track**', woven throughout the coverage of grammar, presents a succinct recap of complex rules.

New feature called '**A Closer Look**' expands on ideas that students may want to learn more about. Topics of interest include metre, irony, research disciplines, and writing indirect thesis statements.

Focus on the three most common types of **student essays**—expository, argumentative, and literary—has been expanded to include more and new coverage of rhetorical analysis and response forms.

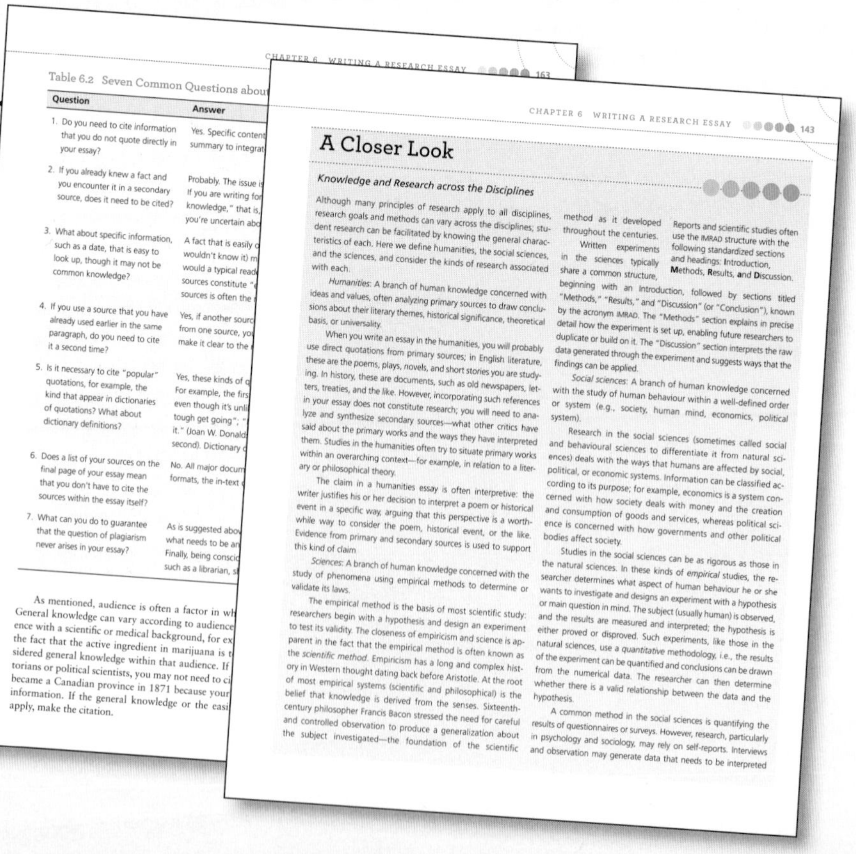

Expanded sections on electronic research, source reliability, and writing across the disciplines make this the perfect choice for today's student.

Table 3.2 Four Common Reading/Writing Assignments

Type of Assignment	Purpose	Audience/Style	Typical Activities/Structure
Rhetorical Analysis	To examine how a text is constructed and assess its importance/ influence; better understand types of texts, their uses, and their effectiveness	Written in formal style/ objective voice for audience knowledgeable about rhetorical practices and strategies	Focused reading; comprehension and critical thinking; analyzing and evaluating used throughout; stating main features of source text in thesis Breaks down text to provide support for thesis; focuses on source text
Critical Response	To explore your views on a topic and share them with others	Readers interested in the topic who might also have opinions/ observations about it; semi-formal style but use of first-person point of view usually acceptable	Critical thinking; expressive/ personal writing; stating your agreement/ disagreement in thesis; moving back and forth between text and your views/ experiences
Research Paper	To answer a question, solve a problem, or test a hypothesis; to better understand the research process and evaluate a source	Written in formal style/ objective voice for audience varying in interest in and knowledge of the topic; may include jargon (specialized terms and concepts)	Scanning potential sources; focused reading for main ideas/findings; synthe- sizing used throughout; using logical order of points to arrive at conclusion Uses fact-based thesis; evaluates sources; examines issue/ problem/ hypothesis
Précis Summary	To demonstrate comprehension, concision, and ability to establish hierarchy of ideas	Writer must use own words and write clearly so a reader unfamiliar with the original text could understand its essence	Scanning and focused reading; compre- hension; rephrasing and using synonyms; informing main points Follows order of points in source text

> Does the author include any particular stylistic features (analogies, meta-
>   phors, imagery, anecdotes, non-standard sentence structure)?
> Does the author use reason effectively? Are there flaws in logic?
> Does the essay appear free of bias? Is the voice objective?
> Has the author acknowledged the other side? How has he or she responded
>   to the opposing viewpoint?
> Does the author make emotional appeals? Any extreme or deceptive?

Writing Strategies

> In your introduction, name the text and author, and give information con-
>   cerning the author's background and/or publication information, if relevant.
> Briefly summarize the author's approach and/or thesis.
> Conclude your introduction with a thesis statement that comments on the
>   essay's main features and/or significance; you may also explain what makes
>   the essay effective or ineffective, significant or insignificant, etc. Be specific;
>   simply saying that the essay is effective/ineffective is not enough.

Sa...

Reading 4

Sample Rhetorical Analysis o...
by Stephen Hen...
by Doug Stu...

"White Curtains," by Stephen Henighan, is designed to...
as Canadians and to expose the optimistic beliefs of th...
ficial or naïve." Henighan does this very effectively by t...
makes his own arguments. However, his thesis and ma...
nothing more than a few observations and personal e...
somewhat deceptive allure, Henighan's lack of support...

In his anecdotal introduction concerning the behavi...
immigrant neighbour, the author's subject is indirectly rev...
block steps overlooking the parking lot" and the symbo...
may represent the pressure immigrants in Canada experie...
diction—"darkness," "illusions," "second-hand cars," a...
hardships of the immigrant life in Canada. During a p...
Yugoslav immigrant, begins to cook a steak on a kerosene...
he no doubt learned to do in similar circumstances durin...
nighan tells us that he and the rest of Dragoslav's neighb...
Up to that point, they had accepted him as an ordinary n...
denly, his action characterized him as a foreigner. Heni...
when they behave like the majority, but we merely tolera...
fort, when they behave in unfamiliar ways. This storytell...
journalistic experience, focusing on one individual to illus...
utilize this background to add human interest to his artic...

While the tone established in the essay's introduction...
by proponents of the multicultural ideal, Henighan's infere...
to look at Dragoslav because they were embarrassed at H...
Perhaps the condominium owners didn't "look in Dragos...
was doing" because they did not want to disturb the man...
also account for their behaviour, or lack of response. Hen...
currence that the power outage and provides no direct c...
therefore, it almost seems as if he made an inference tha...
multiculturalism. Of course, Henighan's inference might...
proven assumption as a springboard into the core of an a...

Henighan uses several journalistic techniques in an...
keeps his readers' attention by writing concisely without...
ment is one that many readers would disagree with, he...
the essay. In this way, a potential adversary would rea...
nighan's views. As well, the introduction is very effective...
subtly slanted, can persuade someone who might not a...
author. The section of the essay that attacks Pico Iyer'...

Table 6.2 Seven Common Questions abou...

Question	Answer
1. Do you need to cite information that you do not quote directly in your essay?	Yes. Specific content... summary to integra...
2. If you already knew a fact and you encounter it in a secondary source, does it need to be cited?	Probably. The issue i... If you are writing for... knowledge," that is... you're uncertain abo...
3. What about specific information, such as a date, that is easy to look up, though it may not be common knowledge?	A fact that is easily c... wouldn't know it) m... would a typical read... sources constitute "... sources is often the...
4. If you use a source that you have already used earlier in the same paragraph, do you need to cite it a second time?	Yes, if another sourc... from one source, yo... make it clear to the...
5. Is it necessary to cite "popular" quotations, for example, the kind that appear in dictionaries of quotations?	Yes, these kinds of q... For example, the firs... even though it's unli... tough get going"; "... it." (Joan W. Donald... second). Dictionary o...
6. Does a list of your sources on the final page of your essay mean that you don't have to cite the sources within the essay itself?	No. All major docum... formats, the in-text c...
7. What can you do to guarantee that the question of plagiarism never arises in your essay?	As suggested abou... what needs to be an... Finally, being consci... such as a librarian, s...

As mentioned, audience is often a factor in wh...
General knowledge can vary according to audienc...
ence with a scientific or medical background, for ex...
the fact that the active ingredient in marijuana is t...
sidered general knowledge within that audience. If...
torians or political scientists, you may not need to ci...
became a Canadian province in 1871 because your...
information. If the general knowledge or the easi...
apply, make the citation.

A Closer Look

Knowledge and Research across the Disciplines ● ● ● ● ●

Although many principles of research apply to all disciplines, research goals and methods can vary across the disciplines; stu- dent research can be facilitated by knowing the general charac- teristics of each. Here we define humanities, the social sciences, and the sciences, and consider the kinds of research associated with each.

Humanities: A branch of human knowledge concerned with ideas and values, often analyzing primary sources to draw conclu- sions about their literary themes, historical significance, theoretical basis, or universality.

When you write an essay in the humanities, you will probably use direct quotations from primary sources; in English literature, these are the poems, plays, novels, and short stories you are study- ing. In history, these are documents, such as old newspapers, let- ters, treaties, and the like. However, incorporating such references in your essay does not constitute research; you will need to ana- lyze and synthesize secondary sources—what other critics have said about the primary works and the ways they have interpreted them. Studies in the humanities often try to situate primary works within an overarching context—for example, in relation to a liter- ary or philosophical theory.

The claim in a humanities essay is often interpretive: the writer justifies his or her decision to interpret a poem or historical event in a specific way, arguing that this perspective is a worth- while way to consider the poem, historical event, or the like. Evidence from primary and secondary sources is used to support this kind of claim.

Sciences: A branch of human knowledge concerned with the study of phenomena using empirical methods to determine or validate its laws.

The empirical method is the basis of most scientific study: researchers begin with a hypothesis and design an experiment to test its validity. The closeness of empiricism and science is ap- parent in the fact that the empirical method is often known as the *scientific method.* Empiricism has a long and complex hist- ory in Western thought dating back before Aristotle. At the root of most empirical systems (scientific and philosophical) is the belief that knowledge is derived from the senses. Sixteenth- century philosopher Francis Bacon stressed the need for careful and controlled observation to produce a generalization about the subject investigated—the foundation of the scientific

method as it developed throughout the centuries.

Written experiments in the sciences typically share a common structure, beginning with an introduction, followed by sections titled "Methods," "Results," and "Discussion" (or "Conclusion"), known by the acronym IMRAD. The "Methods" section explains in precise detail how the experiment is set up, enabling future researchers to duplicate or build on it. The "Discussion" section interprets the raw data generated through the experiment and suggests ways that the findings can be applied.

Social sciences: A branch of human knowledge concerned with the study of human behaviour within a well-defined order or system (e.g., society, human mind, economics, political system).

Research in the social sciences (sometimes called social and behavioural sciences to differentiate it from natural sci- ences) deals with the ways that humans are affected by social, political, or economic systems. Information can be classified ac- cording to its purpose; for example, economics is a system con- cerned with how society deals with money and the creation and consumption of goods and services, whereas political sci- ence is concerned with how governments and other political bodies affect society.

Studies in the social sciences can be as rigorous as those in the natural sciences. In these kinds of *empirical* studies, the re- searcher determines what aspect of human behaviour he or she wants to investigate and designs an experiment with a hypothesis or main question in mind. The subject (usually human) is observed, and the results are measured and interpreted; the hypothesis is either proved or disproved. Such experiments, like those in the natural sciences, use a *quantitative* methodology, i.e., the results of the experiment can be quantified and conclusions can be drawn from the numerical data. The researcher can then determine whether there is a valid relationship between the data and the hypothesis.

A common method in the social sciences is quantifying the results of questionnaires or surveys. However, research, particularly in psychology and sociology, may rely on self-reports. Interviews and observation may generate data that needs to be interpreted

Reports and scientific studies often use the IMRAD structure with the following standardized sections and headings: Introduction, **M**ethods, **R**esults, **a**nd **D**iscussion.

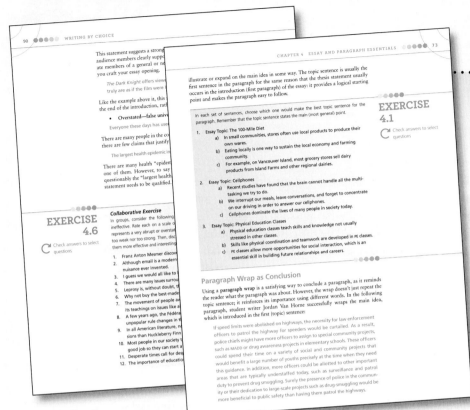

More exercises, including both individual and collaborative activities, provide students with opportunities to practice their skills. An 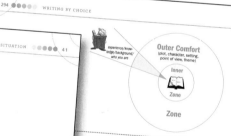 indicates those exercises that have corresponding answers at the back of the text.

Greater use of visuals such as figures, tables, and illustrations makes the information more accessible.

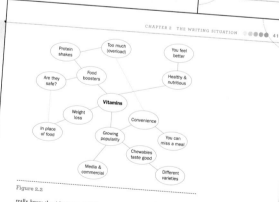

Preface

Writing by Choice is designed to improve writing skills and empower the student writer. While the first objective might seem modest, the second might seem somewhat overreaching, though in most other pursuits, empowerment is an inevitable consequence of improvement. This should be the case with writing as well.

By the time students begin post-secondary study, they are familiar with the do's and don'ts of writing essays. They may expect that university writing will give them more of the same or may be surprised when instructors give them rules that contradict what they have been told. First and most frequent questions instructors face are those of limits: "Do you want the essay to have five paragraphs?" "Are we allowed to use *I*?" "How many words does it have to be?" Such questions, and many others, imply that students have previously been taught stringent guidelines for the writing of essays. While guidelines are essential, they should not hamper thought or expression. They should not deprive writers of choices, but enhance their ability to make *informed* choices given the wide range of variables affecting different kinds of writing tasks.

At the university level, student writers are capable of, and should assume responsibility for, making informed choices. Only by doing so can they take up the challenges offered by their disciplinary studies and by the wide variety of workplace writing tasks that may lie ahead. In a world that increasingly values solutions to its problems, the knowledgeable, adaptable writer will always be in demand, since written forms of communication are likely to reach the widest possible readership—to be heard, considered, and acted on.

Writing by Choice provides students with a detailed, holistic, and widely applicable approach to developing writing skills at the university level—and beyond. Writing at university can be considered goal-centred, but in this text the goals are approached more often through questions that student writers can ask themselves than by a series of conditions or requirements that must be satisfied. The approach to many topics in *Writing by Choice* is through open-ended questions rather than definitive statements. Thinking and writing are treated as closely connected; reflection should inevitably precede selection.

The text's developmental approach stresses the steps involved in any writing project. It enables instructors or students to choose to omit specific steps in a process. For example, a class in intermediate or advanced composition may possess a level of knowledge that makes it redundant to focus on paragraph unity; but the instructor may focus extensively on the more complex area of paragraph and/or essay development. The same approach can be used in the grammar section, which begins by identifying the parts of speech and proceeds through to the complexities of parallel structure. On the other hand, in most introductory composition courses, a full review of the structure of English, as it is provided here, is the necessary starting point.

As the Contents pages reveal, the composition sections of *Writing by Choice* are not organized around the teaching of the traditional rhetorical modes. Detailed treatment is given to three kinds of essays: expository, argumentative, and literary—the kinds typically assigned in first-year composition and literature courses. Specialized writing contexts also considered in *Writing by Choice* include the in-class or examination essay and online writing.

The common belief that students have difficulty applying the grammar rules they learn to their own writing is countered here by an incremental approach to the acquisition of grammar skills that is designed to enable students to assimilate these crucial skills. The grammar and the composition sections stress the developmental approach of identifying, applying, and integrating. Almost all of the many examples in the text are taken from students' writing, allowing students of this text to see the relevance of its material to their own writing. Sentences and paragraphs from students' writing also are used in the exercises, which reinforce rules and concepts as they apply to realistic, everyday writing contexts—ones that have occurred and will occur to students as they write.

Some of the exercises in *Writing by Choice* narrow the focus to one learning objective while others require students to integrate several objectives. Exercises are designed to engage students on their own as well as in group or collaborative environments. Many instructors consider editing by peers an indispensable part of collaborative learning; peer edit forms are included in an appendix. An important feature of this text, full-length student essays illustrate expository, argumentative and literary essays, as well as critical analyses and responses. The importance of summarizing is reflected in the text as well. MLA and APA documentation styles are outlined in a separate chapter, along with the rudiments of the notes style. The writing by students represents a wide variety of disciplines, reflecting the diverse interests of today's students. Several selections from the academic, business, and professional worlds of the kind that students encounter in their research also are included as teaching/learning devices.

Writing by Choice seeks to instill the basic principles of effective writing and to give student writers the knowledge they need to make successful and empowering choices in their writing in college and university and in their future business, professional, and personal lives.

Acknowledgements

Preparing the second edition of *Writing by Choice* has given me an opportunity to reflect on the privilege of working with many knowledgeable and enthusiastic experts at Oxford University Press Canada in editorial, management, marketing, and sales over the last seven years; I particularly want to thank editors Jodi Lewchuk and Eric Sinkins for their guidance in the development of the second edition of this textbook, my first with *OUP*. Most appreciative thanks go to copyeditor Leslie Saffrey, whose work was a marvel of proficiency and professionalism.

Several named and anonymous reviewers offered detailed comments, which proved invaluable in planning the many changes and additions for the second edition. I would like to thank the following reviewers, as well as those who elected to remain anonymous, for their thoughtful feedback:

Trevor Arkell, Humber College
Ann Braybrooks, University of Lethbridge

Sally Hayward, University of Lethbridge
Roneen Marcoux, University College of the Fraser Valley
Darren Miller, University of Ottawa
Barbara Rose, Brandon University
Mark Spielmacher, University of Waterloo
Kelly St-Jacques, University of Ottawa

I also thank the students in my composition and literature classes at the University of Victoria who agreed to have their work published here; I can show no greater appreciation than by noting their alacrity in responding to my emails long after classes had ended!

Some ten years ago, amid self-doubts occasioned partly, perhaps, by too many years teaching continuing education, I at last took up the suggestion of Madeline Sonik that a 40-page writing text called "The Gremlins of Grammar" could aspire to something more; for that challenge, I will always be grateful.

Chapter 1

Developing "3-D" Skills: Thinking, Reading, and Writing

A Choice-Based Approach

Many students fear writing, believing that they lack the skills to write successfully, that what they write will be imperfect and result in a poor grade. Once you set words down in concrete form, they can be analyzed and judged—by you and, perhaps ultimately, by someone else, such as your instructor. When writing an essay as a course requirement, you *know* your writing is going to be analyzed, evaluated, commented on, and graded. If your writing can be seen as a *concrete* representation of your thoughts, those thoughts, now concretized in the form of your essay, receive a *concrete* mark. A mark given for a paper, like the pin that fixes a butterfly to a display backing, suggests something permanent and possibly not to be challenged.

Making that commitment to a "public" form of discourse is difficult and often intimidating, but it need not be traumatic. Most first-year writing courses are designed to give you the information you need, much of it as general rules applicable to a wide variety of writing that lies ahead; other information will be specific to tasks such as report writing or summarizing another writer's work.

As important as they are, general rules and guidelines can take you only so far. They are best thought of as a foundation for the writing you will do throughout your academic and professional careers, when you will not always be aware of, or governed by, rules, standards, or conventions, and when there may not be someone like a teacher to tell you what to do. In such cases, you will need to make choices that reflect your understanding of your task. These choices are crucial in both developing writing skills and using these skills to best advantage throughout your writing life.

Two basic factors that influence writing choices are **purpose** and **audience**. Purpose refers to your reason for writing—for example, to respond to a reading or to summarize a source. Audience refers to the person or people you are writing to—for example, fellow students, members of another peer group, or a knowledgeable expert. Considering both factors is crucial *before* you begin writing, since many of your choices will depend on the *why* and the *who* of the writing process (see Writing Purpose and *A* is for Audience in Chapter 2, page 28).

Writing and Reading

Where does reading fit into the writing process? What actually happens when we read? Researchers are uncertain, but they do know that reading involves more than determining the meaning of each successive word. When we read, we look at units larger than individual words, constantly anticipating content based both on our familiarity with the reading experience and on the reading context. When we read, we are in effect processing, or "translating," the thoughts of the writer, using both language and our understanding of the way it operates. Like writing, it is a complex process.

Some studies have shown that good readers tend to be good writers. Thus, studying other writers can improve your own writing. This means you must first clearly understand the writer's language, both the individual words and their combined meaning. "Active reading" usually involves more than simple comprehension, and most university-level assignments will require you to do more than read for understanding. Studying the works of other writers can also sharpen your critical thinking skills, as discussed below.

Most of what you read is in a finished form (exceptions include rough drafts or similar "works in progress"). In other words, you read a "product." Although the product is "finished," it is usually possible to see how it was put together. For example, in any well-constructed piece of writing, you should be able to identify the main ideas. This ability is especially important if you are summarizing a work, perhaps in order to use the summary in your own essay. Also, there may be other features of the work's construction that you can study: in addition to identifying the writer's purpose in writing and whom the work was written for, you can analyze the writer's style or specific strategies used to communicate meaning or tone. By examining any of these features in a written work, you can enlarge your understanding and appreciation of the writing process and become a more effective writer. Many of these points are discussed under Critical Thinking, below (see page 14).

Writing and Thinking

Essay writing gives student writers the opportunity to exercise different kinds of thinking. To come up with and develop a topic, you will probably begin with a concept or abstraction; by free association or other strategies, you will try to make connections that will narrow the topic's scope and increase its manageability. Most kinds of writing activate different skills at different times. In addition to linear and associative thinking, you might use your abstract or your concrete perceptual capabilities and such cognitive skills as analysis (breaking down) and synthesis (putting together). Each of the various approaches to the thinking–writing process may stress one activity over another, but they all have one aim in common: to make you more conscious of how you write in order to make your writing more successful and, hopefully, more enjoyable. The remainder of this chapter gives an overview of the writing, reading, and thinking processes, stressing the connections among them.

The Composing Process

The Traditional Linear Model

University-level writing has been the subject of much inquiry in the last 40 years. Writing teachers, along with writing theorists and researchers, have put forward valuable models to help explain the writing process and assist the student writer. But no model has emerged as the "best" or "right" one, owing partly to the variability and complexity of writing tasks today and to the inability to explain precisely how our internal processes enable us to create and communicate meaning through written texts.

One of the most common models used in teaching writing is the linear one that asks the student for a written "product," usually an essay or report, after clearly defining its goal (purpose), thinking about it (pre-writing), planning it (researching and outlining), drafting it, and revising it. The five-paragraph essay is the best-known example of such a written product. With an introduction containing a thesis statement, three body paragraphs with clear topic sentences, and a conclusion that restates the thesis, the five-paragraph essay has proven adaptable to many different situations. Remember, however, that there is no "magical" number of paragraphs for an essay; several interrelated factors—for example, your writing purpose and topic—could determine how many paragraphs are needed.

This model teaches writing as a linear, sequential process. To a large degree, it is. Even when, say, the writer discovers in the first draft that the order of points isn't logical and must return to the outline and reorder these points, the process can still be considered linear—going backwards before going forwards again. The traditional linear model recognizes that in virtually all writing, the writer has a purpose or goal.

This traditional approach to essay writing divides it into several stages, beginning with what is sometimes called *inventing*, an explorative stage in which you may start with a subject or a topic, but no thesis. This is the point where pre-writing strategies come in—systematic methods to generate ideas (see Chapter 2, Subjects versus Topics, and Pre-writing Strategies, pages 36 and 38). When you have enough ideas and have made connections among some of them, you may be ready to write a thesis statement.

As you continue expanding and exploring the topic, you will soon be able to construct an outline, which will clarify the relationships among the main points. The further you proceed in the traditional linear model, the less you will be *thinking about* a topic and the more you will be relying on specific methods and forms with measurable objectives. After constructing an outline, you will begin your rough draft in which you will work towards unified, coherent, and developed paragraphs. After you have completed the draft, you will revise it, paying particular attention to grammar, punctuation, sentence structure, and mechanics.

Practical benefits of learning and using this traditional model are that it applies directly to many university and workplace tasks in which objectives are clearly defined and form is important—such as scientific experiments and business letters—and that it can be adapted to a variety of specialized functions.

Process-Reflective Writing

Typically, composing involves periods of intense writing balanced by periods of reflection, which may lead you to further develop an idea, to qualify it, or perhaps to abandon it in favour of another line of thought. You may stop to recall, analyze, or reconsider. Another characteristic activity is looking over what you have written.

As you write, your thinking is affected in two related ways: a choice, once made, excludes options that may have existed before, but it also creates new options. In this way, what you *have written* directs what you *will* write. By writing down your thoughts, you become conscious of them, and they become subject to your control. As a result, your thinking becomes clearer. It is said that clear thinking produces clear writing—likewise, writing (especially clear writing) produces clearer and more directed thinking. In process-reflective writing, you *reflect on* your process in order to make both your writing and thinking clearer.

Process-reflective writing encompasses the necessary connection between writing and thinking, the back-and-forth nature of the composing process in which thinking alternates with writing, and rethinking with rewriting. In-class writing and other kinds of timed writing require your immersion in the writing experience, during which you may ask yourself: "Where have I been going? Is my purpose the same as it was when I started? Where am I going now? How does what I have said affect what I need to say? What do I need to say (or do) to draw closer to my goal? How can my previous idea be expanded, illustrated, or linked to my next idea?"

After you have provided the bridge to the next idea, you can consider the same questions to guide you to your next point. As the draft proceeds, you become more conscious of structure by building on what has come before. In this way, too, transitions provide the stepping stones for your reader to follow. Here are some tips for process-reflective writing:

> Look for appropriate transitions (word or phrase connectors—see Chapter 4, Transitions between Sentences, page 78), since they reveal shifts in thought.
> Ask if your transitions reflect the relationships between ideas that you want to convey.
> If you are uncertain that your words reflect your intended meaning, try rephrasing the point and choose the passage that best captures your meaning.
> Don't worry about grammatical or mechanical errors; focus on clarity and the complete expression of your ideas.
> Don't worry about length; unneeded details or less important points can be deleted during the next draft.
> If you are unsure where a point is going, consider leaving some blank space and use a previous sentence or point as a new starting place.
> Keep your thesis in mind throughout, but don't be afraid to depart from it if necessary; it can be changed or reworded later.

Typical activities of process-reflective writing are questioning, clarifying, expanding, and emphasizing. Process-reflective drafts are often longer than final drafts, since the purpose of reflection is to generate clearer thinking, and a trial-and-error approach may be needed to achieve this clarity. The rough draft will probably need polishing. In addition to correcting grammar, word choice, and mechanics in later drafts, you may need to rephrase your ideas to make them clearer. You may also eliminate what seems incompatible with the thesis or explain an idea further to bring it in line with your thesis.

In the process-reflective approach, you may not need a formal outline, but you should have a clear purpose and thesis before writing. These can be developed through pre-writing. You may want to construct an outline after writing the rough draft, though an outline often is discovered within the draft itself. Instead of submitting an outline or a rough draft for written feedback, you can submit a partial draft, consisting of at least an introduction and a first body paragraph. You and your peer editors can discuss further development of the paragraph, such as what links could be used to connect it to a hypothetical following paragraph. Reflecting on purpose, audience, thesis, and your main points with a peer is one way to clarify your thinking.

Table 1.1 compares the two approaches to the composing process. Although each method's distinctive qualities are stressed here, in practice, writers often use different composing methods at different times without consciously choosing one or the other.

Table 1.1   The Two Approaches to the Composing Process

	Traditional Linear	Process-Reflective
Content	Focused on what you need to write	Focused on what you are writing
Typical Activities	Following an outline, developing sub-points, giving detail, illustrating, completing	Clarifying, evaluating, reflecting, questioning, emphasizing, filling gaps, connecting
Typical Questions	Are my points relevant? Do my sub-points develop my main points? Are they ordered logically?	How did I get here? Where am I going from here? How can I get there? What will make my thinking clearer?
Typical Number of Drafts	Two: a rough draft getting down ideas and a draft focused on the revision processes, including clarity	Two: a first draft focused on content and clarity and a second focused on revision, mechanics, and cutting repetition
Potential Uses	Typical workplace writing tasks; some academic writing; business and science reports; research essays	Exam writing; some professional and academic writing

Thinking and Writing + Reading

Most of us read for pleasure, at least sometimes. We choose what, when, and where we want to read. Even when you read for pleasure, though, the process is not simple. Most of the time, you read words whose **denotations** (literal meanings) are known to you; however, at other times, words have **connotations** (associations) that may also affect your reading. You are continually determining and re-determining context as you follow the pattern of the words, their meanings, and their associations, as words combine into syntactical structures to create an overarching pattern of meaning.

This kind of reading is primarily a one-way activity; reading to grasp content is essentially "passive reading." But this one-way activity becomes two-way when you begin responding to the text. In a literary text, you may make personal associations—recollections, emotions, desires—or experience the simple pleasure of escaping into another world that is, in some way, like your own. Consider, for example, the beginning of the short story "Friend of My Youth," by Alice Munro:

> I used to dream about my mother, and though the details in the dream varied, the surprise in it was always the same. . . . In the dream I would be the age I really was, living the life I was really living, and then I would discover that my mother was still alive. . . . Sometimes I would find myself in our old kitchen, where my mother would be rolling out piecrust on the table, or washing the dishes in the battered cream-colored dishpan with the red rim. But other times I would run into her on the street, in places where I would never have expected to see her.
>
> —Munro, Alice. *Friend of My Youth*. Toronto: Penguin, 1991. Print.

In theory, someone could read this passage merely by focusing on the meanings of the words and trying to grasp the literal meaning of the passage. But most readers will find themselves engaged in some deeper way, forming associations that depend on their own experiences and outlook. Now, consider the beginning of another text, also about dreams, roughly the same length as the first:

> Religion was the original field of dream study. The earliest writings we have on dreams are primarily texts on their religious and spiritual significance. Long before psychoanalysts, sleep laboratory researchers, and content analysts arrived on the scene, religious specialists were exploring dreams in a variety of ways: using dreams in initiation rituals, developing techniques to incubate revelatory dreams and ward off evil nightmares, expressing numerous dream images in different artistic forms, and elaborating sophisticated interpretive systems that related dreams to beliefs about the soul, death, morality, and fate.
> —Doniger, W. & Bulkley, K. (1993). Why study dreams? A religious studies perspective. *Dreaming: Journal of the Association of Dreams*, *3*(1), 69–73.

Did you read this paragraph differently from the fictional one? There may have been specific words or phrases, such as "content analysts" or "incubate revelatory dreams," that caused you to reach for a dictionary; in the first paragraph, the language was probably more familiar.

In reading the second paragraph, you no doubt went beyond one-way reading. Though you may have formed some personal associations, you probably reacted more critically; the writers were making general statements about the use of dreams in religious societies and cultures, and you were probably beginning to consider the use of dreams in this or a similar context. If you had continued to read the article, you would have made certain inferences and drawn conclusions based on the writers' statements and the way they were presented. You would have begun, perhaps, to test the claims and propositions based not only on your own experience but also on your sense of their logic and consistency: Is the claim logical? Is it valid considering the circumstances? Is it truthful? Reliable? Is it consistent with previous claims? When you engage in this process and ask these kinds of questions, you are responding *critically* to a work.

A writer may say something directly or may present evidence from which the reader can draw a conclusion. For example, Doniger and Bulkley provide factual evidence that ancient societies developed highly sophisticated methods for studying dreams—perhaps just as complex as the methods today of psychoanalysts and dream researchers. The writers don't directly *say* that the ancient methods were as complex, but readers could legitimately make that **inference**.

The main point is that while both passages above require you to react at some level beyond that of simple comprehension, the second passage calls forth a more critical response. In critical thinking, you use two-way reading to determine the validity of an author's statements, to test them by considering the logic and consistency behind them, and to determine whether the evidence supports the author's claims. Of course, if you were interested in creative writing, you could read the Munro text critically also, focusing on her writing strategies and techniques.

The main difference between what we usually call "reading" (that is, "two-way reading") and what can be called "three-way reading" or *3-D* (three-dimensional) *reading* is that in the latter you respond *consciously and analytically* to the text.

Inference

When a reader infers, or makes an inference, he or she draws a conclusion based on the evidence presented (i.e., the reader is not directly told what to conclude *from* the evidence). See Applying Critical Thinking, page 15.

Reading actively forges the connection between the *what* and the *how* of an essay. Fully engaging in the reading–thinking–writing process is a valuable way to augment your writing skills, as well as your reading and thinking skills. A critical analysis of a literary work involves both a critical *and* an analytical focus: you employ the vocabulary of literary criticism to analyze the writer's theme and the strategies used to convey it. For example, as part of a critical analysis of Munro's story "Friend of My Youth," you might consider her use of the first-person (*I*) point of view.

As a homework assignment, you may be asked to write a response based on a 3-D reading of an essay you've studied. As you respond in writing following this method, you complete the cycle that incorporates reading–thinking–writing: you read a text; you think about it critically; you write about those thoughts, making them conscious and thereby closing the cycle of learning that started with reading. You can then go back and begin the cycle again by rereading the piece, rethinking it, and, perhaps, responding to your more developed perceptions by writing about it again. Responding to essays and other texts and thinking about the conscious choices that the writer made will lead you to reflect on your own writing processes and enable you to make sound and *conscious choices* in your own writing.

Active Reading

Reading to Understand Meaning (Content)	One-Way Reading
Reading to Respond (Associative/Critical)	**Two-Way Reading**
Reading to Analyze Techniques (Analytical)	3-D Reading

The model above is not intended to illustrate levels of greater difficulty or complexity. In many challenging texts, for example, it may be quite difficult to grasp content; in fact, understanding the precise meaning of certain terms might be the key to analyzing such a text. What is usually true, though, is that these levels represent a "progressive" approach to reading where it is first necessary to understand content before proceeding to respond critically or analytically. Thus, active reading *at all three levels* is essential to your success in responding to the kinds of challenging texts you encounter in university.

Two Kinds of Selective Reading

The process of analyzing a work may sound intimidating, and you may think that a lot is being asked of you in an analysis. Different kinds of reading may be needed depending on subject matter: for history, attentive reading dominates; poetry often requires intensive analysis at the level of letters in words; sociology necessitates seeking particular patterns of information, often of the kind that can be outlined; mathematics and chemistry may have to be read even more closely than poetry; and so on. But university-level reading is not always detailed, microscopic reading. Rather, there are purposes for which scanning is useful just as there are purposes for which it is necessary to read for detail. It is more accurate to say that university-level reading is governed by choices; it is selective. In other words, *how* you read depends on both what you read and your purpose for reading. Thus, it is important to distinguish between different types of **selective reading**, such as scanning and focused reading, in which you have a clear purpose in mind.

When you **scan**, you read for the gist of an essay or its main points, or to identify another specific feature. To scan effectively, you often need to know where to look. For example, if you want to get the gist of a reading, you might scan the introduction to find

Selective reading

a reading strategy designed to meet a specific objective, such as scanning for main points or reading for details

Scanning

a reading strategy in which you look for key words or sections of a text the thesis, which contains the gist of the essay. For main ideas, you might look at the first sentences of paragraphs (they are often topic sentences). You could also scan a table of contents or list of references for keywords. Note that scanning as defined here is not the same thing as idle browsing where you casually scan a webpage or magazine to see what interests you. Like focused reading, scanning is reading with a purpose.

When you practise **focused reading**, you concentrate on smaller blocks of text. Sentences are read carefully for detail, and sometimes for tone or style. In this sense, focused reading is specialized reading—it asks you to become a specialist (historian, literary critic, sociologist, mathematician) in your reading of the text.

In university-level reading, scanning is often combined with focused reading. Following specific stages will help you conduct research thoroughly:

> When you begin research, you need to *scan* catalogue entries, journal indexes, book content pages and indexes, reference books, and other types of sources in order to find materials to support your essay topic.
> Once you have located most of your sources, you need to *scan* them to determine which are the most valuable for your purpose, so that you begin your focused reading with the most useful.
> Then, *scan* the most valuable articles, books, and websites to identify the main ideas.
> After identifying the ideas most relevant to your topic, practise *focused reading* to understand them and see how they fit with your thesis or with the ideas of other writers. You can then begin the process again with step 2 or 3.

Scanning and focused reading are most effective when you employ them as deliberate strategies, asking specific questions in order to get as much from the reading as possible without wasting your time. Guidelines and strategies for selective reading are discussed in Responding Critically and Analytically through Questions, page 10. Some basic strategies for scanning and focused reading are outlined in Table 1.2.

Focused reading

a close and detailed (i.e., word-by-word) reading of a specific, relevant passage

Table 1.2 Basic Strategies for Scanning and Focused Reading

Scanning	Focused Reading
Scanning begins when you know your purpose for reading and what you are looking for	Focused reading begins when you have identified important or relevant passages
Knowing *where* to look will help you scan efficiently	Breaking down the passage will help you access complex material—for example, separating main points from sub-points, and claims from supporting details and examples
In scanning, you will skip much of the text, isolating only the most relevant areas	Read the passage first for comprehension; then, apply active-reading skills
With practice, scanning can be done quickly	Although focused reading is a methodical process, frequent practice will enable you to read faster and at a greater depth
Activities associated with scanning include note taking and cross-referencing (see Chapter 6, Research Note-Taking, page 149)	Activities associated with focused reading include summarizing, paraphrasing, and direct quotation (see Chapter 6, Using Sources in the Composing Process, page 160)

EXERCISE 1.1

Find a one-sentence definition of a topic using a book index. A book index is an alphabetical listing of content found at or near the end of a book. Choose one of your textbooks or another book and scan its index, looking for a general topic that interests you (for example, in a sociology text, you could look for "sexuality" or "deviance"; in a psychology text, you could look for "depression" or "motivation"). Scan the entries under the topic you have chosen; then, scan the referenced pages themselves to locate a definition of the topic. (An introductory textbook is probably your best choice because it will likely include definitions of both general and specialized terms.)

Responding Critically and Analytically through Questions

Focused, active reading can be triggered by asking questions about a written work. These can be asked before you read, while you read, after you have completed the first reading for content, or during later readings. Some questions can relate to content, such as one asking for the specific date of a historical event; others require you to read critically or analytically, such as one asking about the causes of a historical event. Active reading typically involves responding to different kinds of questions at different times. Of course, your response to any of the questions can change at any point in the reading process as you gather more information.

Before Reading

If you wanted to go on a trip somewhere far away, you probably wouldn't just head for the nearest terminal and purchase a ticket for your destination; you would learn about that place before you risked your money. Pre-reading questions can lead you to valuable information to help you plan your reading; they can give you an agenda, just as planning a trip enables you to prepare an itinerary. When you select a text, ask yourself, "How much and what parts of it are useful to me?"

If your assignment is to write about a common theme in two Canadian novels, you must read actively the two primary works with an eye to that theme. In addition, you may need to read other works by the same writers. You also need to find critical works dealing with that theme, preferably in the Canadian context and relating directly to your primary authors and the specific works you are examining. The secondary texts can be scanned and read quite selectively for what they have to contribute to an understanding of the theme.

If you are researching a topic such as changes in subsidized housing policy during the last 50 years in Toronto, you need primary documents from the City of Toronto Archives, journal and newspaper articles, and books that may treat the subject in a wider fashion but bring Toronto policy into the discussion.

If you are researching an aspect of Aboriginal history in Saskatchewan from the 1900s, there may be no primary texts on the subject. You need to consult a range of texts, documents, newspaper archives, journal articles, and university archives to compile primary information on your subject. Secondary sources could provide you with methods and points of view for analyzing these sorts of data. From some secondary authors, you might need little more than their research plans.

Various pre-reading questions can help you determine how appropriate a text is for your needs. Questions about the writer could alert you to his or her qualifications, the audience for whom the book or essay was written, and possible biases of the writer. In the sciences and social sciences, an abstract (a concise summary) may precede the article, giving an overview of the writer's hypothesis, method, and results. Abstracts direct readers to those articles most relevant to their own reading or research interests (see The Abstract in Chapter 6, page 161).

> *What information is given by the work's title?* Even a work's title can convey much useful information about content, organization, tone, or rhetorical purpose. For example, consider the assumptions you would make about works with the following titles—both deal with the settlement of Canada's Prairies:
>
> Buckley, Helen. *From Wooden Ploughs to Welfare: Why Indian Policy Failed in the Prairie Provinces.*
>
> Owram, Doug. *Promise of Eden: The Canadian Expansionist Movement and the Idea of the West, 1856–1900.*

Both titles contain words that inform their readers about rhetorical purpose, as well as the time and place they address. The title of the first book suggests its author analyzes, and perhaps criticizes, the causes of the failure of Indian policy. In the second title, the words "Promise of Eden" and "idea" suggest Owram focuses on perception and ideology behind the movement during the years indicated. As opposed to those of literary works, the titles of non-fiction works—including many academic books and articles—need to inform readers about content. Often, as with the two titles above, the main title encapsulates the work through an appealing image or stylistic device (Buckley uses the alliteration of "Wooden" and "Welfare"), while the subtitle (following the colon) gives specific information about content.

EXERCISE 1.2

Many of your textbooks include references to journal articles, books, and other media. These could be found in the content, or under "Notes," "Bibliography," or "Suggestions for Further Reading." Using a textbook in your favourite subject, choose the titles of two journal articles or books referred to and analyze them word for word. In at least one sentence for each title, describe what you think the work is about.

Other pre-reading questions include:

> *How long is the text?* Few people begin an essay without leafing through the pages to find the ending; this impulse reveals how much reading time it will require. It is best, whenever possible, to complete the reading at one time, since general impressions are important. With a book, you can follow the same procedures with chapters or sections.
> *Who is the author?* Do you know anything about him or her?
> *What is his or her profession?* Nationality? Are any other important or defining characteristics apparent or notable?
> Does he or she belong to or *have affiliations* with a specific organization, group, or community?
> Docs he or she seem to be *an expert* in the field? What shows you this?

> *Why was the work written?*
> Is the work *divided into parts*? Extra spacing between paragraphs could indicate divisions. Are there headings throughout the essay? Sub-headings? Do they inform you about content or organization? In a book, you would look for chapter titles and, perhaps, headings within individual chapters.
> *When was the work written?* In an essay, the date could be found in the beginning, in a footnote at the bottom of the first page, or at the end. In a book, the publication date usually appears on the copyright page (the back of the title page). The most recent date is not necessarily the relevant one for your purpose; for example, if you want to know when the book was first published, you need to look for the date of the first edition, and not the dates of reprints or subsequent editions. On the other hand, changes or updates in a second or revised edition make it more current, and possibly most useful to you. Essays in an edited collection will probably have earlier publication dates than the collection itself (though essays are sometimes commissioned for a volume and will then bear the same date).
> *To whom is the work addressed?* Who was it written for? For an essay, what publication does it appear in, and what does this information tell you? If the publication is a journal, it could be a refereed scholarly journal or one that is not refereed. In a refereed journal, the articles have been evaluated by knowledgeable peers and will be seen as more reliable by your instructors if you are writing a research essay.
> For a book, *who is the publisher*? An academic or university press? Again, if you are writing a research essay, a scholarly publication might be a more reliable source than a trade publication, since the latter is usually designed for a wide, non-specialized audience.
> What is the *level of language* used? Does it seem difficult, specialized? If the answer is "yes," you may have to do a little background reading or exploratory research—and ensure you have your dictionary handy.
> Is there *an abstract* that summarizes the entire essay? Usually, the abstract precedes the essay; occasionally, it can be found after the essay. In a book, the "Preface," "Introduction," or "Foreword" might give you a summary, thus saving you from unneeded reading. The editor of an essay collection may summarize each essay in an introduction or foreword.

EXERCISE 1.3

Using the same material as in Exercise 1.2, choose five of the above questions and further analyze the book or journal article. Write a short response (no more than one or two sentences) to each question.

First Reading

It's a good idea to first read the essay or chapter for content and general impressions. Some people like to underline or highlight important passages; but ensure that you don't underline or highlight too much, or on the second reading it will be hard to discriminate between the main ideas and the less important ones. You may prefer to leave highlighting until your second reading, when you have a better idea of the relative importance of the various passages.

Other people prefer to make annotations, such as comments, thoughts, associations, criticisms, questions, or additions, in the margin of the text (assuming they own the text!). Still other people prefer to respond to the text on a separate piece of paper, keeping their own responses and the source text apart. If you don't know which method works best for you, experiment. Responding in some way to the text is the most natural way to make it relevant to you, even if that means you just write abbreviations or symbols, such as ?, ??, !, N.B., or *, **, or ***, in the margin to denote levels of importance. Also see Research Note-Taking in Chapter 6, page 149.

Questions to ask yourself during and after the first reading might include:

> What are your impressions of the first few paragraphs?
> Is there a distinct introductory section?
> What is the tone (i.e., the writer's attitude to the subject matter—for example, familiar, objective, detached, casual, humorous, ironic, formal, informal)? Tone can vary greatly from discipline to discipline or even from journal to journal, with scientific writing typically sounding the most detached.
> What kinds of words are used? More specifically, what is the vocabulary level (simple, sophisticated, general, specific, specialized)?
> Is jargon used? Jargon consists of words and expressions used among members of a designated group or in a particular discipline that those members would understand, but that people outside those groups would not necessarily understand. Jargon is a kind of specialized diction.
> If an essay, what kind of essay is it (persuasive, expository, personal, narrative, descriptive, combination of different kinds)?
> What is the work about? Do you know anything about the subject? Do you know of, or have you read, other works on the subject?
> What is the work's main point or thesis? Is it readily identifiable?
> Are the work's main points identifiable (in paragraph topic sentences, for example)?
> Do the points seem well-supported? Is enough detail always provided?
> Are secondary sources used? Does the writer use footnotes, endnotes, or parenthetical references?
> Is the text easy to follow? Are the points clearly expressed or is the meaning sometimes unclear? Note areas where the meaning is unclear to you. You can underline unclear passages with a different coloured pen or place question marks in the margin.
> Does the author always seem confident and certain about what he or she is saying? Does he or she ever express reservations or doubt? Does he or she ever appear to contradict him- or herself?
> Does the author seem to change his or her position at any point?
> Does the work shift its focus—if so, is there an apparent reason for this?
> Does the work seem to build? Does it get stronger or weaker? Where?
> Is there a distinct concluding section? Is it satisfying?

For an example of a passage annotated by a student, see Chapter 3, Sample Précis, page 67. Note that the purpose for reading helps determine the kinds of questions you ask of a reading. In the sample annotated passage on page 67, the student was reading the work in order to summarize it.

Second Reading

In your second (and later) readings of a work, your ability to apply critical and analytical skills is crucial. With practice, these skills will become active in all your reading.

> Is the introduction effective? What makes it effective or not?
> What specific strategies does the writer use to draw you into the work (question, quotation, anecdote, narration, description, analogy)?
> Is the author's purpose in writing the work clear from the start?
> What audience is the work written for? Is the choice of words always appropriate for the intended audience?
> Why does the writer use the tone or voice that he or she does?
> Is the main thrust of the work argumentative (does it try to persuade you to change your mind about something?), or does the writer intend to explain or explore something? Or is it something different—to describe something or tell a story, for example?
> Is the main point of the work (the thesis statement) announced in the introduction? If so, what is the thesis statement? Can you put it in your own words?
> How, specifically, are the points backed up? What kinds of evidence are used (examples, illustrations, facts, statistics, authorities, personal experience, analogies)?
> How does the writer organize the work? Is one method used more than any other (compare/contrast, definition, cause and effect, narration, description, division, other)?
> Does the author appear reliable? Trustworthy? Fair?
> How are the main points arranged? Is the strongest point placed near the beginning, middle, or end? Are the points arranged in the most effective order?
> Does the work depend more on logic or on emotion?
> Does the writer appeal to a set of values or standards?
> What inferences are readers called on to make? Do there appear to be any lapses in logic? Is deductive reason used effectively? Is inductive reason used effectively?
> If the points are not always clear, what are the reasons for this lack of clarity (specialized language, insufficient background given, poorly constructed paragraphs, faulty or ineffective writing style, inconsistencies or contradictions in the argument)?
> Is the conclusion effective? What makes it effective or not?

Critical Thinking

What Is Critical Thinking?

One meaning of the adjective *critical* is "making a negative comment, criticizing." However, the root of *critical* comes from a Greek word that means "to judge or discern, to weigh and evaluate evidence." When you apply critical thinking, you weigh the evidence and come to a conclusion. **Critical thinking** can be defined as *a series of logical mental processes that lead to a conclusion*. Critical thinking may involve

> analyzing
> comparing
> evaluating
> questioning
> rethinking
> synthesizing (putting together)
> other activities.

Much of what we do today is done quickly. This is true not only of video games, text messages, and email but also in business, where "instant" decisions are often valued (especially if they turn out to be good decisions!). However, because critical thinking involves many related activities, speed is not usually an asset. Leaders may sometimes need to make quick decisions, but more often, their decisions arise after carefully weighing an issue and receiving input from diverse sources. Since critical thinking is a process, the best way to succeed is to slow down, to be more deliberate in your thinking so you can complete each stage of the process.

This section is not designed to *make* you think critically, since you probably would not be at university if you did not use critical thinking daily. Rather, it is to *make you more conscious of the process*, especially when you read and analyze an essay or when you write one. Many of your assignments will require you to form conclusions about what you have read. Critical thinking skills are triggered whenever you read a work in order to comment on it, such as during a classroom discussion or debate, or to use it for support in your essay. The previous section, Responding Critically and Analytically through Questions, provides guidelines to help you become a careful reader who asks important, relevant questions.

Applying Critical Thinking

Critical thinking skills also apply to many everyday situations—from deciding what courses to take to what clothes to wear. Although choosing clothes might seem trivial, consider the importance of comparing, questioning, weighing, and rethinking if you were deciding on an outfit for an important job interview. What factors might affect your choice? These could range from the type of job you are applying for, the dress code of the company, the clothes you feel most confident in, or the weather on the day of the interview.

Critical thinking, then, involves making choices, but the most highly developed critical thinking is more than simple choice-making: it involves making the *best* choice from a range of possibilities. When you are reading an essay or a book, or evaluating a real-life situation, you are often not directly told what to think. You might be presented with evidence and left to infer the meaning. When you infer, you arrive at a probable conclusion based on what you read (or see). The *best* inference is the *most probable* one after all the evidence is weighed.

Much research relies on inferences: astronomers, for example, study the phenomenon of black holes by observing the behaviour of matter that surrounds the black hole. They know that before gas is swallowed up by a black hole, it is heated

Consider the following situation:

You invite a new friend for a coffee, but she does not show up. The next day, you meet her unexpectedly and ask her what happened. She pauses for a few seconds and then says matter-of-factly, "Well, actually, I was abducted by aliens, and they just released me." What do you make of her statement? What inferences are possible? Which are more likely? What could you say or do to ensure that your conclusion was the most probable one?

Possible inferences:

Probable inferences:

How to ensure that your inference is correct:

to extreme temperatures and accelerates. In the process, X-rays are created, which escape the black hole and reveal its presence. Scientists cannot actually see black holes, but they can *infer* their existence through the emission of X-rays.

You use critical thinking as you read whenever you evaluate and draw conclusions about claims, and the evidence or sources of these claims. It is important to remember that **critical thinking** is a *process of engagement* with a text (or a situation) that may change as you read (or learn more about the situation).

A Closer Look

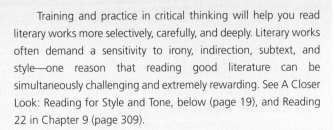

Critical Thinking in Literature Classes

Learning how to analyze literary works means learning how to apply specific reading strategies to interpret literature (i.e., how to arrive at the best inferences to make your reading more complex and/or subtle). When you read a poem, short story, or novel, the writer doesn't explicitly tell you the work's theme, explain how a symbol is being used, or list the traits of the main character. Instead, he or she embeds theme, symbol, and character within the work, enabling you to draw conclusions about their significance.

Training and practice in critical thinking will help you read literary works more selectively, carefully, and deeply. Literary works often demand a sensitivity to irony, indirection, subtext, and style—one reason that reading good literature can be simultaneously challenging and extremely rewarding. See A Closer Look: Reading for Style and Tone, below (page 19), and Reading 22 in Chapter 9 (page 309).

Reading closely, then, means becoming more conscious of how you interact with an unfamiliar text, being open to challenges to your own ways of thinking, but not being swayed by other views unless they stand up to the tests of logic and consistency. The critical thinker questions assumptions, tests the evidence, and accepts (or rejects) conclusions after careful analysis. When questions arise, the critical thinker seeks answers within the text itself, but may also consider relevant knowledge from personal experience or from outside sources. For example, in the coffee situation described in the box above, you might ask the woman's friends about her belief in aliens—or about her sense of humour.

In analyzing arguments, the critical thinker should carefully evaluate all claims made by the writer and look for failures in logic or misuse of emotion (see Logical, Emotional, and Ethical Fallacies in Chapter 8, page 244). He or she should also consider points that the writer *does not* raise. Is the writer avoiding certain issues by not mentioning them?

Expository (fact-based) writing can also produce disagreement and contradictory findings. For example, different researchers determining the effectiveness of a new drug or investigating the connection between television viewing and violence may arrive at very different conclusions though their methods appear credible. What can account for the differing results? Attempting to answer this question involves critical thinking, too.

Reading and Critical Thinking

As we read, we may not be aware that we are thinking critically. However, at times, critical thinking is clearly employed, such as when a writer makes a claim about a topic that experts have debated for years—for example, that cats are smarter than dogs. Making the best inference could involve weighing a number of factors:

> *The writer's credibility*. Is the writer considered an expert? What is the nature of his or her expertise? Is he or she a researcher into animal behaviour? A veterinarian? An animal trainer? Someone who has owned both dogs and cats? Someone who has owned cats only? Could the writer have a bias against dogs? Are there any errors in logic, such as "My neighbour's dog jumps up on me all the time; therefore, dogs are not smart"? Has fact been carefully distinguished from opinion?

> *Nature of the thesis or main points*. Specific points are stronger than general ones, and they are often easier to prove. Since there are many different dog breeds, it would be difficult to generalize about the intelligence of *all* dogs.

> *Basis of the statement*. Some claims are more straightforward than others. A claim may depend on an underlying assumption, such as a particular definition. There are various ways to define and measure intelligence: physiologically (e.g., the weight of the brain in proportion to the weight of the body) and behaviourally (e.g., trainability, adaptability, independence). Those who think dogs are more intelligent may point to trainability as the intelligence factor, while cat fanciers may point to adaptability or independence.

> *Method*. How does the writer attempt to prove his or her point? Since intelligence can be measured, a method that measured it scientifically would be more credible than one that relied on personal experience—especially since many pet-lovers are opinionated about their pets' intelligence and may not always distinguish between fact and opinion.

> *Support*. A credible writer would need to provide more than opinion to back up a claim, though research alone does not ensure a writer's credibility. In critical thinking, you must evaluate the nature of the evidence and the way the writer uses it. Typical questions might include: "What kind of evidence does the writer use? Does the writer rely too much on one kind of evidence or one source? How many sources are used? Are they current sources (recent studies may be more credible than older ones)? Does the writer ignore some sources (e.g., those that found dogs more intelligent than cats)?"

> *Conclusion*. While analyzing and questioning are important during your reading of the work, as you complete your reading you should be synthesizing (putting together) information in order to say something definitive about the work, the writer, or both. *Your goal is to determine whether the weight of evidence supports the writer's claim.* You might consider how weaker points affect the validity of the findings. Are there any gaps or inconsistencies in the chain of reasoning? Is the writer's conclusion logically backed up?

EXERCISE 1.4

↻ Check answers to select questions

As discussed in this section, we use critical thinking and inferences every day. The following scenarios call for critical thinking skills by asking us to make inferences.

A. What inferences could be made in each case?

B. Is there a best (i.e., most probable) inference? Justify your choice of the most probable inference. If you believe no inference can be made, explain what kind of information you would need to make an inference.

1. You arrive at your 8:30 a.m. class after missing yesterday's class because you overslept. You are surprised to see an empty classroom. As well, there is no one you recognize from class hanging around outside, and there is nothing posted on the wall or door to show that the instructor is ill.
   Inferences:
   a) You have mistaken either the time or the room.
   b) The instructor announced class cancellation yesterday.
   c) The instructor is ill, but no one put up a notice.
   d) No inference is possible. (What further information is needed?)

2. It was Todd's roommate's turn to cook dinner, but when Todd got home, his roommate was glued to the tv and the kitchen looked untouched. "Wow! Something smells great," enthused Todd.
   Inferences:
   a) Todd has a poor sense of smell.
   b) Todd is sarcastically voicing his displeasure.
   c) Todd is trying to give his roommate a hint that he should start dinner.
   d) No inference is possible. (What further information is needed?)

3. The students at the school work in isolated workstations; their desks face the walls. Social interaction is structured and supervised. Time-out rooms are small, windowless areas without furniture or carpeted floors; the doors have keyed locks. The cells are painted bright colors: pink, yellow, and blue; the light switch for each cubicle is on the outside.
   Inferences:
   a) The students at the school are thoroughly dedicated to their studies.
   b) School designers have provided the optimal conditions for study.
   c) The school has been designed for students with behavioural problems.
   d) No inference is possible. (What further information is needed?)

4. All was not eager anticipation for Meghan. She chose to attend the largest university in the province, and she found herself frequently feeling lost, both geographically and socially. She had to take a campus bus to get to some of her classes on time. Most of her classes were large with well over 100 students; one class had 250 students. She was used to smaller class sizes in high school with support from her resource teacher. Although she arranged for support through the university's Office of Disability Services, Meghan realized that she would have to approach the professors to describe her learning problems and request accommodations. Meghan also felt disorganized. Although her roommates had purchased their texts, yearly organizational calendars, and other materials, Meghan had no idea where to begin; her fear of failure was increasing by the moment.

Inferences:
   a)   Meghan will likely face many challenges at the university.
   b)   Meghan will likely give up and go home.
   c)   Meghan's fears are likely unfounded, as the many resources available at the university will help her adjust to her new life.
   d)   No inference is possible. (What further information is needed?)

5.   Binkley paid for all the travel and expenses, and what was only twelve months ago a very new and controversial transaction has today left Binkley a healthy man—and the first of 16 people who have successfully received organs through MatchingDonors.com.
   Inferences:
   a)   The author believes that this method of soliciting donors is wrong.
   b)   The author believes that this method of soliciting donors is, at the very least, ethically questionable.
   c)   The author sees nothing wrong with this method of soliciting donors.
   d)   No inference is possible. (What further information is needed?)

A Closer Look

Reading for Style and Tone

Straightforward, direct writing is rightly praised (especially by writing instructors!). However, a writer may deliberately employ a more complex, indirect style in aiming for an other effect than simple, direct communication. Why would a writer choose to use *indirect* means to get his or her points across?

The simple answer is that such a style can make writing more effective or interesting and the thesis more convincing. Alert readers will understand that the writer's indirectness is serving a purpose and read the essay in light of that purpose. Readers who do not notice this may be confused by the essay or misinterpret it.

A writer's style consists of features that (1) make the writing distinctive—for example, a descriptive style might use many adjectives—and (2) reflect the audience or purpose in writing. For example, an informal style could indicate familiarity with average readers or their values; if a writer's purpose was to parody (make fun of) someone, the style might reflect this through exaggeration. Features of style, then, can range from diction (word choice) to the use of literary devices, such as imagery or metaphors, to the appearance of words on the page. Note that *style* has other meanings in writing (see Chapter 7 and Chapter 12).

Sometimes readers need to use their critical thinking skills to "read between the lines" and understand the author's **tone**—his or her attitude towards the subject matter or audience.

Tone is usually revealed through language and style, including features like diction or specific stylistic choices, like the use of metaphors or humour. For example, in **satire**, a writer uses humour and an ironic tone to poke fun at an individual, group, or society itself—the target of the satire.

What is the author's tone in the following passage? Is it one more of amusement or of contempt? What, specifically, shows you the writer's attitude?

They're the impulse buys piled up next to the cash register. They're the books stocked by Urban Outfitters and hipster gift stores. They're the books you pick up, laugh at, and figure would be just about right for that co-worker who's into sci-fi (*The Space Tourist's Handbook*) [or] the friend who watches too much TV (*Hey! It's That Guy!: the Fametracker.com Guide to Character Actors*). . . .

Pop-culture-inspired handbooks for situations you're never going to face featuring information you're never going to need, these gimmicky, kooky, sometimes just plain stupid books have at least one thing in common: There are more and more of them out there, because they sell.

—Hal Niedzviecki, *The Globe and Mail*, 2005

EXERCISE 1.5

Think of a recent episode of a TV comedy, an article in a magazine, or a webpage in which satire was used. Can you identify the target of the satire (i.e., whom it was directed against)? Was the target announced or did a reader/viewer have to infer it? Consider specific features that contributed to the satire and write a short response in which you identify the target of the satire, along with passages, images, dialogue, and so on, that pointed to the target.

Before reading the essay below, consider any relevant questions from Before Reading or First Reading (pages 10–13) that might apply to this essay. After reading "Embrace the Mediocrity Principle," answer the questions that follow, focusing on making inferences based on content and credibility, along with tone and style, where applicable.

Sample Professional Essay

Reading 1

Embrace the Mediocrity Principle
By Daniel Wood
The Tyee, 24 December 2008

[1]   The shoe has dropped. But few are inclined to embrace the implications of the discoveries in the last few years that there are, almost certainly, millions of Earths out there and that the big rock you inhabit is as ordinary as phlegm.

[2]   Welcome to The Mediocrity Principle—astrophysicists' scary gift to the third millennium. Unlike the famous Peter Principle that says people rise to fulfill their incompetence, the new and very real Mediocrity Principle says that wherever astronomers look, the universe—and, by extension, all its constituents—sinks into trans-galactic commonness.

[3]   The Earth isn't the least unique. Ipso facto: neither are you. You're unalterably average.

[4]   It's an idea that, cosmologically speaking, has been a long time coming. But, its acceptance as a guiding 21st century paradigm, say pundits of impending environmental and economic apocalypse, just might save humankind from its own bloated sense of superiority and greed.

[5]   Welcome to 2009: Year of the Hairshirt. SUVs are officially DUM. Sardines trump swordfish. Mediocrity begins to replace excess. Frugalism is the new black.

[6]   In a Very Brief History of Time (169 words), this is how the Earth and its occupants have fallen into disgrace. A few centuries ago, people in the West thought this planet was the centre of the universe, that it began in 4004 B.C. (on Saturday, Oct. 22, to be exact), and that humans were made in the image of God. Copernicus, Galileo, and Darwin put large holes in these beliefs.

[7]   In the early 20th century, astronomer Edwin Hubble said a lot of those stars out there aren't stars at all. They're distant galaxies—billions of them, each containing billions of stars.

[8]   To make matters worse for humankind's sense of uniqueness, it soon became clear that time didn't start with The Big Guy in 4004 B.C., but with The Big Bang in 15 billion B.C.

[9]   Now, using information from the Hubble telescope, the first 300 of what's-predicted-to-be millions of distant planets have been found. There are almost certainly tens of millions of life-sustaining, Earth-like rocks out there. We live, it appears, on a commonplace hunk of granite, Coca-Cola, and chop suey surrounded by 10,000,000,000,000,000,000,000 stars and innumerable solar systems.

"Why should we assume there is anything special about us? Mediocrity is the universal rule," says Alexander Vilenkin, the Boston cosmologist who in 1995 coined the phrase The Mediocrity Principle. [10]

As this was happening, the late Harvard University paleontologist Stephen Gould pilloried Darwin's theory, saying evolution comes about, in part, through fluke and global catastrophe, not just through a species' inherent superiority. Now, humans can no longer claim to be Heavenly or even evolutionarily blessed; we're the result—in part—of renegade luck. [11]

Headed for newt status?

And the realization couldn't come at a more crucial moment. The Earth today is facing one of those planetary catastrophes that Gould and his doom-saying associates have often spoken about. Is our luck running out? [12]

The planet's systems are breaking down: global warming, economic disintegration, energy and food crises, the accelerating extinction of species, rampant pollution, AIDS, regional economic ghettoization, and the threat of worldwide terror. The list is long and familiar. [13]

Sixty-five million years ago, the dinosaurs failed to adapt to change and became, in time, newts. Mediocrity was forced on them. Today, there are creepy species waiting in the wings—rats, blackberries, cockroaches, lawyers—ready to claim humanity's position atop the Pig Pile. (Remember, the planet's dominant life-form throughout history is slime.) [14]

It's beginning to look as if the wackos carrying the placards reading "The End Is Nigh," are right. Unless...UNLESS: This planet's brainiest inhabitants accept that The Mediocrity Principle applies to them. [15]

Tad Homer-Dixon is no wacko. He's a 52 year-old University of Waterloo professor of international affairs and author of the 2001 Governor-General award-winning book *The Ingenuity Gap*. [16]

In it he describes how the current convergence of global crises can no longer be dismissed by the "Don't Worry, Be Happy" voices of hucksters promoting status, wealth, and consumption. [17]

"The conceit of sustainable development," says Homer-Dixon, "is you can have your cake and eat it, too. You can't. There's only so much. The cliff-edge is out there." [18]

As Homer-Dixon sees it, there are two human options for the future: 1) capitulation to drastic worldwide regulations and limits...or 2) chaos. [19]

To achieve the former, there'd have to be restrictions on consumption and on freedoms that—to use Homer-Dixon's phrase, "would be Holland—times 10." It would be a world of unimaginable technocratic order, enforced mediocrity, and eco-police. Flagrant extravagance would be a crime. [20]

That is the good option. To achieve the latter—chaos—Earthlings just have to keep doing what we're doing now. This route leads to fortified enclaves of wealth scattered amid widespread political and environmental collapse, plus the quarantine of entire sections of the planet. It would be—again using Homer-Dixon's analogy, "a patchwork of global anarchy—like many, many Haitis." [21]

Which option would you choose? [22]

Selling mediocrity

The point man for global mediocrity is Vancouver's Kalle Lasn, the 66-year-old founder of award-winning *Adbusters* magazine, and creator of the unlikely "Buy Nothing Day." His is not an easy task. In a world of exceptionalism, glitz, and vacuous spectacle, the satisfactions of the ordinary are, he knows, made to appear third-rate. [23]

For example, recent ad copy hyping the Nissan Altima read: "May Promote Feelings of Superiority." There are no ads anywhere promoting the virtues of mediocrity. Lasn knows this because he has produced 25 anti-commercials and sought to air them on the three big American TV networks. His success rate? Zero for 25. [24]

[25]   "Consumption is the mother of all evils," he says as he studies the foyer of a big-box Toys 'R' Us near his office. Colourful, inflated swimming pool animals float overhead. "People think business and technology will save us. But that's science fiction. Calamities lie ahead. Ordinariness will be resisted. In time, there'll be hell to pay. This over-consumptive culture of ours is going to die very hard."

[26]   As he leaves the store, he admits that he doesn't have much hope for the future. But he does, he says, have faith . . . in the potato. He'd dug one that morning in his backyard garden and fried it up for breakfast. At the memory, he smacks his lips.

Embrace our boringness

[27]   There are, cynics acknowledge, a few hopeful signs that mediocrity might take root amid a society that has, since the corporate scandals and economic turmoil of recent years, grown disenchanted with excess.

[28]   But first, we need to move past the idea's negative implications. Mediocrity is not about tastelessness. It's not about bad. It's not the Lada or carpet bowling or people who say, "Yo!" Mediocrity eschews the snobbishness of Calvin Klein for the practicality of Sears. Mediocrity does not go ga-ga over miniature summer squashes, when there are plenty of zucchinis—grown locally, of course.

[29]   Mediocrity embraces home haircuts, tap water, elbow patches, Scrabble nights, and naps. Mediocrity celebrates the winners of the annual Darwin Awards for their fatal stupidity. They are the true heroes!

[30]   Mediocrity looks for guidance to Despair, Inc.—a real business whose motto is: "Increasing Success by Lowering Expectations" and whose logo features the Leaning Tower of Pisa.

[31]   Mediocrity has as its most respected voice the man who gave the commencement address at his Yale University alma mater in 2001 and said there was nothing wrong with getting Cs. He'd done it himself. The usual venue for his speeches has been The White House.

[32]   There are some who'd argue that the Truth is out there and that extraterrestrials lurk at the periphery of our vision. The Mediocrity Principle provides a simpler explanation.

[33]   Mediocrity says there are no aliens nearby in their flying saucers because—despite humankind's efforts to simultaneously Disneyfy and destroy the planet—the Earth is a boring destination for intergalactic travellers.

[34]   Now let's make sure it remains a liveable place for ourselves.

EXERCISE 1.6

1. Sum up the Mediocrity Principle in one to two sentences using your own words.
2. How effectively does Wood support his thesis concerning the Mediocrity Principle? What would you consider his strongest point?
3. What is the only way, according to Wood, that global catastrophe could be prevented? Do you think he is generally hopeful about humanity's future?
4. What do you think "anti-commercials" are (see paragraph 24)? How could you find out if your inference is correct?
5. Analyze paragraphs 1–3 for their style. You could consider word choice/level of language, sentence structure, use of the second-person pronoun (*you*), or other strategies that reveal the author's style.
6. Identify the author's tone (i.e., apparent attitude towards his subject) in paragraph 14. Does it seem the same in paragraph 27? Identify the author's tone in one other paragraph in which it seems different from that in paragraphs 14 and 27.
7. What are the Darwin Awards?

8. Why does Wood not give the name of the man who, he says in paragraph 31, is the voice of mediocrity?

9. Why do you think Wood chooses the particular examples he does in the last section, "Embrace our boringness"? Do you believe they help support his thesis?

10. Do you agree with Wood's thesis? Write a 500-word response in which you explain your agreement or disagreement, using your critical thinking skills and referring specifically to the essay itself.

Word Meanings

Dictionaries are indispensable tools for writing, whether you are a professional writer or a student writer, whether you do your writing mostly by hand or use a word-processing program from start to finish. They are also an essential part of the reading life, and every student needs at least one good, recently published dictionary—two are preferable: one mid-sized dictionary for the longer, more complex writing you do at home and a portable one for when you are at school (you may also be able to access reliable online dictionaries through your library). But while a good dictionary is part of the key to understanding challenging texts, it is not the only one—often it is not even the best one.

The texts you read in university may be more challenging than those you are used to. To look up every word whose meaning is unclear would require too much time. If you interrupt your reading too often, it is hard to maintain continuity, reducing your understanding and retention of the material. Thankfully, you don't need to know the precise meaning of every word you read; you need to know the exact meanings of the most important words but only approximate meanings for many of the others.

We all have three vocabularies: a speaking vocabulary, a writing vocabulary, and a reading, or *recognition*, vocabulary. The speaking vocabulary is the smallest—2000 words is sufficient for most of our conversational needs. The recognition vocabulary is the largest, but it includes words we would not use in our writing. If you are asked the meaning of a word from your recognition vocabulary, you might struggle to define it, though you might *think* you know what it means; however, you know it only within the contexts in which you have read it.

Since relying *only* on a dictionary is both inefficient and unreliable, you should cultivate reading practices that minimize—not maximize—the use of a dictionary. Refer to a dictionary when needed, for example, to confirm a word's meaning; otherwise, try to determine meanings through contextual clues or by noting similarities with words you *do* know.

Important nouns, verbs, adjectives, and adverbs are often revealed through context—the words around them. Writers may define difficult words, or may use synonyms or rephrasing to make their meanings easy to grasp; such strategies are used if the author thinks the typical reader will not know them. On the other hand, authors may use an unfamiliar word in such a way that the meanings of the surrounding words clarify the meaning and connotation of the unfamiliar word.

Using Context Clues

In the following sentences from "Embrace the Mediocrity Principle," words before or after the italicized words can be used to determine their meanings:

> [The principle's] acceptance as a guiding 21st century *paradigm* . . . just might save humankind from its own bloated sense of superiority and greed.

A paradigm is something that guides, such as a pattern; "21st century" could further suggest that a paradigm is an enduring pattern.

> [Homer-Dixon] describes how the current convergence of global crises can no longer be dismissed by the "Don't Worry, Be Happy" voices of *hucksters* promoting status, wealth, and consumption.

With the words that follow "hucksters," the writer appears to be criticizing people who sell consumer goods. You might conclude that the word refers to people who take advantage of others' naivety to make a sale.

Particularly important concepts may be defined. In paragraph 2, two important principles are defined:

> Welcome to The Mediocrity Principle . . . . *Unlike the famous Peter Principle that says people rise to fulfill their incompetence,* the new and very real *Mediocrity Principle says that wherever astronomers look, the universe . . . sinks into trans-galactic commonness.*

When a writer does not define a word, you may be able to infer its meaning through context—by looking less at the words around it than at the idea the writer is trying to express. In the following example, it is apparent that Gould has challenged a major finding of Charles Darwin. In fact, the verb *to pillory* means something stronger than simply "challenge"—"to hold up to public ridicule." Since Darwin's theories are publicly accepted, the choice of "pilloried" seemed a suitable one.

> . . . the late Harvard University paleontologist Stephen Gould *pilloried* Darwin's theory, saying evolution comes about, in part, through fluke and global catastrophe, not just through a species' inherent superiority.

The meanings of words can often be determined because they look like other, familiar words. One could guess that "ghettoization," part of the phrase "regional economic ghettoization," is related to *ghetto*, a place in which a minority group lives, cut off from the more privileged.

After you have inferred the word's meaning through its context, you should look up the word in a dictionary to confirm that it means what you think it does; however, remember that a word's denotation, its "official" dictionary definition, may be different from its connotation, the word's meaning as determined by its context. A word may have more than one denotation, but most have several possible connotations.

Reading carefully to determine both the immediate context and the encompassing idea of the sentence or passage can help you determine a word's meaning. Remember that the object is not necessarily to make the word part of your writing vocabulary but to enable you to know how the author is using it—to recognize its particular connotation. However, by examining a word's denotations and at least one of its connotations, you are well on the way to making it part of your writing vocabulary.

EXERCISE 1.7

From the following list, choose three words you're unfamiliar with and try to determine their meaning by their context in "Embrace the Mediocrity Principle." When you've written a short definition of the word, look it up in a reliable dictionary to confirm its meaning. Then, use the word in a sentence of your own that would enable another writer to guess its meaning. Finally, give the sentence to a classmate and have him or her determine the meaning by context.

bloated
capitulation
convergence
cosmologist
disenchanted
enclaves
flagrant
inherent
pundits
renegade
vacuous

Chapter 2

The Writing Situation

Writing Purpose

Before you begin writing, you need to consider all the factors that influence your writing task, including your purpose for writing and your audience. Purpose refers to more than your reason for writing. It could include many related areas, such as the skills that the assignment is intended to develop. Assessing purpose could involve any number of the questions below and address either broad concerns or more specific ones. If you are uncertain about writing purpose, seek clarification—either by asking your instructor or by using techniques, such as pre-writing, designed to clarify purpose.

> Will you be choosing your own topic or have you been given a specific topic? If the latter, will you have to narrow the topic?
> What kind of writing will you be doing? What form will it take (response, formal essay, research proposal, lab report)?
> What main activities are involved (informing, explaining, arguing, narrating, describing, summarizing)?
> Does the assignment stress learning objectives or does it ask you to apply concepts and practices already taught?
> What specific skills will you need to demonstrate? How important is each to the overall assignment? For example, will you have to define, summarize, synthesize, analyze, compare and contrast, or classify? If the assignment includes a specifically worded question or statement, pay particular attention to verbs, such as *evaluate* or *assess*, *summarize*, *explore*, *explain*, *argue for or against*, *discuss*, *describe*. These each indicate a different purpose for the assignment.
> Will you be using your own ideas? Will you be basing these ideas on recollection, observation, opinions, readings, or class or group discussions?
> Where do your interests lie relative to the topic? How can you find out what they are and develop them further, if necessary?
> What level of knowledge does the assignment require? What level of specialization?
> Will the assignment test originality—new approaches to an old problem (inventiveness, imagination, creativity)?
> Should your language be formal, like that of most academic disciplines? Will some informality be acceptable—the use of contractions and/or some informal diction?
> Will you be using other people's ideas? Will you get these from books and articles or other secondary sources (interviews, surveys)?
> How much preparatory reading do you expect to do? What kind of reading?
> Will you be submitting work in progress, such as pre-writing assignments, a self-survey, a proposal, an outline, a plan, or a rough draft?
> Is there a specified length? Is it a word or page range? Will penalties be applied (i.e., marks deducted), if you write outside this range?
> How much time have you been given for the assignment? For example, an in-class exam would require a different assessment of purpose than that of an essay assigned weeks in advance.

●●●●●

EXERCISE 2.1

A good way to prepare for an assignment is to think about the questions discussed above so that you understand what is required of you. You can do this as a self-survey by dividing a page into three columns. In the first column, write abbreviated forms of the most relevant questions above (these could vary, depending on the assignment); in the second column, write your responses; and in the third column, briefly state what you know and/or what you need to find out to satisfy the writing purpose. This activity could be used either before or after writing a research proposal; see Chapter 6, The Research Proposal, page 145.

●●●●●

Table 2.1 is an example of the beginning of a self-survey on the topic "Is Internet Piracy Wrong? Agree or Disagree." A longer, more complex assignment, such as a research essay, would probably require a more detailed self-survey than that of a response.

Table 2.1 Sample Self-Survey

Relevant Question	My Response	Where to Begin/What Needs to be Done
Kind of writing	Response	Need to review the section of the text on response
Main activity	Arguing	As responding is a form of arguing, I need to know if I have to include a rebuttal
Specific skills	Definition, analysis	It will be necessary to define "Internet piracy," using a reliable current source as the definition has probably changed over time and definitions may conflict or overlap
Interest/knowledge	High level of interest, am unsure about my knowledge level; topic is of interest to me because I and most of my friends have committed Internet piracy, but I do not believe it is ethical if other options exist	Knowledge questions: What is the legal definition of "Internet piracy"? How does one know if one is doing something illegal? What are the possible repercussions? Has anyone ever been fined or jailed for this?

A is for Audience

Almost everything is written for an audience—readers with common interests, attitudes, reading habits, and expectations. There are many ways to test this statement. For instance, pick up a children's book with one hand and the closest textbook with the other. Note the many differences. Likely, the textbook weighs more than the children's book; it has more pages, and the print is smaller. The cover of the children's book is likely colourful; the cover of the textbook is designed to give basic information in a pleasing form—no more.

Publishers have expectations about their readers: children's book publishers expect their readers to look for something to catch their interest. If the cover is appealing, a child or parent might turn to the first page and begin reading. A typical textbook reader might read no further than the title, or might turn to the index or table of contents to get a general idea about content or to see how thoroughly a specific topic is covered. If the first few sentences of the children's book do not intrigue the reader, the book will be put back on the shelf; if the index of the textbook doesn't meet the reader's needs, the textbook will be put back.

Student writers need to "design" their essay for an audience or typical reader. Therefore, the kinds of questions that apply to publishers and book designers also apply to student writers.

When physicist Stephen Hawking set out to write his popular book on cosmology, *A Brief History of Time*, audience concerns were taken into account, as is evident in his first paragraph. Italics show where readers are specifically addressed:

> Where did the universe come from? How and why did it begin? Will it come to an end, and if so, how? These are questions that are of interest to *us all*. But modern science has become so technical that only a very small number of specialists are able to master the mathematics used to describe them. Yet the basic ideas about the origin and fate of the universe can be stated without mathematics in a form that *people without a scientific education* can understand.

How does Hawking tell you what kind of audience he is writing for? He begins with straightforward questions that he says interest us all, meaning curious people with no scientific training. He chooses direct language and simple sentence structure. If he were addressing his book to specialists, he probably would not have used the phrase "a very small number of specialists." Perhaps he would have said, "cosmologists, astrophysicists, and mathematical physicists," specifically addressing these readers.

The tone of the passage also shows his concern with audience. It is inviting and implies that a non-specialist reader can understand difficult concepts. Clearly, Hawking wrote the way he did because he wanted to meet the expectations of his target audience.

EXERCISE 2.2

Writers want their message—their communication—to be received and to be accepted. Looking at the writer–reader relationship this way, you could consider it a kind of contractual arrangement with responsibilities on both sides. What responsibilities would a writer have in this relationship to make it more likely that the message will be received and accepted? What responsibilities, ideally, should a reader have in this relationship? Add to the list in Table 2.2, assigning additional responsibilities in this contractual arrangement.

Table 2.2 Responsibilities of Reader/Responsibilities of Writer

Responsibilities of the Reader	Responsibilities of the Writer
1. to read attentively and closely	1. to use appropriate language and a clear, readable style
2. to test the writer's claims for logic and consistency	2. to reason fairly, logically, and with consistency
3.	3.
4.	4.
5.	5.

Reader-based Prose: Writing *to* an Audience

Reader-based prose is focused on the reader. It makes clear communication a priority and acknowledges the role of the reader in the communication process. Reader-based prose is geared towards the particular audience the essay is designed for. It can be a good idea to visualize an audience made up of typical readers before you begin composing; in this way, your reader will not be just an abstraction but a specific person or group. If your essay is written for your instructor, visualize a group of instructors as your readers. This will help you avoid the mindset of writing *for* a particular reader (your instructor); instead, you will be writing *to* individuals like your instructor.

However, remember that in formal writing you should not address your audience directly using the second-person pronoun, *you*. Using *you* implies you know your reader well or that he or she is a member of a specific group whose characteristics you know well. For example, the second-person pronoun is often used in this book because it is written to a specific group: university students in writing and composition classes. But even in formal writing, although you do not know your typical reader well enough to address him or her as *you*, you do need to consider the audience and determine where the reader's interests and values lie, as you will see below under Audience Factors.

In contrast with reader-based prose, **writer-based prose** is much less directed to its audience: private journal writing is one example of a writing activity where there is no need to acknowledge and accommodate a reader. Another example is freewriting (see Freewriting and Clustering, page 39); after you have used freewriting to uncover your thoughts and feelings about a topic, you then need to begin shaping that topic to a specific reader.

Because reader-based prose is directed to an audience, you must ensure it is error-free and clear in its meaning. Ideas need direct and concise expression. In addition, there should be no obvious gaps in logic, nor should you assume a reader knows something just because you know it. In some cases, you may have to define terms or clarify specific points. Even if the intended audience has specialized knowledge about a subject, it is best to assume that *the reader knows a little less about the subject than you do.*

Readers should not have to fill in gaps. In the following example, the writer should have accommodated a general reader by giving more information. A reader could legitimately ask what a "deer tag" is and how it is "filled":

> In 1998, there were more than 1 million deer tags handed out in Pennsylvania; of these, only 430,000 tags were actually filled.

Audience Factors

An audience can be characterized or profiled in a variety of ways. You should bear these in mind when you assess your essay's purpose and when you choose what to include or not to include, what level of language and tone to use, how to develop your ideas, how much background to provide, what kind of support to use, and other rhetorical concerns.

You can characterize an audience according to four criteria:

> *Knowledge*: the background, expertise, or familiarity with the subject
> *Interest level*: the extent of audience interest or potential interest

> *Reader–writer relationship*: the way an audience would be expected to respond to the writer
> *Orientation*: the attitudes and emotional/ethical positions that define a typical reader.

Awareness of an audience's level of knowledge and interest, its relationship to the writer, and its orientation to the subject, writer, or the argument can be determined through various questions (see Knowledge and Interest Questions below).

Knowledge and Interest

> A **general audience** is one with no special defining characteristics; thus, a general audience is usually quite large. Such readers may have little knowledge about the topic, and their interest may vary—for example, the students at your university; readers of *The Globe and Mail* newspaper.
> An **implicit audience** has both more knowledge about and interest in the subject than a general audience but less than an explicit audience—for example, first-year science students at your university; readers of the business section of *The Globe and Mail*.
> An **explicit audience** has specific assumptions and may have a more in-depth knowledge of and interest in the topic. When writing to this audience, you can use specialized terms and expect to be understood. Some typical explicit audiences are chemistry students at your university or readers of the stock market reports of *The Globe and Mail*.

Usually, readers with some knowledge about a topic are also interested in the topic, with an *explicit* audience being more interested than either *general* or *implicit* audiences; however, there is not always a correlation between knowledge and interest, and they can often be considered separately.

Remember that meeting the expectations of an audience does not necessarily mean telling its members what they *want to hear*, but, rather, doing everything you can to make it more likely they *will hear* you and understand you. For example, if you do not meet their expectations by using familiar terms or explaining unfamiliar ones, they will be less likely to "hear" you and understand you; hence they may not pay attention to the points you make. That is why it is more accurate to speak about writing *to* your audience than *for* your audience.

By asking these questions and trying to find accurate answers, you will be better able to create reader-based prose.

Knowledge and Interest Questions

1. How much do you know about your potential readers? How much do you need to know? What assumptions can you make about them? What might they value? What ambitions and goals might they possess? How could your writing appeal to their values and goals?
2. In what ways might the members differ from you? From one another? Consider such factors as their location, age, gender, occupation, education, ethnic and/or cultural background, social status, politics, religion, hobbies, and entertainment.
3. Is there a specific group of individuals you want to reach (other students, scientists, people your age, people of different ages)?

4. If your readers' knowledge about a subject is less than your own, what would help them better understand the topic (background information, facts and figures, examples, analogies or comparisons, references to experts)?

5. If your readers' interest in a subject is less than your own, what could help them better relate to the topic (examples, questions, anecdotes or short narratives, personal experience)?

EXERCISE 2.3

In terms of their knowledge and interest, what general or specific assumptions could you make about readers of the following?

- a blog
- a trendy e-zine
- a trade journal
- an academic English journal
- a book about recent discoveries in palaeontology
- a best-selling book on a topical subject

EXERCISE 2.4

Explore the databases your university subscribes to. The journals and trade publications found on these databases are written for explicit audiences. For example, the *International Journal of Clinical Practice* is written for people in the medical field, and most of the articles use terminology that these professionals are familiar with. Find an article that was written for an explicit audience. Then, using the databases, find an article about the same topic, but which was written for a general or implicit audience (you might try searching magazines or newspapers). Compare the prose and writing styles. How are different words used to convey the same information? How would you include some of the information if you were going to write for your professor who is an expert in the field? Which article would you cite more if you were writing to your peers in the classroom?

Writer–Reader Relationship

Although it's useful to visualize an audience that consists of more than just your instructor, of course it's also important to acknowledge your instructor as a reader by following directions given for the assignment. For example, if you are required to include a title page with the instructor's name beneath the name or number of the course, not including this information would be failing to meet his or her expectations. The presentation of your essay demands your careful attention since instructors vary in their requirements; for instance, one instructor may require you to use 12-point size type while another may say that a point size between 10 and 12 is acceptable. At the very least, you will not make a favourable impression on the first instructor if you use 10-point type.

Writer–Reader Relationship Questions

1. What is your relationship to the audience? Student to instructor? Student to student? Another kind of peer-based relationship, such as individual to professional

associates or members of a group or community you are part of—for example, an organization of rock-climbers? Architects? Members of the union you belong to? Employee to employer? Employer to employee?

2. Do your readers expect you to conform to the conventions of a particular form or discipline? What are the specific formal requirements? (These questions are important when considering purpose as well.)

Audience Orientation

An audience can have *positive*, *neutral*, *negative*, or *mixed* orientations towards the subject, the writer, or the writer's thesis.

> ❯ *Positive*: holds the same view as the writer, or is more likely to agree than disagree
> ❯ *Neutral*: does not feel strongly one way or the other
> ❯ *Negative*: differs from the writer's view or is more likely to disagree than agree
> ❯ *Mixed*: is divided between those who agree and those who disagree

Assessing audience orientation to your thesis is especially vital in argument. Will most of your readers agree or disagree with your viewpoint, or will they have no opinion? Many people form attitudes about matters of common interest, though they may be open to other views. As an arguer, part of your job is to convince those whose views differ from yours, or who have no particular opinion, that your view is worth supporting.

Consider the subject of cloning. How might the opinions of members of a scientific community differ from those of a religious community? Would all scientific or religious communities have identical attitudes? What could affect differences? What about an audience of first-year philosophy students?

Orientation Questions

1. What is your audience's attitude towards your topic or viewpoint? If you are unsure, how could you find out? What preconceived opinions might its members hold? What has informed these opinions (any of the factors mentioned above, such as education or where they live)? Do you need to be sensitive to the audience's background? For example, are you a vegan writing to an audience of cattle farmers?

2. If you expect your readers to be unsympathetic to your views, how could you make them more receptive? How could you bridge the gap between you and them? (See Chapter 8, page 238, Refuting the Opposing View.)

Finally, the following questions could be relevant to all the above areas: What kind of writing does your audience expect or appreciate—simple and direct? complex? subtle? original? Could you use humour? Would they understand or value irony? How could your knowledge of audience affect your writing style or your tone?

Check answers to select questions

EXERCISE 2.5

Five topics are given in Table 2.3 with a group of potential readers for each. From what you know or can assume about the topic and audience, complete the third column indicating the probable orientation of the audience (positive, neutral, negative, or mixed) to the topic.

Table 2.3 Topic/Audience Table

Topic to Argue	Audience	Orientation
Mandatory physical education in school	high school history teachers phys-ed teachers high school students	
Abolishing NHL hockey fights	NHL hockey fans referees' union NHL team owners	
Compulsory pet neutering	pet owners city council pet breeders	
Use of taser guns by the RCMP	a citizens' rights group RCMP officers dentists	
Laptops in the classroom	students who own laptops students who do not own laptops instructors who have taught for 20 years or more	

EXERCISE 2.6

Collaborative Exercise—Assessing the Writing Situation

From Table 2.4, select one Purpose variable and one Audience variable from each category of column three (Knowledge, Interest Level, Relationship, and Orientation). Discuss how you would approach writing an essay if you were given one of the Topics from column one. How could you ensure that your message is received and accepted? How could you meet audience expectations? Try to be as specific as you can about approach and strategy. Hint: Start with Purpose, follow with Topic, and then choose Audience variables, considering assumptions about that audience and the way they would affect your writing choices.

Table 2.4 Topic/Purpose/Audience Table

Topic	Purpose	Audience
		Knowledge
smoking in public places	formal essay	general knowledge
schizophrenia	in-class essay	implicit (moderate knowledge)
abolishing final exams	tell something that happened to you (narration)	explicit (specialized knowledge)

(continued)

Table 2.4 (Continued)

Topic	Purpose	Audience
		Interest Level
snowboarding	to explain (exposition)	low interest
conservation	to persuade (argument)	moderate interest
downloading music from the Internet	to summarize (put ideas in your own words)	high interest
		Relationship
the structure of DNA	to use research	superior–subordinate relationship
age discrimination	to explore or discover	peer–peer relationship
		Orientation
victims' rights	to describe	positive orientation
weblogs ("blogs")	to define	neutral orientation
		negative orientation

EXERCISE 2.7

Collaborative Exercise—Formulating an Audience Profile

Create an audience profile by considering the four criteria characterizing an audience. In a group of three, take turns interviewing the other two members of your group, asking them questions that will enable you to assess your audience according to its knowledge, interest level, and orientation (you can omit Writer–Reader Relationship). Assume your purpose is to persuade your audience. Therefore, if you follow Table 2.4 in Exercise 2.6, you could use one of the following topics: smoking in public places, abolishing final exams, downloading music from the Internet, victims' rights, or blogs. You can also come up with a topic of your own that you feel strongly about and would like to argue for or against.

Write a four-paragraph profile based on the results of your interviews. Devote a paragraph to each variable of knowledge, interest, orientation, and strategies to consider in order to appeal to your specific audience. (You may also choose to create headings for each of the categories and then use bulleted lists to create an informal profile.) If you wish, you can pre-read Two Strategies for Refutation in Chapter 8, page 238.

In many cases, your instructor will inform you of the intended audience for your essay—perhaps a general audience or first-year students.

Assessing Your Own Attitude

Remember that you should consider not only what you know or need to know about your audience, but also your own attitude to them. Is it positive? Neutral? Cautious? Mistrustful? What attitudes will the audience expect you to hold? What attitudes might disturb or offend its members, making them less likely to "hear" you? Again, such questions are especially pertinent to argument where any suggestion of bias will undermine the strength of your argument. If you hope your audience will respect your point of view, you must respect their point of view and take care to consider it objectively. Otherwise, those with opposing views will quickly realize your bias and may read no further.

Stages in Essay Writing

Once you have considered purpose and audience, you are ready to begin narrowing your topic. Whichever composing method works best for you, writing an essay inevitably means working steadily towards a goal. Although you may allot more time and energy to one stage or another, you will generally write an essay in five stages.

1. **Pre-writing** (**Inventing**): thinking about and coming up with a topic
2. **Research**: finding background information and supporting evidence (This stage could involve intensive library resources or simply consist of examining your knowledge about a topic.)
3. **Organization**: determining the order of points; outlining
4. **Composing** (**first draft**): getting down your ideas in paragraph form
5. **Revising** (**final draft**): revising and editing to achieve the finished version

External factors could determine how much time you devote to the pre-writing stage. If you are assigned a specific topic, you won't have to spend as much time at this stage as someone who is simply told to "write on a topic of your choosing." Similarly, if you have the option of not writing a formal outline, you may spend much less time on outlining—perhaps by writing only an informal scratch outline—than would someone asked to complete a formal outline. However, when you revise your essay, you should always plan for enough time to ensure your writing is grammatical, mechanically correct, and clear.

Pre-writing

Subjects versus Topics

In your assignment, you may be told to choose your own topic or be given various broad subject categories and asked to narrow one down to a manageable topic. A **subject**, then, contains many potential topics. Consider your school subjects: history is a subject, but it can be broken into many different topics—for example, different time periods (the Middle Ages, the Industrial Revolution), which might correspond to different history courses you can enroll in. Other subjects, like psychology or English literature, can be similarly broken down.

"Modern technology," "global warming," and "energy sources" are examples of essay subjects. A subject could also be more specific than these examples ("the Internet," "species extinction," and "alternative energy sources" could also be considered subjects). A **topic** differs from a subject in being narrower or more focused. Similarly, a **thesis** is more focused than a topic because it makes a specific comment on the topic or tells the reader how you will approach the topic. A statement that contains a thesis will need support; a statement that consists of only a subject or topic will usually not need support.

Below we will consider using pre-writing strategies to come up with a topic. These strategies sometimes result in a thesis and even in some main points for your essay, but at other times, your thesis is not clear to you until after you've begun your research. However, your topic *should always* be clear before you begin your research. There may not always be a clear line between a subject and a topic, but there should be one between a topic and a thesis.

Thesis

A **thesis** is a formal statement that includes both your topic and your approach to, or a comment on, the topic. A thesis could be expanded to include your main points. See Chapter 4, The Thesis Statement, page 91.

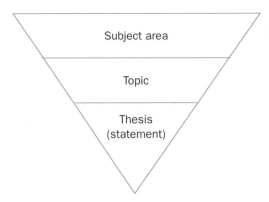

Figure 2.1

●●●●●

EXERCISE 2.8

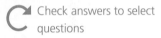

Check answers to select questions

Read through the following list. Decide whether each statement is a subject, a topic, or a thesis. If it is a topic, identify the subject; if it is a thesis, identify the topic and the subject. There may be more than one possible topic or subject, as in the example below:

> The discrepancy between men's and women's golf coverage is due to sexism.
> It is a *thesis* (the statement makes a comment about a topic)
> *Topic*: men's and women's golf coverage
> *Possible subjects*: golf, sports coverage, sexism in society

1. Video games are bad for youth.
2. Borderline Personality Disorder is a controversial condition.
3. The federal government should change the drinking age across Canada to 18.
4. More hybrid cars are on the market than ever before.
5. Whales are one of many threatened species today.
6. "Managed trade" involves government intervention, such as the imposition of tariffs.
7. Cruelty to animals often goes unpunished.
8. Studying the classical languages in school is unnecessary today.
9. Many varieties of dance and dance styles exist today.
10. Enrolling in a dance class can help people with disabilities.

Topic Hunting

Your instructor may tell you to find your own topic or to narrow a given subject to a manageable topic. In the first case, you would start from scratch. Here are some questions you can consider if you need to come up with a topic from scratch:

> ❯ Where do your interests lie (hobbies, leisure pursuits, reading interests, extracurricular activities)?
> ❯ What would you like to find out more about? Curiosity is a good motivator. A topic you are very familiar with does not always make a good one for a research essay, as your knowledge could inhibit your ability to fully explore the topic.
> ❯ Are there are sufficient sources available? Consider not only research sources but also questionnaires, interviews, experts, statistics, and so on.
> ❯ What topic do you think readers might like to learn about? Thinking of *other* people's interests can guide you to a worthwhile topic. What topic

could benefit society or a specific group in society (for example, students at your university)?

> Can you think of a new angle on an old topic? Neglected areas of older topics can be new opportunities for exploration.

By using pre-writing techniques, you can narrow down a subject to a usable topic. However, not all topics can be turned into effective thesis statements. Some are too broad while others are too narrow. If the topic is too broad, it will be hard to do more than provide a general overview. Your essay may also be difficult to plan and write because there will be so much you could say about the topic. On the other hand, if your topic is too specific, you could feel yourself limited by the topic's scope; you may also have problems researching it if there's not much available.

Pre-writing Strategies

Pre-writing strategies should clarify your thoughts about the subject and enable you to generate useful ideas, some of which you will use in your essay; others can be discarded as you further clarify your topic. Pre-writing often brings you to the point where you can write a tentative thesis statement and, in many cases, determine your main points.

Pre-writing strategies include *asking questions* about the topic; *brainstorming*, alone or with others; *freewriting*, in which you write continuously for a specific time without editing yourself; and *clustering*, or *mapping*, in which you graphically represent your associations with a subject.

All these pre-writing techniques work by association—using one or more of questioning, brainstorming, freewriting, or clustering enables you to trigger associations, to tap into subconscious ideas and feelings. By employing these methods, you are taking a step towards writing your essay. Pre-writing is an especially worthwhile activity in the traditional linear model, since it may help generate the ideas that could lead to an outline of your main points.

Although all pre-writing techniques work similarly, each has unique strengths, and one may be more useful than another for a particular kind of writing. Table 2.5 (page 41) lists possible uses of pre-writing techniques. The most important thing is that you learn to work with whatever methods serve you well.

Questions and Brainstorming

Asking questions and brainstorming are tried-and-true approaches for finding out more about a subject. Although you can pose any **questions**, asking the traditional journalistic questions—"Who?," "What?," "Why?," "When?," "Where?," and "How?"—can be helpful for almost any subject, such as "roommates":

Who? Who make the best roommates? (worst?)
What? What are the qualities of an ideal roommate?
Why? Why are roommates necessary? (or not?)
When? When is the best time to start looking for a roommate?
Where? Where can you find a roommate? Where can you go for privacy when you have a roommate?
How? How do you go about finding a good roommate? How do you get along with a roommate?

In **brainstorming**, you write down words, phrases, or sentences that you associ-ate with a subject. You can then begin looking for what some of the items have in common. How can they be connected and categorized? You can often combine brainstorming with one or more pre-writing methods. For example, if you began by asking the journalistic questions about the subject "roommates," you could brainstorm the qualities of an ideal roommate, using the question "What?" to generate a list. You could continue to use these two methods by then asking why these important qualities contribute to a good roommate.

Although brainstorming can produce a list that looks something like an outline, the object is to come up with as many points as possible and then to connect them in some way; you don't need to begin with logical connections between any one item and the next.

In addition to listing random associations on one subject, you could set up the brainstorming session by applying different criteria to a topic. For example, using a topic like "private versus public health care," you could list your associations under *pro* and *con*; you could also list similarities and differences between two related items, such as two addictive substances, two movie directors, or two racquet sports; or you could divide a general category, such as contemporary music, into sub-categories and list your associations with each. These specific kinds of lists are useful when you know that your essay will employ a primary method of organization such as cost-benefit, compare and contrast, or division/classification.

Freewriting and Clustering

In **freewriting,** you write for a span of time without stopping, usually five to ten minutes. You can freewrite without a topic in mind and see where your subconscious leads you, or you could begin with a specific subject or topic, though you may well stray from the topic and end up writing about something else. That is fine. You do not need to censor or edit yourself, or concern yourself with spelling or grammar. You are concerned with flow and process and should not worry about mechanics or content. In some freewriting, you do not punctuate or use capital letters: you just write without lifting your pencil from the page, or just continue typing without worrying about spacing. Many people, though, prefer to use punctuation occasionally and to write mostly in sentences. The important principle is that you do not stop writing. If you can't think of anything to say, you write something anyway, such as "I can't think of anything to say," "what's the point in this?" or even "blah, blah, blah" until another idea or association comes to you.

If you enjoy freewriting and find it beneficial, you can follow it with a looping exercise. In **looping,** you underline potentially useful words, phrases, or sentences; then, you choose the best one to focus on as the beginning point for more freewriting. You can also take the most useful phrase, sum it up in a sentence, and begin freewriting using this sentence as a starting point. Although freewriting is a popular pre-writing strategy, you can use it at any point in the composing process—if you get stuck on a particular point or experience "writer's block" when drafting your essay.

Freewriting has several functions:

> It can free you from writer's block. A typical problem in beginning to write is feeling you have nothing to say.
> It enables you to express undiscovered feelings and associations; in other words, it gives you access to areas of your thinking or belief you might not have known about.
> Combining freewriting with looping can help you narrow down a topic and, sometimes, come up with a thesis and main points.

The freewriting sample below is the result of 10 minutes of freewriting in which the writer chose the topic "inspiration." It shows how, through a series of stops and starts, doubts and questions, the writer arrived at an insight about herself and what she values (ellipses [. . .] represent places in the freewrite where irrelevant words have been omitted). To further narrow her topic, she could then underline her statement that research inspires her and use it as a beginning point for another freewriting session.

How can a person get inspired? On many occasions i have found myself in front of a perfectly blank page. I stare at the ridges the fine lines that are created by the drying process the paper undergoes the fine blots of perhaps ink or some sort of goop that you constantly see in recycled paper (which i hope is just ink and try not to think about toilet paper and how it too gets recycled and put with the rest of it. Then i stop and think about the environment and say well things could be worse). . . . So how does a person get inspired? Will the change of pencil to ink make a difference? Does a person think about all the goals they have to accomplish then panic when their mind draws a blank? Does it happen often? I believe so my experience has taught me that my mind does not work like most minds. It is unorganized, it speaks to itself yes i often do find myself talking when no one is around. So you can now see how hard it is to get inspired with a mind like that. Can i inspire someone else? Perhaps! Do I have a source of inspiration? Not at the moment! . . . And here i am writing nonsense and trying to just think i hope this isn't worth part of my grade. . . . I'd say that most students do just that. They probably stop and think about how much it will count in their final grade and from there they give their time a value. "Is this worth an all nighter?" . . . So how does a person get inspired? At some point, someone must have stopped and thought about this, maybe even written a book. You see for a person like me it's not a question of time for writing. It's more of the breakthrough that inspiration gives and also the research i conduct in order to receive this inspiration. Now after all this ranting i have found my source of information. RESEARCH. Now i can worry about the time i've wasted just thinking about that. Trying to build a decent essay with proper grammar and spelling that will get a good mark.
—I.H.

Clustering, or mapping, is an associative technique that is represented graphically rather than linearly. Near the centre of a blank piece of paper, write down and circle your subject and then think of related words or phrases, which you record and circle, connecting each with the word or phrase that gave rise to it. The clustering method can help you develop your main points and provide a structure for your essay. Unlike questioning, brainstorming, and freewriting, clustering produces distinct groups of related words and phrases, which may be developed into main points. You can often see other relationships between circles in one cluster and those in another. In the example in Figure 2.2, dotted lines represent other possible connections.

Figure 2.2 is the result of a group clustering exercise that began with the subject "vitamins," and produced this thesis statement: "Due to media hype and the promise of good health, more people than ever are taking vitamins before they

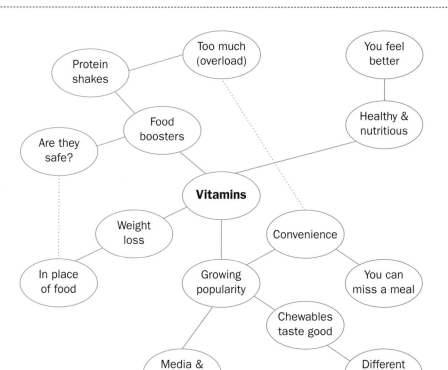

Figure 2.2

really know the risks involved." The statement needs further work, but it is a solid start.

All the pre-writing methods could be considered meeting places between you and your topic. Because they are designed to "free up" your thoughts and feelings, do not hesitate to experiment with variants on these methods.

Table 2.5 Pre-writing Strategies

Pre-writing Strategy	Description	Uses
Questioning	asking questions about subject/topic	expository (informational) essays in the sciences or social sciences where thesis can be framed as a specific question or series of questions you will try to answer
Freewriting	timed writing in which you write without stopping or editing yourself	personal essays in which you try to make unconscious or emotional connections with the topic
Brainstorming	writing down in point form associations with a subject/topic	collaborative work in which all group members can give input; exam questions in which you need to generate main points quickly
Clustering	representing ideas by series of circles and connecting lines, showing their relationships	argumentative essays, which rely heavily on logical connections; good for those who prefer spatial to linear representations

Research

If your essay is research-oriented, you will do most of your research in a library or in a similar environment where you have access to written and electronic material. However, not all research is library research, because not all evidence comes from secondary sources; personal interviews and personal observation can be carried out elsewhere. Also, research may involve determining what you already know about a topic and consolidating this information or adapting it to your particular topic. Research is indispensable to university-level reading, thinking, synthesizing, and writing. For a detailed analysis of research methods, see Chapter 6.

Organization

Students rightly associate organization with an outline. Knowing how to construct a usable outline is a valuable skill that can save time, as referring to an outline in the drafting stage can keep you on track. As an outline gives you a specific plan, it can be reassuring, instilling confidence as you draft your essay. Three kinds of outlines are discussed below: scratch, formal, and graphic. Sample outlines can be found on pages 43 and 45.

Scratch (or Sketch) Outline

A scratch (or sketch) outline represents only your main points, usually just by a word or phrase. The scratch outline provides a rough guideline and gives you flexibility in developing your points. It can be used for a discovery draft, where the purpose and most of the essay's substance are unknown; it may also be perfectly adequate for a short essay; as well, it is helpful for planning an in-class essay, where limited time can make a formal outline impractical.

Graphic Outline

A graphic outline show connections through spatial, rather than linear relationships. A flow chart is a kind of graphic outline that represents complex, multi-layered plans or procedures. For example, it can show the sequence in a scientific experiment or clarify the steps in a procedure, such as the steps in approving a loan or conducting a survey. A graphic outline is especially useful for writers who work best with visual aids. One way to construct a graphic outline is to put your main points in rectangular boxes and use vertical arrows to show the order of the points. Horizontal or diagonal arrows can show sub-points or supporting points.

A graphic outline typically looks more like a working outline than a formal outline does. As needs are redefined, changes can be shown through arrows, parentheses, crossings-out, or additional boxes (or other shapes). You can think of a graphic outline as a set of temporary road signs, aiding and guiding the traffic of your thoughts during construction.

Figure 2.3 shows a graphic outline applied to the five stages of essay writing. Vertical arrows represent the sequence of stages (the main points), while diagonal arrows indicate sub-points—composing choices for writers. The two-pointed arrow shows the interrelationship between questioning and brainstorming discussed previously.

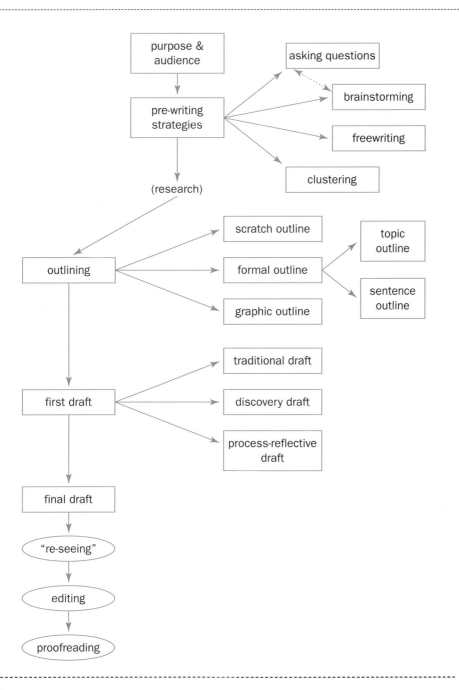

Figure 2.3

The parenthesis around "research" indicates that research may or may not be part of the composing process. Finally, the vertical arrows under "final draft" show that each activity in the oval is performed in the order indicated. The arrows, then, show sequence, while the use of ovals, rather than rectangles, calls attention to the fact that "re-seeing," "editing," and "proofreading" should not be treated as major stages like "pre-writing," "outlining," "first draft," and "final draft." Graphic outlines must be logical but, as mentioned, can be customized to reflect the writer's needs.

Formal Outline

The formal outline includes sub-points as well as main points, so you are able to represent more of your essay's structure. In a formal outline, you can see at a glance how the parts interrelate—which is especially useful in a longer essay and in one employing a complex structure, such as a compare-and-contrast or research essay. A formal outline is also a good choice for a writer who lacks confidence in his or her organizational skills: the writer's points and sub-points can be consulted often during the composing stage to remind him or her of the original plan.

Using an outline effectively is really a matter of timing. You would not put together an outline without having a thesis or a central idea in mind. A formal outline would be less useful if you had not thoroughly researched your topic and decided on your main points. The outline is the skeleton from which the fleshy contours of your essay takes shape. Your audience will notice these contours and will not likely stop to think about the planning and structure that went into the essay; but in any organized and coherent piece of writing, the outline will always be apparent to anyone who looks for it. In this sense, any well-written formal document will contain an *implied outline*. Summarizing (see Chapter 3, page 65) is one way of discovering the implied outline in the work of another writer.

A formal outline usually shows the relationships between the different levels of points (main point, sub-point, sub-sub-point, etc.), using co-ordination and sub-ordination. Co-ordinate (equal) and subordinate (not equal) elements are shown through the numbering system common to formal outlines:

I.
    A.
    B.
        1.
        2.
            a.
            b.
II.
    A., etc.

Points I, II, etc. are co-ordinate or equal, as are sub-points A, B; 1, 2; etc. However, sub-points A and B are subordinate (not equal) to main points I and II, just as 1 and 2 are subordinate to A and B.

The first level (main) points are not indented, but each successive level is indented one or more spaces from the previous level. An outline made up of main and sub-points is a two-level outline; one with main points and two levels of sub-points is a three-level outline. It is not usually necessary to go beyond a three-level outline unless the essay is very long or some points need considerable development.

Although an outline typically proceeds from the general (main) points to the specific (sub-) points, another ordering principle is involved: **emphasis**. You can order your main points and your sub-points according to the strength of the argument presented in each. Order of points is particularly important in an argumentative essay. You can begin with your weakest, or least important point and proceed to the strongest, most important point: the **climax order**. You can use the **inverted climax**, or **dramatic order**, beginning with the strongest point and ending with the weakest.

You can also use a **mixed order** in which you begin with a moderately strong argument and follow with the weakest argument, before concluding with the strongest. The number of main points and the strength of opposing arguments can help you determine which method is best for your topic and your approach to it.

There are two kinds of formal outlines: **topic** outlines and **sentence** outlines. A topic outline shows paragraph topics and their development, usually through just a word or phrase. A sentence outline shows more detail and uses complete sentences in parallel format. You may be asked to submit a formal outline either before or when you submit the final version of your essay. A formal outline can be compared to an engineer's blueprint, revealing how a structure will be put together. For an example of formal sentence outlines, see page 171. An example of a two-level topic outline follows. This outline was used as the basis for a student essay, the final draft of which appears on page 254. Inevitably, the writer made a few changes when she drafted the essay; for example, she changed paragraph order, switching II and III.

Topic Outline for "Arts and the BC Government: The Deepest Cut"
I. Introduction
   A. Public appreciation of the arts
   B. Thesis: budget cuts to the Arts in BC are a bad decision
II. History
   A. History of arts cuts in BC
   B. History of Canadian artists' earnings
III. Facts and Figures: 2010/2011 Budget Cuts
   A. Current status of arts funding
   B. Government's response to budget cut disputes
IV. Economic Factors
   A. Global arts budgets
      1. Comparisons to other provinces
      2. Comparisons to other countries
   B. Studies that support investment in the arts
      1. Revenue
      2. Employment
V. Community
   A. Public response to the cuts
   B. Why Canadian should care
VI. Conclusion
   A. Summary of main points
   B. Future consequences
   C. Emotional appeal

General Guidelines for Outlining

1. Decide on your topic and the main point you want to make about your topic; you can use brainstorming, question/answer, clustering, or freewriting to develop ideas.
2. Divide outlines into introduction, paragraphs for development, and conclusion.

3. Plan for a *minimum* of five paragraphs altogether unless told otherwise. For longer essays, five will probably not be enough.
4. Ensure you have one main idea per paragraph.
5. Divide your main ideas (points) into sub-points (at least two per paragraph) that develop the main idea.
6. Represent the relationship between main ideas and their points of development (or sub-points) graphically by indenting sub-points or, more formally, use a combination of letters and numbers.
7. Ensure that the main points themselves are ordered logically and effectively.

Composing: First Draft

Getting words on paper in sentence and paragraph form is the most challenging stage for most writers. The different approaches to writing the first draft have been discussed in Chapter 1. The traditional rough draft is based on the outline, while the process-reflective draft is really an essay-in-progress that works towards a more finished form.

In the first draft, your focus should be on setting your ideas down. In the case of the essay-in-progress, though, you may sometimes find yourself reordering sentences, providing transitions, or working on other "road-clearing" activities to eliminate obstacles to clear thinking. If you find it difficult to paraphrase (put into your own words) something you have written, your thinking may not be clear about that point and you should consider revising it.

Composing on the Computer

Computer labs packed with students hunched over keyboards are a familiar sight across campuses today. While not all students accessing school computers are working on papers for their courses, many find this an efficient use of spare time between classes. At school or at home, most students today have made computers a large part of their academic life.

Unlike students educated before the advent of the personal computer, students today have options besides paper, pen, and typewriter. Some may prefer to do at least some of their work, such as brainstorming, outlining (especially graphic outlines), and perhaps even composing on paper where everything is before them and mistakes are easy to spot and to fix. Even students who do most of their work on the computer often print a rough draft and make pen or pencil revisions or marginal notes. They may find this a convenient way to experiment with wording or to make suggestions to follow up on. For example, it may be easier to see that one paragraph is shorter than the rest and that the point needs to be researched further.

On the other hand, computers are being increasingly used for all stages of the process from outlining to revision, and almost all university instructors today require a computer-generated final draft. Outlines are easily created by using the function found under View/Outline in Microsoft Word. When you are working on your outline or draft, it's important to manage each stage of the process carefully so you're not confused by the different versions on your computer or by the many edits on one page.

For many, composing on the computer is both fast and efficient. Sentences, paragraphs, or entire sections can be moved to improve coherence. Many writers like to move text they're unsure about to the end of the document where they have access to it later. In addition, you can use different fonts or colours, or include graphics, if your instructor permits them. But all these benefits come with potential pitfalls: most computer users know the pain and frustration when a computer crashes, a file gets lost, or a printer runs out of ink.

Organizing Computer Files

The keys to successful composing on the computer are careful planning and organization. After completing a stage in the process, create a folder and save the latest version (file) of your notes, outline, drafts, etc. to this folder, labelling it for later use. You will appreciate being able to identify the most recent file, especially if your work on a paper is interrupted by other course work and you can't resume work until later. The following file, which includes the course code, project name, version, and date, will be easy to retrieve: *ENGL135_ResearchDraft1_15March*. When you call up the file, use the Save As function after you make your first change to the document (for example, a deletion or addition); then, rename the document—for example, *ENGL135_ResearchDraft2_19March*, and proceed with the draft.

When you create successive versions of a document, you create an electronic "trail." If, for example, in your second draft, you want to refer back to your outline to locate a source that you didn't use in your first draft, or a paragraph that you deleted from the first draft, you can do so. Although most word-processing programs have the auto-save feature, you should save your document every few minutes in case your computer crashes or power is lost. Also, consider backing up files to a mass-storage device, such as a USB flash drive. This will ensure that, even if your hard drive crashes, the document is saved to a permanent location.

Another way to create a trail is to use the Track Changes function (found under the Review tab in Word 2007). This enables you to make multiple edits and keep track of them by having all text—the original and the new text—in one place. If you delete or change material, you will see this material with strike-through marks, along with any replacement text. Using the Track Changes function through many different versions of the same document can be distracting, however. Consider saving different versions if one version becomes hard to follow.

Many word-processing programs also include a Comments function. By highlighting a portion of text and clicking Comment, you can use pop-up boxes to make notes to yourself, such as areas to follow up on. This feature is especially useful in collaborative work where comments by individual group members appear in different colours, with each user identified.

Most universities today have temporary network storage space available for students' university-related work, which you can access from the institution's workstations as well as your personal laptop or home computer. Instructions for accessing and using this space is usually available through your institution's computing help centre or similar site. Avoid frustration by making sure you know the proper channels and procedures for saving and retrieving your documents.

Even if most of your work is done on the computer, it's strongly recommended that you print a final version of your essay and carefully check your hard copy for typos and spelling and grammar errors. Spell-checkers do a good job for obvious spelling errors but will not catch spelling errors that depend on context or usage—for example, they may fail to flag misspellings of *their/there*, *to/too*, or *woman/women* (see Proofreading, Chapter 12, page 435).

Revising: Final Draft

The final draft probably is the most undervalued stage of the writing process. Many student writers think the final draft is the place to apply a few necessary touch-ups. They may have assumed they were supposed to "get it right the first time." However, professional writers almost never do, so why should this be expected of student writers?

Remember that most first and even second drafts are essentially rough efforts to put your thinking into words. To change the rough into final requires a new focus: the written document. When you revise, you want to build on its strengths as well as repair any weaknesses. This process could involve any or all of the following:

Fine tuning
Overview of purpose and audience
Clarifying meaning
Underscoring ideas
Solidifying structure

The acronym FOCUS can serve as an aid to memory. It is important to remember that while there is no "right" order in revision, proofreading should always be the final stage.

Overview of Purpose and Audience

Conduct an overview of purpose and audience. Ask yourself honestly whether the essay fulfills its purpose and whether it speaks to your intended audience. These questions seldom result in major changes, but you may decide you need to adjust your introduction or make minor changes in the body of the essay. For example, you might find a point that seemed relatively unimportant in your outline turned out to be very important. You might then need to rewrite a part of the introduction to be consistent with this new emphasis. On the other hand, you might find that you have over-developed a point that is only slightly related to your thesis. You might then decide to delete a part of a body paragraph. You might also now find that some of your words were too informal for your audience and you need to find new words to replace them.

Clarifying Meaning

Try reading complicated or unclear parts of the essay aloud. Will your audience understand your meaning? These unclear passages should receive your close attention. Wherever a sentence seems awkward or just overly long, consider rephrasing for directness and clarity.

It is hard to be objective when you look back at what you have written, especially if you have just written it. Allotting some time between completing the first draft and revising will help you see your essay more objectively. Also, getting someone else to read over your paper can give you valuable input, especially if he or she can point to unclear passages. Seeing the places where other people have difficulty will highlight those specific places for close attention. The problem may be as small as a word out of place or one that means something different from what you thought. Such seemingly small errors can obscure the meaning of an entire sentence and affect the impact of a paragraph. Work on these unclear or awkward passages.

Underscoring Ideas

In your body paragraphs, your main ideas are introduced and developed. These paragraphs should reinforce your thesis and support your points. Reviewing your body paragraphs might mean going back to your notes, outline, or early drafts to see if you can further support an idea that now strikes you as undeveloped. Or, you might include an example, illustration, or analogy to make an abstract or general point more concrete and understandable. Do not settle for *almost*. Ask yourself if all your points are as strong as they *could* be.

What if you now see that a point is underdeveloped but you do not know how to go about developing it further at this stage? Remember that pre-writing strategies can be used at any point in the process; their main purpose is to generate ideas. Try a brief freewriting session (or whichever method works best for you) to help you expand on the undeveloped point.

Solidifying Structure

In order to solidify your structure, return to your outline. Does your essay's structure reflect your original plans for it? Do you see any weaknesses in the outline you didn't see before? Can the structure of the essay be made more logical or effective? If the essay's structure seems strong, look at each paragraph as an essay in miniature with a topic sentence, full and logical development of the main idea, and a concluding thought. Not all paragraphs need to be constructed this way, but all do need to follow a logical sequence. Is the paragraph unified and coherent as well as adequately developed? Are paragraphs roughly the same length, or are some conspicuously short or long?

When you revise, you want to make your essay strong*er*, clear*er*, and *more* readable. When writers make changes to their drafts it is often because they discover better ways to say what they wanted to say. After all, you know much more about your topic now than you did at any other stage in the composing process.

Fine-Tuning

Working on the final draft could involve some large-scale adjustments, as described above, and it will almost certainly involve some small-scale ones. In the first stage of final drafting, focus on large, global concerns. Ask yourself whether you have addressed the audience and purpose for your essay. The crucial second stage—editing—shifts the focus to the sentence and to individual words. This means ensuring that each sentence is grammatical, that your expression is clear and concise, and that you have used appropriate transitions between sentences. You can also refine your style, for example, asking if there is enough sentence variation. Can you combine sentences to produce more complex units, or can you use different sentence types to make your prose more interesting? Finally, the mechanics of presentation should be double-checked during the editing stage. The third stage is the final review—proofreading for mechanical errors and typos. For a full treatment of efficient writing and editing strategies, as well as proofreading guidelines, see Chapter 12.

Chapter 3

Kinds of Essays

Rhetorical Modes of Discourse

Essays can be classified according to the traditional ways of organizing information for written or verbal communication. These are known as the **rhetorical modes of discourse**: argument, exposition, narration, and description. Because argumentative and expository essays are discussed in detail in later chapters, they will be introduced here only briefly. Narration and description are discussed more fully in Chapter 5, Essay and Paragraph Development, as well as briefly below.

Expository versus Argumentative Essays

Often, expository writing is contrasted with persuasive or argumentative writing. **Exposition** explains; **argument** attempts to persuade your audience to change its mind or to see your point of view. An expository research essay in the sciences doesn't usually state the writer's opinions (if it does, it is considered an argumentative essay); its conclusions result from the use of fact-based sources of information, such as scientific studies. There may be an element of argument involved or implied, but the expository essay, unlike an argumentative essay, takes an objective stance towards issues of argument. The writer of an expository essay may consider different or contrary views on a controversial issue without taking sides; in argument, the writer takes sides.

Although these seem like fundamental differences, the dividing line between exposition and argument is not always a solid one, and many of the same skills and strategies are applicable to both.

Here are some elements that exposition and argument share:

> Both can use factual information and reliable sources to support main points.
> Critical thinking is essential to successful expository and argumentative writing.
> In both, your voice should remain objective and your language neutral.

Table 3.1 lists some ways that exposition differs from argument.

Sample topic for an expository essay:

How the skeletal evolution of the penguin enabled it to adapt to an ocean environment

In this case, the writer will inform and explain.

Sample topic for an expository essay that might use some argument:

What we can do to alleviate the impact of global warming on the emperor penguin habitat on Roosevelt Island

How do you think argument might be involved—either directly or indirectly? What assumption is the writer making about the topic that the reader would be expected to agree with?

Sample topic for an argumentative essay:

Nations must act quickly and collectively to put an end to global warming, which is destroying penguin habitats in the Antarctic sub-continent.

Verbs like *must* and *should* usually signal an argumentative thesis.

Table 3.1 Expository versus Argumentative Writing

In expository writing	In argumentative writing
You use a fact-based thesis (see page 51)	You use a value- or policy-based thesis (see page 51)
You begin with an open mind and see where your exploration takes you	You begin by considering where you stand on an issue and how you can support your position
In your body paragraphs, you look at the available evidence and rely on critical thinking for your conclusion	In your body paragraphs, you draw the reader's attention to supporting evidence but do not ignore or distort contradictory evidence
Research is usually an integral part of expository writing	Research is not always necessary in argumentative writing (although your instructor may ask you to include research to strengthen your argument)
If you are writing on a controversial topic, you do not take sides, though you may explain the position of both sides using objective language	You take a side and try to win your argument fairly, by using logic and using emotion where appropriate

Narration and Description

Recall the excerpt by Alice Munro in Chapter 1 (page 6) in which the writer is telling a story. That is what **narrative** does: it tells about something that has happened or is happening, relating incidents (usually, but not always, chronologically) and revealing character. The narrative pattern is commonly used in fiction and in personal essays; it can be used occasionally in fact-based essays as well.

The Munro excerpt is also descriptive as it gives the reader concrete, sensual information. **Description** mainly evokes the sense of sight, but it can also make use of the other senses. If you use description in an expository essay, it is important to be as concrete as possible and avoid general, abstract words or phrases. Words such as "dank, dirty, and dreary," used in the second excerpt below, help readers see details clearly in their mind.

Narration and description are often used to convey immediacy. The selective use of either in factual writing can lend drama, directness, and impact to your essay. Consider the following as sample openings of fact-based expository essays. In the narrative paragraph below, the writer uses short, simple sentences with repetitive openings to suggest an endless cycle of suffering.

Narration:

Pali is five years old. She lives in sub-Saharan Africa in a small hut made of straw, mud, and cow manure. She lives with her two sisters, 13 and 15, and a brother, 2. She awakes at 2 a.m. Her older sister has returned home from her occupation—selling herself as a prostitute—in order to make enough to feed Pali and her siblings. She is now caring for Pali's brother who has severe diarrhoea. He has AIDS; he was born with it. Both of their parents are dead. Their father died of AIDS two years ago; their mother was beaten to death one year ago after admitting that she, too, had AIDS. Such stories are not uncommon in sub-Saharan Africa today.

—Student writer James Pascoe

The writer of the paragraph below uses many adjectives and strong verbs to create a stereotypical city scene, then reverses the reader's expectations by the question at the end of the paragraph.

Description:

The alleyway is dank, dirty, and dreary. In its ill-lit past, it has harboured many of society's outcasts, providing temporary shelter to the homeless, out-of-the-way encounters for the prostitute and her customer, and, for the junkie, a convenient and anonymous place to shoot up. Tonight, it shrouds only four 16-year-olds, nervously sharing a brown-bagged bottle of vodka. The dinginess of the alley makes it hard to see that these teenagers are dressed in designer jeans and dark hoodies. What are respectable, middle-class young males doing in a place like this?

—Student writer Levi Newnham

The In-Class Essay or Examination Essay

You will likely have to do in-class writing, at least occasionally, during your academic career. Timed activities, typically, are seen as stressful, as you need to demonstrate both your knowledge of a subject and your writing skills. You may be able to use a text, notes, or a dictionary; or it may just be you, your pen, and some paper (or a computer).

In some respects, this kind of situation is artificial. Where but in a college or university classroom are you compelled to sit immobile for up to three hours as you urge your reluctant pen across a piece of paper in pursuit of the "best" answer? At the end of this time you know your answers will be analyzed and a grade assigned—a grade which, possibly, will affect your future. This scenario is a recipe for stress.

Although in-class writing—especially exams—might be considered a necessary evil for many, it serves several practical purposes, demonstrating your ability to think, read, and write under pressure. Although these kinds of essays usually test recall, they also test other important qualities, such as organization and time management, discernment, and adaptability, as well as, possibly, creativity and imagination.

Recall

In-class or examination essays require you to remember information from lectures, textbooks, and discussions; however, other factors may also be crucial. Being familiar with the *terminology* of your discipline is vital. This means that you need to be able to communicate effectively in the language of the discipline. For example, if you are writing an English literature exam, you will need to be able to understand and refer to terms such as *metaphor* or *analogy* that are used to analyze prose, poetry, and drama.

You also need to be aware of *basic principles*, *procedures*, and *methods* stressed throughout the year. If you are asked to write one or more essays, you will need to know the basics of essay format and structure. If you are asked to write a summary of a text, you will need to know how to summarize; if you are asked to write a critical response to an essay, you will need to know how to analyze and think critically.

Nobody can remember everything that was taught, so you should allow enough time for a complete and leisurely review of your notes, highlighted sections of course texts, and instructor comments on term essays and tests. The goal is to distinguish the essential from the less-than-essential and to focus on what you *need* to know. Although it's important to have a grasp of basic facts and details, essays more often test the *application* of facts than simple recall. For example, in English literature, applying key terms like *irony*, *point of view*, or *dramatic structure* may be more important than defining them. Use whatever methods you're comfortable with to commit facts to memory. Writing out important material, reading critical points aloud, making personal associations, using verbal or visual aids, or using self-testing strategies can be effective methods of study and reinforcement.

Organization and Time Management

It is important to spend a few minutes planning your approach to the questions. The advantages are twofold: beginning the in-class assignment with a general plan ensures you will write a complete exam according to the exam instructions; second, planning the exam will give you a sense of control over circumstances that, otherwise, have been determined by someone else. Once you have decided how you will divide up the exam and how much time to spend on the various parts, stick to your plan. It is common to spend too much time on the first question. If you find yourself doing this, jot one or two points in the margin to follow up on, time permitting, and move on to the next question.

Do you begin with the longest question, the shortest one, the hardest or the easiest one, the one worth the most marks or those worth fewer marks? It is probably safest to begin with the question you feel most comfortable with. Writing a confident answer can make you feel at ease when responding to the other questions.

Obviously, you should read the general exam instructions carefully before beginning. Resist the urge to dive right in. Read every word and underline key words or phrases to reinforce their importance and to keep them in mind as you write. Of course, the same applies to each question (see Discernment and Adaptability, below). Remember that writing skills are connected to reading and thinking skills. The student who misreads loses credibility as a writer because he or she has not followed directions. This is especially important when the question makes a distinction of some kind: "answer *three* of the following five questions"; "respond to *either* question one *or* question two." Also pay attention to the verb used to introduce or frame the question; *discuss*, *compare and contrast*, and *explain* give you three different instructions. Dictionaries are useful for interpreting questions and helping you find the right word. Ask your instructor if they are allowed. Once again, make sure your dictionary is suitable for university and that it is up-to-date.

Finally, plan for at least five minutes per question to look over the exam after you have finished writing to ensure that nothing has been omitted and that the marker will be able to follow your ideas. Final checks and careful proofreading are important—as are small additions, such as transitions to connect ideas. Instructors prefer to read a thoughtfully revised and carefully proofed essay, even one that has a couple of deletions and, perhaps, even an arrow showing a re-organization of ideas, to one that is meticulous-looking but unclear in places. Neatness is important, but completeness and accuracy are more so.

Discernment and Adaptability

Once you have done the necessary planning and are focusing on the individual question(s), you need to

1. distinguish what is important from what is less important, and
2. focus on strong, well-chosen points and supporting details, adapting the question, if necessary.

In the question for the Sample Student In-Class Essay (Reading 2) below, the writer has underlined the important parts of the question and has already begun to shape his answer by attempting to rephrase or elaborate on the question. At this stage, he is looking for clues, hints, and suggestions for writing.

Before he can proceed from topic to thesis statement, he has to decide on his approach. The subject of discrimination is very large, and if he does not put some thought into limiting it, he may find himself becoming too vague. One of the common weaknesses of in-class essays is the tendency to generalize, to be too broad. Therefore, first limiting the topic and finding a distinct area to make your own will result in a more manageable essay.

When you limit or refine a general topic, you want to achieve focus and intensity. Ask yourself the following questions to help limit the topic:

> What do you know about the topic?
> Have you or anyone you know had experience with it?
> How can you relate the topic to your own knowledge base or skills?

The main reason for asking such questions is not to enable you to write using the first-person (*I*, *me*, etc.) but to consider *how you can use your experience as an asset*. Finding where you are knowledgeable is the key to refining the topic in order to use your demonstrable strengths.

Every essay benefits from examples and illustrations that give solid support for your points. Examples and illustrations also turn the general and abstract into the concrete and specific. Details are essential. Consider using a pre-writing technique, such as questioning or brainstorming, to generate detail.

The student who wrote the in-class essay in Reading 2 was given 90 minutes, enough time to develop an approach to his topic and a thesis statement, and to prepare a scratch outline. Of course, you may not be given this much time to write an in-class essay and so may not be able to develop each point as thoroughly as this writer has done. Note that this student was very well-prepared and used a dictionary to help with his revisions; as a result, he wrote an excellent essay.

Sample In-class Student Essay

Reading 2

By Jon Zacks

Exam question: Although Western cultures have striven to identify and eradicate many of the more obvious faces of discrimination today, subtle and covert forms of discrimination, particularly racism and sexism, exist in our lives, which can be activated by day-to-day circumstances. Discuss this form of discrimination as you believe it exists today.

Student's response: Although Western cultures have striven to identify and eradicate many of the more obvious faces of discrimination today, subtle and covert forms of discrimination, (**i.e., that are not acknowledged by society**) particularly racism and sexism, exist in our lives, which can be activated by day-to-day circumstances (**this makes them escape everyday notice**). Discuss this form of discrimination (**i.e., hidden subtle forms**) as you believe it exists today (**"believe" suggests that I can use opinion—as long as it is supported by logic, facts, and examples**).

[1]   Although racism is often not expressed overtly today, it is still very much alive. The fact that it often takes subtle forms makes it no less harmful; in fact, it could be considered more harmful. Our society has embraced a dominant ideology, which, while it accepts and tolerates "others," continues to affirm white, middle-class males as the power bloc. This is particularly obvious in the media, in politics, and in academia.

[2]   Discrimination in the media is perhaps the most difficult form to see, and thus to attack. However, an attentive viewer will realize just how pervasive it is. Perhaps the best examples can be found in film and television culture. Dominant cinema is one of the most powerful ideology mechanisms in contemporary North America. In film, no representation is ideologically neutral. Rather, mainstream cinema is laden with the hegemony that is encoded into the images we see. Films such as the *Die Hard* trilogy and *Indiana Jones* are examples of this. In these films, the white male hero saves the world from the disorder caused by the "others." Using binary oppositions, these "others" are set up as inferior and threatening to our comfortable existence.

[3]   Of course, it is not only the fictional in media that serves to promote this dominant ideology. Contemporary news media is rife with hegemonic treatment of public events. Never has this been more evident than after the terrorist attacks in New York City in September 2001. The media immediately set the terrorism up as the work of radical religious fanatics, Arab extremists, and anti-capitalist fundamentalists. By setting the terrorists up as others, retribution is justified. As well, national security is once again promoted by showing that these others live elsewhere and will be contained. The dominant ideology was thus served by "othering" the Islamic Arabs, and glorifying the (mostly white male) heroes at home. While there have been objections to the mistreatment of minorities in the US, the media has conveyed the message that these minorities must be accepted (superficially) because they are now American. The fact that the media is so successful with this hegemony also suggests that this latent racism is present not only in the powers that be but also in society itself.

[4]   In politics in general, this hegemony is promoted. The incidents since September 11 have shown American politicians trying to accommodate minorities while essentially serving the interests of the majority. Indeed, this is typical of politics in general. We can see regular occurrences of governments making changes to the system so that minorities will feel less oppressed. However, these changes are mere concessions. What is becoming obvious is that the entire

system is built on discrimination, power, and patriarchy. This system must make concessions to accommodate the voices of opposition and avoid losing power. It is not until people realize that the system is indeed built on subjection and patriarchy that true changes can be made.

A final example of discrimination can be seen in academia. Areas such as art history, history, and cultural studies provide examples of discrimination within the educational and academic worlds. For example, History in Art has long been viewed as essentially a history of Western Art. Most of us are familiar with the works of great European artists of the Renaissance, etc. While almost everyone knows of the *Mona Lisa*, very few people are aware of any Aboriginal, African, Indian, Chinese, Japanese, Mesoamerican or Native art. Many see the *Mona Lisa* as the greatest painting created. By contrast, we often see Native American art as ugly or primitive. Not until these marginalized art forms are viewed as equal can they stand alongside dominant art. There are many people who would argue that Native arts, for example, have been accepted in Western culture. However, they have not been truly accepted. Rather, we buy Native arts because we see them as novel and feel good about having a Roy Henry Vickers (a Native-American hybrid) beside a Picasso or a Renoir.

[5]

Western culture continues to endorse the discriminatory hegemony that has plagued it since oppositional voices first began demanding acceptance. Our culture has heard these voices, and rather than changing the very structure upon which it has been built, it has made superficial concessions. As media and culture have shown, oppositional voices are tolerated, but they are still marginalized. It is not until we deconstruct our culture and realize that it is founded on discrimination that this discrimination can be eradicated. And, as always, the hardest thing to fight is complacency. If someone is not aware that the system is unjust, there is no reason that he or she would realize that it needs to change.

[6]

Questions to Consider

A. 1. How did the writer limit the topic? Do you think he has an area of expertise or specialization that he was able to use to adapt the topic to capitalize on his knowledge?
   2. Identify the thesis statement and the main points (the latter take the form of topic sentences for the body paragraphs). Why do you think he used the order of points he did?
   3. Some of the writer's statements could be contested. Do you think that, within the constraints of the in-class essay form, the writer has adequately supported his points? How has he done this? Has he failed to do this anywhere?
   4. Returning to the exam question, do you think the writer directly addressed what he was asked to address? Suggest other viable ways that a student writer could respond to the question.
B. Give yourself 90 minutes to write a 500-word response to the question.

Rhetorical Analysis and Critical Response

In-class and out-of-class assignments often require you to analyze an essay you have never seen before. To do so, you need to exercise your active reading skills, beginning with comprehension. A **Rhetorical analysis** should demonstrate effective critical thinking and your ability to analyze such elements as the writer's purpose, audience, and strategies. A **Critical response** may require some of the same skills, but most responses are balanced between analysis of one or more of the essay's main points and your own opinion or observations about an issue raised in the text you have read. Thus, while applying your analytical skills is central to a rhetorical analysis, applying critical thinking skills to your observations and experiences contributes to the success of a critical response.

An analysis or a response is focused mainly or exclusively on the source text itself. In this way, these differ from another kind of common assignment in universities, the research paper, whose main purpose is to investigate how an issue or problem has been dealt with by experts. Although a research paper uses analysis, it also uses **synthesis**; that is, you "put together" your essay by combining your own words and critical thinking skills with the findings of reliable sources to help guide you to a conclusion about the issue or problem.

A fourth type of assignment based on a source text, the **summary**, is also important in many of the writing projects you will undertake at university. You need to understand the main ideas in an article you read before you can use it for different purposes—for example, as part of a research paper. Thus summarizing a complete essay or major section of an essay is an important skill in itself. The "stand-alone" summary, the **précis**, is discussed in Summary: The Précis, page 65.

The four kinds of writing assignments vary in their purpose, audience/style, and typical activities/structure, as shown in Table 3.2; each also highlights specific writing skills. However, selective reading is crucial in each.

Below are some of the objectives and conventions that can help you read texts as well as plan and write rhetorical analyses and critical responses. Remember, though, to pay careful attention to the guidelines your instructor gives you, as they can vary greatly from instructor to instructor and from assignment to assignment. For example, rhetorical analyses may be much longer than the sample here, or you may be asked to compare and contrast two essays on a similar topic. (For general guidelines for reading challenging essays, see Responding Critically and Analytically through Questions in Chapter 1, page 10).

The Rhetorical Analysis
Reading and Other Planning Strategies

> What do you know about the author? Does he or she appear to be an expert in his or her field or otherwise qualified to write on the topic? How is this apparent (if it is)?
> What is the essay's thesis? Can you identify the essay's main points?
> Are the thesis and main points well supported by specific and relevant detail? Do all the sources seem reliable?
> What inferences are readers called on to make? Are they reasonable and valid?
> Does the author manage to create interest in the topic? How is this done? Would other strategies have worked better?
> Is it important that the author makes the issue relevant to the reader? Does he or she appeal to the reader's concerns and values? How?
> How is the essay organized? What kinds of strategies and techniques does the author use to facilitate understanding? Are they effective? Are there other ways that organization or content could have been made clearer?
> What audience was the essay written to? What level of language is used? Is the voice or tone appropriate given the kind of essay and the audience? Does the author make it clear that he or she is using a distinctive voice/tone for a specific purpose?

Table 3.2 Four Common Reading/Writing Assignments

Type of Assignment	Purpose	Audience/Style	Typical Activities/Structure
Rhetorical Analysis	To examine how a text is constructed and assess its importance/ influence; better understand types of texts, their uses, and their effectiveness	Written in formal style/ objective voice for audience knowledgeable about rhetorical practices and strategies	Focused reading; comprehension and critical thinking; analyzing and evaluating used throughout; stating main features of source text in thesis Breaks down text to provide support for thesis; focuses on source text
Critical Response	To explore your views on a topic and share them with others	Readers interested in the topic who might also have opinions/ observations about it; semi-formal style but use of first-person point of view usually acceptable	Critical thinking; expressive/ personal writing; stating your agreement/ disagreement in thesis; moving back and forth between text and your views/ experiences
Research Paper	To answer a question, solve a problem, or test a hypothesis; to better understand the research process and evaluate a source	Written in formal style/ objective voice for audience varying in interest in and knowledge of the topic; may include jargon (specialized terms and concepts)	Scanning potential sources; focused reading for main ideas/findings; synthesizing used throughout; using logical order of points to arrive at conclusion Uses fact-based thesis; evaluates sources; examines issue/ problem/ hypothesis
Précis Summary	To demonstrate comprehension, concision, and ability to establish hierarchy of ideas	Writer must use own words and write clearly so a reader unfamiliar with the original text could understand its essence	Scanning and focused reading; comprehension; rephrasing and using synonyms; inferring main points Follows order of points in source text

> Does the author include any particular stylistic features (analogies, metaphors, imagery, anecdotes, non-standard sentence structure)?
> Does the author use reason effectively? Are there flaws in logic?
> Does the essay appear free of bias? Is the voice objective?
> Has the author acknowledged the other side? How has he or she responded to the opposing viewpoint?
> Does the author make emotional appeals? Are any extreme or deceptive?

Writing Strategies

> In your introduction, name the text and author, and give information concerning the author's background and/or publication information, if relevant.
> Briefly summarize the author's approach and/or thesis.
> Conclude your introduction with a thesis statement that comments on the essay's main features and/or significance; you may also explain what makes the essay effective or ineffective, significant or insignificant, etc. Be specific; simply saying that the essay is effective/ineffective is not enough.

> Provide a brief summary of the essay, giving any background information that would help a reader understand what it is about.

> Use most of your body paragraphs to support your thesis with clear and well-supported points; ensure that each paragraph focuses on one main point and that points are connected appropriately so your analysis is easy to follow.

> Refer directly to the text as often as possible; use direct quotation for major points and summarize or paraphrase less important points (see Methods of Integrating Sources, Chapter 6, page 60).

> Keep your tone (attitude) neutral and your voice and language objective.

For a sample student analysis, see Reading 4, below, Sample Rhetorical Analysis of "White Curtains," on page 63.

The Critical Response

Many of the questions for a rhetorical analysis can also apply to a critical response, so you should read them before looking at the questions below. Although in most university writing assignments you will not use a first-person point of view, in a critical response, you are not just recalling something or expressing a viewpoint: you are using personal experience and observation as a critical thinking tool to explore the implications of a topic. Thus from the first-person point of view you can make valid and relevant claims about the topic.

Reading and Other Planning Strategies

> Are you familiar with the topic? If not, consider freewriting about it or exploring it through background reading or by asking questions of experts or knowledgeable peers.

> Have you had any personal experience with the topic? If not, can you think of a related or similar topic with which you have experience? For example, while not everyone has the ethnic background of student Daniela Dima, who wrote the sample critical response below (Reading 5), many of us have experienced different aspects of Canadian multiculturalism or have informed views on this topic.

> Plan on focusing on no more than two or three points connected to the reading to avoid covering points superficially; ensure that you connect each point to the essay's thesis and/or to other related points—do not discuss them in isolation.

Writing Strategies

> In your introduction, name the text and author, and give relevant information about the author's background and/or publication information.

> Your first sentences could include an overview or generalization about the text or the central issue it raises.

> If your reader is unfamiliar with the text, briefly summarize its main ideas (or plot, if the text is a literary work or a movie) (check with your instructor whether this is necessary).

> At the end of your introduction, include a thesis statement in which you succinctly state *why* you agree or disagree with the author or one of his or her points; simply saying that you agree or disagree is not enough.

> ❭ Do not lose sight of the fact that you reacting to a *text*. Your careful use of opinion, personal experience, or observation should relate directly to points raised by the source text.

> ❭ In some critical responses, you may be required to respond to something other than just the text—for example, to another student's response to the text. In that case, you will need to filter your perspective through that of another reader, considering the validity of both his or her views, and your agreement or disagreement. Sometimes, instructors will help get you started by posing specific questions about the text.

> ❭ In addition to analyzing what is in the essay, you can consider what is *not* in the essay and explain why you think it should have been included.

Remember that the essay you respond to may be written more informally than your critical response to it. For example, the writer may not have cited sources or may have used slang or colloquial language. You should check with your instructor before using an informal style. For an example of a sample student response, see Sample Critical Response to "White Curtains," Reading 5, page 64.

Sample Essay for Rhetorical Analysis and Critical Response

The short essay below is the source text for a sample student rhetorical analysis and a sample student critical response. Note the differences between them; for example, the rhetorical analysis evaluates using objective standards and language; the critical response uses personal experience and observations. Again, your instructor may have different requirements for your assignment.

Sample Professional Essay

Reading 3

White Curtains
by Stephen Henighan
Geist, 2004

During the power cut that paralyzed Ontario in August 2003, the residents of my townhouse condominium complex began talking to each other. It was an event that took me by surprise. Under normal circumstances, human interaction in our development is limited to someone reporting a neighbour to the condominium authorities for putting up curtains of a colour not permitted by regulations. (This means any colour other than white.) But, facing darkened apartments, darkened television screens, darkened stoves—a darkness that even pristine white curtains could not repel—we wandered out to sit on the hard cinder-block steps overlooking the parking lot. In the fading light we traded wild-eyed rumours about the power outage. People who habitually passed each other on the way to the mailbox without stopping to speak progressed from discussions about the power cut to stories of childhoods spent in countries where electrical power was a luxury. I was at the point of succumbing to the illusion that the mood of communal bonding might outlast the blackout when, all at once, conversation stopped. [1]

My neighbour Dragoslav walked out to the patch of grass next to his parking spot carrying a small kerosene stove, a frying pan, some cooking implements and a steak. He sat down in the grass and coaxed [2] a muted roaring from his stove. Crouched in the shadow of his high-fendered 1970s sedan, he began to fry the steak. The gush of kerosene and the sizzle of tenderloin carried across the parking lot. No one spoke. We did not look in Dragoslav's direction and we did not comment on what he was doing. The Dragoslav we knew was a man who drove a second-hand car, lived with a woman who spoke less English than he did and walked his dog when he came home from work. The Dragoslav who was cooking in the grass next to the parking lot was a foreigner: a Yugoslav who had learned survival skills in a grisly war.

[3]   Contrary to custom, no one reported Dragoslav to the condominium authorities. We sat on the steps in the dusk, mute and embarrassed. All of us had arrived in Canada as immigrants (even though some, such as I, had been here since childhood). We were happy to talk about the countries in our pasts, but we were mortified to see one of our neighbours acting as though he were living in the past. It was normal to be an immigrant; it was unacceptable to act like one. As proven members of southern Ontario multicultural society, we knew how to respond to Dragoslav's lurch into antediluvian behaviour: we tolerated him. We neither reproached Dragoslav nor approached him. We kept our distance and turned conversation to other subjects. When darkness fell, we all went back inside to sleep behind our white curtains. Two days later, when our television screens lighted up again, we stopped talking to each other.

[4]   In 1994 Neil Bissoondath published *Selling Illusions: The Cult of Multiculturalism in Canada*. At the time I joined the chorus denouncing Bissoondath's book as a silly right-wing tract. Since moving to southern Ontario, where the idea of multiculturalism is more dominant than in eastern Ontario or Quebec (my earlier Canadian residences), I have modified my view. There is silliness in Bissoondath's book, but there is also wisdom. Bissoondath's analysis of "tolerance," the central tenet of Canadian multiculturalism, is particularly trenchant. Tolerance, Bissoondath writes, "requires not knowledge but wilful ignorance, a purposeful turning away from the accent, the skin colour, the crossed eyes, the large nose . . . . Understanding, in contrast, requires effort, a far more difficult proposition, but may lead to acceptance." To tolerate people is to fail to engage with who they are and how they differ from you. The fact that we define our multiculturalism in terms of tolerance may help to explain why it is so rare for Canadians who live in multicultural neighbourhoods to write multicultural novels.

[5]   According to an overprivileged globetrotter named Pico Iyer, Toronto is the global capital of cost-free multiculturalism. (Iyer bestows an honourable mention on Vancouver; he ignores Montreal.) Last winter, when I was invited to teach a "Topics in Canadian Literature" course for M.A. students, I assigned an article by Iyer in which he claims to find a laudatory shedding of cultural baggage in Canadian novels that disdain Canadian material. I was surprised (though, I'll admit, not disappointed) that my students, whom I had expected to embrace this hymn of praise to the city where most of them had grown up, disliked Iyer's vision of Toronto. They saw his omission of the ethnic retaining walls that channel daily interaction in urban Canada as superficial or naïve. Iyer's article sparked a discussion of the students' experience of cultural barriers: of how little they knew their neighbours; of the scant communication among the various cultural cliques present in student life; of all that Iyer overlooked; of the doctrine of tolerance that makes us turn away from the accent, the skin colour, the man who cooks in the parking lot.

[6]   The writer, of course, faces the danger that dramatizing cultural differences will descend into stereotyping. But the literary writer must take risks: must challenge and extend popular understanding, not just mimic the status quo. By averting their creative gaze from the cultural dissonance that clatters around us in the shopping malls of Mississauga, the ruelles of Montréal-Nord, the street corners of Winnipeg, the leaky condos of New Westminster, writers actually may contribute to prolonging a polite, latent racism. You do not overcome racism by avoiding the issue and changing the subject. Racism dissolves only when you ask the awkward, embarrassing question: do all Chinese women behave that way, do all Yugoslav men cook in parking lots? Until you voice this gut reaction, or, better yet, dramatize it in a scene, you cannot begin to question your own chauvinism. Such uncomfortable yet revealing moments abound in our daily lives. Our fiction could be feasting on them if fewer of our writers chose to sleep behind white curtains.

Sample Student Rhetorical Analysis

Reading 4

Sample Rhetorical Analysis of "White Curtains" by Stephen Henighan
by Doug Stuart

"White Curtains," by Stephen Henighan, is designed to challenge our notion of multiculturalism as Canadians and to expose the optimistic beliefs of the followers of multiculturalism as "superficial or naïve." Henighan does this very effectively by relating a story to his audience before he makes his own arguments. However, his thesis and main points are unsubstantiated, based on nothing more than a few observations and personal experience. Despite a well-structured and somewhat deceptive allure, Henighan's lack of support reduces his credibility as an arguer.   [1]

In his anecdotal introduction concerning the behaviour of condominium residents towards an immigrant neighbour, the author's subject is indirectly revealed. Henighan refers to the "hard cinder-block steps overlooking the parking lot" and the symbolic white curtains on the windows, which may represent the pressure immigrants in Canada experience to meld with white society. Henighan's diction—"darkness," "illusions," "second-hand cars," and "embarrassment"—help illustrate the hardships of the immigrant life in Canada. During a power outage, his neighbour Dragoslav, a Yugoslav immigrant, begins to cook a steak on a kerosene stove in the condominium parking lot, as he no doubt learned to do in similar circumstances during the civil war in his country of origin. Henighan tells us that he and the rest of Dragoslav's neighbours do their best to avoid staring at him. Up to that point, they had accepted him as an ordinary neighbour, often seen walking his dog; suddenly, his action characterized him as a foreigner. Henighan's point is that we accept immigrants when they behave like the majority, but we merely tolerate them, with a distinct feeling of discomfort, when they behave in unfamiliar ways. This storytelling approach suggests that Henighan has journalistic experience, focusing on one individual to illustrate his general concept; also, he is able to utilize this background to add human interest to his article.   [2]

While the tone established in the essay's introduction is very effective in critiquing the views held by proponents of the multicultural ideal, Henighan's inference that the condominium owners refused to look at Dragoslav because they were embarrassed at his "antediluvian behaviour" lacks support. Perhaps the condominium owners didn't "look in Dragoslav's direction . . . [or] comment on what he was doing" because they did not want to disturb the man as he made his dinner. Other reasons could also account for their behaviour, or lack of response. Henighan does not mention discussing the occurrence after the power outage and provides no direct quotations from the condominium owners; therefore, it almost seems as if he made an inference that would illustrate his preconceived views of multiculturalism. Of course, Henighan's inference might have been correct; however, using an unproven assumption as a springboard into the core of an argument is not credible.   [3]

Henighan uses several journalistic techniques in an attempt to convince his readers. First, he keeps his readers' attention by writing concisely without ornamentation. As his pessimistic argument is one that many readers would disagree with, he holds back his thesis until near the end of the essay. In this way, a potential adversary would read the entire essay before realizing Henighan's views. As well, the introduction is very effective: stories attract audience attention and, if subtly slanted, can persuade someone who might not agree with the thesis to think more like the author. The section of the essay that attacks Pico Iyer's views, while impolite, even scathing, is   [4] forceful and supported by references to the views of Toronto students. The very last paragraph, however, is the weakest part of the essay. Instead of presenting a nuanced version of the thesis he has been developing throughout the essay, Henighan voices a plea to writers to "challenge and extend popular understanding" of Canadian racism. His focus on such a plea does not seem to fit in with the logical chain of points developed in this essay. If the topic of the essay had been how writers affect Canadian beliefs, this final paragraph would have been relevant; however, the essay had focused on a different topic. In short, Henighan's essay is ineffectually argued as he either chooses not to or is not able to support his own argument by logical and valid points.

Sample Student Response

Reading 5

Sample Critical Response to "White Curtains" by Stephen Henighan
by Daniela Dima

[1] As a Romanian-born immigrant with Italian and Croatian parents who observes Canadian society from the outside, I found the lack of communication between neighbours in Stephen Henighan's "White Curtains" accurate. People are polite and even helpful at times, but they seldom engage in more than brief, superficial conversations. Many of them hide indifference behind the white curtains of respectful, yet meaningless interaction. However, this is not necessarily a bad thing because politeness is, in fact, a crucial component of civilized behaviour. To some degree, politeness is the norm in Canada, which may be the main reason for the relative lack of racist attitudes here compared to other countries, but whether this norm has managed to erase racism or the "ethnic walls" within people's minds is another story.

[2] The reaction of the condominium residents to Dragoslav cooking steak in the condominium parking lot struck me as unpleasant and difficult to accept, but nonetheless real and relevant to Canadian society. People do seem to turn a blind eye instead of correcting or at least verbally questioning behaviour in order to understand it. I often ask myself on the bus why nobody says anything to the parent whose child is screaming uncontrollably, although everyone is bothered by it. Do they fear breaking the unwritten rule? Is there no polite way to signal that something is wrong?

[3] Every day at my university I see the "ethnic islands" that Henighan refers to. They are more obvious when it comes to some Asian students and less noticeable with Europeans. I had no problem interacting and making friends with my Canadian colleagues. However, I was the one who made the first step, as I thought this is the way it should be. I must try to fit in, not the other way around; otherwise, people would seldom initiate contact with me. Nevertheless, Canadians who interact are genuinely interested in knowing other cultures. Maybe some Asian students stick together because they, too, fear breaking the invisible wall. I remember a student from Taiwan complaining she had a hard time making Canadian friends. She felt as if there was her on one side and the rest of the class on the other.

[4] Undoubtedly, Canada is a successful multicultural society. Although there is often a difference between how people act towards other ethnicities and how they really feel, tolerance does not equal indifference for all Canadians. The fact that Canada is spending so many resources and human effort to promote dialogue in a world torn apart by ethnic, religious, and economic differences, makes its multicultural policies something more than just a thin surface; the fact that

Canadians elect politicians that stand for these policies suggests that as individuals they endorse such unifying policies. In the end, as Henighan may realize, tolerance is just the first step required for peaceful cohabitation. Finally, has complete and shared understanding of "the other" ever existed? "White Curtains" tackles a subtle, yet valid aspect of ethnic tolerance we do not always consider in our relationships with "the other." However, as beautiful and desirable as acceptance with understanding may be, the history of the human race and our knowledge of human nature teach us that it is a goal we may strive for but may never fully reach.

Summary: The Précis

The Value of a Summary

In contrast to a rhetorical analysis or critical response, a summary does not interpret or comment on the source text. When you summarize, you include the main points and discard less important information. A précis is a specific kind of summary. It contains the main ideas of a complete work, or a major section of a work, and can be thought of as a miniaturized version of its longer, more detailed original.

Writing full-length summaries sharpens both your reading and writing skills. As you read a work for summarization, your first concern is understanding its meaning. A summary may be unclear because the writer began summarizing without clearly understanding the source. As always, clear thinking helps produce clear writing. The best way to test the effectiveness of a summary you've written is to have others read it and ask them if they can grasp the essence of the original from your summary. If they cannot do this, you need to work on clarity and precision.

However, a précis summary does more than test comprehension skills. To summarize successfully, you must order the main points by their importance. In other words, you must distinguish the more important ideas from the less important ones. To help you see the relationship between main points and sub-points, it can be useful to make a two-level outline before you begin writing your summary.

Finally, a précis must be written concisely, using simple constructions and plain language. Stress basic sentence elements, like nouns and verbs. If you waste words, your summary will be inefficient, but if you write concisely, you can include more points from the original, making your summary better than one that includes fewer points.

Pointers for Précis Writing

A précis

> is accurate and retains the essence of the original
> includes all the main ideas
> includes only the most important developments of these ideas (a very short précis wouldn't include any developments at all)
> omits examples and illustrations, unless very important
> follows the same order of ideas as the original
> does not add anything to the original
> uses succinct prose
> is in your own words but may retain significant words from the original; *place quotation marks* around any phrases (more than *three* or *four* consecutive words) or sentences that you cite directly

A Summary Caution

Although summary writing is an invaluable skill throughout university and in many jobs, like most skills, its value depends on the purpose of the task before you. In most writing, summarizing should supplement, not replace, analysis. Concisely summarizing the results of outside sources in your research paper will help establish your credibility. A succinct summary of the source text in a rhetorical analysis or a critical response will set the stage for your own analysis. In a literary analysis, the plot summary should be kept to a minimum. You can usually assume that the reader of your analysis is familiar with the work and does not need the kind of content that a summary provides.

> › uses brief transitions where necessary to connect ideas, but does not overuse transitions; avoids wordy phrases—e.g., "the writer goes on to say that . . . "
> › is approximately 20–25 per cent the length of the original, unless you have been told otherwise.

Rhetorical Stance

If the essay you are summarizing aims to persuade its reader, rather than to present factual information, you need to acknowledge its rhetorical purpose. In such a case, you should carefully distinguish between fact and opinion. For example, one professional writer begins an essay thus:

> In the course of two years' research for a book on how we think about pain, I've spoken to neurologists, doctors, artists, therapists of every stripe, as well as psychologists—the frontline workers. And frankly, I preferred the people selling healing magnets to most of the psychologists. They were bad communicators. They couldn't make eye contact. They seemed more interested in certain folds in the brain than in helping human beings cope with pain.
> —Marni Jackson, "Every Breath You Take: A Former Hospital Pain Specialist Puts His Faith in the Powers of Meditation," *Maclean's* (16 August, 1999).

If, in such a case, you did not acknowledge the writer's words as opinion, you would seriously misrepresent her:

> *Misleading*: Psychologists generally communicate badly and are shifty-eyed.

However, you could acknowledge the author's rhetorical purpose this way:

> Marni Jackson preferred "the people selling healing magnets" to the majority of psychologists she spoke to.

In expressing rhetorical purpose, whether through appropriate verbs or phrases like *according to*, you are showing the writer's attitude towards the subject. But do not characterize the writer's stance as negative or make assumptions from what you know about the writer's background that refer to his or her possible bias. Summaries should *represent*, not judge. Therefore, choose your words carefully. The writer may be opinionated; when representing those opinions, you should not express your own opinions.

Be especially careful *not* to

> › become too general or vague; be *specific* but *not detailed*
> › distort the writer's meaning in any way; use *your words* but *the writer's ideas*.

Planning Your Summary

You can summarize using three steps:

1. Read the work for the first time to learn its purpose, thesis, intended audience, rhetorical stance, etc.
2. When you re-read it, note its major points, along with the most important sub-points and/or key examples, and from these points write an outline. You can underline main points on a second reading, but underlining when you read it the first time is not advisable. Look up any words you're unsure about; remember

that accurate representation is essential. Also, make any annotations that might help you clarify the writer's ideas, but because you are not annotating in order to analyze, your annotations should mainly rephrase content.

3. Following your outline closely, write a summary that includes the thesis statement and all the main points. If you are writing a summary of a specific length and have room for more than the main points, pick the most important subpoints or developments of ideas to reach the required word range. When you've completed the first draft, refer to Pointers for Précis Writing on page 65 before writing the final version. Importantly, ensure that the summary is essentially in your own words and that you have put quotation marks around any words or phrases taken directly from the source.

Where to Find Main Ideas

When you write a full-length summary, you can begin by scanning the essay, looking for important ideas in the most likely places: the thesis statement at the end of the introduction and the main ideas in topic sentences of major paragraphs, usually the first sentence of a paragraph. However, not all topic sentences are the first sentences of paragraphs—indeed, not all paragraphs have topic sentences. Furthermore, not every paragraph will contain a major idea, so there will not necessarily be a predictable relation between the original's number of paragraphs and the number of points in your outline.

Sample Précis

In the example below, the main ideas are presented in the form of an outline before which the writer underlined important points and wrote comments in the margin; a summary was then written from the underlined sentences and comments. The summary is approximately 20–25 per cent of the length of the original.

"How Should One Read a Book?" is excerpted from Virginia Woolf, "How Should One Read a Book?" *The Second Common Reader* (New York: Harcourt, 1986), 258–70.

Sample Professional Essay Excerpt

Reading 6

How Should One Read a Book?
by Virginia Woolf

The chapters of a novel—if we consider how to read a novel first—are an attempt to make something as formed and controlled as a building: but words are more impalpable than bricks; reading is a longer and more complicated process than seeing. Perhaps the quickest way to understand the elements of what a novelist is doing is not to read, but to write; to make your own experiment with the dangers and difficulties of words. Recall, then, some event that has left a distinct impression on you—how at the corner of the street, perhaps, you passed two people talking. A tree shook; an electric light danced; the tone of the talk was comic, but also tragic; a whole vision, an entire conception, seemed contained in that moment.

[1]

Woolf begins by drawing an analogy between writing a novel and constructing a building, but then points out the crucial difference.

impalpable = without substance

[2]

But when you attempt to reconstruct it in words, you will find that it breaks into a thousand conflicting impressions. Some must be subdued; others emphasized; in the process you will lose, probably, all grasp upon the emotion itself. Then turn from your blurred and littered pages to the opening pages of some great novelist—Defoe, Jane Austen, Hardy. Now you will be better able to appreciate their mastery. It is not merely that we are in the presence of a different person—Defoe, Jane Austen, or Thomas Hardy—but that we are living in a different world. Here, in Robinson Crusoe, we are trudging a plain high road; one thing happens after another; the fact and the order of the fact are enough. But if the open air and adventure mean everything to Defoe, they mean nothing to Jane Austen. Hers is the drawing room, and people talking, and by the many mirrors of their talk revealing their characters. And if, when we have accustomed ourselves to the drawing room and its reflections, we turn to Hardy, we are once more spun around. The moors are round us and the stars are above our heads. The other side of the mind is now exposed—the dark side that comes upper-most in solitude, not the light side that shows in company. Our relations are not towards people, but towards Nature and destiny. Yet different as these worlds are, each is consistent with itself. The maker of each is careful to observe the laws of his own perspective, and however great a strain they may put upon us they will never confuse us, as lesser writers frequently do, by introducing two dif-ferent kinds of reality into the same book . . . .

[3]

But a glance at the heterogeneous company on the shelf will show you that writers are very seldom "great artists"; far more often a book makes no claim to be a work of art at all. These biog-raphies and autobiographies, for example, lives of great men, of men long dead and forgotten, are we to refuse to read them because they are not "art?" Or shall we read them but in a different way, with a different aim? Shall we read them in the first place to satisfy that curiosity which possesses us sometimes when in the evening we linger in front of a house where the lights are lit and the blinds are not drawn, and each floor of the house shows us a different section of human life in being? Then we are consumed with curiosity about the lives of these people—the servants gossiping, the gentle-men dining, the girl dressing for a party, the old woman at the window with her knitting. Who are they, what are they, what are their names, their occupations, their thoughts, and adventures? Biog-raphies and memoirs answer such questions, light up innumerable such houses; they show us people going about their daily affairs, toiling, failing, succeeding, eating, hating, loving, until they die.

Woolf is saying that only by trying to write (and fail!) can you turn to the "great novelists" and see what they are doing. You then can admire the way they master their medium.

Much of the detail in this paragraph expands on the main point about how great writers create realistic and distinct world. Detail should not be included in a summary.

heterogeneous = varied

Woolf introduces biographies and autobiographies to contrast with the "art" of the novel. Although they do not represent art, according to Woolf, they do have value.

Woolf asks questions rhetorically.

These kinds of books are given as examples, but they are important examples as Woolf discusses them fully.

innumerable = numberless, many

Outline: How Should One Read a Book

—Woolf compares writing a novel to shaping something solid like a building, but bricks are more substantial than words
  —reading is more difficult than grasping a solid object
—to understand the process of novel-writing, Woolf says to write about a mem-ory that affected you powerfully
  —this will lead you to experiment with words and their "dangers"
—when you try to reconstruct your experience, you will probably lose the sense of the emotion you felt at that moment
  —you will have to decide which impressions to keep and which to omit
—having tried your hand at writing from experience, Woolf suggests that you then start reading novels by great writers; you will be more aware of the way they have "mastered" their medium
—each novelist represents a word to discover
  —in each novel, the setting, characters, and conflicts differ markedly
—in spite of differences, each world represents a consistent entity that is true to and consistent with its own reality

—the great writer never confuses the reader by presenting two worlds in the same book, as a lesser writer might do
—most books, such as biographies and autobiographies, don't pretend to be "art"
—we read biographies differently from novels, basically to satisfy our curiosity about the lives the subjects lived
—they answer the questions we ask about lives of "real" people

When you decide on the main points of the source you are summarizing, you can paraphrase them either as you construct an outline or after you have your outline in place. In the example above, most of the paraphrasing was done *during* the outline stage. Also, notice that when drafting the summary, the writer added a few transitions to make the points easier to follow.

Much was omitted from the lengthy second paragraph (see the summarizer's annotation). Paragraph length is not always a reliable clue to importance of ideas; in this instance, the second paragraph contained much descriptive detail and many examples—but few important points. These details are vital to our appreciation of Woolf's writing; in fact, it is partly her evocation of specific writers' "worlds" that supports her main point, but when summarizing a passage, you are not concerned with details. If the reader wanted the details, he or she could read the original. *Your job, as a summarizer, is to represent the gist of the work you are summarizing in clear and concise sentences.*

Summary: How Should One Read a Book

Woolf says a novel is something given shape, like a building, but bricks have more substance than words, and reading is more difficult than grasping a solid object. To understand the novelist's art, Woolf suggests you write about an emotional experience. As you write, you will probably feel the emotion slipping away; however, if you start reading the work of great novelists, you will then appreciate their ability to render unique worlds. The best novelist respects the laws that have created this world, and never baffles the reader by presenting more than one world. In contrast, most books, such as biographies and autobiographies, don't pretend to be "art." We read them differently, to satisfy our curiosity about the lives of real people.

↻ Check answers to select questions

●·●·●●●

EXERCISE 3.1

Summarize Reading 7 below in about 100–110 words; a sample summary appears in Appendix D, page 458. The essay is excerpted from Charles E. Taylor's "Life As We Don't Know It" (Reprinted with permission from 1993 Yearbook of Science and the Future, © 1992 by Encyclopaedia Britannica, Inc. 172–87).

●·●●●●

Sample Professional Essay

Reading 7

Life as We Don't Know It
by Charles E. Taylor

What is alive and what is not? How large is the class of objects that possess life? The answer from humankind's deep past—from its oldest myths and ancient religions and cosmologies—has been that life extends beyond plants and animals and permeates all nature and the universe. "We are part   [1] of the earth and it is part of us. The perfumed flowers are our sisters. The bear, the deer, the great eagle, these are our brothers. The rocky crests, the juices of the meadow, the body heat of the pony, and man, all belong to the same family," said Seattle, chief of the Suquamish. As far as can be determined, most hunter societies have similar beliefs.

[2]   For Western culture, that traditional view began to change with the Greek philosophers, particularly Aristotle. Animate and inanimate came to be viewed as fundamentally different. Over the centuries the separation continued to grow, culminating in the theory of vitalism, which lasted well into the 20th century. During the 17th and 18th centuries, building on the discoveries of Galileo, Newton, and others, Descartes and other philosophers made various attempts to view animals as "nothing but" machines. None of their theories proved satisfactory, however, especially for biologists.

[3]   The trend toward separation has now reversed itself. The distinction between living and nonliving is thoroughly blurred. In fact, scientists are building artificial systems—some of them far removed from the common perception of living organisms—that possess most or all of the properties and behaviours that traditionally have been associated with life. These characteristics include self-assembly and self-reproduction, development and differentiation, adaptation and evolution, and complex ecological interactions. Such scientific efforts are defining a new area of research termed artificial life, or a-life. The field attempts to extract the logical properties from naturally occurring organisms and then to provide them to characteristically nonliving systems, like computer processes or robots. It has also begun to seek signs of life in such unlikely places as the abstract realm of ideas and theories.

[4]   A variety of human-made systems now being studied have properties that one commonly attributes to living systems. Investigating these systems is making it possible to understand life in the broader sense, that is, life-as-it-can-be, and through this effort to better appreciate life-as-it-is. The consequences of research in artificial life are likely to be profound: they will challenge, perhaps fundamentally alter, our view of humankind's place in nature; they will dramatically enhance our ability to control our environment; and they may even endow other systems with the ability to control us.

EXERCISE 3.2

Take a section from one of the readings in this textbook, such as "Headed for newt status?," from "Embrace the Mediocrity Principle," (Reading 1, page 20) or "Recommendations for evaluating the suitability of Olympic bids," from "'No Olympics on stolen native land'" (Reading 19, page 257) and write a summary of it approximately 20 per cent of the length of the original.

Essay and Paragraph Essentials

Essay and Paragraph Structure

Like an essay itself, a paragraph must be organized to serve specific functions:

> ⟩ to introduce an important point
> ⟩ to develop that point
> ⟩ to convey both the important point and its development clearly to the reader
> ⟩ to provide a smooth and logical connection to what precedes and follows the paragraph (introductory and concluding paragraphs are discussed as special cases, below).

A paragraph and an essay both have a beginning, middle, and end. The beginning announces what is to follow, usually in the **topic sentence** (paragraph) or the *thesis statement* (essay). Without a clear topic sentence, the paragraph will lack force and unity. The middle of the paragraph develops the main point, while the ending provides a satisfying conclusion. The concluding sentence may act as a *wrap* by summarizing the main idea in the paragraph, in this way functioning much like the conclusion of an essay.

The difference between an essay and a paragraph is, of course, that the essay ends with the conclusion. A successfully constructed paragraph not only provides a satisfying ending but also leads the reader into the following paragraph. This is often done through a transition—a word or phrase that provides a logical connection.

Topic Sentence

A topic sentence introduces the main idea in the paragraph. Therefore, the topic sentence is usually the most general sentence, while the other sentences in the paragraph

A Closer Look

●●●●●

At the paragraph–essay level, the topic sentence is comparable to the thesis statement in that both are generalizations that apply to the paragraph and the essay, respectively. At the paragraph–sentence level, the topic sentence functions similarly to an independent clause: the topic sentence expresses the main idea in the paragraph just as the independent clause contains the main idea in the sentence; typically, the other sentences in the paragraph illustrate or expand on the main idea by giving more detail, just as dependent clauses and phrases give more detail within the sentence. The interconnectedness of essay, paragraph, and sentence is thus underscored through these kinds of coordinate (equal) and subordinate (unequal or dependent) relationships.

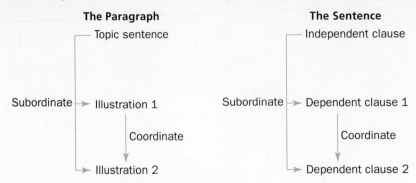

Figure 4.1

illustrate or expand on the main idea in some way. The topic sentence is usually the first sentence in the paragraph for the same reason that the thesis statement usually occurs in the introduction (first paragraph) of the essay: it provides a logical starting point and makes the paragraph easy to follow.

In each set of sentences, choose which one would make the best topic sentence for the paragraph. Remember that the topic sentence states the main (most general) point.

1. Essay Topic: The 100-Mile Diet
    a) In small communities, stores often use local products to produce their own wares.
    b) Eating locally is one way to sustain the local economy and farming community.
    c) For example, on Vancouver Island, most grocery stores sell dairy products from Island Farms and other regional dairies.

2. Essay Topic: Cellphones
    a) Recent studies have found that the brain cannot handle all the multi-tasking we try to do.
    b) We interrupt our meals, leave conversations, and forget to concentrate on our driving in order to answer our cellphones.
    c) Cellphones dominate the lives of many people in society today.

3. Essay Topic: Physical Education Classes
    a) Physical education classes teach skills and knowledge not usually stressed in other classes.
    b) Skills like physical coordination and teamwork are developed in PE classes.
    c) PE classes allow more opportunities for social interaction, which is an essential skill in building future relationships and careers.

EXERCISE 4.1

↻ Check answers to select questions

Paragraph Wrap as Conclusion

Using a **paragraph wrap** is a satisfying way to conclude a paragraph, as it reminds the reader what the paragraph was about. However, the wrap doesn't just repeat the topic sentence; it reinforces its importance using different words. In the following paragraph, student writer Jordan Van Horne successfully wraps the main idea, which is introduced in the first (topic) sentence:

> If speed limits were abolished on highways, the necessity for law enforcement officers to patrol the highway for speeders would be curtailed. As a result, police chiefs might have more officers to assign to special community projects, such as MADD or drug awareness projects in elementary schools. These officers could spend their time on a variety of social and community projects that would benefit a large number of youths precisely at the time when they need this guidance. In addition, more officers could be allotted to other important areas that are typically understaffed today, such as surveillance and patrol duty to prevent drug smuggling. Surely the presence of police in the community or their dedication to large-scale projects such as drug-smuggling would be more beneficial to public safety than having them patrol the highways.

A wrap is especially effective in a longer paragraph (five to eight sentences) where the reader might lose track of the main idea.

Connecting Paragraphs by Using a Transition

Whether or not the paragraph contains a wrap, it's important that the reader can connect it to what follows. A well-constructed paragraph not only states the main point, develops it, and reinforces it, but also leads the reader smoothly to the next point (paragraph), like a well-oiled hinge connecting two solid objects. This is can be done through a transition: a word, phrase, or clause that links ideas. Theoretically, a transition can occur at the end of one paragraph as a form of a wrap or at the beginning of the next paragraph as part of the topic sentence.

The question to ask yourself is whether the reader can follow your train of thought from one paragraph to the next. Most readers expect a new paragraph to introduce a new topic. However, the precise relationship between the two topics may not always be clear. If not, consider using a transition to clarify it. In the following excerpt from a student essay, Marissa Miles began her new paragraph with a dependent clause transition (underlined) before introducing the topic for the paragraph (no underlining). From the transition, you can see that the previous paragraph focused on the fostering of independence through home schooling.

> <u>Although the qualities of independence and self-motivation are important in a home-schooled education</u>, its flexibility enables the child to learn at his or her own pace, matching progress to the child's natural learning processes.

The writer of the following paragraph has combined an indirect reference to the preceding paragraph with the topic sentence of the current one:

> Another crucial function of genetic engineering is its application to the pharmaceutical industry.
> —Student writer Neil Weatherall

In general, avoid the kinds of transitions used to connect sentences *within* paragraphs, such as *consequently*, *for example*, *moreover*, and similar words and phrases (see Transitions between Sentences, page 78 below). They are not usually strong enough to connect main ideas from one paragraph to the next. Using transitions to connect ideas within a paragraph is discussed below under Coherence.

Good paragraphs are unified, coherent, and well-developed. Unity and coherence are discussed below. Because there are many different ways that main points can be developed in a paragraph or throughout an essay, paragraph development is discussed separately in Chapter 5.

Unity

As mentioned, each paragraph should focus on *one* central idea announced in the *topic sentence*. Although it's usually best to place your topic sentence at the beginning, *the topic sentence anchors thought in the paragraph*, so this anchoring *could* occur in the beginning, middle, or end. In a unified paragraph, all sentences in the paragraph relate to the main idea, wherever that idea occurs.

Paragraphing, however, is not a mechanical process. Although the principle of one idea per paragraph is sound and logical, it may sometimes be difficult to tell where one idea ends and the next one begins. This is especially true in a rough draft where you are trying to get your ideas down and may not always be attentive to paragraph structure. Therefore, when you revise your essay, an important question to ask is whether each paragraph contains one main idea.

Also, in revising, you may see that one paragraph is much longer than the others. In such cases, you can determine a logical place to divide the paragraph into two smaller paragraphs. In the case of short paragraphs, you should consider combining them, as short paragraphs may come across as simplistic and underdeveloped. When combining short paragraphs ensure that logical transitions are used to connect sentences.

Paragraph Exercises: Unity

The lengthy paragraph below needs to be broken up into several smaller unified paragraphs. Determine the natural paragraph breaks and mark where the new paragraphs should start. Remember to avoid a succession of very short paragraphs; occasionally, short paragraphs may be acceptable, but too many of them make for choppy and disconnected writing.

> In an argumentative essay, defining something is often the first stage of an argument in which you go on to develop your thesis statement through means other than definition. On the other hand, a definition essay can expand and elaborate on a subject, using a variety of organizational methods to do so. Definition often provides a necessary starting point for an argument. The success you have in getting your reader to agree with your definition will help establish your credibility as a writer and, in this way, strengthen your argument. Defining something also enables you to set the terms on which you want your argument to rest: successful definition enables you to take control of a potentially contentious, controversial, or abstract topic. Although definition in an argumentative essay can be effective, it is often an essential part of an expository essay. An essay in the natural sciences and social sciences often begins by defining terms that the writer will employ throughout the essay. It may be crucial for the writer to establish the sense or connotation of one or more terms that have been subject to a variety of definitions in different studies in the writer's discipline. An academic text—above all, an introductory textbook—often includes a glossary or index of common terms that is designed to make it easier to apply terms correctly. It is important to provide an accurate definition in your paper, as definitions often change over time and according to place, as well as according to cultural, national, social, and other variables. For example, the way you would define privacy today would likely be different from the way it would have been defined 25 years ago, due partly to technologies that have made it easier for others to access personal information.

When you have decided on logical paragraphing, look at the way the paragraph was divided in this text (the revised paragraphs are in Chapter 5, page 112).

In the following paragraphs, one sentence is off-topic, affecting the paragraph's unity. Identify the sentence that doesn't belong and explain why it is off-topic.

1. The requirement to display the N (new driver) sign on your vehicle is a reasonable one. It allows other drivers to recognize that the driver may be inexperienced. These drivers may drive more cautiously around the novice driver. It also alerts law

EXERCISE 4.2

↻ Check answers to select questions

enforcement officials to the fact that the driver is learning how to cope in traffic. However, officers have been known to pull over an N driver even if they have no legitimate reason to do so. Since alcohol consumption is often high in teenagers, the N sign in the rear window enables police to monitor for drunk driving more effectively. The requirement is therefore beneficial for both other drivers and the police.

2. The ability to concentrate during classes can easily be affected by a student's lack of activity. Most students find it difficult to sit around for six hours each day with only a lunch break, during which they might also do nothing but sit and eat. Exercise gives students relief from simply passively taking in information hour after hour. It especially helps children with high energy levels who find it hard to sit still. In addition, exercise is a solution to the ever-growing problem of obesity. By breaking up the day by at least one compulsory period of activity, students will be able to retain more information and perform better academically.

Coherence

It is often easy to identify a paragraph that contains more than one main idea or an off-topic sentence, but identifying a paragraph that lacks coherence may be more difficult. The word *cohere* means "stick together." Someone who is incoherent doesn't make sense; his or her words or ideas don't stick together. By contrast, someone who is coherent is easy to follow. It is the same with a paragraph: one that lacks coherence is hard to follow. The words and the ideas might be jumbled or disconnected. They do not stick in the reader's mind.

Here is the opening of an essay about the need for a nutritional diet. Although the ideas are quite simple, the passage isn't easy to follow. Try to determine why this is the case.

> Most children throughout Canada depend on their parents to provide them with the proper nutrients each day. There are many contributing factors that make this ideal unachievable, and this lack can cause children to cultivate a serious disease known as obesity.

Now consider a rewritten version of this passage. Do you find it easier to follow? Why?

> Most Canadian children depend on their parents for adequate daily nutrition. However, many factors can prevent them from achieving their nutritional ideal, which may result in obesity, a serious medical disorder.

Part of the problem with the original passage lies in the words themselves: "cultivate" and "disease" are not the best words in this context. However, what also helps the words and ideas stick together is the careful use of repetition and transitions. In the rewritten version, the writer has replaced "this ideal" with "their nutritional ideal," linking "ideal" to "nutrition" in the first sentence. By adding the transition "however" and replacing "and" by "which," the relationship between the ideas becomes clearer.

> Most Canadian children depend on their parents for adequate daily *nutrition*. *However*, many factors can prevent them from achieving *their nutritional ideal*, *which* may result in obesity, a serious medical disorder.

Consider in the following two examples of how a professional writer and a student writer achieve coherence through balanced structures. The professional writer is speaking about the plight of today's teachers; she repeats words and phrases, and uses rhythmical patterns and figures of speech to make her point more effective. The student writer evokes the new awareness of his friend during a camping trip after the death of his friend's grandfather; coherence here is achieved largely through repetition, rhythm, and balanced structures.

> . . . literary study today is a profession simultaneously expanding intellectually and contracting economically like some Spenserian snake. So many books, so little time; so many conferences, so few jobs. The list of articles and books to master gets longer every year, and the gap between the academic star—the frequent flyer—and the academic drudge—the freeway flyer—gets wider. Those who do not have jobs feel angry; those who do feel guilty.
> —Elaine Showalter, *Teaching Literature*

> On previous trips, we had noticed the smell of nature when we woke and filled our lungs with fresh air, but this time he noticed the smell of the water and of the rain-sprinkled flowers. We had often looked at the stars on a clear night, but this time he spoke of the deep darkness of the sky; we had always seen the ground we stepped on, but this time he saw the footsteps left behind us.
> —Student writer Walter Jordan

You can use specific methods to ensure your paragraphs are coherent, or easy to follow.

Word Choice

Probably the main cause of incoherence is the fundamental problem of choosing the word that best conveys your meaning. In rough drafts, you may write the first word that comes to mind without even considering whether it is the best or most precise word. If left uncorrected in the final version, your readers may struggle to grasp its meaning and fail to understand the sentence, or at least part of it. Reader-based prose focuses on using the words that best convey your thoughts. Consider the following passage in which the writer is discussing the complex phenomenon of change. What word should the writer have used instead of the italicized word?

> Change is a natural process resulting from interconnected systems in the biosphere, hydrosphere, lithosphere, and atmosphere. However, there is evidence today that human activity, including consumption and urbanization, is *exasperating* such changes.

When you consider what words to use, remember that it is not always a case of the right word versus the wrong word. Often, more than one word can convey your intended meaning, so it may be a question of choosing the best word for the given context. Whenever you use a word that is not part of your everyday vocabulary, you should confirm its meaning by looking it up in a dictionary. For written assignments, it's helpful to exchange your writing with someone else and pay attention to any passages that strike your reader as unclear.

Understanding the meaning of words is important for both reading and writing. If you do not understand a word when you are reading, this can affect *your understanding* of the essay. As mentioned, if you do not understand the meaning of a word when writing, this can affect *your reader's understanding* of your essay. Strategies for learning word meanings are discussed in Word Meanings in Chapter 1, page 23; see also Chapter 12, Working toward Precision: Wise Word Choices, page 417. Common usage errors are listed in Common Words That Confuse, in Chapter 12, page 422.

Patterns of Development

Coherent paragraphs often follow a distinct pattern. Paragraphs can be given a spatial, chronological, cause and effect, division, compare and contrast, or other pattern. Developmental patterns are discussed in detail in Chapter 5.

Logical Sentence Order

Recall that your writing is closely connected to your thinking and that you need to make your thought process clear to your reader. If one idea does not logically proceed from the previous one, then the paragraph will not be coherent. Similarly, there may be one or more gaps in a paragraph that need to be filled in, perhaps by inserting a sentence.

Repetition and Synonyms

Repeating key phrases can help the reader follow the main idea in the paragraph. Using synonyms (words that mean the same thing as, and can therefore replace, other words) can also help you reinforce key words without sounding repetitious; ensure that the replacement word does mean the same thing as the word it replaces. Experienced writers often consider the rhythm of the sentence, placing key words at strategic points in the paragraph. Many writers number their main points in order to make the sequence of ideas easy to follow.

Parallel Structures

Experienced writers also use parallel and/or balanced structures to achieve coherence. One of the reasons why so many readers can remember the beginnings and endings of Charles Dickens's novels is that Dickens often employed balanced structures: "It was the best of times; it was the worst of times" (*A Tale of Two Cities*). See The Parallelism Principle, Chapter 11, page 392, for more information about grammatical parallelism.

Transitions between Sentences

Transitional words and phrases guide the reader from one sentence to the next, signalling the exact relationship between them. Often, just adding the right transitional words gives the paragraph the coherence that is needed. However, if you fail to use a transition to connect two ideas, the reader may find it hard to follow the paragraph's development. Some of the most useful transitions are listed below.

Note how the word *However* in the paragraph above tells the reader that the idea in the second sentence contrasts with the idea in the first one. *However* is a transition of contrast.

Types of Transitions

> **Limit or concession:** admittedly, although, it is true that, naturally, of course, though
> **Cause and effect:** accordingly, as a result, because, consequently, for this reason, if, otherwise, since, so, then, therefore, thus

> **Illustration**: after all, even, for example, for instance, indeed, in fact, in other words, of course, specifically, such as
> **Emphasis**: above all, assuredly, certainly, especially, indeed, in effect, in fact, particularly, that is, then, undoubtedly
> **Sequence and addition**: after, again, also, and, and then, as well, besides, eventually, finally, first . . . second . . . third, furthermore, in addition, likewise, next, moreover, similarly, too, while
> **Contrast or qualification**: after all, although, but, by contrast, conversely, despite, even so, however, in spite of, instead, nevertheless, nonetheless, on the contrary, on the one hand . . . on the other hand, otherwise, rather (than), regardless, still, though, whereas, while, yet
> **Summary or conclusion**: in conclusion, in effect, in short, in sum, in summary, so, that is, thus

When you use transitional words or phrases to connect one idea to the next, be careful to punctuate correctly. In some cases, a comma may be correct, but in many other instances, you should begin a new sentence or use a semicolon before the transitional word or phrase. See Chapter 11 for punctuation rules governing transitional words and phrases. Furthermore, do not begin a sentence with the transitions *and*, *but*, *or*, *so*, or *yet*. They should be used to connect two main ideas *within* a sentence.

In spite of their helpfulness, transitional words and phrases can be overused. Too many can clutter your writing. In addition, try to avoid wordy transitions as they, too, produce clutter (examples include *due to the fact that*, *in spite of the fact that*, *finally in conclusion*, *first and foremost*, *in the final analysis*). See Chapter 12, Rabbit Words, page 407, for further information.

A transitional word or phrase, by itself, does not provide a link in thought—it cannot be a *substitute* for that link; it can only assist the reader to move from one idea to the next. As mentioned above under Logical Sentence Order, a writer needs to be careful that there are no gaps in thought and that he or she has written with the reader in mind. The reader needs to be able to follow the writer's logic every step of the way. In the following passage, the writer has left something out, and no transitional word alone could bridge the gap:

> Society relies on an unbiased newscast in order to gain a true perspective on current events. Front-line employees are entering the TV news field underage and under-educated, thus often producing ill-informed reporting.

The writer has quickly moved from a generalization about the need for "unbiased" reporting to an example of one of the causes of "ill-informed reporting" but has not linked the generalization and the example. One logical link would be that newscasts today are sometimes biased or ill-informed. Then the writer can proceed to give examples of or solutions to this problem. As it is, the problem has not been stated clearly.

> Society relies on an unbiased newscast in order to gain a true perspective on current events. *However, newscasts today are sometimes biased or ill-informed. This may be because* front-line employees are entering the TV news field underage and under-educated, thus often producing ill-informed reporting.

EXERCISE 4.3

Paragraph Exercise: Coherence

The following passage contains a gap; provide a logical link to make it coherent.

The surprise attack on Pearl Harbor forced the US to be more aggressive in world politics. This interventionist policy has recently evolved into a policy of pre-emptive strikes on those perceived as a threat to US security.

In the following paragraphs, student writer Grace Chau uses transitional words and phrases, repetition, and balanced constructions—all of which serve to make the paragraphs more coherent. If these words and phrases were taken away, much of the paragraphs would be unclear. Transitions are in boldface type, repetitions are in italic, and balanced constructions are underlined.

In contrast to allopathy, in Traditional Chinese Medicine (TCM), organs are viewed as "networks"—**that is**, functional physiological and psychological domains—**rather than** discrete anatomical structures. All our organs are related; **in fact**, our body, our behaviour, and the environment we are in are also interconnected. **In other words**, TCM focuses more on the *context* where the disease exists than on the disease itself. **Such emphasis** on *context* implies that the way people get sick and can be treated are highly personalized.

People with different *symptoms* may have the same underlying problem, requiring similar treatments; yet people with the same *symptom* may need completely different remedies. While we are equally endowed with our basic parts, our lungs, heart, kidneys, liver, and so on, our way of coordinating these parts is individualized. **For example**, if arthritis is due to an invasion of "heat" (inflammation), it is different from the same condition with a different cause—**for example**, "cold" (reduced circulation) or "dampness" (accumulation of fluids). **In the first case**, practitioners would administer cooling herbs; **in the others**, warming or diuretic herbs would be used.

A unified paragraph refers to one central idea; in a coherent paragraph, one sentence leads logically to the next sentence. Figure 4.2 shows two diagrammatic representations of unity and coherence in which the sentences are represented by arrows.

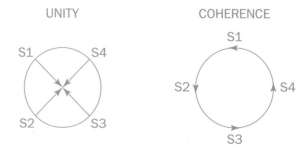

Figure 4.2

Paragraph Exercises: Coherence

I. Coherence through word choice

In the sentences below, replace the italicized words with words that better convey the intended meaning.

1. Today's prospective car buyers should consider buying a hybrid electric vehicle as the benefits clearly outweigh the *detriments*.
2. The *volume* of competition and training that goes into golf requires a high level of physical fitness.
3. The recent *expansiveness* of the Internet frees shy adolescents from the constraints of a face-to-face relationship.
4. The narrow *physique* of glacial fjords protects them from the effects of high waves and storm damage.
5. The safest way to protect the principles of democracy is to keep the division between church and state *tangible*.
6. Sports today have become more competitive, and parents may *enlist* their children in competitive sports at too young an age.
7. One obvious *factor in* anorexia is the stressful environment many youths grow up in.
8. Adopting a vegetarian lifestyle would no doubt have a major *impact towards* ending world hunger.
9. The fashion industry today *distributes* the idea that young women should conform to one *implausible* ideal.
10. To *assure* that teenagers do not drive drunk, the drinking age should be raised to 19, when teens are mature enough to deal *respectably* with alcohol.

II. Coherence through paragraph development

You can organize paragraphs in different ways: by chronology (time order), by spatial order (to describe a person, object, or scene), by comparing and contrasting, by division (dividing a general category into specific ones), and other methods (see Chapter 5).

1. How are the ideas organized in these paragraphs?
2. Besides the main organizational method(s), find other ways that the writer has achieved coherence.
3. What do you think the writer might have written about in the third paragraph?

They came over the land bridge connecting Asia with Alaska, those first men of the Western Hemisphere. The date was between 20,000 and 30,000 years ago. They were hunters, dressed in the skins of the animals they hunted. Their weapons were stone-tipped spears. All this was long before Homer, before the dynasties of Egypt, before Sumer and the Land of the Two Rivers, and, of course, long before the Christian Bible was written. At that time, the glaciers that covered Canada and parts of the northeastern United States during the last ice age were melting. They melted first along river valleys, which turned into great misty, fog-haunted corridors between receding walls of ice.

The hunters roamed south along those corridors, pursuing animals for food and clothing. They died eventually, as all people do, and their children came after them in the long stammering repetition of humanity everywhere. The animals they hunted were principally caribou, bear, and mammoth—the latter long since extinct in North America. Camps of those early men have been discovered recently. They are the ghostly forbears of modern Indians and Eskimos.

—Al Purdy, "Aklavik on the Mackenzie River"

EXERCISE 4.4

↻ Check answers to select questions

III. Coherence through sentence order

Combine the sentences below in the most logical order to form a coherent paragraph; one sentence is not relevant to the topic of this paragraph and should be discarded. Supply any necessary links between one sentence and the next. More than one order may be possible. Be prepared to justify the particular order you used to achieve coherence.

1. The disaster was caused by several safety procedures not being followed.
2. Nuclear energy power plants, although very potent and about 50 to 80 times more efficient than coal-burning plants, produce wastes that are more hazardous than those of coal-burning plants.
3. The explosion at Chernobyl not only contaminated the immediate surroundings but also contaminated areas several hundred miles away.
4. The effects of radioactive wastes are long-lasting and may affect the environment for thousands of years.
5. The disaster at the Chernobyl power plant in the Ukraine occurred in the summer of 1986.
6. A lack of respect for potential disaster led to one of the biggest human-made disasters our planet has known.
7. Nuclear energy will be able to meet the energy requirements of our society.
8. This contamination was due to the nuclear fallout.
9. Because of this disaster, a large area will no longer be habitable to human life for thousands of years.
10. Radioactive wastes are very damaging to the environment.
11. As is the case with everything on this planet, with great power comes an even greater responsibility.

IV. Coherence through transitions

Using transitions can help sentences cohere, or stick together. The following paragraph lacks transitions. Provide logical connections between the sentences by choosing the appropriate transitions from the list below, filling in the blanks. In part b, one transition has been given to you.

1. _____ many educators and parents have praised the Harry Potter series, some Christian parents have called for a ban on the books in their schools and libraries. Some churches have even gone as far as burning the books, citing biblical injunctions against witchcraft, _____ those in Exodus and Leviticus. _____, some Christians believe the books are compatible with Christianity, _____, that they embody basic Christian beliefs.
   although
   however
   indeed
   such as
2. Massive energy consumption is having a negative impact on the planet. _____, in the summer of 2006, western Europe experienced some of the hottest weather on record. _Moreover_, this temperature increase is not an isolated occurrence. _____, almost every credible scientist today believes that the earth is experiencing climate change due to the emissions of greenhouse gases from cars and coal-burning power plants. Ninety per cent of the energy used in the US comes from fossil fuels such as oil, coal, and natural gas (Borowitz 43), _____ problems arise

from other sources, too. _____, nuclear power plants leave radioactive by-products, making storage difficult. _____, dams are not much better as nearby populations must be relocated, and the surrounding habitat is destroyed.

~~moreover~~

but

for example

in fact

unfortunately

for example

V. Coherence through use of repetition, parallel structures, and transitions

1. Read the paragraph below to determine how the writer has used transitions and repetition to achieve coherence. Underline transitions and repetitive devices. Identify the topic sentence. One of the ways to achieve coherence is to number your points, though unnecessary numbering can add to clutter. Do you think that it was a good choice for the writer of the passage below to number his points? If so, why?

Critics of the World Trade Organization argue that its approach to globalization causes more harm than good because it undermines democracy. The WTO is undemocratic in several respects. First, ambassadors from member nations are appointed, not elected. Second, the coalition known as the "Quad," comprising the European Union, the United States, Japan, and Canada, holds almost all the real power. In theory, at least, such decisions as new membership, rule changes, and rule interpretations of WTO rules should be voted for with a three-quarters majority. In practice, however, the "Quad" determines the WTO agenda. Third, WTO trade talks are held in secret to avoid public criticism and scrutiny. Furthermore, an organization that is not elected controls trade so effectively that it possesses the power to supersede the power of elected communities, states, and even nations on any issue, however ambiguous, related to trade.
—Student writer Tao Eastham

2. Read the paragraph below to determine how the writer has used transitions and repetition to achieve coherence. Underline transitions and repetitive devices. Identify the topic sentence. This paragraph is an introductory paragraph to a chapter of a book. What topic do you think will be developed in the next paragraph? Why?

The news media's power to trivialize anything that comes to their attention is almost magical. News service advertisements talk about providing a "window on the world" or a report on "history in the making." But the nightly television newscast and the daily newspaper fall far short of these ideals. Instead, we get a fast-paced smorgasbord of unconnected and disembodied news stories where meaning and context are lost in the rapid-fire delivery of colourful prose and dramatic pictures. As a result, much of what passes for news is instead isolated, unconnected, and almost meaningless bits of information—in effect, the news is trivialized. This trivialization operates at both the structural level of news gathering and dissemination, and at the level of individual news stories. We have termed this style "the trivialization effect."
—adapted from R.A. Rutland, *The Newsmongers*.

Specialized Paragraphs: Introduction and Conclusion

The Introduction

Almost everything you read begins with an introduction. Even if it is not called the "introduction," it acts as one by previewing what follows. It presents the main idea and, probably, the organization pattern of the document—whether it is a book, an article in a scholarly journal, a class essay, a sales proposal, or a résumé. The introductions students are asked to write consist of one or more paragraphs that fulfill specific functions, and that should, like all paragraphs, be unified, coherent, and well-developed.

It's useful to compare the preparations for writing the essay's introduction to the care you would take when meeting someone for the first time. Just as there are people you don't notice because they don't present themselves well, or whom you notice for the wrong reasons, so there are introductory paragraphs that aren't noticed or are noticed for the wrong reasons. As the introduction is one of the most important parts of your essay, it is worth spending time crafting it to meet the requirements discussed below. It will draw the reader into the essay and provide necessary information, satisfying the expectations of your audience.

Catching the Reader's Interest: Logical, Dramatic, and Mixed Approaches

The introduction should create reader interest while informing the reader of the essay's topic. Although most of your essay's "substance"—your main points and subpoints, the supporting details—will be placed in the middle (body) paragraphs, an ineffective introduction could mean that these details are wasted as the rest of the essay may not be read. Keeping the reader's interest while introducing the topic can be achieved through two main methods.

Logical Introduction

The logical approach is the most common and traditional way to create interest. You begin with the general and proceed to the specific; the most specific is your thesis statement. This is also called the *inverted pyramid* structure.

Writers of expository, argumentative, and literary essays often use this method. A logical opening enables you to situate your own approach to a topic within a larger context. In this way, you can establish the topic's relevance and where it fits in as you progressively become more specific. Your thesis statement is usually the last sentence of the introduction. You use the first part of the introduction to build your emphasis.

In the following introduction, student writer Ian Stock begins with a general claim and gradually brings the topic into sharp focus—Laos's dependence on hydroelectric power. The pyramidal development is important for the general readers who may not know much about Laos and the topic.

Rivers have always been a central part of civilization. From the banks of the Tigris and Euphrates was born the idea of civilization, and almost all subsequent peoples have relied on rivers for trade, transportation, irrigation, fishing, and

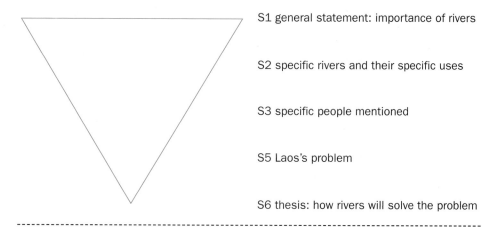

S1 general statement: importance of rivers

S2 specific rivers and their specific uses

S3 specific people mentioned

S5 Laos's problem

S6 thesis: how rivers will solve the problem

Figure 4.3

drinking water. The Lao of Southeast Asia are one such people, living for thousands of years in villages by the many rivers of that country. They have depended on their waterways for clean drinking water, irrigation for their crops, and fishing. The heart of the Lao river system lies in the Mekong River, the longest river in Southeast Asia. Laos is a landlocked country and is therefore doubly reliant on its rivers as a source of trade. Impoverished by war and political turmoil, Laos has turned to its rivers to provide a new, modern resource: electricity.

In another kind of logical approach, you begin by mentioning something *familiar* to the reader and proceed to the *unfamiliar*. The following opening illustrates this approach:

While intelligence quotient (IQ) has long been a useful tool to determine one's intelligence, a new development in the study of human intellectual experience has expanded to include one's emotional state. It is called Emotional Intelligence, or EQ.
—Student writer Chin-Ju Chiang

Dramatic Introduction

The *dramatic* approach can be used in various ways: you could begin with an interesting quotation (citing from a dictionary is *not* a good example of the dramatic approach), a thought-provoking question, a personal experience, an illuminating statistic, a description of a scene, or a brief narrative.

In the dramatic approach, you begin with something quite specific. The object is to surprise or intrigue your reader. Advertisers and marketing specialists often use this approach to catch the attention of the reader or viewer in order to try to sell their product. Remember, though, that the object is to gently surprise, not to shock or startle. Although it is used more often in argument than in exposition, it can prove effective in some expository essays as well, as the example below illustrates. In the following paragraph, the student writer creates a scenario that enables the reader to experience an unfamiliar martial art first-hand, just as she experienced it:

Imagine a circle of adults and children dressed in white pants with different coloured cords around their waists. Everybody is clapping and singing in an

unfamiliar language—entranced by what is unfolding within the circle. Musicians are playing drums, tambourines, and an instrument that looks like a stringed bow with a gourd attached. There is an inescapable feeling of communal energy within the circle. Uncontrollable curiosity lures the unknowing spectator; peering into the circle exposes two people engaged in an intense physical dialogue. Kicks and movements are exchanged with precision and fluidity, which create a dance-like choreography. What is being witnessed is called a *roda* (pronounced ho-da, it means "circle" in Portuguese). A person's first encounter with this intriguing display of physicality and grace is an experience not easily forgotten. I did not forget my first *roda*, and, consequently, I later began training in this Brazilian form of martial arts—*Capoeira* (pronounced cap-where-a).
—Student writer Kerry Hinds

The main function of the dramatic introduction above is to evoke a scene, but the dramatic introduction has other uses, such as evoking an emotional response from the reader. In the *emotional* approach, you begin with a claim or statement designed to arouse an emotional response. Although some of the same strategies as those mentioned above might apply, the stress here is not on surprise or directness but on the shared feeling between writer and reader. However, if you use this approach, you need to ensure that the typical reader will respond in the way you wish. An emotional opening needs to be sufficiently broad so that most people will share your feelings about the issue (unless, of course, you are addressing an audience that feels the way you do). An emotion-based introduction is sometimes used by a writer who wants to alert the public to an important concern—for example, a serious health risk or the incidence of missing children.

EXERCISE 4.5

Rewrite the two complete student paragraphs above using other approaches—i.e., use the dramatic approach for the first paragraph and the logical approach for the second one. (In order to do so, you might have to do some research.)

Mixed Approaches

A writer using the *mixed approach* combines different methods to attract interest.

> *Dramatic-logical*: The writer could begin with a question or challenging statement and then proceed to develop the rest of the paragraph through the logical approach.
> *Logical-dramatic*: The writer could use a "reversal" strategy, beginning with a general statement before dramatically turning the tables and arguing the opposite.

The writer of the paragraph below employs the *logical-dramatic* strategy to introduce her topic, the use of fur in today's society. After explaining the practical function of fur in humanity's past, in the second half of the paragraph she turns the tables and begins her argument that using fur today is wasteful and unnecessary:

Since the beginning of time, people have depended on fur. Cavemen wore animal skins as clothing; furthermore, after an animal, such as a buffalo, was killed, the flesh would be eaten and the bones would be used in tool-making.

They used as much of the animal as possible due to their spiritual beliefs and because with few other resources, it made sense to waste as little as possible. Wearing fur in that age was a necessity: it was warm, practical, and readily available. Today, it is a far different story. Fur is part of the upscale fashion industry, but killing wild animals for their skin extends beyond fur fanciers; it is a luxury product for many different consumers today, such as owners of cars with leather upholstery. There are more than 40 different animal species that are killed for their skin, and not a single one needs to be.
—Student writer Grace Beal

Whatever approach you use, the way you choose to create interest should be relevant to your topic, your purpose in writing, and your audience. For example, if you were trying to argue in favour of euthanasia, or another issue with a built-in emotional aspect, and you knew your audience opposed it, a strongly emotional opening might not be a good approach, because you would risk alienating your readers.

A Closer Look

The Introduction in Scholarly Writing

Writers in the academic disciplines often use a slightly different approach in an introduction, since their essays, typically, are much longer and more complex than those you will write. For example, their research might consist of dozens of relevant sources. They might begin by giving necessary background, such as an overview of the major works in the field or the various positions relevant to the topic. The writer will then link these studies, particularly the last ones discussed (usually the most recent ones), to his or her own approach, directly showing what he or she expects to add to the knowledge about the topic.

As in a student essay, the introduction concludes with a thesis statement, but this may take a different form from the kind you will be asked to write (see The Thesis Statement, below). For example, it might be a question or hypothesis (prediction) about the results of the study, particularly if the study is an experiment. For examples of academic introductions, see readings 9 and 19 on pages 118 and 257.

As a student, you will likely be asked to *read* scholarly studies that begin with a direct and concise statement of the problem or purpose and may even include the study's findings in the introduction. This is often the case with scientific articles designed for those with specialized knowledge of the subject area. However, unless you are writing a report for a science or business course, the essays you are asked to *write* will have introductions similar to what is laid out in this section.

Other Features of the Introduction

The introduction serves three other important functions:

> To announce your topic and the main point. The thesis statement, occurring near or at the end of the introduction, gives the main point of the essay and must have two parts: the topic itself plus a comment on the topic (see The Thesis Statement on page 91, below).

> To introduce the writer. The introduction is the place where the reader first comes to know that he or she is in competent hands. The introduction is the writer's first chance to establish *credibility*, presenting him- or herself as knowledgeable about the topic as well as reliable and trustworthy. One of the ways this comes across is through good writing; another way is by appearing rational, fair, and in control.

> ❯ To indicate *how* the writer plans to develop the main points. What organizing method will be used throughout the essay? Examples of organizational patterns include description, narration, definition (saying what something is), chronology (using time order), compare and contrast, and cause–effect, along with several other patterns discussed in Chapter 5, Essay and Paragraph Development.

Introduction Length

There is no fixed length for an introductory paragraph. Some successful introductions are quite brief; others are longer. The length may depend partly on the length of the essay itself; it may also depend on your decision whether to list the main points of your essay in an expanded thesis (but you should not *develop* your main points here) or give background information. In general, an introduction should not be more than 10–15 per cent of the length of the essay, but you should check with your instructor for specific guidelines.

Student writer Scott Fedyshen chose to use a relatively lengthy introduction to set up his thesis. He also chose to mention two specific sources that required citations, following a common practice in introductions to scholarly articles. Because he planned to focus on "new studies" in grief theory, he felt it necessary to summarize "traditional theories" before moving on to his thesis in the final part of the introduction. Read the paragraph below and suggest sentences that *could have been omitted* if he had wanted to write a more concise introductory paragraph. Where would you have put this material?

> Anyone who has experienced the death of a loved one knows the emotional pain that can follow. When bereaved, it is common and natural to go through the grieving process as part of mourning. However, each one's grief experience will be different; there is no universal concept that defines the truly individualized experience of grief. Traditional bereavement theorists have claimed that it is necessary to deal with the emotional pain caused by a death in order to resolve one's grief (Bonanno & Field, 2001). These theorists also suggest that those who do not follow the normal grieving process are likely to experience complicated grief symptoms—in particular, delayed grief in which grief symptoms will arise later in more severe forms. However, new studies suggest that avoiding grief may be an adaptive and effective form of coping with a loss. Such studies also claim that a delayed grief construct, as suggested by traditional theorists, is invalid, and that the importance of grief counselling is minimal (Stroebe, Stroebe, Schut, & Bout, 2002). New research related to bereavement and the grieving process provides important information on acceptable ways to grieve and appropriate methods of coping. These new findings allow for better understanding of the way people handle loss.

Starting at the Beginning

You could think of the introduction as gradually building up to its last sentence, your thesis statement. However, you should not focus all your energy on the last sentence at the expense of the first sentence. Your opening sentence needs to be carefully crafted too. An ineffective opening may be too general, obvious, irrelevant, too abrupt, or overstated (making a false universal claim). Using the analogy of meeting someone for the first time, you could say that a general, obvious, or irrelevant opening is the equivalent of a weak handshake and an averted glance rather than a firm handshake and direct eye contact. An abrupt or overstated opening could be compared to an overly aggressive greeting and vice-like, rapid hand pumping.

Weak Openings

A weak opening may fail to engage a reader's interest. A generalization is a broad statement, but when used as an opening sentence, it should not be too broad; it needs to be directly related to your topic (see "Overstated—false universal claim" below, where generalizations lack validity). Similarly, obvious and irrelevant claims may bore a reader.

- **Too general or broad:**

This is the technology age.

In the twentieth-century, many historic events have occurred around the globe, especially in Europe, Asia, and America.

The "especially" phrase in the second statement does nothing to make this assertion less broad.

- **Obvious:**

As population continues to rise around the world, the need for transportation will also increase.

Many people consider hockey Canada's sport.

- **Irrelevant, or "so what?":**

Few people know that sea otters can live to the age of 15 years.

This could be an effective opening if the statement really fell into the category of "believe it or not"—but it doesn't.

When I attended high school, I took every opportunity to be actively involved in all the physical education classes and sports organizations available.

Although there are legitimate uses of personal experience in some kinds of essays, a reader might well wonder how the writer's experience is relevant to the reader. One variant of a dramatic opening is asking the reader to imagine a specific scenario. If you use the "imagine" opening, ensure what you are asking the reader to imagine is realistic and interesting to a general audience.

Imagine you are behind the wheel of a formula racing car, about to complete the final lap for your first NASCAR victory.

Such an opening would likely interest a reader only if he or she were interested in stock car racing.

- **Too abrupt:**

First Nations' self-determination and self-government must come from within.

This statement suggests a strongly partisan point of view that would be acceptable if audience members clearly supported this kind of self-government; but it could alienate members of a general or neutral audience. Bear audience in mind, then, when you craft your essay opening.

> *The Dark Knight* offers viewers a chance to see themselves and society as they truly are as if the film were holding up a mirror to our faces.

Like the example above it, this statement might better serve as a thesis statement at the end of the introduction, rather than as the opening.

- **Overstated—false universal claim:**

> Everyone these days has used a computer at one time or another.

There are many people in the country where you live who have not used a computer; there are few claims that justify the use of "everyone."

> The largest health epidemic in today's society is obesity, especially among children.

There are many health "epidemics" today, and obesity among children is certainly one of them. However, to say without proof that obesity among children is unquestionably the "largest health epidemic" detracts from the writer's credibility. The statement needs to be qualified.

EXERCISE 4.6

↻ Check answers to select questions

Collaborative Exercise

In groups, consider the following opening statements and what makes each effective or ineffective. Rate each on a scale of 1 to 5, where 1 represents a very weak opening and 5 represents a very abrupt or overstated one. Give a 3 rating if the opening seems good, neither too weak nor too strong. Then, discuss how those with a 1 or 5 rating could be revised to make them more effective and interesting.

1. Franz Anton Mesmer discovered hypnosis in the 1770s.
2. Although email is a modern communications miracle, it is also the biggest nuisance ever invented.
3. I guess we would all like to look like Angelina Jolie if we could.
4. There are many issues surrounding end-of-life treatment of terminally ill individuals.
5. Leprosy is, without doubt, the most brutal disease known to humanity.
6. Why not buy the best-made sports car the world has to offer?
7. The movement of people away from the Catholic Church today is mostly due to its teachings on issues like abortion, women's equality, and homosexuality.
8. A few years ago, the Fédération Internationale d'Escrime (FIE) passed several unpopular rule changes in the sport of fencing.
9. In all American literature, no character ever gave more thought to moral decisions than Huckleberry Finn does.
10. Most people in our society today dream of growing up, marrying, and getting a good job so they can start a family.
11. Desperate times call for desperate measures.
12. The importance of education has been reiterated many times.

13. It is said that ignorance is bliss.
14. Fighting is a part of hockey—no ifs, ands, or buts.
15. Health and academic success have long been considered interrelated.
16. Mixed martial arts is the best entertainment value available today.
17. What is a bylaw?
18. Imagine that you are a woman standing before a mirror.
19. Western society today increasingly accepts different lifestyles and personal choices, giving many marginalized individuals greater freedom to live as they choose.
20. High school students should have the chance to participate in a wide variety of non-competitive activities in their physical education classes.

Writing an introduction requires time and patience. You should not feel discouraged if, after having produced an outline, you cannot quickly come up with a strong introduction. It may be best to return to your introduction *after* you've written the rest of the essay. In fact, some instructors believe that the introduction should be the last part of the essay you write.

The Thesis Statement

Nearly all essays need a thesis statement—the main point of your essay, or what you will be attempting to prove. A thesis statement has two parts: the *topic* and the *comment*. It does not just state a topic. Consider this example:

My essay will be about life in residence at the University of the South Pole.

The sentence above states a topic and does not comment on it. But a thesis might be as follows:

Life in residence at the University of the South Pole helps prepare you for life after university.

This sentence makes a comment about the topic. "Life in residence at the University of the South Pole" is the topic; "helps prepare you for life after university" is the comment. It tells the reader how you will be addressing the topic, what your focus will be.

Kinds of Thesis Statements

Simple Simple thesis statements have the two required parts, like the example above.

Expanded Expanded thesis statements give more detail, usually by including your main points. "Life in residence at the University of the South Pole helps prepare you for life after university" is a simple thesis statement. However, it can be turned into an expanded thesis statement by including the main points:

Life in residence at the University of the South Pole helps prepare you for life after university by making you independent, by reinforcing basic life skills, and by teaching you how to get along with other penguins.

Just as a simple thesis statement goes further than a topic, so an expanded thesis statement goes further than a simple thesis statement by answering questions like

"How?" or "Why?," by accounting for or justifying the main idea. *How* does life in residence prepare one for life after university?

Here's an example of a topic, followed by a simple thesis statement and an expanded one that answers the question "Why?":

> *Topic*: School uniforms
>
> *Simple thesis statement*: Making school uniforms mandatory has many advantages for students.
>
> *Expanded thesis statement*: Making school uniforms mandatory has many advantages for students because they eliminate distractions, encourage a focus on academics, and reduce competition based on appearances.

Should you use a simple or expanded thesis statement in your essay? There is no easy answer, but simple thesis statements may be sufficient for short essays, such as those fewer than 500 words. Simple thesis statements are sometimes used in fact-based (expository) essays in which you attempt to answer a question or solve a problem. In argumentative essays, you try to convince your reader of something. An expanded thesis that announces all your points in the introduction gets you off to a forceful start. Check with your instructor for specific guidelines about simple versus expanded thesis statements.

A Closer Look

Indirect Thesis

In an indirect thesis statement, the main point or thrust of your argument is not explicitly stated but is implied in your introduction. Writers of expository essays do not often use indirect thesis statements, though experienced writers may sometimes use them in personal or argumentative essays. One of the best-known examples of an indirect thesis statement is in Jonathan Swift's satiric essay "A Modest Proposal," published in 1729. Swift advocates the sale of one-year-old children to the wealthy, who will buy them to eat! The "modest proposal" is designed to call attention, in an absurdly callous way, to the problem of poverty in Ireland, which Swift felt was being ignored by the wealthy.

Effective Thesis Statements

An effective thesis statement should be interesting, specific, and manageable.

> › *Interesting*: The thesis is likely to attract the reader, especially the general reader, to the topic and the essay.
> › *Specific*: The thesis isn't so general, broad, or obvious that it lacks relevance; it informs the reader about what follows.
> › *Manageable*: The thesis sounds as if it can be reasonably explored in the space of the essay; the writer can successfully carry out what is promised in the thesis.

Ineffective Thesis Statements

Although a thesis statement may be ineffective because it is not interesting, specific, or manageable, it may have other problems. An unclear thesis statement may confuse, not inform. For example, the following thesis statement doesn't clearly express the main points of the essay. In this case, the writer needs to be more detailed and precise:

> Pets are important in that they can unify, heal, and are an inevitable part of human nature.

Do we know what the writer means by these items? As an expanded thesis statement that includes the main points of the essay, it is inadequate because it will likely baffle readers, not inform them.

> *Revised*: Pets are important in bringing people together, helping them recover from an illness or depression, and enabling them to express important human values, such as love.

A thesis statement may be unclear because it seems to straddle two topics rather than centring on one. This could be the result of the writer's early uncertainty: he or she may not yet know the essay's major focus. In revising your essay, you should always ensure that your thesis accurately reflects the essay's main point. In this example, we don't know whether this essay will be about excessive dieting or body image:

> *Ineffective*: Many youths are obsessed by dieting today due to the prominence our society places on body image.

To successfully revise this thesis, the writer needs to narrow the topic to one specific area, such as one of the following:

- unhealthy diets and the problems they create
- the effects of body image on youths
- the relationship between body image and dieting.

The last topic would likely involve extensive research and might not be manageable within the scope of a medium-length essay.

Avoid a stiff and self-conscious thesis statement that refers directly to the writer or to the essay's purpose:

> *Ineffective*: I (or, This essay) will examine the phenomenon of online gambling and argue in favour of strict government regulation of this growing industry.

> *Revised*: Online gambling is an increasing concern to governments today and should be subject to strict regulations.

When you use an expanded thesis statement, you need to express your main points in parallel structure; otherwise, the thesis could be hard to follow (see The Parallelism Principle in Chapter 11, page 392).

Thesis statements can be difficult to write. A clear thesis begins with the writer's clear thoughts. As in all writing, clear thinking produces clear expression. On the other hand, the thesis you start with shouldn't be considered fixed. As you write your outline or rough draft and uncover areas about your topic you weren't aware of before, you may want to go back and revise your thesis.

Fast-Track

●●●●●

Thesis Statement Checklist

☑ Have you written a complete thesis statement, not just a topic?

☑ Does it have two parts (simple thesis statement)?

☑ Have you included your main points in the order they will appear in your essay (expanded thesis statement)?

☑ Is there enough detail to enable the reader to understand your main points (i.e., it is clearly phrased and not confusing)?

☑ Is it clear what *one topic* the thesis will focus on (i.e., it does not appear vague or appear to straddle two topics)?

☑ Is it worded objectively and not self-consciously (i.e., by mentioning the writer or the essay itself)?

☑ In arranging your main points, have you applied parallel structure?

EXERCISE 4.7

⟳ Check answers to select questions

A. If you were asked to write an essay on how the computer influences people, which of the simple thesis statements below would be suitable? Rate each according to whether it is interesting, specific, and manageable. Be prepared to explain your decisions.

1. The computer is one of the most entertaining pastimes we have today.
2. Violence in computer games is affecting children these days by increasing the number of shootings in schools.
3. The computer has helped change the way we live today compared to the way our grandparents lived 50 years ago.
4. Computers take away our free time by creating a dependency that is very hard to escape once we are hooked.
5. The computers is a great babysitter for pre-school-aged children.

B. Write an effective thesis statement on the topic of the computer's influence, using any pre-writing technique you feel comfortable with and making sure that you include the requirements of a good thesis statement.

C. The following thesis statements are either simple or expanded. Identify the type. If they are simple thesis statements, add detail, turning them into expanded thesis statements.

1. Regular, moderate doses of stress not only are inevitable in today's world but also can be good for you.
2. As consumers, we must keep ourselves informed about the activities of the industries we support.
3. Although poor waste management has already had a significant impact on the planet, through recycling, waste reduction programs, and public education, future damage can be minimized.
4. Education is viewed as a benefit to individuals, but too much education can have negative results.
5. Many people today misunderstand the meaning of success.

Collaborative Exercise

In groups, use a pre-writing technique to formulate a simple thesis statement that has all three criteria discussed above. Begin with a choice of broad subject areas, such as the ones suggested below. When each group has come up with a thesis statement and written it on a piece of paper, exchange it with another group's and have that group evaluate it according to the three criteria. One mark should be given for an interesting thesis statement; another mark should be awarded for being specific; and a third mark should be given if it seems manageable (half marks are possible). When each group has completed the evaluation process, discuss the ratings and the rationale behind them.

After each group has received feedback on its thesis statement and revised it accordingly, use another pre-writing technique to come up with three main points. Then reword the simple thesis statement so that it is an expanded thesis statement. The thesis statements can again be marked. Expanded thesis statements can be given three marks by awarding a mark for points 4, 5, and 6 in Fast Track: Thesis Statement Checklist on page 94.

Possible topics: aliens, backpacking, clothes, diet, energy, Facebook, ghosts, humour, indie rock, justice, karma, luck, malls, nature, organic food, pets, Quebec, relationships, science, taboos, (the) unconscious, virtual reality, waste, xenophobia, youth, Zen Buddhism

EXERCISE 4.8

EXERCISE 4.9

↻ Check answers to select questions

Evaluate the following introductory paragraphs according to the criteria discussed in the previous pages. Does each function as an effective introduction? Specifically consider the following:

- Which method(s) did the writer use to create reader interest (logical, dramatic, mixed)?
- Is the opening effective? What makes it effective (or not)?
- Identify the thesis statement. Is it interesting, specific, and manageable? Simple or expanded?
- Has the writer established credibility (shows knowledge, seems reliable/ trustworthy)?
- Is the essay's main organizational pattern (e.g., chronology, compare and contrast, cause–effect, problem–solution, cost–benefit) apparent? If you wish, you can look ahead to Chapter 5, page 100, where organizational patterns are discussed.

1. Clothing has always reflected the times, and a prime example is the bathing suit. From their most cumbersome and unattractive beginnings to the array of styles we see today, bathing suits have always reflected the lives of the women who wore them and the society in which they lived. In the last hundred years, roles of the sexes, improvements in women's rights, changes in the economy, and perceptions of body image have all played a part in bathing suit design.
   —Student writer Stephanie Keenlyside

2. What is it about the Italian Mafia that fascinates millions of people? Could part of the answer lie in Hollywood's depiction of a 5′ 9″, 275-pound Italian named Bruno Francessi who drives a black Cadillac, wears $3,000 silk suits, and claims to have "two" families; or is it the way the media creates celebrity status for Mafiosi people and events? The media and film industry portray a mobster's lucrative lifestyle as the result of thoughtless killings, a regimen of violence and

corruption. But to fully understand the mob lifestyle, one must understand how mobsters operate—not what they appear to be on the surface, but the structure, conduct, and economic realities that created their power and enable them to maintain it. As someone who lived close to this power, I know that behind the media perception lies a fundamental belief in and adherence to a system.
—Student writer Dino Pascoli

3. Two 20-year-old Vancouver men were street racing three years ago when one of the cars, a Camaro, struck and killed Irene Thorpe as she crossed the street. The car was going so fast that Thorpe was thrown 30 metres into the air. Both men were convicted of criminal negligence causing death. They were given a two-year conditional sentence to be served at home, put on probation for three years, and had their drivers' licenses revoked for five years. Like most street-racing tragedies, this one was preventable. Though the street-racing phenomenon has been around for decades, it is growing exponentially. Recent movies have glorified this activity, enticing young, inexperienced drivers. The increase in street racing has led to an increase in the injuries to racers, spectators, and innocent bystanders. In addition, racing often results in property damage and is associated with assault, weapons offences, and drug and alcohol abuse. To help combat this growing problem, anti-racing legislation needs to be introduced and strictly enforced. Furthermore, an education program needs to be implemented and legal racing venues created.
    —Student writer Maureen Brown

4. The sport of bodybuilding has evolved considerably through the ages. Starting with muscle man competitions, it has now turned into what some would call a "freak show." Bodybuilding is a sport that requires its athletes to display their best aesthetically pleasing physiques on stage; they are judged according to specific criteria. Many factors leading up to the judging itself contribute to the outcome of the competition; for example, nutrition from whole foods and supplements, and low body fat percentage from proper diet and cardiovascular training all contribute to the success of the competitors. Steroids, too, are a major factor in professional events like the International Federation of Bodybuilding and Fitness (IFBB) competitions, where athletes are not tested for drug use. Anabolic steroid abuse plays a large role in bodybuilding, often resulting in adverse health effects.
    —Student writer Mike Allison

5. Why does my cellphone not work? Why do I get radiation poisoning when I travel by plane? Why is the light switch not working? These are the kinds of questions we ask ourselves when solar flares are striking the Earth. Solar flares originate from the sun. Every 11 years, the sun switches its magnetic poles, causing the magnetic fields to twist and turn in the atmosphere above sunspots, which are eruptions on the sun's surface. The magnetic field seems to snap like a rubber band stretched too tightly. When one of these fields breaks, it can create energy equal to a billion megatons of TNT exploding. The magnetic fields seem to flip and reconnect after they break. Solar flares occasionally head towards the Earth, and even though we are 1.5 million kilometres from the sun, these flares can

reach us in fewer than two days. While the Earth is experiencing a solar flare, multiple problems can occur—from malfunctions of orbiting objects to disruption in power systems and radio signals. Yet, while the flares can produce these problems, they can also create the most beautiful and unusual auroras seen around the world.
—Student writer Nicholas Fodor

EXERCISE 4.10

Evaluate the following introduction according to the criteria discussed under Introductions. For example, you could consider whether the opening is successful, whether the writer creates interest and appears credible, and whether the thesis statement is effective. Then, rewrite it, correcting any weaknesses you find. You can use your own material or ideas, but try not to increase the length of the paragraph (approximately 130 words).

Something drastic needs to be done about obesity among teenagers today! Over the last decade, there has been a disturbing trend toward teenage obesity. Teenagers today would rather lodge themselves in front of the TV or play video games for hours on end than get some form of physical exercise. This problem becomes pronounced in high school because physical education is not compulsory in most schools. However, PE classes have a lot to offer. Participation can reduce the risk of heart failure, improve overall fitness, promote good health habits, improve self-discipline and skill development, boost self-confidence, increase academic performance, and enhance communication and co-operative skills. Obesity is an alarming trend among high school students today and should be a concern to both students and their parents.

The Conclusion

Unlike the surprise ending of some short stories, the conclusion of an essay should be prepared for every step of the way—both by the introduction and by the points that are developed within the essay itself. So, a surprise ending to an essay indicates serious structural problems in the body.

Although you will prepare the reader for your conclusion, it should not be boring or merely repetitive. A conclusion that simply repeats the thesis statement is predictable and redundant. It will leave the reader with the impression of a static, undeveloped argument.

In your conclusion, you need to find a way to bring the reader back to reconsider the thesis statement in light of how you have developed the thesis through your main points. The conclusion *recalls both* the thesis statement and what has been discussed in the body paragraphs.

Two Kinds of Conclusions

The introduction and the conclusion are not like identical bookends with the body paragraphs like books between them. The conclusion can underscore the importance of the thesis in two ways: (1) it can reiterate the thesis using different words that stress its importance, perhaps by a call to action if you are arguing for a practical change of some kind; (2) it can suggest a specific way that the thesis could be applied, ask further questions, or propose other ways of looking at the problem. These two strategies for concluding an essay suggest two fundamental patterns:

> *circular conclusion*: recalls and reinforces the thesis
> *spiral conclusion*: refers to the thesis but also leads suggestively beyond it

A **circular conclusion** "closes the circle" by bringing the reader back to the starting point. It is particularly important that a circular conclusion does not simply repeat the thesis statement word for word but shows how it has been supported. A circular conclusion might reinforce the importance of the thesis by making an ethical or emotional appeal, for example, by reminding the reader that the action argued for in the thesis is morally the best choice. A **spiral conclusion** might point to ramifications or results of the thesis or suggest follow-up research.

Whereas the introduction often starts with the general and works towards the specific (the thesis statement)—the "inverted pyramid" structure—the conclusion often works from the specific to the general, as shown in Figure 4.4.

Specific things to avoid in the conclusion are

> restating the thesis statement word for word
> mentioning a new point; conclusions should reword the old in an interesting way, not introduce something new
> giving an example or illustration to support your thesis; examples belong in your body paragraphs
> writing a conclusion that is very much longer than your introduction. Exceptions sometimes occur—especially in scholarly articles in the sciences and social sciences, which may end with a lengthy discussion.

Set your conclusion beside your introduction to check that it fulfills all the functions of a conclusion discussed above and relates to your introduction in a satisfactory way.

Introduction

Conclusion

Figure 4.4

EXERCISE 4.11

Introduction and Conclusion Exercises

Consider these sets of paragraphs, which form the introduction and the conclusion of two essays. Is it clear from the introduction what the writer will be discussing? What kind of introduction did the writer use? Is it clear from the conclusion what the writer has discussed? What kind of conclusion is each writer using?

Write a brief analysis of how the two parts of the essays intersect yet, at the same time, operate independently. Consider strengths and possible weaknesses. Remember that the paragraphs should not only function as effective specialized paragraphs but also display unity, coherence, and development.

A. **An expository essay:** Topic: a racial incident in Canada's past

Introduction

One of Canada's most important features, which figures prominently in its self-presentation to the world, is as a peaceful nation that respects the individual and celebrates multiculturalism. The country is known for its cultural and ethnic diversity. Often, however, Canadians idealize their image and push inequality out of their presentation of their country. However, if we look carefully at the history of Canada, there have been many occasions when the clean image of national tolerance has been seriously undermined, such as in the Komagata Maru incident in Vancouver in 1914.

Conclusion

Although much has changed for the better since the beginning of the twentieth century and Canada is justifiably proud of its diversity today, people sometimes ignore past incidents of racial discrimination. Since the Komagata Maru incident is not well-known, it is important that people hear about it so they can be aware that even in a democratic country like Canada injustice and intolerance have occurred in the past and will continue to occur unless people learn from the past and guard against such incidents.

—Student writer Ruth Wax

B. **An argumentative essay:** Topic: smoking and organ transplantation

Introduction

The atmosphere grew tense in the cramped hospital room as eight-year-old Marla looked up through frightened eyes, trying to be strong for her mother. Everyone was trying to be hopeful, but Marla instinctively knew that she would not be getting a heart transplant in time; the waitlist was long, and an organ match was unlikely. Although Marla was an otherwise healthy girl, there were others on the transplant list who were ahead of her, though not all of them had as good a prognosis. Due to the scarcity of organ donations in comparison to many in need, serious debates have arisen concerning the suitability of some potential heart and lung recipients. Some feel that everyone should have equal right to a transplant and that there should be no pre-conditions relating to what they see as lifestyle choices, such as smoking. Others advocate that smokers should be refused transplants on medical or moral considerations since smokers are more likely to experience complications after surgery. Given the current crisis of long waitlists and variable success rates, lung and heart transplant candidates should be required to quit smoking at least six months prior to surgery in order to reduce smoking-related complications and maximize transplant success.

Conclusion

The scarcity of organ donations and the length of waitlists have placed an increasing obligation on the part of health care professionals to ensure the best outcome for their patients. Denying transplants to those who refuse to quit smoking may appear to discriminate against smokers and their lifestyle choice. However, doing so would result in better odds for post-transplant success and would involve the most efficient use of limited health care services and resources. In short, health authorities should move to institute clear guidelines on pre-surgery smoking restrictions for the benefit of both individuals and the health care system.

—Student writer Annie Gentry

Chapter 5

Essay and Paragraph Development

Developing Your Essay through Substantial Paragraphs

As discussed in Chapter 4, an effective paragraph is unified, coherent, and well-developed. A unified paragraph focuses on one topic. A coherent paragraph makes sense and includes logical connections so the reader can follow the writer's train of thought. Finally, a well-developed paragraph contains supporting information organized by consistent patterns. A well-developed paragraph, then, not only thoroughly expands on a point but also increases the essay's coherence, contributing to the essay as a whole.

The writer may choose to use one main method of organization for the essay itself and other methods in supporting roles. For example, an essay may set out to examine a cause–effect relationship but may use different methods from paragraph to paragraph to introduce, clarify, illustrate, or expand the main points.

Choosing the appropriate organizational or developmental patterns is one of the keys to writing a complete and interesting essay. Which patterns should you use for your essay? Your choice will depend on the kind of essay, your purpose in writing, your topic, your audience, your essay's primary organizational method, your main points and their order (climax, reverse climax, or some other), and other factors.

In this chapter, we are concerned mainly with developing paragraphs to ensure the essay will contain substantial points. First, we will consider the many ways that writers can develop their key points through paragraphs that use different rhetorical patterns. However, because definition is an excellent starting point for many essays, using definition is discussed separately on page 112. Also, because organizing an essay by the compare and contrast method can be more complex than by other methods, compare and contrast essays are discussed beginning on page 113.

Rhetorical Patterns

A topic may lend itself to a particular method of development. In fact, in some cases, your main organizational method is given to you by the topic itself, so from that you will know how your points should be developed. For example, for the topic "Which is more important at college or university: acquiring skills or getting good grades?" you might guess that the essay should be organized by compare and contrast. For the topic "Solutions to the problem of homeless people," you would know that the essay should be organized as problem–solution where you briefly describe the problem and then suggest ways to solve it. On the other hand, if the topic question were "Do you believe that homeless people today are a problem?" you might develop your essay in a similar way, but the *problem* of homelessness would be much more important than the solutions. Even if the topic determines the *main* way that the essay should be developed, there will likely be opportunities to consider different methods for developing individual paragraphs. These methods, which are often referred to as **rhetorical patterns,** are discussed below, with examples, beginning with Definition— What Is It? on page 102.

Being aware of the various rhetorical patterns can help not only in developing paragraphs but also in generating points and sub-points by ordering your thoughts into specific, useful patterns. For example, the following paragraph, from the student essay (Reading 14) on page 176, is annotated to show how it was developed using the **chronological pattern.**

> After using a transitional phrase, the writer announces the topic of the paragraph: the rise of the CD.

> In his second sentence, the writer gives the starting point for the time period covered in the paragraph.

> The writer begins by referring to the original purpose of the CD; in the next sentence, he builds on the idea by accounting for its growing popularity, suggesting why the CD came to be a popular medium. Notice that the writer doesn't explain how music quality was enhanced or what made CDs a more convenient medium; doing so might have affected the paragraph's unity.

> The year 1993 was significant in the history of the CD. In this sentence, the writer introduces the cassette tape; for the rest of the paragraph, he uses compare and contrast, along with chronology, to help trace the relationship between the cassette's decline and the CD's rise in popularity.

> The writer uses statistics and several secondary sources to develop this paragraph.

> Although the writer uses paraphrase for most of the paragraph, he concludes forcefully with a direct quotation.

As the music industry's expansion was slowing, however, the compact disc was gaining in popularity. In 1990, while fewer music stores were opening, companies halted the production of record albums and began to concentrate completely on the compact disc ("Record and Prerecorded Tape Stores"). Originally designed to be strictly a music carrier, the CD marked a revolution within the music industry (Pohlmann 313). The quality of recordings on a CD was greatly enhanced, and it was a much more convenient medium on which to record songs. Where cassette tapes and records had once coexisted, in 1993 there was a 7 percent drop in cassette tape shipments, and the Recording Industry Association's (RIA) statistics showed an increase of 21 percent in the shipments of CDs worldwide. In that same year, the RIA also compiled information indicating that nearly half of all American households had CD players. For the first time, the music industry had reached unit sales of more than $10 billion. As CDs became available in more and more retail outlets and, starting with Amazon.com, became purchasable online, cassette tape sales began to decline steadily. In 1998, cassette shipments dropped 8.2 percent, and their dollar value decreased by 6.8 percent ("Record and Prerecorded Tape Stores"). By 2004, Matt Phillips of the British Phonographic Industry (BPI) reported that the year had seen only 900,000 cassette tapes sold in the UK. "[Since] their peak in 1989," said Phillips, "[it's] clear to see that cassette sales are dwindling fast" (BBC News).

Analysis, meaning "loosening" or "dissolving," as well as "separating" or "breaking up," is sometimes considered a distinct method of development. When you analyze, you are loosening, then separating something in order to look at it closely. You analyze when you divide and classify, compare and contrast, consider problems and solutions, identify costs and benefits, and the like. Not all the rhetorical patterns truly involve analysis—description and narration, for example, do not—but most of them do. Analysis is one of the keys to critical thinking.

One way to generate methods of development is to ask questions about the topic. Each question in Table 5.1 leads to a particular method for developing a paragraph. If, for example, your topic is "fast foods," you could use any of the methods below to help develop an essay on this topic, depending on the question you choose to focus on in each paragraph.

Definition: What Is It?

Define something in an essay in order to tell the reader precisely what you will be talking about. Defining a term, such as an abstract concept, can also help you understand your topic better and, perhaps, help you organize your main points. By "fast foods," do you mean something like a "Big Mac?" Do you mean food that you can buy at a store that is quickly heated and eaten? Both could be considered "fast foods," but they are not the same. Below, the writer concisely defines "peer-to-peer file sharing" for his general audience and then uses the division pattern to expand the definition. (For more about definition in essays, see Using Definition in an Essay, page 112.)

Table 5.1 Methods of Development

Question	Method of Development
What is it?	definition
When did it occur?	chronology
What does it look like?	description
How can it be told?	narration
How do you do it? or How does it work?	process/"how to"
Why should/does it affect me?	personal
What kinds/categories are there?	classification/ division
What causes/accounts for it?	cause–effect
What is the result/effect?	cause–effect
What is the answer?	question–answer
How can it be shown?	example/illustration
How can it be (re)solved?	problem–solution
What are the advantages/disadvantages?	cost–benefit
How is it like something else?	analogy
How is it like and/or unlike something else?	compare and contrast

Peer-to-peer file-sharing (P2P) is a technology that enables users to share files among themselves without the use of a central host of the files (traditionally called the client–server model). In P2P, each client acts as a "mini server" and can both send and receive files. The information regarding the files on each client usually is distributed in one of three ways. The first involves the use of a central server to store this information and the use of a protocol for clients to update the central server with file information whenever they connect or disconnect from the network. A more modern method for distributing information about files on different hosts, "hybrid P2P," involves the use of certain hosts on the network to maintain the information and distribute it. The third approach, called "decentralized P2P," is similar to hybrid P2P, but differs because it uses each individual host on the network to store and share file information.

—Student writer Mik Nuotio

Chronology: When Did It Occur?

In the **chronological** method, you do more than simply look back to a specific time: you trace the topic's *development over time*. (If you looked back to a specific time and compared an aspect of the subject to that aspect today, you would be using compare and contrast.) For example, when did fast foods begin, and when did they truly begin to affect people and society? Tracing the evolution of fast foods in the last 15 years might provide evidence that many fast-food restaurants have been forced to expand their choices and reduce their portion sizes to counter the perception that these foods are unhealthy. Applying this method of development, then, could also involve a cause–effect or problem–solution approach.

> The earth shook as father and son wrestled high above the clouds; Kronos, the dreaded father who ate his children, battled his powerful son to rule the Earth. However, Zeus, whom the Fates had protected as a child from Kronos's mighty jaws, triumphed once again, becoming, in the words of Homer, "father of gods and men"; his children would honour his victory as a celebration known as Olympia. From 776 BCE, the Olympic Games occurred every four years to celebrate Zeus's success. By 260 CE, the Games' importance had deteriorated so much that they were held only occasionally, until the Roman Emperor Theodosius outlawed them completely in 394 CE. The Olympic Games were founded on a profound religious significance, specific ideals about athletes, and strict rules that enabled the Games' long existence and prohibited the inclusion of women. As Olympia changed, the founding principles that had originally made Olympia so significant were disregarded, eventually leading to the end of the ancient Games.
> —Student writer Courtenay O'Brien

For another example of a paragraph developed mainly through chronology, see page 102.

Description: What Does It Look Like?

You can use **description** at any point in your essay to add concrete, physical detail, but description should play a limited role unless you are writing a personal essay or a creative writing piece. You could describe something by using the **spatial** method, a particular kind of descriptive pattern. In the spatial method, you describe something in a systematic manner—for example, from left to right, or as you approach the object. For example, you could describe a fast-food burger from the sesame-seed top bun, through its assorted condiments and extras, to the plain lower bun.

> The Parc Guell, constructed between 1900 and 1914, was originally intended as the setting for a garden city. The park is fairy tale–like in appearance: the first building one sees on entering the site resembles a gingerbread house. The rounded corners on the brown façade and colourful decoration of the window sills give the building a magical, playful appearance. Other structures that stand out within the park include a giant fountain shaped like a lizard and a mile-long bench that winds along one path in the park. The most

remarkable feature, though, is Gaudí's use of beautiful, multi-coloured tile work throughout.
—Collins, George R. *Antonio Gaudí and the Catalan Movement 1870–1930*. Charlottesville: American Association of Architectural Bibliographers/University Press of Virginia, 1973. Print.

For another example of a paragraph developed mainly through description, see Chapter 3, page 53.

Narration: How Can It Be Told?

A story can lend drama to an argument or illustrate a point. **Narrating** an incident, or even including some dialogue, can effectively introduce or reinforce your topic. For example, through observation and a little imagination, a visit to a fast-food restaurant could produce interesting stories about those who eat or work there. Narration is a natural method in a personal essay but can also be used in an argumentative essay, and even in an expository essay, as in the example below about the legendary origins of coffee. Because description and narration are generally considered more informal, you should ask your instructor before using them extensively in a formal essay.

Legend has it that one day, Kaldi, an Ethiopian goat-herder, noticed his goats were so frisky when they returned from grazing that they "danced." Curious about the source of their excitement, Kaldi followed them the next day and observed the animals eating the berries of a nearby tree. Kaldi grabbed some berries himself and soon experienced a slow tingle that spread throughout his body. According to the legend, Kaldi was soon "dancing" alongside his goats.
—Pendergrast, Mark. *Uncommon Grounds: The History of Coffee and How It Transformed Our World*. New York: Basic Books, 1999. Print.

For another example of a paragraph developed mainly through narration, see Chapter 3, page 52.

Process Analysis: How Does It Work?

Although **process analysis** usually appears in a fact-based essay that relates the chronological, step-by-step stages of a *process*, you can also use this method of development in an argumentative essay—for example, if you wanted to convince a reader that one games system was easier to operate than another. This method can also be used for non-technical subjects—for example, "How to Impress Your Boss, or Professor, in Ten Easy Steps." Remember that relating a process focuses specifically on the successive steps in a *sequence*. For example, since the production of fast-food burgers is often a regimented process, you could describe this process from the time a customer places an order to the time it is handed to him or her.

The traditional method of painting icons is a long process, requiring a skilled and experienced painter. The artist takes a wooden panel, one with the least amount of resin, knots, and risk of splitting, and covers it with cheesecloth. A gesso is then made from rabbit-skin glue and calcium carbonate (chalk). It is applied to the panel seven to ten times and then polished by hand until it is mirror-like. The original is traced to perfection and then transferred onto the gessoed surface. After this, gold leaf is laid on everywhere it is required (backgrounds and halos, for example). Egg tempera paint is freshly made from powdered pigment and egg yolk and is applied from the darkest dark to the lightest light with an egg-white glaze spread on between each coat.

—Student writer Magda Smith

Personal: Why Should It Affect Me?/How Does or Did It Affect Me?

A **personal** essay is focused on the writer—an aspect of his or her life or a relevant experience. Personal experience in an essay contributes immediacy and, sometimes, drama. But don't use personal experience extensively, unless you are writing a personal essay. In a successful personal paragraph or essay, the writer is able to make personal experience seem relevant to the reader.

For example, to apply your personal experience to fast-food restaurants, you might consider your visits to such restaurants as a child when the busy and exciting atmosphere was more important to you than the food. Below, the writer began his expository essay on student binge drinking by citing a recent personal experience; such an approach would be particularly appropriate if his audience were composed mostly of university students.

Exam time is approaching at my university, and stress levels are at an annual high. For this reason, when Friday night arrives, I know I will be drinking—and I definitely will not be alone. Last weekend, my friends and I went to a typical residence party. If I can remember correctly, there were about 15 people noisily crowded into a room the size of a large closet, and many more were herded in the hallways. According to a study in the *American Journal of Public Health*, today's North American college students have the highest binge drinking rate of any group, even when compared to their peers who do not go to school; furthermore, alcohol is associated with many social problems on college campuses and is the most widespread and preventable health issue for the more than six million students in America (Wechsler et al., 1995, p. 921).

—Student writer Brian Gregg

Classification/Division: What Kinds Are There?

Humans, apparently by nature, tend to classify things. In **classification**, you begin with a large number of items—for example, commonly known members of the animal kingdom—which you organize into more manageable groups: mammals, birds, fish, reptiles, and amphibians. Each category, such as mammals, could in turn be organized into still smaller units, such as rodents, primates, and carnivores. Fast-food burgers can easily be classified as well: hamburgers, chicken burgers, fish burgers, veggie burgers. In the example below, the writer uses classification to break down movies into five designations; the differences could then be analyzed by applying the same criteria to each category.

> Ontario has five categories for rating movies: general, parental guidance, 14A (those under 14 must be accompanied by an adult), 18A (those under 18 must be accompanied by an adult), and restricted. In the "general" category, the language must be inoffensive, though words like "damn" and "hell" can occur occasionally. Violence must be limited and permissible; sexual activity includes only embracing and kissing "in a loving context"; horror is defined by genre—for example, fantasy giants, ogres, and dragons are acceptable.
> —Ontario Film Review Board, http://www.ofrb.gov.on.ca/english/page6.htm

In **division**, you are more concerned with how the individual parts relate to the whole. You break a topic down into parts in order better to understand or explain the whole (the topic). For example, to illustrate how essay structure works, you can divide the essay into introduction, body paragraphs, and conclusion. Under Definition—What Is It? above (page 103), the writer divides peer-to-peer file sharing into three different kinds.

Cause–Effect: What is the Cause? Or, What is the Effect?

You can use the **cause–effect** pattern to organize an entire essay, or you can use it in one or more paragraphs to explore and analyze a main point. When you deal with causes, you consider the reasons for an occurrence. A cause–effect essay or paragraph might focus on one effect, which would be accounted for by one or more causes; similarly, you could focus on one cause and consider one or more effects or results arising from this cause. For example, since fast food has often been blamed for obesity, you could look at studies that link obesity (effect) to unhealthy diets (cause). Cause–effect studies are particularly common in the sciences. The **antecedent–consequent** organizational method uses time–order relationships in a similar way to cause–effect relationships (think of "before and after" photographs). The following essay excerpt discusses one cause for stress in first-year students:

> A major cause of stress in first-year students is the need to establish a new social base. Students not only find themselves among strangers, but also often have to rely on these strangers for moral support. Consequently, friendships tend to be forged rapidly but superficially. When students inevitably find themselves dealing with midterms, assignments, and an increasingly heavy course load, they need close friends and family for support but are forced to turn to these new acquaintances instead. Great friendships may be formed during such times, but often the stress is insurmountable, leading students to give up and head home.
> —Student writer Alexis Parker

Question–Answer: What Is the Answer?

The **question–answer** method is effective when you ask the question in the topic sentence and then answer it in the paragraph. Questions—including the journalistic questions *Who?, What?, When?, Where?, Why?, and How?*—can be applied to most topics: "How did fast foods become so popular?"; "Are fast foods to blame for the 'obesity epidemic'?". Posing a relevant question is a good way to engage the reader since it directly invites his or her answer to the question. Below, the writer began his essay by asking two questions, suggesting that his essay will focus on two related areas of foreign policy:

> In the post–Cold War era, do military solutions still have a place or is diplomacy able to solve all our foreign policy questions? Does the United Nations still have a useful purpose or will military coalitions like NATO usurp its role entirely? With increasing world tensions and the current Anglo-American–led war in Iraq, many people around the world are asking these questions.
> —Student writer Robert Tyre

Example/Illustration: How Can It Be Shown?

Using a concrete **example** is an excellent way to support a point and clarify an abstract idea. This method of development can often be combined with other methods, such as cause–effect, cost–benefit, or compare and contrast. For example, if you were using the cause–effect method to develop the point that fast foods save valuable time (an effect), you might discuss the convenience of drive-through lanes at fast-food restaurants as one example; another example might be the use of an assembly line to prepare the food. Examples are indispensible in most writing and may consist of brief expansions of a point or more-fully developed explanations:

> *Brief expansion*: Graffiti art can be seen as a political message on a sidewalk, a limerick on a bathroom wall, a doodle on a desktop, or even a digital image on the Internet.

> *Fully-developed explanation*: During the 2002 Commonwealth Games, Kelly Guest was suspended from participating in the triathlon by the International Olympic Committee (IOC). Guest tested positive for nandrolone, a substance banned by the IOC. Guest argued that he had never intended to use nandrolone to enhance his performance, but had ingested the banned substance through the natural supplements he was taking.
> —Student writer Tim Dewailly (from his introduction to an essay on the use of natural supplements by elite athletes)

Problem–Solution: How Can It Be (Re)Solved?

The **problem–solution** pattern could focus on a problem, a solution to a problem, or both a problem and its solution. For example, a problem with fast foods is their dubious nutritional value. After stating this problem, you could propose ways that fast foods could be made healthier or perhaps give examples of how this is being done today; in this case, you would be combining problem–solution with example/illustration. Studies focusing on problem–solution and cost–benefit (see below) are particularly common in the social sciences where human behaviour is the focus. In the following conclusion, the author restates his thesis that Canada's Confederation in 1867 was not so much an effect, or consequence, of various causes, but the best solution to unanticipated political problems:

> Politicians were not entertaining the idea of uniting the British North American colonies until numerous problems arose. Political alliances, foreign raids, railway expansion, industrial booms, and the termination of long-standing agreements would have been significant events on their own, but their convergence before 1867 helped push Canada towards Confederation. The most logical solution to these problems was union. Macdonald, Brown, and other nineteenth-century politicians did not strategically plan Confederation, but rather Confederation offered itself as a solution to the problems imposed on them.
> —Student writer Chris Hoffart

Cost–Benefit: What Are the Advantages and Disadvantages?

Analyzing something often involves weighing the advantages and disadvantages, the pros and cons. **Cost–benefit analysis** can be applied to almost any topic, since few things in life come without some costs or negative consequences. You could apply cost–benefit analysis to fast foods, for example, by focusing on the individual, community, or perhaps even global costs or benefits. In an expository essay, cost–benefit analysis involves the objective weighing of pluses and minuses. However, if you were *arguing* that the benefits were more important than the costs, you might well consider the costs first and *then* the benefits, leaving the strongest argument for the last. If you took the opposing position, you might begin with benefits, as the writer does below in her argumentative essay on genetically modified organisms:

> Some scientists believe that releasing GMOs into the environment could reduce pesticide use since crops could be genetically modified to produce a toxin against the pests. Unfortunately, such a toxin could have adverse effects on other organisms, such as the pollinator species of the plant. Some believe that genetic engineering could reduce hunger in third-world countries by allowing more food production. However, after growing genetically modified crops, the farmer would be unable to sow the seeds to grow more crops because GMO seeds are sterile, forcing the farmer to buy new seeds every year—an unrealistic expense. Furthermore, introducing GMOs in third-world countries would be risky as most countries have limited resources and few safety measures in place for controlling GMOs.
> —Student writer Jutta Kolhi

Analogy: How is It Like Something Else?

An **analogy** is a comparison between one object and a second object that, except for the point of comparison, is unlike the first one. The analogy helps the reader better understand the original object. For example, you could compare fast foods to the fast pace of society itself. Below, the author began his essay on water resource management by using the analogy of a desert to stress the importance of water management in North America:

> Imagine a hot, torturously dry desert. Throughout this arid wasteland, no life exists—not a tree, shrub, or animal alive. Though to many residents of Europe

and North America this scenario may seem highly abstract and incomprehensible, it is the reality faced by many equatorial nations, such as China, Africa, Saudi Arabia, and parts of India.
—Student writer François Beaudet

Like any comparison, an analogy is effective only if the second object truly can be compared to the original object—if the comparison is *valid*, in other words. However, when arguing, a writer might deliberately use an extreme comparison to surprise the reader and make the point more convincing. The author below uses a colourful analogy to appeal to his audience, many of whom will have seen or know about the movie he refers to:

Watching a fight in the National Hockey League is reminiscent of the 2002 movie *Gladiator* in which two people fight to the death while the crowd yells from above for blood. Although fighters in the NHL are obviously not trying to maim or kill their opponents, the reaction of the crowd as they stand, raise their arms, and scream in unison is similar. Fights in the NHL serve primarily as a crowd pleaser and outlet for spectators' frustrations.
—Student writer Erik Lehman

How does the analogy convey which side of the "fighting in the NHL debate" the writer is on?

Compare and Contrast: How is It Like and/or Unlike Something Else?

To **compare and contrast** is to systematically draw similarities and identify differences between two things. When you compare and contrast, you begin by finding logical bases of comparison, and then analyze similarities and differences. In arguing that one hamburger restaurant is better than another, for example, you could use as bases of comparison their prices, their food quality, their hygienic values, and the friendliness of their staff. Early in her compare and contrast essay, the writer below contrasts two different environmental philosophies by defining each, according to the beliefs of an influential philosopher:

Conservation is a "shallow ecology" approach to viewing the environment and the role of humans within it. Conceived by Norwegian philosopher and linguist Arne Naess in the early 1970s, "shallow ecology" begins with "an assumption, often unexamined, that human beings are [the] central species in the Earth's ecosystem, and that other beings, as parts of systems, are of less importance or value." Preservation, on the other hand, is based on Arne Naess's "deep ecology" movement, which places humans within ecosystems and holds that humans are different from, but not more valuable than, other species.
—Student writer Bree Stutt (quotation from The Living Awareness Institute, http://lebendig.org/deep.htm)

For an example of a compare and contrast essay, see page 116.

In the following paragraph, the writer announces the developmental method in the topic sentence; however, she uses other rhetorical patterns as well. Along with the main rhetorical pattern, identify two other patterns in the paragraph.

> Vegetarianism, derived from a Latin word meaning "to enliven," was practised in ancient Greece as early as the sixth century BCE by the Pythagoreans, and its reputation has spread to many other countries since then. It is a way of life in China, India, Japan, Pakistan, and even in North America with more than 14 million vegetarians. Since its beginnings, many well-known people have been non-meat eaters, including Socrates, Plato, Leonardo da Vinci, Charles Darwin, Thomas Edison, Albert Einstein, and Isaac Newton. The term "vegetarian" refers to someone who does not eat any flesh; however, there are many varieties of vegetarianism. If one eats no flesh (red meat, poultry, fish), but consumes dairy and egg products, one is said to be a lacto-ovo vegetarian (the most popular type in North America). Pesco-vegetarians eat seafood but avoid red meat and poultry. Vegans are "strict vegetarians," who not only avoid consuming any type of animal but also avoid anything manufactured from animals (soap, leather, wool, honey, gelatine). Any form of vegetarianism is a healthy way of living, which not only benefits humans but also benefits animals and the planet itself.
> —Student writer Jessica Charbonneau

EXERCISE 5.1

↻ Check answers to select questions

Find two body paragraphs from the same student or professional/academic essay in this textbook. (Do not use an introduction or conclusion.) Identify the rhetorical pattern used and analyze the effectiveness of the paragraphs' development. Try to come up with at least three relevant points for each paragraph.

EXERCISE 5.2

Below are 15 general topics. Using at least three different organizational methods per topic, come up with at least three different topic sentences for each topic. Here are some examples using the topic "rap music":

1. *Cause–Effect*: Rap music, with its reliance on ever-changing slang, has expanded people's vocabulary; for instance, one's boyfriend is now called one's "boo."
2. *Definition*: Rap music is defined by some as being no more than talking over someone else's music.
3. *Description or Narration*: The lights were dim, and the crowd, writhing to the rhythm of the bass, was pressing forward to the stage.
4. *Chronology*: The style of rap music has evolved considerably since it first gained popularity with North American youth in the early 1990s.
5. *Question–Answer*: How does rap music manage to offend such a broad demographic group while maintaining such a strong fan base?
6. *Problem–Solution*: It may seem somewhat ironic, but it is possible that many of the problems addressed in rap lyrics could be solved through this very same medium.
7. *Compare and Contrast*: Rap and hip hop music of the late 1980s and early 1990s, with its offensive lyrics and radical counter-cultural appeal, can be compared in terms of its sociological implications to the rock'n'roll revolution of the late 1960s and early 1970s.

EXERCISE 5.3

8. *Personal*: When I first heard rap music I found the lyrics offensive and sexist.
9. *Cause–Effect*: Living in the ghetto, surrounded by "booty" and the "brothers," can sometimes cause young men to chant words to a particular rhythm that has no melody.
10. *Cause–Effect*: Rap music has been used as a vehicle for an oppressed minority to get its voice heard.
11. *Process*: To create rap music you need a DJ to provide the beats by mixing records, and an MC who takes the beats and contributes the vocals to make the finished product.
12. *Classification*: There are many different forms of rap; these include hip hop, hard core, and R&B.
13. *Definition and Division*: Rap is a unique form of music that is built around heavy bass beats mixed with sharp, quick lyrics. There is a whole spectrum of rap music, ranging from slow love ballads to fast-paced dance songs.
14. *Cost–Benefit*: Though rap may lead young people to openly and healthily question authority and the status quo, it can lead some adolescents to commit acts of violence against society.
15. *Analogy*: Rap can be compared to the insistent and repetitive chants of an evangelistic preacher.

Topics:

sports violence	email	privacy
animal rights	exercise	stress
Internet piracy	organ transplants	public speaking
eating disorders	alternative schooling	evolution
gas prices	same-sex marriages	global warming

Essays Using a Primary Method

Primary versus Secondary Methods

If you use one of the patterns above as the primary method to support your thesis statement, you will likely use other methods of development in supporting roles. Some of these methods are almost always used to develop paragraphs rather than as a controlling pattern for the entire essay. It is difficult to write an essay using *only*, or even primarily, question–answer, example/illustration, or analogy. Similarly, unless you set out deliberately to write a definition, process, chronological, or personal essay, likely none of these methods will be used exclusively in your essay. Although much writing, especially creative writing, uses narration and description, these are used less often in a fact-based essay.

Using Definition in an Essay

In an argumentative essay, defining something is often the first stage of an argument in which you go on to develop your thesis statement through means other than definition. On the other hand, a definition essay can expand and elaborate on a subject, using a variety of organizational methods to do so.

Definition often provides a necessary starting point for an argument. The success you have in getting your reader to agree with your definition will help establish your credibility as a writer and, in this way, strengthen your argument. Defining something also enables you to set the terms on which you want your argument to rest: successful definition enables you to take control of a potentially contentious, controversial, or abstract topic.

Although definition in an argumentative essay can be effective, it is often an essential part of an expository essay. An essay in the natural sciences and social sciences often begins by defining terms that the writer will employ throughout the essay. It may be crucial for the writer to establish the sense or connotation of one or more terms that have been subject to a variety of definitions in different studies in the writer's discipline (see the cloning example below). An academic text—above all, an introductory textbook—often includes a glossary or index of common terms that is designed to make it easier to apply terms correctly.

It is important to provide an accurate definition in your paper, as definitions often change over time and according to place, as well as according to cultural, national, social, and other variables. For example, the way you would define *privacy* today would likely be different from the way it would have been defined 25 years ago, due partly to technologies that have made it easier for others to access personal information.

In each of the first two examples below, the writer defines a concept, consumerism, in order to use it in a specific way in his or her essay. Each definition is affected by the writer's purpose. In the first example, the writer makes it clear he will argue that consumerism plays a negative role in society. In the second example, taken from the introduction to an expository essay, the writer defines consumerism as a basic economic principle. She then connects the definition to one aspect of consumerism—consumer protection, her topic.

Our lives today are defined by consumerism and revolve around it. We seem to constantly be purchasing or planning to purchase an item that will somehow make our lives easier or more enjoyable. Indeed, consumerism is the culture that promotes excessive shopping and buying without considering the use or importance of the products we buy.
—Student writer Rob McDannold

Most people use money as an exchange between goods and services, and it is essential to understand one's rights as a customer. Nowadays, most products require labelling because they inform the customers about the contents and specifications of the product, giving customers the right to choose between different products and not be affected by misleading advertising. Consumerism is a modern movement to help protect the consumer against useless, inferior, or dangerous products, misleading advertisement, unfair pricing, and other important concerns.
—Student writer Kelly Kao

A writer may sometimes give a broad or common definition to lead up to the definition most pertinent to the essay. It would have been misleading if the writer of the paragraph below had cited only the broad definition and not defined the specific way he is using the term *cloning*.

In the past decade, cloning has been scrutinized by the media, yet cloning has been going on in nature since the origins of life. By definition, clones are "a group of two or more individuals with an identical genetic makeup derived, by asexual reproduction, from a single common parent or ancestor" (Haran, 2008, p.13); cutting a worm in half, in fact, creates a clone. However, for the purpose of this essay, "cloning" will refer to the artificial production of a genetically identical cell or tissue. Cloning is broken into two main categories: reproductive cloning, the production of a whole duplicate being, and therapeutic cloning, creating cloned tissue from stem cells harvested from a cloned embryo.
—Student writer Chris Batt

Definition is a fundamental part of many of the academic essays you will read, and grasping a definition can help you know how to read the essay itself. In the following paragraph from the introduction of an academic essay, the writers use detailed criteria established by a creditable organization to help explain the methodology of their own essay.

According to the Association for Experiential Education (AEE), experiential education is an educational process whereby a learner "constructs knowledge, develops skill, and clarifies values from direct experiences and reflection on that experience" (AEE, 2007). Principles associated with this definition include involving a learner on multiple levels (e.g., intellectually, socially, and emotionally); having a learner contemplate and examine her or his personal values; encouraging a learner to become aware of her or his own biases, judgements, and preconceptions, and to reflect critically on these; and promoting a personal learning process that has implications for future learning (AEE, 2007). The educator's role is to provide experiences that facilitate learning and are congruent with these principles.
—Rye, B.J., Elmslie, P. & Chalmers, A. (2007). Meeting a transsexual person: Experience within a classroom setting. *Canadian On-Line Journal of Queer Studies in Education, 3*(1).

The Compare and Contrast Essay

Compare and contrast can be used as the controlling organizational method in either an argumentative or an expository essay. As these kinds of essays can be more challenging to write than other kinds, consider using the three-step approach:

1. Ensure that the topics you want to compare are, indeed, comparable. For example, it is not possible to compare the health-care system in the United States to the educational system in Canada. While it might be possible to compare the health-care systems of the two countries, such a topic might be too broad and complex to be manageable. However, it would be manageable to compare the health-care systems of two Canadian provinces.
2. After you have determined that the topics are comparable and that the essay is manageable, carefully choose at least three bases of comparison for the main points of your essay, ensuring that each basis of comparison is logical and can be applied to both subjects being compared.

3.   Organizing a compare and contrast essay is especially crucial. To ensure the essay is clearly laid out with the points easy to follow, you can choose between the block and the point-by-point methods.

Block and Point-by-Point Methods

In the **block method**, you consider all the points that relate to your first subject of comparison (which becomes your first block of material). Next, you consider all the points as they apply to the second subject of comparison (your second block). When you are comparing the second subject, you use the same order as you did with the first.

In the more commonly used **point-by-point method**, you consider one basis of comparison as it applies to each subject and continue until you have considered all the bases of comparison. In the following outline, "A" and "B" represent your subjects, or what you are comparing, and the numbers represent your points, or bases of comparison:

Block Method

A: SUBJECT OF COMPARISON

   1. Basis of comparison

   2. Basis of comparison

   3. Basis of comparison

B: SUBJECT OF COMPARISON

   1. Basis of comparison

   2. Basis of comparison

   3. Basis of comparison

Point-by-Point Method

1. BASIS OF COMPARISON

   A: Subject of comparison

   B: Subject of comparison

2. BASIS OF COMPARISON

   A: Subject of comparison

   B: Subject of comparison

3. BASIS OF COMPARISON

   A: Subject of comparison

   B: Subject of comparison

Below, the two methods are applied to the identical topic and bases of comparison.

Topic: Compare and contrast benefits of walking to benefits of cycling.

Block Method

A: CYCLING

   1. transportation

   2. exercise

   3. health

   4. cost

B: WALKING

   1. transportation

   2. exercise

3. health

4. cost

Point-by-Point Method

1. TRANSPORTATION

    A: Cycling

    B: Walking

2. EXERCISE

    A: Cycling

    B: Walking

3. HEALTH

    A: Cycling

    B: Walking

4. COST

    A: Cycling

    B: Walking

Sample Student Essay: Compare and Contrast

After reading this essay, answer the questions that follow, which focus on audience, paragraph development, and essay organization.

Sample Student Essay

Reading 8

Why Is the Rum Gone?
Carolyn Hardy

[1] It is unclear who fired the first shot or who threw the first shuriken; however, it is apparent that there is a serious, ongoing conflict between the pirates and the ninjas of this generation, a conflict that rages on the Internet and, no doubt, other places where reality and fantasy meet. Primarily, the tension between the two groups revolves around the question of superiority in battle. To determine the answer to this question (and to end the seemingly endless debate), several factors will be considered: the battlefield, lifestyle, weapon choice, training, and the intimidation factor. Although pirates may have the advantage when fighting at sea, ninjas are mysterious killing machines specially trained in a variety of unorthodox arts of war, thus making ninjas the ultimate victors.

[2] The outcome of the battle between pirates and ninjas is based partly on the location of the battlefield. Land covers approximately 30 per cent of the Earth's surface, whereas water covers about 70 per cent. Although on land, pirates would be greatly disadvantaged because of their long established "sea legs," a pirate's life is confined mostly to water. Fighting on a ship would be to a pirate's advantage and to a ninja's disadvantage due to the pirate's ability to adjust to the movement of the ship. However, it is important to remember that for pirates and ninjas to battle, either the pirates would have to dock on land, or ninjas would have to set sail to find the pirates, at which point the ninjas would probably adjust to the movement of a ship. In either

case, no matter the location of the battlefield, the pirate's advantage at sea could not be considered a constant or reliable one.

Physical fitness is a key attribute in any battle. Pirates are prone to scurvy, and they drink a lot of alcohol. The constant drinking makes pirates confused, disorientated, and susceptible to anterograde amnesia (loss of consciousness resulting in memory loss). In addition to drinking, their lifestyle includes excessive smoking and eating. If a pirate is injured, it does not stop him from fighting, even though there is rarely a proper medical doctor on board. Although this commitment to the job is highly commendable, injuries that frequently occur without proper medical attention can lead to a severe disadvantage in the battlefield. For example, if an eye injury occurs, the eye will most likely remain untreated, leading to either its removal or to the need for an eye patch. Needless to say, a pirate's depth perception is severely limited with an eye patch, reducing his ability in battle. Although ninjas are prone to vitamin D deficiency due to their lack of exposure to sunlight, they take excellent care of themselves with daily exercise and healthy eating habits; a ninja remains in top physical condition at all times. Furthermore, since ninjas live on land, they have access to proper medical attention if such an injury occurs, making recovery significantly faster and more effective than that of a pirate.

[3]

The weapon of choice says a lot of things about the fighting skills of the warrior. Pirates battle with swords, daggers, pistols, and gun powder, and command a ship equipped with cannons. Ninjas also battle with swords, but include several weapons unknown to the pirate, such as hallucinogenic powder, flash-bangs, katana, throwing stars, nunchucks and the sais. Although the ninja's ranged weapon, the shuriken, lacks the striking distance of a pirate's gun, a ninja has many more stealthy-ranged weapons, such as poisoned darts. Furthermore, the creativity of the ninja's weapons makes for over ninety nine ways to be killed at the hands of a ninja alone; pirates can't top ten, and that includes the plank.

[4]

Like the samurai, ninjas were born into the profession, where traditions were kept in and passed down through the family. Unlike the ninja, pirates do not have any proper training. This is because pirates are not interested in preparing for combat, but rather interested in seeking out buried treasure without recognizing the consequences. This constant hands-on learning technique is no match for ninjas, who are trained professional assassins. As well as training, it is important to note the practice of stealth. Daisuke and Doshi, the creators of ninja warfare, based the training on *nonuse*, the art of stealth (Szczepanski). In other words, ninjas are the masters of discretion. Pirates, on the other hand, have no idea what stealth means: they wear heavy outfits with clunky jewellery, have peg legs, and don't believe in hygiene; therefore, they can be smelt long before they are seen. Furthermore, ninjas can go undercover, if need be, and would not promote suspicion on arrival at a fancy dinner. Pirates, in contrast, are far too gruff to get away with any type of undercover activity without attracting any attention to themselves.

[5]

Finally, intimidation can be a vital psychological factor in warfare. It is true that pirates are physically more intimidating than ninjas because of their large boats, aggressive crew, and their sheer number. Seeing a group of pirates stagger onto the mainland would be quite nerve-wracking. On the other hand, ninjas would also be really quite intimidating if one dropped behind you in a dark alley and let you look at him for a split second; however, anyone who has been assassinated by a ninja probably did not see it coming.

[6]

In a battle between pirates and ninjas, each side has its own strengths and weaknesses. Both groups have coexisted for a long time; therefore, they must each be excellent fighters in their own way. When battling at sea, it may appear that pirates have the advantage over ninjas; when battling on land, it also appears that pirates' sheer numbers would be highly intimidating.

[7]

However, ninjas are the masters when it comes to the element of surprise; therefore, it would not matter if the pirates outnumbered the ninjas or if the battle took place on land or sea. In the end, due to a ninja's stealth, a pirate cannot win against a battle with a ninja who is a trained assassin. Clearly, a pirate is no match against an opponent that cannot be seen until it is too late.

Work Cited

Szczepanski, Kallie. "History of the Ninja." *About.com: Asian History*. The New York Times Company, 2010. Web. 5 Oct. 2010.

EXERCISE 5.4

1. The title is a quotation from the movie *Pirates of the Caribbean* (2003). Why do you think the author used this as her essay's title? What does it tell you about her intended audience?
2. Briefly analyze the essay's introduction. Consider the effectiveness of the opening and thesis statement. Is Hardy successful in establishing her approach to the topic of pirates and ninjas?
3. How could you characterize the writer's tone? Give specific examples.
4. Analyze one of the body paragraphs, using criteria discussed in this chapter; you may also use criteria discussed in Chapter 4.
5. Identify the compare and contrast method Hardy uses and the bases for comparison. You can use the appropriate diagrammatic model on page 115, above, to show method and bases for comparison.

Sample Scholarly Essay (Excerpt): Compare and Contrast

The following excerpt is from the journal article "The Worlds We Live In: Gender Similarities and Differences," by Meredith M. Kimball (*Canadian Psychology/ Psychologie canadienne* 35.4 [1999]). The one-paragraph introduction provides background to the topic, after which the essay is broken down into sections. The questions that follow focus on reading strategies and the organization of the excerpted passage.

Sample Professional Essay

Reading 9

[1] Throughout the history of feminism, from Wollstonecraft to the present, two views of gender differences have been advocated (Cott, 1986). In one, similarities between the sexes have been emphasized, whereas in the other women's special characteristics that differ from men's have been emphasized. These two different intellectual views have been used by feminists to support different but important political goals. Arguments proposing gender similarities have most often been used to support goals of political and social equality for women. Gender differences have been used to support the creation of special spheres or separate institutions for women. Within psychology, these

two traditions of feminist thinking have been visible since the beginning of the discipline. In this paper, I will explore the tensions between them, and develop the example of moral theory as a way of exploring and using this tension.

The Similarities Tradition. The similarities tradition has focused on intellectual skills and social competencies that have been assumed to explain the preponderance of men in positions of power and prestige. By showing that gender differences in these skills and competencies are either non-existent or far too small to explain existing gender differences in the labour force, feminist psychologists have sought to provide the scientific justification for political equality. This work has occurred largely within academic experimental psychology and relies on statistical techniques as the main source of proof. Historically, this tradition can be traced to the earliest work in experimental psychology. Helen Thompson was one of the first women to obtain a Ph.D. from the University of Chicago. Her thesis, *The Mental Traits of Sex* (1903), illustrates the main arguments in the similarities tradition. These include the importance of overlap between genders, the requirement of highest methodological standards to demonstrate difference, the search for social explanations of difference, and the demonstration of the specificity of difference. In 1914 Leta Stetter Hollingworth published a series of papers that undermined the hypothesis of male superiority through greater variability (Hollingworth, 1914a) and arguments that women were dysfunctional during their menstrual cycle (1914b). Work in this tradition died out around 1920 and did not become a focus within academic psychology again until the early 1970s. [2]

Beginning with the publication of Eleanor Maccoby and Carol Jacklin's *The Psychology of Sex Differences* in 1974, work in the similarities tradition again came to the fore of academic psychology. Feminist psychologists working within the similarities tradition have consistently emphasized the small magnitude of behavioural gender differences. Research reporting gender differences is examined for androcentric bias (e.g., Eichler, 1980; McHugh, Koeske, and Frieze, 1986; Stark-Adamec and Kimball, 1984). Statistical significance is supplemented with effect size calculations and meta-analytical techniques in order to eliminate the problem that very small and meaningless differences are assumed to be important because they are statistically significant (e.g., Hyde and Linn, 1986; Hyde, Fennema, and Lamon, 1990). Overlap between distributions of female and male scores is emphasized (Favreau, 1993). Another important theme is that it is not gender per se but the interaction of gender with situational variables that explains reported differences (e.g., Deaux and Major, 1987; Eagly, 1987; Kimball, 1989). Finally, the lack of choice and the role of coercion in determining women's behaviour are emphasized. Coercion may occur through either ideology and socialization or through violence and threats of violence (Epstein, 1988). In either case choice, especially a choice of traditional roles and behaviours, is viewed as largely illusory. [3]

The Differences Tradition. In contrast to the similarities position, the differences tradition has focused on positive human characteristics that have been undervalued because they are associated with women and with the symbolic feminine. Central to the concerns of this tradition are the sense of connectedness, concern with human relationships, and care-giving that women, more than men, bring to human culture. The political goal is not equality, but rather the creation of a different, more humane world that incorporates traditional feminine values as a central human focus. Most of the work in this area is qualitative, and much of it exists within a psychoanalytic framework. That women and men are different is accepted; what is questioned is the traditional devaluation of women and the symbolic feminine. Historically this tradition can be traced to the early work on gender differences in psychoanalysis. Karen Horney's (1926) critique of Freud's ideas about female development illustrates the main focus of the differences tradition. She did not question that women were different from men, but did question the reduction of this difference to mere compensation on the part of women. [4]

[5]   With the publication of Nancy Chodorow's *The Reproduction of Mothering* in 1978, a consciously feminist psychoanalytic theory began to be developed and used, which continued the tradition begun by Horney of emphasizing the importance of a particular female development and psychology that differed from the male. The three main themes of the differences tradition are present in Chodorow's work. The first is an emphasis on gender asymmetry in early child development. As a result of the social fact that infant girls are mothered by a same-sex person, issues of intimacy and autonomy become gendered. The second is an emphasis on subjective experience. For example, it is not so much mothering behaviour but rather women's desire to mother that needs explanation. Related to the emphasis on subjective experience is the theme of choice. In contrast to the emphasis on coercion and determination in the similarities tradition, theorists operating in the differences tradition emphasize and explain how it is that women make choices, in particular, choices that include traditional roles and behaviours. Indeed, Chodorow argues that mothering cannot be coerced, that the activity must be voluntary in order for a genuine emotional relationship to develop between the mother and the infant.

[6]   *Tensions between the Traditions*. The exchange of views and ideas between these two traditions has been minimal. The criticisms that have been levelled have an arrogant or extreme quality and thus the nature of the exchange when it has occurred has been adversarial. Feminist psychologists have, by and large, sided with one tradition over the other. Those working in the similarities tradition have tended to dismiss the differences viewpoint as empirically naïve and reinforcing of political conservatism. These criticisms are often quite extreme in assuming that work in the differences tradition is not only scientifically incorrect but politically antithetical to the goals of the women's movement (Kahn and Yoder, 1989). For example, Mednick (1989) describes Gilligan's (1982) theory as a conceptual bandwagon that lacks empirical support but remains popular because of the simplicity of the ideas. Sometimes critics do allow that difference theorists, such as Gilligan, do not intend to support conservative political views (Lott, 1989; Mednick, 1989). However, either this is not followed with an analysis of how these theories might be feminist (Mednick, 1989) or their work is described as empowering but for the wrong reasons and is therefore of dubious value (Lott, 1989). In one critique the feminist work of Gilligan (1982) on women's moral development and the work of Belenky and her colleagues (Belenky, Clinchy, Goldberger, and Tarule, 1986) on women's ways of knowing are grouped with the work of Benbow and Stanley (1980) on women's inferior math performance as examples of research biased towards differences (Kahn and Yoder, 1989) without any consideration of the differences in value that inform the work on these authors. Gender differences are not denied; however, the underlying assumption is that they are not real but rather correlates of the power differences between genders (e.g., Lott, 1990). Because "behavior has no gender" (Lott, 1990, p. 79) to think in terms of gender differences is to reinforce stereotypes (Bohan, 1992; Greeno and Maccoby, 1986; Lott, 1990).

[7]   The critique of similarities by theorists in the differences tradition is much less frequent; indeed, with a few exceptions it is absent. Sometimes there is a feeling one is experiencing an arrogance of silence, that there is a refusal to refute a view seen as so trivial or shallow. Although the reasons for silence are hard to document, the flavour of this shows in some of the criticisms. Gilligan (1986) implies that her critics reduce questions about sex differences in moral development to arguments about Kohlberg test scores, and sex differences in violent fantasies to disagreements over picture classifications (p. 331). In her psychodynamic theory of the development of mothering, Chodorow (1978) acknowledges, but then dismisses the importance of social reinforcement and ideology in constructing women's mothering. The implication is that such external factors are too shallow to be anything more than the social frosting on a psychodynamic cake.

Questions for Active Reading

Answer each of the short questions below. Then, determine and schematize the method used to compare and contrast.

1. How can the section of this article be divided? On what basis did you determine this?
2. What assumptions about audience are evident in the first sentence of the paper?
3. Identify the thesis statement.
4. Define *androcentric* (The Similarities Tradition, paragraphs 2–3) and *gender asymmetry* (The Differences Tradition, paragraphs 4–5).
5. What does the author consider the key work in the similarities tradition? In the differences tradition? How is this indicated in each case?
6. Explain what Kimball means by "an arrogance of silence" in paragraph 7 and consider how this concept helps shape Kimball's argument in this paragraph.
7. Which of the two methods for organizing a compare and contrast essay did the writer use? Why do you think she chose this method? Construct a schematic representation of this method. You can use the appropriate diagrammatic model above (page 115) to show method and bases for comparison.

The Essay: An Analytical Model

An essay can be analyzed, or "broken down," in different ways. For example, you can divide an essay's structure into introduction, body paragraphs, and conclusion, or you can divide essay writing into five chronological stages. When you are asked to write a critical analysis, you may discuss such areas as the writer's use of logic and reason, the number and reliability of sources, the tone or style of writing, the writer's background or bias, and the like.

Examining a generic model of the essay will help you know what to look for when you analyze another essay. It will also help with your own writing since the elements discussed below are common to most essays—from scholarly studies for specialized readers to the kinds of essays you will write. But whether you are reading an essay or writing one, you will often begin by identifying the claim, a general assertion about the topic on which the essay is based.

Kinds of Claims: Fact, Value, Policy, and Interpretation

Every essay makes some kind of **claim**, usually expressed in the thesis (see page 36), and then proceeds to prove the claim by various means of support. Thus, there are two main parts to an essay, whether it is argumentative or expository: the *claim* and the *support*. The essay writer may use a claim of fact, value, policy, or interpretation.

Claims of Fact

A **claim of fact** is usually an **empirical** claim that uses the evidence-gathering methods of observation and measurement, a claim that can be proven by facts and figures or through the results of prior studies relating to the claim. Claims of fact are used in most expository essays.

Claims of Value

A **claim of value** is an ethical claim and appeals to one's sense of values or a moral system; such values could be inherent in a religious, philosophical, social, cultural, or other system. A claim of value is supported largely through a process of **deductive reasoning** where certain standards of good or bad, right or wrong, are accepted as **premises**.

Claims of Policy

A **claim of policy** is usually a call for some kind of action to rectify a problem or improve a situation. Although a claim of policy does not have to be grounded in a claim of value, it often will be; for example, a proposed change to a law or regulation that gives people more control over something in their lives may be presented as a claim of value, and could involve the argument that the change will produce a more democratic society in which people have greater freedom to assert their rights.

Most topics can be explored through any of these three claims, depending on the way the claim is presented. In an expository essay, the claim will be presented as factual. In an argumentative essay, the claim will usually be presented as one of value or policy. If you were asked to write an essay on the topic of "homelessness," for example, your claim could take a form similar to one of the following:

Factual claim: Due to the unsettled economic climate, homelessness is increasing in most Canadian provinces.

For support, the writer might use economic data to help prove a relationship between economic instability and incidence of homelessness.

Value claim: In a society of excess, our indifference to the problem of the homeless on our doorsteps is an indictment of our way of life.

For support, the writer might make emotional and ethical appeals to the reader.

Policy claim: To solve the problem of homelessness in our city, council needs to increase the number of permanent shelters, erect temporary shelters in downtown parks, and educate the public about this escalating social problem.

For support, the writer could appeals to the reader's values but would focus more on practical, "real-world" solutions.

Claims of Interpretation

A **claim of interpretation** is a more specialized type of claim. A literary essay will often use a claim of interpretation, which is supported through references to the primary (literary) text itself, as well as to secondary sources if research has been done. A writer in a discipline such as history, philosophy, or cultural studies also may use a claim of interpretation if the main purpose is to weigh and interpret the evidence found in either primary or secondary sources. For example, a writer could claim that the defeat of Athens in the Peloponnesian War was inevitable due to the internal conflicts within

Athens itself. In such an essay, the writer would likely use the interpretations of experts to help formulate the essay's claim. Because a claim of interpretation can often be challenged, it can be considered as a kind of argumentative claim.

Tentative and Conclusive Claims

Although the reader expects your claim early in your essay, usually at the end of the introduction, you may find yourself rewriting your claim *after* you have written your body paragraphs. This is because a claim is a generalization based on specific evidence or careful reasoning. You are often better able to make a generalization after you've thoroughly explored your topic, gathered details, and analyzed all the evidence.

Thus, a claim can take one of two forms. A *tentative* (temporary) claim is a generalization that seems true or applicable to your topic but which could change as you become aware of new information. A claim made in a research proposal or outline—even sometimes in a rough draft—can be considered tentative. A *conclusive* claim acts as a conclusion: you can express it with confidence in your introduction because the evidence you've uncovered has pointed to it (see Chapter 4, The Thesis Statement, page 91).

Support: Evidence and Credibility

A claim will not be accepted without **support**—in other words, without **evidence** to back it up. But evidence alone is not enough. To convince your reader that your claim is justified, you need to demonstrate your **credibility**. Although many student writers believe that evidence is more important than credibility, the effort of gathering and arranging evidence may be wasted if you do not present yourself as credible. When you produce support in your body paragraphs, you then need to present ample evidence and do so in a credible way.

Organization of Evidence

You support your claim through your main points and sub-points. These points function effectively when appropriate organizational methods are used and when the points are ordered logically (climax, inverted climax, or mixed order). Organizational methods include definition, division/classification, cause–effect, compare and contrast, problem–solution, and chronology (see pages 102–103 earlier in this chapter).

Kinds of Evidence

The effectiveness of your argument also depends on the specific *kinds* of evidence you use. Depending on your topic, the instructions for the assignment, and the discipline in which you are writing, you may use some kinds of evidence more than others in your essay. Writing in the humanities often relies on primary, or original, sources. If you write an English essay, for instance, you will probably use many quotations from literary works. The primary sources commonly used in historical research are autobiographies, newspapers, letters, and other records from the era being studied.

Social sciences writing tends to focus on facts and figures, statistics and other numerical data, case studies, interviews, questionnaires, and observation. Scientific studies may use similar kinds of evidence but frequently rely on direct methods that involve experimentation. Examples are important in just about every discipline.

Using a variety of evidence, rather than relying solely on one kind, will likely produce a stronger essay. However, it's important, especially if you are using research, to find **hard evidence** to support your key points. Hard evidence includes facts, statistics, and statements from authorities (experts). **Soft evidence** alone, such as examples and illustrations, might make your essay readable and understandable, but hard evidence will make it more convincing. Hard evidence is essential in a factual claim. It is also effective in a policy claim because this claim advocates specific actions. It may be less important in a value claim, in which appeals to reason, emotion, and ethics, along with examples, analogies, brief narratives, description, or personal experience in themselves could produce an effective argument.

Facts and Statistics

It is hard to argue with facts. For this reason, factual information is the strongest kind of evidence in an essay. Its effective use will also enhance your credibility by making you appear knowledgeable. Although facts from reliable sources are always relevant to a research essay, they can provide support in an essay not involving research if you are arguing a topic you know a lot about. The student writer of the essay on page 56 in Chapter 3 cites facts, such as the September 2001 tragedy in New York City, and mentions works of art, artists, and art periods. When you use research sources, you should ensure that the conclusions are based on factual data tested under controlled conditions. Reliable findings from research can be treated as factual.

You probably have heard people say that statistics lie or that numbers can be twisted to mean whatever you want them to mean. It's important that you take statistics from reliable sources. Although a statistic may not be an outright falsehood, you should pay attention to the wording of the passage that it comes from in order to assess possible bias or distortion. Use caution with statistics cited by people or organizations promoting a particular cause or viewpoint. For example, surveys conducted by special interest groups can be deceptive (see Chapter 6, Reliability of Internet Sources, page 140).

Consider the case of a union that wants to put pressure on the government by making its case public. The group's executive pays for a full-page ad in major newspapers, claiming 93.7 per cent support among the public. The questions to ask are, "Who were the survey's respondents?" "How many were surveyed?" "How was the survey conducted?" Perhaps in this situation a small number of people who happened to be walking by the picket lines were stopped and surveyed. Reliable sources disclose their information-gathering methods, which you can evaluate.

It is often apparent whether the source is trustworthy or not. For example, although People for the Ethical Treatment of Animals (PETA) strongly opposes practices like animal testing, many statistics they publish can be considered reliable because they come from reliable sources. In a PETA factsheet criticizing animal research, for instance, the writer cites a 1988 study that appeared in the refereed journal *Nature*, which "reports that 520 of 800 chemicals (65 per cent) tested on rats and mice caused cancer in the animals but not in humans (Lave et al. 631)." In sources like this, however, remember that statistics and factual data are being used for a specific purpose; evaluate them individually and keep this purpose in mind. Also bear in mind that sources like PETA may report only on those studies that agree with the organization's mission or viewpoint, ignoring contrary findings.

All the essays in Chapter 6 make effective use of facts and statistics.

Authorities and Experts

When you apply for a job, you may be asked for letters of reference. Unless your prospective employer asks specifically for a character reference, you would normally submit letters from knowledgeable experts—perhaps from your former bosses or those you have worked with. They would be considered authorities who could support your claim of competence and testify that you are a good candidate for the job.

Authorities can be used to support your claim if they have direct knowledge of your subject. Authorities who are not experts have less credibility. For example, in an essay that argues a scientific or mathematical point, citing Albert Einstein would provide hard evidence. In an essay about vegetarianism, citing Einstein would provide soft evidence as he is not considered an expert on the topic. You will usually locate experts as you research your topic. However, it's also possible to conduct an interview with an expert, asking questions pertinent to your claim. See Chapter 6, Field Research: Interviewing, page 159.

Examples, Illustrations, Case Studies, Precedents

While hard evidence provides direct support, **soft evidence** indirectly supports your points and makes them more understandable to the reader. Indirect support includes examples, illustrations, case studies, and precedents. Analogies, description, and personal experience may also be used if your instructor approves.

We use **examples** in both speech and writing. To support his argument, a teenager arguing for his independence might give several examples of friends who live on their own. Examples should always be relevant and representative. The teenager's parents might refute the examples by pointing out that they are not representative—for example, that one friend, Shawn, has a full-time job and that another, Giovanna, spent the summer travelling throughout Europe before moving out of her parents' house.

In most writing, examples bring a point home to the reader by making it specific and concrete. Examples are especially useful if you are writing for a non-specialist reader, as they make it easier to grasp a difficult or an abstract point. Illustrations, case studies, and precedents are extended examples that can help to explain or reinforce important points.

Illustrations are detailed examples that often take the form of anecdotes or other brief narratives. In this example, the writer uses an illustration to support his point that logic can be used to draw different conclusions from the same premise (a statement assumed to be true):

Consider the example of the hydroelectric dam that the Urra company constructed in Colombia. The dam provides electricity to industry and profit to the companies and people who invest in it. The area flooded by the dam was inhabited by indigenous peoples. The river was a source of fresh water and fish, and on the river's now flooded banks were food plants that sustained them. . . . If an analysis of this situation were based on the premise that all people should be treated equally and with respect, then through reason, the conclusion would be that this was a bad thing for the indigenous peoples living along the river. If, however, the basic premise was that business interests are primary, then the logical conclusion would be that the hydroelectric dam was a good thing.

—Student writer Graeme Verhulst

Case studies are often used as support, particularly in the social sciences, education, and business; they can also be the focus of research studies. A case study is a carefully selected example that is closely analyzed in order to provide a testing ground for the claim the writer is making. Because case studies are practical, real-life examples, they can be used to support a **hypothesis** (a prediction). For example, to find out if involving youth in decision-making could produce a safer school environment, a Vancouver school planned a series of student-led initiatives and activities. The results showed that that the students felt safer and had improved their pro-social and conflict resolution skills. The outcome supported the hypothesis concerning the effectiveness of youth self-governance.

Precedents are examples of how particular situations were dealt with in the past. Judgments in courts of law establish precedents that influence future court decisions. Once you have established some course of action as a precedent, you then apply it to your argument. Successfully using precedents as evidence depends on your ability to convince the reader that

1. similar conditions apply to your topic today, and
2. following the precedent will produce a desirable result.

For example, if you were arguing that Canada should offer free post-secondary studies to all academically qualified individuals, you could refer to the precedent of Denmark, one of the first countries to provide universal access to post-secondary schooling. Then you must make it clear that

1. the situation in Denmark is comparable to that in Canada, and
2. Denmark has profited by this system, so Canada will also likely benefit from a similar course of action.

Analogy, Description, Personal Experience

Analogy, description, and personal experience as evidence are suggestive and indirect; they cannot in themselves prove a claim.

Analogy, a kind of comparison (see page 109), and **description** (see page 104), can be used to make a point easier for the reader to understand and relate to. Like narration, description may also play a limited role in argument, perhaps to attract interest in the essay's introduction or to set up a main point.

Personal experience could take the form of direct experiences or observation. Recounting an experience can help the reader relate to your topic. You should keep your voice objective when using personal experience; any bias will undermine your credibility. Personal experience can effectively support a value claim. For example, if you had witnessed a dog fight, your observations on dog fighting could support the claim that dog fighting is cruel. Similarly, if you have had personal experience with homeless people by working in a food bank, you could use your experience to help support a related policy claim. Student writer Rob Wilkinson uses it to help introduce his topic (see page 148).

Credibility

Demonstrating credibility as a writer strengthens your claim. Three factors contribute to credibility: knowledge of the topic, reliability/trustworthiness, and fairness. Your knowledge by itself doesn't make you credible. Consider again the analogy of job-hunting: when you send out your résumé, you want to impress prospective employers with your experience and knowledge; however, during the interview, the employer will likely ask questions that pertain more to your reliability as an employee than to your knowledge—for example, "Why do you want to work for us?" "Where do you see yourself in five years?" "Why did you quit your last job?" Furthermore, when employers check your references, questions of your reliability are bound to arise. Similarly with essay writing, once you have conveyed your knowledge, you must convince the reader that you also are reliable.

You demonstrate **knowledge** through the points made in the essay and the kinds of evidence you use to support them. But you can present yourself as knowledgeable without being thought reliable. You instill confidence in your **reliability** or trustworthiness when you can answer "yes" to questions like the following:

> Is your essay well-structured?
> Are your paragraphs unified, coherent, and well-developed?
> Is your writing clear? Is your grammar correct? Is your style effective?
> Have you used the conventions of your discipline?
> Have you used critical thinking skills effectively? Are your conclusions logical and well-founded?

You must demonstrate **fairness** in an argumentative essay, where it is often important to consider opposing views. To strengthen your claim, you can pinpoint the shortcomings and limitations of these views. A writer who is fair comes across as objective in addressing the other side, avoiding slanted language that reveals bias. While you can demonstrate reliability by avoiding misuse of reason, you can demonstrate fairness by using emotional appeals fairly and selectively (discussed in more detail in Chapter 8). The question of fairness can also arise in an expository essay if you are not objective in your use of the evidence.

The Unity of the Essay

Student writers sometimes have the impression that an effective essay comprises parts that function in isolation. But the opposite is true: it is really one entity with many interdependent parts. In Figure 5.1 below, each part coexists with the other parts; none is an isolated entity that you can simply inject into an essay mechanically or without considering where it fits in. This inter-relatedness is evident in many places in a successful essay. In writing your own essays, you can ask questions like, "Am I using the kinds of evidence favoured by my discipline?" "Am I organizing this evidence logically?" "Have I used enough sources?" "Is my essay well-structured and is my writing clear and grammatical?" "Have I used evidence fairly?"

When reading an essay in order to analyze it, you can ask similar questions about the writer and the essay. When you analyze, you break something down into parts so you can look closely at each part. The interdependence of the various parts of the essay can then be clearly seen. For example, grammatical errors affect the writer's reliability, thus reducing credibility and weakening support for the claim. Understanding the relatedness of the different parts should enable you to approach your own writing critically and give you the tools to analyze other writing.

The Essay

Claim — Support

Claim:
Fact   Value   Policy   Interpretation

Support:
Evidence — Credibility

Evidence:
Organization/Order of Evidence   Kinds of Evidence

Kinds of Evidence:
Knowledge   Reliability   Fairness

Figure 5.1   The Essay: An Analytical Model

EXERCISE 5.5

Check answers to select questions

It is important that you be able to distinguish between a factual claim and a value or policy claim. Although there may not always be a firm line between exposition and argument, you may be asked to write an essay that is clearly either one or the other; and, of course, your reader should recognize what kind of essay he or she is reading.

Determine whether the statements below are most suited to argument or exposition by putting an *A* or *E* beside them.

1. British Columbia's environmental policy is better than Alberta's policy.
2. Legislators should impose an outright ban on smoking in indoor public establishments and places of business.
3. Diplomacy and militarism are the two main approaches to foreign policy which, though sometimes used independently, are much more effective when used in combination.
4. 3M's tradition, strategy, and corporate image have helped it maintain its top-ten ranking in *Fortune* magazine year after year.
5. Organic farming has many costs, but the benefits seem much greater as this farming method is becoming more popular.
6. Hip hop today acts as a cultural bridge for widely diverse groups of young people to communicate across racial, class, religious, linguistic, and national divisions.
7. In spite of ethical concerns, can the human race really afford to ignore the tremendous potential benefit of embryonic stem cell research to find cures for many diseases?
8. The government should take steps to regulate the monopolistic practices of airlines today.
9. Probably nobody in the history of psychology has been as controversial—sometimes revered, sometimes despised—as Sigmund Freud.
10. What are the physical effects of artificial and natural tanning? What are the risks involved, and what can be done to educate the public about both?

EXERCISE 5.6

Each of the 15 simple thesis statements below contains a claim of fact, value, or policy. Identify the kind of claim, and then turn the original claim into the two other kinds of claims (one sentence for each new claim). You may make any changes in wording you wish as long as the topic remains the same.

Example

Thesis Statement: Cellphones are a wonderful modern convenience, but they can be dangerous in cars because they often distract the driver.

Kind of Claim: Claim of value: the statement asserts that cellphones can be dangerous (a bad thing).

A. The recent use of cellphones in cars has increased the number of accidents in many urban centres—especially during rush hour.

Kind of Claim: Claim of fact: the statement asserts that the number of accidents has increased.

B. Cellphones in cars should be prohibited as they are dangerous both for the user and for other drivers.

Kind of Claim: Claim of policy: the statement advocates an action, although this action is based on a value, i.e., that cellphones in cars are dangerous (bad).

1. It is increasingly necessary to be bilingual in Canada today.
2. The lyrics of rap music are inherently anti-social and encourage violence.
3. Women should not be allowed to serve in the military in anything but administrative roles.
4. Whatever one may think of same-sex marriages, it is evident that they are here to stay.
5. After completing high school, it is best to travel for at least a year before proceeding to college or university.
6. It is necessary to provide more funding for technology in today's classroom and to spend less on teachers' salaries.
7. The current practice of appointing Supreme Court judges in Canada is undemocratic.
8. With the number of sports teams, clubs, and cultural groups on campus, students who do not participate in extra-curricular activities are not getting good value for their education.
9. School uniforms provide many benefits to students and their parents.
10. The government should subsidize organically grown food.
11. Recreational use of steroids can cause physical and psychological damage to the user.
12. Before committing more resources to space exploration, we should work to solve global problems, such as poverty, that affect people every day.
13. The growing popularity of Eastern medicine today shows that society is tending towards a more natural approach to health care.
14. Parents should have the right, within reason, to discipline their child as they see fit.
15. While advocates of a shorter work week believe that this measure will help our troubled economy, opponents say it will only weaken it and create social problems.

EXERCISE 5.7

Collaborative Exercise

Taking one of the claims for each statement in Exercise 5.6 above, determine how you would most effectively support it in the body of an essay. This exercise could take the form of a group discussion, or your group could write out a strategic approach, referring as specifically as possible to those parts under Support in Figure 5.1 above.

Strategies to Consider

Organization of Evidence: Which patterns of organization/development would you likely use? Which could be used?

Kinds of Evidence: Which kinds of evidence would most effectively back up your claim?

Credibility: Which of the three categories of credibility—knowledge, reliability, fairness—seem the most important? Why? What general or specific strategies could you use to ensure your support is credible?

Writing a Research Essay

Exposition, Synthesis, and Research

When you are assigned to write a research essay (often called a research paper or research project), you will be exercising a number of valuable and interrelated skills, including planning, various kinds of selective reading, critical thinking, evaluating and summarizing sources, analyzing, synthesizing, organizing, integrating, and documenting your sources. Because of the breadth of activities involved, research essays can be a vital learning experience and are a hallmark of university writing.

Research is associated with expository writing. **Exposition** is an inclusive term for writing concerned with *informing* or *explaining*, as distinct from arguing or persuading. However, arguments can often be bolstered by research: using secondary sources, such as facts and statistics from a government website, the results of an academic study, or the opinion of an expert can make your value or policy claim more convincing (see Chapter 8). Similarly, if you are asked to use research in a literary analysis, in addition to analyzing primary sources—the works themselves—you will be analyzing the views and opinions of experts to give more credibility to your thesis (see Chapter 9).

Research comes from the French *rechercher*, "to seek again." Most researchers can attest to the fact that when they conduct research, they look and *look again*—exploring, checking, and re-checking are integral to research. In an expository research essay, **claims of fact** are generally used, and you don't set out to argue for one side or the other; instead, after determining your research question, you analyze and assess the validity of the conclusions of various researchers on the topic and, from these findings, come to a reasoned conclusion.

However, if you went no further, if you contented yourself *only with finding out*, your learning would not be complete. You might know a lot, but you would not necessarily be able to apply your knowledge unless you also were able to **synthesize**, or integrate, your new-found learning. Thus, while exposition implies research, research, in turn, implies synthesis—putting together what you have learned.

Exposition is an inclusive term for writing concerned with *informing* or *explaining*, as distinct from arguing or persuading.

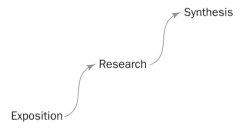

As a philosophical term, synthesis is the third, higher stage of truth that results from the combination of thesis and antithesis. In chemistry, synthesis refers to the formation of a more complex compound from two or more chemical elements. These definitions suggest what you do when you use the findings of others to help explain your topic: you create a synthesis, or "a higher stage of truth."

Building and Using Knowledge: Learning the Research Craft

What we call progress in the sciences, the social sciences, and the humanities is cumulative. Like apprentice researchers, experts rely on the previous research of others; the research they do themselves, in turn, adds to the common store of knowledge, enabling them to contribute to their field. For example, the authors of the article "Social Consequences of the Internet for Adolescents" (page 184) rely on previous research; this reliance can be seen in their list of sources and by the way they use the sources within the article itself. Although online communication technologies is a current topic, Valkenburg and Peter use a measurement scale devised in 1985. They also analyze many studies from the 1990s and compare them to more recent studies; finally, the authors suggest several hypotheses to explain the differences, which future researchers can use to further explore the topic.

In their research projects, students, too, will build on work done by others. Although undergraduate student researchers do not, typically, further knowledge in the sense that established scholars and researchers do, the research project provides a useful and enduring model (outlined below). It might be more accurate to say that student researchers are like artisans learning a craft, building future skills by following in the footsteps of others in pursuit of a goal:

> Artisans pursue the creative blending of materials, tools, techniques, design, form, and function, often to enable them to realise the vision which inspired them. . . . Likewise, the academic researcher starts with a question, which can only be satisfactorily answered by blending appropriate data, concepts, research design, research methods, analytical techniques, and so forth. . . .

> Whether it is a completely original outcome or a new representation of something familiar, the finished work of both the artisan and the researcher should resonate with their intended audience, as capturing and explaining some aspect of their subject. Although the finished research product must be rigorously informed, the unique fusion of method, data, and the researcher means that it is, in many ways, as much art as science.
> —Guthrie, Cathy. "On Learning the Research Craft: Memoirs of a Journeyman Researcher." *Journal of Research Practice* 3.1 (2007): 1–2.

Although the research process is not always linear, it can be broken down into distinct stages. As you work toward your goal of investigating a problem, there are specific questions you can ask yourself to monitor your progress, perhaps using the questions below as a checklist. At the end of each stage, you should sense that you are building towards your goal and have completed the tasks before proceeding to the next stage in what Cathy Guthrie above calls a "journey."

Research: Finding and Exploring

This step involves determining your topic and relevant sources (see Subjects versus Topics in Chapter 2, page 36). Once you have selected your topic, you may have to narrow it down so that your essay is not too general, perhaps by thinking about your own interests in relation to the topic. For example, student writer Rob Wilkinson was in a band and attempting to distribute his music (see his proposal, Reading 11, page 134). Initially, he considered writing on illegally downloading music. Recalling his childhood experience with cassette tapes, he began to wonder whether the CD would survive the advent of the MP3 player. The more he explored the topic, the more curious he became. (See his essay, Reading 14, page 176.)

Student writer Iain Lawrence wanted to research some aspect of sports. As he had a four-year-old son, he began thinking about the value of children's sports and sports leagues. Preliminary research in textbooks and other general sources guided him to the topic he eventually settled on: the relationship between participation in sports and childhood aggression. See his proposal (Reading 10, page 147), outline (Reading 12, page 171), and essay (Reading 13, page 173).

After you have a topic and have begun your research, it is helpful to write a *research proposal* (page 145), which could include your purpose, topic, thesis and main points, as well as a tentative list of source material. To get to this stage, of course, you will have had to think about the topic and use the pre-writing strategies you find the most effective.

Questions to Ask

> Where do your interests lie?
> Do you have a knowledge base you can use to begin exploring the topic?
> If the topic is unfamiliar, how can you obtain background information?
> What are you hoping to contribute to this subject?
> How can you narrow down your topic?
> To whom are you writing? Who is your audience?
> What kinds of sources are appropriate given your topic and audience?
> Where should you look to find your source material?
> Do you know of the major authors in the field, or how you can find these authors?
> Have you given yourself sufficient time to research, synthesize, organize, compose, document, and revise?

Synthesis (I): Assimilation

After you have found your sources, your mental process becomes one of **assimilation**; by taking notes and summarizing where appropriate, you are demonstrating that you can accurately represent another person's ideas and use them (assimilate them) with your own ideas. This vital stage of the research essay is discussed on pages 165–170; summarizing is discussed in Summary: The Précis in Chapter 3, page 65 and below, Summary, page 160. When you have done these tasks, you are ready to begin to organize your points and structure your essay.

As Rob Wilkinson and Iain Lawrence recorded information, they were already beginning to evaluate its usefulness and connect information from different sources. For Wilkinson, who relied on facts and statistics, part of the challenge was avoiding being overwhelmed by the surfeit of data. Although Wilkinson knew he would be using summary and paraphrase a great deal, he carefully recorded significant and colourful direct quotations, which he planned to use to vary his essay's flow and maintain reader interest. In reading peer-reviewed journals on child development, Lawrence came across several definitions of aggression and had to decide on the relative importance of each. He then sorted them into categories and focused on the most relevant ones.

During this stage, as you decide how the material is going to be used and where it belongs in your essay, your goal should be much clearer than in the finding and exploring stage. You should begin to see your essay "coming together" as you work towards building your essay's structure, the next stage.

Questions to Ask

> Is your research geared towards supporting your points?
> How do the sources help you in your exploration of the topic?
> Have you understood the results of the studies you've looked at and/or the positions of the experts whose works you have read?
> Are all your sources credible? Are there many recent ones?
> Have you summarized adequately and/or quoted accurately all sources you might use?
> Have you recorded the authors' names, titles, page numbers, and other bibliographic information accurately?
> Which sources are the most important? Which are most relevant to your topic and thesis?
> How do the different experts' views or conclusions fit together?
> Are there opposing positions? Do some findings challenge others, for example?
> Has your research changed your approach to the topic? If so, how? Do you need to change your thesis?

Organization: Arranging

Every essay needs a structure; often this will be shown through an outline, a kind of blueprint for the writing stage. Strategies for outlining are discussed in Chapter 2; an example of a topic outline is given on page 45. An example of a detailed sentence outline follows on page 171.

Coming up with an outline was easier for Wilkinson than for Lawrence: because Wilkinson was organizing by chronology, the order of points was straightforward. For Lawrence, a comprehensive outline was essential, and the composing stage was directly linked to his detailed outline. Although he relied on the outline, he continued to develop some of his points as he worked on his rough draft. Although a formal outline can be useful, it shouldn't be considered unchangeable.

Questions to Ask

> Do you have enough support to begin an outline? If so, what kind of outline should you use?
> Is there a natural organizational method you should use (chronological, cause–effect, problem–solution) ?
> Do your points thoroughly explore the topic?
> Are any points inadequately developed? How can they be further developed?
> Do all your points include sub-points? If not, should these points be discarded or should you try to find ways to develop them?
> Are all areas of your research relevant to the points you want to make?
> What points are most essential and what sources are most relevant?
> Are you off topic anywhere?
> How should the points be ordered (e.g., from least important to most important)?
> Does your chosen structure reflect your purpose? Does it reflect your audience? Is it logical?

Synthesis (II): Composing

During the first-draft stage, synthesis takes place at the linguistic or the textual level, as you are now concerned with integrating your sources into your essay. Thus, how you use direct quotations, summary, and paraphrase will be crucial (see Using Sources in the Composing Process, pages 160 and 161). Wilkinson decided to use selected portions of the direct quotations he recorded to keep his audience interested, whereas Lawrence makes minimal use of direct quotation, preferring to summarize findings in his own words and reserve direct quotations only for key phrases that could not easily be paraphrased. His choice was determined partly by the assigned word length of the essay: summary enabled him to convey information efficiently and he could therefore include more sources in his essay, enhancing his credibility.

When Wilkinson was integrating direct quotations into his essay, he too was concerned with efficiency, choosing to use ellipses to omit less important content. For clarity, he also used square brackets to indicate changes and additions to the source material. (See pages 176–179.)

Questions to Ask

> Have you used sources consistently to support your points? Have you overused one or more sources (i.e., depended too much on it/them)?
> If you are working directly from an outline, can you see any points that need further development? Do any overly long paragraphs need to be subdivided?
> Which sources should be summarized, which paraphrased, and which quoted directly? (This will depend on various factors including length, importance, and phrasing of the source.)
> Have you attributed (cited) all sources that need to be cited?
> Is there any danger that you have unintentionally plagiarized by failing to cite a source or by citing it incorrectly? (If in doubt, check with your instructor.)
> Can you use ellipses to omit less important parts of a direct quotation?
> Have you provided smooth transitions between quotations and your own writing?
> Is the language level roughly consistent throughout? Is it appropriate for your audience?
> Are direct quotations grammatically integrated and easy to read?
> Have you double-checked quotations for accuracy?
> Is your own writing clear, grammatical, and effective?

Documenting: Following Procedures

In this final stage of the research essay, you follow the documentation guidelines as laid down by the authority of your discipline. The two main scholarly methods for parenthetical referencing are those of the Modern Language Association (MLA) and the American Psychological Association (APA). Some journal and book publishers use notes as a referencing system, following, for example, the Chicago Manual of Style (CMS) or the Council of Science Editors (CSE); still others use variants of one of these systems. The major documentation methods are outlined in Chapter 7.

Lawrence, whose disciplines are Biology and Psychology, used APA style (see pages 173–176). Wilkinson, a Humanities student, used MLA style.

Questions to Ask

> What documentation style is expected for the essay?

> Where can you find reliable information on documenting? (Sources of information on documentation must be both accurate and current.)

> If you have used electronic sources, are you clear on acceptable methods for documenting them? In addition to using current editions of documentation guides and/or reliable websites, such as those of university libraries, look for current guidelines on documenting non-print sources on the websites of organizations like the APA and MLA.

> Do you know exactly what needs to be documented and what does not?

> Is it possible that the reader could confuse your ideas or observations with those of a secondary source?

> Have you carefully documented other people's words and ideas without cluttering the essay with unnecessary citations?

> Have you included *all* the sources in your essay in your alphabetical list at the end of your essay? (Note that some citation styles may not require you to include sources that cannot be accessed by someone else, such as informal interviews, even if you do use them in your essay.)

Table 6.1 summarizes the five stages discussed above. Remember to pay attention to grammar, style, and clarity at all stages of the process, particularly the last two. As you revise, these matters should always be uppermost. Demonstrating your knowledge of previous research on your topic will help convey your reliability as a researcher; paying strict attention to the formal writing standards of the academic disciplines will help convey your reliability as a writer.

Table 6.1   Stages in Writing a Research Essay

Stage	Activities	Writing Tasks	Textbook Readings
Research	finding, exploring, scanning	Pre-writing, narrowing topic Research proposal	The Research Proposal (page 145); Writing a Research Essay (page 131); Where Experts Are Found (page 140)
Synthesis (I)	focused reading, assimilating ideas from sources	1. Note-taking 2. Summarizing	What Is Research? (page 138) Summary: The Précis (page 65)
Organization	arranging, determining structure	Formal outline	Formal Outline (page 44)
Synthesis (II)	integrating at textual level	1. Summary 2. Paraphrase 3. Direct quotation 4. Mixed format	Source Citation and Plagiarism (page 162) Methods of Integrating Sources (page 165)
Documentation	following guidelines	1. In-text citations 2. Bibliography section	Why Document Your Sources? (page 193); Source Citation and Plagiarism (page 162)

Coming Up with a Title

Your research essay's title, like all essay titles, should be informative, reflecting the essay's content and the approach you take to your topic. Clearly, a title like "Major Research Paper" conveys neither. The title "Attention Deficit Disorder" announces only the topic; it says nothing about content or approach. Titles must also be clear to readers who might know little about the topic. For example, "The Mozart Effect and Cognitive Processing" may be informative, but may mean little to its audience. "Treating Attention Deficit Disorder without Drug Interventions" and "Does Listening to Classical Music Enhance Intelligence?" are both informative and clear.

Although the title of an argumentative essay is often designed to arouse interest, the title of an expository essay should focus on conveying information efficiently. Do not wait until you have finished your essay before choosing a title. As possible titles occur to you as you research, outline, or compose, write them down for further consideration. A blank title page and a looming deadline can make a last-minute decision difficult; remember that your title will be the first part of your essay that is read. Here are some suggestions to make title selection easier:

> Nouns are usually the keywords in titles. If you are stuck for a title, choose three or four important nouns in your essay or ones that sum up your main points; then, look for the best way to connect them (e.g., *videogames+children+aggression*; "The Effects of Video Games on Childhood Aggression").

> If your title seems too long, consider dividing it into two parts with a colon in between (e.g., "The Negative Impacts of the International Monetary Fund's Policies on Argentina's Social Disparities" could become "The Impacts of the International Monetary Fund's Policies on Argentina: Fanning the Flames of Social Disparity").

> A "two-part" title could pose a central question that the essay will answer (e.g., "Laptops in Today's Classroom: Distractions or Educational Tools?").

> Although an expository essay title may not need to attract a reader's interest, a catchy title may convey information more efficiently than one that is more straightforward (e.g., "Airbrushed to Perfection: Media and Teenagers' Self-Esteem" conveys essentially the same information as, and is more interesting than, "Unrealistic Images in the Media and Their Effects on Teenagers' Self-Esteem").

What Is Research?

Although you may not realize it, research is probably familiar to you. It is unlikely you will have made many important life decisions without researching them beforehand, whether deciding which MP3 player to buy or which post-secondary schools to apply to. In the case of an MP3 player, you may have asked friends or simply browsed through the selection on the store shelves, noting the features of each model. In the case of schools, you may have read brochures, talked to other people—perhaps current students, graduates, or school counsellors—and considered various academic and non-academic criteria. However, you probably placed the highest value on *factual evidence*: programs, prerequisites, tuition fees, housing, and campus size. You may have consulted objective experts, such as people who have researched the different MP3 players or schools, ranking them according to different criteria.

Decision-making based on research is a life skill, and analysis, judgment, and evaluation are involved in the decision-making process. Research assignments in university ask you to analyze, compare, assess, and/or synthesize the scholarship of experts in your subject area, generally by discussing multiple positions on a problem. Simply rephrasing these sources is not necessarily research, nor is summarizing your own opinions or experiences.

One common approach to organizing a research paper is to compare and contrast the similarities and differences between two or more ideas. Another method is to evaluate the strengths and/or weaknesses of an idea based on criteria that you create or borrow from experts. The following step-by-step example involves both compare and contrast and evaluation to draw a conclusion about each source.

1. Identifying a problem:

   The effect of playing video games on aggressive or violent behaviour.

2. Stating a claim or hypothesis about this problem (what the writer will explore or prove):

   Violent video games can cause aggression in teenagers.

3. Describing the points made by one or more "experts" concerning the claim:

   Researcher A's research shows a significant increase in emotional arousal and a decrease in brain activity in areas responsible for self-control after teenagers played a violent video game for 20 minutes. Researcher A used brain scans to detect changes in activity in different areas of the brain.

   Researcher B's research shows a small but significant relationship between playing violent video games and thoughts and behaviour after the period of game playing. She studied young teenagers who completed questionnaires about their video playing habits and their aggressive thoughts and behaviour.

4. Reaching a decision on the merits of these experts' approaches to the thesis:

   Researcher A's finding is more convincing than that of Researcher B because his method provides direct evidence that playing video games altered parts of the brain associated with aggressive behaviour. However, it did not investigate aggressive acts; therefore, his study did not attempt to link video game playing and aggressive behaviour.

   Researcher B's study found a positive correlation (association) between games playing and aggression, but it was small and was based on self-reports, which may not always be reliable.

5. Concluding with your judgement on the thesis, either by rating the experts' approaches or by suggesting a new way of thinking about the problem:

   Researcher A has convinced you that there is physical evidence linking violent video games and aggressive impulses. Even though Researcher B's finding suggests a link between game playing and aggressive thoughts and behaviour, the evidence is less compelling due to the study's method. Clearly, though, both studies could be viable sources in an essay that explores the effects of violent video games.

Where Experts Are Found

Experts are highly experienced or highly educated people who have produced significant work on a subject. A documentary filmmaker may be an expert; watching his or her film could enable you to gather information for your essay. A magazine or newspaper writer may also be an expert; so, too, could a person interviewed on radio or television be very familiar with a topic, either through his or her background knowledge, research, or personal experience. Library shelves are laden with the publications of experts, and the Internet may be another source of expertise. Since the number of experts on your subject may be enormous, you need standards for screening the quality of their information. In the case of the filmmaker, you could consider the following criteria for credibility:

> An important part of research is to select experts whose work has been scrutinized by their colleagues. Anyone who can run a camera can make a documentary film. Are there any reviews in journals or other comments you can read about the film? This will help you know what the filmmaker's colleagues think about this film.
> Is the film part of your institution's collection or available through a reputable organization like the National Film Board?
> Since you are writing a research paper in an educational context, you may wish to consider the filmmaker's academic credentials.

University library websites provide a wealth of accurate scholarly information, so an excellent strategy for beginning researchers is to use them to guide you towards appropriate online material. A website's Universal Resource Locator (URL) can help you identify academic websites. The web addresses of degree-granting American educational institutions always end with ".edu" as the domain. Canadian schools' web addresses generally contain a shortened version of their name, followed by ".ca" as the domain. Similarly, Canadian government websites end in ".ca" preceded by the level of government (i.e., federal, provincial, municipal); more specific domain information, such as department, office, commission, or other agency may also be included in the URL.

Reliability of Internet Sources

When assessing the credibility of a secondary source, especially an Internet source, consider the words of the porcine dictator in George Orwell's *Animal Farm*: "[S]ome animals are more equal than others." The ease with which anyone with basic computer skills can publish online has created both new opportunities and new challenges for researchers.

Searching the Internet for MP3 prices and using it for academic research require different criteria; research is focused on the trustworthiness of the author. The Internet has countless sites created by individuals, companies, and institutions with very few controls to guarantee the accuracy or fairness of the information placed online. To retrieve quality information, you must assess the reputation of a site's creator and double-check the information in other sources. Many thoughtful and well-respected authors use the Internet to reach others who share their interests; however, it is important to judge a website author's motivation carefully. Some information on the Internet merely expresses the author's point of view without supporting evidence, or contains inaccurate information. Therefore, its usefulness is limited. Ask yourself, "Is the author providing a reasoned argument or just an opinion?" Be aware that personal blogs and Internet forums, by and large, are designed for opinion and conversation rather than the promotion of academic research.

The Internet has increasingly become an arena for personal opinion, some of it informed, much of it uninformed. Moreover, "digital advocacy" has rapidly become a form of mass protest. Individuals or groups garner support for a cause in order to argue for their position (for example, by having visitors "sign" petitions) against government and other policy makers. Visual appeal and a sophisticated design may help make such sites *appear* credible and reliable.

Today's student researcher must be able to distinguish between reliable and unreliable sources, as well as objective ones and those with a viewpoint to promote. In general, assess a website or any non-library source by ensuring that it satisfies the four "Re's" of research:

1. *Reputable*
2. *Reliable*
3. *Recent*
4. *Relevant*

1. *Reputable*: Reputable websites make their purpose known to readers (many have an easily accessible "mission statement" or an "About Us" page). They also support their statements with verifiable facts and figures, and make known their evidence-gathering methods. Most reputable websites are associated with a well-established organization. Reputable websites clearly distinguish between fact and opinion (see Opinion, Facts, and Argument in Chapter 8, page 230).
2. *Reliable*: You can trust the information posted on reliable sites. To determine the reliability of a website with no stated connection with familiar organizations, verify the information in another source that you know is reliable. Checking and double-checking are signs of good research.
3. *Recent*: Since attitudes and analyses change over time, recent information allows you to consider the latest developments in your field. Internet information is often current (in some cases, currency applies to hours or days rather than weeks or months!), and content several months old may be outdated. This can be true even of reputable and reliable sites, like some government websites. Always check the date of the website's creation or its most recent update.
4. *Relevant*: As your research develops, it is common to discard some sources that you uncovered early in the research process. General sources, which are useful in the early going, often suggest more specific ones, which, in turn, may refer to other specific sources *more closely connected to your research question*. It is tempting to keep all the sources you used in your essay, even if they become superseded by more relevant sources. One reason may be that a long list of sources on your bibliography page looks impressive! However, using sources that are not directly relevant to the point you wish to make disrupts your essay's unity; a "padded" "References" or "Works Cited" page also reduces your

credibility. Ask if there is a *direct* connection between your point and its support and whether it is the *best* support you can find.

These criteria apply particularly to open-access resources, from Google Scholar to the enormously vast array of commercial, governmental, and personal websites that anyone can view. These contrast with the more predictably authoritative resources accessed through your institution's library home page.

The way you use these open-access resources, or whether you use them at all in your research (your instructor may specify whether they are legitimate sources for your essay), depends on what kind of information you are looking for. You should first consider your purpose for seeking out a source. Is it for reliable information from an objective source with evidence-gathering methods beyond reproach (Statistics Canada, for example), or is it to learn about a particular viewpoint? In the latter case, it might be acceptable to use a website that advocates a position or supports a cause as long as you make that position clear in your essay.

Formulating a Research Question

Research often begins with the statement of a problem or with a **research question**. It could also take the form of a **hypothesis**, as it does in many scientific experiments where the researcher states the expected or probable result of the experiment; the experiment is set up to test the hypothesis. Student researchers, too, could then conduct research to determine whether their prediction is valid. For example, you could hypothesize that there is a causal relationship between children playing violent video games and aggression. However, if no such causal relationship is discovered, your original hypothesis is still valuable. Whether hypotheses are proven or not, you have discovered something new about your topic.

EXERCISE 6.1

Choose five topics from the list below and formulate a research question or hypothesis for each. Make sure it is specific enough to serve as a thesis statement in an essay.

Example

Topic: organic foods

Question: Do organic foods hold measurable health benefits for humans?

Hypothesis: Although organic foods have environmental benefits, they do not hold measurable health benefits for humans.

alternate energy sources	genetic engineering
bullying	globalization
campus housing	hybrid vehicles
cosmetic surgery	over-the-counter medications
deforestation	pet overpopulation
early development of humans	private health care
educational spending	religious education
endangered species	social networking
fashion industry	traditional media
file-sharing	weight-loss methods

A Closer Look

Knowledge and Research across the Disciplines

Although many principles of research apply to all disciplines, research goals and methods can vary across the disciplines; student research can be facilitated by knowing the general characteristics of each. Here we define humanities, the social sciences, and the sciences, and consider the kinds of research associated with each.

Humanities: A branch of human knowledge concerned with ideas and values, often analyzing primary sources to draw conclusions about their literary themes, historical significance, theoretical basis, or universality.

When you write an essay in the humanities, you will probably use direct quotations from primary sources; in English literature, these are the poems, plays, novels, and short stories you are studying. In history, these are documents, such as old newspapers, letters, treaties, and the like. However, incorporating such references in your essay does not constitute research; you will need to analyze and synthesize secondary sources—what other critics have said about the primary works and the ways they have interpreted them. Studies in the humanities often try to situate primary works within an overarching context—for example, in relation to a literary or philosophical theory.

The claim in a humanities essay is often interpretive: the writer justifies his or her decision to interpret a poem or historical event in a specific way, arguing that this perspective is a worthwhile way to consider the poem, historical event, or the like. Evidence from primary and secondary sources is used to support this kind of claim

Sciences: A branch of human knowledge concerned with the study of phenomena using empirical methods to determine or validate its laws.

The empirical method is the basis of most scientific study: researchers begin with a hypothesis and design an experiment to test its validity. The closeness of empiricism and science is apparent in the fact that the empirical method is often known as the *scientific method*. Empiricism has a long and complex history in Western thought dating back before Aristotle. At the root of most empirical systems (scientific and philosophical) is the belief that knowledge is derived from the senses. Sixteenth-century philosopher Francis Bacon stressed the need for careful and controlled observation to produce a generalization about the subject investigated—the foundation of the scientific method as it developed throughout the centuries.

Written experiments in the sciences typically share a common structure, beginning with an Introduction, followed by sections titled "Methods," "Results," and "Discussion" (or "Conclusion"), known by the acronym IMRAD. The "Methods" section explains in precise detail how the experiment is set up, enabling future researchers to duplicate or build on it. The "Discussion" section interprets the raw data generated through the experiment and suggests ways that the findings can be applied.

Reports and scientific studies often use the IMRAD structure with the following standardized sections and headings: **I**ntroduction, **M**ethods, **R**esults, **a**nd **D**iscussion.

Social sciences: A branch of human knowledge concerned with the study of human behaviour within a well-defined order or system (e.g., society, human mind, economics, political system).

Research in the social sciences (sometimes called social and behavioural sciences to differentiate it from natural sciences) deals with the ways that humans are affected by social, political, or economic systems. Information can be classified according to its purpose; for example, economics is a system concerned with how society deals with money and the creation and consumption of goods and services, whereas political science is concerned with how governments and other political bodies affect society.

Studies in the social sciences can be as rigorous as those in the natural sciences. In these kinds of *empirical* studies, the researcher determines what aspect of human behaviour he or she wants to investigate and designs an experiment with a hypothesis or main question in mind. The subject (usually human) is observed, and the results are measured and interpreted; the hypothesis is either proved or disproved. Such experiments, like those in the natural sciences, use a *quantitative* methodology, i.e., the results of the experiment can be quantified and conclusions can be drawn from the numerical data. The researcher can then determine whether there is a valid relationship between the data and the hypothesis.

A common method in the social sciences is quantifying the results of questionnaires or surveys. However, research, particularly in psychology and sociology, may rely on self-reports. Interviews and observation may generate data that needs to be interpreted by the knowledgeable specialist. Thus, some social science studies differ from those in the natural sciences in the form of a specialist interpreting primary sources (for example, school children's comments about bullying). In fact, observing groups or individuals is a commonly used method in the social sciences.

Rather than seeing studies in the humanities, social sciences, and sciences in isolation, however, some writers today focus on their similarities, or how thought in the humanities can inform thought in the sciences and vice versa. As well, much research today is cross-disciplinary, concerned with issues that transcend the traditional divisions. Other disciplines, such as law, business, and education are intrinsically interdisciplinary in their nature or scope.

Researching Your Topic

Beginning to Explore

The first stage in researching a topic is to determine the major authors in your subject area and what they say about your topic. As well, you need to know where they provide this information so that you can quote or paraphrase what these experts have to say and so that you can accurately document your sources.

In most cases, especially if you are free to choose your own topic, beginning and narrowing the search for material related to your topic will be something you do yourself. Looking for a general work, such as a textbook, in your subject area is a useful first step. A general work likely includes a bibliography (alphabetical listing of sources), which you can scan for relevant titles and authors. Consult works on your subject in the library's Reference section, such as indexes, encyclopedias, dictionaries, and comprehensive guides. Most library reference books can't be borrowed, but they can direct you to more specific sources that can be taken out; increasingly, many such library resources are available online. Internet search engines and subject directories can also provide excellent starting points, providing you with general topics that you can narrow down.

When you find potentially useful sources, you can add them to your **working bibliography**, a list of books and articles you plan to look at. For a book, scan the index and the table of contents to determine how helpful the source will be. If it looks promising, but you're still uncertain, read the writer's "Introduction," "Preface," or "Foreword." The author often summarizes his or her approach, and may provide chapter-by-chapter summaries in an introductory section. For an article, read the abstract (short summary that precedes a science or social science journal article).

Your working bibliography will likely not exactly match the final list of works you actually use; the purpose of a working bibliography is to lead you to directly relevant sources. Remember to note the date of a book's publication from the copyright page (the back of the title page). Prefer more recent works, not only because they will be up to date but also because they may draw on relevant previously published works and provide you with other useful sources. Sometimes just scanning the "Works Cited" or "References" section at the end of a recent work will suggest potential sources. However, it is also wise to consider the most enduring experts in your subject alongside the latest trends in order to understand whether outlooks about the subject have changed, and why or how.

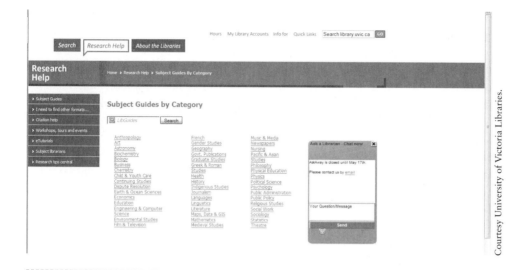

Courtesy University of Victoria Libraries.

Figure 6.1

Most university libraries have user-friendly interfaces that enable you to begin with a subject area that provides fast links to more specific information. In the sample shown in Figure 6.1 above, clicking the link in a subject category takes you to a list of resources for that subject, for example, journal collections and useful databases.

EXERCISE 6.2

Choose one question/hypothesis that interests you from the list you made in Exercise 6.1, above. Using a textbook, encyclopedia, or subject guide available from your library, generate three specific questions related to the main question/ hypothesis you came up with. You could use one of the four pre-writing methods discussed in Chapter 2, Pre-Writing Strategies, page 38, to help generate the questions.

EXERCISE 6.3

Using a general reference work, such as an encyclopedia or subject dictionary, locate the entries for the topic you used in Exercise 6.2. One source common to most university libraries is *Oxford Reference Online*, which includes many guides in 20 subject areas, such as Biology, Computing, Economics and Business, and Environmental Sciences. For example, if your topic is organic foods, *The Oxford Encyclopedia of Food and Drink in America* is a possible source. When you have located an entry:

summarize it in about 100 words

or

use some of the information to help answer one of the three questions in Exercise 6.2. Your instructor may specify a length for this answer.

The Research Proposal

Proposals are common in university research and in workplace writing, especially in engineering, business, and education. Non-profit organizations and individuals also use them to apply for grants. The ability to make the proposal sound worthwhile may convince the granting agency that the writer is the best person for the project. Similarly, as an essay writer, you want your subject to appear worth investigating, and you want to be perceived as credible.

In the professional world, a proposal can be detailed and complex. It can be divided into introduction/overview, background information and/or statement of the problem, goals and objectives, methods, available resources, needed resources, and conclusion. Not all your instructors will require you to write a proposal before you begin a project like a research paper. However, even if you are not asked to submit one for approval, choosing to write a proposal can help clarify your thinking about the topic and provide a rough plan. Sometimes writers include dates for the completion of specific parts of the process—for example, the date to finish preliminary research.

A proposal may mark the initial stage of the project, consisting of just an "expression of interest," perhaps a paragraph or two explaining your topic and why you are interested in exploring it. Or, it may be submitted later in the process and include a formal outline.

What Could Be Included in the Proposal?

> topic and thesis statement
> importance/significance of topic (to others/society)
> relevant background (if any)
> kinds of sources you are likely to use
> possible problems that might arise and how to deal with them
> main organizational method
> your main points/subtopics

A Simple Proposal: Purpose and Methodology

A research proposal should include, at a minimum:

> purpose: a statement about your topic, along with your research question, hypothesis, or problem to be investigated; and
> research methodology: a brief description of how you plan to locate the major sources.

Part One: Purpose

1. Announce the area you want to explore. You can also briefly state why you want to explore this area and/or why it might interest other people or be of concern to them.
2. Include a tentative thesis statement; of course, you can amend it later.
3. Outline at least three to four main points (or questions) in addition to your thesis.

Part Two: Research Methodology

1. Relevant background could include anything you need to find out about before you begin writing.
2. Mention the *kinds of sources* you will likely be using; what resources are suggested by the topic or your discipline? Which are likely to be most useful to you:

books, journals, magazines, Internet sources? What kind of preliminary research are you planning? In addition to primary and secondary sources, consider whether alternate sources, such as interviews or surveys, might be useful; name book/journal titles and specific names of articles, if possible.

3. You should anticipate what organizational methods you will be using (e.g., cause–effect, compare and contrast, division, problem–solution).

Sample Research Proposals

Here are the two research proposals for the student essays that appear in this chapter (pages 173 and 176, respectively). Wilkinson's proposal is more detailed and includes a list of key questions that will guide his research, but both satisfy the requirements of research proposals as discussed above. By giving details and specific references to research sources, each writer demonstrates his credibility as a researcher.

Sample Proposal Student

Reading 10

The Impact of Sport on Levels of Inappropriate Childhood Aggression
By Iain Lawrence

Purpose

Parents are often told that involvement in aggressive sports such as martial arts will help shy or passive children develop a sense of self-esteem and confidence; at the same time, they are told that such sports will promote respect for others and function as a channel for inappropriate aggression in anti-social or aggressive children. Are such claims warranted, and do other "aggressive" sports, such as lacrosse, hockey, or perhaps even soccer, provide a healthy outlet for aggression, or do they simply encourage further inappropriate behaviour? The central question for this research project is "Does involvement in 'aggressive' sport mitigate inappropriate childhood aggression?"

Methodology

Key terms, such as "inappropriate aggressive behaviour" and "aggressive sport," will be defined and distinguished where necessary from their counterparts, such as "acceptable aggressive behaviour" and "high-energy sport." Since this research paper is only about 1,500 words, it will be important to remain focused on the task of answering the general question described above, rather than narrowing the focus too much, for example on one particular sport. Further research could examine whether *specific* sports reduce or control inappropriate aggression in children. In addition to defining key terms, this research project will provide a literature review to try to determine the current knowledge about the relationship between children and aggressive sports.

Key sources will be found primarily in peer-reviewed journals devoted to childhood development. Those with a focus on child psychology will likely be relied on heavily. An example of such a source is "A Qualitative Study of Moral Reasoning of Young Elite Athletes," by Long, Pantaléon, Bruant, and d'Arripe-Longueville, published in the journal *The Sport Psychologist*. Textbooks discussing the proven emotional and social benefits of different sports will also be useful for this project, especially as starting places. An example of a book containing such information is Gatz, Messner, and Ball-Rokeach's *Paradoxes of Youth and Sport* (2002), an authoritative collection of essays on youth and sports.

Sample Proposal Student

Reading 11

The Compact Disc: Its Effect on Music and Music Recording, and its Future
By Rob Wilkinson

Topic and Main Points: The presence the compact disc has in 2010, the impact it has had on the development of music recording when it was designed to replace the cassette tape, and the possibility that it could become obsolete in the near future.

Purpose: To determine how and why the CD replaced the cassette tape and compare them to how MP3 players could potentially replace CDs entirely. I personally favoured the cassette tape when I was young for the ease in recording specific songs that I liked from the radio. It became much simpler, as CDs and CD burners began to become cheap and easily obtainable, to burn a CD. Now, some may argue that it is even easier to put music onto your MP3 player and listen to it anywhere, on your person, in the house, and even in your car. That said, it seemed like only a few years went by before the CD completely overtook the cassette, and yet in 2010, even though MP3 players are easier than ever to obtain and load with songs, the CD is still a popular way for consumers to listen to music and for artists to distribute it. Why is this the case, and how long will it last?

Central questions/ topics:
- Why are compact discs still often used in the age of the MP3 player, and how long until the former is completely replaced by the latter?
- What were the advantages of the CD over the cassette tape, and how long did it take the cassette tape to be completely replaced by the CD?
- What were the stages of development of the CD?
- What was the most popular design of CD?
- What is the appeal of the CD versus the MP3 player?
- How did the MP3 player develop and how could this development affect the production of CDs?
- What are musicians' opinions about this matter?

Organization: I'll provide information on the mediums of storing recordings involved (cassette, CD, MP3 player) and then compare and contrast them based on research and examples. I'll then find opinions of artists and the public on MP3 players versus CDs, and also research the increasing convenience of using MP3 players over CDs. I hope to find enough information to determine whether the MP3 player will completely replace the CD as the standard medium for storing and playing recorded audio.

Projected Research: As I'm currently performing in a band and am working to distribute my own recorded tracks via several mediums, I am both very interested and moderately informed on certain aspects of the topic. Searching on Google Scholar, I've encountered the articles "Will MP3 downloads annihilate the record industry? The evidence so far" and "Measuring the effect of file sharing on music purchases." I've also scanned several encyclopedia articles on both CDs and MP3 players that will assist in the compare and contrast process, and I'm aware of several musicians and musical groups with strong opinions on the pros and cons of MP3 distribution versus the distribution of CDs.

Research Note-Taking

Keeping clear records during the research phase of the essay-writing process allows you to read material efficiently as well as save time (and your sanity) when you write your paper. You should make notes as you research your sources, ensuring that you record the following information:

1. The complete names of the authors
2. The names of editors or translators, if applicable
3. The name of the book, journal, magazine, newspaper, or website affiliation or sponsor
4. The name of the specific article, chapter, section, or website with the full publication details, including date, edition, or translation; for a journal article, this could be the volume and issue number; for Internet sites, this could be the date the site was created or updated
5. For books, the name of the publisher and the company's location (including province or state)
6. For Internet sites, the day you viewed the page and either the URL or the **digital object identifier** (DOI)
7. The call number of a library book or bound journal for later reference, if needed
8. A direct quotation, a summary or a paraphrase of the writer's idea; *if it is a direct quotation, make sure you put quotation marks around it*
9. The page numbers you consulted, both those from which specific ideas came and the full page range you looked at (for unnumbered online documents, use some other marker, such as paragraph numbers or section headings)

Digital object identifier (DOI) is a number-alphabet sequence that begins with the number 10 and is often found on documents obtained electronically through databases. In APA documentation style, it is the last element in the citation.

Organizing Research Notes

One time-honoured method is to write your notes on index cards (remember to number them). You can also record notes in a journal and use tabs to section the book into particular headings. If using a computer, you can create a record-keeping system, either by using a database program like Access or by simply creating multiple document files in a folder (see Chapter 2, page 47). In addition, there are a number of software programs that can help you organize your research. Programs such as Scribe (http://www.scribes.com) imitate the card file system. Others, like EndNote (http://www.endnote.com), Bibliographix (http://www.bibliographix.com), and Nota Bene (http://www.notabene.com) are databases.

Another program you can use to keep track of source material is RefWorks (http://www.refworks.com). You can enter the bibliographic information into the system and it will create a "Reference" or "Works Cited" page (depending on whether you specify APA or MLA style, which are discussed in Chapter 7). Creating such a document can help you retrieve information if you lose or misplace it. Before submitting a final paper, review all the entries to ensure you have eliminated any sources you have decided not to use in your essay.

Learning programs such as these take time, but they generally offer beneficial extra features like the automatic formatting of citations and references or bibliographies. If you choose to record your notes electronically, you should back up your work regularly in case of technical failure.

Cross-Referencing

Cross-referencing your notes can increase the ease with which you retrieve your information when you are writing your essay. You can create a list of key words, names, or themes, perhaps on index cards, and record where in your notes these occur. Some students draw themselves a visual aid like a mind map (graphic organizer) on a large sheet of paper to connect their key words and their locations. You can indicate cross-references in the margins of hand-written notes, or use a commenting feature within computer files. Some word-processing programs let you make cross-references within a single documents (in Word 2007, for example, this is found under Insert, then Cross-reference, in the drop-down menu). The computer databases mentioned previously often have built-in, key word–based cross-referencing systems.

Some Useful Research Strategies

Assimilating

> Begin the research by gathering definitions of the key words and phrases in your thesis statement.
> Read or view potential sources with the thesis statement always in mind. Resist getting sidetracked by unconnected material, however interesting it might be.
> Judge whether or not a book will be worth your time by looking up your key words and phrases in the index at the back of the book. Read the abstracts of articles to similarly determine their usefulness.
> Consider how the information you take from your sources can be strung together using transitional words and phrases like *as a result of*, *because*, *on the other hand*, or *in contrast*. This will help you select points that flow logically.
> Try to find an example to support every major statement you wish to make. An example can be a quotation, a paraphrased reference, or a larger concept like an author's comment on or solution to your thesis statement.

Arranging

> When you've finished your first round of research, write an outline that lays out the structure of your paper by creating primary and secondary headings corresponding to the major elements of your thesis statement. Under the headings, list the lines of reasoning that support these points and the examples that support each of them.

> Decide how many pages you will allot for each section of the paper, taking the instructor's requirements for paper length into serious account.

> Look over your outline. Do you have sufficient examples to support all your major statements? Review the assigned word count. Do you have enough material in your study notes to fill the pages? If neither of these things appears to be true, perhaps you need to do more research. On the other hand, if you have too many key points and several examples for each one, now is the time to choose the strongest ones in order to meet length requirements.

> Consider laying out your paper in a word-processing program according to the suggested page number count. Use manual page breaks (under Insert in most programs) to create document sections that follow your outline, and to judge whether you're writing too much or too little for any portion of the paper.

> Design a timeline for each of the steps in your paper, if you haven't already done so in a research proposal. This will help ensure that you don't spend a disproportionate time on any one segment of the paper.

Using Contradictory Evidence

In the initial research stage, you will need to find sources relevant to your topic; however, not all studies on a given topic come to the same conclusion. If your primary purpose is to explain or investigate a problem, you will have to assess the different findings, trying to discover why the findings are different, perhaps by analyzing their respective strengths and weaknesses. This process of weighing the conclusions involves critical thinking and is a fundamental part of the research process.

In the humanities, your thesis is often based on your interpretation of the findings, so you must carefully show how the interpretations of other academics differ from your own. An excellent strategy when discussing conflicting results is to acknowledge another interpretation and use it as a springboard into your own interpretation. Contradictory interpretations should not simply be dismissed without explanation; it is better to acknowledge them and qualify them, possibly by briefly discussing their limitations.

If you do not address contradictory studies, the reader may wonder why. For example, there have been many recent studies that attempt to show the health benefits of vitamins. If you are investigating the benefits of vitamin E in preventing heart disease and have found that credible evidence exists, you still need to acknowledge contradictory studies, especially recent ones, and explain how these findings fit into your claim about the value of vitamin E.

Sources of Research Material

Until a generation ago, a student began researching a paper by going to a library and checking out books written about the topic. However, almost all research can now be electronically mediated in some way, and libraries have progressed from being physical repositories of paper into new roles as interactive and virtual clearing houses for information storage and distribution. Thus, a "library source" today doesn't always mean a hard copy version but one that could also exist electronically as a library holding—or perhaps that exists only electronically but is accessible through your library.

The Range of Sources

Rather than dividing the world of knowledge into cyber versus paper categories, we can define some types of information sources used for research, which may be available either online or at a library. There are many different kinds of source materials available; most of the important ones are discussed below.

Primary and Secondary Sources

The distinction between primary and secondary sources is crucial to you as a student researcher for two reasons. A major goal of university-level research is to read or view original material, known as **primary sources**. The ability to analyze and integrate **secondary sources**, the literature that has grown up in response to the original work, is also a principal goal of post-secondary learning. You need to be able to distinguish between **original** authors and the **commentary** on their work. Sometimes authors function in both roles, as authors of primary literature and as commentators on other original works. Essay assignments frequently include a requirement that both primary and secondary sources be identified and referenced.

Primary sources are the original compositions of authors. For example, the First Folio edition of Shakespeare's plays published posthumously in 1623 provides the earliest available text of *As You Like It* and would be considered the primary source for this play. A scholarly edition of the play, such as one in the Oxford series of Shakespeare's works, would be acceptable as a primary source in an undergraduate's work because the First Folio editions are rare. Personal documents, such as letters and journals, and initial scientific articles reporting on a work are also considered primary sources. A secondary source for *As You Like It* would be another writer's analysis of and commentary on the play, material about Shakespeare's theatre or Elizabethan English, and so on. An encyclopedia entry is also considered a secondary source.

You can obtain a copy of a primary source like *As You Like It* by searching a library's catalogue (in person or online) and taking the book home to read. *As You Like It* and other Shakespeare plays also are available in "full-text versions" from several different sources on the Internet.

Kinds of Secondary Sources

As mentioned above, an efficient way to construct a general framework of research from your thesis statement or research question is to access reference sources such as indexes, almanacs, encyclopedias, dictionaries, and yearbooks. These compendiums can provide you with concise summaries of statistics, definitions, and biographies, and they also generally provide a reading list of the principal primary and secondary sources. Although these books generally can't be taken home, this type of broad-spectrum information is widely available on the Internet. For instance, a Google search of "black hole" and "encyclopedia" returns results that include the

Encyclopaedia Britannica, the *Columbia Encyclopedia*, *Encarta Encyclopedia*, and numerous library-based sites offering further links to information on the subject. The *Britannica* entry includes a listing of relevant books, articles, websites, magazine articles, and videos on black holes.

Books and Articles

Once you've developed a basic understanding of your topic, you can look for books and journal articles that specifically address your research question/thesis statement. Continue your research by locating the books and periodicals mentioned in your preliminary search of reference materials.

A book can be a unified work written on a single theme; a compilation of articles, essays, or chapters by a number of authors around a topic; or a collection of pieces by a particular author that have already been published individually. Books can be located by searching a library's card catalogue; they can also generally be found online through an author or title search or through a database. For instance, Project Gutenberg has digitally published more than 33,000 e-books, ranging from the contemporary *Human Genome Project, Y Chromosome*, by The Human Genome Project, to the nineteenth-century novel *The Hunchback of Notre Dame*, by Victor Hugo.

Today's libraries increasingly have e-book collections that can often be accessed from your library's home page. As with print resources, you can scan the table of contents and index in order to find references to your key words and phrases; you may also be able to do a keyword search within the full text of the book.

Periodicals are published regularly—for instance, monthly, yearly, or daily. Examples include newspapers, magazines, journals, and yearbooks. Unless you are writing about an extremely current aspect of contemporary culture, you will probably be concentrating on **journals**, which publish articles written by academics, scientists, and researchers. The most respected journals are **peer-reviewed**, which means that other experts in that field have assessed the work prior to its being published. Peer-reviewed journal articles are expected to describe the authors' original research.

The articles published in scholarly journals are the "products" that researchers create in order to advance their ideas—and their careers. Thus, there are thousands of scholarly journals publishing a wealth of current and authoritative research on just about any topic you can imagine. However, finding these articles can be a challenge because the journals generally are distributed only through very expensive subscriptions. University libraries subscribe to some of the journals that they consider most useful to their institutions and then allow students, faculty, and staff access to them either in paper editions or online.

Locating a **hard copy** (paper copy) of a journal article generally begins with a library's electronic catalogue, either in the library or via the Internet. Let's say you want to find an article listed in the bibliography of a well-known textbook on your topic. You'll need the detailed information that makes up what is called a **citation**, which includes much more than the author's name and the name of the journal:

Author(s) Name(s): Zigler, E. F. & Gilman, E.

Publication Year: 1993

Article Title: Day care in America: What is needed?

Journal Name: Pediatrics

Volume and Issue Number: 91, 2 (an issue number is not always required in your citation, but you should record it in case it is needed)

Page Numbers: 175–178.

The complete citation written in APA style (see Chapter 7, page 206) looks like this:

Zigler, E. F., & Gilman, E. (1993). Day care in America: What is needed? *Pediatrics, 91*(2), 175–178.

Most library catalogues let you select "journals only" in the search options and then search for the journal name (as opposed to the article title or author name). You'll be given a call number that will direct you to a location in the library where you'll find issues of the journal (either unbound or bound into a book). Look up the volume month or issue, and then follow the page numbers to the article. If you are unsure how to do this, ask for help. The librarians or library technicians are trained (and usually have lots of personal experience) to show you how to search quickly and efficiently.

Online Searches

What happens if your university doesn't subscribe to a paper version of the particular journal you want? This is where the Internet has revolutionized the research process. University libraries generally subscribe to databases and indexes that contain the full texts of journal articles, which you can download to your computer. Supplied by private companies, these services are called **aggregator databases**, since they collect or aggregate many different journals together in searchable interfaces that give you access to many more journals than any individual library could ever afford to subscribe to or find the space to store.

A full-text journal article accessed through a database is almost always the same as in the print version of the journal. Databases also may house a blend of scholarly and non-scholarly information, including popular magazines, newspapers, and non-peer-reviewed journals, along with government-produced documents. In addition, databases supply links to the growing number of journals that don't publish a paper version at all, and are available only online: electronic journals, or **e-journals**.

Although database interfaces can vary, most function on the principle of keywords (including authors' names). For instance, EBSCO*host* hosts a number of databases, including *Academic Search Complete*, providing links to several thousand journals and millions of articles by using a combination of keywords, search limiters, and search expanders.

By entering your keywords in the **find** or **search** box, you can retrieve any article that contains your keywords in either the title or the body of all of the thousands of periodicals available through EBSCO*host*. (If you want to use a phrase such as "homeless teens," you must use quotation marks unless the field provides the option to search two or more words as a phrase.)

The number of hits can be enormous and overwhelming. For this reason, EBSCO*host* allows you to select **limiters** on your search, including a time period of publication and the option to search only peer-reviewed journals (see Figure 6.2). There is also an advanced search window, which permits you to define various

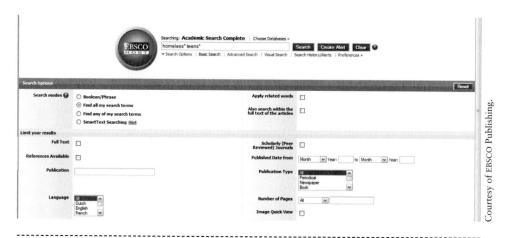

Courtesy of EBSCO Publishing.

Figure 6.2   An EBSCO*host* **page showing basic search options, including limiters like peer-reviewed journals, publication date ranges, and publication type**

combinations of keywords and **search limiters** or **expanders**. Each academic discipline has specialized databases and indexes that concentrate on publications that are particularly relevant to that field. You can ask your instructor to direct you to the most appropriate databases or search your library's website for discipline-related listings. All databases have a link to online help. When you need help in your search, use the **help** button.

Boolean operators are used to customize your search. Search limiters include the words AND and NOT. If you type AND between two or more search terms, your results will combine search terms; if you type NOT between search terms, your results will omit what follows NOT. If you use OR as a search expander, your results will include **at least one** of the terms.

Let's say you were undecided about the topic you wanted to explore but were seriously considering researching either caffeine or alcohol. A database search on "caffeine OR alcohol" using EBSCO*host* turns up 27,388 entries. This is far too many to be useful, so you then enter only one search term, "caffeine"; this yields 1,658 entries. Thinking that you might want to compare caffeine and alcohol, you use the limiter AND, which produces 116 results. In order to exclude "tobacco" from your search, you add a second limiter, "NOT tobacco" and hit Search. Using the two limiters (caffeine AND alcohol NOT tobacco) produces 93 results—a more manageable start.

Finally, many databases will now allow you to combine your keywords without using the Boolean operators at all. You simply enter your terms and choose the correct search mode. For example, in Basic Search in EBSCO*host*'s Academic Search Complete, the search mode *Find all of my search terms* is equivalent to AND, and the search mode *Find any of my search terms* is equivalent to OR. Many other databases and catalogues now work in a similar manner, including Google Scholar.

Truncation and Wildcards

Boolean searches often allow truncation and wildcard symbols. Truncation symbols enable you to include all variants of a search term. For example, using the asterisk as the truncation symbol in "teen*" will ensure that your search results include the terms *teen*, *teens*, and *teenager*. Wildcards are used within a word, for instance in "colo#r" to include alternative spellings (*colour* and *color*), or in "wom?n" to include variable characters (*woman* and *women*). Most databases and catalogues use the asterisk (*) or question mark (?) as the truncation or wildcard symbol. Some databases may also use the pound sign (#) or another symbol. If you are not sure what symbol to use, check the help menu. This will usually be located in the upper right-hand corner of your screen. The help menu will also provide information on other advanced search strategies that can be used in that particular catalogue or database.

Saving Search Results

Most databases and online catalogues let you save your search results. You can mark a result to be saved by checking a box or adding it to a folder, and then choose from several options—usually print, email, save, or export. Export often includes an option to download or export to the bibliographic management software of your choice, such as RefWorks or EndNote. Some databases also allow you to create a personal account so that you can customize your preferences, save and retrieve your search history, organize your research in folders, or set up email alerts and RSS feeds. Again, the help menu for each database will provide information on special features.

Some Popular Databases

Academic Search Complete, on the EBSCO*host* platform, is the leading comprehensive multi-disciplinary database for academic research. In addition to more than 7,000 full-text periodicals, including 6,300 peer-reviewed journals, it provides indexing and abstracting for over 12,000 publications including journals, monographs, reports and conference proceedings.

Bibliography of the History of Art (BHA) is the premiere database for scholarly research in the history of Western art. BHA includes coverage for over 1,200 journals related to art history.

Business Source Complete provides indexing and abstracting for more than 1,300 scholarly journals and business periodicals dating back to 1886. It includes full-text journal articles for all business disciplines, including marketing, management, accounting, and economics. Additional non-journal full-text content includes financial data, books, monographs, major reference works, conference proceedings, case studies, investment research reports, industry reports, market research reports, and more.

The Canadian Periodical Index (CPI.Q) features full-text content with a Canadian focus from Canadian and international periodicals, magazines, and newspapers. It includes *The Globe and Mail* and *Maclean's* magazine, Canadian News Facts, and reference sources.

ERIC (Education Resource Information Center) is the bibliographic database for scholarly education journals and other education-related information. In addition to journal articles, ERIC includes records for books, research syntheses, conference papers, technical reports, policy papers, grey literature, and other education-related materials. It is best known for its sizable series of short synopses on pertinent topics (ERIC Digest Records) written by educational experts under the auspices of the US Department of Education.

Google Scholar is a website for scholarly research in all disciplines. It enables basic and advanced searching across the web for scholarly content like books, articles, abstracts, theses, and other sources from academic publishers, universities, scholarly websites, and more. Many sources link to abstracts and previews or to full text available freely online or through your library.

Historical Abstracts and **America: History and Life:** Historical Abstracts is the most comprehensive, scholarly database for researching the history of the world, excluding North America, from 1450 to the present. America: History and Life is a key database for the History of North America. It indexes literature back to 1964 on the history and culture of the United States and Canada from pre-history to the present.

IEEE Xplore provides full-text access to high quality information in electrical engineering, computer science, and electronics produced by the Institute of Electrical and Electronics Engineers and its publishing partners. It encompasses over 2 million articles from more than 12,000 publications, including the most highly cited technical journals and magazines, conference proceedings, and standards.

JSTOR is a full-text scholarly journal archive of more than 1,000 leading academic journal titles in the humanities, social sciences, and sciences. It also includes selected books and other materials for scholarly research. Journals are full-text from the first volume and issue, but recent issues (the last three to five years) are generally not available.

LexisNexis Academic contains full-text articles from over 9,000 news, business, and legal sources, including national and regional newspapers, wire services, broadcast transcripts, and international news. A Company Dossier module provides detailed company and financial performance information. The database also provides extensive legal sources including law review articles, legal news, US federal and state court decisions, and legal reference materials. Canadian legal content includes Canadian law journals, court cases from 1876, and legislation from 1988.

Literature Online (LION) is a fully searchable library of more than 350,000 works of English and American poetry, drama and prose, 312 full-text literature journals, and other key criticism and reference resources.

MLA International Bibliography is the leading bibliographic database for research on modern languages, literatures, folklore, and linguistics. In addition to print and electronic journal articles in these disciplines, MLA provides citations for books and e-books, book articles, dissertation abstracts, and websites, and links to full-text items available online or through your library.

Project Muse provides full-text articles from hundreds of scholarly journals in the humanities and the social sciences, including many titles from leading university presses and scholarly societies.

Sociological Abstracts provides abstracts and indexing for over 1,800 journals in sociology and related disciplines in the social and behavioural sciences. It also provides abstracts for books, book chapters, dissertations, and conference papers with coverage back to 1952. Cited reference linking is provided for articles added to the database since 2002, showing how many times an article has been cited in other papers.

Statistics Canada is the country's National Statistics Agency with national and provincial statistics on population, resources, economy, society, and culture. In addition to conducting a census every five years, 350 active surveys can be accessed on most aspects of Canadian life. Statistics Canada also provides government reports, profiles, data tables, and other publications.

Web of Science consists of six comprehensive citation databases in the sciences, social sciences, arts, and humanities, including Science Citation Expanded, Social Sciences Citation Index, and Arts & Humanities Citation Index. It provides coverage back to 1900 of thousands of scholarly journals, books, book series, reports, and conference proceedings. Web of Science is also the leading database for cited reference searching.

WorldCat is a global union catalogue of holdings from more than 70,000 member libraries. It lists books, audiovisual materials, government documents, electronic resources, archival materials, and more from libraries around the world.

The Value of Library Research

With the wealth of research information available electronically, it may seem redundant to go to a university or public library in person. But libraries continue to be valuable resources for researchers at all levels of expertise; they have materials not available online and are staffed by professionals who understand how information is organized and interrelated. Most libraries have reference librarians who can save you time and direct you to sources you might never come across on your own. Furthermore, libraries hold many important records, including

> Indexes for many periodicals, images, films, microfiche files, and videos
> Theses and dissertations (book-length documents written by university students as part of their advanced degree requirements)
> Historical documents, including maps and public records
> Collections of textual and graphic material on special subjects, sometimes including original documents
> Clipping files from newspapers and magazines
> Bound volumes of journals
> Collections of audio and film/video recordings

In addition, libraries store print information, sometimes gathered over centuries, that is too expensive or fragile to digitize. The gradual transition to electronic record-keeping means that some important compilations of information made before 1985 are available only in paper form at a library.

Using electronic sources to access journals that also publish paper versions has another wrinkle that can frustrate inexperienced researchers: these publications often withhold recent issues or volumes from databases in order to maintain their subscription lists; the delay can be anywhere from a few months to several years. This means that it's still necessary to view the most current issues in person; and remember, accessing recent studies is vital, especially if your subject is a topical one.

Although the nature of research has changed dramatically with the increasing availability of online resources, it is best to think of the cyber–paper relationship as complementary. An Internet source's reliability may be difficult to assess, and some instructors may specify how much—if any—electronic research is permitted.

For example, he or she may not permit the use of Wikipedia, because the accuracy of its content cannot be guaranteed.

Alternative Information Sources

Although we have emphasized written research, many disciplines accept support for your thesis from visual or audio media, such as television, film, video, works of art, performances, surveys/questionnaires, interviews, and observations. Using these alternative sources of information requires the same attention to detail in note-taking as when using traditional materials, and most citation styles provide instructions for citing and referencing non-textual research information. As these approaches to research are more accepted in some disciplines than in others, it is wise early in the writing process to review with your instructor an essay paper outline that leans heavily on alternative information sources.

A Closer Look

Field Research: Interviewing

When you conduct **field research**, you go beyond written sources such as you find in libraries or online. The purpose in field research, such as interviews, questionnaires, and personal observation, is to generate useful primary sources to augment secondary source material. The results of this research, whether field or interview notes or questionnaire results, can be interpreted and integrated along with your other findings. Field research, however, may be invalid if you have not researched your topic thoroughly in advance by looking at what experts have discovered about your topic—in other words, if you are not prepared for the field research you do.

If you have direct access to a noted authority in your area, interviewing can be an effective form of field research. For example, if your topic is "organic foods" and you want to objectively evaluate both sides of the issue, you might want to search out representatives of both the organic and the non-organic food industries. Possible interview subjects could include spokespeople for organizations, growers of both kinds of food, or researchers like university professors.

The principle advantage of an interview, whether face-to-face, by telephone, or by email, is that you can ask questions directly relevant to your topic and subtopics. Interview subjects can be treated the same way as other expert sources of knowledge; that is, their words can be summarized, paraphrased, or quoted directly. There are also specific methods for documenting interviewees. The university community—including, perhaps, one of your professors—is an ideal place to look for experts.

Tips for Effective Interviewing

> Determine the *purpose* of the interview; for example, is it to obtain information? What kind and level of information do you need? How does the information differ from the kind of information available through books or articles (more detailed, precise, current)? Is the interviewee a researcher in the field or a knowledgeable expert?

> Do you want the interviewee's informed opinion about something (for example, if the findings related to your topic are controversial—e.g., the benefits of chocolate, coffee, or red wine; links between TV viewing and violence)? An *informed* opinion is different from just opinion: it implies that the person knows enough about the topic to understand the strengths and weaknesses of both sides.

> Choose your expert carefully; in addition to professors, there may be other experts both inside and outside your community. You may be able to get a list of experts through your library or your faculty/department office.

> Choose the interview medium (of course, the interviewee may prefer one medium over another):

• *Telephone* interviews are quickest—for example, if you want to ask only one or two specific questions or to confirm information

• *Personal/face-to-face* interviews are flexible—for example, if you want your subject to expand on an answer. Sometimes letting an interviewee go slightly "off track" can produce useful information or a colourful quotation, but make sure you *always* use quotations fairly and do not quote out of context.

- *Email* interviews are convenient for the interviewee, who can take time to consider the question and respond at his or her own convenience.

> Carefully explain to the subject *why* you would like to interview him or her; assure the interviewee of your interest in the topic and that his or her comments are *integral to* your research.

> *Always ask* before recording an interview.

> The form of the interview will also help shape the interview itself, including the kinds of questions you ask:

- In face-to-face interviews, remember that you should take notes even if you use a recording device; questions should be clear and direct.

- Email interviews tend to be more formal than personal or phone interviews. Although the responses may seem more "thought out," they also may be more general. Phrase the questions to encourage specific and detailed answers—avoid general, open-ended questions such as "What do you think about . . .?", or those that could result in simple "yes" or "no" answers.

> In face-to-face interviews, consider giving the subject a list of questions in advance to enable him or her to think about them; however, it's usually acceptable to add follow-up questions during the actual interview.

> Structure your interview logically; for example, begin with more general questions before becoming more specific. Having a logical *order* of questions can also help create coherence in the responses.

> Don't overburden your interview subject with unnecessary questions; make sure *each question has a specific purpose* that is connected to your research question or a subtopic.

> Before leaving a personal interview or when you present your list of questions in an email interview, ask politely if you can contact the subject again, if necessary, for brief clarifications; don't forget to express your gratitude for the subject's time and expertise.

Using Sources in the Composing Process

Summary and paraphrase are integral parts of the composing process in a research essay. When summarizing or paraphrasing, you are acting partly on behalf of the original writer. Scrupulous representation of the writer's ideas is the hallmark of good summarizing and paraphrasing.

Summary

Summary is the general term for the rephrasing of somebody else's ideas essentially or completely in your own words. Summarizing a book, article, or Internet source puts the main points before you when you come to write your essay, enabling you to demonstrate your understanding of the source and its applicability to your research question/thesis. Summarizing the main points from a source also avoids the unfortunate practice of *too much* direct quotation. A summary can cover anything from the content of a sentence (occasionally less) to several pages. The précis (see Chapter 3, page 65), the abstract, and the annotated bibliography fulfill different summarizing functions.

Paraphrase

A **paraphrase** is a restatement of someone else's idea entirely in your own words, and structured differently from the original. It is usually about the same length as the original. You would normally paraphrase an important part of a text, perhaps a significant sentence or paragraph. Because a paraphrase doesn't omit anything of

While a *summary* includes only the main point(s) of the source, using the same order as the original and putting it in your own words, a *paraphrase* includes all the original, changing the order of points, if possible, and putting it in your own words.

substance from the source, it is unlike a summary, which is meant to condense the original, retaining only its essence.

The differences between a summary and a paraphrase are illustrated by the passage below, taken from Reading 19 on page 257 in Chapter 8. In the summary, the gist of the original is the focus, and less important information in the passage, such as the experience of prior Olympic hosts and the reference to the 1976 Montreal Olympics, is omitted. In the paraphrase, the entire passage is rephrased, the order of the ideas is changed, and the sentences are structured differently.

Original: In its hosting of Olympic Games, Canada has also grappled with the appropriateness of including indigenous peoples and their complementary imagery within the programming of the Games. Similar to Australia and the United States, Canadian Olympic Games organizers have appropriated indigenous imagery. In response to the contentious inclusion of indigenous imagery within the programme of the 1976 Montréal Olympic Summer Games, Janice Forsyth notes the paradox that exists between the celebratory promotion of indigenous peoples within the Olympic context, and the everyday lived realities such populations experience in Canada. (89 words)

Summary: As an Olympic host, Canada has incorporated indigenous groups into the Games' programming, but celebrating Native culture seems at odds with the reality of the lives of indigenous peoples. (29 words)

Paraphrase: Janice Forsyth comments on the controversial use of indigenous symbols in the Montréal Olympic Summer Games of 1976, questioning the contradiction inherent in celebrating indigenous peoples to publicize the Olympics while the fact is that many Native Canadians experience ongoing hardships in their daily lives. The most recent Olympics, like its predecessors in the United States and Australia, are also exploiting indigenous symbolism, and, as the current host, Canada is struggling with the legitimacy of integrating indigenous peoples and the imagery that represents them into the Games' programming. (88 words)

A Closer Look

Other Types of Summaries

The Abstract

While a research proposal states your purpose for exploring a topic and, perhaps, what you hope to find out about it, an **abstract** is an overview of your purpose, methods, and results; you write it *after* you have finished your essay, or, at least, after you have arrived at your conclusions. However, the abstract precedes the finished essay on the page; it is placed after the title and author notation and before the Introduction, enabling readers to decide whether they wish to read the whole essay.

An abstract should be able to stand on its own, clearly but briefly representing the entire essay. It should include most or all of the following: background or overview of the field of study; the specific problem and your purpose in investigating it; methods or procedures; results; and a discussion of the results. It may end with a brief consideration of the significance or implications of the findings. An essay abstract should be approximately 100–150 words, unless your instructor tells you otherwise. An abstract for a scientific paper is typically at least twice as long (200–300 words).

Many abstract writers incorporate key phrases or even complete sentences from the full work into the abstract. The following abstract by student writer Kathy Dawson preceded her essay that compared the usefulness of two online sources of information. It includes the topic, problem, criteria for evaluation, and findings. (For an example of an abstract in an academic article, see Reading 16 on page 184.)

> This report compares and contrasts the quality of two online sources as academic research tools. They were chosen for their information on endangered languages and the increasing concern with language extinction and conservation. Maffi's (2002) journal article "Endangered language, endangered knowledge" and Crawford's (2002) Web site article "Endangered Native American languages: What is to be done, and why?" were evaluated on their credibility, organization, and content. While Maffi's essay was found more credible, Crawford's Web-essay was better organized. Both provided excellent content and proved equally valuable as research sources. (89 words)

The Annotated Bibliography

An **annotated bibliography** is an expanded bibliography (*annotate* = "to + note") that often accompanies large research projects, such as books, dissertations, or major compilations relevant to a particular field. It can take the form of a critical survey, demonstrating the variety of approaches that other writers/researchers have taken to the subject, as well as the relationship of the work in which the bibliography is situated to the research area being studied. While an abstract concisely summarizes your own work for potential readers, an annotated bibliography concisely summarizes similar works in the field of study—they tell your readers where each writer's piece of the puzzle fits into the whole.

Generally, each entry in an annotated bibliography provides a very brief summary of content, focusing primarily or exclusively on thesis statement and major points and findings. If the entry refers to a book-length study, the main points may take the form of major section or chapter headings. Frequently, an annotated bibliography contains an appraisal of each study's usefulness, contribution to the field of study, or limitations. The 102-word example below is an entry from the essay by Iain Lawrence (see page 173), in which he concisely summarizes the source's main points and ends with a brief evaluation.

> Emery, McKay, Campbell, and Peters studied the attitudes of young hockey players to aggression and empathy in relation to their participation in either a non-body-checking league or body-checking league. Emery et al. discussed the differences between instrumental aggression and hostile aggression. They found that young body checking players showed little difference in their level of empathy when compared to their non-body checking counterparts; however, they did demonstrate a greater degree of aggression. The major limitation of the study was that the players themselves selected the league in which they would participate, meaning that no conclusion as to cause and effect can be drawn.

Source Citation and Plagiarism

Plagiarism is the unacknowledged borrowing of someone else's words or ideas. Intentional plagiarizing, such as using someone else's essay, buying an essay, or copying verbatim from a website, is considered by many the most serious academic crime, for which there are equally serious repercussions. The consequences for plagiarizing can range from a zero for that particular paper to failing the course or being expelled from your school.

It is often easy for an instructor to detect plagiarism through a shift in tone or word use. When an obvious clue like this shows up, many instructors will then type the questionable phrase into a search engine and see if the exact wording matches anything on the Internet. Many colleges and universities now subscribe to services such as Turnitin, which maintains an electronic copy of your essay and compares it to thousands of documents. If any matches are found, the results will be posted electronically for you and your instructor to see, along with the sources that match.

Unintentional or inadvertent plagiarizing usually leads to the same repercussions, even if the reason for the plagiarism was careless note-taking, improper documentation, or a lack of knowledge about plagiarism itself. The questions and answers in Table 6.2 are designed to prevent unintentional plagiarism. Examples of plagiarized content follow.

Examples of intentional plagiarism include

1. copying another's work
2. buying an essay
3. using another student's essay or reusing your own essay from another class
4. not following the guidelines set down by your institution about plagiarized material; such information is usually included in the university calendar or similar document.

Table 6.2   Seven Common Questions about Plagiarism

Question	Answer
1. Do you need to cite information that you do not quote directly in your essay?	Yes. Specific content requires a citation, whether you use direct quotation, paraphrase, or summary to integrate it into your essay. Even general information may need a citation.
2. If you already knew a fact and you encounter it in a secondary source, does it need to be cited?	Probably. The issue isn't whether you know something but whether your reader would know it. If you are writing for an audience familiar with your topic, you may not need to cite "common knowledge," that is, knowledge that all or almost all readers would be expected to know. If you're uncertain about the common knowledge factor, make the citation.
3. What about specific information, such as a date, that is easy to look up, though it may not be common knowledge?	A fact that is easily obtained from a number of different sources (even if a typical reader wouldn't know it) may not need to be cited. Other factors could be involved (for example, would a typical reader know where to look?). Your instructor may be able to tell you how many sources constitute "easily obtainable" information; three common, accessible, and reliable sources is often the minimum.
4. If you use a source that you have already used earlier in the same paragraph, do you need to cite it a second time?	Yes, if another source, or your own point, has intervened. If all the content of the paragraph is from one source, you may not have to cite it until the end of the paragraph. However, always make it clear to the reader what is taken from a source.
5. Is it necessary to cite "popular" quotations, for example, the kind that appear in dictionaries of quotations? What about dictionary definitions?	Yes, these kinds of quotations should be cited unless the quotation has entered everyday use. For example, the first quotation below would not need a citation, though the second would—even though it's unlikely a reader would know either source: "When the going gets tough, the tough get going"; "Making your mark on the world is hard. If it were easy, everybody would do it." (Joan W. Donaldson is the author of the first quotation; Barack Obama is the author of the second). Dictionary definitions should be cited.
6. Does a list of your sources on the final page of your essay mean that you don't have to cite the sources within the essay itself?	No. All major documentation methods require both in-text and final-page citations. (In some formats, the in-text citations consist only of numbers.)
7. What can you do to guarantee that the question of plagiarism never arises in your essay?	As is suggested above, honesty alone is not enough, but it is a good start. Knowledge about what needs to be and what may not need to be cited is also essential and can be learned. Finally, being conscious of "grey areas" and checking with your instructor or another expert, such as a librarian, should almost guarantee that this serious issue doesn't arise.

As mentioned, audience is often a factor in whether a citation is given or not. General knowledge can vary according to audience. If you are writing for an audience with a scientific or medical background, for example, you may not need to cite the fact that the active ingredient in marijuana is tetrahydro-cannabinol; it is considered general knowledge within that audience. If you are writing a paper for historians or political scientists, you may not need to cite the fact that British Columbia became a Canadian province in 1871 because your readers could easily obtain this information. If the general knowledge or the easily obtainable standards do not apply, make the citation.

In the following examples, italicized words indicate sections of the original that are plagiarized.

Example 1

Original:

Anybody who will look at the thing candidly will see that the evolutionary explanation of morals is meaningless, and presupposes the existence of the very thing it ought to prove. It starts from a misconception of the biological doctrine. Biology has nothing to say as to what ought to survive and what ought not to survive; it merely speaks of what does survive.
—Stephen Leacock, "The Devil and the Deep Sea: A Discussion of Modern Morality"

Language of the source unchanged:

A person willing to see *the thing candidly* would realize that morals cannot be accounted for through evolution.

Sentence structure unchanged:

Biology does not distinguish between *what should and should not survive; it simply tells us "what does survive."*

Acceptable paraphrase:

An honest appraisal can tell a person that morals cannot be accounted for through evolution . . . . Biology tells us only "what does survive," not what should and should not survive (Leacock 57).

Example 2

Original:

Similar to Australia and the United States, Canadian Olympic Games organizers have appropriated indigenous imagery.
—Christine M. O'Bonsawin, "'No Olympics on stolen native land': contesting Olympic narratives and asserting indigenous rights within the discourse of the 2010 Vancouver Games" (see Chapter 8, Reading 19, page 257).

Language of the source unchanged:

Organizers of the Canadian Olympic Games *have appropriated indigenous imagery*, just as organizers of previous Games have done.

Sentence structure unchanged:

Much like Australia and the U.S., organizers of the Canadian Olympic Games have exploited imagery of indigenous peoples.

Acceptable paraphrase:

The most recent Olympics, like its predecessors in the United States and Australia, are also exploiting indigenous symbolism.

Decide whether the following paraphrases are acceptable or if they unintentionally plagiarize their originals. Rewrite them, if necessary.

↻ Check answers to select questions

1. *original*: "The power of cultural standards of beauty emphasize slenderness as a key feature of feminine identity" (Haworth-Hoeppner 212).
   paraphrase: The strength of our culture's standards of beauty stress thinness as a major aspect of feminine identity (Haworth-Hoeppner 212).

2. *original*: "Restorative justice involves the victim, the offender, and the community in a search for solutions which promote repair, reconciliation, and reassurance" (Zher 5).
   paraphrase: Restorative justice brings victim, offender, and community together in an attempt to find ways to fix damage, create harmony, and build confidence (Zher 5).

3. *original*: "Changes in the atmospheric concentration of a number of air pollutants over the last century are hallmarks of the magnitude and extent of human impact on the environment" (Taylor et al., 1994, p. 689).
   paraphrase: Variations in the atmospheric concentration of several contaminants during the last century highlight the extent of the impact of people on the environment (Taylor et al., 1994, p. 689).

4. *original:* "The support of an outside role model, like a coach, helps improve an athlete's self-esteem as well as lower the chance of depression" (Stewart 17).
   paraphrase: An athlete's self-esteem is improved and chance of depression is lowered if he or she can receive support from an adult role model like a coach (Stewart 17).

5. *original*: "No matter how intense curiosity about public figures can be, there is an important and deep principle at stake, which is the right to some simple human measure of privacy" (Ostrow).
   paraphrase: The basic right of public figures to a degree of privacy should be considered more important than the public's obsessive need to know every detail of their lives (Ostrow).

Methods of Integrating Sources

❭ You can *summarize* the source, or the section of the source that is most directly relevant to your point.
❭ You can *paraphrase* the source.
❭ You can use a *direct quotation*.
❭ You can use *mixed format*—paraphrase and direct quotation combined.

One of the choices you have in using sources is deciding how to integrate the information with your own ideas. Using a variety of methods is a good rule of thumb. However, there are general guidelines that can help you make choices. With any method, remember that the source must be identified either in a signal phrase (see below), or in a parenthetical reference if you do not use a signal phrase (MLA and APA styles).

Summary

Summarize if you want to use a source's main ideas to provide background information, to set up a point of your own (to show similarity or difference, for example), or to explain positions relevant to your argument. You can summarize passages of just about any length—from one sentence to several pages of a source.

Paraphrase

A paraphrase restates the source's meaning using only your own words. Paraphrase when you want to cite a relatively small amount of material that is directly relevant to the point you wish to make. When you paraphrase, you include *all* of the original thought, but rephrase it.

Direct Quotation

Direct quotation is used when both the source itself and the exact wording are important. You might want to preserve specialized vocabulary in the cited passage or the unique way that the source uses language or expresses the idea. You can directly quote a few words or one complete paragraph; overly long direct quotations should be avoided. If you choose to quote four or more consecutive lines, use the **block format**: set the quotation in a separate paragraph indented one-half inch from the left margin. You double-space the text, *but do not use quotation marks*. The block quotation is usually introduced by a complete sentence followed by a colon. See also Mixed Format.

Use single quotation marks to indicate a word or passage in your source that is in quotation marks in the original. In this example, the single quotation marks around *elsewhere* inform the reader that quotation marks were used in the original:

> "In a number of narratives, the (usually female) character finds herself at a significant crossroad between home and a problematic 'elsewhere'" (Rubenstein 9).

Avoid a direct quotation if there is no compelling reason to use it; use summary or paraphrase instead. A direct quotation is most effective when used *selectively* to preserve the wording of the original. You more clearly demonstrate your ability to understand and synthesize sources when you summarize and paraphrase.

Avoid using a direct quotation if

> the idea in the passage is obvious, well-known, or could be easily accessed
> the material is essentially factual and does not involve a particular interpretation of the facts
> the passage can be readily paraphrased.

The following are examples of direct quotations that are unnecessary or ineffective. The preferable alternatives are given after them.

> "About one-third of infants are breast-fed for three months or longer."
> *Paraphrase*: Approximately 33 per cent of infants receive breast-feeding for at least three months.
> "The greenhouse effect is the result of gases like carbon dioxide, nitrous oxide, and methane being trapped in Earth's atmosphere."
> *Paraphrase*: The accumulation of such gases as carbon dioxide, nitrous oxide, and methane in the atmosphere has led to the greenhouse effect.

The following are examples of direct quotations that are necessary or effective.

> Albert Einstein once said, "It always seems to me that man was not born to be a carnivore."

Quoting someone as well-known as Einstein, even though he is speaking from personal opinion, would make direct quotation a good choice—though not an essential one.

In the following example, precise wording matters:

> "Neither capital punishment nor life imprisonment without possibility of release shall be imposed for offenses committed by persons below 18 years of age"(UN Convention on the Rights of the Child).

Mixed Format

Using a mixture of paraphrase and direct quotation can be an effective means of showing your familiarity with a source and confidence in your ability to integrate words and ideas smoothly into your essay; it also is an efficient method since you include only the most essential words and phrases from the source, as in this example:

> Although in his tribute to Pierre Elliott Trudeau in *The Globe and Mail*, Mark Kingwell recalls the former Prime Minister as "the fusion of reason and passion, the virility and playfulness, the daunting arrogance and wit, the politician as rock star," behind this he finds "the good citizen."

Compare this paragraph with the original text below. The text crossed out shows what was not used.

> It's hard to say anything about Trudeau now that has not been said a thousand times before: the fusion of reason and passion, the virility and playfulness, the daunting arrogance and wit, the politician as rock star. All true; all banal. Butunderneath all that I find a more resonant identity, one which is at once simpler and more profound: the good citizen.

When you integrate a direct quotation using mixed format, you can remove the quotation marks and just look at the portion of the quoted text as words, phrases, or sentences that, like all sentences, must be written grammatically. Don't forget to put the quotation marks back in when you've integrated it grammatically, and also ensure that any changes you made to the original are indicated through brackets or ellipses (see Signal Phrases, Ellipses, and Brackets below).

When you use direct quotations, ensure that the quoted material is integrated grammatically, clearly, and gracefully. The examples below show poorly integrated quotations followed by corrected versions:

Ungrammatical: Charles E. Taylor discusses the efforts of scientists "are defining a new area of research termed artificial life" (172).

Grammatical: Charles E. Taylor discusses the efforts of scientists to "[define] a new area of research termed artificial life" (172).

Unclear: Art critic John Ruskin believes that the highest art arises from "sensations occurring to *them* only at particular times" (112).

Clear: Art critic John Ruskin believes that highest art arises from "sensations occurring to [*artists*] only at particular times" (112).

Or: Art critic John Ruskin believes that *artists* produce the highest art from "sensations occurring to *them* only at particular times" (112).

Signal Phrases, Ellipses, and Brackets

Signal Phrase

The examples above under Mixed Format use **signal phrases** to introduce direct quotations. A signal phrase contains the source's **name** (Taylor, Ruskin) and a **signal verb**, such as *believes*, *discusses*, or *recalls*. A signal phrase alerts the reader to exactly where the reference begins. It can also guide the reader through the complexities of an issue that involves different findings or interpretations. The following paragraph contains two citation formats: the first reference contains a signal phrase; the second one does not:

> *Richard Goldbloom states* that a surveillance video taken in Toronto showed that in more than 20 per cent of incidents where bullying was involved, peers actively became part of the bullying (2). Furthermore, recent statistics show not only the pervasiveness of the problem but that outsiders perceive bullying as a problem in schools today (Clifford 4).

The reader of this paragraph could easily separate the two sources, so a second signal phrase is unnecessary, though certainly not incorrect. Signal phrases are not always necessary if the context is clear without them; they can clutter an essay and make the writing seem mechanical if they are overused. However, it's often helpful to "signal" your intentions.

Omitting Material: Ellipses

In direct quotations, you can use points of ellipsis (. . .) to indicate that you have omitted one or more words from a direct quotation. Three spaced dots (periods) show an ellipsis (omission). Four dots with a space at the beginning of the sequence (e.g., "childhood requires . . . .") indicate that the omitted text includes all the remaining words up to and including the period at the end of the sentence. The fourth dot is also used if you omit one or more complete sentences.

If a parenthetical citation follows an ellipsis, the fourth dot (i.e., the period) follows the citation:

> "Going green might cost a lot, but refusing to act now will cost us the Earth . . ." (*BBC News*, par. 5).

You can use points of ellipsis before or after the original punctuation to show exactly where you have dropped material, as in the following example, where the comma following *head* is left in:

> "But some damage to the head, . . . occurs from fighting as a player's head is struck, either by a fist or when he falls against the ice."

When you omit significant amounts of material, such as entire paragraphs, or lines of verse, the points of ellipsis should occupy a line to themselves:

> . . . but were there one whose fires
> True genius kindles, and fair fame inspires;

. . .

> View him with scornful, yet with jealous eyes,
> And hate for arts that caus'd himself to rise;
> Damn with faint praise, assent with civil leer,
> And without sneering, teach the rest to sneer; . . .
> —Alexander Pope, "Epistle to Dr. Arbuthnot," ll. 193–4, 199–202.

An ellipsis before a direct quotation: Do not use an ellipsis at the beginning of a direct quotation, except, as in the example above, when part of a line of poetry has been omitted or if you break off a direct quotation and resume the same quotation later in the sentence or paragraph.

An ellipsis after a direct quotation: In general, do not use an ellipsis at the end of a direct quotation. However, if what follows the direct quotation in the original completes the thought, it may be advisable to use an ellipsis in order to avoid a potentially incomplete statement. In the following sentence, an ellipsis would be optional:

> "[If] what follows the end of the direct quotation is significant in the meaning of the sentence, use an ellipsis . . . ."

> *Or*:

> "[If] what follows the end of the direct quotation is significant in the meaning of the sentence, use an ellipsis."

In the first sentence, what follows "ellipsis" is treated as completing the thought; in the second sentence, it is not considered essential, so no ellipsis is used.

Brackets

Square brackets (or just *brackets*) are used to indicate a change or addition to a direct quotation. Brackets can indicate a stylistic change (e.g., upper case to lower case), a grammatical change (e.g., the tense of a verb), or a change for clarity's sake (e.g., adding a word to make the context clearer). The following illustrates these kinds of changes (although you would probably paraphrase a passage that contained as many brackets and ellipses as this one):

> The text states that "[a]ll secondary sources require parenthetical citations and an alphabetical listing . . . at the end of [the] essay . . . . [Students] must cite secondary sources, whether [they] quote from them directly, summarize them, paraphrase them, or just refer to them in passing by using the [MLA or APA] style . . . ."

> *The original text*:

> All secondary sources require parenthetical citations and an alphabetical listing in the "Works Cited" section at the end of your essay (MLA) or the "References" section (APA). You must cite secondary sources, whether you quote from them directly, summarize them, paraphrase them, or just refer to them in passing by using the style preferred by your discipline.

Parentheses would be incorrect in the passages above. Parentheses are a form of punctuation (they enclose text that explains or expands on something, as these parentheses do); brackets tell the reader that a change has been made to the original passage or that something has been inserted.

You may occasionally use brackets to explain an unfamiliar term within a direct quotation:

> Emergency room nurse Judith McAllen said, "We triage [prioritize by severity of injury] patients if it's a non-emergency, and don't treat them on the basis of their arrival time."

Avoid the use of brackets any more than is strictly necessary.

Inserting *sic* (which means "thus") between brackets—[sic]—tells the reader that what immediately precedes [sic] occurs in the original exactly the way it appears in your quotation. One use of [sic] is to call attention to an error in the original:

> As people often say, "vive le différence" [sic].

[Sic] here calls attention to the article error: "le" should be "la." In APA style, italicize *sic* within brackets: [*sic*].

Punctuate a direct quotation exactly as it is punctuated in the original, but do not include any punctuation in the original that comes *after* the quoted material. Note the omission of the original comma after *recklessness*.

> *Original*: "Any accounting of male–female differences must include the male's superior recklessness, a drive, not, I think, towards death . . . ."

> *Directly Quoted*: In his essay "The Disposable Rocket," John Updike states that "[a]ny accounting of male–female differences must include the male's superior recklessness."

Outline for a Research Essay

How do you know when you have sufficient support for your points and can begin an outline? The answer may depend on the assignment itself, as your instructor may be expecting a specific or minimum number of sources. Otherwise, as suggested above, you should probably have at least one citation (direct quotation, paraphrase, idea, or example) to support each of your major points. Whereas an argumentative essay depends on effective reasoning and various kinds of evidence—including examples, illustrations, analogies, anecdotes, and *perhaps* the findings of secondary sources, the expository essay relies heavily on outside authority as support. Therefore, your outline may benefit from such sources. Being specific in your outline will make it easier to write your first draft, where your main concern is integrating the sources with your own words.

Iain Lawrence's formal sentence outline is reproduced below (see his final draft, Reading 13, which follows on page 173; see also his research proposal, Reading 10, page 147). Lawrence closely followed the outline of his points when writing his essay. This was possible due to the detail included in his outline. In addition to providing detail, Lawrence spent a great deal of time organizing his points, so that his structure could be clear. However, he made some changes when composing; for example, he combined the material in points I and II in his introductory paragraph, dropping a sub-point (II, B) in the interests of an efficient introduction.

Other writers prefer less detailed outlines (see, for example, Erica Isomura's topic outline in Chapter 2, page 45 and her essay, Reading 18, in Chapter 8, page 254). Choose the kind of outline—topic, sentence, or graphic—you feel most comfortable with.

Sample Student Outline

Reading 12

Outline for "The Impact of Sport on Childhood Aggression"
By Iain Lawrence

I.   Hypothesis: Participation in aggressive sport can mitigate inappropriate childhood aggression.

   A.   Proponents of martial arts claim that participation encourages passive children to become more confident, while at the same time promotes respect for others and functions as a channel through which to direct inappropriate aggression for more hostile or violent children.

   B.   Reasons why parents might have their children take part in organized sports are "enhanced self-esteem," "improved social interactions," and "development of leadership skills" (Emery, 2009, p. 207).

   C.   Are such claims warranted, and do other "aggressive" sports, such as lacrosse, hockey, or perhaps even soccer, provide the same opportunity for a healthy outlet for aggression or do they simply encourage further inappropriate behaviour?

II. There are two reasons why parents of aggressive children might have them participate in organized sport:

   A.   Sports may be thought to provide an outlet for unhealthy aggression.

   B.   Aggressive behaviour may be modeled in such a way that the child learns environments in which aggression is appropriate.

III. Key terms and their definitions

   A.   Three categories of aggressive behaviour within sport have been identified (Maxwell, 2004):

      1.   *Instrumental aggression*: aggression used strategically within the rules of the game with no intent to cause physical harm to the opponent.

      2.   *Hostile aggression*: aggressive acts engaged in the aim of injuring the opposing player.

      3.   *Reactive aggression*: aggressive act resulting from an instinctive response to the act of another player. Reasoning plays little role in whether or not the act takes place.

      4.   Maxwell argues that these terms are less useful than they appear because an athlete may have more than one motivation.

         i.   Example: An athlete may be strategically aggressive in order to gain tactical advantage within the rules of play, but may take pleasure in causing injury at the same time.

Lawrence's beginning point is a hypothesis, something that he believes might be true. However, his thesis, his final sub-point, is phrased as a question. Notice that the wording is identical to the wording of his thesis in his essay, page 173.

Lawrence does not provide the names of all authors of this study in his outline; the first author's name will enable him to locate the reference when he writes his draft.

Lawrence does not use this point in his introduction, probably in the interests of space and efficiency; however, he does consider this point in later paragraphs.

Notice the important role that definition plays in Lawrence's essay. Discussing the complexities of aggression and sport requires a grounding in clear terminology.

B. Definitions of aggressive sport can be arrived at through a summary of the literature:
1. Aggressive sport has a high level of physical contact between participants.
   i. Examples would include tackling in rugby or football, body-checking in ice-hockey, and punching and kicking in the martial arts.
   ii. Aggressive sport makes use of instrumental aggression, although differentiating between instrumental and hostile types may become blurred.
2. Non-aggressive sport has little or no physical contact.
   i. Examples would include competitive cycling, running, swimming.
   ii. Such sports may be high-energy and intensely competitive in spite of the absence of physical contact in order to gain an advantage.

IV. What aspects of emotional well-being are affected by aggressive behaviour?
   A. No difference was found in levels of *empathy* between body-checking and non-body checking leagues (Emery, 2009).
   B. Negative outcome of contact sport (i.e., hockey) may be increased aggression (Emery, 2009).

In his essay, the writer focuses only on the result of the study and does not give details about the level of hockey or where the study of the children was carried out.

   1. A study of midget hockey league players in Calgary indicated that those in the body checking league had higher levels of aggression than those in a non-body checking league.

V. There appear to be beneficial emotional aspects of aggressive sports for aggressive children.
   A. Benefits do not necessarily come from aggressive sports, but from sport in general.
   1. Sports helps socialize children (Nucci).
      i. They learn how to compete, cooperate, and role-play.
      ii. They learn discipline regarding rules, regulations and goals.
   2. Both shy and aggressive children showed greater self-esteem when participating in sports (Findlay).
   3. Aggressive children demonstrate greater anxiety, loneliness and negative affect than "normal" children.
      i. They are less likely to have high physical ability and self-esteem.
      ii. There are links between these characteristics and "acting out" behaviour.
      iii. Sports are positively correlated with "higher positive affect and well-being and greater social skills" (p. 160). Decreased social anxiety has also been noted.

In developing his outline, Lawrence has carefully considered the order of his points. After defining key terms, he briefly summarizes the literature on the pros and cons of sports and childhood aggression. He then turns to social learning theory to help explain some of the discrepancies in the findings. Finally, he notes some of the limitations in the research he has discussed. In his essay, he follows this same logical order, providing appropriate transitions to guide the reader from one point to the next.

VI. Social learning theory can be used to account for the mixed results of research.
   A. The social learning theory of Albert Bandura can help explain the relationship between sports and aggression (Berk, p. 17).
   1. The theory emphasizes modeling and observational learning.
   2. It has been updated to reflect the recognition that children think about themselves and others. It is now referred to as the social-cognitive approach.
   3. Nucci & Young-Shim stress the important role of coaches and parents in the use of strategies to reduce unsportsmanlike behaviour and increase moral reasoning:
      i. Coaches should use instruction with praise, modeling, and a point system.
      ii. There is evidence that athletes who have received coaching that demonstrates moral reasoning and promotes sportsmanship are better equipped than their non-athletic counterparts to effectively handle aggressive situations.
      iii. Further evidence suggests that under trained leadership, combative sports may be of benefit to athletes when faced with hostile situations.

VII. Discuss possible limitations in the current studies.
   A.   Most studies examine the attitudes of children who already are participating in a particular sport, whether an aggressive sport, a full-contact sport, or simply a high energy, non-contact sport.
   B.   Children self-select for their sports, meaning that a child scoring highly on an aggression test may naturally choose a full contact sport.
   C.   Randomized studies are required in order to gain a more accurate picture.
   D.   The effect of culture on the outcome of various studies is unclear, as suggested by Maxwell's study of Hong Kong Rugby Union participants.
VIII. Conclusion
   A.   Participation in sports, even aggressive sports, provides the opportunity for hostile children to receive proper instruction for dealing with misplaced aggression.
   B.   Sports in which positive modelling and reinforcement are present encourage sportsmanship and appropriate displays of aggression.
   C.   Some evidence suggests that combative sports better equip athletes to handle aggressive and hostile situations.

> In this section, the writer uses critical thinking to discuss possible flaws in the studies he has used. This leads directly to his brief conclusion in which he provides an overview of and final comment on his topic.

> The writer changed the order of sub-points in his essay, as the point about the need for randomized studies (C) follows more logically from A, B, and D.

Sample Student Essays

To conserve space, these student essays are not double spaced and References and Works Cited sections are not on separate pages; in addition, the essays do not follow essay format requirements for title pages or identification information (see Chapter 12, Essay Presentation, page 437).

Sample Student Expository Essay—APA Style

The author of this essay uses reliable journal studies to explore and help answer his research question. Lawrence also wisely uses current sources; all had been published in the previous five years. He uses the results of the research and his own critical thinking skills to explore a much-debated topic.

Sample Student Research Essay

Reading 13

The Impact of Sports on Childhood Aggression
By Iain Lawrence

Participation in sport has been recognized as an important source of childhood development: children involved in sports may learn to work with others to achieve a common goal, develop self-confidence, learn to abide by a set of rules, and acquire a sense of fair play. In some cases, parents of children with behavioural challenges, such as excessive shyness or aggression, look to aggressive sport as a means of helping their child integrate successfully into his or her peer group. Such solutions to social and emotional challenges like these have some support within both the scientific literature and the sporting community. Emery (2009), for example, identified three benefits realized by children taking part

[1]

in organized sports: "enhanced self-esteem," "improved social interactions," and the "development of leadership skills" (p. 207). On the practical side, martial arts schools often claim that participation in their discipline will encourage passive children to become self-confident, while teaching aggressive children to become more respectful of others. These schools typically suggest that the martial arts function as a channel through which to direct inappropriate aggression in more hostile or violent children. Are such claims warranted, and do other "aggressive" sports such as lacrosse, hockey, or perhaps even soccer, provide the same opportunity for healthy outlet for aggression, or do they simply encourage further inappropriate behaviour?

[2]   Within the field of psychology, two major categories of aggressive behaviour have been identified (Berk, 2008, pp. 386–387; Maxwell, 2004, p. 238), instrumental aggression and hostile aggression. In a sporting environment, instrumental aggression is characterized by behaviour that includes a high level of purposeful physical contact between opposing players. The participants use such aggression strategically with actions confined to those permitted under the rules of the game. In addition, players have no intention of causing physical harm to their opponents. Examples of this type of aggression include bodychecking in hockey and punching in boxing. The second type of aggressive behaviour, hostile aggression, is typified by acts engaged in with the intent of injuring an opposing player. Examples of this type of aggression include hitting an opposing player in the face with a stick in hockey or biting one's opponent in boxing. Maxwell (2004) includes a third type of aggression in his discussion: reactive aggression. As the name implies, this type of aggression involves instinctive acts in response to the action of another player. Reasoning plays little role in whether or not the athletes act aggressively. However, while these terms are useful for an introductory discussion on aggression, Maxwell argues that they have less value than initially thought since an athlete may have many different motivations for acting in a particular way (p. 238). For example, an athlete might be strategically aggressive in order to gain tactical advantage within the rules of play, but in addition, he or she may take pleasure in causing injury.

[3]   Two additional terms help provide a context for a discussion on childhood aggression and sport: aggressive sport and non-aggressive sport. An aggressive sport includes one with purposeful, physical contact between participants, such as tackling in rugby or football, bodychecking in ice hockey, or punching and kicking in the martial arts. An aggressive sport makes use of instrumental aggression, although as noted by Maxwell, determining when instrumental aggression spills over into hostile aggression may become difficult (p. 238). A high-energy, non-aggressive sport, on the other hand, has minimal or no purposeful contact between opposing players. In fact, any form of physical contact with the opposition may be prohibited under the rules of play. While a non-aggressive sport may seem "tame" at first glance, these sports remain highly competitive and can require a level of physical exertion equal to or higher than many aggressive sports. Examples of such high-energy activities include competitive cycling, running, and swimming.

[4]   Psychologists and other researchers have examined a possible link between emotional well-being and aggression in sports. In their study of minor hockey players, Emery, McKay, Campbell, and Peters (2009) described two major findings related to hockey where bodychecking is permitted and the child's emotional development. The first was that children in a league that permitted bodychecking showed similar levels of empathy as did their counterparts in a league that prohibited bodychecking (p. 213). At the same time, Emery et al. noted players in the bodychecking league demonstrated increased aggression in comparison to those in the non-bodychecking league. They suggested that increased aggression results from prolonged participation in the league with greater physical contact (p. 213).

[5]   Can it be said, then, that there are positive outcomes for children who participate in aggressive sports? Several researchers have highlighted a number of beneficial socio-emotional

outcomes for aggressive children through participation in sports (Emery et al., 2009; Findlay & Coplan, 2008; Nucci & Young-Shim, 2005). However, these benefits come not from aggressive sports *per se*, but from sports in general. In terms of socialization, Nucci and Young-Shim (2005) point out that children enrolled in sports have the opportunity to learn how to compete, cooperate, and role-play. They also have the chance to develop an ethic of discipline as it relates to following regulations and pursuing goals. In addition, McHale et al. (2005) reported that both shy and aggressive children showed greater self-esteem after participating in sports (p. 130). These children share increased feelings of anxiety, loneliness, and negative affect more than their more confident and even-tempered peers (Findlay & Coplan, 2008, pp. 158–159). Such feelings also correlate with a greater likelihood of decreased physical ability and self-esteem, along with misbehaviour. By contrast, after participation in sports, they tend to experience "higher positive affect and well-being and greater social skills" (p. 160).

[6] An important model for understanding the relationship between aggressive sport and the outworking of aggressive behaviour in children is the social learning theory developed by Albert Bandura in 1977. His theory emphasizes the importance of modeling by parents, teachers, and, in sport, coaches. The theory recognizes that children are likely to imitate the behaviour of their mentors (Berk, 2008, p. 17). Following Bandura's model, it is important that coaches and parents understand their contribution to the development of a child's social and emotional well-being. Specifically, Nucci and Young-Shim (2005) outline several strategies to reduce unsportsmanlike behaviour and increase moral reasoning. These include instruction and praise, modeling, and a points system, whereby children earn points for good behaviour. It follows that athletes who have received coaching that exemplifies moral reasoning and promotes sportsmanship are better equipped than non-athletic counterparts to effectively handle aggressive situations. Moreover, under trained leadership, combative sports may be of benefit to athletes when faced with hostile situations outside the sporting arena (pp. 128–129).

[7] While research on aggression and sport seems to be divided on whether or not aggressive sports are beneficial for the development of children's social and emotional well-being, most of the studies themselves suffer from a number of limitations. The Emery (2009) study, for example, examined the attitudes of children who were already participating in one of two respective leagues. This was also true for other studies, whether focused on aggressive, full-contact sport, or simply high-energy, non-contact sport. With rare exception, children and their parents self-select the sports in which the children will participate. This means that a child scoring highly on an aggression test may naturally choose a full contact sport. In addition, the effects of culture on the outcome of various studies are unclear. Maxwell's (2009) study of Hong Kong Rugby Union athletes suggested that there is some correlation between culture and aggression as it relates to sport. Therefore, in order to gain a more accurate picture of precise relationship between sport and aggression, randomized studies are required. In such studies, participants would be assigned to aggressive sport and high-energy, non-aggressive sport groups based on research design criteria, rather than self-selection.

[8] While opinion is divided on whether or not participation in aggressive sport contributes to or mitigates aggression, the act of participation provides the opportunity for hostile children to receive proper instruction for dealing with misplaced aggression. In accordance with the social learning theory, activities where positive modelling and reinforcement are present encourage sportsmanship and appropriate forms of aggression. What should concerned parents of aggressive children seek in sports programs if they wish to provide the best opportunity for social integration? At the present time, the most widely accepted answer appears to be a coach who is well-trained and is sensitive to both the needs of aggressive children and the potential of the sport to foster further aggression.

References

Berk, L. E. (2008). *Infants and children: Prenatal through middle childhood* (6th ed.). Boston: Pearson.

Emery, C. A., McKay, C. D., Campbell, T. S., & Peters, A. N. (2009). Examining attitudes toward body checking, levels of emotional empathy, and levels of aggression in body checking and non-body checking youth hockey leagues. *Clinical Journal of Sport Medicine*, 19(3), 207–215. doi:10.1097/JSM.0b013e31819d658e

Findlay, L. C., & Coplan, R. J. (2008). Come out and play: Shyness in childhood and the benefits of organized sports participation. *Canadian Journal of Behavioural Science*, 40(3), 153–161. doi:10.1037/0008-400X.40.3.153

Maxwell, J. P., & Visek, A. J. (2009). Unsanctioned aggression in rugby union: Relationships among aggressiveness, anger, athletic identity, and professionalization. *Aggressive Behavior*, 35(3), 237–243. doi:10.1002/ab.20302

McHale, J. P., Vinden, P. G., Loren, B., Richer, D., Shaw, D., & Smith, B. (2005). Patterns of personal and social adjustment among sport-involved and noninvolved urban middle-school children. *Sociology of Sport Journal*, 22(2), 119–136.

Nucci, C., & Young-Shim, K. (2005). Improving socialization through sport: An analytic review of literature on aggression and sportsmanship. *Physical Educator*, 62(3), 123–129.

Sample Student Expository Essay—MLA Style

The following student essay presented challenges due to the currency of the topic: there were relatively few print sources available. The writer, therefore, had to rely mostly on Internet sources. To ensure his information was from reputable and reliable sources, he used mainly established online magazines associated with the entertainment and computing industries, along with websites with creditable sponsors. The result was a well-researched essay of interest to many people of Wilkinson's generation.

Sample Student Research Essay

Wilkinson's title, like that of many academic essays, is informative: what precedes the colon announces his topic, while what follows it includes his main focus (thesis) and the question he hopes to answer through his research. [1]

Although the use of personal experience is not common in expository essays, the writer uses it to establish a bond with his audience, many of whom likely had similar experiences.

Reading 14

Evolution of the Compact Disc: Its Role in the Development of Music Recording and Its Future
By Rob Wilkinson

When I was young, in the 1990s, and when I was not at school, I clearly remember spending much of my free time by the radio with a cassette tape in the player. I waited, impatient and excited, for my favourite song to be played so I could record it. The thrill was such that sometimes I would even record a song twice on the same tape, just because it was so rare that I would actually get the song I wanted from the very beginning to the end. Catching even a part of a song I liked was good enough, however: at the time, there was no other way that I could listen to it whenever I wanted to without going out and buying the entire CD. Years later, when I had heard that individual songs could be downloaded online for free, a friend of mine told me his parents had bought an external CD-burner. It was half the size of a shoe box and took about an hour to burn 15 songs to a disc, but I was more than thrilled.

These days, it is almost impossible to buy a computer without a built-in CD burner; full CDs take minutes to write. Why bother to record a cassette tape off the radio when any song one desires can be found online, and with superior sound quality? Cassette tapes and their players have practically disappeared, and the reason is obvious: the compact disc was an improvement over the cassette tape in every way, making the latter obsolete. Now that the MP3 player has been invented, will the compact disc face the same fate?

In the 1960s, Dutch electronics perfected the cassette tape. The ease with which artists and listeners could record music on a tape presented such a large advantage over its predecessors that the music industry became concerned. At the time of the cassette tape's release, the market was monopolized by reel-to-reel tape recorders and vinyl LPs, and despite the obvious advantages of the cassette tape, the new medium did not meet worldwide success immediately. It was not until the 1980s that tapes began to dominate the industry. In the mid-to-late 80s, 900 million cassette tapes were being sold annually, accounting for 54 percent of total global music sales ("Not Long Left"). In 1989, cassette tape sales peaked, with 83 million tapes sold in the UK alone, but soon afterward record producers raised the cost of cassette tapes. As a result, in 1990, sales began to take a turn for the worse. From a 10 per cent industry growth rate in 1989 (in terms of new store openings), there was only a 3 per cent growth rate in 1990 ("Record and Prerecorded Tape Stores").

As the music industry's expansion was slowing, however, the compact disc was gaining popularity. In 1990, while fewer music stores were opening, companies halted the production of record albums and began to concentrate on the compact disc ("Record and Prerecorded Tape Stores"). Originally designed to be strictly a music carrier, the CD marked a revolution within the music industry (Pohlmann 313). The quality of recordings on a CD was greatly enhanced, and it was a much more convenient medium on which to record songs ("Record and Prerecorded Tape Stores"). Where cassette tapes and records had once coexisted, in 1993 there was a 7 per cent drop in cassette tape shipments, and the Recording Industry Association's statistics showed an increase of 21 per cent in the shipments of CDs worldwide. In that same year, the RIA also compiled information which indicated that nearly half of all households in America had CD players. For the first time, the music industry had reached unit sales of more than $10 billion. As CDs became available in more and more retail outlets and, starting with Amazon.com, became purchasable online, cassette tape sales began to decline steadily. In 1998, cassette shipments dropped 8.2 per cent, and their dollar value decreased by 6.8 per cent. By 2004, Matt Phillips of the British Phonographic Industry (BPI) reported that the year had seen only 900,000 cassette tapes sold in the UK. "[Since] their peak in 1989," said Phillips, "[it's] clear to see that cassette sales are dwindling fast" ("Not Long Left").

In 1998, as the compact disc was enjoying the peak of its success, a United States patent was issued to the German company Fraunhofer-Gesellschaft for the MP3 file format. Any company that wished to develop MP3 encoders, decoders, rippers, or players, now had to pay a licensing fee to Fraunhofer-Gesellschaft. The record company SubPop was the first to adhere to these patent rights, and in 1999, the first portable MP3 players began to appear in the US. The audio compression standard of the MP3 makes any music file smaller while losing little to none of the sound quality in the process. The development of the MP3 player meant mass storage of music on a small device with sound quality equivalent to that of the music on a CD. Slowly, beginning with a device dubbed the "MP Man," more and more MP3 players with increasing

[2] Unlike the writer of the previous essay, Wilkinson uses the dramatic method in his introduction to create interest. His thesis is displaced to his second paragraph.

[3] By contrasting the present with the past, the writer skillfully introduces his thesis and his research question. In the next paragraph, he reveals his controlling organizational method: chronology.

[4] In contrast to the preceding essay and the one that follows it, in which books and journals are used as sources, Wilkinson uses several websites, the most current sources for his topic. Many short online documents do not have page or paragraph numbers; hence, this information can't be included in parenthetical references. For MLA Style, see p. 195.

The use of brackets indicates that changes were necessary to integrate the direct quotation.

[5] Wilkinson does not explain these terms. He may have assumed his reader would know them or that they weren't important enough to define.

It is important that Wilkinson does not just string together different facts and dates but explains the major advantages of the MP3 over the CD. In the following sentences, he uses parallelism effectively to summarize reasons for the growth of the MP3 at the expense of the CD.

storage and user-friendly interfaces began to appear (Bellis). With the release of the iPod in October 2001, the device becoming Windows PC compatible in 2002, and Apple's partnership with HP on its 4th generation model release (the HP brand allowed the iPod to be sold in many more locations, including Wal-Mart), Discmans were fast becoming a rare sight (Hornby and Knight). The compact disc was beginning its decline.

In 1999, Musicland Stores Corporation dominated the retail music industry. Together with MTS Inc and Wherehouse Entertainment, they accounted for more than $3 billion in CD sales that year. In the early 2000s, just as it had done in the early 1990s, the recorded music industry entered a state of crisis. CD sales were falling annually, dropping a billion dollars in 2001 from 2000, and another 9 per cent in 2002 ("Record and Prerecorded Tape Stores"). The Recording Industry Association of America (RIAA) blamed file sharing and digital downloads for the increasing speed with which CD sales were falling. By 2005, after having spent over $1 billion fighting online file sharing through legislative and court actions, the RIAA recorded that the sales of CD singles had dropped a staggering 80 per cent since 2000. Since the peak of Napster users in 2001, "illegal file-sharing sites . . . spread through the net like wildfire" (Jones and Benzuly 27). In the same year, the once-powerful Musicland Stores Corporation was sold to Best Buy; in 2002, as a result of faltering sales, Best Buy closed 160 Musicland outlets, and put the company up for sale. In 2003, the founder and CEO of Echo Networks, Dan Hart, said that the major record labels had to make a decision: "It's a choice of do nothing online and let free file swapping destroy your business, or embrace online and save your business. It's an obvious choice" (Jones and Benzuly 72).

The International Federation of the Phonographic Industry (IFPI) first recorded digital music as a statistic in 2004, when digital sales accounted for only 2 per cent of total music revenue. In 2005, the revenue of online music sales increased by roughly five percentage points, and continued to do so every year until 2007; in 2008, the revenue of digital music sales grew by 12 per cent. This impressive growth data indicated not only that digital music would account for most of US major record label revenue by 2010, but also that worldwide digital revenue is predicted to equal worldwide physical sales revenue by 2016 (Johnston).

In 2003, vice-president Russ Crupnick of the marketing-information firm NPD Group told *Spin* magazine that "price is at the top of the list every time" when customers are asked why they're buying less music (46). As if to thwart the looming statistics given by the IFPI, in March 2010 the Universal Music Group announced its plan to drop CD prices to a maximum of $10 (Foresman). President and CEO of Universal Music Group Distribution Jim Urie told *Billboard* magazine that the company believed the pricing program would "really bring new life into the physical format." However, while physical CD sales still account for about 65 per cent of Universal's revenue, it seemed likely that lowering prices would serve to only slow the inevitable replacement of CDs by digital media as the primary format for recorded music (Foresman).

Many people continue to buy CDs almost solely for use in their cars; in this century, most new cars, however, are designed with MP3 player compatibility in mind. Car companies Cadillac and Infiniti have begun to produce cars with built-in hard drives, allowing the owner to keep thousands of songs permanently stored in the car (Mateja). Newer generations have become accustomed to convenience in their lifestyles, and the potential convenience of obtaining music is no different. Steve Grady, general manager of Emusic.com, believes that people who grew up purchasing physical copies of CDs did so out of familiarity with that

---

In contrast to most of his paragraphs, the writer here uses the final sentence as a topic sentence, summarizing the paragraph's main idea. [6]

In this well-developed paragraph, the writer summarizes the effects of illegal downloading on CD sales. Note that he does not discuss this controversial issue but confines himself to his topic, using facts and figures, and the words of an industry expert.

The use of an ellipsis here indicates one or more words were omitted from the middle of the sentence.

In contrast, with the previous essay, but like the one that follows, Wilkinson uses direct quotation selectively. Doing so stresses the point that the CD did not evolve in a vacuum but due to a conflux of human factors; here, its development is linked to human agency and the choices we make. [7]

As he does in the previous paragraph, Wilkinson first gives the full name of an organization, then uses the abbreviation in future references. [8]

In this paragraph, the writer might have found a way to rephrase sentences 1 and 3 to stress the important information, the direct quotation, at the expense of distracting nouns.

Wilkinson uses mixed format twice in this paragraph, effectively combining direct quotation with paraphrase. [9]

medium. File sharing and obtaining music online, Grady explains, have become natural for recent generations. "It's not that [newer generations are] not willing to pay for something," Grady told *Mix* magazine in 2003. "[T]hey [just] don't associate the same kind of value with something that they're downloading over the Internet as they do a CD that's bought in the store" (Jones and Benzuly 73).

To me, there is something special about having the music in a physical form—a feeling, I have found, that many others share, including musicians and many of their fans. Some believe that vinyl albums have exceptional sound quality, whereas others from previous generations prefer the method of recording that cassette tapes present. "I liked it when I sat in front of my stereo, my tape deck, with a big pile of CDs, deciding on the fly which songs to put in what order," musician Joel Keller told BBC news in 2005. The songwriter said that he saw the act of burning a CD as "simply less fun" than the making of a mix tape had been: "[It] seemed like more of a labour of love than it is to do CDs now," he explained. I, too, have grown accustomed to the convenience of MP3s, but if I really like a particular group, something compels me to buy the physical CD. Forrester research analysts believe that CDs are a dying format and that lowering the price of physical-format music will not change that fact (Foresman; Milner 46). The statistics and trends seem to indicate the same, but personal preference and values may allow recorded music, in all forms, to linger.

[10] Wilkinson returns to first-person in his conclusion, recalling his introduction. However, he also uses other sources to suggest a possible answer to his question: whether CDs will continue or will die out.

Works Cited

Bellis, Mary. "The History of MP3: Fraunhofer Gesellschaft and MP3." *About.com*. Web. 9 Apr. 2010. <http://inventors.about.com/od/mstartinventions/a/MPThree.htm>.

Foresman, Chris. "Years Late, Universal Cuts CD Prices to Combat Poor Sales." http://arstechnica.com. *Ars Technica*, 18 Mar. 2010. Web. 02 Apr. 2010. <http://arstechnica.com/media/news/2010/03/years-late-universal-cuts-cd-prices-to-combat-poor-sales.ars>.

Hornby, Tom, and Dan Knight. "A History of the iPod: 2000 to 2004." *Low End Mac*, Sep. 2007. Web. 4 Apr. 2010. < http://lowendmac.com/orchard/05/origin-of-the-ipod.html>.

Johnston, Casey. "US Digital Music Sales to Eclipse CDs by 2010." http://arstechnica.com. *Ars Technica*, 14 Aug. 2009. Web. 02 Apr. 2010. <http://arstechnica.com/media/news/2009/08/global-digital-music-sales-to-overtake-physical-by-2016.ars>.

Jones, Sarah, and Sarah Benzuly. "What Can Save the Music Industry? Paying to Play." *Mix*. 27. 6 (May 2003): 72–74. Print.

Mateja, Jim. "Mobile MP3." *Cars.com*. 7 Aug. 2009. Web. 9 Apr. 2010. <http://www.cars.com/go/advice/Story.jsp?story=mp3&section=gdgt&subject=mp3&referer=advice&aff=jconline>.

Milner, Greg. "Cost in Translation: Will Lower CD Prices Help Stop Illegal File Sharing?" *Spin*. Dec. 2003: 46. Print.

"Not Long Left for Cassette Tapes." *BBC News*. BBC News, 17 June 2005. Web. 02 Apr. 2010.

Pohlmann, Ken C. *McGraw-Hill Encyclopedia of Science & Technology*. 9th ed. Vol. 4. New York: McGraw-Hill, 2002. Print.

"Record and Prerecorded Tape Stores." *Gale Encyclopedia of American Industries. Answers.com*, 2005. Web. 02 Apr. 2010. <http://www.answers.com/topic/record-and-prerecorded-tape-stores>.

Sample Student Expository Essay—MLA Style

In the following student essay, the writer analyzes the arguments on both sides of an important issue. By using critical thinking and keeping her voice objective, she is able to write an effective expository essay on an arguable topic. A series of questions related to the essay follow the Works Cited page.

Sample Student Research Essay

Reading 15

Multiculturalism in Canada: Controversial Consequences of the Multiculturalism Act
by Reneé MacKillop

[1] What does it mean to be Canadian? The act for "the preservation and enhancement of Multi-culturalism in Canada" declares recognition and promotion of understanding racial and cultural diversity as important parts of the Canadian identity (Bissoondath 36–37). The Multiculturalism Act allows all Canadians to freely safeguard and develop their cultural heritage (36). This act, however, has evoked questions concerning its validity, acceptance, and limits as well as questions of national unity and identity. According to supporters of multiculturalism, being Canadian means being a part of a cultural mosaic in a pluralistic society; according to critics of the Act, there is no conclusive answer to what it means to be Canadian because multiculturalism hinders the national quest for unity and identity. The Multiculturalism Act has required government involvement in cultural affairs and has extended accommodations to immigrants. The absence of restrictions on multiculturalism has blurred lines between what is acceptable and what is not. The ambiguity of the Act has forced questions about what unites Canadians as a national community and what makes this country Canadian.

[2] The validity of government involvement in the cultural affairs of Canadians is a debatable issue. Opponents of the Multiculturalism Act believe that, similar to religion, culture should be a private matter left to individuals and families (Bissoondath 112). They argue that the state has no jurisdiction in the cultures of Canadians. Opponents refer to Canada's past foundation based on "white supremacy" and on the shift from Canada as an "ethnic nation" to a "civic nation" (Kymlicka 25). After World War II, individuals became included in the national community by becoming legal citizens as opposed to past inclusion based on ethnicity; the Citizenship Act of 1946 provided a new way to be Canadian (James). Therefore, in the declaration that Canada is a "civic nation," ethnic and cultural neutrality in the government is implied. Supporters believe that government involvement, namely the Multiculturalism Act, is vital to ending racism and discrimination. They feel that it is the Canadian government's duty to redress past wrongs by ensuring equality to present-day ethnic minorities. However, both opponents and supporters agree that the true motives behind government involvement in the cultural affairs of the nation are unclear.

[3] Although the policy of multiculturalism was established with the equality of all Canadian citizens in mind, Richard Gwyn has accused policy-makers of creating a "slush fund to buy ethnic votes" (as cited in Bissoondath 25). Moreover, due to "internal globalization" and the neo-liberal shift in Canadian society, emphasis is diverted from the original intentions of the policy to national competitiveness and economic gain (Abu-Laban and Christian 119–23). Ethnic entrepreneurs

provide valuable trading and investment connections to the global community (111). The government issued an evaluation of the Multiculturalism Act, the Brighton Report, in 1996, which reviewed the program through literature, media coverage, and interviews, along with providing a statistical analysis of funding for the policy. The Brighton Report stated that past funding reinforced attendance to special interests and not to all Canadians (113). However, the Report did not mention ulterior motives for government funding of multiculturalism. Nonetheless, some Canadians are questioning whether the support and funds for multiculturalism are government strategies for attaining an international competitive advantage and not primarily for nation-building.

The Multiculturalism Act is a renegotiation of immigrant integration (Kymlicka 37). Critics feel that the policy has created excessive accommodations for immigrants, instead of integration, while advocates feel that accommodations are necessary. Critics hold the opinion that immigrants expect integration and that newcomers are responsible to learn an official language, abide by Canadian laws, and accept Canadian society (Bissoondath 23). However, advocates believe that multiculturalism is not intended to create new nations within Canada for individual cultures (Kymlicka 37). Proponents of multiculturalism feel that in response to problems of social marginalization and historically stigmatized communities' political inequality, it is necessary to redress past injustices and ensure a better and more equal future; the Multiculturalism Act encourages victims of stigmatization to seek redress (Dyck 117). After progress recognizing ethnic minorities, providing funding, and confronting past wrongs (wrongs frequently authorized by the government) ethnic minorities had endured in Canada, critical opposition surfaced in the 1990s (Dyck 120–21). Critics of multiculturalism believe that immigrants are threatening job security. They cite as an example the "instant Liberals" who were welcomed into the party based solely on their ethnicity, which undermined hard-working members who had been active in the party for considerable lengths of time (Dyck 121). Opposition has grown as Canada continues to increase accommodations for ethnic minorities. Political and legal protections of cultural expression allow the open-ended policy constantly to be stretched (Bissoondath 134). Some critics fear the direction that multiculturalism is taking in Canada by legitimizing all forms of cultural expression.

[4]

The official recognition of minority contribution, personal freedom, and diversity, namely pluralism, has declared that society is best served by the contribution of varied components (Bibby 2). Tolerance and respect are enforced, and coexistence has become a national objective. Canadian critics do not consider pluralism beneficial, however, because it entrenches relativism, "the inclination to see the merits of behaviour and ideas as universal or absolute, but as varying with individuals and their environments, and, in the end, as being equally valid because they are chosen" (Bibby vi). According to the critic, "pluralism establishes choices; relativism declares the choice valid" (10). The essential concern is the lack of restrictions limiting what is socially acceptable in Canada.

[5]

The thorny question of restrictions is difficult because relativism has validated all viewpoints, eliminating cultural expectations (Bibby 10). Hopeful advocates of multiculturalism believe that boundaries would enable the multiculturalism policy to be successful. However, critics continue to caution the "slippery slope" of relativism that is leading towards acceptance of all forms of cultural expression and away from civic and political integration, regardless of the impact on Canada (Kymlicka 60). They believe that "rights [are] outstanding rules" and "relativism has slain moral consensus" because there are no authoritative instruments capable of measuring Canadian social life (Bibby 10–11). On the contrary, a pluralistic nation, which entails relativism and individualism (the tendency to stress the individual over the group), is notably rewarding because Canadians are free to live out their lives as they see fit, resulting in high standards of living, peaceful existence, and, ultimately, freedom (Bibby 90). However, what is

[6]

best for Canada is no longer relevant because everything is equal and, therefore, no particular way can be better than another, according to opponents (14).

[7]   A clear example of the feared results of relativism is the continued practice of female circumcision by some African minorities in Canada. In spite of western society's view of female circumcision as a form of mutilation and a health risk, it is a vital, traditional rite of passage to womanhood for some African women (Bissoondath 134–35). The questions are whether this practice should be acceptable in Canadian society and how far, in the Canadian context, should Canada go in accommodating these kinds of cultural expressions? Detractors of the Multiculturalism Act believe that the policy ends where notions of human rights and dignity commences (135). Critics fear that Canadians are "not differentiating between being judgemental and showing sound judgement and between exhibiting discrimination and being discriminatory" (Bibby 101).

[8]   Despite the concerns over relativism and individualism in a pluralistic society, supporters of multiculturalism claim that the policy provides external protection to minorities, possibility for redress, access to mainstream institutions, and protection from discriminatory and prejudiced conduct (Kymlicka 65). These advocates believe that, despite the lack of explicit restrictions limiting the policy, the preamble to the Act emphasizes human and individual rights and sexual equality (66–67).

[9]   Multiculturalism encourages accepting the rights of others to be different and, consequently, national togetherness (Bibby 90). However, critics pose the following question: "If what we have in common is our diversity, do we really have anything in common at all?" (92). There is freedom for the individual, but how are people brought together into the national community? This implicit criticism suggests that a group needs an identity because individualism brings freedom and equality, but it also removes persons from the guidance of the group and the security of tradition. Thus, the identity of merely being an autonomous Canadian is forced upon citizens (96). Whereas proponents advocate the policy's ability to instil pride in Canadians and a sense of belonging to a mosaic of cultures, opponents call the policy a "song and dance" affair that encourages stereotyping and national divisiveness (96–98). Proponents acknowledge multiculturalism as officially recognizing the reality that Canada has never been unicultural; opponents see it as extenuating national minorities. Aboriginal and Francophone Canadians, two national minorities, are offended by being categorized with other minorities and not being recognized as founding peoples (James). René Lévesque called multiculturalism "folklore" and named the policy a "'red-herring' . . . devised to obscure the 'Quebec business', to give an impression that we are all ethnics and do not have to worry about special status for Quebec" (Bissoondath 37). Some Canadians propose officially declaring Canada multinational along with multicultural as a solution to the problem of national unity. The problematic criticism remains, however, that multiculturalism is divisive and prevents Canadians from establishing a national identity.

[10]   The Multiculturalism Act, like all political policies, is not above criticism, and the concept of multiculturalism has both supporters and detractors. It is essential that a democratic state be constantly analyzed, critiqued, and questioned. Diversity is a reality in Canada; however, government involvement in immigration integration is controversial. The outcomes of a pluralistic society, officially recognized as being polyethnic, are uncertain as Canada diverges from the melting pot standard. Not surprisingly, there have been unexpected consequences of The Multiculturalism Act, such as relativism, individualism, and division. In the words of the Brighton Report, critics "misunderstand and misrepresent Canada's multiculturalism policy." However, the report concluded that the policy is in need of amendments (Abu-Laban and Christian 113). In summary, the Multiculturalism Act is progressive, yet in need of revision to allow Canada to flourish as a unified country with a strong national identity.

Works Cited

Abu-Laban, Yasmeen, and Gabriel Christian. *Selling Diversity: Immigration, Multiculturalism, Employment Equity, and Globalization*. Peterborough: Broadview, 2002. Print.

Bibby, Reginald. *Mosaic Madness: The Poverty and Potential of Life in Canada*. Toronto: Stoddart, 1990. Print.

Bissoondath, Neil. *Selling Illusions: The Cult of Multiculturalism in Canada*. Toronto: Penguin, 1990. Print.

Dyck, Rand. *Canadian Politics: Critical Approaches*. 4th ed. Toronto: Thomson Nelson, 2004. Print.

James, Matt. Political Science 101. Department of Political Science. Elliott Building, University of Victoria, Victoria. 25 Nov. 2004. Lecture.

Kymlicka, Will. *Finding Our Way: Rethinking Ethnocultural Relations in Canada*. Don Mills: Oxford UP, 1998. Print.

Questions to Consider

1. Summarize the arguments of the two sides as they are presented in the first body paragraph (paragraph 2).

2. MacKillop uses direct and mixed citation to support her points, along with some paraphrase and summary. Why does she choose to use a variety of methods? What is the role and importance of direct quotation in an essay that presents two opposing views of a topic?

3. Explore the writer's credibility. Does her essay demonstrate knowledge, reliability, and fairness?

4. Explain her use of secondary sources. Do you think she uses them well (for example, is there an over-reliance on any source)? Do the sources themselves appear reliable?

5. MacKillop's essay compares and contrasts two positions on multiculturalism and the Multiculturalism Act. Which of the two methods for organizing compare and contrast essays does she use (see Chapter 5, page 115)? Are the two positions always clearly separated from one another? Give specific examples.

6. Does the first paragraph function as an effective introduction? Does the last paragraph provide a satisfactory conclusion? What kind of introduction does the writer use? What kind of conclusion? Do they work well together? (See Chapter 4).

Sample Scholarly Essay

Scholarly essays, which usually appear in academic journals and can be accessed electronically through your school's databases, are longer and more complex than the kinds of essays you will be asked to write. Many of the challenges they present, however, can be overcome by knowing where to look for information. Following the steps below will make the reading process easier:

1. Read the title and abstract to get an idea of the essay's purpose, topic, and results or findings. If the essay includes specific headings, they may also give useful information.

2. Read the introduction, especially the last paragraphs, where important information is placed.
3. Read the conclusion section (called "Conclusions and Future Research" in this essay), in which the findings are summarized and made relevant, applying the strategies discussed in Chapter 1, Two Kinds of Selective Reading, page 8.
4. If you can see that the essay will be crucial to your own research, you can now go back and read the other sections closely.

The essay that follows represents a particular kind of scholarly essay, a **literature review**, or critical evaluation, in which the authors analyze previous studies on a particular topic. Their purpose is to assess what researchers have uncovered about a significant area of investigation, to disclose aspects that need further research, and, to suggest ways to go about this research. Like most literature reviews, the authors discuss the results of previous studies throughout their essay, organizing their essay by logical sections.

Before reading this essay, you can also review the questions discussed in Chapter 1, Responding Critically and Analytically through Questions, page 10.

Pre-Reading Questions/Activities

1. Recall that an abstract gives an overview of the paper. After reading the abstract, determine the purpose of the essay. Scan the headings. In your opinion, are the headings and subheadings helpful? Why or why not?
2. Without reading the article, come up with your own definitions of *social competence* and *social connectedness* as they relate to social networking.
3. Collaborative or individual activity: As a group, consider what you think (a) the "Internet-enhanced self-disclosure hypothesis," referred to in the abstract, might involve; and (b) the reasons might be why use of the Internet is no longer considered "detrimental." As an individual activity, you could answer parts (a) and (b) in paragraph form or as freewriting activities.

Sample Scholarly Essay

Reading 16

Social Consequences of the Internet for Adolescents: A Decade of Research
Patti M. Valkenburg and Jochen Peter

ABSTRACT—Adolescents are currently the defining users of the Internet. They spend more time online than adults do, and they use the Internet for social interaction more often than adults do. This article discusses the state of the literature on the consequences of online communication technologies (e.g., instant messaging) for adolescents' social connectedness and well-being. Whereas several studies in the 1990s suggested that Internet use is detrimental, recent studies tend to report opposite effects. We first explain why the results of more recent studies diverge from those of earlier studies. Then, we discuss a viable hypothesis to explain the recent findings: the Internet-enhanced self-disclosure hypothesis. Finally, we discuss some contingent factors that may deserve special attention in future research.

KEYWORDS—Internet; Internet effects; adolescents; wellbeing; social competence; social connectedness

When online communication technologies, such as e-mail and chat rooms, became popular in the 1990s, several authors believed that these technologies would reduce adolescents' social connectedness and well-being. Social connectedness refers to adolescents' relationships with others in their environment (e.g., friends, family members). At the time, it was assumed that (a) the Internet motivates adolescents to form superficial online relationships with strangers that are less beneficial than their real-world relationships (e.g., Nie, 2001) and (b) time spent with online strangers occurs at the expense of time spent with existing relationships (Kraut et al., 1998), so that (c) adolescents' social connectedness and well-being are reduced (e.g., Kraut et al., 1998).   [1]

This reduction hypothesis received considerable empirical support in the second half of the 1990s. Several studies in the early years of the Internet, conducted among adolescents and adults, demonstrated that Internet use was negatively related to social connectedness and well-being. For example, a longitudinal study by Kraut et al. (1998) showed that Internet use reduced adolescents' social connectedness and well-being within a period of 1 year. In addition, Nie (2001) demonstrated that adults who spent more time on the Internet spent less time with friends. Finally, Mesch (2001) found that adolescents who had fewer friends, particularly fewer "friends who always listened to them," were more likely to be Internet users. However, while these reduction effects were demonstrated consistently in the early stages of Internet adoption, at least two changes in Internet use may render such effects less likely now. First, in the second half of the 1990s, it was hard to maintain one's existing social network on the Internet because the greater part of this network was not yet online. For example, in the study by Mesch (2001), only 11% of adolescents were online. In the Kraut et al. (1998) study, none of the respondents had Internet access before they participated in the study. At the time, online contacts were separated from offline contacts. But at present, the vast majority of adolescents in Western countries have access to the Internet (e.g., Lenhart & Madden, 2007). At such high access rates, a negative effect of the Internet on social connectedness is less likely because adolescents have more opportunities to maintain their social network through this medium.   [2]

Second, communication technologies that were popular among adolescents in the 1990s, such as MUDs (Multi-User Dungeons) and public chat rooms, were typically used for communication between strangers. However, in recent years, several communication technologies, such as Instant Messaging (IM) and social networking sites like Facebook, have been developed that encourage adolescents to communicate with existing friends. European and U.S. studies have shown that 84% (e.g., Gross, 2004) to 88% (e.g., Valkenburg & Peter, 2007a) of adolescents use IM for communication with existing friends.   [3]

A Time-Related Shift from Negative to Positive Internet Effects

Obviously, when media use changes, its outcomes may change. Because adolescents now predominantly use the Internet to maintain their existing friendships, the condition for negative effects of the Internet on social connectedness and well-being no longer exists. It is no surprise, therefore, that most recent Internet studies have demonstrated that adolescents' online communication stimulates, rather than reduces, social connectedness and/or well-being. For example, in a 2-year follow-up study based on their initial sample of Internet novices, Kraut et al. (2002) found that Internet use   [4]

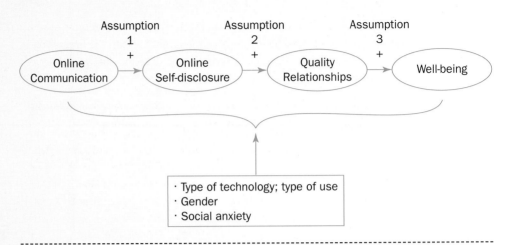

Figure 1   The Internet-enhanced self-disclosure hypothesis. Assumption 1 is that online communication stimulates online self-disclosure. Assumption 2 is that this higher online self-disclosure leads to higher-quality relationships, which in turn (Assumption 3) increase adolescents' well-being. This stimulation effect depends, however, on (a) the type of technology that is used, (b) the user's gender, and (c) the user's level of social anxiety. All three assumptions of the Internet-enhanced self-disclosure hypothesis have been confirmed in several studies.

improved social connectedness and well-being. Several other recent studies have demonstrated significantly positive relationships between online communication (mostly IM) and adolescents' social connectedness and/or well-being (e.g., Bessière, Kiesler, Kraut, & Boneva, 2008; Valkenburg & Peter, 2007a). However, these positive results are only found for adolescents who use the Internet predominantly to maintain existing friendships (Bessière et al., 2008). When they use it primarily to form new contacts and talk with strangers, the positive effects do not hold (Bessière et al., 2008; Valkenburg & Peter, 2007b).

Identifying Underlying Processes

[5]   Although changes in Internet use may plausibly explain changes in the social effects of the Internet, the question remains why online communication is positively related to social connectedness and well-being. Unfortunately, earlier studies on the effects of the Internet have typically investigated direct relationships between the independent variables (i.e., different types of Internet use) and dependent variables (i.e., social connectedness or well-being) without exploring the processes that may underlie these relationships. In the past years, we have conducted several studies to identify the underlying processes of the relationship between the Internet and social connectedness. On the basis of these studies, we have formulated a hypothesis that may explain the Internet's positive effects—the Internet-enhanced self-disclosure hypothesis. This hypothesis states that the positive effects of the Internet on social connectedness and well-being can be explained by enhanced online self-disclosure. Online self-disclosure refers to online communication about personal topics that are typically not easily disclosed, such as one's feelings, worries, and vulnerabilities. The three assumptions of our hypothesis are summarized in Figure 1.

Assumption 1: Online Communication Stimulates
Online Self-Disclosure

The first assumption of our hypothesis is that online communication stimulates online self-disclosure. [6] This assumption is based on earlier computer-mediated communication (CMC) theories in general and on Walther's (1996) hyperpersonal communication theory in particular. According to hyperpersonal communication theory, CMC is typically characterized by reduced visual, auditory, and contextual cues (e.g., social status cues). An important consequence of these reduced cues is that CMC interactants become less concerned about how others perceive them and, thus, feel fewer inhibitions in disclosing intimate information. In other words, their communication becomes hyperpersonal—that is, unusually intimate. These liberating processes are particularly relevant to adolescents, for whom shyness and self-consciousness are inherent to their developmental stage.

The assumption that CMC stimulates self-disclosure has received ample support. A series of [7] studies have shown that CMC and online communication result in more and/or more intimate self-disclosures (e.g., Tidwell & Walther, 2002; Valkenburg & Peter, in press). In fact, the finding that online communication enhances self-disclosure is one of the most consistent outcomes in CMC research.

Assumption 2: Online Self-Disclosure Enhances
Relationship Quality

A second assumption of our hypothesis is that Internet-enhanced online self-disclosure enhances the [8] quality of adolescents' relationships (see Fig. 1). It is long-standing wisdom in interpersonal communication that offline, face-to-face self-disclosure is an important predictor of adolescents' friendships (Berndt, 2002). Several studies have demonstrated that face-to-face self-disclosure is related to the closeness and quality of adolescent friendships (e.g., McNelles & Connolly, 1999). Adolescents identify the mutual disclosure of intimate topics as a vital characteristic of high-quality friendships and as one of those friendships' highest rewards (Buhrmester & Prager, 1995).

There is also evidence that online self-disclosure is related to friendship formation (McKenna & [9] Bargh, 2000) and to the quality of existing friendships (Valkenburg & Peter, 2007a). A recent longitudinal study showed that, within 1 year, adolescents' online self-disclosure resulted in higher-quality friendships (Valkenburg & Peter, in press). This study also found that the direct relationship between online communication and the quality of friendships disappeared when online self-disclosure was added to the analysis. The disappearance of this direct effect implies that online self-disclosure mediates the relationship between online communication and the quality of friendships. It also means that it is not just online communication (or mere exposure to IM) that leads to higher-quality friendships; Internet-enhanced self-disclosure accounts for the positive effect of online communication on the quality of friendships.

Assumption 3: High-Quality Relationships
Promote Well-Being

The final assumption is that Internet-enhanced self-disclosure indirectly promotes adolescents' well- [10] being—specifically, by enhancing the quality of their relationships (see Fig. 1). This assumption is based on the repeated finding that the quality of adolescents' friendships is a powerful predictor of their well-being (Erdley, Nangle, Newman, & Carpenter, 2001). High quality friendships can form a powerful buffer against stressors in adolescence, and adolescents with high-quality friendships are often happier than adolescents without such friendships (Hartup & Stevens, 1997).

However, although there is evidence that online self-disclosure enhances the quality of adoles- [11] cent friendships (e.g.,Valkenburg & Peter, in press) and that the quality of friendships promotes wellbeing (e.g., Erdley et al., 2001), it is unclear whether the quality of adolescents' friendships mediates, and thus accounts for, the relationship between online self-disclosure and well-being. However, a recent study did provide circumstantial evidence for our final assumption (Valkenburg & Peter, 2007b). It was demonstrated that the quality of adolescents' friendships mediated the relationship between their online communication with existing friends and their well-being: Online communication stimulated the quality of adolescent's friendships, and via this route, it improved adolescents' well-being, measured with the five-item satisfaction-with-life scale developed by Diener, Emmons, Larsen, and Griffin (1985).

Who Benefits Most From The Effects Of Online Communication?

[12]   The effects of the Internet may be contingent upon many factors, such as the type of technology, the adolescent who is using the technology, and his or her social environment. Although the literature on Internet effects has rapidly grown in the past decade, knowledge about the factors that may influence any Internet effect is still scarce. At least three moderating factors deserve more attention. These factors, which are presented at the bottom of Figure 1, have not yet been investigated in an integrated effects model. Therefore, their function in the effects model cannot yet be decisively specified.

Type of Technology, Type of Use

[13]   Online communication and online self-disclosure can stimulate adolescents' social connectedness and, thereby, their well-being. However, several studies have found that this positive Internet effect holds only when (a) adolescents predominantly talk with their existing friends (Bessière et al., 2008; Valkenburg & Peter, 2007a) or (b) when they use IM (Valkenburg & Peter, 2007b). IM is a text-based technology that is predominantly used to talk with existing friends. Therefore, self-disclosure via IM inherently means self-disclosure to existing friends. Communication technologies that are predominantly used to communicate with strangers (e.g., chat in a public chatroom) or more solitary forms of Internet use (e.g., surfing) have no effects or even negative effects on social connectedness and well-being (Bessière et al., 2008; Valkenburg & Peter, 2007b). Future research should, therefore, differentiate between types of Internet use and formulate hypotheses that are based on the functions that these technologies have for adolescents.

Gender

[14]   Adolescent boys seem to benefit more from online communication with existing friends than girls do. About one in three adolescents are able to self-disclose better online than they are offline. This holds more for boys than for girls (Schouten, Valkenburg, & Peter, 2007). Especially in early and middle adolescence, adolescents are inhibited in disclosing themselves in face-to-face settings. At this stage, IM may be particularly helpful to encourage self-disclosure. In face-to-face settings, adolescent boys generally have more difficulty self-disclosing to friends than girls do (McNelles & Connolly, 1999). Therefore, boys especially benefit from online communication to stimulate their self-disclosure and, thereby, their social connectedness and well-being (Schouten et al., 2007).

Social Anxiety

[15]   In the 1990s, it was often believed that the Internet would especially attract socially anxious adolescents. Social anxiety implies that one is worried about the self and consequently is inhibited in face-to-face social interactions. There are two hypotheses on the relationship between social anxiety and online communication. The social compensation hypothesis assumes that it is mainly socially anxious adolescents who turn to online conversation. The reduced audiovisual cues of the Internet may help these

adolescents overcome the inhibitions they typically experience in real-life interactions. The opposite hypothesis—the rich-get-richer hypothesis—states that it is primarily socially competent adolescents who use the Internet for online communication. These adolescents, who already have strong social skills, may consider the Internet as just another venue to get in touch with peers (Kraut et al., 2002).

Most studies seem to support the rich-get-richer hypothesis rather than the social compensation hypothesis (for a summary, see Valkenburg & Peter, 2007a). Adolescents who are socially competent in offline settings also more often use online communication technologies, such as IM, to stay in touch with these friends. These adolescents typically also often use other communication technologies, such as social networking sites and text messaging through their cell phones (Bryant, Sanders-Jackson, & Smallwood, 2006). However, in comparison with their socially competent peers, socially anxious adolescents do more often prefer online self-disclosure to offline self-disclosure. Because socially anxious adolescents are inhibited in face-to-face social interactions, they may prefer a more protected environment in which they feel less inhibited to reveal their concerns. The Internet provides them with such an environment. The reduced auditory and visual cues of online communication diminish the constraints that socially anxious adolescents typically experience in offline settings (Schouten et al., 2007). Furthermore, because socially anxious adolescents often prefer settings in which their interactions can be prepared ahead of time, they find the control over message construction, which is possible in online communication, more important than less socially anxious adolescents do (Schouten et al., 2007).

[16]

Conclusions and Future Research

Based on the evidence presented in this article, it is plausible to assume that online self-disclosure accounts for the positive relationship between online communication and social connectedness. However, Internet research is still young and does not yet allow us to draw decisive conclusions. Several alternative explanations may be possible. For example, in comparison with face-to-face communication, online communication may result in greater positivity of interaction, in enhanced liking of online partners, and in more breadth of interaction. These processes may all qualify as alternative explanations for the positive relationship between Internet use and social connectedness found in recent studies. In addition, other moderators may have to be added to our model. For example, in face-to-face interactions, self-disclosure is often only effective for the development of close friendships when the communication partner is responsive and supportive. It is important to investigate whether these results also hold for online self-disclosure.

[17]

We hope that future research will pay attention to additional variables that may explain the social consequences of the Internet and that they will compare the validity of our hypothesis with that of other explanatory hypotheses. Future research should also investigate the simultaneous effect of different communication technologies. Most research has focused on the effects of IM and chat in public chat rooms. However, the advent of IM and chat technologies coincided with all kinds of other technologies, such as text messaging through cell phones. For an encompassing view on the differential effects of current communication technologies, it is important to compare the effects of these different technologies.

[18]

The positive effect of online communication with existing friends may be attributed to enhanced online self-disclosure. However, the same liberating or disinhibiting mechanisms of online communication that have led to the positive outcomes that were the focus of this paper can also have negative consequences for adolescents. For example, flaming (hostile and insulting interactions between Internet users), online harassment, and cyberbullying may all be associated with the disinhibition that results from the reduced auditory and visual cues in CMC. Our article must not be misunderstood simply as a glorification of the Internet. There is definitely a need for more research to identify the conditions under which adolescents may experience potential positive or adverse effects of different forms of online communication and how adolescents can be educated about such effects.

[19]

References

Berndt, T.J. (2002). Friendship quality and social development. *Current Directions in Psychological Science*, *11*, 7–10.

Bessière, K., Kiesler, S., Kraut, R., & Boneva, B.S. (2008). Effects of Internet use and social resources on changes in depression. *Information, Communication, and Society*, *11*, 47–70.

Bryant, J.A., Sanders-Jackson, A., & Smallwood, A.M.K. (2006). IMing, text messaging, and adolescent social networks. *Journal of Computer-Mediated Communication*, *11*(2), article 10. Retrieved January 2, 2009, from http://jcmc.indiana.edu/vol11/issue2/bryant.html

Buhrmester, D., & Prager, K. (1995). Patterns and functions of self-disclosure during childhood and adolescence. In K.J. Rotenberg (Ed.), *Disclosure processes in children and adolescents*. Cambridge, UK: Cambridge University Press.

Diener, E., Emmons, R.A., Larsen, R.J., & Griffin, S. (1985). The satisfaction with life scale. *Journal of Personality Assessment*, *49*, 71–75.

Erdley, C.A., Nangle, D.W., Newman, J.E., & Carpenter, E.M. (2001). Children's friendship experiences and psychological adjustment. *New Directions for Child and Adolescent Development*, *91*, 5–24.

Gross, E.F. (2004). Adolescent Internet use: What we expect, what teens report. *Journal of Applied Developmental Psychology*, *25*, 633–649.

Hartup,W.W., & Stevens, N. (1997). Friendships and adaptation in the life course. *Psychological Bulletin*, *121*, 355–370.

Kraut, R., Kiesler, S., Boneva, B., Cummings, J., Helgeson, V., & Crawford, A. (2002). Internet paradox revisited. *Journal of Social Issues*, *58*, 49–74.

Kraut, R., Patterson, M., Lundmark, V., Kiesler, S., Mukopadhyay, T., & Scherlis, W. (1998). Internet paradox: A social technology that reduces social involvement and psychological well-being? *American Psychologist*, *53*, 1017–1031.

Lenhart, A., & Madden, M. (2007). *Teens, privacy & online social networks*. Washington, DC: Pew Internet & American Life Project.

McKenna, K.Y.A., & Bargh, J.A. (2000). Plan 9 from cyberspace: The implications of the Internet for personality and social psychology. *Personality and Social Psychology Review*, *4*, 57–75.

McNelles, L.R., & Connolly, J.A. (1999). Intimacy between adolescent friends: Age and gender differences in intimate affect and intimate behaviors. *Journal of Research on Adolescence*, *9*, 143–159.

Mesch, G. (2001). Social relationships and Internet use among adolescents in Israel. *Social Science Quarterly*, *82*, 329–340.

Nie, N.H. (2001). Sociability, interpersonal relations and the Internet: Reconciling conflicting findings. *American Behavioral Scientist*, *45*, 420–435.

Schouten, A.P., Valkenburg, P.M., & Peter, J. (2007). Precursors and underlying processes of adolescents' online self-disclosure: Developing and testing an "Internet-attribute-perception" model. *Media Psychology*, *10*, 292–314.

Tidwell, L.C., & Walther, J.B. (2002). Computer-mediated communication effects on disclosure, impressions, and interpersonal evaluations. *Human Communication Research*, *28*, 317–348.

Valkenburg, P.M., & Peter, J. (2007a). Preadolescents' and adolescents' online communication and their closeness to friends. *Developmental Psychology*, *43*, 267–277.

Valkenburg, P.M., & Peter, J. (2007b). Online communication and adolescents' well-being: Testing the stimulation versus the displacement hypothesis. *Journal of Computer Mediated Communication*, *12*(4), article 2. Retrieved January 2, 2009, from http://jcmc.indiana.edu/vol12/issue4/valkenburg.html

Valkenburg, P.M.,& Peter, J. (in press). The effects of instant messaging on the quality of adolescents' existing friendships: A longitudinal study. *Journal of Communication*.

Walther, J.B. (1996). Computer-mediated communication: Impersonal, interpersonal, and hyper-personal interaction. *Communication Research, 23,* 3–43.

Post-reading questions/activities

1. After reading the essay, look back at your definitions in pre-reading question 2 and see if either needs revision; revise as necessary, using your own words. Do the same for question 3a.

2. In the section with the heading "Identifying Underlying Processes," explain in a couple of sentences how the authors justify their study?

3. Like researchers conducting an experiment, the authors of this study propose a hypothesis. How do they set out to "prove" this hypothesis?

4. In a paragraph, explain how the three assumptions (paragraphs 7–12) are related to one another.

5. It is evident that the authors often cite studies that they co-authored; explain why you believe this (a) increases their credibility, or (b) decreases their credibility.

6. Summarize the section "Social Anxiety" in 75 words: it is 302 words (excluding citations), so 75 words is 25 per cent of the original.

7. Suggest one hypothesis that might follow from the statement in paragraph 13 that "[f]uture research should, therefore, differentiate between types of Internet use and formulate hypotheses that are based on the functions that these technologies have for adolescents";

   Or:

   Suggest a hypothesis arising from one of the suggestions for future research mentioned in the final section, "Conclusions And Future Research."

8. Do you think the statement "[o]ur article must not be misunderstood simply as a glorification of the Internet" in the final paragraph is necessary or appropriate? Why or why not?

Collaborative or Individual Activity

This paper discusses a change in the results of the early versus late studies on Internet use.

1. What possible factor(s) or conditions do you think could affect the results of future studies conducted, say, between 2010 and 2020?

   Or:

2. Do you think networking sites will continue to offer more benefits or detriments for users in the coming years? Defend your position.

Documentation Styles

Why Document Your Sources?

Documentation is usually the final stage of research, but that doesn't mean you shouldn't prepare for it long in advance. In fact, carefully recording *all* relevant bibliographic details of the sources you will or may use in the early stages of research is essential, as it is time consuming to go back and retrieve these details later.

When you document your sources, you are confirming that the information used in your essay comes from verifiable documents; thus, careful documentation of sources *gives you credibility as a researcher*. Other reasons for documenting include

> giving appropriate credit to the work of others
> showing where your own work fits into other work in the field
> avoiding plagiarism, a form of theft, and certainly one of the most serious academic crimes, with severe penalties for anyone who knowingly or unknowingly plagiarizes
> enabling interested readers and knowledgeable experts (such as your instructor) to trace or verify your sources
> finding the reference again if you need it for further research.

Necessary versus Unnecessary Citations

Parenthetical references are intended to give the reader as *much* information as possible about the source while interfering as *little* as possible with the essay's content and readability. This is an especially important principle in the Modern Language Association (MLA); however, in both MLA and American Psychological Association (APA) documentation styles, you should not include unneeded citations or parts of citations.

You can avoid citing the same source repetitively in one paragraph if it is clear you are referring to that one source throughout. Thus, you can combine a few references from the same source in one comprehensive citation. For example, let's say you used three pages from your source, Jackson; when you were finished drawing from that source, you could indicate your use of Jackson this way: (Jackson 87–89). This citation would tell the reader that you used that one source continuously for three of her pages—perhaps one idea from page 87, two facts from page 88, and a paraphrased passage from page 89.

Another strategy for direct and economical documentation is to use a signal phrase to indicate a forthcoming reference. After naming the source and following with the material from the source, for example, a direct quotation or paraphrase, provide the page number. The reader can then clearly see the beginning and end of the source material. Since you have named the author(s) in your own sentence, you do not repeat the name in the citation (see Signal Phrases in Chapter 6 on page 168).

A third strategy is combining in one citation sources that contain the same point. This method is useful when you are summarizing the findings of several studies in the same paragraph and want to avoid excessive citations:

(Drinkwater, 2008, p. 118; Hovey, 2007, p. 75).

Choosing Your Documentation Style

Handbooks are published for the major documentation styles and contain extensive guidelines. However, usage rules are updated every five years or so. This is

---

In addition to *documentation*, the following terms apply to this stage of research:

Reference and **citation** both refer to a brief acknowledgement of the source of your information, whether paraphrased, summarized, or quoted directly. You show that you have made a reference to an outside source by use of a citation.

A documentation (citation) **style** refers to the system used in academic disciplines and by publishers to identify the kinds of documents that can be cited. Disciplines often favour one system over another and publish their guidelines in **style manuals** or **handbooks**.

An **in-text citation** or reference occurs in the text of your essay, usually immediately after the information from that source.

A **bibliography** is usually (but not always) an alphabetized list at the end of the essay of all the sources used in the essay. The title of this list varies depending on the style.

done for a variety of reasons. For example, in the 1980s, the Internet did not exist as the research tool we have today. Therefore, rules had to be adapted to fit the changing technology and the ways people retrieved information. Even the emergence of Web 2.0 has created new procedures, as websites are increasingly less static and contain a broader range of materials that can be used as sources for essays.

University libraries provide a range of current style manuals. When using a manual, ensure that you have the most up-to-date edition. If you want to purchase your own book, be aware that older editions and second-hand copies may not provide the latest rules.

Different areas of academia favour distinct styles. Below is a list of the styles used in common areas. However, your department or your instructor should be the final guide in your choice of documentation style.

> APA (American Psychological Association): business, education, psychology, many other social sciences and some sciences
> MLA (Modern Language Association): English literature, philosophy, religion, modern languages, some interdisciplinary subjects
> CSE (Council of Science Editors): biology and other sciences
> CMS (Chicago Manual of Style) notes and bibliography system/Turabian: history, some humanities
> In addition to the major styles, some subject areas, such as chemistry, engineering, mathematics, medicine, music, and sociology, have their own style specification.

Although there are many subtle differences among the various styles, the main elements of an in-text citation may include

> the name(s) of the author(s)
> the page number or a similar locator of the information cited
> the year of publication.

Most styles require an abbreviated citation in the sentence where the referenced material appears. In parenthetical styles, the information is enclosed in parentheses.

Further details on each cited work are given in an alphabetized list at the end of the essay under a heading such as "References" or "Works Cited." The following references have been styled according to the rules of each handbook or manual:

> **Humanities**
  The Modern Language Association. MLA *Handbook for Writers of Research Papers*. 7th ed. New York: the Modern Language Association, 2009. Print.

> **Social Sciences**
  American Psychological Association. (2010). *Publication manual of the American Psychological Association* (6th ed.). Washington, D.C.: Author.

Unlike the MLA and APA style guides, some other prominent documentation styles, such as the CMS notes and bibliography system, use numbered, detailed citations either at the bottom of the page or at the end of the essay (see pages 217–219 for common examples).

The Major Documentation Styles: MLA and APA

In the following MLA and APA sections, the basic standards for documenting sources are shown with examples to illustrate format. For cases where an example is not given below, you can check updates on the APA and MLA websites. As well, you can consult a reference librarian, reliable website, or your instructor for hard-to-find formats. However, if you use a "non-official" website for help, always double-check the information with one or more other sites, noting when each was last updated. If you have run out of resources, or simply do not have more time to spend on the citations chase, common sense suggests you adapt the rule closest to your particular case.

> APA and MLA are both parenthetical styles, meaning that parentheses are used to enclose brief bibliographical information about the source.

MLA Documentation Style

In the humanities, the principal documentation style has been developed by The Modern Language Association of America. The MLA publishes two manuals that define its style. The *MLA Style Manual and Guide to Scholarly Publishing* is designed for publishing academics. The *MLA Handbook for Writers of Research Papers*, 7th edition (2009), is compiled specifically for student researchers. The association also maintains a website (http://www.mla.org) that offers guidelines on Internet citations and updates. If you use an online source for documentation other than the MLA website, ensure it is reliable and follows the guidelines of the *Handbook*'s 7th edition.

MLA style is parenthetical, meaning that whenever you directly quote or paraphrase an author in your essay, or otherwise use an author's idea, you give the author's last name and the location of the reference (usually a page or paragraph number) in parentheses. Then, you provide a more complete description of all the sources in the last part your paper, titled "Works Cited" (see pages 198–206).

MLA In-text Citations

General Guidelines

> MLA in-text formats include author(s) and page number(s) (e.g., Ashton 17). If the author is named in a signal phrase (e.g., Ashton found that . . . .), only the page number will be in parentheses (17).

> Drop the redundant hundreds digit in the second page number (e.g., 212–47, *not* 212–247), but use both tens digits (e.g., 34–37).

> Leave one space between the author's last name and the page number. Do not use commas to separate items unless you need to include both an author and title in the citation or if you need to separate author from paragraph number in an electronic source.

> Readability and efficiency are key principles in MLA style: parenthetical references should not intrude in the text but should clearly indicate the cited sources.

> MLA in-text formats include author's last name(s) and page or paragraph number(s).

Specific Examples

A citation including a direct quotation, paraphrase, or summary. Give the last name of the author and the page number in parentheses.

No signal phrase:

> During World Wars I and II, the Canadian government often employed masseuses because surgery and medical care were insufficient "to restore severely wounded men" (Cleather ix).

Signal phrase. Since a signal phrase names the author, the citation requires only the page number:

> Gillam and Wooden argue that Pixar studio films show "a kinder, gentler understanding of what it means to be a man" (3).

Block quotation. A quotation longer than four typed lines is indented one inch from the left margin. Quotation marks are not used, and the quotation should be double-spaced. The author's name and the page numbers appear in parentheses at the end of the quotation and *after* the final period:

> . . . and older children. (Gillam and Wooden 7–8)

A citation referring to an indirect source. If it is necessary to refer to a source found in another work, include the name of the original author in the sentence, along with the source of the information in parentheses. This is preceded by the abbreviation "qtd. in" and followed by the page numbers:

> Francis Bacon observed that language affects our thinking when he said "words react on the understanding" (qtd. in Lindemann 93).

In "Works Cited," list details for the indirect source.

Personal communication, including interviews and emails. This kind of communication needs the interviewee's last name only, in parentheses:

> (McWhirter)

Multiple sources in one citation. You may cite more than one relevant source in a single citation if the point you are making applies to both. Order the sources alphabetically by last name and separate them by a semicolon:

> The practices of teaching composition in college have not radically changed in the last few decades (Bishop 65; Williams 6).

However, if the citation is lengthy, consider moving the entire citation to a note (see MLA Notes, page 206).

If you cite two sources in the same sentence, placing the citation after each source may help with clarity:

> One study looked for correlations between GPA and listening to music (Cox and Stevens 757) while another study related academic performance to three types of music (Roy 6).

An indirect source is one that is cited in another source—not the original one. If you have to cite information from an indirect source, use the phrase "as qtd. in" ("qtd." is an abbreviation for "quoted") followed by the place where you got the information.

MLA In-text Citations by Format

Kinds of Authors

Work by one author (book or article). Give the author's last name and page number. Note that a book with both an author and an editor is typically cited by author:

(Bloom 112)

Work by two authors needs the last names of both authors with the word *and* between them, in addition to a page number:

(Higgins and Wilson-Baptist 44)

Work by three and by more than three authors. Include the last names of all authors with commas between them. To cite three authors, use the word *and* between the second and third names in the list in addition to the page numbers. For more than three authors, include all names as above or give only the last name of the first author with the abbreviation "et al." and page numbers:

(Higgins, Wilson-Baptist, and Krasny 102); (Terracciano et al. 96)

> For four or more authors, you may give last name of first author followed by "et al."

Two or more works by the same author. If you have used two or more works by the same author in one essay, give the author's last name, along with a shortened version of the work's title separated by a comma, and a page number:

"self-enforced discipline" (Foucault, *Power/Knowledge* 37)

Two authors with the same last name. Include the authors' first initials along with page numbers:

(S. Taylor 225)

(D. Taylor 17)

Use first names if their initials are the same.

Group or organization as author (corporate author). Documents published by companies and other groups may not list an author. MLA style recommends including the entire name of the organization in the sentence itself, if possible, in order to avoid overly long citations. For example, the organization commonly known as UNICEF would appear in the sentence as The United Nations Children's Fund (along with a page number in parentheses). However, it is also acceptable to shorten the organization's name, accompanied by the page number in the same manner as a standard author citation:

> If no author is given, use the name of group or organization in place of author's name—in the sentence itself, if possible.

The United Nations Children's Fund reports that indigenous children are at exceptional risk of becoming refugees (204).

Some child protection advocates suggest that indigenous children are at exceptional risk of becoming refugees (UNICEF 204).

Work by an unknown author (including many dictionary and encyclopedia entries). Begin with the title, if it is short, followed by the page number. When the title is lengthy, a shorter version can be used. Distinguish articles from complete works by placing article titles in quotation marks:

("Plea to City Hall" 22).

MLA *In-text Citations: Electronic Sources*

The most challenging aspect of citing online documents is that they often lack page numbers. If your source is the entire website, use the author's name in the sentence without a citation. If you are citing a specific quotation or paraphrasing and the document uses paragraph numbers, use these (preceded by the abbreviation "par." for one paragraph, or "pars." for more than one, with a comma and space between author's name and "par."). If sections are numbered, you may use these numbers (preceded by the abbreviation "sec."). If the reference is specific but the document has neither numbered pages nor paragraphs nor section headings, the work must be cited without a page, paragraph, or section reference.

Many articles retrieved from a database are viewed as Portable Document Format (PDF) files. In such cases, use the page numbers in the document. They are usually the same as the page numbers of the print version if one exists.

Citation of entire website. Give the author's last name within the sentence:

> In his article, Dillon compares reading practices for print media to those for electronic media.

Citation from specific passage. The specific location is given in the parenthetical citation:

> One firmly entrenched belief is that reading screens will never replace reading books and other print media (Dillon, sec. 1).

Website by an unknown author. A site without an author's name follows the guidelines for a print document by an unknown author and uses the site title or an abbreviated form to direct readers to the source of any information:

> ("LHC Machine Outreach")

MLA *In-text Citations: Non-textual Sources*

Film, video, audio, TV broadcasts, musical recordings, and other non-textual media. Give the name of the individual most relevant to your discussion in the text. In the case of a film, this could be the director, performer, screenwriter, or other contributor, or several of these:

> Francis Ford Coppola's film *The Conversation* explores the psychology of surveillance.

If your focus is on the whole work, use only the title. In the "Works Cited" section, the entry would be alphabetized under *C* for Coppola, the film's producer.

MLA Entries in the "Works Cited" Section

The "Works Cited" section containing complete retrieval information appears at the end of your essay and on a new page that continues the numbers of your essay. The "Works Cited" list is double-spaced, with a one-inch margin. Omit words like "Press," "Inc.," and "Co." after publisher name (but university presses should be abbreviated "UP"). Common abbreviations used in MLA style include

For specific references from electronic documents without page numbers, use paragraph number(s) if visible, separated by a comma from the author's name; the abbreviation for "paragraph(s)" is "par(s)." If sections are numbered, use these, preceded by a comma and the abbreviation "sec."

If you are referring to a website itself, rather than a specific part, include author's name within the sentence and do not use any numbering.

assn. (association)

ch. (chapter)

ed. (editor[s], edition)

fwd. (foreword)

introd. (introduction)

P (Press)

par. (paragraph)

pars. (paragraphs)

pt. (part)

rev. (revised)

rpt. (reprint)

sec. (section)

trans. (translator)

U (University)

vol. (volume)

General Guidelines

> The title, "Works Cited," is centred an inch from the top of the page without underlining or bolding.

> The list is alphabetized by author's last name; each entry begins flush with the margin with subsequent lines indented half an inch.

> The standard MLA citation begins with the author's last name, followed by a complete first name (unless the author has published only initials). Italicize book titles and titles of other complete works, such as plays, films, and artistic performances—along with journal titles and websites; place quotation marks around titles of articles, essays, book chapters, short stories, poems, web pages, and TV episodes.

> The first letter of every major word in the title is capitalized, even if the initial source did not do so.

> The medium of publication or a similar descriptor is included, usually as the last element, unless date of access is required in an electronic source.

Specific Examples

Sample book entry: List book (or pamphlet or brochure) data in this sequence: author; title (italicized); place of publication; shortened version of the publisher's name (remove articles *A* or *The* and abbreviations); year of publication; publication medium:

Fries, Charles, C. *Linguistics and Reading*. New York: Holt, Rinehart and Winston, 1962. Print.

Sample journal entry: List journal article data in this sequence: author; title of article (in quotation marks); title of journal (italicized); volume number; issue number; year of publication; inclusive pages; publication medium:

Valkenburg, Patti M, and Peter Jochen. "Who Visits Online Dating Sites? Exploring Some Characteristics of Online Daters." *CyberPsychology and Behavior* 10.6 (2007): 849–52. Print.

Kinds of Authors

Work by one author (book). See above, "Sample book entry."

Work by two or three authors. Only the first author's complete name is inverted with a comma before *and*:

Luckner, John, and Reldan Nadler. *Processing the Experience*. Dubuque: Kendall/Hunt, 1992. Print.

The order for most Works Cited entries is author's last name and first name; title of work; publication details, which vary depending on whether the work is a book, journal article, or electronic document; and medium of publication.

Work by more than three authors. MLA style provides two possibilities: (1) the complete names of all authors, reversing the name of the first author only and including a comma between the authors' names; or (2) the complete name of just the first author plus the abbreviation "et al." ("and others"):

> Festial, Lawrence, Harold Inch, Susan Gomez, and Komiko Smith. *When Economics Fails*. Minneapolis: U of Minnesota P, 1956. Print.

> *Or:*

> Festial, Lawrence, et al. *When Economics Fails*. Minneapolis: U of Minnesota P, 1956. Print.

Two or more works by the same author. Works by the same author are arranged chronologically from earliest to most recent publication. The author's name appears in the first listing only, with three dashes substituted for it in the additional citations:

> Foucault, Michel. *Discipline and Punish: The Birth of the Prison*. Trans. Alan Sheridan. New York: Random, 1977. Print.

> ---. *The History of Sexuality*. Trans. Robert Hurley. 3 vols. New York: Random, 1978. Print.

Different works by two authors with the same last name. Alphabetical order of first names determines sequence:

> Taylor, Dylan. "The Cognitive Neuroscience of Insight." *Psychological Inquiry* 18.4 (2009): 111–18. Print.

> Taylor, Sara. "Creativity Unbound: New Theoretical Approaches." *Creative Being* 2.1 (2009): 14–23. Print.

One work with two authors. If two works have the same first authors, the order is determined by the last name of the second author:

> Srivastava, Sarita, and Margot Francis. "The Problem of 'Authentic Experience.'" *Critical Sociology* 32.2–3 (2006): 275–307. Print

> Srivastava, Sarita, and Mary-Jo Nadeau. "From the Inside: Anti-Racism in Social Movements." *New Socialist* 42 (2003): n. pag. 18 May 2006. Web. 8 Dec. 2009.

Group or organization as author (corporate author). Use the full group name in place of the author's name (if the organization name begins with an article [e.g., *The*], omit it):

> Education International. *Guide to Universities & Colleges in Canada*. Victoria: EI Education International, 2000 ed. Print.

Work with unknown author, publisher, or publication location (non-electronic). If the work being cited does not provide an author's name, list it alphabetically by the title. For missing publication details, use the following abbreviations: Before the colon, "N.p." means "no place," and after the colon it means "no publisher"; "N.d." means "no date." Use square brackets to identify any information that isn't from the source; if the information may be unreliable, add a question mark.

No author name (unsigned encyclopedia entry):

> "Interveners." *Canadian Encyclopedia*. 1985 ed. Print.

In a work by two or three authors, all authors are listed with only first author's name inverted. Use a comma between first author's first name and the word "and." With more than three authors, you may name all authors or only the first and use abbreviation "et al." to indicate there are at least three more authors.

When a work has a group, rather than an individual, author, the group name takes the place of author's name.

No publisher. In this example, the publisher is unknown; the place of publication is tentatively identified as Ontario:

Webb, Noah. *The Great Haileybury Forest Fire*. [Ontario?]: n.p. 1971. Print.

No publishing place or date:

Case, Michael. *Opus Dei*. N.p.: Slipshod P, n.d. Print.

Source Type

Work by author with an editor or translator. Begin with the author's name unless you refer primarily to the work of the editor (for example, his or her introduction or notes); original publication date can be included after the title. Follow the same format for a translated work. "Ed." is used for one or more editors.

Referring primarily to the text. The first date indicates the year the book was originally published:

Hawthorne, Nathaniel. *The Scarlet Letter*. 1850. Ed. John Stephen Martin. Peterborough: Broadview, 1995. Print.

Referring primarily to editor's work:

Martin, John Stephen, ed. *The Scarlet Letter*. By Nathaniel Hawthorne. 1850. Peterborough: Broadview, 1995. Print.

Translated work. The abbreviation "Trans." precedes the translator's name after the work's title:

Calvino, Italo. *Why Read the Classics?* Trans. Martin McLaughlin. New York: Pantheon, 1999. Print.

Chapter or other type of selection, such as an essay, in edited volume. Begin with the author's name and chapter (or essay) title. Follow with the book title and book editors' names, not inverted and preceded by "Ed." The citation concludes with publication information, the complete page range, and publication medium:

Sanders, Douglas E. "Some Current Issues Affecting Indian Government." *Pathways to Self-Determination: Canadian Indians and the Indian State*. Ed. Leroy Little Bear, Menno Boldt, and J. Anthony Long. Toronto: U of Toronto P, 1984. 113–21. Print.

> In an edited volume, including an anthology, begin with author's name and work title. Follow with book title and editor name, not inverted and preceded by "Ed." If you use more than one selection from the volume, you can create one entry for the work as a whole and abbreviated entries for specific works.

If you use more than one work from the same collection, you can economize by creating one entry for the work as a whole and abbreviated entries for specific works.

Main entry:

Little Bear, Leroy, Menno Boldt, and J. Anthony Long, eds. *Pathways to Self-Determination: Canadian Indians and the Indian State*. Toronto: U of Toronto P, 1984. Print.

Specific entry using Sanders, above; other essays in the work would follow the same format:

Sanders, Douglas E. "Some Current Issues Affecting Indian Government." Little Bear, Boldt, and Long. 113–21.

Introduction, preface, foreword, or afterword. Begin the entry with the name of the author of the section, followed by the section name (not in quotation marks). The title of the complete work comes next, then the work's author preceded by *By*:

Scholes, Robert. Foreword. *The Fantastic: A Structural Approach to a Literary Genre.* By Tzvetan Todorov. Trans. Richard Howard. Ithaca, NY: Cornell UP, 1975. v–xi. Print.

Volume in multivolume work. State the volume number if you use just the one volume:

Bosworth, A. B., ed. *A Historical Commentary on Arrian's History of Alexander.* Vol. 1. London: Oxford UP, 1980. Print.

If you use more than one volume, give the number of volumes in the whole work instead of the specific volume numbers:

Bosworth, A. B., ed. *A Historical Commentary on Arrian's History of Alexander.* 2 vols. London: Oxford UP, 1980. Print.

In your essay, the parenthetical reference would include author's name, volume number followed by a colon; after a space, include the page numbers:

(Bosworth 1: 212)

Second or subsequent edition of a work. Include the edition number after the title (or editor, translator, etc.):

Suzuki, David, Aaron Griffiths, and Rebecca Lewontin. *An Introduction to Genetic Analysis.* 4th ed. New York: Freeman, 1989. Print.

Book published before 1900. The publisher's name can be omitted; between the place of publication and year, insert only a comma:

Baring Gould, S. *Old Country Life.* 5th ed. London, 1895. Print.

Article in a journal. Whether the numbering of the journal continues with each succeeding issue in a volume (continuous pagination) or begins at *1* in every issue, you should include both volume and issue number:

Trew, Johanne Devlin. "Conflicting Visions: Don Messier, Liberal Nationalism, and the Canadian Unity Debate." *International Journal of Canadian Studies* 26.2 (2002): 41–57. Print.

If the journal does not use both volume and issue in its numbering, follow the journal's numbering system.

Article in a magazine. Cite the complete date (day, month, year) if the magazine is issued every week or every two weeks; if issued monthly or every two months, include month and year:

Knapp, Lonny. "Licensing Music to the Film and Television Industries." *Canadian Musician* Sept./Oct. 2007: 49–56. Print.

If the article breaks off and continues later in the work, cite the first page number followed by a plus sign—not the page range (e.g., "12+" indicates the article begins on page 12 and continues somewhere after page 12).

> After the name of the journal, always include volume and issue number in your citation, and follow with year (in parentheses), colon, page range, and medium.

Article in a newspaper. Cite the author if given; if no author, begin with the title. Give the day, month, and year; give the page number, preceded by section number or letter if the newspaper contains more than one section:

> "Lawyer seeks mistrial for client accused of illegal midwifery." *National Post*
>   20 April 2003: A8. Print.

If the article breaks off and continues later in the work, cite first page number followed by a plus sign—not the page range. A letter to the editor follows the same format and includes "Letter" after the title.

Book/Movie review. Follow reviewer's name by title of review; if there is no title, continue with "Rev. of" and the book or movie title followed by *by* and the author's or director's name. Conclude with publication information:

> Mihm, Stephen. Rev. of *Swindled: The Dark History of Food Fraud, from
>   Poisoned Candy to Counterfeit Coffee,* by Bee Wilson. *Business History
>   Review* 83.2 (2006): 379–81. Print.

Government document. If the author is unknown, begin with the name of the government followed by the agency (e.g., ministry, department, crown corporation) and document name:

> British Columbia. Office of the Auditor General. *Salmon Forever: An Assessment
>   of the Provincial Role in Sustaining Wild Salmon.* Victoria: Office of the
>   Auditor General of British Columbia, 2005. Print.

Indirect source. Cite the work where you found the citation rather than the original text:

> Lindemann, Erika. *A Rhetoric for Writing Teachers.* 4th ed. New York: Oxford
>   University Press, 2001. Print.

See "MLA In-text Citations, A citation referring to an indirect source," for the in-text format.

Personal communication, including interview. Include a description of the communication. *TS* in this example stands for "typescript":

> Carr, Emily. Letter to Lawren Harris. 12 December 1940. TS.

MLA Web Publication Citations

As online sources often change or even disappear, the MLA recommends that you download or print research material that may become inaccessible later. In cases where some relevant information is unavailable (such as page or paragraph numbers), cite what you can to enable the reader to access the source. Note that a URL, enclosed in angled brackets, is given only if the specific page of the website would be otherwise hard to locate. (If you need to divide the URL between two lines, break it after single or double slashes.) The date of access, however, is an essential part of web citations.

Sample electronic citation. Give the title of the website after the work's title, followed by the site's publisher or sponsor; if unavailable, use "N.p." The first date is

When you type in a URL, most word processing programs automatically flag it as a hyperlink. This means that the URLs are underlined and usually show up in blue. If you are reading the document electronically and click on the hyperlink (and if you are connected to the Internet), you will automatically be taken to that URL. However, in print documents, you must delete the hyperlink. Therefore, before printing your essay, make sure all URLs show up as plain text and not as hyperlinks.

that of the creation of the website or its latest update. The date that follows publication medium (Web) is the date of your latest access:

> Czekaj, Laura. "Promises Fulfilled: Looking at the Legacy of Thousands of Black Slaves Who Fled to Canada in the 1800s." *InnovationCanada.ca.* Canada Foundation for Innovation, 7 Feb. 2009. Web. 19 Apr. 2010.

The first date in a web entry is the date of the site itself or most recent update; the second is the date you last accessed the site. Medium of publication precedes access date.

Group, organization (e.g., corporate or government) **website**. If there is no author, list the entry by the organization's name. In this example, the URL is included because the page might be hard to locate otherwise:

> Environment Canada. "10 Things You Should Know About Climate Change." 12 Aug. 2009. Web. 15 Aug. 2010. <http://www.ec.gc.ca/cc/default.asp?lang= En&n=2F049262-1>.

Article in online-only journal. Online-only journals may not include page numbers, in which case use the abbreviation "n. pag." (no pagination) after the website date:

> Rye, B. J., Pamela Elmslie, and Amanda Chalmers. "Meeting a Transsexual Person: Experience within a Classroom Setting." *Canadian On-Line Journal of Queer Studies in Education* 3.1 (2007): n. pag. Web. 21 Oct. 2010.

Internet article based on a print source and retrieved from a database. In addition to the information required for the print version of a journal article, the name of the database and date of access are included:

In addition to the information included in the print version, journal articles retrieved from a database require database name and date of access, which follows medium of publication.

> Barton, Sylvia S. "Discovering the Literature on Aboriginal Diabetes in Canada: A Focus on Holistic Methodologies." *Canadian Journal of Nursing Research* 40.4 (2008): 26–54. *Ingenta.* Web. 11 May 2010.

Work found online that originally appeared in print. Include details of the print source and follow with the title of the website, publication medium, and date of access:

> Douglass, Frederick. "My Escape from Slavery." *The Century Illustrated Magazine* Nov. 1881: 125–31. *Electronic Text Center, University of Virginia Library.* Web. 14 Jan. 2011.

Letter or email. If the letter is published, cite it as you would a work in an edited volume, adding the date of the letter. If it is a personal letter or email, include a description, such as *Message to the author* and date:

> Barrett, Anthony. "Re: *Lives of the Caesars.*" Message to the author. 15 Aug. 2009. Email.

If the message is a typed letter, use *TS* (typescript) as publication medium.

Message posted to online forum, discussion group, or blog post. Follow the guidelines for "Sample electronic citation," above. If no title is given, the entry should include a generic label after the author's name. In this example, the author did not include a first name, so this information cannot be given:

> Koolvedge. Online posting. *Adbusters.org.* Adbusters Media Foundation, 8 Aug. 2009. Web. 30 Aug. 2010. <https://www.adbusters.org/blogs/dispatches/ massacre-peru.html#comments>.

MLA Citations for Non-textual Sources

MLA style has been updated to include specific citation formats for a variety of non-textual information sources. As a general rule of thumb, the persons most relevant to your discussion should be featured in your citation, along with an abbreviated description of their role. For example, if your paper is about actors, you can cite their contribution in a film either alongside or instead of naming the director.

Lecture or other oral presentation. Begin with the name of the speaker, the title of the presentation, the meeting and/or sponsor (if applicable), location detail, and date. Conclude with the equivalent of publication medium (e.g., *Lecture*, *Reading*):

> Armstrong, Nancy. "Darwin's Paradox." Department of English. David Strong Building, University of Victoria, Victoria. 2 April 2010. Lecture.

Film or video. Begin with the work's title unless you are referring mainly to one person's contribution (for example, a performer or writer). Follow with the names of the most relevant individuals and conclude with the distributor's name and year of release.

Citing the film:

> *Apocalypse Now*. Dir. Francis Ford Coppola. United Artists, 1979. Film.

Citing a specific individual (the abbreviation "perf." stands for "performer"):

> Brando, Marlon, perf. *Apocalypse Now*. Dir. Francis Ford Coppola. United Artists, 1979. Film.

Performance (e.g., play, concert). Begin with the title of the performance and follow with relevant information, usually the names of the writer, director, and main performers. Conclude with the company name, theatre, city, date of performance, and the word *Performance*:

> *Macbeth*. By William Shakespeare. Dir. Des McAnuff. Perf. Colm Feore and Yanna McIntosh. Stratford Shakespeare Festival Company. Festival Theatre, Stratford, ON. 1 June 2009. Performance.

If you are citing one individual's contribution, begin with that person's name (see "Film or video," above).

Episode of a television or radio series. Use the following order: title of episode (in quotation marks), title of program (italicized), network, call letters of local station, and city, if relevant. Conclude by giving the broadcast date and medium of reception:

> "Man of Science, Man of Faith." *Lost*. Dir. Jack Bender. CTV. CFTO, Toronto, 21 Sept. 2005. Television.

Information relevant to the episode (e.g., the writer or director) follows the episode title; information relevant to the series follows the series title. If you are citing one individual's contribution, begin with that person's name (see "Film or video," above).

Music. Use the following order: performer (or other most relevant individual), recording title, label, year of issue, and medium (e.g., CD, LP):

> Morrison, Van. *Too Long in Exile*. Polydor, 1993. CD.

If you are citing a specific song, place its name in quotation marks after the performer's name; use a period before and after the song's name.

Work of visual art. Use the following order: artist, title (italicized), date of composition (or "n.d." if this is unavailable), medium of composition, name of the institution that contains the work, and city:

> Escher, M. C. *Drawing Hands*. 1948. Lithograph. Cornelius Collection, National Gallery of Art, Washington.

Interview. Begin with the name of the interview subject and follow with the interviewer's name preceded by "Interview by." Conclude with the publication details:

> Murakami, Haruki. Interview by Maik Grossekathöfer. *Spiegel Online International* 20 Feb. 2008. Web. 8 Dec. 2009.

If you are the interviewer, give the name of the interview subject followed by the interview medium and date:

> McWhirter, George. Email Interview. 2 June 2010.

MLA Notes

MLA permits either footnotes (at the bottom of the page) or endnotes (at the end of the document) as a way of including information you feel is valuable but which does not fit well within the text. You may use notes to further explain a point, to cite multiple sources, to suggest additional reading, or to cite related points of interest. These notes are indicated by a superscript (raised) number directly to the right and above the word most related to the note, or at the end of a phrase; they are numbered consecutively through your paper. Format the notes to match the rest of the document by double-spacing and indenting each note.

APA Documentation Style

In the social sciences, the principal documentation style has been developed by the American Psychological Association (APA). It is sometimes used in the sciences as well. The APA publishes a manual (*Publication manual of the American Psychological Association*, 6th ed.) and maintains a website (http://www.apastyle.org) that offers updates, FAQs, and specific information on Internet citations.

APA style is parenthetical, meaning that whenever you directly quote or paraphrase an author in your essay, or use an author's idea, you give the author's last name and the year of the work in parentheses; you will usually include page numbers as well. Then, you provide a more complete description of all the sources in the last section of your essay, titled "References."

APA In-text Citations

General Guidelines

APA in-text style includes author's last name, year of publication, and, usually, page number(s).

> ❭ APA in-text formats include authors and year. If the author is named in a signal phrase (e.g., "Ashton found that . . ."), the year follows the author's name and precedes the verb: "Ashton (2008) found that . . . ." Otherwise, the publication year follows the author's name in the end parentheses: (Ashton, 2008).

> A specific reference, such as a direct quotation or paraphrase, requires a page number. Use the abbreviation "p." for "page" and "pp." for "pages."
> Use commas to separate items in the citation.

Specific Examples

Citation including a direct quotation. Give the last names of authors, a comma, year of publication, a comma, and page number(s) all in parentheses.

No signal phrase. In this example, the author, Cleather, is not named in a signal phrase, so the parenthetical citation includes the author's name:

> During World Wars I and II, the Canadian government often employed masseuses because surgery and medical care were insufficient "to restore severely wounded men" (Cleather, 1995, p. ix).

Signal phrase. You can use a signal phrase to set up your reference. After the author is named in the signal phrase, follow with the year in parentheses. Place the page number at the end of the reference. In this example, the authors, Gillam and Wooden, are named in the signal phrase, so the parenthetical citation consists only of the page number. Note that the year follows the authors' names:

> Gillam and Wooden (2008) argue that Pixar studio films show "a kinder, gentler understanding of what it means to be a man" (p. 3).

When you name the source in a signal phrase, publication year (in parentheses) follows author's name.

Block quotation. A quotation of 40 words or more is placed on a new line and indented one half-inch from the left margin. Quotation marks are not used, and the quotation is double-spaced. The author's name, the year of publication, and the page number appear in parentheses at the end of the quotation *after* the final period:

> . . . and older children. (Gillam & Wooden, 2008, pp. 81–82)

Citation including a specific reference (such as a paraphrase). Give the last name of the authors, year of publication, and the page numbers:

> Most of the profits from BC's aquaculture industry go to Norwegians, who control 92 percent of the industry (Macdonald, 2009, pp. 148–149).

Citation for a non-specific reference. A non-specific reference might be an author's topic or thesis or the main findings of a study. It applies to the essay as a whole rather than to a specific page in the work. Give the last name of the author and the year of publication:

> Conservation biologists agree that protecting habitats is the most effective way to conserve biological diversity (Primack, 2000).

You do not include the page number(s) in a citation that refers to the work as a whole rather than to a specific page(s).

Citation referring to an indirect source. If it is necessary to refer to a source found in another work, include the original author in the sentence. In parentheses, use the phrase "as cited in," followed by the name of the source of the information and the year of publication:

> Francis Bacon (as cited in Lindemann, 2001) observed that language affects our thinking when he said that "words react on the understanding" (p. 93).

An indirect source is cited in another source. If you have to cite information from an indirect source, use the phrase "as cited in" followed by the place where you got the information.

In the References section, list the details for the indirect source.

Personal communication, including interviews. Give the author's name, including initials, the phrase "personal communication," and a date:

(J. Derrida, personal communication, September 20, 2000).

Note that personal communications are cited only in the text of your essay; they are not listed in the References section.

Multiple sources in one citation. You may cite more than one source in a single citation if the point you are making applies to both. Order the sources alphabetically by last name and separate them by a semicolon:

> You may include more than one source in a single citation. Order alphabetically and separate by semicolons.

The practices of teaching composition in college have not radically changed in the last few decades (Bishop, 2005; Williams, 2007).

APA In-text Citations by Format

Kinds of Authors

Work by one author (book or article). Give the author's last name, a comma, year of publication, a comma, and the page numbers (if required):

(Bloom, 2002, p. xviii).

Note that a book with an author and an editor is usually cited by author.

Work by two authors. Give the last names of both authors with an ampersand (&) between them, a comma, a date, a comma, and the page numbers (if required):

> When you refer to a work with more than one author, use an ampersand (&) to separate last author's name from preceding name.

(Higgins & Wilson-Baptist, 1999, p. 44).

When naming the authors in the text of your essay, as in a signal phrase, use the word *and* instead of an ampersand:

Higgins and Wilson-Baptist (1999) argue that "a tourist exists outside of experience. A traveller, though, submerges herself in the new" (p. 44).

Works by three, four, or five authors. List the last names of all authors for the first citation. For later citations, give the last name of the first author followed by the abbreviation "et al." with the publication year. If the authors are mentioned more than once in a paragraph, the year of publication is not included after the first reference:

> For three to five authors, list the last names of all authors in parentheses for the first citation with name of first author and abbreviation "et al." in later citations. For six or more authors, name first author followed by "et al."

(Higgins, Wilson-Baptist, & Krasny, 2001); later citations in the same paragraph: (Higgins et al.)

Work by six or more authors. Give the last name of the first author followed by the abbreviation "et al.," a comma, and the publication year:

(Terracciano et al., 2005)

Two or more works by the same author in the same year. Add alphabetical letters in lower case (a, b, c) to distinguish works chronologically in that year. In this example, the *a* after the year indicates that this is the first of at least two works by the same author in 1980 that you have used:

> . . . self-enforced discipline (Foucault, 1980a, p. 37)

Two authors with the same last name. Include the authors' initials separated from the last names by commas:

> (Sinkinson, S. & Sinkinson, B., 2001, pp. 225–237)

Group or organization as author (corporate author). Documents published by companies and government departments may not list an author. If the group title is long, or is well known by an acronym or abbreviation of the name (for example, The United Nations Children's Fund is commonly known as UNICEF), for the first citation include the entire title where the author's name would appear; also give the acronym in square brackets, a comma, and the year of publication. Use the abbreviation with the year of publication throughout the rest of the paper. If the group name is not well-known, use the full name with publication year each time:

> (American Educational Research Association [AERA], 2001);
>
> later citations: (AERA, 2001)

Work by an unknown author (including many dictionary and encyclopedia articles). Put the first few words of the title of an article or chapter in quotation marks followed by a comma and the year of publication:

> ("Plea to City Hall," 2003)

Author designated as "Anonymous." Cite in the same way as a named author:

> (Anonymous, 1887, p. 12)

Republished book. Give both the original and current publication dates:

> (Lacan, 1966/1977)

APA *In-text Citations: Electronic Sources*

The most challenging aspect of citing online documents is that they often lack page numbers. If paragraph numbers are given, cite by paragraph number preceded by the abbreviation "para." If neither page nor paragraph numbers are given but the document includes section headings, cite the heading title in quotation marks, count the paragraphs, and include the paragraph number(s) in which the material occurs:

> (Kao & Choi, 2010, "Economic Variables," para. 5)

Many articles retrieved from a database are viewed as Portable Document Format (PDF) files. In such cases, use the page numbers in the document. They are usually the same as the page numbers of the print version if one exists.

Sample in-text Internet citation. Include author's last name, a comma, the year the site was mounted or updated, a comma, the title (if applicable), a comma, and page or paragraph number:

> (Gregoire, 2000, "Bones and Teeth," para. 5)

If no author is given, use name of group or organization in place of author's name.

If you cannot locate page or paragraph numbers in an electronic document, include section heading in quotation marks and count by paragraphs from heading to the appropriate paragraph(s).

Internet site with an unknown author. Give the title (abbreviated if needed) in quotation marks, a comma, the year the site was created or updated, a comma, and a page or paragraph reference:

("Muchinfo's Poll," 2002, para. 16)

Internet site without a date. Use the abbreviation "n.d." if no date is available:

(Hannak, n.d., para. 2)

APA In-text Citations: Non-textual Sources

Film, video, audio, tv broadcasts, and musical recordings. Give the most senior production person's name, a comma, and the year of public release or broadcast:

(Coppola, 1979)

Installation, event, performance, or work of art. Give the name of the artist, a comma, and a date of showing or creation:

(Byrdmore, 2006)

APA Entries in the References List

In APA style, the References section containing complete retrieval information appears at the end of your essay and begins on a new page that continues the page numbering of your essay. The References list is double-spaced, with a one-inch margin. Omit words like "Publishers," "Inc.," and "Co." after publishers' names, but write out complete names of associations, corporations, and university presses. Some of the most common abbreviations include

ed. (edition)	para. (paragraph)
Ed. (Editor)	Pt. (Part)
Eds. (Editors)	Rev. ed. (Revised edition)
No. (Number)	Trans. (Translator[s])
p. (page)	Vol. (Volume)
pp. (pages)	Vols. (Volumes)

General Guidelines

> The title is centred an inch from the top of the page.
> The list is alphabetized by author's last name; each entry begins flush left with the margin; subsequent lines are indented one inch from the margin. Items are not numbered.
> The standard APA reference begins with the author's last name followed by initials, not given names. Titles of full-length works are italicized.
> Capitalize only the following elements of book and article titles: the first letter of the first word, the first letter after a colon, the first letter of all proper nouns, and acronyms like NFB or CBC, regardless of how the original is capitalized. Capitalize the names of journals exactly as they appear in the published work, however.

Specific Examples

Sample book entry. List book and report data in the following sequence: author, date of publication, title of book, place of publication, publisher:

The order for most final-page citations is author's last name and initial(s); publication date; title of work; and publication details, which vary depending on whether the work is a book, journal article, or electronic document.

Fries, C. C. (1962). *Linguistics and reading*. New York, NY: Holt, Rinehart & Winston.

Sample journal entry. List journal article data in the following sequence: author, date of publication, title of article, title of journal, volume number, issue number (if required), page range, and DOI or URL:

Valkenburg, P. M. & Jochen, P. (2007). Who visits online dating sites? Exploring some characteristics of online daters. *CyberPsychology and Behavior, 10,* 849–852. doi:10.1089/cpb.2007.9941

A "DOI" (digital object identifier) is included in many journal articles whether in print or electronic format; it is not followed by a period. A DOI enables readers to locate documents throughout the Internet.

Kinds of Authors

Work by one author. See above, "Sample book entry."

Work by two authors. Use an ampersand (&) to separate the authors, and invert the names of both authors with commas between last name and initial and a period at the end:

Luckner, J., & Nadler, R. (1992). *Processing the experience*. Dubuque, IA: Kendall/ Hunt Publishing.

> With two to seven authors, invert all authors' names and use an ampersand (&) between last and second-last name.

Work by three to seven authors. List all the authors:

Festial, L., Ian, H., & Gomez, S. (1956). *When economics fails*. Minneapolis, MN: University of Minnesota Press.

Work by eight or more authors. List the first six authors and the last author with three ellipsis points between the sixth and the final author:

Terracciano, A., Abdel-Khalek, A. M., Ádám, N., Adamovová, L., Ahn, C.-K., Ahn, H. N., . . . McCrae, R. R. (2005). National character does not reflect mean personality trait levels in 49 cultures. *Science, 310,* 96–100. doi:10.1126/ science.1117199

> With eight or more authors, list first six authors and last author with three ellipsis points between the sixth and the final author.

Two or more works by the same author. Works by the same author are listed chronologically, earliest to latest:

Foucault, M. (1977). *Discipline and punish: The birth of the prison*. A. Sheridan (Trans.). New York, NY: Random House.

Foucault, M. (1980). *The history of sexuality*, (Vol. 1). R. Hurley (Trans.). New York, NY: Random House.

> Arrange works by same author chronologically from earliest to latest.

Works with the same publication year are listed alphabetically by first major word of the title; lowercase letters follow the year within the parentheses. Below, the earliest article is listed first; the *h* in *history* precedes the *P* in *Power*:

Foucault, M. (1980a). *The history of sexuality*, (Vol. 1). R. Hurley (Trans.). New York, NY: Random House.

Foucault, M. (1980b). *Power/Knowledge: Selected interviews and other writings 1972–1977*. C. Gordon (Ed.). Brighton, England: Harvester Press.

Different works by two authors with the same last name. Alphabetical order of first names determines sequence:

> Taylor, D. (2009). The cognitive neuroscience of insight. *Psychological Inquiry*, *18*(4), 111–118.

> Taylor, S. (2009). Creativity unbound: New theoretical approaches. *Creative Being*, *2*(1), 14–23.

One work with two authors. If two works have the same first authors, the order is determined by the last name of the second author:

> Jason, L. A., & Klich, M. M. (1982). Use of feedback in reducing television watching. *Psychological Reports*, *51*, 812–814.

> Jason, L. A., & Rooney-Rebeck, P. (1984). Reducing excessive television viewing. *Child & Family Behavior Therapy*, *6*, 61–69.

Group or organization as author (corporate author). Use the full group name in place of the author's name (f the organization name begins with an article [e.g., *The*], omit it):

> Education International. (2008). *Guide to universities & colleges in Canada.* Victoria, BC: EI Education International.

Work by an unknown author (non-electronic source), such as an entry in a reference book. List alphabetically by the first major word in the title:

> Interveners. (1993). In *Canadian Encyclopedia* (Vol. 11, pp. 344–348). Ottawa. ON: Smith Press.

When an author is listed as "Anonymous," alphabetize by the letter *A*.

Work with no date. Replace the date with "n.d.":

> Gaucher, D. (n.d.).

Source Type

Work with an editor. Begin with the name of the editor(s) followed by "Ed." (one editor) or "Eds." (more than one editor) in parentheses:

> Corcoran, B., Hayhoe, M., & Pradl, G. M. (Eds.). (1994). *Knowledge in the making: Challenging the text in the classroom.* Portsmouth, NH: Boynton/Cook.

Chapter or other type of selection, such as an essay, in edited volume. Begin with author name, year, and chapter or essay title. Follow with *In* and the name(s) of book editor(s), not inverted, and the abbreviation Ed. or Eds. The citation concludes with the book title, page range in parentheses, and publication information:

> Sanders, D. E. (1984). Some current issues affecting Indian government. In L. Little Bear, M. Boldt, & J. A. Long (Eds.), *Pathways to self-determination: Canadian Indians and the Indian state* (pp. 113–121). Toronto, ON: University of Toronto Press.

Translated work. The translator's name is placed in parentheses after the work's title, followed by "Trans."

> Lacan, J. (1977). *Écrits: A selection.* (A. Sheridan, Trans.). New York, NY: W. W. Norton. (Original work published 1966)

When a work has a group author, rather than an individual author, use group name in place of author's name.

The usual order for an essay or other selection in an edited book is author name, year, essay title, book editor's name preceded by "In," the abbreviation "Ed.," book title and page range, and other publication details.

Volume in multivolume work. Include the volume number after the title:

> Bosworth, A. B. (Ed.). (1995). *A historical commentary on Arrian's history of Alexander* (Vol. 1). London, England: Oxford University Press.

If referring to more than one volume, give the specific volumes or range (e.g., Vols. 1–3).

Second or subsequent edition of a work. Include the edition number after the title:

> Suzuki, D. T., Griffiths, A. J., & Lewontin, R. C. (1989). *An introduction to genetic analysis* (4th ed.). New York, NY: W. H. Freeman.

Article in a journal with continuous pagination. If the numbering in each issue continues from the previous issue, include the volume but not the issue number. Page numbers in journals are not preceded by "p." or "pp.":

> Garner, R. (2003). Political ideologies and the moral status of animals. *Journal of Political Ideologies, 8*, 233–246.

If the article is assigned a DOI, it should be included after the page range (see "APA Internet Entries in the References Section," below).

Article in a journal that is paginated by issue. If every issue begins with page number "1," include both volume (italicized) and issue number (in parentheses and not italicized):

> Trew, J. D. (2002). Conflicting visions: Don Messier, Liberal nationalism, and the Canadian unity debate. *International Journal of Canadian Studies, 26*(2), 41–57.

Article in a magazine. Cite the complete date beginning with the year; follow with a comma and the month or month and day. Include the volume and issue number if available:

> Knapp, L. (2007, September/October). Licensing music to the film and television industries. *Canadian Musician, 29*(5), 49–56.

Article in a newspaper. List the author if given; if no author, begin with the title. For page numbers, use the abbreviation "p." or "pp." If the article breaks off and continues later in the work, give all page numbers, separated by commas, or the page range:

> Lawyer seeks mistrial for client accused of illegal midwifery. (2003, April 20). *National Post*, p. A8.

A letter to the editor or an editorial follows the same format and includes specific information in square brackets after the title (e.g., [*Letter to the editor*]).

Book/movie review. Follow the article format but in brackets include the title of the book and the reviewer's name, preceded by *Review of* and the medium (e.g., "Review of the DVD . . ."):

> Mihm, S. (2009). Swindled: The dark history of food fraud, from poisoned candy to counterfeit coffee [Review of the book *Swindled: The dark history of food fraud, from poisoned candy to counterfeit coffee*, by B. Wilson]. *Business History Review, 83*(2), 379–381.

Whether you include issue number depends on whether each journal issue is numbered separately (include issue number) or numbering continues from previous issue (do not include issue number).

If author is unknown, begin with the name of the government followed by agency (e.g., ministry, department, crown corporation) and document name. Report numbers can be included in parentheses right after work's title.

Government document. If the author is unknown, begin with the name of the government followed by the agency (e.g., ministry, department, crown corporation) and the document name. In this example, because the publisher is the same as the author (i.e., Office of the Auditor General of British Columbia), *Author* replaces the publisher's name:

> British Columbia. Office of the Auditor General. (2005). *Salmon forever: An assessment of the provincial role in sustaining wild salmon*. Victoria, BC: Author.

For government reports, along with similar documents, like issue briefs and working papers, the report number can be placed after the work's title: (e.g., "Research Report No. 09.171").

Indirect source. List the work the citation comes from, not the original text:

> Lindemann, E. (2001). *A rhetoric for writing teachers*. (4th ed.). New York, NY: Oxford University Press.

Personal communications (including emails, phone calls, interviews, and conversations) are not included in list of references.

Personal communication. Because they cannot be verified by the reader, personal communications (including emails, phone calls, interviews, and conversations) are not included in the list of references.

APA *Internet Entries in the References Section*

Include DOI (digital object identifier) for journal articles if available; otherwise, cite the URL of the home page of the journal or book publisher. Date of access is not usually required.

The 6th edition of the APA manual recommends that online sources include the elements of print sources in the same order with exact location information added as needed. If it is available, include the DOI, which is found with other publication information, such as journal title and volume number, and/or on the first page of the article. The DOI is a number-alphabet sequence that begins with "10." It forms the last element in your citation sequence and, like a Uniform Resource Locator (URL), is *not* followed by a period.

Since not all publishers use this system, cite the URL of the home page of the journal or book publisher if the DOI is unavailable or if your instructor tells you to do so. If the document would be hard to locate from the home page, provide the exact URL or as much as is needed for retrieval. APA does not usually require your date of access for Internet sources, but you should confirm electronic links before including them in your paper. More information on electronic reference formats recommended by the APA is available at http://www.apastyle.org/elecref.html.

Sample electronic reference. Citation formats follow those of print sources with the title of the website replacing the journal title:

> Czekaj, L. (2009, February 7). Promises fulfilled: Looking at the legacy of thousands of black slaves who fled to Canada in the 1800s. *InnovationCanada.ca*. Retrieved from http://www.innovationcanada.ca/en/

Note the absence of a period after the URL. If it is necessary to break the URL from one line to the next, break *before punctuation*, such as the period before "innovationcanada" above; never use a hyphen to break a URL unless it is part of the URL. Remember to always remove the hyperlink from the URL before printing your essay.

Group or organization (e.g., corporate or government) **website**. If there is no author, list by the organization's name. In this example, the complete URL is given because it might be hard to locate the document from the organization's home page:

Environment Canada. (August 12, 2009). 10 things you should know about climate change. Retrieved from http://www.ec.gc.ca/cc/default.asp?lang= En&n=2F049262-1

Article in online-only journal. In this example, the home page of the journal has been used for retrieval information:

Rye, B. J., Elmslie, P., & Chalmers, A. (2007). Meeting a transsexual person: Experience within a classroom setting. *Canadian On-Line Journal of Queer Studies in Education*, *3*(1). Retrieved from http://jps.library.utoronto.ca/ index.php/jqstudies/index

Article from a database (with a DOI). The name of the database is not usually required. In this example, the first part of the article is in quotation marks, indicating that a direct quotation is part of the title:

Martel, M. (2009). "They smell bad, have diseases, and are lazy": RCMP officers reporting on hippies in the late sixties. *Canadian Historical Review*, *90*, 215–245. doi:10.3138/chr.90.2.215

Article from a database (no DOI). The home page of the journal is used; the name of the database is not usually required:

Barton, S. S. (2008). Discovering the literature on aboriginal diabetes in Canada: A focus on holistic methodologies. *Canadian Journal of Nursing Research*, *40*(4), 26–54. Retrieved from http://cjnr.mcgill.ca/

No author or date. Place "n.d." in parentheses:

Hegemony. (n.d.). In *Merriam-Webster online dictionary*. Retrieved from http://www.merriam-webster.com/dictionary/hegemony

Electronic-only book. In this example, the hyphen after the first "mod" is part of the URL:

Radford, B. (n.d.). *Soil to social*. Retrieved from http://on-line-books.ora.com/ mod-bin/books.mod/javaref/javanut/index.htm

Electronic version of print book. Do not include publication details of the print version but include reader version, if applicable, in brackets, and either the DOI or URL:

Douglass, F. (1881). My escape from slavery [MS Reader version]. Retrieved from http://etext.lib.virginia.edu/ebooks/

Message posted to online forum, discussion group, or blog post. Give the format of the message, such as *Web log message* or *Video file*, in brackets:

Koolvedge. (2009, August 8). Reply to massacre in Peru [Web log message]. Retrieved from https://www.adbusters.org/blogs/dispatches/massacre-peru. html#comments

APA *Citations for Non-textual Sources*

Lecture or other oral presentation. Include the name of the lecturer, the date (in the format: year, month day), the title (or topic) of the lecture, followed by *Lecture presented at* and location detail, such as the sponsoring agency or school department and/or the building name, name of the school, and location of the school:

Armstrong, M. (2009, April 2). *Darwin's paradox*. Lecture presented at David Strong Building, University of Victoria, Victoria, BC.

> If there is a DOI or if there is no DOI and you include the journal home page, name of database can be omitted.

Film, video. Use the following order: producer, director, year, and title of the film, followed by *Motion Picture* in square brackets. Conclude with the country of origin and studio:

> Coppola, F. F. (Producer & Director). (1979). *Apocalypse now* [Motion picture].
> USA: Zoetrope Studios.

Episode from a television series. Use the following order: writer, director, year, and the title of the episode, followed by *Television series episode* in brackets. Conclude with the city and broadcasting company:

> Lindelof, D. (Writer), & Bender, J. (Director). (2005). Man of science, man of
> faith [Television series episode]. In J. J. Abrams (Executive producer), *Lost*.
> New York, NY: American Broadcasting.

Music. Use the following order: writer, copyright year, and the title of the song, followed by the recording artist in brackets (if different from the writer). Conclude with the album title preceded by *On*, the medium of recording in brackets, the city, and the label:

> Morrison, V. (1993). Gloria. On *Too long in exile* [CD]. UK. Polydor.

If the recording date is different from the copyright year, provide this information in parentheses.

CMS Documentation (Notes) Style

The Chicago Manual of Style (CMS) numbered notes and bibliography system is used primarily in history and other humanities disciplines. This CMS style may also include at the end of the essay a list of sources in alphabetical order by last name. Sometimes the bibliography is omitted, when the notes provide all the details; however, you should include it unless told otherwise.

If you take history courses, you may be asked to document your essays using the CMS notes style (or a variant, Turabian Style). You may also encounter this documentation style in your research. For this reason, the rudiments of CMS notes style are discussed below. You can consult a reliable online source, such as a library website, for information about hard-to-find formats. The Chicago Manual of Style website offers updates and sample formats at http://www.chicagomanualofstyle.org/home.html.

Guidelines are found in the 16th edition of *The Chicago Manual of Style* (2010), published by the University of Chicago Press, and *Chicago Manual of Style Online*. (These manuals also describe a scientific style that closely resembles APA with an MLA-style bibliography). The CMS style for humanities uses footnotes (at the bottom of each page) or endnotes (at the end of the paper) to direct readers to the sources of the information cited. Most word-processing programs will format these notes for you (under Insert—Footnote/Endnote). A superscript number (in a smaller point size raised above the level of the rest of the sentence) immediately follows the final punctuation of the reference (e.g., appears after the last word and quotation mark of a direct quotation). This number refers to a note at the bottom of the page or the end of the document.

General Guidelines

> ❭ Each note is single-spaced with the first line indented 5 spaces and successive lines flush left.

> Full bibliographical details are given for first references: author's name (first names followed by surname); work's title; place of publication, publisher, date (in parentheses); and page number(s). Successive references are condensed. Unlike in-text numbers, corresponding footnote/endnote numbers are the same point size as the rest of your text.
> Block quotations should be used for important passages of at least 100 words. Indent them 5 spaces from the left margin and do not include quotation marks.
> The final section, usually titled "Bibliography," alphabetically lists by last name all works used in the essay. Not all works cited in notes are included in the bibliography—for example, personal communications, brief dictionary/encyclopedia entries, and newspaper articles may be omitted.
> Bibliography entries are single-spaced. Leave a blank line between each entry.

Sample Notes and Bibliographic Entries

Book: One author

In-text reference:

Pringle believed "there is real need of authentic information" about social usage in Canada as distinct from the U.S. or Britain.[1]

Note for first reference:

1. Gertrude Pringle, *Etiquette in Canada: The Blue Book of Canadian Social Usage* (Toronto: McClelland & Stewart, 1932), vi.

Note for subsequent reference to same work:

3. Pringle, 28.

If more than one work by Pringle had been used, the title of the work (or a short form of it) would follow the author's last name with a comma to separate it from the page number.

Note for successive reference to same author:

4. Ibid., 16.

"Ibid." means "in the same place." If the page number is the same as in the preceding note, only "Ibid." is used; do not use "Ibid." unless the reference that *immediately* precedes is from the same source.

Bibliography:

Pringle, Gertrude. *Etiquette in Canada: The Blue Book of Canadian Social Usage*. Toronto: McClelland & Stewart, 1932.

Book: Two or three authors

Note:

2. Jung Chang and Jon Halliday, *Mao: The Unknown Story* (London, Vintage Books, 2005), 53.

Bibliography:

> Chang, Jung, and Jon Halliday. *Mao: The Unknown Story*. London: Vintage Books, 2005.

Book: More than three authors. In the note give the name of the first author and follow with "and others" or "et al." All authors are named in the Bibliography entry. See "Journal Article" below for examples.

Journal Article

Note:

> 5. Todd G. Morrison et al., "Canadian University Students' Perceptions of the Practices That Constitute 'Normal' Sexuality for Men and Women," *The Canadian Journal of Human Sexuality* 17, no. 4 (2008): 163.

Bibliography:

> Morrison, Todd. G., Travis A. Ryan, Lisa Fox, Daragh T. McDernnott, and Melanie A. Morrison. "Canadian University Students' Perceptions of the Practices That Constitute 'Normal' Sexuality for Men and Women." *The Canadian Journal of Human Sexuality* 17, no. 4 (2008): 161–71.

If the journal is **paginated by issue** (i.e., each issue begins with page 1), the issue number is included after the volume number; see example above. The season or month should be included if the issue number is not given: e.g., 165 (Spring 2010).

If the article is **accessed from a database,** follow the format above, but also include the DOI (if available) or URL, preceded by a comma (note) or period (bibliography entry). Include your date of access only if your instructor requires it. (Examples below include access dates.)

Note:

> 6. Peter John Loewen, "Affinity, Antipathy and Political Participation: How Our Concern For Others Makes Us Vote," *Canadian Journal of Political Science* 43 (2010): 666, accessed October 2, 2010, doi:10.10170500084239100065X.

Bibliography:

> Loewen, Peter John. "Affinity, Antipathy and Political Participation: How Our Concern For Others Makes Us Vote." *Canadian Journal of Political Science* 43 (2010): 661-87. Accessed October 2, 2010. doi:10.10170500084239100065X.

Magazine Article

Note:

> 7. Katelyn Friel, "Seven Tips for a Winning Website," *Dance Magazine*, August 2009, 12.

Bibliography:

> Friel, Katelyn. "Seven Tips for a Winning Website." *Dance Magazine*, August 2009.

Newspaper articles follow a similar format, but section (sec.) number or name replaces page number(s) as the last element. If the author of the article is unknown, begin with the newspaper's name and follow with article title. Newspaper articles are not included in the bibliography unless your instructor requires it.

Selection in an Edited Work

Note:

> 8. David Henry Feldman, "Creativity: Dreams, Insights, and Transformations," in *The Nature of Creativity: Contemporary Psychological Perspectives*, ed. Robert J. Sternberg (New York: Cambridge University Press, 1988), 275.

Bibliography:

> Feldman, David Henry. "Creativity: Dreams, Insights, and Transformations." In *The Nature of Creativity: Contemporary Psychological Perspectives*, edited by Robert J. Sternberg, 271–97. New York: Cambridge University Press, 1988.

If you are referring to the collection as a whole, the name(s) of the editor(s) would replace article author's name at the beginning of the citation and would be followed by ed(s). Use a comma for a note and a period for a bibliographic entry.

Electronic Reference

Note:

> 9. The Internet Encyclopedia of Philosophy, "Deductive and Inductive Arguments," accessed October 7, 2009, http://www.iep.utm.edu/d/ded-ind.htm.

Bibliography:

> The Internet Encyclopedia of Philosophy. "Deductive and Inductive Arguments." Accessed October 7, 2009. http://www.iep.utm.edu/d/ded-ind.htm.

If the author is known, both the note and bibliography entry begin with his or her name. In the Bibliography, the item should be alphabetized by the first major word in the title ("Internet"). The access date is added before the website URL with a comma before the URL. Encyclopedia articles and dictionary entries are not usually included in the bibliography; however, your instructor may require them.

The following exercises ask you to apply information from Chapters 6 and 7. They test your ability to use summary, paraphrase, direct quotation, mixed format, block format, signal phrases, ellipses, brackets, and MLA and APA in-text citations.

1. Following the instructions given in this text, complete parts (a), (b), and (c), creating sentences that show your understanding of how to use sources. The excerpts are from the website article "Comets May Have Led to Birth and Death of Dinosaur Era," by Hillary Mayell. It was published in *National Geographic News* on 16 May 2002. The information for part (a) is taken from numbered paragraphs 1 and 2 of the source; part (b) is taken from paragraph 4; part (c) is taken from paragraph 3.

   a) Paraphrase the following in one or two sentences. Do not use a signal phrase or any direct quotations. Use MLA style for the parenthetical citation.

   > Comets slamming into the Earth may be responsible for both the birth and the death of the dinosaur era, an international group of

EXERCISE 7.1

Check answers to select questions

researchers report. There is a considerable amount of evidence that a bolide [a comet or asteroid] collision with Earth triggered the end of the dinosaur era 65 million years ago.

b) Paraphrase the following sentence, but include one direct quotation that is no more than eight words (choose the most appropriate words for the quotation). Use a signal phrase to set up the paraphrase (i.e., source's name and signal verb).

"We have been able to show for the first time that the transition between Triassic life-forms to Jurassic life-forms occurred in a geological blink of an eye," said Paul Olsen, a geologist at the Lamont-Doherty Earth Observatory of Columbia University.

c) Using brackets, grammatically integrate the direct quotation into the complete sentence. Do not use a signal phrase.

The cause of the end of the dinosaur age might have been "a giant ball of ice, rock, and gases smashed into the supercontinent Pangaea."

2. a) Integrate the passage below as if you planned to use it in your essay, following the instructions. Use a signal phrase and APA style, which includes source's name, year, and signal verb, followed by a direct quotation of the passage. In sentence three, omit (i) "oral contraceptives, transoceanic phone calls" and (ii) "just to mention a few," indicating to the reader that material is omitted. Format the quotation in the most appropriate way—i.e., either as part of the text or in block format. The author is David Suzuki; the name of article is "Saving the Earth"; the date of publication is June 14, 1999; the quotation is from page 43 of *Maclean's*.

In this century, our species has undergone explosive change. Not only are we adding a quarter of a million people to our numbers every day, we have vastly amplified our technological muscle power. When I was born, there were no computers, televisions, jet planes, oral contraceptives, transoceanic phone calls, satellites, transistors or xerography, just to mention a few. Children today look at typewriters, vinyl records and black-and-white televisions as ancient curiosities.

b) Paraphrase the passage below, which is from page 45 of the same Suzuki essay as in part (a), and cite using APA style. Include one direct quotation no longer than three words as part of your paraphrase. Do not use a signal phrase.

In biological terms, the globe is experiencing an eco-holocaust, as more than 50,000 species vanish annually, and air, water and soil are poisoned with civilization's effluents. The great challenge to the millennium is recognizing the reality of impending ecological collapse, and the urgent need to get on with taking the steps to avoid it.

c) Summarize the above passage in one sentence of no more than 20 words (there are 54 words in the original); begin with a signal phrase and use APA style. Do not use any direct quotations.

3. The following passage appeared as a block quotation in an essay on video game addiction. Reduce the word count of the quotation by one-third (i.e., reduce it to approximately 100 words from the current 155). Your answer should include (a) at least two ellipses indicating material omitted; and (b) at least one use of square brackets, indicating a grammatical or stylistic change, or added words.

Example: The game offers an experience many other activities cannot offer. . . . [with] stimulating auditory and visual components.

> The game offers an experience many other activities cannot offer. There are stimulating auditory and visual components, as well as "raids" that keep the players coming back. The players always want to be on top. I can understand why they would want to stay home from work or school to play. To 'keep up with the Joneses,' you have to raid four days a week, but the company that oversees *World of Warcraft* recently cut it down to two or three because players were burning out. The rewards totally help too. It is set up so you get better rewards depending on the difficulty of the content. I would say a good number of *WoW* players are enslaved by it; it just adds purpose to their lives. A lot of people get depressed when they have to stop playing. I quit cold turkey a few years ago, but since I moved, I started playing again. (Castigliano)

4. **Collaborative activity.** Decide which of the following direct quotations should be paraphrased and which should be left as direct quotations; then, write a paraphrase for each that should be paraphrased. To justify your choices, you could refer to the criteria in Chapter 6, page 160. (For the purposes of this exercise, you can omit the citation; source information is provided to help you decide or help in a paraphrase if one is required.)

Example:
    "A person would need to gain an additional 75 to 100 pounds in order to equal the health risks associated with smoking one pack of cigarettes a day." (John Polito)

- is easily paraphrased
- is factual information

Paraphrase: According to John Polito, by consuming only one pack of cigarettes daily, you are doing as much damage to your body as you would by gaining 75 to 100 pounds.

a) "In Canada, over 26 percent of children and youth (1.6 million in all) are considered overweight or obese." (Childhood Obesity Foundation)

b) "Everything great that we know has come from neurotics. Never will the world be aware of how much it owes to them, nor above all what they have suffered in order to bestow their gifts on it." (French novelist Marcel Proust)

c) "The hippocampus is a component of the brain's limbic system that is crucial for learning, memory, and the integration of sensory experiences with emotions and motivations." (Council on Alcohol & Drug Abuse)

d) "Research shows that children raised by same-sex parents are just as healthy as those raised by heterosexual parents because stable family relationships are more important in the long run than parental sexual orientation." (Alyssa Judd)

e) "Our media and entertainment industry remains vibrant and ripe with opportunity; you just have to look in the right places. Television has never been better; the audiences have never been bigger, programming has never been more diverse, or distribution more available. And, as a result, our industry has never had greater potential for growth." (John Foote, Research Manager, Department of Canadian Heritage)

f) "The increase in carbon dioxide–related air pollution is posing a serious health risk threat to residents of inner-city communities, especially children." (Gale Jurasek)

g) "Although there are signs of mild cognitive impairment in chronic cannabis users, there is little evidence that such impairments are irreversible or that they are accompanied by drug-induced neuropathology." (Leslie L. Iversen)

h) "In 2006, 11 million cosmetic plastic surgeries were performed in the United States, where any doctor, no matter what the specialty, may perform these procedures." (Martin Anderson).

i) "It is a well-known fact that dramatic musical scores and operas written by Richard Wagner, with their intense, romantic and mythic qualities, heavily influenced the Nazi party and its idealism." (Leopold von Konigslow)

j) "Congress shall make no law respecting an establishment of religion, or prohibiting the free exercise thereof; or abridging the freedom of speech, or of the press; or the right of the people peaceably to assemble, and to petition the Government for a redress of grievances." (US Constitution: First Amendment)

Chapter 8

The Argumentative Essay

Everyday Arguments

Argument is so ingrained in our lives that it might seem strange to devote space to what people do naturally and usually believe they do well—few people would say they argue poorly. A teenager argues with his parents that he is old enough to live on his own; a lawyer argues a complex point of law before a Supreme Court judge. What is the difference between these arguments? Complexity might be one difference, but another lies in the likelihood that both the teenager and the parents will present the argument at least partly in emotional terms—especially if the two sides are firmly opposed and equally determined.

This is not the case with the lawyer who knows that her credibility is built more on logic, precedent, and other rational variables than on emotional ones. It could be a good strategy for a defence lawyer to create sympathy for a defendant, but the lawyer would have to do this indirectly, perhaps through the emotional testimony of character witnesses—not by displaying emotion herself. Whereas the teenager and the parents have only a goal in mind and may be willing to use all available means to achieve it, the lawyer's goal is firmly supported by an overarching design. The kind of arguing you will do at the university level has more in common with that of the prudent lawyer than that of the passionate parent.

The roots of argument are embedded in public discourse in which highly trained and proficient orators did battle with one another in assemblies, in courtrooms, and at public events in ancient Athens and Rome. Many of the argumentative strategies used today reflect these roots; even the terminology sometimes used to teach effective argument reveals classical origins: *argumentum ad hominem*, *petitio principii*, *post hoc*, and *non sequitur* are Latin names for some of the fallacies in argument (see page 244).

Although argument is rooted in antiquity, it has been adapted to many contemporary functions: for example, editorials and letters to the editor, proposals advocating change, and the language of mediation all rely on argument. Advertising tries to influence us through argument, though more often by manipulating reason than by using it. When you design your résumé, you are presenting a case for your abilities in order to persuade an employer to hire you over someone else. Thus, the argumentative essay exercises the logical and critical thinking skills you use every day.

Rhetoric and Argument

Rhetoric has taken on a range of meanings today. The word can have negative connotations, as when someone speaks of empty or meaningless rhetoric—*just* words; similarly, if someone asks a question without expecting an answer, but in order to produce an effect, he or she has posed a rhetorical question. On the other hand, you can admire a person's rhetorical skills, meaning the sophisticated way he or she uses words. Greek philosopher Aristotle (384–322 BCE) used the word *rhetoric* to stress a speaker's awareness of the choices available in any given situation to persuade an audience. He believed that a general audience would often need to be persuaded—that showing knowledge alone was not enough. Aristotle identified specific **topoi** (strategies or, literally, places) that could help accomplish this aim.

Aristotle, who laid much of the groundwork for classical and even modern argument in his book the *Rhetoric*, divided arguments into three kinds: those founded on reason (**logos**), on morality (**ethos**), and on emotion (**pathos**). Of the three, the most important appeal is to a reader's reason and logic. Ethical appeals play a major role, too, mostly in establishing your credibility as an arguer, though Aristotle connects ethical appeals to the moral worth of the arguer, reasoning that an audience will be more convinced by an argument if the arguer is seen as "understand[ing] human character and goodness in their various forms." Aristotle also stresses the connection between emotional appeals and knowledge of one's audience. He believes this consists not only of knowing the audience's "hearts" but also of understanding the causes of the different kinds of emotions and how they work.

Although rhetoric can be defined broadly as the use of effective modes of communication, in this chapter, we will work within the narrower meaning of **rhetoric** as the structure and strategies of argumentation used to persuade the members of a specific audience.

Argument and Persuasion

Some people make a distinction between argument and persuasion, but at other times these terms are used synonymously. If there is a difference, it lies in the degree of stress on the logical argument compared to that of the appeal to emotion. Faulty or distorted reasoning may, to the unsuspecting, seem convincing, and, as Aristotle acknowledges in the *Rhetoric*, may even seduce the unwary, inattentive, or uncritical reader to a point of view; but it will not produce a good argument. It fails not only the test of logic but also the test of fairness.

While **argument** focuses on reason by employing the strategies and structures of logic, **persuasion** focuses on the feelings of the audience through emotional appeals. Among ways to get people to change their minds are rewarding a change of thinking or behaviour in some way, or, more sinisterly, by appealing to emotions like anxiety, fear, or nationalism. These methods may sound extreme, but the news frequently exposes viewers to political speakers whose persuasion stresses these elements more than logic.

A Closer Look

Two Modern Models of Argument

The approach of **Carl Rogers** emerges out of communication theory and involves "see[ing] the expressed idea and attitude from the other person's point of view." Rogerian strategies include framing your argument in terms that will be acceptable to the other person who may otherwise resist it. The main strength of the Rogerian system is its focus on the audience. In traditional arguments, arguers may be encouraged to "imagine" a community of critics, and thus to anticipate counterpoints and sharpen one's *own* points, but not to genuinely engage with one's critics, as the Rogerian model invites. The Rogerian approach encourages establishing common ground—points of agreement—with your audience. Rogerian argument discourages a "winner takes all" approach; successful arguments can be signalled by a willingness to engage in debate.

The system of **Stephen Toulmin** is a direct response to the limitations of traditional arguments, which begin with or depend on a generalization, a universal statement. The Toulmin model, based on the way lawyers present their cases before courts, was designed for a full range of arguments, from sophisticated written ones to casual oral ones. In particular, Toulmin realized that claims alone aren't enough; they need some kind of underlying basis. In other words, there has to be a justification for the claims one makes; one can't simply argue in a vacuum. One of Toulmin's important contributions is the concept of the *warrant*, the basis or foundation of an argumentative claim (see Solidifying the Claim, page 237).

Another aspect of Toulmin argument is the need to qualify claims, to avoid absolute statements. A qualified general claim will be more acceptable to a reader, who may simply reject a claim that is too broad. With or without a qualifier, though, a claim, says Toulmin, must have something behind it to justify it, to make it reasonable and acceptable to its audience. So asking of the arguer, "Why do you say so?," "Why is this true/what makes it true?," or even "So what?" leads to the warrant. Looking at *if* and *how* your claim is justified helps prevent the kind of reasoning that sees argument simply as stating your opinion and backing it up—an oversimplified approach to argument.

Table 8.1 summarizes the major features of the argumentative models of Aristotle, Rogers, and Toulmin.

Table 8.1 Argumentative Models

Argumentative Model/Theory	Original Uses	Key Concepts/ Terms	Uses in an Argumentative Essay
Aristotle	Oratory/public speaking	Logical, ethical, and emotional appeals	Understanding inductive and deductive kinds of reasoning; using reason effectively; establishing authority and trustworthiness; appealing appropriately to audience emotions
Rogers	Psychology/ interpersonal communication	Common ground, consensus	Acknowledging opposing views; laying grounds for trust and receptivity; reaching consensus and mutual understanding
Toulmin	Law	Claim, warrant, data (support)	Providing foundation for/developing a claim to make it convincing; tying claim to support; qualifying claim to avoid generalizations

Appeals to reason, to emotion, and to ethics all can be used in argument, as can the need to seek common ground with your audience. The following "real-life" scenario demonstrates the various facets of arguments as outlined above:

You are disappointed by an essay grade and arrange to meet your instructor in her office. By your effective use of reason, you try to convince her that your mark does not reflect your true abilities, while conceding the validity of some of her criticisms; *concessions* are used in many arguments. Going through the paper systematically, you focus on points that seem arguable, asking for clarification or elaboration and presenting your counterclaims. As you do, you appear a responsible, conscientious student: you make an *ethical appeal*.

You appeal to her fair-mindedness, reiterating her helpfulness, your interest in the course, and your desire to do well. In this way, you establish *common ground*, as you would try to do with the reader of your essay. As well, you do not come across merely as one who wants a better mark, but as one who is interested in learning how to write a better essay. In doing so, you are giving a valid *foundation to your claim* much more than you would be if you said something like "I need a B− in this course so I can get into my program."

If you argue with integrity, you will leave a good impression. Emotional appeals, such as tearfully bemoaning your stressful life, are apt to be less successful, but subtle appeals may have influence.

What Is an Argument?

Approaching argument as a "one size fits all" is limiting. An argument can have many purposes, large or small, as was suggested above in the examples of the Supreme Court lawyer and the teenager. These include

> ❯ defending your point of view
> ❯ seeking to change a situation
> ❯ promoting affiliation
> ❯ drawing attention to a problem or raising awareness
> ❯ reaching a compromise.

Defending your Point of View

The most common reason for everyday arguments is probably to defend a viewpoint or express an opinion. Such an argument often uses a value claim, asserting that the arguer's point of view is fair or right, in order to convince the reader or listener to adopt a new position on the issue. In her comparison essay, student writer Carolyn Hardy supports her value claim that ninjas are better warriors than pirates (see Chapter 5, Reading 8, page 116).

Seeking to Change a Situation

When you seek to change a situation, you advocate a specific action. Such claims are referred to as action- or policy-based, since they are often directed to those in a position to make changes (for example, governments and similar bodies). Student writer Bain Syrowik argues for a specific change in his essay, Reading 17, page 252.

Promoting Affiliation

On the surface, it might seem strange to use argument if an audience already agrees with you, but many written arguments appear in publications whose readers share core values or opinions about a controversial issue. Argument implies agreement, as well as disagreement, and we often form relationships on the basis of our agreement; in this sense, argument can be used to affirm bonds of affiliation. An arguer may also seek to solidify common bonds with a reader in order to change a situation, as student writer Erica Isomura tries to do in her essay on arts funding (see Reading 18, page 254).

Drawing Attention to a Problem/Raising Awareness

An arguer may seek to draw attention to a problem that has been ignored or overlooked. Instead of attempting to effect change, the writer is more concerned with "raising consciousness," perhaps as a first step in instituting change. Part of your job is informing and explaining (i.e., exposition); above all, you need to convince the reader that the problem is urgent and that attention is crucial. Christine M. O'Bonsawin, the writer of the scholarly essay, Reading 19, on page 257, uses exposition and argument in order to draw attention to an important issue.

Reaching a Compromise

To argue for compromise, or a "middle ground," is often more practical than asserting a one-sided claim. Such an "argument" may not seem much like an argument at all, but, like any other argument, it has a specific objective requiring the use of deliberate strategies and an objective voice—both of which are crucial in any successful argument. Although arguing for a compromise might not entirely convince either side, it may well shift the attitude of *both* sides from rigid determination to flexibility; at the very least, they may see the need for compromise.

Combining Argumentative Purposes

As suggested above, intended audience goes hand-in-hand with argumentative purpose. Just as you would not begin planning an argument without a topic, you should not begin planning without a purpose and audience in mind. For example, if a bargaining committee were planning a strategy for improving the conditions for its workers, an article that appeared in the union newsletter would probably be designed to *promote affiliation*, to solidify union members. If it took out advertising space in a local newspaper, the purpose might be to *raise awareness* of issues they considered important. However, when the members of the committee sat down with management, they would have to adopt a new objective: knowing that neither side is likely to get its way on all issues, they might try to plan a strategy that would give them many or most of their key points without giving up too much, by reaching a *compromise* solution.

Of course, an argumentative essay can combine two or more purposes. For example, student Erica Isomura (Reading 18, page 254) uses emotional appeals throughout her essay to seek affiliation, as well as to seek to change the government's policy towards the arts.

Although a writer of a scholarly essay will not likely employ the kinds of argumentative strategies discussed in this chapter, he or she may use argument to raise awareness in order to affect policy. To this end, the writer may make recommendations to governments or other governing bodies. For example, the writer of the academic essay (Reading 19) on page 257 makes recommendations to the IOC (the International Olympic Committee, the governing body of the Olympic Games).

A Sample Argument

In the scenario below, Ivannia Herrera argued with her roommate over what might seem a trivial issue, a so-called "tempest in a teapot"; however, the underlying issues are not trivial. Although this is an informal argument, it contains many of the features of a formal argument as described above—for example, a claim, supporting evidence, and warrants that link the evidence to the claim. Refutation and concessions, particular argumentative strategies, also are involved.

Read the argument carefully to find the appeals to reason, emotion, and ethics. Does the essay make an appeal to common ground? Can you identify the warrant (assumption) that underlies the main claim?

Tempest in a Teapot

Background: My roommate and I share a kitchen and utensils. Each day I make tea in a small stainless steel pot, which has a glass cover and a pouring spout with tiny holes that serve as a strainer. I pour two cups of water into the pot, let it boil, then add the leaves. When the tea is ready, I strain the tea water from the pot, leaving the tea leaves behind. I leave the pot on the counter until the next time I make tea. The reason for the argument: My roommate has made it plain she does not enjoy seeing the pot with drenched tea leaves in the bottom.

Which points in the argument seem the most convincing to you? Why? Do you think there are any irrelevant points? Are points missing that might have been made?

My Side

If I leave the pot with the tea leaves on the counter, I can reuse them three times. Since I make the same type of tea several times a day, it makes sense that I reuse the leaves rather than throw them out, which will cost me more money in the long run.

I bought all the pots and pans in this household, and I am happy to share them; however, if you need a pot like this to use regularly, you should consider buying one yourself.

I think of myself as a clean person, and I contribute greatly to the cleanliness of the household. I think that your having to look at a small pot is a small "defect," considering . . . . Drinking tea is part of my daily life, and I enjoy it. As well, it costs me $6 per month; if I were to discard the tea each time, I would be spending $18 per month, and I can think of better ways to spend those extra $12!

We both agree on the need to compromise. I'm willing to compromise and buy a ball strainer that can hold the tea leaves inside for as long as need be. It is a small ball attached to a chain; the ball divides in half, the tea leaves are put in one half, the ball is closed, and it is placed inside a cup filled with boiling water. I suggest we compromise and each pay half for the ball strainer.

Roommate's Side

The pot is left on the counter for many hours. Though it's okay to reuse the leaves, the kitchen looks messy. I don't like the kitchen looking dirty with an unclean pot sitting there every day. Furthermore, I can't use this pot because it is always filled with tea leaves that I can't throw away.

I also bought utensils for the household—and even the computer. I share these things and understand the concept of sharing. I think that having roommates means having to compromise.

I am not saying that you should throw away the tea leaves, but just find a better way to use them so they are not in sight and taking over the pot. I think that the cleanliness of my living space is a reflection on me, which is why I want a clean environment. I do not like seeing a messy pot, and that is my "defect." I also think I should be able to use the pot if I like, and I can't with the leaves in it.

I'm happy to pay for half of it, as long as you keep the ball with the tea leaves in a cup in your own room. That way, you can bring it out anytime you want tea, but it will be out of my sight.

Recall a recent argument. Begin by briefly describing the circumstances that led to it. Then, divide a page in half vertically and summarize each point raised by "your side" and "the other side" (as shown for "Tempest in a Teapot"). Simply report what was said (do not embellish with interpretations of the meaning of what was said)—each side's point of view and the counter-argument, if there was one. When a new point begins, draw a horizontal line to separate it from the previous point. Finally, analyze the strengths and weaknesses of each point. Did the point make an appeal to reason? An emotional appeal? An ethical one? Was an opinion supported? Were facts used to support an opinion? Were the points logically related to one another? Was the argument resolved? If so, how? Write a paragraph response to the argument, analyzing its flaws, such as simplifications and generalizations. In your analysis, try to be as objective as possible to *both* sides.

Opinion, Facts, and Argument

Opinions are not the same as facts, which can be verified by observation or research. Opinions can be challenged. As you will see, you cannot argue a position on a topic that has no opposing view—in other words, that cannot be challenged. On the other hand, facts can be interpreted differently and used for different purposes. Facts, therefore, can be used to support the thesis of an argumentative essay. However, effective arguers are always clear about when they are using facts and when they are using opinion. In reading, use your critical thinking skills to ask if the writer always clearly separates facts from opinion. If not, he or she might be guilty of faulty reasoning (see page 244).

The following statement is a fact that is therefore not changeable:

Fact: The moon is 378,000 kilometres from earth's equator.

Now consider the following two pairs of sentences, each consisting of a fact (not changeable) and a related opinion:

Fact: According to moon landing conspiracy theories, the 1969 Apollo moon landing was faked.

Opinion: The Apollo moon landing didn't actually take place; it was all a hoax.

Fact: On November 13, 2009, NASA announced that water had been found on the moon.

Opinion: Now that water has been found on the moon, humans should set up colonies at the moon's poles by 2050.

Collaborative Exercise

Consider the two pairs of statements above on the topic of humans on the moon. Discuss the ways that fact differs from opinion in each case. Come up with two other topics and write two statements for each, one of which represents a fact and the other of which represents an opinion.

Staking Your Claim: Argument versus Exposition

Like other formal essays, argumentative essays need a claim, usually made in the thesis statement near the beginning of the essay (see Kinds of Claims: Fact, Value, Policy, and Interpretation in Chapter 5, page 121, for types of claims). The body paragraphs should provide good reasons in support of the claim. Many kinds of evidence can be used for support, including facts, authorities, research studies, statistics, examples, and personal experience, as discussed in Kinds of Evidence, in Chapter 5, page 123.

Claims in argument can be about value (something is good or bad, right or wrong) or policy (something requires change through action). You can also argue a fact-based claim if you *interpret* the factual support for the claim in a particular light, rather than simply *present* the evidence as you would in an expository essay. For example, you could use a cause–effect claim to argue that aspartame is an unsafe sugar substitute. You would use the results of research but, without suppressing contradictory information, interpret the findings in a specific way that supports your claim.

If you were writing an expository essay on the same topic, you would mediate the two sides of the debate, presenting and weighing the evidence to come to a conclusion. Perhaps you would find that there is no conclusive evidence that aspartame is dangerous at moderate levels of consumption but that further research needs to be done. You could also write a fact-based essay about the aspartame controversy, perhaps using the chronology organizational method to trace its development over time. Your thesis statement should clearly indicate whether you will mainly be arguing or explaining.

The following is the conclusion of an *expository* essay by student writer Rick Jew in which he objectively presents and analyzes the two sides of the debate over genetically modified organisms:

> There is no simple answer to this issue. Biotechnology is a double-edged sword. On one side, we are faced with feeding the growing population of the world, and on the other, we have to contend with the possible impact this new technology might have on our planet. Biotechnology may be able to give us the means to combat the growing malnourishment problem that persists in our world. Can we, however, turn back if we go too far by constantly modifying food to fit our needs? Does this biotechnology solution to our food shortage raise other unforeseen problems that can only be answered with another technology? The questions are many, and the answers are few. One thing certain is that genetic modification is in our future.

Arguable Claims

What is needed for a valid argument? First, you need an *arguable topic*. Let's say you see two friends emerging from a showing of a popular movie. With raised voices and exaggerated gestures, friend A states categorically that *Avatar* is the best movie of the year. Matching friend A gesture for gesture, friend B insists that *Harry Potter and the Half-Blood Prince* was a much better movie. To support her claim, friend A cites *Avatar*'s "awesome special effects." Friend B's counter-claim is that Daniel Radcliffe is the most "awesome wizard ever." Who is right?

Obviously, neither is "right," because the topic is not arguable: you cannot base a rational argument on purely subjective standards. On the other hand, you might be able to base an argument on the superiority of one movie over another if they had similar plots or were in the same genre: perhaps you could compare the elements of suspense in both, or the quality of the acting or directing—if you could apply measurable standards to both.

There are other kinds of claims that are not arguable. You could not easily write an argumentative essay on the virtues of good health, as there is no competing viewpoint. Similarly unarguable are obvious claims, such as "computers have changed a great deal in the last decade." A controversial subject does not always translate into an arguable one. For example, an argument that justifies computer hacking or the writing of viruses likely is not valid.

You also need to ensure that the claim, like all thesis statements, is **specific, interesting**, and **manageable**. Below, we focus on a sample argumentative claim, showing the kinds of questions you can ask to help you develop a strong and effective thesis for an argumentative essay. To review thesis statements, see The Thesis Statement, Chapter 4, page 91.

> Arguable claims must (1) be based on more than subjective standards; and (2) have an opposing viewpoint. In addition, successful claims should be specific, interesting, and manageable (see below).

Specific Claim

A specific claim states clearly and precisely what you will be arguing. The reader should know whether the claim is one of fact, value, or policy. In addition, a specific claim is worded precisely.

> *Vague claim*: Parents of children who play hockey would like to see fighting eliminated from the game at all levels.

Is this claim specific? Although it technically satisfies the two conditions for an arguable topic, it is not specific enough to suggest what kind of argument will follow or even if the essay will focus on argument rather than exposition: "parents," "would like to see," and "at all levels" are vague. Also, the phrase "eliminated from the game at all levels" does not seem connected to the rest of the claim. What has this got to do with the parents who presumably don't like seeing their children fight? Expanded thesis statements that include your main points can be useful in arguments, as the reader will see at a glance that you have supported your claim. In the following revised thesis statement, the claim is expressed more clearly through specific words as well as the inclusion of main points. As well, "should" clearly reveals a policy claim:

> *More specific argumentative claim*: Fighting should be prohibited in hockey, since violence gives young hockey players a negative model and reinforces a "win at all costs" mentality.

Although a claim may be specific if it is precisely worded, it is often a good idea, as mentioned above, to follow the claim by defining concepts central to your argument. In the claim above, the writer might define what is meant by "fighting." Does the dropping of hockey gloves or excessive physical contact constitute the beginning of a fight? Does a fight begin when there is a third player involved? Definition enables the writer to narrow the topic, to make it more specific.

An "all or none" claim is also non-specific. Where your claim is too broad, you should either use qualifiers to restrict its scope or reword it to make it more realistic.

Examples of qualifiers include *a few, in part, many, often, several, some, sometimes,* and *usually*. In addition, you can use verbs and verb phrases that qualify and limit, such as *contribute to, may, play a role in,* and *seems*.

Interesting Claim

Is this claim interesting? To help make your claim interesting, draft it with a specific audience in mind. In the claim about fighting in hockey, the intended audience is hockey parents as well as coaches, managers, and other hockey executives—people who can make changes. Many die-hard fans of professional hockey would not be interested in the main point of the argument, as it applies mostly to children. Those who never watch hockey or don't have children playing hockey probably would be even less interested. Similarly, an argument concerning the best measures to prevent eutrophication and growth of single-celled algae in China's lakes and reservoirs might be interesting to marine biologists, but probably not to the average reader.

Along with audience interest, an important consideration is the viewpoint of your audience. Are most people to whom the argument is addressed likely to agree with you? Disagree? Be neutral? Will they possess general knowledge of the topic? Is the topic a current one that most will have heard of? These kinds of questions will be even more relevant when you come to structure your essay and support your claim. For example, if your audience includes many opponents, it may be important to establish common ground and to convince them that you have similar values and goals. See below, Refuting the Opposing View, page 238, for specific audience strategies.

Manageable Claim

Although the manageability of a claim will be determined partly by whether it is specific and interesting, it will also depend on essay length, availability of support, and the complexity of the issues raised by the claim. A claim that promises more than the writer could reasonably achieve in a medium-length essay would not be manageable.

Policy-based claims, which try to persuade people to take action, go beyond simply proving something is bad or unfair. Often needed are realistic solutions or at least suggestions that these kinds of solutions exist. Is the proposal realistic? To say that a government should increase funding to post-secondary education by 25 per cent is probably not realistic given the current economy. If the change you propose isn't realistic, it may be best to change your claim to one of value or else reword it. Your supporting points may be complex, but the thesis statement itself must be workable and clear to the reader.

The claim about hockey violence was found to be arguable, specific, and interesting (to its intended audience), but is it *manageable*?

> Fighting should be prohibited in hockey, since violence gives young hockey players a negative model and reinforces a "win at all costs" mentality.

The issue of banning fighting throughout hockey, especially at the professional level, seems too complex to be manageable if the issues relating to young hockey players are also addressed. Realistically, would the fact that many hockey players act as role models for younger players motivate those who manage the game to ban fighting? To make the statement manageable, the writer could focus *either* on the way that fights in professional hockey undermine hockey players as role models *or* on the consequences of fighting in minor hockey:

Value claim: Fighting in professional hockey gives young hockey players a negative model since violence reinforces a "win at all costs" mentality.

Reworded policy claim: Fighting should be prohibited in minor hockey at and below the midget level since violence reinforces a "win at all costs" mentality.

Remember that all claims need to focus on one main topic, not to straddle two related topics. In addition to specific, interesting, and manageable claims, all claims must clearly express the essay's focus.

EXERCISE 8.3

◯ Check answers to select questions

Collaborative Exercise

In discussion groups, evaluate the 10 claims below, determining whether they would make good thesis statements for an argumentative essay. Are the claims arguable, specific, interesting, and manageable?

1. Cloning should be prohibited as it will mean the end of natural selection.
2. Since underage drinking is a major problem today, it wouldn't make sense to lower the drinking age any further.
2. *Futurama* is a much funnier sitcom than *Family Guy*.
4. Email is a very useful form of communication today as it is accessible, fast, and far-reaching.
5. Sex education needs to play a greater role in schools so that the number of pregnancies can be reduced and teenagers will practise safer sex.
6. No-fault insurance has made it easier for insurance companies to stay in business.
7. Internet dating services are innovative, convenient, and affordable alternatives to the singles scene.
8. It is better to have a summer job in retail than in customer service; though the pay is less, you meet nicer people.
9. Legal guidelines are needed for genetic testing as it may threaten our privacy, lead to harmful gene therapy, and have dangerous social costs.
10. Due to the dangerousness of the sport utility vehicle, people should have to prove they really need an SUV before being permitted to purchase it.

Working Your Claim: Kinds of Evidence

Value and policy claims, like factual claims, need support. In Chapter 5, evidence was divided into two main categories: hard evidence and soft evidence. Fact-based essays, not surprisingly, depend mostly on facts, statistics, and the findings of empirical studies. In argument, factual sources may be important as support, along with soft evidence, such as examples or analogies, or perhaps the selective use of anecdotes, narration, or personal experience. However, what will always be crucial regardless of your purpose for arguing is the careful use of reason and logic.

Two strategies often used to support an argument are **definition** and **comparison**. It can be important to define a concept in order to control how you use it in your essay. For example, if you want to argue that dance should be considered a sport, you can define precisely what is meant by "sport." A definition most readers would agree with could be a springboard into your thesis, showing how dance skills reflect your definition of sport.

Comparisons can make a claim more concrete. For example, if you establish criteria for judging the excellence of a film (perhaps by using definition), you could argue that *Harry Potter and the Half-Blood Prince* satisfies those criteria. However, you might be able to strengthen your points by comparing this film with another in the series, say, *Harry Potter and the Order of the Phoenix*, which does not satisfy your criteria. Similarly, you could compare *Half-Blood Prince* favourably with a classic fantasy film, such as *The Wizard of Oz*, noting similarities between them.

Working Your Claim: The Rational Basis of Argument

A logical argument consists of assumptions and premises, which may not be explicitly stated. Two kinds of reasoning methods are used in logical arguments: through *inductive* or *deductive* reasoning, the assumptions and premises can be validated and a conclusion can be made. An argument, then, is a set of premises that show logical relationships with one another. Supported by various kinds of evidence, they attempt to prove a claim, usually of value or policy.

In reality, reasoning often involves the use of both inductive and deductive methods, rather than one method exclusively. In the section that follows, each is considered separately, as each involves a different method for arriving at a conclusion.

Inductive Reasoning

Induction, or **scientific reasoning**, arrives at a conclusion based on specific occurrences, which are observed and recorded. The conclusion, then, is the result of the accumulation of evidence through controlled and objective methods of evidence-gathering.

People like to make jokes about the weather by using faulty inductive reasoning. How often have you heard someone say, "Whenever I wash my car, it rains," or "Every time I bring my umbrella, it's a sunny day, but the first day I forget it, it rains"?

Inductive reasoning is called scientific reasoning because scientific research frequently relies on the collection and analyzing of specific data to arrive at a conclusion. We also use inductive reasoning daily to draw conclusions. Consider the following example:

Recorded observations:

on June 5 the sun set at 9:16

on June 6 it set at 9:16

on June 7 it set at 9:17

on June 8 it set at 9:17

on June 9 it set at 9:18

Prediction/Claim:

on June 10, the sun will set at 9:18.

It is possible to make this prediction because we have observed specific data relating to this phenomenon. (Of course, knowledge of the motion of the earth around the sun would also be needed to ensure the accuracy of the predictions.)

If we had simply recorded the times that the sun set on June 5 and 6, we might conclude that the sun would set at 9:16 on June 7, which would be incorrect: we would be *drawing a conclusion without an adequate sample*. On the other hand, if we made our first set of observations in Edmonton, Alberta, on June 5 and 6 and the second set in Regina, Saskatchewan, on June 7 and 8, the conclusions would also be incorrect because *the methodology for evidence-gathering would be faulty*.

Conclusions arrived at through inductive methods are said only to be likely or probable, even after many observations have been made and evidence-gathering has been reliable. Most research studies focusing on causes and effects, such as clinical trials to test a new drug, work by induction, not to arrive at an absolute truth but to discover a *probable cause or effect*. Thus, further studies may seek to duplicate the results of the original study in order to make the findings more reliable. For example, according to the most recent Intergovernmental Panel on Climate Change (2007), human agency is 90 per cent likely the major cause of global warming since 1950. Further inductive evidence may change this percentage.

Two questions to ask yourself when using inductive reasoning are (1) Have you provided enough support for each statement you make? and (2) Have you been logical and consistent in applying your reasoning method? Several examples of faulty inductive reasoning are given under Logical, Emotional, and Ethical Fallacies on page 244—for example, "hasty generalization" and "doubtful causes."

Deductive Reasoning

The deductive reasoning process can be broken down into two parts, each of which can be represented by two statements, one general and the other specific: a **major premise** and a **minor premise**. The third step involves combining the two to reach a conclusion. Below is an example of a three-part structure, known as a **syllogism**, that illustrates the deductive method:

> *Major premise:* All property owners in the municipality must pay taxes.
>
> *Minor premise:* I am a property owner in the municipality.
>
> *Conclusion:* I must pay taxes.

However, consider the following syllogism:

> *Major premise:* All people who live on the west coast of North America are in danger from earthquakes.
>
> *Minor premise:* Nancy lives in California.
>
> *Conclusion:* Nancy is in danger from earthquakes.

If one of the premises is wrong, as is the major premise above, the conclusion will be invalid. Incidents of faulty deductive reasoning can be used to exclude or even persecute minorities, and many forms of stereotyping are based on faulty deductive reasoning.

Logical fallacies in inductive reasoning can develop (1) where there is not enough evidence to make a generalization; or (2) where the means for gathering the evidence are faulty or biased.

Two questions to ask yourself when using deductive reasoning are (1) Does the major premise (general statement) apply to the people or situation described in the minor premise (specific statement)?; and (2) Is it a valid generalization?

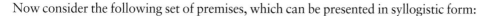

Now consider the following set of premises, which can be presented in syllogistic form:

Major premise: It is wrong not to treat all people with respect.

Minor premise: In building the dam, the Urra company did not treat the indigenous peoples with respect.

Conclusion: The Urra company was wrong to build the dam.

Major premise: It is right to treat business interests as primary.

Minor premise: In building the dam, the Urra company treated business interests as primary.

Conclusion: The Urra company was right to build the dam.

Even though the conclusions are contradictory, in each syllogism the conclusion is logical according to its premises. As an arguer, you need to ensure that any general claims you make will be ones your audience will accept.

> Sound use of inductive and deductive reasoning will help produce a logical argument and increase your credibility as an arguer. However, making logical fallacies (see page 244), which involve faulty use of reason, such as drawing a conclusion despite a lack of evidence or making a generalization that isn't true, will reduce your credibility.

EXERCISE 8.4

↻ Check answers to select questions

Collaborative Exercise

Detective Work

Read the following short scenarios and analyze how the police reached their decision (i.e., analyze their reasoning methods) or why the investigation failed. Were *inductive* methods involved? If they were flawed, was the problem due to a lack of evidence or faulty methods of evidence gathering? Were *deductive* methods involved? If so, what generalization was made?

1. *Scenario*: After a robbery at an expensive and seemingly burglar-proof home, the police investigation settled on two possible suspects. One suspect had been seen near the house near the time of the robbery, but had never previously been arrested. The second suspect had not been seen near the home but was not able to account for his movements that night; furthermore, he had two prior robbery convictions. *Result*: Police brought the second man in for further questioning.

2. *Scenario*: Police believed they would easily be able to identify the suspect of an assault when they discovered blood samples on the floor and wall of the crime scene. But the crime scene officer, who was working on his first case, neglected to prepare the samples correctly, and they deteriorated. *Result*: Police were unable to come up with a suspect.

Solidifying the Claim through the Warrant

One way to test the logical connection between your claim (or any important point), and its support is through the underlying rationale for the claim, the **warrant**. A warrant solidifies the connection between claim and support. If the warrant is self-evident to the reader, it does not have to be announced. The following warrant is clear without being stated:

Claim: I have to buy a new watch.

Evidence: It says the same time as it did 30 minutes ago.

Warrant: My watch is broken.

A warrant can arise from various sources, including physical laws, human laws, assumptions, premises, common knowledge, aesthetic values, or ethical principles. For an argument to be successful, the reader must agree with the warrant, whether stated or implied. Student writer Erica Isomura (Reading 18, page 254) announces her claim that arts funding should not be cut. Much of the evidence she supplies is based on the warrant that underlies her thesis: the arts make a valuable contribution to society (an aesthetic or ethical principle), which she begins her essay by establishing. She then provides the statistical and other kinds of evidence to try to persuade her readers that her claim is valid. However, those who disagree with her assumption about the value of the arts may not be convinced by her evidence.

See also Figure 8.1, "Please Sign Our Petition": A Case Study, on page 241, which illustrates how claims, warrants, and support work together to produce an effective argument in the workplace about the need for a company's health services.

Refuting the Opposing View
Two Strategies for Refutation
Strategy A: Acknowledgement

Acknowledging the other side is important in most arguments, although sometimes it may not be necessary, as in Erica Isomura's claim that government cuts to arts and cultural program are wrong (Reading 18, page 254). In cases where you need only acknowledge the opposition, you will have to decide how much space to devote to this. In the following example, student writer Laura Benard briefly characterizes the opposing viewpoint using only a prepositional phrase ("Despite their aesthetic value") ahead of her thesis statement. She presents no real rebuttal, but treats the opposing argument, that people use pesticides to make their lawn look attractive, as obvious:

> Despite the aesthetic value of weed-free, green lawns, the negative impacts of maintaining lawns by means of pesticide, lawn mower, and water use are so great that lawn owners should adopt less intensive maintenance practices or consider lawn alternatives.

If you use the acknowledgement strategy, you can put the acknowledgement in the form of a dependent clause that contains the less important (opposing) information, followed by your own claim in an independent clause. "Although some may argue . . . [major point of opposition argument], the fact is/I believe that . . . [your thesis]."

You may need to provide background or a brief summary of the opposing view. In this case, you can begin with this view, then follow with your own argument. Deciding how much space to spend on the opposing view requires striking a balance between the desires to demonstrate your fairness and to present a strong argument of your own. When you give background information or summarize the opposing view, make sure you use an objective tone and neutral language: summarize concisely and state the other side's points clearly and fairly.

Strategy B: Point-by-Point Refutation

You should consider responding thoroughly to the other side if it has strong support or if your purpose is to arrive at a compromise; in the latter case, you will try to find common ground. In either case, you would raise individual points, usually beginning with an opposing point, and respond to its weaknesses. If your purpose is to win the argument, you will stress the opposing point's inadequacies and inconsistencies, and draw attention to any fallacies. If your purpose is to find common ground, you will point out the inadequacies of the opposing point but assume the role of a constructive critic rather than that of a strong opponent. In either case, though, your voice should be unbiased and objective.

In the excerpt below, student writer Spencer Cleave addresses an opposing point concerning the US embargo against Cuba. After a concession (italicized below), he introduces two counter-claims, developed in the succeeding paragraph, that attempt to undercut the original claim:

> Many supporters of the maintenance of the trade embargo against Cuba contend that the Cuban government fails to uphold the human rights of its population. *It is true that Cuba has had a number of human rights violations in its past. Thus, it is conceded that Cuba is also morally at fault on certain issues.* However, many reforms have recently been made by the government in an attempt to remedy its human rights problems. These efforts show that the government has a desire to improve the conditions within its own nation. Furthermore, it would be in the best interest of the US to applaud the Cuban government in any human rights improvements, thus giving the image of a co-operative partner.

Conditions for Rebuttal

For every valid argument there must be an opposing argument, and you need to consider how you can respond to the opposing view. The **rebuttal** (also called the refutation) is that part of your argument in which you raise the points on the other side, usually in order to strengthen your argument and to appear fair. Whether and how you choose to make a rebuttal will depend on

> ❭ the topic itself
> ❭ your purpose in arguing
> ❭ your audience.

Topic

If the reader is likely familiar with the topic and the major points of debate (such as arguments about legalizing marijuana, abolishing capital punishment, and other often-debated topics), it is a good strategy to raise all opposing points and rebut each one; see Strategy B above. If a topic is likely to be less familiar to a reader, it may be best to acknowledge only the major counter-arguments, while ensuring that your points are stronger and more numerous. In his argumentative essay, student Bain Syrowik (Reading 17, page 252) focuses on one main opposing point, the strongest argument against his own claim, which he then refutes. If the main arguments on the other side are self-evident, however, there may be little point in giving space to them in your essay.

Purpose

The primary goal of an argumentative essay is not always to win the argument, and an argument should not be judged successful purely because it manages to silence the opposition. An argument may be an opportunity to engage in dialogue with others who share your concern about the topic, or to enable your reader to see another side of a problem or another dimension to an issue in order to view it with greater tolerance. Long-lasting change is often a result of an attitude of openness and flexibility on the arguer's part, while a "pin the opponent" approach may result in nothing more than a fleeting victory. The open approach to arguing can be particularly effective with value-based claims.

The purpose of an argument should be clear in the introduction, which should be shaped according to purpose, as well as the topic and audience. The writer of the scholarly essay on page 257 (Reading 19) summarizes her essay's purpose of raising awareness about an important issue:

> This essay contributes to the ongoing narrative of the 2010 Vancouver Olympics as it provides an historical framework for understanding the fragile tensions that exist between present-day Olympic programming and indigenous activism.

Audience

You should bear in mind the stance of the audience towards your claim. If your audience is likely composed of mild dissenters and the undecided, it may be wise simply to acknowledge the other side and oppose it by a strong argument, employing Strategy A, Acknowledgement. If, however, you are addressing those strongly opposed to your claim, acknowledging their side and perhaps even admitting concessions would be advisable. An important aspect of rebuttal is anticipating your opponents' objections so that you can refute such points in advance. Acknowledging your opponents' views should show that, having analyzed them, you find them inadequate. Consider using Strategy B, Point-by-Point Refutation, then, if your audience likely supports the opposing view.

A related strategy in the case of moderate opponents is to stress ways that such a reader can benefit—either personally or as a member of a community—from considering your view. In her essay on safe injection sites, student writer Kerry Hinds first addresses the mild dissenter by pointing out the disadvantages drug users must overcome; when she argues that these sites would reduce health care costs, she addresses another kind of dissenting reader, one, perhaps, motivated more by practical than humanitarian concerns:

> If we wish to control the spread of AIDS, we cannot look at AIDS as strictly a drug-user's disease; many non-users get infected also. If money is not put into [safe injection] programs such as these, our health-care system will be further burdened with the care of chronically ill patients, costing the taxpayers even more money than the cost of opening a clinic. Without foresight and action, the health of non-users will be further compromised and our health-care system will be further debilitated.

Whether the reader is undecided, mildly opposed, or strongly opposed, you should work to establish **common ground**. This can be done by demonstrating that you share basic values with your reader, though you may disagree with the action suggested by an opponent. Making concessions and agreeing in part with an opponent's argument, shows your reasonableness and willingness to compromise.

Summary of Argumentative Strategies

Common ground: Getting your readers to see that you share some of their values or concerns.

Concession: Acknowledging the validity of an opposing point in order to appear fair.

Appeal to reader interests: Showing how opponents might benefit by adopting your claim.

Emotional appeal: Appealing subtly to the feelings of your readers.

This chapter began by noting the importance of argument in all aspects of our lives. What follows is adapted from an information campaign of a medical service company in response to a government decision to restructure the services provided by the company. Although the form of the argument is very different from that of an essay, notice that the necessary parts of an argument are included and that in other respects, too, it conforms to the basic argumentative model discussed above. The document also uses argumentative strategies, such as concessions and common ground. Numbers and letters have been added in order to make it comparable to body paragraphs in an outline.

WE NEED YOUR SUPPORT! PLEASE SIGN OUR PETITION

The government plans to fundamentally change how laboratory services are delivered. These plans jeopardize the lab services you depend on.

These plans could also compromise one of the best lab systems there is—one that has been serving patients in communities across our province for more than 45 years.

I. WHAT THE GOVERNMENT IS PLANNING

A. It has already announced a 20 per cent cut in the fees it pays to community labs for the testing services we provide.

B. It is planning to dismantle the existing province-wide system and create six independent lab delivery systems—one within each of the health authorities.

C. It is planning to establish a bidding process that would see each health authority going to tender for all outpatient lab services.

II. WHAT THIS MEANS TO PATIENT CARE

A. 1. Alone, the magnitude of the fee cuts will affect patients and patient care.
A. 2. The government's other plans will bring a period of complete instability, turning today's system upside down.

B. The government's plans will result in six fragmented systems—potentially providing six levels of service and access—and six new bureaucracies to manage them.

C. Applying a competitive bidding process to laboratory medicine comes at a very high risk. Price is always a major factor in competitive bidding process, and lowest bids come with reduced access service levels.

III. OUR CONCERNS

A. The government based its plans on flawed, faulty, and unsubstantiated data.

B. We don't understand why the government chose to dismantle a system that works well, instead of building on its strengths.

C. We fully support the government's goals. However, we don't agree with the way it is trying to achieve these goals.

As with most arguments, the claim is announced early. It is a policy claim, asking the reader to take an action—: sign a petition; however, it is grounded in a value claim, that government plans could "compromise one of the best lab systems." To support this, the company cites various facts and statistics in a list; these purport to show that the labs provide essential services. Underlying the claim and connecting it to the evidence is the warrant: the premise that people are happy with and care about the service the lab provides. If the warrant is not accepted by the reader, the claim will be ineffective.

The argument begins by summarizing three points of the opposing position. Systematically, the points are refuted in the next two sections. For example, point A above is countered by two points under "What this means to patient care" (point A below). The argument is developed through cause and effect: a 20 per cent cut (cause) will affect patients and patient care.

Figure 8.1   "Please Sign Our Petition": A Case Study (*Continued*)

In addition to countering the major points of the government's argument, the company is concerned with establishing its credibility. Topic II addresses "patient care," focusing concern directly on the reader. Topic III Point C attempts to find common ground in an effort to show fairness to the government side: "We fully support the government's goals."

IV serves as a conclusion to the argument. The information in Points A, B, and C in effect summarize the claim by rewording it: in the claim/thesis, the phrase "jeopardize the lab services you depend on" is used; compare—"affect lab services and service levels," "value the services we provide," and "protecting the lab services you rely on." Point C makes an emotional appeal with its deliberate choice of the words "care" and "protect."

IV. WHAT WE'VE DONE

A. 1. We've told the government repeatedly that we support its goals and can help them achieve them. We've told the government to put its plans on hold so that we can talk to them about less disruptive alternatives.

A. 2. We've told patients and physicians about the government's plans and how they could affect lab services and service levels.

WHAT WE'RE DOING NOW

B. 1. We're asking people who value the services we provide to show their support by signing our petition.

B. 2. If you want to know more about the government's plans and our concerns, please visit our website.

C. *If you care about protecting the lab services you rely on—please sign our petition.*

Community Lab Facts:

- For more than 45 years, physicians and their patients have relied on the quality cost-effective diagnostic testing and information services community labs provide.
- The testing and information services we provide help doctors diagnose, treat, and monitor their patients.
- **Every day,** the 1,600 people working in community labs
- provide a selection of several hundred different tests, from routine to specialty diagnostics.
- support early discharge hospital programs by providing access to lab testing at home and in the community.
- perform more than 55,000 tests on the 16,000 patients who visit one of our labs.
- visit more than 700 patients in their homes and in long-term care facilities, at no charge to the patient or health-care system.
- deliver more than 5,000 specimens to public testing agencies at no cost to the patient, agency, or health care system.
- transmit lab results electronically via PathNET to more than 3,000 physicians.
- support our services through an extensive collection and transportation network, information technology, and analytical expertise that's taken years to develop.

Figure 8.1 *(Continued)*

In groups or individually, analyze the argument presented in Figure 8.1 and evaluate its effectiveness, using the questions below as guidelines.

1. Consider your own position towards the issues. Do you have any knowledge about this or similar issues relating to government decisions about health care (or education)? How do government decisions affect you and/or other consumers of these kinds of services? What are the sides of the debate? Which side do you support? How might your prior knowledge and opinions affect your response to this argument or others like it?

2. Is there anything that would have made the argument more effective? Be as specific as possible.

3. Are there any questionable appeals to emotion or ethics? Are there any logical fallacies? Why do you think the company does not give specific information in main point III, sub-point A: "The government based its plans on flawed, faulty, and unsubstantiated data"?

4. Analyze the refutation, bearing in mind topic, audience, and purpose. Why do the authors employ Strategy B to refute the three points mentioned in main point I, which gives background about the government's position?

5. What specific changes would you make if you were writing this argument as a formal essay? In what ways does it differ from a formal essay? (See Chapter 12 for some of the characteristics of informal writing.)

6. Imagine that one year has passed. The government is proceeding with its plans; some lab employees have lost their jobs, and there are dire predictions in newspaper editorials that our health care will be directly affected. How do you think the company's argument might change in response? Write a revised claim that reflects the new current conditions. Choose one specific form: informal brochure for distribution, letter to the editor/editorial, or argumentative essay.

EXERCISE 8.5

Categories of Faulty Reasoning

Many arguments are based on opinion, but in order to be convincing, the arguer should not come across as *opinionated*. Argument at the university level is not just writing with an "attitude"; in fact, in effective arguments, writers express themselves objectively, using neutral language.

Consider the following passage in which the writer makes it clear to the reader that he is opinionated; however, if the reader is overwhelmed by opinion, he or she may well miss the points:

Institutions of higher learning are meant for people hoping to broaden their interests and knowledge in order to contribute to society. I, myself, agree with this principle, and I also agree that a degree can help me acquire a job and be good at it. Along with this, I do not doubt that these institutions facilitate higher cognitive functioning. What I do not agree with is the approach that these institutions have towards the sciences. In fact, I oppose the favouritism that is always shown to the sciences whenever financial matters are considered.

EXERCISE 8.6

Rewrite the paragraph above, eliminating the references to opinion and changing pronouns from *I*, *me*, etc., to *one* or a suitable noun. Does the revised paragraph sound more forceful? How is the writer's credibility enhanced?

Logical, Emotional, and Ethical Fallacies

Some kinds of arguments are effective; others are not. Ineffective arguments that use logical, emotional, or ethical fallacies detract from the writer's credibility. Misuse of reason affects reliability: we don't trust someone who misuses logic or reason. Misuse of emotional or ethical appeals shows unfairness to the other side: emotional fallacies *exploit* emotions, so are very different from legitimate appeals to emotion.

Some fallacies are founded on faulty inductive reasoning (for example, cause–effect fallacies); others are grounded in the faulty use of deductive reasoning (where invalid generalizations are made).

Table 8.2 lists common argumentative fallacies. Avoid these errors of reasoning in your own writing and look for them in the arguments of your opponents. Identifying them and analyzing their faults will enhance your own credibility. Although these categories may enable you to identify the misuse of reason, emotion, or ethics, this list is not all-inclusive; in many instances, more than one type of fallacy may be involved.

These fallacies were categorized many years ago, and you may hear them referred to by their old Latin names. In Table 8.2, their Latin names have been replaced by more modern descriptive labels.

Table 8.2 Common Logical, Emotional, and Ethical Fallacies

Term	Description	Example
Authority worship	Accepts unquestioningly the argument of an authority not on the basis of what is said but solely on the basis of who says it. It's important that you exercise critical thinking and do not accept claims without thinking them through, especially if bias could be involved.	He spent 17 years on the Atomic Energy Board. He must know everything there is to know about his subject.
Bandwagon	An emotional fallacy; it argues in favour of something because it has become popular.	Everyone has seen the movie. We have to see it tonight.
Certain consequences ("slippery slope")	A common fallacy with many other names. It insists that a result is inevitable based on an oversimplified cause–effect relationship.	If we legalize marijuana, other, more dangerous drugs are going to end up being legalized as well.
Desk-thumping (dogmatism)	A common type of argument that asserts a claim without supporting evidence on the basis of what the arguer firmly, perhaps passionately, believes.	It is everyone's moral obligation to oppose the new tax. (In argumentative essays, it's best to avoid opinionated statements; instead, you should let your points talk for you.)

(continued)

Table 8.2   *(Continued)*

Term	Description	Example
Doubtful causes	Insists that a result is inevitable and cites too few causes to support that result; it bases an argument on a relationship that may not exist.	He looked unhappy after the exam; he must have failed miserably. (This argument assumes there was only one cause for his unhappiness—if, indeed, he was unhappy.)
Either/or (false dilemma)	Suggests that there are only two available options.	Either I borrow the car tonight or my life is over. (Consider that notorious cry "you're either with me or against me," which takes the logical either/or fallacy and gives it a strong emotional thrust.)
False authority	Argues on the basis of a presumed or unspecified authority.	All the studies show that people would support a law for raising the drinking age. (The writer generalizes: what specific studies show this?)
False analogy	Compares two things that are, in fact, not alike. While true analogies can provide support for a point, to draw a true analogy, there must be a real basis for comparison.	How can people complain about circuses that use wild animals in their acts? We keep animals, such as cats, that were once wild in small spaces in our homes.
False cause	Another cause–effect fallacy; asserts that simply because one event preceded another one there must be a cause–effect relationship between them.	Neesha wore her favourite socks to class the day she failed a test; consequently, she threw the socks away. (Superstitions can arise when people assume a causal relationship between two events. Of course, there are causal relationships between many events; for example, if Neesha walked in front of a car and was hit, then obviously her action resulted in her injury. A false cause assumes a connection without valid evidence.)
Filling the void	Argues that since no plausible explanation for something has been offered, the one the writer puts forward must be accepted.	No one has ever been able to explain how the pyramids got built, so obviously it must have been done with the help of aliens.
Finite categories	Asserts that something belongs in a certain category on the basis of only one characteristic.	I finally passed my driver's test, so where are the keys to the car? (The illogical assumption here is that legality alone determines the right to drive a car.)
Fortune-telling	Denies an effect as arising from a cause on the basis that it hasn't happened yet—therefore, it's not going to. In this distorted cause–effect fallacy, the arguer projects into the future without considering probability or other evidence.	Uncle Harry has smoked two packs of cigarettes a day for 20 years, and he hasn't died yet, so smoking obviously is not that dangerous.
Fuzzy categories ("argument of the beard")	So named because of the difficulty of deciding how many hairs on a chin constitute a beard; insists that there is no fundamental separation between two ideas or objects, or no point where one clearly becomes the other. This fallacy appears when terms are imprecisely defined.	A student argues with Professor Fuddle that there is no precise reason why his English essay was given a C. After the professor agrees to a C+ grade, the student repeats the argument that there is no clear distinction between a C+ and a B- and eventually works his mark up to an A!

(continued)

Table 8.2 (Continued)

Term	Description	Example
Guilt by association	Takes a view contrary to that of a supposedly disreputable person or group, based only on the arguer's opinion of that person or group.	How bad can whale hunting be when an extremist group like Greenpeace opposes it?
Hasty generalization	Forms a conclusion based on little or no evidence.	I talked to two people, both of whom said the text was useless, so I will not buy it. (Perhaps many people bought the text, so two people may not be a good sample.)
"It does not follow"	This suggests that there is a logical connection (such as cause–effect) between two unrelated areas.	If we hadn't built planes to conquer gravity, the NY tragedy of September 11 wouldn't have happened.
		I worked hard on this essay; I deserve at least a B+. (Unfortunately, working hard at something does not guarantee success, even if it does make it more likely.)
Longevity	Argues the validity of something solely because it has existed for a long time.	How can war be wrong when people have been fighting each other since the dawn of civilization?
Name-calling	Assigns base motives to or insults an individual or group (see "slanted language"). An individual or group can be assigned a negative label, which then becomes grounds for attack. Recently, the Western definition of terrorism has been challenged for its narrow applicability to subversive anti-Western groups. In such cases, applying the label of terrorist may also be an example of an unproven assumption (i.e., a narrow definition of terrorism).	Pharmaceutical companies' long hold on patents denies needed medicines to the poor and is just plain greedy.
Name-dropping	Uses the fact that some popular person or group supports something as an argument in its favour; such spurious authorities can include entertainment and sports celebrities who endorse a particular product for financial gain; compare with the **guilt by association** fallacy.	
Red herring	A fallacy of irrelevance that attempts to distract or sidetrack the reader, often by using an ethical fallacy. In the first example, there may be some validity to the point, but it should not form the basis of an argument. In the second example, the writer does not address the racism issue.	My honourable opponent's business went bankrupt. How can we trust him to run the country?
		Heart of Darkness is not racist because Conrad's target was the greed of Europeans.

(continued)

Table 8.2 *(Continued)*

Term	Description	Example
Straw man	Another fallacy of irrelevance. It misrepresents an opponent's main argument by substituting a false or minor argument in its place. The point is to get the audience to agree with the minor argument, making it easier to criticize the opponent's overall argument. The "straw man," then, is a flimsily constructed argument that is substituted for a valid one.	Thaddeus Tuttle points out that while women have not achieved wage parity with men, they often take maternity leaves, which means they don't work as much as men. (Among its flaws, this argument ignores the basic principle of equal pay for equal work.)
Tradition ("that is the way we have always done it")	Argues for a course of action because it has been followed before, even if the same conditions no longer apply.	You shouldn't ask if you can go to Toronto for the Thanksgiving weekend. This is a time you always spend with your family.
Treadmill logic	An argument that does not move forward or that continues in a circle. The main point is just repeated, but not expanded.	Applied degrees are now available at some community colleges in Canada. They are only offered there because community colleges teach applied skills.
Two wrongs make a right	A closely related ethical fallacy to the **bandwagon**.	There are far worse crimes than smoking weed, especially as hundreds of millions of people do it worldwide.
Unproven assumption	An argument based on an unproved assumption, as if it didn't need proving, or one that ignores a question or issue that needs to be answered before the conclusion can be drawn (sometimes called "begging the question").	Charlotte saw a blue van drive past her house three times yesterday. She phoned the police to report the incident. (This is not an argument, because the issue of whether or not the driver of the blue van is engaging in suspicious or illegal activity has not been addressed—the argument begs [asks] that the question of legality be answered.)

Determining context is vital in deciding whether the writer has used fallacious reasoning or has misused emotion. There are certainly many occasions when, for example, there are only two alternatives to consider (either/or). At other times, the fallacy represents a distortion of a legitimate form of support; for example, an analogy can become a false analogy if there is no true basis of comparison between the object compared and what it is being compared to. False analogies often implicitly address the question of scale and may seek to compare the very small to the very large; for example, when a baseball strike loomed in 2002 and was scheduled to begin on 11 September, an analogy was made between the parties involved in the strike and the terrorists that perpetrated the events of 11 September 2001. As well, the tradition fallacy should be carefully distinguished from the legitimate use of precedent as a form of evidence (see Chapter 5, page 126).

All lines of argument work most effectively when they are combined with other arguments. In fact, you could think of fallacies as unwarranted generalizations or oversimplifications that, as such, fail to do justice to the complexities involved in an issue. Fallacies embody identifiable evidence of poor reasoning. In addition, the writer using them weakens his or her argument, as a reader could easily think, "Wait a minute; that doesn't make sense." When you argue, you want your statements to be forceful and effective—not to provoke suspicion or mistrust. Otherwise, the reader might commit the fallacy of rejecting your entire argument (hasty generalization) because in one instance you misused reason.

A writer needs to look closely and objectively at *how* he or she argues and ensure that arguments are always founded on logic and that appeals to emotion and ethics are always moderate—avoiding excessive praise or condemnation. Watching out for the first will make the writer appear reliable and trustworthy; watching out for the last two will make the writer appear fair.

EXERCISE 8.7

↻ Check answers to select questions

A. **Silencing.** A writer sometimes resorts to logical or emotional fallacies to silence those against whom they are directed. No logical response is possible, since the reasoning behind the fallacies is flawed. Each of the following statements is based on faulty reasoning. Try to determine why it fails the test of reason and why it would not be effective in an argumentative essay. If it seems to afford an example of one of the fallacies listed above, decide which one; in some cases, more than one fallacy might be involved. More important than being able to identify the precise label is being able to see why the statements, as they are, are not logical or make unfair appeals to emotion.

1. The premier made a promise during his election campaign that he has failed to keep. He is a liar and his word can no longer be trusted.
2. He's already a full professor, and he's only 44 years old. He must possess a brilliant mind.
3. In our family, males have always been named "Harold" and females "Gertrude"; therefore, you should name your twins "Harry" and "Gerty."
4. If you don't get a degree in law, medicine, or business these days, you're never going to make any money.
5. Murder in Oman is almost non-existent because Oman has capital punishment, but murders occur every day in Canada because Canada doesn't have it.
6. When I serve you dinner, it's terrible not to eat all of it when you consider that one-third of the world's population goes to bed hungry.
7. The teacher hasn't called on me to answer a question for three consecutive days; it looks like I don't need to do the reading for tomorrow.
8. Television has changed so much over the years; there can be little doubt that it will survive the invasion of the computer.
9. Believing that women should serve in combat roles in the military is like believing that men should be able to bear children.
10. I know I went through the red light, officer, but the car in front of me did too.

B. **Find the Fallacies.** The following story by student writer Alison James contains at least five errors in reasoning. Try to classify them according to the logical and emotional fallacies referred to above:

Last week, Tina and her boyfriend, Steve, were running late for a reservation at their favourite restaurant. They were trying to figure out the quickest route so they would not lose their table. Tina suggested taking the side streets in order to avoid the traffic lights. Steve suggested that, while there are traffic lights on the main street, there was a chance they would hit all the green lights; but if they took the side streets, they would have to stop at all the stop signs. He added that the speed limits were faster on the main street than on the side streets where the speed limit was 30 km/h.

Tina rebutted, "But nobody actually drives 30 on those streets!"

Steve replied, "But we could get stuck behind a little old lady, and everybody knows how slowly they drive. Besides, we can speed on the main street; there are never any cops on that street, so we won't get a ticket."

Tina said, "No, let's take the side streets: we always go that way. And there have been two accidents recently on the main street, so the side streets are safer."

Neither of them was convinced by the other's argument (perhaps because they were so faulty), and they missed their reservation after all!

Slanted Language

In addition to misusing logic and emotion, a writer can show a lack of objectivity by using **slanted** or **loaded language**. Such language shows that the writer is not objective and detracts from his or her credibility. Slanted language can take many forms from extreme statements to qualifiers (adjectives or adverbs) that convey, sometimes subtly, a bias. When slanted language is direct and offensive, it is easy to spot. For example, if you dismissed the other side as "evil" or their argument as "horrible" or "disgusting," you would reveal your bias. When you use slanted language, a reader could easily take offence and question your fairness.

However, slanted language can be less obvious, for example, when words play unfairly on the connotations, rather than the denotations, of language—in other words, on the negative *implications* of particular words, rather than on their literal meanings. A writer's careful and conscious use of a word's connotations can be effective in an argument, but if the purpose is to distort the truth, then the writer's credibility is at stake. For example, in the passage below, "removed from office," rather than the more neutral "voted out of office," plays unfairly on the connotations of the first phrase. The italicized words in the following reveal slanted language:

> In the recent election, the *reigning* political *regime was removed from office* as a result of the *atrocities they had committed* against the people of the province. The voters believed the new government would improve things, but when you achieve such easy victory there is a tendency to overlook the reason for your victory: the people who elected you. Today, the government is ignoring the middle class, *betraying* the very people who *naively* voted them into office.

Collaborative Exercise

The following paragraphs suffer from faulty logic and/or emotional appeals, as well as examples of slanted language. In groups, analyze each argument, determine what fallacies and inconsistencies make it ineffective, and suggest improvements to make the argument stronger. More important than being able to identify the precise fallacy is being able to see that the statements are illogical or make unfair appeals to emotion.

EXERCISE
8.8

 Check answers to select questions

1. Genetically engineered foods are being sold in most supermarkets without anyone knowing that we are being used as guinea pigs for the corporations developing this technology. The general public is being kept in the dark entirely, and the way that this food is being sold is through one-sided advertising. The public is being told that genetically engineered foods are a safe and effective way to grow a lot of food faster by inserting genetic material of one species into another. Though the proponents of genetically engineered foods attempt to convince the public that this technology will save lives, the reality is that major biotechnology companies are developing genetically engineered food crops to maximize their profits. Corporations would have us believe that the reason why 19,000 children starve to death daily is because of inefficient agricultural practices, but the world currently produces enough food today to provide a decent diet for every person on this planet. In spite of this fact, genetically engineered foods are being sold as the cure for Third World starvation. This, however, is simply not true. The motives of the companies selling genetically engineered foods are not to save the lives of starving people, but to line their own pockets by profiting from the biotechnological industry. As a society, we should move to force governments to ban the development of genetically engineered foods before it is too late.

2. The legalization of marijuana would destroy society as we know it today. The typical Canadian would be exposed to many harsh drugs, such as coke, crack and heroin, due to the increased acceptance of drugs within the community. Rehabilitation clinics for chronic drug users would be a huge drain on the economy. There would have to be new laws and screenings implemented to prevent people from working with heavy machinery or operating a motor vehicle while impaired by marijuana. Canadian business owners would be dissatisfied with many of their employees, and then discrimination would rear its ugly head. Firing someone for smoking marijuana and not being productive at work is not discrimination; however, the point would be made that it is. Clearly, our society would sink to a despicable level if this drug were legalized.

Organizing an Outline for Argument

When outlining and drafting an argumentative essay, you should pay attention to the order of your main points. Ensure that they are ordered logically—i.e., from least to most important point—**climax order**—or from most important point to least important—**inverted climax**—whichever is most relevant for your argument; other orders are possible. You do not have to include all the elements listed below nor follow the same order of parts; for example, it may not be necessary to include background if the issue is well known to most readers. The rebuttal may not require a lot of space. Depending on the topic and other factors, you might choose to place it before your main points. If you use rebuttal Strategy A to acknowledge the other side, you could place the acknowledgement in either the Introduction or the Background section. Using Strategy B, you could begin a point-by-point refutation in Part III.

Rhetorical Function of Parts

The most common pattern in formal writing is the classical model (or its variants) described here. This pattern is based on the five-part argumentative model used from the time of the orators of the ancient world to the present day. Other patterns are possible, including **holding back the claim,** which can be useful if you expect strong opposition or if your opening is dramatic or memorable in another way. In this pattern, you do not announce your claim until you have provided the evidence, so your claim, in effect, acts as the conclusion.

I. **Introduction**
   - gains reader's attention and interest
   - includes your claim
   - may suggest the primary development method (if there is one)
   - establishes your credibility (knowledge, reliability, and fairness)

Body Paragraphs: II, III, and IV

II. **Background**
   - presents background information, if relevant

III. **Lines of Argument**
   - presents good reasons (logical, emotional, and ethical appeals) in support of thesis; draws on assumptions, premises, and warrants
   - uses all relevant evidence—facts, statistics, examples, views of experts/authorities
   - presents reasons in specific order related to argument

IV. **Refutation**
   - considers opposing points of view
   - notes both advantages and disadvantages of opposing views
   - argues that your thesis is stronger than opposing view and more beneficial to the reader

V. **Conclusion**
   - summarizes argument
   - expands or elaborates on the implication of your thesis
   - makes clear what you want reader to think or do
   - may make final strong ethical or emotional appeal

Sample Student Essays

The first of the following argumentative student essays, Reading 17, uses minimal research. The second essay, Reading 18 on page 254, uses research extensively. For an example of an argumentative essay that does not use research at all, see Reading 2 on page 56.

To conserve space, the essays are single-spaced and "References" and "Works Cited" sections are not on separate pages. The essays do not follow essay format requirements for title pages or identification information. For the correct ways of dealing with these issues, see Chapter 12, page 437, Essay Presentation.

Sample Student Argumentative Essay—APA Style

For another example of an essay using APA style, see Reading 13 on page 173.

Sample Student Essay

Reading 17

The Penny: Still Good for Art Projects
By Bain Syrowik

[1] Many years ago, when you could still make a one-cent purchase, the penny was vital to both the consumer and the retailer. Today, the penny is largely considered a nuisance: it is tossed into fountains, collected in cars and couches, and even thrown away. Very few people even use pennies, so why do we still have them around? In fact, attempts have been made to discontinue the use of the penny in Canada, including a private member's bill that is still on the table ("Senate Debates"). By contrast, many other countries have already eliminated their one-cent pieces. Even though eliminating the penny would make our lives easier, we continue to spend hundreds of millions of dollars annually on these coins. The costs of the penny are too great to warrant its continued production; eliminating the penny would have many personal, economic, and environmental benefits.

> The writer uses an expanded thesis statement, summarizing his main points concisely and forcefully.

> The writer raises what he considers the main argument against his claim, refuting it by using the results of an academic study.

> Here Syrowik uses precedent for support, effectively arguing that other countries have already eliminated the equivalent of the penny, so Canada should too. Note that the writer stresses the importance of this point by referring to it in his introduction.

[2] Consumers and retailers would be better off without the penny. All cash transactions would be automatically rounded to the nearest five cents, while all credit and debit card transactions would remain un-rounded. Many people opposed to abolishing the penny are concerned that they would be paying more for items; however, this concern is not borne out by research, which shows that a rounding strategy will result in a net rounding of zero cents (Chande & Fischer, 2003, p. 516), since approximately half of transactions would be rounded up, and half would be rounded down. This is fundamentally the same as the "give a penny, take a penny" trays at many convenience stores. Abolishing the penny would make it easier to give the correct change and also reduce the time needed for cash transactions. Australia, the Czech Republic, Finland, France, the Netherlands, New Zealand, and Spain have all successfully phased out their one cent or equivalent pieces and now use a rounding strategy. There is no reason such a plan would not work in Canada. Removing the penny from circulation would mean that it would no longer weigh down people's pockets and change purses, and would not accumulate in bowls, jars, and furniture around the house. Discontinuing penny production would be advantageous for everyone.

> As he does in all his body paragraphs, the writer uses a paragraph wrap to summarize the main point in the paragraph: here, he reiterates that discontinuing the penny would have many personal benefits.

> Syrowik raises his main points in the same order they are mentioned in his thesis.

> To cite this online source, the writer follows the APA's most recent guidelines, including a heading and paragraph number.

> Most of the evidence in this paragraph is statistical, taken from reliable sources.

[3] To continue the production of the penny is economically unsound. It is estimated that it may cost as much as four cents to produce a single penny (Chande & Fischer, 2003, p. 513). In some years, 95 percent of the coins produced in Canadian mints have been pennies and it may cost over $130 million each year to keep the penny in circulation (Bowman, 2008, "Inflation and the Penny," para. 5). Although only one-third of Canadians use pennies, the government produces about 25 pennies per Canadian each year. This is in addition to the estimated $200 million worth of pennies already in circulation (Bowman, "Canada's Farthing," para. 7), many of which are sitting unused in homes, fountains, cars, streets, and even landfills. This is an enormous waste of resources. All of the pennies the Royal Canadian Mint produces need to be

distributed all over the country, incurring huge transportation costs. Pennies are not always associated with financial losses. Many charitable and non-profit organizations rely on money collected in penny drives. For this reason they are often opposed to abolishing the penny; however, a nickel or dime drive should be at least as profitable. As long as these organizations are collecting money, they should easily accept the absence of the penny. It is unreasonable that so much money and natural, non-renewable resources go into producing a coin that is scarcely used. Halting the production of pennies could save millions of tax dollars and conserve precious resources.

The continued production of pennies has a huge environmental impact. Today, pennies contain 94 percent steel, 1.5 percent nickel, and 4.5 percent copper (Royal Canadian Mint, 2008). Mining these metals is very harmful to the environment: the production of steel releases large quantities of greenhouse gases, especially carbon dioxide, into the environment while the mining and processing of steel, nickel, and copper releases significant quantities of heavy metals into the environment. Heavy metals can leech into ground water and contaminate rivers, wells, and soil. Heavy metal contamination can lead to poisoning and death for animals, plants, and people. A lot of energy is needed to process the metals in pennies; producing this energy releases greenhouse gases as well. Once the metal has been purified and refined further, energy and resources go into minting and transporting the pennies. With the current environmental situation, we must do as much as possible to reduce our influence on the Earth. Stopping the production of pennies is a quick and easy way to minimize our environmental impact.

Our modern way of life, economy and environment call for the penny to be discarded. The lives of consumers and retailers would be simpler without the penny. The economy and environment would profit as well. Some argue that eliminating the penny would mean eliminating a national icon. However, the benefits of abolishing the penny outweigh the benefits of keeping it: our lives would be simpler, tax dollars would be saved, and we would minimize our impact on the environment. Even if the penny is not discarded, at least it is still good for art projects.

The writer again briefly raises a point on the other side and uses reason to refute it.

Syrowik, an engineering student, assumes his reader would know the effects of mining on the environment. If his intended audience did not know this, they could easily obtain this [4] information. (See pp. 250.) Hence, he does not give a citation.

The writer uses an ethical appeal, furthering his credibility.

Syrowik does not mention this point in his body paragraph, probably because he doesn't consider it important enough. By acknowledging it here, however, he attempts to come across as fair, leaving the reader with the sense of a balanced and objective argument.

[5]

After referring to his main points, Syrowik chooses to close with a brief humorous line that echoes his title. However, if his audience had been composed of strong opponents, this probably would not have been a good ending.

References

Bowman, J. (2009, April 1). Save the penny or leave the penny? *CBC News*. Retrieved from http://www.cbc.ca

Chande, D., & Fischer, T. (2003). Have a penny? Need a penny? Eliminating the one-cent coin from circulation. *Canadian Public Policy, 29*(4), 511–517.

Royal Canadian Mint. (2008). Circulation currency. Retrieved from http://www.mint.ca/

"Senate debates the penny's future." (2010, May 28). *CBC News*. Retrieved from http://www.cbc.ca

Sample Student Argumentative Essay—MLA Style

For another example of an essay that uses MLA style, see Reading 15 on page 180.

Sample Student Essay

Reading 18

Arts and the Provincial Government: The Deepest Cut
By Erica H. Isomura

[1] Arts and culture have always been an inevitable aspect of day-to-day living: in its many varieties and forms, the arts decorate our homes, sit on our bookshelves, and perform on our televisions, iPods, radios, and CD players. Despite the fact that arts are a necessity to Canadian well-being, the provincial government has slashed the budget of arts and culture in British Columbia. The government tried to cover up some of these cuts and, at the same time, introduced 2010 Legacies Now, an Olympic by-product that will receive arts funding. With BC artists' earnings declining, many more jobs within the BC arts industry are now at stake. Despite recent government studies that have related arts to the economy and proved the assets of a solid arts community, the government does not heed its own results. The budget cuts to the arts are a bad decision on the behalf of British Columbia.

[2] Arts enhance one's quality of life. With more than 25,600 working artists, BC has the largest percentage of artists in the labour force of any province. BC has also had the largest growth rate of artists in the work force in Canada in recent years (British Columbia Arts Council, *Strategic Plan* 18). According to Vancouver mayor Gregor Robertson, "the arts are at the core of . . . identity and spirit [and] beyond that, arts and culture are a huge economic driver. . . . There [was] an expectation that [BC] artists [would] shine alongside athletes [during the Olympics]" (Werb). Robertson's statement was realized during the 2010 Olympic Games when the Vancouver Art Gallery received 95,000 visitors in 17 days, its highest visitor attendance in history (CBC News, "Olympic Visitors"). At that time, most of the gallery's displays were dedicated to art from its own collection of distinguished BC artists, notably Emily Carr, Jack Shadbolt, Jeff Wall, B.C. Binning, and Bill Reid.

[3] Through its concern for BC arts, public disapproval forced the government to re-evaluate its arts funding. The government released the 2010–2011 budget in September 2009, in which 90 per cent of funding was cut from the BC Arts Council. It re-released a budget in March 2010 that allotted $46.1 million to the arts (CBC News, "Cuts"). This new budget appeared to fully restore funding; however, appearances are not always as they seem. Amir Ali Alibhai, the executive director of the Alliance for Arts and Culture, claims that the BC government has cut BC Arts Council funding by almost 50 per cent. In previous years, the BC Arts Council received around $14 million each year; this year they will be receiving only $7.9 million to distribute to BC artists. This year's budget also received $8.5 million less from gambling funds compared to past years, which also means less funding for non-profit arts organizations (Pablo and Smith).

[4] In addition to these cuts, many other changes are being criticized. Finance Minister Colin Hansen noted that this year's budget included the $12.2 million operating funds for the Royal BC Museum. These funds were not mentioned in past years' budgets and critics have taken this inclusion as a subtle funding reduction. Another addition that artists are approaching with caution is the funding for the new three-year art and sport Olympic legacy program; over 20 per cent of the funds from the new budget are being allocated to this program. Since this program is unfamiliar, as well as government-induced and promoted, nobody in the arts community is

certain of how this money will be spent. NDP MLA Spencer Herbert says that "the people in the arts community…never asked for [the new fund] and are concerned that [it is] just more bureaucracy taking away from program funding." Critics are skeptical about the new funds because this new program is receiving more money than the BC Arts Council, British Columbia's major art agency (Lederman, "Money Restored" S3).

According to the Canadian Conference of the Arts, British Columbia's provincial government was the only one to make budget cuts to its province's arts and culture sector. However, even though British Columbia's arts community was the hardest hit of the provinces, other provinces have been negatively affected by arts cuts. In 2008, the federal government cut $45 million in arts and culture funding; as a result, CBC announced television and radio programming reductions, which included prime time cancellations. In response to the outrage expressed by Canadians across the country, Prime Minister Stephen Harper said that "ordinary people" do not resonate with artists at "a rich gala . . . subsidized by taxpayers [while] claiming [that] their subsidies [are not] high enough" (Campion-Smith). Harper seems to be severely misinformed on the financial status of Canadian artists, particularly of BC artists. In 2006, BC artists were working for wages at almost poverty level. Statistics Canada has defined annual earnings of $20,800 as the low-income cutoff. The average annual earnings of a BC artist in 2006 were $21,069; the average BC worker earned $36,000. Although BC has the highest percentage of artists in Canada, a BC artist's earnings in 2006 were less than those of the average Canadian artist in 2005, who earned $22,731. Unfortunately, artist earnings do not appear to be improving, especially with the current lack of arts funding. BC artists' earnings decreased by 5 percent between 1991 and 2005 (Adams R1).

[5]

Despite the low income of Canadian artists, there are always exceptions, such as Margaret Atwood, one of Canada's most renowned writers. In response to Harper's comment about rich artists who whine about their grants at galas, in a *Globe and Mail* article, Atwood declared that while she is one of the few moderately wealthy writers in Canada, she does not receive grants; instead, she "[whines] about other grants—grants for young people, that may help them to turn into [a writer like her]" (Atwood A17). Even though BC has the largest Canadian artist growth, these cuts will not help up-and-coming artists pursue their art. Rather, they may need to spend more time at part-time jobs to raise their earnings while trying to keep up with other artists (British Columbia Arts Council, *Strategic Plan* 18). Atwood's career was boosted by Ontario arts funding; rising artists need support to succeed in their industry, just like any other labour-specific worker.

[6]

Although budget cuts seem an obvious solution in a recession, cuts to the arts are unwise not just for the artists but also for the government: revenues that the arts reap prove that British Columbia's arts sector is strong and vibrant. However, before money is earned, money needs to be spent. A government-funded study for the Ministry of Tourism, Sports and Arts of BC reported that for every dollar spent by the government in grants for arts and culture, it received $1.36 in return in provincial taxes (Sandhu 9). The arts generate a multiplier effect: it is estimated that $13 in spin-off economic activity can be produced by every dollar spent on the arts at the municipal level (Cernetig). According to the BC Arts Council, more than $5.2 billion annually is contributed to our provincial economy from BC's arts and culture sector (British Columbia Arts Council, "Facts"). The government's actions fail to acknowledge that the arts are not a luxury, but an industry like any other. BC's arts and culture industry employs 80,000 people, many of whom are not artists, but operate artists' entailment jobs. If government reports acknowledge the advantages of supporting the arts community, why does the provincial government not heed these benefits?

[7]

[8]   Although Harper claims that "ordinary people" do not seem to care about the arts, reports contradict this statement. In 2007, 759,000 Canadians donated approximately $101 million to non-profit art and culture organizations. Donors from BC were more likely to give to arts and culture organizations than those in all other provinces (Hills Strategic Research). BC's level of donations to the arts could imply that BC residents are aware of the benefits arts bring to the community and the economy. A 2006 government report stated that "arts and cultural organizations make a broad contribution to society. . . . These organizations help preserve heritage, facilitate arts and cultural education, identify, develop, and recognize artistic talent, and encourage . . . participation" (Sandhu 1). Since the budget cuts, many successful BC artists have spoken out against the government's rash decision, including actress Kim Cattrall and writer Douglas Coupland (Lederman, "Atwood" S1).

[9]   Perhaps Harper believes that "ordinary people" do not care for the arts, and yet if the arts cuts continue, as many have predicted, they may soon increasingly affect the everyday lives of these ordinary people. They will begin to care as their daily television and radio programs vanish due to funding loss or when their children's after-school art classes are cancelled. However, British Columbians are not ordinary; they are extraordinary. They care about the future of their arts and culture, vital factors that define their province and their country. They take preventative measures and will not wait for the government to reduce their arts funding to nothing. The provincial government will not be able to take away funds without a good fight from its citizens. These extensive budget cuts have sparked a battle that the government will not be able to win; whether they lose economically or from public retaliation, BC citizens will challenge the government to, wisely, make its next move.

Works Cited

Adams, James. "Starving Artists? Study Shows That's Not Far from the Mark." *Globe and Mail* 5 Feb. 2009: R1+. Print.

Atwood, Margaret. "To Be Creative Is, in Fact, Canadian." *Globe and Mail* 25 Sept. 2008: A17. Print.

British Columbia Arts Council. "B.C. Arts and Culture Facts." *British Columbia Arts Council*. 2010. Web. 5 Apr. 2010.

British Columbia Arts Council. *B.C. Arts Council: Strategic Plan 2009–2013. British Columbia Arts Council.* 11 Dec. 2009. Web. 6 Apr. 2010.

Campion-Smith, Bruce. "Arts Uproar? Ordinary Folks Just Don't Care, Harper Says." *Toronto Star* 24 Sept. 2008: A1+. *Canadian Newsstand Major Dailies*. Web. 2 Apr. 2010.

CBC News. "CBC Cuts Hit News, Drama, Sports, Radio." *Canadian Broadcasting Corporation*. 26 Mar. 2009. Web. 7 Apr. 2010.

CBC News. "Olympic Visitors Also Lined up to View Art." *Canadian Broadcasting Corporation*. 2 Mar. 2010. Web. 6 Apr. 2010.

CCA Bulletin. "Provincial Initiatives to Help the Arts Weather the Recession—An Overview." *Canadian Conference of the Arts*. 20 May 2009. Web. 6 Apr. 2010.

Cernetig, Miro. "Games' Cultural Legacy Will Disappear if Arts Funding Cuts Continue." *Vancouver Sun* 29 Jan. 2010: A4+. *Canadian Newsstand Major Dailies*. Web. 5 Apr. 2010.

Hill Strategies Research. "New report shows that 759,000 cultural donors gave a total of about $101 million to arts and culture organizations in 2007." *Hills Strategies Research Inc.*, 25 Feb. 2010. Web. 6 Apr. 2010. <http://www.hillstrategies.com/docs/Donors2007_summary.pdf>.

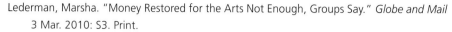

Lederman, Marsha. "Money Restored for the Arts Not Enough, Groups Say." *Globe and Mail* 3 Mar. 2010: S3. Print.

Lederman, Marsha. "Atwood, McLachlan, Coupland Join Campaign against Arts Cuts." *Globe and Mail* 25 Sept. 2009: S1. Print.

Pablo, Carlito, and Charlie Smith. "Arts Alliance Says B.C. Budget Cuts Arts Funding, but Liberals Cover It Up by Including Museum Funds in Total." *Georgia Straight* [Vancouver] 2 Mar. 2010. Web. 2 Apr. 2010.

Sandhu, G.S. and Associates. *Socio-Economic Impacts of Arts and Culture Organizations in BC: Grant Applicants to the BC Arts Council*. Ministry of Tourism, Sports and Arts. Dec. 2006. Web. 2 Apr. 2010. <http://www.tca.gov.bc.ca/arts_culture/docs/dec2006_socio_economic_impacts.pdf>.

Werb, Jessica. "Why Do the Arts Matter?" *Georgia Straight* [Vancouver] 17 Sept. 2009. Web. 6 Apr. 2010.

Sample Scholarly Essay (CMS Style)

Before reading this essay, you can also review the questions discussed in Chapter 1, Responding Critically and Analytically through Questions, page 10. For general strategies for reading scholarly essays, see Chapter 6, page 184.

Pre-reading Questions

1. Had you heard of the debate referred to in the first paragraph of the essay or of the anti-Olympic campaigns before? Access the website "Olympic Resistance Network" or websites featuring the anti-Olympic Slogan "No Olympics on Stolen Native Land." Then, look up two additional websites or blogs, one that supported this campaign and one that opposed it. Do all the websites raise reasonable points? Are the authors objective and/or fair? Provide specific examples.

2. Look up the issue in which this article appeared and read the abstracts of at least three of the other articles. What other perspectives on sport (and on sport and Canada) are represented in this issue?

Sample Scholarly Essay

Reading 19

"No Olympics on Stolen Native Land": Contesting Olympic Narratives and Asserting Indigenous Rights within the Discourse of the 2010 Vancouver Games
Christine M. O'Bonsawin
Sport in Society 13, no. 1 (2010):143–56

At present, organizing initiatives for the 2010 Vancouver Olympic Winter Games have caused tension and dissonance within local, provincial, national and international factions. As expected, the issue of indigenous rights, and the infringement on such rights, has once again come to the forefront of Olympic debates as indigenous peoples, communities, activists and scholars openly critique and [1] resist the hosting of the XXI Olympic Winter Games in Vancouver, British Columbia—or what some consider "Stolen Native Land." For indigenous communities, opposition to the Games rests in the historical exploitation and, arguably, the ongoing disregard for the rights of indigenous peoples within Canada. The reality is that the 2010 Vancouver Olympic Games will take place, and in the midst of national celebrations there will be indigenous protest and activism as indigenous peoples and groups attempt to "grapple" with the "legacy of the past."[1]

[2]   The purposes of this essay are threefold: (1) to conceptualize the paradox between Olympic principles and indigenous rights in Canada, and elsewhere, through an examination of previously hosted Olympic Games on contentious indigenous lands; (2) to provide a framework of indigenous/settler political history in British Columbia in the context of current opposition to the Vancouver Olympics; and (3) to offer recommendations for evaluating the suitability of Olympic bids from cities, and thus nations, which attempt to govern over indigenous populations. Accordingly, this essay contributes to ongoing debates surrounding the 2010 Vancouver Olympic Winter Games as it provides an historical framework for understanding the tensions that exist between present-day Olympic programming and indigenous activism.

Olympic principles, indigenous rights and representation: an historical overview

[3]   The Baron Pierre de Coubertin (1863–1937), a French aristocrat who was highly influenced by his memories of the Franco-Prussian War, the British Public School tradition of physical education, and the integrity of the nation-state, is the individual most often credited for the "revival" of the modern Olympic Games. Coubertin meticulously oversaw the adoption and introduction of the Olympic principles, which eventually came to be branded as "Olympism." Olympism, by definition, is a "philosophy of life" that praises a balance of body, will and mind. Through the unification of "sport with culture and education, Olympism seeks to create a way of life based on the joy found in effort, the educational value of good example and respect for universal fundamental ethical principles."[2] As a universal philosophy, Olympism is generally understood to be global coherent that speaks in truisms of equity, anti-discrimination, mutual recognition and respect, tolerance and solidarity. For Coubertin, the Olympic Games represented a site for world progress, diplomatic co-existence, global understanding, and for instilling social and moral values. By the early twentieth century, the philosophy of Olympism had been infused into the Olympic project, thereby entrenching a social ideology that would serve as the raison d'être for the movement itself. However, it remains unclear on what grounds this abstract concept serves as the marker, or "core value," which elevates the Olympic Games above all other sport competitions. As Wamsley argues, "in many respects the two [Olympism and the Olympic Games] are incongruous, . . . and during the twentieth century, the nebulous concept of Olympism became the structural apologetic for the Olympic Games."[3]

[4]   By the early years of the twentieth century, the emerging philosophy of Olympism became the structural apologetic for a deeply politicized and xenophobic Olympic movement.[4] Since its revival, the Olympic movement has renounced Olympic-like athletic competitions that embody racial, political or religious undertones. It is believed that such events have the potential to undermine Olympism and its perceived virtues of peace, brotherhood and humanity. However, the Olympic Games, on all levels, are deeply politicized. Under the moral guise of Olympism, participants (in the capacity of athlete, builder, spectator, global citizen or otherwise; in short, universal participation in the Olympics is expected) are encouraged to cast aside everyday lived experiences, which are undeniably shaped by such factors as race, gender, sexuality, religion, culture and ideology, and class. The reality for marginalized peoples is that their everyday experiences are lived not on equitable, anti-discriminatory, tolerant, respectful and harmonious terms.

In the Olympic context, spectators have to look no further than the ceremonies to appreciate the discordant historical and contemporary realities of indigenous peoples around the world. It is in this context, the ceremonies, that the allure of the Olympic spectacle is most evident. And it is in this same medium where the plight and hardships of indigenous peoples within colonial and settler societies become most sensationalized. In the opening ceremonies of both the 2000 Sydney and 2002 Salt Lake City Olympic Games, organizers followed informal tradition, thereby taking this opportunity to recount, and in many instances reinvent, national narratives. In both examples, indigenous peoples were relegated to nominal and inconsequential roles. The foundations of both nations rest heavily on the hardships and sufferings of indigenous peoples, yet their contributions to these national histories are by no means nominal or inconsequential. [5]

For the 2000 Sydney Olympic Summer Games, Australian organizers promoted and endorsed their Games under a national campaign which called for "Reconciliation" between aboriginal and settler Australia. Despite tense relationships at home as well as international scrutiny from abroad, the Sydney Olympics opened in celebration of national reconciliation. For example, in its media guide, the Sydney Organising Committee for the Olympic Games (SOCOG) described the opening ceremony to have been [6]

> [a] celebration of Australia that begins by the sea and returns to the harbour city after a journey through our land and history . . . . [W]e are taken on a journey through Australian history, environment and culture by two characters; a little girl and the traditional Aboriginal dancer, Djakapurra . . . her dream [the little girl, Nikki Webster] gives way to Djakapurra, Aboriginal dancers and members of tribes from all corners of the country, forming circles around burning eucalyptus leaves. They conjure a giant Wandjina, a creation myth spirit symbolizing the unity of Indigenous people . . . a segment that takes us on a journey through European settlement . . . . [T]his is a cue for a series of groups to sweep into the area. This represents the successive waves of immigration that has transformed Australia into the cosmopolitan and diverse society it is today. With 2,000 people in the centre of the arena, Sydney's landmark Anzac Bridge rises, and Djakapurra and our little girl meet again amid a crescendo that celebrates the city of Sydney.[5] [7]

As the ceremony moved forward, it was revealed that Cathy Freeman, a highly celebrated yet controversial aboriginal athlete and political figure in Australia at this time, would light the Olympic cauldron. Symbolically, the message was "reconciliation," and the international audience was led to believe that a gesture of respect and an opportunity for healing was being offered to aboriginal Australia. However, in the years and months leading up to the 2000 Sydney Olympic Summer Games, Australia was anything but reconciled. [8]

In the late seventeenth century, the concept of terra nullius—land belonging to no one—had been employed during these early years of settlement in the new colony. In 1901, at the time of Confederation, terra nullius was firmly embedded within the political and legal governance of Australia. It was not until 1992, in the case of Mabo and Others v. The State of Queensland that the High Court of Australia finally rejected the concept of terra nullius and ruled that native title—the right to exclusive use and occupation of land—had not previously been extinguished in Australia. In 1993 the Keating government responded by enacting the Native Title Act, a legislative document that established criteria for dealing with native title, particularly by validating the interests of non-indigenous land holders. In the 1996 case of Wik Peoples v. The State of Queensland, Australia's High Court once again ruled in favour of aboriginal rights, and decided that pastoral leases could co-exist with native title. In 1998, the Howard government amended the Native Title Act through its "Ten Point Plan," which removed aboriginal rights to negotiate on pastoral leases. Consequently, in 1999, at its 54th session in March of 1999, the United Nations Committee for the Elimination of Racial Discrimination (CERD) placed Australia on an "urgent business" priority as it brought down "damaging [9] findings" against the government concerning its treatment of an aboriginal population. These findings were once again supported in August of 1999 at the 55th session.[6] This was the first time in its history that CERD expressed "serious concerns" about a Western nation going backwards on the land rights of indigenous people.

[10]   For the opening ceremony, Australian organizers altered historical and national narratives in an attempt to promote a reconciled and united Australia. Magdalinski argues that that the hosting of these Games provided the nation with an opportunity to explore

[11]   Australian identity and nostalgic remembering in a climate of economic restructuring and social turmoil. In a growing era of political disquiet, where right-wing fundamentalism [was] increasing, where indigenous and migrant issues [were] threatening the homogeneity of Australia's political and social landscape and where the Asian economic crisis threatened national economic security, the Olympic Games provided a useful cultural focal point around which images of the Australian nation could be generated.[7]

[12]   Magdalinski further argues that during times of rapid social change, national celebrations, such as hosting the Olympic Games, become increasingly significant as nations attempt to "project themselves into the future" while struggling with the "legacy of the past." In the closing ceremony of the Sydney Games, Olympic and political officials were publicly embarrassed, and ultimately criticized, as the Australian band, Midnight Oil, took the stage wearing "SORRY suits." The apology was directed to aboriginal Australians. The band publically criticized Prime Minister Howard's (who was in attendance at the closing ceremony) refusal to apologize to aboriginal Australians for the treatment they had received under white rule, particularly the survivors and families of the Stolen Generations (Stolen Children).[8] An apology was eventually offered by Prime Minister Kevin Rudd in February of 2008.[9]

[13]   In many respects, the hosting of the 2002 Salt Lake City Olympic Winter Games also brought the matter of indigenous rights to the forefront of national and international politics. By comparison, indigenous opposition to the Games appeared to have been silenced, or at least overshadowed. Certainly the events of September 11th, 2001, which led to increased anxieties and considerable monies directed at security efforts, reduced adversarial response to the Games. Despite increased tensions, the festivities of the Salt Lake City Olympics thrived and the Games opened in national celebration. The opening ceremony was a celebration of the American west, with organizers seeking to feature the five tribes of Utah, including the Shoshone, Ute, Paiute, Goshute and Dine-Navajo. For this ceremony, members of these nations danced into the stadium in traditional regalia followed by drummers who were positioned on planks, which were sequenced to match the five colours of the Olympic rings. At the end of their performance, tribal representatives from the five Nations welcomed Olympians, and in return received gift bundles; however, American broadcasters failed to translate these blessings or explain the significance of indigenous gift-giving practices. Consequently, the deeper cultural meanings of the welcomes and gift exchange were lost, and viewers were left with appropriated and mythological images of "all things Indian." While an otherwise uninformed audience was left with messages of a fabled past, indigenous critics publically asserted their dissatisfaction.

[14]   Susan Shown Harjo, a prominent Cheyenne and Hodulgee Muscogee writer and activist, claimed that

[15]   [after the Indians had their moment in the spotlight], they danced back into history, making way for miners, cowboys and settlers of all races to do-se-do together (as if that ever happened in that place and time). Only the Indians were missing from the hoedown in Salt Lake . . . . But these are just symbols, you say? Well, yeah. Mega-bucks worth of symbols. Symbology that reaches millions of people around the world and leaves a lasting impression in place of reality.[10]

As Harjo suggests, Native representatives should have welcomed Olympic dignitaries. This would have [16] served as an important contextual point that affirmed the sovereignties and rights to the lands that Natives American peoples possess today. However, the failure to do so confirmed tensions within the current relations between indigenous peoples and the American state.[11] Furthermore, Native American concerns rest with the hypocrisy of parading the tattered American flag from the September 11th bombings of the World Trade Centre [sic]. For many Americans this display provided assurance that by bravely going forward and hosting the Olympic Games, the United States was reclaiming its security in the face of terrorism. However, as Judith Lowry, a painter of Maidu and Pit River ancestry, suggests, Native Americans "would like to live with the illusion that we are safe, but for those of Native heritage, that is impossible. The reminders stay with us from generation to generation."[12]

In its hosting of Olympic Games, Canada has also grappled with the appropriateness of includ- [17] ing indigenous peoples and their complementary imagery within the programming of the Games. Similar to Australia and the United States, Canadian Olympic Games organizers have appropriated indigenous imagery. In response to the contentious inclusion of indigenous imagery within the programme of the 1976 Montréal Olympic Summer Games, Janice Forsyth notes the paradox that exists between the celebratory promotion of indigenous peoples within the Olympic context, and the everyday lived realities such populations experience in Canada. Forsyth argues that

> although Olympic organizers stated publicly that the Closing Ceremony was being held to [18]
> honor Canada's Aboriginal peoples, the organizers did not consult with the populations
> who they proposed to respect in the construction of the program. From start to finish, the
> celebration was designed by Olympic organizers for Aboriginal peoples.[13]

The most blatant disregard for indigenous peoples occurred during the closing ceremony with the [19] participation of nine First Nations, including the Abenaki, Algonquin, Atikamekw, Cree, Huron, Mi'gmiq [sic], Mohawk, Montagnais and Naskapi nations. Olympic organizers invited representatives from these nations to participate in what was proposed to be a "commemoration ceremony." In the end, 200 representatives from the nine First Nations were escorted into the arena and led in "traditional" dance by 250 non-indigenous performers who were painted and dressed to look like "Indians." Despite proposals that this performance was being held to honour indigenous peoples, the choreography was under the direction of Canadian choreographer Michel Cartier, the musical inspiration was based on the works of Canadian composer André Mathieu, which included La Danse Sauvage, and due to financial constraints, over half of the "Indian hosts" were, in fact, local nonindigenous people who were painted and dressed to look like "Indians."

In the case of Calgary, organizing efforts attempted to appropriate indigenous imagery for the [20] purpose of promotional gain. Wamsley and Heine identify the various ways in which the Olympiques Calgary Olympics '88 (OCO) used indigenous culture to present a "Western" character of Calgarian hospitality. In doing so, they utilized the international prestige of the Calgary Stampede and based their cultural programming around the Stampede's symbolic use of the Mountie, the cowboy and the Indian.[14] Indigenous peoples within Alberta and throughout Canada took offence to a number of suggestions and actions taken by the OCO that involved the use of indigenous imagery for Olympic programming. For example, the composition of the Olympic medals displayed winter sporting equipment protruding from a ceremonial headdress, an enormous teepee at McMahon Stadium supporting the Olympic cauldron, and the Calgary Stampede Board's suggestion that an "Indian attack and wagon-burning" be a part of the opening ceremony (this was ultimately rejected). For Olympic organizers, programming [was] also encroached upon by indigenous activism, notably the Lubicon Lake Cree Nation who opposed federal, provincial and corporate funding in support of indigenous Olympic programming. The Lubicon Cree initiated boycotts of the Petro Canada sponsored torch relay run, and the Shell Canada/Federal co-sponsorship of "The Spirit Sings" Olympic exhibit, which was hosted by the Glenbow Museum. The debate centred upon the presence of these oil corporations on contested indigenous territories, as well as the federal and provincial governments' unwillingness to engage in honourable treaty negotiations with the Lubicon Cree.

[21]   In July 2003, Jacques Rogge, the president of the International Olympic Committee (IOC), announced Vancouver's successful candidacy to host the XXI Olympic Winter Games. Vancouver's successful bid was the result of the formation of a 500-plus-member committee, a four-year preparation effort, a multi-million dollar investment from public and private entities, the development of a 460-page Bid Book, and a municipal plebiscite vote that went in favour of the Games. Incorporated within The Sea to Sky Games: Vancouver 2010 Bid Book was the clear recognition of indigenous peoples. S. 1.1 of the Bid Book states, 'Canada is a living mosaic of peoples and cultures from around the world. Virtually every nation has *joined* [emphasis added] Canada's First Nations, making us a truly multicultural society."[15] In this context, bid organizers fomented a wider confusion about indigenous peoples as an ethnic minority within Canada's multicultural milieu. Furthermore, as explained in the Vancouver 2010 Bid Book, organizers claimed that the four political institutions of Canada include the federal government, the provincial and territorial governments, the municipal/regional governments, and the "First Nations." However, a national policy has yet to be developed that recognizes First Nations as an official political institution within Canada. This leads one to question the integrity, or at the very least, the organizational creditability of an international movement that permits a few individuals, normally members of the political and corporate elite, to provide the IOC with an abridgment of complex national structures. In the case of Vancouver 2010, bid members positioned First Nations as an official political institution of Canada. Beyond the erroneous nature of this claim it is important to note that indigenous peoples continue to live in disadvantaged, and in many instances, desperate conditions within this very nation. This IOC process, arguably, sustains indigenousness as "an identity constructed, shaped and lived in the politicized context of contemporary colonialism."[16]

[22]   With its successful candidacy to host the XXI Olympic Winter Games, the bid committee quickly dissolved and the Vancouver Olympic Organizing Committee for the 2010 Olympic and Paralympic Winter Games (VANOC) was established. Throughout the entire process, organizers have made significant attempts to ensure that indigenous participation and imagery are prominent and visible expressions of the Vancouver Olympics. For example, there has been the implementation of the Four Host First Nations (FHFN) Protocol Agreement, the adoption of the inukshuk logo, indigenous representatives in the 2006 Torino handover ceremony, the inclusion of the indigenous inspired Olympic mascots, the creation of a Sustainability and Aboriginal Participation programme, a torch relay schedule that includes stops in over 300 aboriginal communities, and significant aboriginal programming administered through 2010 Legacies Now (an official partner of VANOC).[17] VANOC has made considerable efforts to ensure indigenous visibility and economic support in the organizing and hosting of the Games. Large sums of Olympic dollars are being directed at indigenous programming and economic projects within communities; however, a troubling reality looms overhead: the Vancouver 2010 Olympic Winter Games are being hosted on unceded and non-surrendered indigenous lands.

Indigenous/settler political history in British Columbia and opposition to the Olympics

[23]   Opposition to the 2010 Vancouver Olympic Winter Games has rallied under the Olympic Resistance Network and the anti-Olympic campaign calling for "No Olympics on Stolen Native Land." This Olympic Resistance Network is based in Vancouver and works in solidarity with communities across British Columbia, "particularly indigenous communities who have been defending their lands against the onslaught of the Olympics since the bid itself."[18] This umbrella network represents the continuously growing number of groups and individuals who share common anti-colonial and anti-capitalist understandings, and work in solidarity with those negatively impacted by the 2010 Games. Some of

the associate organizations and groups include 2010 Games Watch, Anti-Poverty Committee, No 2010 Olympics on Stolen Native Land, No One is Illegal, and Our Freedom.[19] The Olympic Resistance Network has been working under a common anti-Olympic campaign that calls for "No Olympics on Stolen Native Land." From this position, it is argued that British Columbia

> remains largely unceded and non-surrendered Indigenous territories. According to Canadian law, BC has neither the legal nor moral right to exist, let alone claim land and govern over Native peoples. Despite this, and a fraudulent treaty process now underway, the government continues to sell, lease, and "develop" Native land for the benefit of corporations, including mining, logging, oil [and] gas, and ski resorts. Meanwhile, Indigenous peoples suffer the highest rates of poverty, unemployment, police violence, disease, suicides, etc.[20]

[24]

Certainly, this campaign must appear one-sided to those unaware of the histories and contemporary realities of indigenous populations whose lands make up present-day British Columbia; and no doubt, this effort must seem insulting to Olympic loyalists who perceive the Games and its virtuous ideals to be humanitarian-centred. The question arises: what do advocates mean when they petition for "No Olympics on Stolen Native Land"?

[25]

The British Columbia land question is a complex legal issue in present-day Canada, which arises from a multifaceted political history between indigenous and settler populations. While this issue has been discussed at length and appropriately critiqued elsewhere, for the purpose of this essay it is important to provide an historical framework for the unlawful transfer of indigenous territories to Crown and provincial lands.[21] In an effort to account for the ongoing conflicts within the historic and present-day treaty process (or lack thereof), the issue of aboriginal title is discussed from two perspectives—a Western perspective and an indigenous worldview—as there is a clear contradiction between the two sides concerning ideological understandings of land ownership.

[26]

From a Western perspective, there is considerable debate as to the origins and continued assertion of aboriginal title in the province of British Columbia. Foster and Grove aptly summarize the brief history of treaty making in British Columbia.[22] Following the signings of the Vancouver Island Treaties (commonly referred to as the Douglas Treaties) in the 1850s, treaty making in the colony arbitrarily ceased. From the 1860s to 1927 the "Indian Land Question" in British Columbia was a significant issue amongst indigenous peoples as they were resisting settler encroachment and exploitation of their lands. With the exception of a small portion of land in northeastern British Columbia, which was negotiated into Treaty 8 in 1899, land cession treaties were never made in the province during this time period, as was the case in Ontario and the Prairies. Furthermore, an amendment to the Indian Act in 1927 temporarily ceased the treaty process throughout Canada as this revision made it illegal for indigenous people to pursue legal counsel, and thus treaty. This amendment would not be overturned until 1951 in a radical rewrite of the Indian Act.[23]

[27]

A commonly held view among legal scholars and historians is that treaty making ceased because aboriginal title was not recognized in the colony. Rationales for this include that Sir James Douglas and his successors were not aware of the 1763 Royal Proclamation, which set up the criteria for treaty making elsewhere in Canada, and therefore did not realize that they were legally obliged to extinguish aboriginal title; that there were instructions from the Colonial Office in Britain informing Douglas that "measures of liberality and justice may be adopted for compensating [the Indians] for the surrender of the territory which they have been taught to regard as their own";[24] and that Douglas and his successors were influenced by policy and judicial decisions in the western regions, notably in the states of Washington, Oregon, Alaska, as well as significant legal decisions being made in New Zealand, which had established an alternative formula—other than treaty—for extinguishing aboriginal title.[25] Despite this rationale, the question of aboriginal title was never addressed in British Columbia. Accordingly, the lands were settled by immigrant families, and laws were established to govern over those inhabiting the territories—indigenous and non-indigenous.

[28]

[29]   It was not until 1973, in the landmark decision of Calder v. British Columbia that the Supreme Court of Canada ruled in favour of indigenous rights as it was decided that aboriginal title had not been extinguished through previous means, and therefore continued to exist in British Columbia. This decision would eventually assist with the establishment of a comprehensive lands claims process in Canada, which set the stage for modern treaty making. Prominent agreements that have been negotiated under the modern treaty process include the James Bay and Northern Quebec Agreement (1975)/Northeastern Quebec Agreement (1978), the Nunavut Land Claims Agreement Act (1999), and the Nisga'a Final Agreement (2000). Furthermore, other judicial landmark decisions, including Guerin v. The Queen [1984] and Delgamuukw v. British Columbia [1997] have since ruled in favour of aboriginal title, and have made definitive statements as to the definitional meaning of this abstract concept. As Kanien'kehaka (Mohawk) scholar, Taiaiake Alfred, explains:

[30]   The Delgamuukw decision is generally seen as progressive, expanding the notion of indigenous rights by ruling that "Aboriginal title"—defined as "the right to exclusive use an occupation of land"—is "inalienable" except to the Crown (that is, such rights cannot be extinguished except by the federal government), and indigenous peoples have a constitutionally protected right to be consulted on and compensated for title infringements that affect their access to or use of the lands for purposes integral to their cultural survival.[26]

[31]   Decisions such as Calder, Guerin and Delgamuukw are often considered positive steps forward for indigenous rights in Canada; however, as Alfred further questions, what does this mean "to people whose traditional territories have for the most part already been alienated from them by law, settled by others, or handed over to corporate interests for resource development"?[27]

[32]   From an indigenous perspective, rights to the land derive from the presence of indigenous peoples on these territories since time immemorial. The concept of aboriginal title does not exist within indigenous philosophies, at least not in the Western concept of land ownership and exploitation of resources. Concepts such as terra nullius and aboriginal title were manufactured and employed under Western capitalist imperialism to validate illegal land grabs and justify the subjugation, containment and mistreatment of indigenous populations. In the case of British Columbia, indigenous peoples maintain that the land was never surrendered, and in recent years, the common law legal system in Canada has supported such claims.

[33]   By the early 1990s, it became clear to provincial and federal politicians that the British Columbia land question could no longer be ignored. Beyond legal reasoning, the province was most likely prompted by external, yet interconnected, events drawing attention to indigenous issues. These events include the violent standoff at Oka in the summer of 1990; the unprecedented allocation of federal funds in 1991 to a Royal Commission that was mandated with the responsibility of investigating the historical and existing state of indigenous affairs; judicial rulings in Canada's high and supreme courts supporting aboriginal title and indigenous rights; and the fact that comprehensive/ modern land claims were being negotiated elsewhere in Canada. In 1991, the British Columbia Land Claims Task Force released its report, which recommended that the province establish a "new relationship" with indigenous peoples through a "made in-BC Treaty Process." In 1993, the British Columbia Treaty Commission (BCTC) officially opened for business. However, since its inception many have questioned the dishonest characterization of this "treaty" process.

[34]   By definition, "A treaty is . . . a formal agreement between two or more recognized, sovereign nations operating in an international forum."[28] However, one must question the sincerity of a "treaty" process that attempts to extinguish indigenous nationhood by bringing such peoples into the Canadian political and legal structures and which refuses to employ the word "treaty" in any of its text "agreements." And it should not be forgotten that the BCTC was founded upon a mistaken premise in Canadian law—that Crown title exists in British Columbia. To assert the authority of

Crown title is to expose an historical intellectual framework based on racist conceptions of "civilized" and "uncivilized" societies. In this capacity, the concept of terra nullius and the application of aboriginal title are prioritized over the rights of indigenous peoples, their nationhoods and respective territories.[29] So we stand at an impasse.

Through the authority of its Charter, the Olympic Movement has the capacity to do many things, particularly contravene national policies and laws of host nations. In the case of Vancouver 2010, the most obvious imposition of IOC rule over national governance is the IOC's decision not to include women's ski jumping on the program. The decision was challenged in BC Supreme Court on the grounds that providing events for men only violated the Canadian Charter of Rights and Freedoms. In rejecting the challenge, the Honourable Madame Justice Fenlon ruled that while VANOC is subject to the Charter, the discrimination that the plaintiffs are experiencing is the result of the action of a non-party (i.e., the IOC) which is neither subject to the jurisdiction of this court nor governed by the Charter.[30]   [35]

A second example of IOC imposition on national policy relates to section 51 (3) of the Olympic Charter, which states, "No kind of demonstration or political, religious or racial propaganda is permitted in any Olympic sites, venues or other areas."[31] This IOC prohibition also conflicts with the Canadian Charter of Rights and Freedoms as this constitutional document guarantees freedom of expression, albeit through a limitation clause.[32] VANOC is once again abiding by IOC regulations and will be creating "Free Speech Zones" (also referred to as "Protest Zones"), which will provide a space for protestors and activists to engage in "lawful protest." However, Royal Mounted Canadian Police Assistant Commissioner Bud Mercer has recently announced that protesters are not limited to these zones as "lawful protest is legal and lawful in Canada."[33]   [36]

With regard to the rights of indigenous peoples, the imposition of Olympic policy and the delivery of programmes have significantly altered the treaty process and treaty making in British Columbia. Since awarding the 2010 Olympic Games to Vancouver, the BCTC has been significantly altered as a result. For example, there are currently 49 sets of negotiations with First Nations communities in British Columbia. Not surprisingly, the only First Nation community to reach a Final Agreement—Stage Six: Implementation of a Treaty—is Tsawwassen First Nation.[34] It is important to note that the Tsawwassen First Nation community will play an active role in the 2010 Games as the traditional territory of this Coast Salish community is not only within 30 kilometres of downtown Vancouver but also because the province of British Columbia, through BC Ferries, has established a major port on Tsawwassen territory. By negotiating this agreement the province has "secured the uninterrupted functioning of the major passenger and shipping ports for the lower mainland. A disruption to either of these ports, with the eyes of the world on Canada, up to and during 2010, would have been a massive embarrassment."[35] Furthermore, the treaty process highly encourages First Nations communities that are engaged in the treaty process to develop tourist centres with the purpose of promoting indigenous cultures and attracting local, national and international visitors. This will greatly assist the cultural programme of the 2010 Olympics as local indigenous culture will provide the city, province and country with a unique local identity.   [37]

The inclusion of colonial narratives has tacitly been enshrined within the Olympic formula, and indigenous peoples have long served the performance needs of nations whose histories rest in imperial conquest. Such storylines position the subjugation and containment of indigenous peoples within national histories, thereby removing them in time and space from present-day realities. Throughout Olympic history, most notably within the last quarter of the twentieth century and the first decade of the twenty-first century, there have been numerous incidences to support claims that indigenous peoples have been proactively, if not productively, incorporated into the cultural programmes of Olympic modules in support of colonial narratives. In this ever-growing global community, the rights of indigenous peoples are coming to the forefront of international political action (i.e.   [38]

the adoption of UN Declaration on the Rights of Indigenous Peoples in 2007 and many state apologies to indigenous peoples) and as an international body with significant global influence, it is the responsibility of the IOC—in the name of Olympism—to adopt new policies that support the rights of indigenous peoples.

Recommendations for evaluating the suitability of Olympic bids

[39]   The Olympic movement has used the medium of sport to educate the youth and the people of the world about honesty, fair play and respect for self and others, despite the fact that through such educational forums cultural imperialism continues to be advanced, cultural dependency is promoted, and sport continues to be abused in order to promote nationalism, sexism, racism and xenophobia.[36] As Lenskyj suggests, there exists, "The strong possibility of a neocolonialist agenda at work when Western sporting practices are imposed on developing countries and when recipients lack the power to negotiate and dialogue with donors."[37] In other words, basic human needs should not be pushed aside in favour of sport, the Olympics, or what Lenskyj terms, "circuses."[38]

[40]   While Olympism "seeks to create a way of life based on the joy found in effort, the educational value of good example and respect for universal fundamental ethical principles,"[39] current Olympic policies do not have adequate structures in place to uphold such virtues. As mentioned in the introduction to this work, the 2010 Vancouver Olympic Games will take place, and in the midst of national celebrations there will be indigenous protest and activism as indigenous peoples and groups attempt to "grapple" with the "legacy of the past." The Olympic industry is too powerful, and consequently, the interests of marginalized groups become lost in the fanfare of Olympic symbolism. It is for this reason that the IOC must adopt a strict process of evaluation for bid and candidate cities (and thus nations) aspiring to host the Olympic Games. As previously mentioned, The Sea to Sky Games: Vancouver 2010 Bid Book correctly followed Olympic bid procedures by outlining the political institutions of Canada. However, no one in Canada, indigenous or non-indigenous, would seriously contend that "First Nations" is a recognized and official political institution of Canada. So why is it that the IOC takes such information at face value and what prevents it from seeking out truths and realities?

[41]   The answers rest within the limitations of the Olympic Charter. As is stated at the beginning of its text, "The IOC is the supreme authority of the Olympic Movement" and "Any person or organization belonging in any capacity whatsoever to the Olympic Movement is bound by the provisions of the Olympic Charter and shall abide by the decisions of the IOC."[40] S. 37 of the Olympic Charter is dedicated to the "Election of the host city," which establishes that this process is the "prerogative of the IOC alone."[41] While there are specific guidelines in place that bid cities are required to follow (i.e. approval from a National Olympic Committee, timelines, and guarantees), there is no process or bylaw in place that allows for external (non-IOC) review of a bid or candidate city. In many regards, the IOC has relied on the United Nations (UN) to assist with sustainability and equity procedures. However, the IOC has fallen way-short of entrenching such measures within the mandate of the Olympic movement, and thus its bid and selection process.

[42]   In 1999 the IOC enacted The Olympic Movement's Agenda 21: Sport for Sustainable Development. This policy was inspired by the UN's "Agenda 21," a global action plan, which was adopted by consensus on 14 June 1992 by 182 governments represented at the UN Conference on Environment and Development (UNCED) Earth Summit in Rio de Janeiro, Brazil. With the inclusion of this global plan into its own framework, sport communities are provided with a reference tool for their respective environmental and sustainable development programmes.[42] According to this plan the Olympic Movement is dedicated to "Strengthening the Role of Major Groups," which includes the advancement of women, promoting the role of young people, and the recognition and promotion of indigenous populations.[43] In consideration of indigenous peoples, it is stated:

Indigenous populations have strong historical ties to their environment and have played an important part in its preservation. The Olympic Movement endorses the UNCED action in favour of their recognition and the strengthening of their role. In this context, it intends: to encourage their sporting traditions; to contribute to the use of their traditional knowledge and know-how in matters of environment management in order to take appropriate action, notably in the regions where these populations originate; to encourage access to sports participation these populations.[44]

[43]

While this reference appears to be vague in substance, it has placed bid, candidate and host cities in fragile positions whereby they must seriously consider establishing cordial (or at least the appearance of) working relations with local indigenous populations, or be dismissed in favour of cities/nations willing to comply with Olympic standards of environmental protection, sustainable development and the promotion of major groups. On the surface, this may be viewed as a positive initiative; however, it must not be misconstrued as having the capacity to assist the very persons or entities which it proposes to advance.

[44]

The adoption of *The Olympic Movement's Agenda 21* is deeply flawed on two levels. First, since it is not entrenched within the Olympic Charter it merely serves as an invitational guide that bid, candidate, and host nations can "take or leave." Second, and perhaps more importantly, it does not consider the basic human needs and rights of marginalized peoples. In order for the latter to be addressed, and the former to be embedded, the IOC's evaluation process for bid and candidate cities must be restructured. Accordingly, the IOC needs to make room for external consultation and evaluation of potential host cities/nations. For example, the UN has implemented various committees, including CERD and the Human Rights Committee, which have both established resolutions for evaluating internal and national treatment of marginalized groups. While the decisions and resolutions of such committees are non-binding, they operate within international philosophical norms of justice. Indigenous beliefs, and the just treatment of such populations, are becoming increasingly eminent within UN and global resolution plans. If the Olympic Movement is to prosper into the twenty-first century, then it must follow suit. For instance, an amendment to S. 37 "Election of the host Nation" of the Olympic Charter could allow for external consultation or at the very least the adoption of an evaluation process, as already developed by UN Committees. Under such an assessment process, bid and candidate cities would be identified as "suitable" or "unsuitable" as they have either succeeded or failed to meet international norms of morality. If a bid or candidate city/nation is in fact deemed suitable, then the guiding principles of a doctrine such as The Olympic Movement's Agenda 21 could sensibly be imposed as the indigenous peoples (recipients) are considered to be on fair terms with Olympic organizers (donors). Under such a process, we can begin to view Olympism as a philosophy that speaks in truisms of equity, anti-discrimination, mutual recognition and respect, tolerance and solidarity.

[45]

Prior to awarding the Games to this city/nation, there was no process in place to determine whether the recipients (i.e. indigenous peoples) held the power to negotiate with its donors (i.e. VANOC and the IOC), and whether or not they would benefit from a policy such as The Olympic Movement's Agenda 21. As it stands, indigenous programming has proven to be a clear priority for VANOC. However, this should not be misconstrued to be anything more than a reinvention of national narratives, as demonstrated in Montréal, Calgary, Sydney and Salt Lake City. A serious flaw exists within the current Olympic structure, particularly the bid process, which continues to play a part in the ongoing marginalization and exploitation of indigenous peoples. In this ever-growing global community, the rights of indigenous peoples are coming to the forefront of international political action. As an international body with significant global influence, it is the responsibility of the IOC—in the name of Olympism—to adopt new policies that support the rights and dignity of indigenous peoples. However, as history has proven itself, it would take nothing short of a World War to cancel the Olympic Games.

[46]

The Olympic Movement is a powerful industry and resistance to it is often deemed unwarranted, and at times, criminal. The Olympic Resistance Network has rallied under a public campaign calling for "No Olympics on Stolen Native Land," and its various factions have engaged in educational, resistance and activist activities to disseminate anti-colonial, anti-capitalist and anti-Olympic messages at home and abroad. However, the reality is that the 2010 Vancouver Games will take place, and in the midst of national celebration there will be indigenous protest and activism. The British Columbia land question remains unanswered, and the very presence of the current Olympic structure on contentious indigenous lands has the potential to temporarily silence, and perhaps permanently alter, the fragile state of indigenous affairs in the province.

Acknowledgements

I am extremely grateful to Adam Barker, Emma Lowman, and Cheryl Suzack for their conceptual and editorial refinement of this essay.

Notes

1. Paul Connerton, *How Societies Remember* (Cambridge: Cambridge University Press, 1989).
2. International Olympic Committee, *The Olympic Charter* (Lausanne: International Olympic Committee, 2007), 12.
3. Kevin B. Wamsley, "Laying Olympism to Rest," in *Post-Olympism? Questioning Sport in the Twentieth-First Century*, ed. John Bale and Mette Krogh Christensen (Oxford: Berg, 2004), 231.
4. Ibid.
5. "Media Guide." *Opening Ceremony of the Games of the XXVII Olympiad in Sydney, September 15, 2000*.
6. United Nations Committee on the Elimination of Racial Discrimination, "Decision on Australia."
7. Tara Magdalinski, "The Reinvention of Australia for the Sydney 2000 Olympic Games," *International Journal of the History of Sport* 17, no. 2/3 (2000): 309.
8. Helen Jefferson Lenskyj, *The Best Olympics Ever?* (Albany, NY: State University of New York Press, 2002).
9. Government of Australia, House of Representatives, "Apology to Australia's Indigenous Peoples," February 13, 2008.
10. Susan Shown Harjo, "Indians in the Opening Ceremony: Postcard from the Past," *Indian Country Today*, February 16, 2002, http://www.indiancountrytoday.com/archive/28187844.html.
11. Ibid.
12. Ibid.
13. Janice Forsyth, "Teepees and Tomahawk: Aboriginal Cultural Representation at the 1976 Olympic Games," in *The Global Nexus Engaged: Past, Present, Future Interdisciplinary Olympic Studies—Sixth International Symposium for Olympic Research*, ed. Kevin Wamsley, Robert K. Barney, and Scott G. Martyn (London, ON: The International Centre for Olympic Studies, 2002), 72.
14. Kevin B. Wamsley and Michael Heine, "'Don't Mess with the Relay—It's Bad Medicine': Aboriginal Culture and the 1998 Winter Olympics," in *Olympic Perspectives: Third International Symposium for Olympic Research*, ed. Robert K. Barney (London, ON: University of Western Ontario, Centre for Olympic Research, 1996).
15. "The Sea to Sky Games: Vancouver 2010 Bid Book," 17.

16. Taiaiake Alfred and Jeff Corntassel, "Being Indigenous: Resurgence against Contemporary Colonialism," *Government and Opposition* 4, no. 4 (2005), 597.

17. For clarification on some of the controversies surrounding the inclusion of indigenous imagery into the programme of the Olympics see, Christine M O'Bonsawin, "The Conundrum of Ilanaaq: First Nations Representation and the 2010 Vancouver Winter Olympics," in *Cultural Imperialism in Action: Critiques in the Global Olympic Trust*, ed. Nigel B. Crowther, Robert K. Barney, and Michael K. Heine (London, ON: International Centre for Olympic Studies, 2006).

18. Olympic Resistance Network, http://www.web.resist.ca/~orn/blog/?page_id=2.

19. Furthermore, the Olympic Resistance Network works in support of an international resolution that was passed by over 1,500 indigenous representatives who attended the Intercontinental Indigenous Peoples Gathering in Sonora, Mexico in October 2007. Resolution No. 2 states, "We reject the 2010 Winter Olympic on sacred and stolen territory of Turtle Island—Vancouver, Canada." Consequently, 2010 resistance efforts are working towards hosting a global anticapitalist and anti-colonial convergence from 10 February to 15 February 2010. See Olympic Resistance Network.

20. "Why We Resist 2010," No Olympics in Stolen Native Lands: Resist the 2010 Corporate Circus. http://www.no2010.com/.

21. Taiaiake Alfred, "Deconstructing the British Columbia Treaty Process," *Balayi: Culture, Law, Colonialism* 3 (2001); Hamar Foster, Heather Raven, and Jeremy Webber, eds., *Let Right Be Done: Aboriginal Title, the Calder Case and the Future of Indigenous Rights*. (Vancouver: UBC Press, 2007).

22. Hamar Foster and Alan Grove, "'Trespassers on the Soil': United States *v.* Tom and a New Perspective on the Short History of Treaty Making in Nineteenth Century British Columbia," *BC Studies* 138/139 (2003).

23. Ibid.

24 Ibid., 63.

25. Ibid.

26. Taiaiake Alfred, *Peace, Power, Righteousness: An Indigenous Manifesto* (Don Mills, ON: Oxford University Press, 1999), 120.

27. Ibid.

28. Alfred, "Deconstructing the British Columbia Treaty Process," 3.

29. Ibid.

30. Sagen v. Vancouver Organizing Committee for the 2010 Olympic and Paralympic Winter Games, Supreme Court of British Columbia, 10 July 2009: 41, 42.

31. International Olympic Committee, *The Olympic Charter*, 99.

32. *Canadian Charter of Rights and Freedoms*, Part I of the Constitution Act, 29 March 1982.

33. "2010 Olympic Security Plans Include 'Free Speech Areas,'" *CBC News*, July 2, 2009, http://www.cbc.ca/canada/british-columbia/story/2009/07/08/bc-olympic-security-plans-free-speechareas.html.

34. There are six-stages in the BCTC including Stage 1: Statement of Intent to Negotiate, Stage 2: Readiness to Negotiate, Stage 3: Negotiation of a Framework Agreement, Stage 4: Negotiation of an Agreement in Principle, Stage 5: Negotiation to Finalize a Treaty, and Stage 6: Implementation of the Treaty. Tsawwassen is the only First Nation community to reach Stage 6: Implementation of a Treaty. See "First Nations & Negotiations," BC Treaty Commission, http://www.bctreaty.net/.

35. Adam Barker, Christine O'Bonsawin, and Chiinuuks Ogilvie, "Business as Usual? Reflections on the BC Treaty Process," *New Socialist* 65, no. 1 (2009), 26.

36. Helen Jefferson Lenskyj, *Olympic Industry Resistance: Challenging Olympic Power and Propaganda* (Albany, NY: State University of New York Press, 2007).
37. Lenskyj paraphrases from Giulianotti, "Human Rights." See Lenskyj, *Olympic Industry Resistance*, 82.
38. Lenskyj, *Olympic Industry Resistance*.
39. International Olympic Committee, *The Olympic Charter*, 12.
40. Ibid., 11. In force as from 4 July 2003.
41. Ibid., 62.
42. This plan of action builds upon proposals put forth in the Rio Declaration on Environment and Development, and is considered to be a theoretical and practical tool for addressing problems of sustainable development concerning "social and economic dimensions," "the conservation and management of resources for development," "strengthening the role of major groups," and offers a "means of implementation." See United Nations Department of Economic and Social Affairs—Divisions for Sustainable Development, "Agenda 21," 14 June 1992.
43. International Olympic Committee, *The Olympic Movement's Agenda 21*, 42–5.
44. Ibid., 45.

Bibliography

Alfred, Taiaiake. *Peace, Power, Righteousness: An Indigenous Manifesto*. Don Mills, ON: Oxford University Press, 1999.

Alfred, Taiaiake. "Deconstructing the British Columbia Treaty Process." *Balayi: Culture, Law, Colonialism* 3 (2001): 37–65.

Alfred, Taiaiake, and Jeff Corntassel. "Being Indigenous: Resurgence against Contemporary Colonialism." *Government and Opposition* 4, no. 4 (September 2005): 597–614.

Barker, Adam, Christine O'Bonsawin, and Chiinuuks Ogilvie. "Business as Usual? Reflections on the BC Treaty Process." *New Socialist* 65, no. 1 (2009): 24–6.

Connerton, Paul. *How Societies Remember*. Cambridge: Cambridge University Press, 1989.

Forsyth, Janice. "Teepees and Tomahawks: Aboriginal Cultural Representation at the 1976 Olympic Games." In *The Global Nexus Engaged: Past, Present, Future Interdisciplinary Olympic Studies—Sixth International Symposium for Olympic Research*, edited by Kevin Wamsley, Robert K. Barney, and Scott G. Martyn, 71–5. London, ON: The International Centre for Olympic Studies, 2002.

Foster, Hamar, and Alan Grove. "'Trespassers on the Soil': United States *v.* Tom and a New Perspective on the Short History of Treaty Making in Nineteenth Century British Columbia." *BC Studies* 138/139 (2003): 51–84.

Foster, Hamar, Heather Raven and Jeremy Webber eds. *Let Right Be Done: Aboriginal Title, the Calder Case and the Future of Indigenous Rights*. Vancouver: UBC Press, 2007.

Giulianotti, R. "Human Rights, Globalization and Sentimental Education: The Case of Sport." *Sport in Society* 7, no. 3 (2004): 355–69.

International Olympic Committee. *The Olympic Movement's Agenda 21: Sport for Sustainable Development*. Lausanne: International Olympic Committee, 1999.

International Olympic Committee. *The Olympic Charter*. Lausanne: International Olympic Committee, 2007.

Lenskyj, Helen Jefferson. *The Best Olympics Ever?* Albany, NY: State University of New York Press, 2002.

Lenskyj, Helen Jefferson. *Olympic Industry Resistance: Challenging Olympic Power and Propaganda.* Albany, NY: State University of New York Press, 2007.

Magdalinski, Tara. "The Reinvention of Australia for the Sydney 2000 Olympic Games." *International Journal of the History of Sport* 17, no. 2/3 (June 2000): 305–22.

No Olympics on Stolen Native Land. "Resist the 2010 Corporate Circus." http://www.no2010.com/node/19.

O'Bonsawin, Christine M. "The Conundrum of Ilanaaq: First Nations Representation and the 2010 Vancouver Winter Olympics." In *Cultural Imperialism in Action: Critiques in the Global Olympic Trust*, edited by Nigel B. Crowther, Robert K. Barney, and Michael K. Heine, 387–94.London, ON: International Centre for Olympic Studies, 2006.

"The Sea to Sky Games: Vancouver 2010 Bid Book." VANOC, 2002.

United Nations Committee on the Elimination of Racial Discrimination. "Decision on Australia." Session (54) of 18 March 1999 and Session (55) of 19 August 1999.

Wamsley, Kevin B. "Laying Olympism to Rest." In *Post-Olympism? Questioning Sport in the Twentieth-First Century*, edited by John Bale and Mette Krogh Christensen, 231–42. Oxford: Berg, 2004.

Wamsley, Kevin B., and Michael Heine. "'Don't Mess with the Relay—It's Bad Medicine' Aboriginal Culture and the 1998 Winter Olympics." In *Olympic Perspectives: Third International Symposium for Olympic Research*, edited by Robert K. Barney, 173–98. London, ON: University of Western Ontario, Centre for Olympic Research, 1996.

"Why We Resist 2010." No Olympics in Stolen Native Lands: Resist the 2010 Corporate Circus. http://www.no2010.com/.

Questions to Consider

1. Paraphrase one of the three stated purposes of O'Bonsawin's essay in paragraph 2; paraphrase the last sentence of the paragraph.

2. Briefly explain the connections between "Olympic principles," "Olympism," and the "modern Olympic Games." Why is it important to introduce these concepts early in the essay?

3. In your own words, explain the "paradox" of the Olympic Games, according to the writer.

4. Focusing on the description of one of the previous (pre-2010) Games, show how the author makes it relevant to the 2010 Games. Cite specific evidence.

5. Identify an example of a primary source in the first section.

6. Analyze the writer's effectiveness in dealing with BC's land question, which she acknowledges is "a complex legal issue . . . [arising] from a multifaceted political history between indigenous and settler populations" (paragraph 26). You could consider the structure of this section (paragraphs 23–38), strategies for comprehension, voice (i.e., objectivity), or other factors.

7. What kind of evidence seems most important in this essay? Analyze one specific example of this kind of evidence, explaining why it is important to the point the writer is making in the paragraph. Briefly consider its importance to the essay as a whole.

8. Explain the importance of the UN's "Agenda 21" and the way it could serve as a model for the IOC.

9. Summarize two recommendations of the author in the last section.
10. Analyze the rhetorical effectiveness of the last paragraph. What kind of appeal does the writer make? Is it successful?

Collaborative Discussion

1. To what extent do you believe the IOC has or should have the responsibility to support indigenous populations?
2. To what extent do you believe that new IOC policies could actually effect change in the way indigenous groups are perceived or treated?

The Literary Essay

General Features of Literary Essays

In today's diverse literature classes, you might study poems, short stories, plays, novels, biographies, autobiographies, journals, diaries, songs, myths, or movies. The close relationship between the works you study and your writing is a defining feature of literature classes.

Although the literary essay has unique characteristics, it has features in common with other kinds of essays you have written or will write. In its structure, the literary essay is like an argumentative or expository essay. It begins with an introduction that contains a thesis statement directly related to the works you are analyzing; it includes several well-developed body paragraphs and ends by summarizing your main points and reiterating your thesis. Attention to grammar, punctuation, and mechanics is important. You will also need to pay close attention to diction (word choice), syntax (word order), and sentence structure. In sum, you will need to give as much thought to clarity, coherence, and concision as you do with other essays.

A literary essay argues for the validity of a claim. You need to adopt a specific viewpoint on the works you analyze and express this in your thesis statement. The claim you make is not one of fact, policy, or value (unless you are evaluating a work as you would in a book report); rather, it is one of interpretation. In the body paragraphs, much of the supporting evidence for your claim comes from the primary texts you are analyzing. You may support your points also through researching the authorities on your text, i.e., through secondary sources.

Literature as a Unique Encounter

In responding to a literary work, you acknowledge a long-established tradition, a kind of tacit agreement between writer and reader: in accepting the conventions of literature, we "willingly suspend our disbelief"—in other words, we collectively agree to consider the work as "real" or "factual," to treat the events that occur in a novel, play, or poem as something that *could have really occurred* to us or people like us. Although poet Samuel Taylor Coleridge applied the phrase "willing suspension of disbelief" in 1817 to his own poetry, it is often used to help explain the process whereby we become receptive to art and allow it to work on us.

In literature, you respond to feelings evoked by a poem, to the thoughts or behaviour of a character in a novel or play, or to a defining moment in the life of a character in a short story. Literature inevitably deals both specifically and generally with human experience. When you respond to a literary work, you find yourself particularizing, exploring what is unique about a character, situation, or feeling, as well as universalizing and synthesizing—making meaning and creating significance. When you write an essay about the work, you, too, focus both on the particular and specific, as well as on the universal qualities of the work.

American poet Emily Dickinson once described the experience of reading good poetry: "If I feel physically as if the top of my head were taken off, I know *that* is poetry." Similarly, fiction writer Vladimir Nabokov said that he feels the appeal of fiction as a "tingling at the top of the spine." Responding to good literature often seems akin to a physical experience, as though you were at the mercy of two gravitational forces, one pulling you towards the familiar and the specific, the other tugging you insistently in the opposite direction, towards the unfamiliar and the abstract or universal.

It often happens that both impulses intensify as you read and reread the work. As many assignments in literature classes ask you to focus on a work's theme, it helps if you can keep the "universal" experience in mind even as you are drawn towards specific images, characters, settings, and situations.

Many of the challenges of writing about literature are related to the practices and procedures of literary analysis. Unless you are writing a personal response to a work, you need to be familiar with the terminology used in analyzing literature. As with other disciplines, a vocabulary and a methodology have developed over the years enabling those who analyze literary texts to converse in a specialized—though certainly not a privileged—linguistic environment.

Unlike students studying disciplines like psychology, anthropology, or women's studies for the first time, however, many students of literature are already acquainted with the rudiments of this vocabulary and with the essential practices of literary interpretation through English courses in high school or, perhaps, through discussions with family or friends of stories, poems, or novels. Many students are also familiar with current movies, which, of course, have plots, settings, characters, and themes similar to those of literary texts: thus, most students are more prepared to read and analyze literary texts than they realize.

Although literary essays often require you to focus on literary devices and techniques, you have likely already served part of your apprenticeship—through your understanding of the "comfort categories" of plot, setting, theme, and character in fiction or through your discussion of movies or television shows. For most students, then, it is not so much a question of learning a new category of discourse than of expanding and refining what you already know to adapt to the more sophisticated analyses you will do at the post-secondary level.

> You should refer to a work's meaning or its **theme**, rather than its *message*. Literary works seldom are written just to communicate a message.

Kinds of Literary Essays

Although the kinds of assignments will vary considerably from instructor to instructor, you can divide literary essays into three types: response, evaluation of a work, and literary or critical analysis.

Response

A "response," such as a journal entry, is concerned with your personal or "gut" reaction to a work: the ways it affects you or makes you feel, or the ways it leads you to reflect on your own attitudes, values, or life experiences. You could be asked to keep a record of your responses to various works you study throughout the term. Although such assignments may not be required, they can still be worthwhile. When you have to choose a topic to write on, looking back at your personal responses can remind you what you enjoyed most—where your interests lie—and perhaps provide a starting point for a more complex analysis.

For example, a student responded to a poem about an elderly woman knitting ("Aunt Jennifer's Tigers," by Adrienne Rich) by recalling his feelings about his grandmother, and the security and comfort he felt around her. When he came to analyze the poem for an assignment, the student returned to the journal entry and, recalling the feeling that the poem evoked, began to explore its ironies and complexities, taking him far beyond his first response to develop a thesis statement related to the deceptions of appearance in a patriarchal society.

Evaluation

Although evaluations often have a subjective element, they should use primarily objective criteria to judge the quality of a work. Because a successful evaluation is based largely on *informed* opinion, it is necessary to support the claims you make about the work's worth or relevance. This can be done by referring directly to the work as well as by basing your comments on accepted standards for assessing a work's achievement, such as plausibility, quality of writing, originality, or universal appeal. In an evaluation, the focus is on the work's meaning and its significance to the reader. It attempts to answer the questions, "What is the importance of this book?"; "How is it like or unlike other works?"; and "Should I recommend this work?" In answering these questions, you may be concerned more with the "what" than with the "how." An evaluation is usually shorter than an analysis and deals less with technique. The most common form of an evaluative essay is a book report or review.

While a response implies a personalized and subjective engagement with the work, an evaluation is typically written for many readers. Because successful evaluations may tread a fine line between opinion and analysis, they are useful for bridging the gap between personal responses and the highly objective literary analysis.

Literary or Critical Analysis

Because an analysis is objective, you should not use quantitative words like *great* and *amazing*; in most analyses, you avoid first-person references: *I believe . . . , I will show . . . , it seems to me . . . .*

While an evaluation is designed for people who haven't read the work, in a critical analysis you are writing for a more knowledgeable reader. A critical analysis focuses more on the author's technique, on the strategies and methods he or she used to create the work. It might seek to show how figurative language contributes to the interpretation of a work, how imagery helps set a work's mood, or how the first-person voice enables us to identify with the narrator. Typically, the aim of an analysis is to support a claim about the work's theme. Like an evaluation, then, a critical analysis comes to focus on theme, but it gets there via a more complex route, potentially giving us a more technical, multi-layered reading of the work.

Research

You can think of the literary research essay as a literary analysis in which you support your thesis statement in part by citing what others have said about the work. In a literary research essay, you will try to use relevant reviews, commentaries, articles, and books—sources that analyze the same work you are analyzing and whose approaches are similar to your own. You may also consider approaches that are different from yours in order to broaden your own approach or argue against these approaches. As in any essay involving research, your concern is to integrate your own ideas and language with the ideas and language of others (see pages 165–170).

Text-Centred and Context-Centred Approaches

Two of the most common approaches to a literary analysis are text-centred and context-centred approaches.

> A *text-centred approach* is focused on the text itself. It usually involves a close, detailed reading of the work, treating it as a self-sufficient entity. This approach could explore a work's structure and how the parts function separately yet unite to form a whole, or it could isolate one or more passages and analyze the writer's techniques, relating them to a specific claim about the work.

> A *context-centred approach* pays careful attention to the text but views the work within an established context of some kind: historical, biographical, ideological/political, aesthetic, sociological, cultural, psychological, feminist, mythic, or sources-based. This approach could also refer to a theory and analyze the work within that framework. Although a text-centred approach may or may not need to be bolstered by secondary sources, it is likely that a context-centred approach will refer to important works in the field.

The text-centred and the context-centred approaches are discussed in more detail below. The three complete essays in this section illustrate these different approaches: the essay on "Stopping by Woods on a Snowy Evening" (Reading 20, page 284) and the student essay on "Metamorphosis" (Reading 21, page 292) illustrate the former; the student essay on "The Yellow Wallpaper" and "My Papa's Waltz" (Reading 22, page 309) is a research paper that combines text- and context-centred approaches.

> *Reading* is a term that can refer to the cognitive act of processing words (the familiar sense of reading a book) or to the more deeply intellectual process of understanding a literary work's meaning through *analysis* (which means a "breaking up" or "loosening"). *Reading*, then, is an activity. *A reading* is an *interpretation* of a work as a result of reading and analyzing it.

A Closer Look

Evaluating a Student Essay

Take a moment to consider the following statements:

"There aren't really any objective criteria for grading a literary essay!"

☐ True
☐ False

"I can say whatever I want as long as I back it up!"

☐ True
☐ False

"There seems to be one reading of a work—and it's the prof's!"

☐ True
☐ False

For the most part, instructors do arrive at grades using objective standards, even if these standards aren't always comparable to those in disciplines where there are clearly right or wrong answers: some readings are better or more complete than others. Although the grading of an English essay is not as straightforward as in many other disciplines, it doesn't follow that standards don't exist. Three standards that pertain to your use of primary texts are discussed at the end of this section, The 3 C's of Criticism; or, How *Not* to Get a C on Your Essay.

It is essential that you support your points by referring directly to the literary work itself, but that doesn't mean that simply referring to a passage provides that support. You need to ensure that you have used the text logically and effectively. The *way* you back up your points is more important than the simple fact that you refer to the text. In other words, by making a point and then directing the reader to a specific passage *in itself* is not sufficient; quotations should not simply be sprinkled across the page. You must show the reader that your reference is *representative* and *relevant*.

Representative and relevant references clearly illustrate the point you are trying to make. In the first example below, the writer has not provided a strong enough context for the quotation; it is not representative. In the second, the quotation does not bear out the claim the writer makes for it; it is not relevant.

In Dickinson's "Because I could not stop for Death," adulthood is depicted in the line, "The Dews drew quivering and chill."

The statement needs elaboration. When you use a direct quotation to support a point, ask "How?", "Why?", or "What?" For example, you could ask "*How* does the line depict adulthood?" or "*Why* is this important to the theme of the poem?"

Revised: In Dickinson's "Because I could not stop for Death," the poet's metaphor for life is a carriage ride that passes through childhood and middle age before arriving, after the sunset of life, at an age in adulthood where the falling of the dew is experienced: "The Dews drew quivering and chill."

The writer could then consider Dickinson's unusual choice of words "drew quivering," asking, perhaps, why these words are important, what effect they have on the reader, or how they relate to the work's theme.

The second quotation below, intended to illustrate the narrator's obsession, reveals only her weariness:

The longer that the narrator is confined to the room, the more obsessed with the yellow wallpaper she becomes: "It makes me tired to follow [the pattern]."

How does the quotation relate to the narrator's obsession? *What* does it show about the narrator or her situation in the isolated room? This version is more revealing:

Revised: The longer that the narrator is confined to the room, the more obsessed with the yellow wallpaper she becomes: "It dwells in my mind so."

A work's meaning is a function of the complex interplay of many factors. Unlike a didactic work (one with a clear message), literary works do not always have a fixed, determinate meaning; instead, they may offer numerous, but certainly *not limitless*, possible readings.

The 3 C's of Criticism; or, How *Not* to Get a C on Your Essay

The best readings of a work are those that demonstrate coherence, consistency, and complexity, using the tools you are given to analyze works of literature.

- *Coherence*: the reading makes sense; the points are clearly made, are well expressed, and can be easily followed by a reader.
- *Consistency*: the reading contains no apparent contradictions nor is one aspect of the whole given much greater prominence at the expense of other equally important elements; it takes into account the entire work. Even a close analysis of a specific passage should be related to the work as a whole.
- *Complexity*: the reading is not superficial or simplistic but is detailed and multi-dimensional, given the guidelines prescribed by your instructor, such as those of word length.

These three factors pertain to your reading and handling of the primary work. Obviously, other factors have a bearing on your grade, such as whether you wrote on topic or strayed from it, or whether you gave equal space to all the texts you used; originality may also be important. Furthermore, paragraphing, grammar, punctuation, sentence structure, appropriate level of language, and mechanics of form and presentation are significant factors, as they are in all essays you write. If you used research in your essay, your effective use of secondary sources and correct documentation methods also is crucial.

On the Road to the Rough Draft

Although there are many ways to proceed to explore the meaning of a literary work, having some guiding principles in mind can be useful. What follows is a step-by-step approach to analysis, but you can go about the steps in any order you wish or omit certain steps.

You may be assigned a specific topic to write on, you may be given a list of topics from which to choose, or you could be asked to come up with a topic based on classroom lectures, class or group discussions, or your own interests. Outlined below are some of the steps to follow to begin and develop a literary research essay.

Method for Developing an Outline or Draft

1. *Read and re-read* the work without preconceptions.
2. *Commit your thoughts and feelings to writing* if necessary to give you confidence when it comes to the more formal stages of the analysis. If you have been keeping a response journal, review it and supplement it with fresh perceptions or expand on what you wrote earlier.

3. *Consolidate your impressions of the work.* Ask the kind of questions referred to in the How to Approach a Poem/Fiction/Drama sections that follow to help you formulate a tentative thesis statement. If you don't think you have firmly grasped the content of the work, try paraphrasing or summarizing it. In novels, plays, long poems, and even short stories, you might construct a section-by-section, chapter-by-chapter, or scene-by-scene breakdown, clarifying precisely what happens to whom when and where. This can also help you locate important textual references later on.

4. *Briefly consider information about the author*: the age he or she lived in; his or her nationality, philosophy, beliefs; and other works he or she has written. Review your class notes about the writer and the works. Briefly review some commentary—even article titles can be useful—or peruse online discussion groups to consider how others have approached the work. In doing this, you are seeing "what's out there," not necessarily gathering material for your essay.

5. *Remember that your task as a student writer is not to say everything you know* or that might be said by an expert about a text, or to consider every important detail. *Selection* is expected. Therefore, try to focus on *one or a few important areas*—for example, structure, point of view, imagery, tone, mood, symbolism—whichever seem important. As you proceed to analyze, you may find yourself exploring more of these areas, but, for now, choosing one or two areas can help you focus on a possible thesis statement.

6. *Make connections and find patterns to formulate a thesis statement.* Connections and patterns in a work of poetry, drama, or literary prose guide you toward a reading that is coherent, consistent, and complex. Literary conventions, such as structure and organization, imagery, poetic devices, locales and settings, points of view, treatments of historical connections, consciousness of philosophical issues, to mention a few, suggest many patterns through which a work can be explored. Thus, analyzing a work means explaining its connections and patterns in terms of the specific literary conventions.

    For example, if you find a striking image in a work, see if you can find similar images; once you find a *pattern* of such images, describe the connections that can be made to larger features of the work, such as characters, structure, or point of view. Now you are well on your way to explaining the patterns of these images in terms of the work as a whole. Next, you should be able to write a tentative sentence or two that includes the main point or theme of the work and connect it to your topic.

7. Although your personal response might have been important in your early reading and thinking about a work, it is now time to step back, to *make the transition from personal feelings and associations to objective, critical analysis.*

8. *Do your research.*

    a) Decide on a method of organized note-taking. See Chapter 6, Research Note-taking, page 149 for help with research note-taking.

    b) Don't worry too much if your language isn't keeping pace with your ideas at this point. Finding the right words, or even the best *terminology*, for critical analysis is less important than getting your ideas down. Precise, correct word choice, style, and grammar can follow. It is important, though, that you record examples and page references as you write.

Move from the general to the specific; moving back and forth as required, from concept to detail, from the large-scale to the small-scale, and from general claims to textual references, may strengthen and support your points and help you weave the wording of your outline or first draft.

9. Continually test your points against your thesis. Work towards expanding points that support and enhance your thesis, but don't necessarily discard valid and important points that don't directly support your thesis, which may be flexible enough for you to amend or expand it.

Technique is the means by which the poet, the dramatist, or the fiction writer expresses his or her artistic vision. Therefore, in your analysis you might consider the kinds of devices the writer has used. The technical aspects of the text you are analyzing will vary according to

> the genre you are analyzing—for example, a poem *may* (but will not always) rely more on stylistic and figurative devices than other genres do; fiction writers rely on specific structural devices and narrative techniques

> the formal properties or conventions of a tradition to which the work belongs (sonnet, elegy, ode, or initiation story, for example). Texts within a tradition can be explored in part through the conventions of that tradition, which the author may follow closely, disrupt, or adapt to suit his or her purposes.

> the topic you have been given; you may be required to write on imagery, setting, point of view, or dramatic structure.

10. You may now have enough information to begin constructing an essay outline or a first draft. Since much of your support likely will come from the primary work itself, sometimes just a scratch outline with page numbers from the literary work beside your main points is all the structure you need, though a formal outline is usually helpful (see Chapter 2, Formal Outline, page 44).

When You Write about Literature

1. Avoid telling what happens in the work; assume your reader knows the work and has read it recently. Give as much information about plot, character, and setting as necessary to provide an adequate context for the point you are making. A summary is not the same thing as an analysis; summarizing too much wastes space.

2. When you refer to the text, *use the present tense* to describe action and character; this is known as the **literary present**. This convention applies generally to the arts. For example, if you were looking at Leonardo DaVinci's *Mona Lisa*, you would say that she *has* an enigmatic smile on her face; of course, you would say that the actual model for the painting *had* an enigmatic smile. Although a literary or artistic work is considered timeless, the author *lived and wrote* at a specific time. In the following passage, from a student essay on Ted Hughes's poem "Hawk Roosting," the verbs have been italicized to illustrate how the literary present is

used to represent the actions in the poem and their textual significance. In the last two sentences, Darcy Smith uses the past tense to depict actions in the past outside of the poem.

> The hawk's flight "direct / Through the bones of the living" *is* a particularly sinister image, reinforcing the hawk's vision that he *controls* all life. All these images *project* a sense of divine, or more likely demonic, power. The imagery in the last stanza *suggests* how the hawk's egotism *represents* human nature. In the first line of this stanza, the hawk *observes* "The sun is behind me." The sun *was considered* a god by many ancient civilizations. Ancient Egyptian pharaohs, for instance, *claimed* their divine right to rule *originated* in being descended from the sun.

3.   Use the present tense, also, to refer to the words of critics: "Levin *claims* . . . ."

Theory into Practice: A Sample Poetry Analysis

Robert Frost's poem "Stopping by Woods on a Snowy Evening" is often included in poetry anthologies. You may want to look at "How to Approach a Poem" on page 286 before reading the analysis here.

Assignment

The *assignment* was to write a 500 to 700–word textual analysis of "Stopping by Woods on a Snowy Evening." A textual analysis focuses largely on the text itself, paying attention to the poet's technique and the relations between techniques and theme.

Stopping by Woods on a Snowy Evening
by Robert Frost

	Metre	Rhyme Scheme
Whose woods these are I think I know.	´ ˇ ´ ˇ ´ ˇ ´ ˇ	a
His house is in the village though;	ˇ ´ ˇ ´ ˇ ´ ˇ ´	a
He will not see me stopping here	ˇ ´ ˇ ´ ˇ ´ ˇ ´	b
To watch his woods fill up with snow.	ˇ ´ ˇ ´ ˇ ´ ˇ ´	a

My little horse must think it queer
To stop without a farmhouse near
Between the woods and frozen lake
The darkest evening of the year.

He gives his harness bells a shake
To ask if there is some mistake.
The only other sound's the sweep
Of easy wind and downy flake.

The woods are lovely, dark and deep.
But I have promises to keep,
And miles to go before I sleep,
And miles to go before I sleep.

Preliminary Considerations

"Stopping by Woods on a Snowy Evening" presents particular challenges to the student writer: its simplicity is deceptive. When you read it over (especially if aloud), you might find its simplicity appealing, its regularity captivating, or you might find it a puzzling poem and wonder how you will be able to write enough words about it. You could begin by asking questions about the poem, first to record your impressions and then to consolidate them, to discover patterns from which you can formulate a tentative thesis statement.

> ❯ *What first strikes you about the poem?* Perhaps its regularity strikes you. The structure of the poem consists of three four-line stanzas each with an identical rhyme scheme and a fourth stanza with identical end-rhymes. In creating the poem, the poet has imposed a strict formal pattern on the poem: stanza length, rhyme, and metre are regular and predictable.
>
> ❯ *What actually is happening in the poem?* Remarkably little is occurring. Surprisingly, there is as much about the poet's horse as there is about the poet himself, who seems lost in his thoughts, having fallen into a kind of trance as he looks into the woods. The poet is portraying an everyday kind of experience. Its ordinariness is noteworthy, though. Most readers at one time or another will have experienced a similar feeling to the poet's: being momentarily arrested by a strong, perhaps undefined or untranslatable feeling on their way somewhere or while performing some worldly task. This might be a good place to begin exploring the poem.

If you chose to begin your analysis this way, your notes about the poem might attempt to connect the experience that the poem's speaker is describing with similar experiences you've had. It might be useful to write down associations with daydreaming or perhaps to freewrite on the topic.

What one main area should you focus on? Rather than being overwhelmed by possibilities at this stage, you should try to narrow your focus. In the poem, an act of contemplation seems important. Since contemplative thought may involve a mood, one area to explore might be the mood the poem evokes. Mood can be defined as the predominant tone of the poem created by the poet's language or approach to character and/or setting. To develop this theme, you might want to focus on the way that language and setting combine to evoke a solemn mood. Remember, you can always return to the thesis statement and refine it later—or even radically change it if you need to.

Consider this tentative thesis statement: "The speaker draws the reader into the poem by creating, through simple rhythms, diction, and the device of repetition, a familiar mood of solemnity while contemplating something mysterious or enticing." This probably wouldn't serve as the final version of a thesis statement; for one thing, it doesn't explain why mood is important or how the mood of the poem contributes to meaning, so it would probably fail the tests of consistency and complexity. But it does identify important elements that you can expand on. It specifies mood, setting, and three technical devices: rhythm, diction, and repetition.

Here are some rough notes about the poem. In the final version that follows, you can see that the writer hasn't used all the points, but has applied the principle of selection, using those points that seem most suitable in supporting the thesis statement.

Stanza 1:

- metre is perfectly regular: there are four iambs (metrical unit with one unstressed followed by a stressed syllable) in each line, making it iambic tetrameter. The rhyming scheme is, likewise, quite regular: aaba bbcb ccdc dddd. Diction: simple words: mostly one-syllable words and a few two-syllable ones
- "His house," "his woods": repetition suggests importance of ownership; "He will not see me stopping here": would not approve?
- sets up opposition between woods and the house in the village: do the woods really "belong" to the man in the village? Nature vs. civilization? Narrator vs. owner?

Stanza 2:

- horse seems to think speaker's behaviour is unusual, not his customary habit to stop like this; he is a man of routine or business, perhaps—horses, too, are creatures of habit, under control of humans: a *work* horse? Action vs. thought?
- setting is particularized: "*between* the woods and the frozen lake": alternatives?
- time is particularized: significance of "darkest evening of the year": winter solstice; the word "dark" recurs in final stanza; but in contrast to the "dark" is the snow: whiteness

Stanza 3:

- "harness" suggests captivity, containment: "bells" suggest celebration: Christmas?
- speaker attributes human qualities to the horse: "thinking" (l. 5), "asking" (l. 10): personification
- the sound of the shaking bells contrasts with the "only other" sound, that of the wind
- "easy" suggests the easy way, the simplest choice? It is easy to give way to what you desire, not so easy to give way to what you *must* do
- "downy" conveys softness, comfort, like a pillow: you don't usually think of wind as "easy," and snowflakes are in reality cold, ice crystals

Stanza 4:

- line 13 contains two repeated words: "woods" and "dark"; besides being "dark," the woods are "lovely" (appealing? tempting?) and "deep"; these words suggest seduction, being drawn towards something potentially dangerous and deceptive; or is he in fact being drawn towards something beautiful, profound, and truthful? Alternatives again! "Lovely" is used abstractly—why are they "lovely?" Is it because they are "dark and deep" or for some additional reason not specified? "Deep" and "dark" are likewise not very specific: deep as what? Dark as what? In what sense is "dark" also "lovely" and "deep" also lovely?

- the speaker abruptly reminds himself that he has "promises to keep": what kind of promises and to whom? to what?
- literally, he has distance to travel before he can sleep; sleep can refer to literal sleep (when the journey is done) or perhaps to death—the end of life's journey?
- why does the speaker repeat the last line? Is he confidently and securely repeating what must be done (reinforcing its importance and his choice) or does the repeated line further the idea of a kind of spell or enchantment that he can't break away from? This seemingly simple poem poses alternatives and tensions throughout!

These notes suggest that the poem is built not just on regularity but also on contrasts, on *oppositions between two worlds*. In the essay itself, the writer stressed both these elements but decided that one is more important than the other. This analysis, of course, is far from the only one possible; nevertheless, it is well-supported by the text and is coherent, consistent, and complex, within the 500 to 700–word requirement.

Sample Student Essay

Reading 20

Mystery or Mastery? Robert Frost's "Stopping by Woods on a Snowy Evening"
By Kaja Vessey

[1] Though most of us prefer a planned and orderly life, we may at times surrender to a spontaneous impulse. The first-person narrator of Robert Frost's "Stopping by Woods on a Snowy Evening" yields to such an impulse, stopping by woods to "watch [them] fill up with snow" and falling deeper into their mystery—or, some would say, their mastery. Similarly, the poet draws the reader into the poem by creating a familiar mood of solemn contemplation, using simple diction and basic rhythms.

[2] By constructing a seemingly straightforward poem that employs a regular iambic tetrameter metre with a relatively predictable rhyming scheme of aaba bbcb ccdc dddd, the poet stresses the ordinariness of his experience. Despite this ordinariness, the poem relies on tensions or oppositions to suggest how our perception can at times transcend the ordinary. However, in the end, the poem's regularity affirms a commitment to worldly routine: although the woods hold a mysterious temptation, "lovely, dark and deep," they do not hold mastery, "But I have promises to keep . . . ."

[3] One of the tensions configured by the poem is between the village, representing civilization, and nature. In the first stanza, the poet tentatively identifies the owner of the woods, but since the man lives at some distance, he will not see the poet "stopping here / To watch his woods fill up with snow." Already, a tension is established between the private world of the poet, who has access to nature, and the public world of ownership or business, which separates even the owner from his legacy in nature. Even the horse seems part of the world the poet has

left behind. The horse "thinks" his stopping is "queer" and "ask[s] if there is some mistake." The poet hears the harness bells shaking, but the impatient call to routine is opposed by the subtler sound, "the sweep / Of easy wind and downy flake." The adjectives "easy" and "downy" could convey comfort, relaxation, sleep—the "easy" succumbing to his tranquil feeling; or the lure of the woods could suggest a treachery in nature, the temptation to drop his responsibilities and simply give himself up to sleep, and inevitable death through exposure to cold, in the winter woods at night.

End rhyme also supports the idea of being drawn to the woods: in stanzas one to three, the rhyme in the third line is picked up in the stanza that immediately follows, creating a hypnotic effect. But as the poet falls deeper under the spell of the woods, he abruptly recalls he has "promises to keep." What are these promises? The "darkest evening" might refer to the winter solstice, and the image of the shaking bells suggests it is near Christmas. Are his "promises" connected to religious or familial duties? Perhaps he is facing some other darkness, a disappointing relationship, awareness of advancing age, sorrow, or pain associated with a loved one.   [4]

The repetition of lines 15 and 16 could suggest the progressive intensifying of the spell; more likely, though, they consciously reassert his need to complete the journey and fulfill his obligations. The poem's regular structure, rhyme, and metre, along with simple diction, suggest that he remains committed to his routines even while he is lured by the woods. Like most people, worldly responsibilities restrain him from falling under the power of an undefined impulse; his deeper commitment, like ours, is to duty to the world he knows. As he continues his physical journey and reaches his goal, he may well recall his "stopping by woods" much more than the journey. Our breaks from routine are usually more memorable than the routine itself.   [5]

The Literary Genres: Poetry, the Short Story, the Novel, and Drama

The practice of classifying literary works by their shared characteristics is a flexible system originating with Aristotle. The **genres** of literature include poetry, drama, the novel, the short story, and nonfiction prose (essays). Smaller divisions, or subgenres, are sometimes made—a short story might be classified as myth, fairy tale, fantasy, mystery, western, horror, or science fiction, each of which might be further subdivided.

Much of what has been discussed to this point relates to what the genres of literary writing have in common. The sections on poetry, fiction (the short story and the novel), and drama that follow focus on the unique characteristics of each and some of the challenges each presents to the student researcher and writer. Various ways to approach your reading and study of each genre are discussed.

Most of us are more familiar with the conventions of prose than of poetry; after all, we use prose to communicate every day. However, we may not be able to identify the conventions we are using when we write in prose or may not recognize that in analyzing literary prose we are using many of the conventions of everyday writing. Learning to analyze literary prose means that you can use the conventions *more consciously*. The awareness of conventions and special techniques applies perhaps more to the analysis of poetry, which typically is more formal and compressed than prose and usually makes greater use of stylistic and figurative devices.

How to Approach a Poem

Approach a poem, if you can, without preconceptions or expectations; read it in spite of what you know *about* it or have been taught to look for *in* it. Read it as if you are the first person to discover it, to engage with it, to catch its moods, its vagaries—to sound its depths. Two approaches, the text-centred approach and the context-centred approach, apply to all the literary genres, so much of the information below is general, even though it is discussed in the context of poetry.

Text-Centred Approach: The "Inside-Out" Approach

The text-centred approach limits itself to the wide range of writing strategies and poetic devices available to the poet. Because it explores the connections between the formal elements of a work and its meaning, it is called the **formalist** method. Following are some strategies that you as a reader and writer can apply to analyze the poem "from the inside out."

> ❯ *Look at the poem's structure.* **Structure** refers to the arrangement of parts, to the way they work independently yet contribute to the whole. Is the poem divided into parts? How is it put together? Are there distinct divisions? What are their functions? Do the parts suggest contrast? Do they suggest a movement or progression of some kind? Do they parallel one another?
>
> Many poems are divided into **stanzas**, units of two or more lines that often share metre, rhyme scheme, etc. Within these units there can be smaller but significant structures such as **parallelism** (simple repetition or "echoing") or **juxtaposition** (words or images placed beside others for effect). **Anaphora** (repetition of words or phrases at the beginning of lines or clauses) and **chiasmus** (inversion in the second of two parallel phrases of the order followed in the first) are specific kinds of parallelism. Examples of smaller structural elements in lines of poetry are the **caesura**, a pause in the middle of a line, and **enjambment**, in which the sense of one line runs into the next one, rather than being **end-stopped** (having a logical and syntactic stop at the end of a line).
>
> ❯ *Listen to the poem.* You discern speaker and voice by listening to what is *between* the lines (see below); you determine sound patterns by looking at and hearing the *lines themselves*. Read the lines aloud. What kind of **rhythm** do they have? Is it regular, with repeated units recurring at predictable intervals? If so, can you characterize the poem's **metre**? **Scansion** is the reading of a line of poetry to determine the pattern of stressed and unstressed syllables. Are there departures from a regular metre? If so, what purpose might they serve?
>
> If the poet uses **rhyme**, where are the rhymes? At the end of each line? Are they ever in the middle of a line (**internal rhyme**)? Do the words rhyme exactly, or do they just sound similar with identical vowel or consonant sounds on the last stressed syllable (**near rhyme**)? If there is a distinctive pattern of rhyme, what is it?

Are there other aural features in the poem, such as closely placed words with repeated sounds at their beginning: **alliteration**? Or with repeated vowels in their midst—**assonance**? Are there examples of **onomatopoeia**, words that sound like their meanings (e.g., *buzz*, *splash*)?

A Closer Look

Metre

Metre refers to repeated patterns of stressed and unstressed syllables as they combine in lines of poetry. The name of the metre is determined by the basic unit of measurement (the foot) and the number of feet in a line. The four most common feet are

the iamb (one unstressed + one stressed syllable) ˘ ´

"On either side the river lie" (Alfred, Lord Tennyson)

the trochee (one stressed + one unstressed syllable) ´ ˘

"Tyger, Tyger, burning bright" (William Blake)

the anapest (two unstressed syllables + one stressed syllable) ˘ ˘ ´

"When the voices of children are heard on the green" (Blake)

the dactyl (one stressed syllable + two unstressed syllables) ´ ˘ ˘

"lurching through forests of white spruce and cedar" (Alden Nowlan)

A line that contains three feet is called a **trimeter**, one that contains four feet is a **tetrameter**, and one made up of five feet is a **pentameter**. Thus, a poem with lines composed of five iambs would be written in **iambic pentameter**. **Blank verse**, the closest to the rhythms of everyday English speech, is written in unrhymed iambic pentameter. Blank verse is used in much narrative and dramatic poetry, including the epic poem *Paradise Lost*, by John Milton, and parts of Shakespeare's plays.

> *Identify the poem's speaker* (the main *voice* in the poem) *or narrator* (if the poem is narrated—told as a story). Remember that the "voice" in the work is not necessarily that of the poet. It may be that of a "persona" adopted by the writer. One cannot assume that a literary work is a reliable form of autobiography. Writers may use facts or apparent truths about themselves, but from the standpoint of criticism, these facts are subordinate to the poem as poetic art. The aspect of the poetic work that concerns the critic is the poet's impulse towards creativity and art, more than autobiography.

Can you determine the speaker? Not just *who* it is, but what is his/her perspective? How is the poem told? Does the poet seem to be addressing anyone or anything? Is the person or object absent, as in an **apostrophe**?

What is the **mood** of the poem, and how does it make you feel? Is a predominant emotion expressed? Is it constant, or is there a shift at some point?

What is the poem's **tone**, or attitude to the subject/audience? Does the poet use **irony**? See A Closer Look: Irony, below.

Is **hyperbole** (extreme exaggeration) used? **Understatement** (drawing attention to something by minimizing it)? These devices may help convey a work's tone. Hyperbole is common in comic works; either can be used to convey irony.

A Closer Look

Irony

Irony, an example of indirection, is the condition of two levels of meaning, the apparent (literal or surface) meaning and another intended (non-literal or deeper) meaning. Irony may differ in degree according to its purpose and, traditionally, is divided into three types.

- In **verbal irony**, the discrepancy is between the literal and intended meanings of language. Verbal irony resembles sarcasm, but irony is usually more indirect than sarcasm, which simply states something as its opposite.

    Sarcasm: Mr. Bennet in Jane Austen's novel *Pride and Prejudice* refers to his worthless son-in-law: "I am prodigiously proud of him."

    Verbal irony: "Yet graceful Ease, and Sweetness void of Pride,/Might hide her Faults, if *Belles* had Faults to hide" (Alexander Pope). The last clause is ironic since the "belle," Belinda, is mortal and, as such, does have faults.

    In his anti-war poem "Dulce et Decorum Est," the irony intended by Wilfred Owen is much harsher. His graphic images of a youth dying from a gas attack render ironic the patriot's claim that "dulce et decorum est"—it is "sweet and right to die for your country." While the title affords an example of verbal irony, the poem, as an indictment of war and the "lie" of those who promote its glory, exemplifies situational irony (see below).

- In **dramatic irony**, the reader/audience possesses an awareness about the character or situation that the character doesn't have. For example, in many of Shakespeare's comedies, people are disguised, and while the audience is aware of these disguises, most of the characters are not. **Tragic irony** exists if the reader/audience is aware of a situation that the hero is oblivious to and that will lead to disaster, as when the audience for Shakespeare's *Othello* learns of Iago's treachery long before Othello does. Dramatic irony can also be found in poetry and fiction—as when in Roethke's short lyric, "My Papa's Waltz," irony is expressed in the desperate love of a child for his father: "Then [you] waltzed me off to bed / Still clinging to your shirt."

- In **situational irony**, a situation appears to point to a particular outcome but results in the reverse of the expected or intended one. Situational irony is often found in drama, fiction, and narrative poetry. It is ironic that Pip, the protagonist of Charles Dickens's novel *Great Expectations*, discovers that his benefactor is not the wealthy Miss Havisham but the convict Magwitch.

> ❯ *Pay close attention to stylistic devices and figures of speech.* Some of the more important devices are **diction, syntax,** and **allusion.** Figures of speech include **metaphor, metonymy, synecdoche, simile,** and **personification.** Other rhetorical elements are logic-centred; they include **paradox** and **oxymoron** (the verbal juxtaposition of contraries, as in "darkness visible" or "terrible beauty"). Oxymoron is also considered a device of compression. Another similar device is an **ellipsis** (words left out).

A Closer Look

Common Devices

A **metaphor** is an implicit comparison between two things not usually considered similar; metaphors call attention to an object in an unexpected comparison:

"Love . . . is the star to every wandering bark" (Shakespeare)

Love is compared to a star and the lover is implicitly compared to a "bark" or ship; "star" and "bark" are metaphors for love and the lover, respectively. Metaphors can be divided into the *tenor* (the object being compared—"love," the lover) and the *vehicle* (the image to which the tenor is linked—"star," "bark").

A **simile** is a comparison using *like* or *as* or a similar word/phrase:
"The holy time is *quiet as a Nun*" (William Wordsworth)

Metonymy is the substitution of an object or idea for a related one:
"A *goose's quill* has put an end to murder" (Dylan Thomas)

The poet refers to a document signed by a king; it is in reality the person, not the quill, who "put an end to murder."

An **allusion** is an historical, religious, mythic, literary, or other kind of outside reference used thematically or to reveal another aspect of the work:

"This man had kept a school/And rode our *wingèd horse*" (W.B. Yeats's allusion to the mythological horse Pegasus, associated with poetry)

> *Look at the poem's imagery*. Try to discover patterns of **images**, words conveying sense impressions, particularly sight. What kind are they? Can you characterize them? Which senses do they refer to? How do the images connect with other elements to lead you to a more complex reading of the poem?
>
> Does the writer use the image as a **symbol**? A traditional symbol, such as the sea, star, or heart, has specific cultural or cross-cultural associations; a **contextual symbol** resides in the way the author uses it and may not have traditional associations.

Context-Centred Approach: The Outside-In Approach

The context-centred approach is another beginning point for a textual analysis. The context-centred analysis employs all of the technical terminology of textual criticism, but relates it to an encompassing context. Literary works can be explored through biographical, historical, cultural, racial, gender-based, or theoretical perspectives. Although the formalist (text-centred) critic tends to take an "art for art's sake" approach to poetic analysis, the context-centred critic employs connections between literary art and the "real" world, and considers many of the oppositions between life and art stressed by the text-centred critic as artificial, arbitrary, or, at the very least, limiting. Some of the most common poetic contexts are discussed briefly below (most of them also apply to other genres).

> **Convention and form in poetry.** You may be concerned primarily or even exclusively with viewing a poem in a larger context, perhaps that of a poetic tradition or a specific poetic form with its **conventions** (set of formal requirements or expectations). You could look at the ways that the poem conforms to conventions, the ways that it departs from them, or the ways that the writer adapts the conventions for his or her own purposes.
>
> Broadly speaking, poetry can be classified as lyric, narrative, or dramatic: **lyric** ("song") poetry expresses strong emotions or thoughts in relatively brief form. **Narrative** poetry tells a story and tends to be longer—it may run to book length. **Dramatic** poetry has drama-like qualities, such as a speaker who addresses an imaginary listener (**dramatic monologue**).
>
> The voice in lyric poetry can be referred to as "the poet" (which is not, however, synonymous with the actual author); in narrative poetry, the voice can be referred to as "the narrator"; in dramatic poetry, the voice can be referred to as "the speaker." Both narrative and dramatic poetry can also be

lyrical in places; as well, a lyric could have narrative or dramatic elements. Although these three divisions were introduced by Aristotle in 350 BCE, they are still used today.

Other traditional poetic forms include the ode, the elegy, the sonnet, the villanelle, the haiku (examples of lyric poetry); the ballad and the epic (examples of narrative poetry); and the dramatic monologue (an example of dramatic poetry). Each form employs specific conventions. For example, the **sonnet** always has 14 lines and has two possible stanzaic arrangements: the *Italian* or *Petrarchan* form with an eight-line **octave** and a six-line **sestet**, and the *English* or *Shakespearean* form with three **quatrains** (four lines each) and a **couplet** (two lines); others, like the haiku and the villanelle, have an even stricter and more exacting form than the sonnet. All three are examples of **fixed forms**, which allow for little flexibility. Still others, like the elegy and the ode, may vary widely in their characteristics from one era to another and from poet to poet. At the other extreme from fixed forms are **open forms**: free verse is an open form that does not conform to any set conventions of stanza, rhyme, or metre.

⟩ **The biographical context.** What was the poet's childhood like? Who/what were major influences in his or her life? Does the poem appear addressed to someone the poet knew or does it mention names or places connected with the writer's life? Does the poem focus on a family member or friend? An **elegy** mourns the death of a well-known person or someone the poet knew, providing consolation and usually celebrating that life.

Although the poet is viewed critically as the creator of the work, and not the autobiographical equivalent of the voice, speaker, or narrator, in **confessional poetry** an autobiographical sensibility is produced through the expression of strong emotions and intense personal experiences characterized by revelations of painful honesty and unsettling rawness. The tone can range from despair to anger. Nonetheless, you should not assume that the voice of the poem is *identical* with the biographical poet. Sylvia Plath, a US confessional poet (1932–1963), said this about the relationship between art and personal experience:

> I think my poems come immediately out of the sensuous and emotional experiences I have, [but] I think one should be able to control and manipulate experiences, even the most terrifying . . . with an informed and intelligent mind.

⟩ **The historical/cultural context.** What historical or cultural factors can be brought to bear on the poem? Does the poem reflect a particular time period? Can it be studied as a historical, social, or cultural document? In the following excerpt, student writer Rory Wizbicki explores Al Purdy's poem "The Country North of Belleville" in a historical context. The poem details the hardships of poor, immigrant, nineteenth-century farmers, who travelled to Canada in the hope of finding prosperity and freedom in a new country:

> Although, geographically, the plots north of Belleville are every farmer's nightmare, within this shallow soil lies their blood, sweat, and tears produced from endless days of work and toil. A farmer becomes so connected to his

land, "plowing and plowing [his] ten acre field" that the "convulsions [begin to] run parallel with his own brain" (57). The land is both his greatest enemy and his most respected companion. Despite his plot's stubborn resistance to human cultivation, a man of this area "might have some / opinion of what beauty / is and none deny him / for miles" (5–8). The timeless beauty and respect for the land are paralleled by the lasting cultural values engraved into the farmer's stony fields.

> **The cultural, racial, or gender-based context.** Awareness of the culture that the poet is part of has been instrumental in extending and broadening the canon of literature in the last few decades. For example, the fact that Dionne Brand and George Elliott Clarke are of black heritage and that Adrienne Rich and Margaret Atwood have strongly identified with the feminist movement can be important in analyzing the ways in which their works give voice to the concerns of the marginalized.

Was the poet a member of a well-defined group that shared certain values? Did he or she contribute intellectually to a social, political, or aesthetic movement? Was the poem written as a radical response to a contemporary reality—does it protest something? Cultural, racial, gender, socio-economic, and class issues can serve political ends in poems of protest or resistance; their object may be to express collective or personal empowerment.

The **traditional (Western) canon** was based on the opinion of critics and readers—mostly, white, middle-class, and male—that particular works exemplified high artistic standards and were the most worthy objects of study and scholarship. Due to the increasing interest today in the productions of other individuals and groups, publishers have become responsive to a broader range of human experience. The **literary canon** is now more inclusive of varied cultural, racial, ethnic, economic, and gendered perspectives.

> **The theoretical perspective.** Like other humanities disciplines, the study of English literature is often informed by a theoretical framework. Was the work written from within an established theoretical tradition or does it try to establish a new theoretical position? Theoretical approaches to literature can be divided into two types: (1) those formulated by artists themselves, who have sought to explain their own goals by theorizing about them, and (2) approaches that represent particular schools of critical thought.

Attempts to systematize poetry and other literary genres have brought about what might seem a confusing array of critical approaches today. The profusion of *-isms* began around the turn of the twentieth century through the attempts of writers and critics to categorize technical innovations of that time. Some of these innovations came to be associated with *literary movements*—for example, **imagism**, with its focus on the concrete image, and **surrealism**, with its focus on the subconscious.

Today, the widely divergent schools of criticism may represent the collaborative efforts of educated theorists whose original training was in non-literary fields. Their theories may seek to incorporate theory and practice from other disciplines—for example, linguistics, visual art, history, education, philosophy, psychology, anthropology, economics, and mythology. If there is a collective goal of modern literary theories, it is to break down the notion of a "centre," to stress the ways that all literary art depends on and engages with aspects of language and culture. The interdisciplinary approach to literature enables us to study it from many different angles and viewpoints. These kinds of approaches are common in literary criticism today.

Sample Student Literary Analysis

The following student essay features a close textual reading of the poem "Metamorphosis" by Canadian poet Leona Gom.

Sample Student Essay

Reading 21

Metamorphosis
by Leona Gom

Something is happening
to this girl.
She stands on one leg
on the third block
of her hopscotch game,
lifts herself forward
to the next double squares,
and, as she jumps,
something changes.

Her straight child's body
curls slowly in the air,
the legs that assert themselves
apart on the squares
curve in calf and thigh,
angles become arches;
her arms pumping slowly
to her sides adjust
to a new centre of gravity,
the beginnings of breasts
push at her sweater,

her braids have come undone
and her hair flies loose
  around her.

Behind her
the schoolhouse blurs,
becomes insubstantial
and meaningless,
and the boys in the playground
move toward her,
something sure and sinister
in their languid circling.

Slowly she picks up the beanbag.
When she straightens,
her face gathers
the bewildered awareness
of the body's betrayal,
the unfamiliar feel
of the child's toy
in her woman's hand.

From *The Collected Poems* by Leona Gom, 1991, Sono Nis Press, Winlaw, BC. Reprinted by permission.

A New Game: Leona Gom's "Metamorphosis"
by Melissa Lee

[1] The most intimate experiences of human existence occur every day, to all of us. Art allows us to publicly engage in these without vulnerability; it recognizes their profound impact on human life without taking away their personal value. Leona Gom's poem "Metamorphosis"

is an example of how art can reveal the significance of common life events. The appeal of this poem is universal because it deals with maturation and change, something all humans experience. Gom focuses attention on details with several techniques. Aspects that may first appear unimportant become essential to understanding. In particular, diction, alliteration, and imagery help create the effect of a time-lapse photograph commonly used to show organic growth. Gom's subtle use of such techniques echo the theme of sensing the amazing in the mundane.

Gom's diction relates to the changes the girl undergoes. Thus, words such as "straight," "squares," and "angles" appear to represent feelings of childhood. They are straightforward, systematic, and even mathematical. There is nothing confusing about them; things are black and white. As the girl moves through the game, the diction shifts. The words "curls," "curve," "arches," "undone," "loose," "circling," and "blurs" are used to symbolize maturation. Her body is literally changing from straight to curvaceous, while her mind is changing from concrete to flexible. The diction is complex and chaotic, reflecting the lack of rules for growing up. A grey area exists now where definitive lines used to be.

[2]

In the beginning, the girl "lifts herself forward," expressing her agency in the changes. The use of alliteration in the poem draws attention to pivotal points. Though she is not yet aware of the meaning of her actions (moving towards maturity), she is actively participating. "The beginnings of breasts" represent the changes, signalling a new beginning, not only an end (to childhood). As her changes are public, her societal role must change. Describing the boys' attraction to her as "something sure and sinister" reveals her feelings of newfound power. At the same time, her "bewildered awareness / of the body's betrayal" suggests her resentment of new burdens and responsibilities that come with changes. Cumulatively, these images show an emerging self-consciousness as she begins to reflect on her identity.

[3]

The imagery that Gom uses also represents the girl's passage into womanhood. The fragmented body parts, "leg," "calf," "thigh," "arms," "breasts," "hair," "face," and "hand" throughout the poem suggest feelings of not being fully formed yet. There are many pieces to her, but they are not quite connected. This awareness of being incomplete is the girl's first step towards maturation. She recognizes that she now must find a force within herself to put the pieces together, in a higher order. Thus, at the end we see phrases suggesting action and decisiveness: "she picks up the beanbag," "she straightens," and "her face gathers." These show the girl taking control over her situation and, at some level, accepting her new role in life: she puts things together with a new insight.

[4]

The image of reaching higher resonates throughout the poem and can be seen in the phrases "lifts herself," "she jumps," "curls slowly in the air," "new centre of gravity," and "flies loose around her." Such images evoke the activity of rising up to challenge one's limits. As the poem continues, the take-off gets easier, which is reflected by the diction ("lifts" becomes "jumps," which becomes "curls slowly" and "flies loose"), suggesting the desire of the girl to push her limits and thus change. It is a very positive and optimistic image, showing that while change may close one chapter in a life, it opens many others. She begins to trust her abilities and takes a leap of faith in herself. Without self-doubt holding her down, she experiences a new gravity; she is transformed, undergoes a metamorphosis.

[5]

While change is essential for life to continue, it can also cause great unease. When people adapt to challenging changes in their lives, they gain meaningful insight into what they can accomplish. A poem like "Metamorphosis" acknowledges these private experiences and their deep impact, enabling people to stay connected to what matters most.

[6]

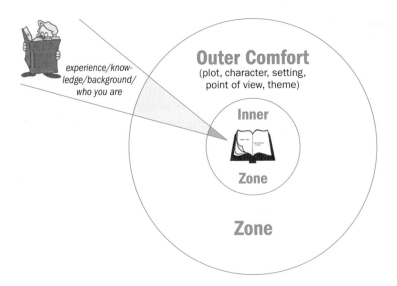

Figure 9.1   A Model for Reading and Interpreting Fiction

Fictional Forms

Fiction is often analyzed according to what you can call the *comfort categories* (these can be applied to any other literary works as well). In fiction, the comfort categories include the traditional areas of plot, character, setting, point of view, and theme. Essentially, the comfort categories relate to basic questions you often ask of a work of fiction or narrative poem in order to begin analyzing it: what, who, where and when, how, and why.

Whether a work of fiction is called a *short story*, a *novella*, or a *novel* depends on its length. In approximate terms, a **short story** is a fictional narrative of fewer than 15,000 words; a **novella** is 15,000–40,000 words; a **novel** is more than 40,000 words.

Explaining or analyzing a work involves exploring its themes, or controlling ideas, along with the other elements mentioned above. A novel's or short story's characters may seem unusual, its plot unlikely, and its setting unfamiliar, but there will always be something familiar about its themes: it might focus on love, death, suffering, renewal, human relationships, social injustice, or spiritual longing. Through the work's themes, the reader can make connections with his or her own experience—themes universalize the writer's work.

As Figure 9.1 shows, a reader's response to a work of fiction will depend partly on his or her experience, knowledge, and background. Because each reader brings a different set of experiences and expectations to a work, no two analyses will be identical. Even though we share the critical tools for analyzing fiction (that "outer zone" containing the comfort categories of plot, character, setting, point of view, and theme), in the "inner zone" one can apply the more complex tools for analyzing fiction discussed below. Being familiar with the many resources for analyzing fiction will enable you to respond more fully and sensitively to the work, to produce an in-depth reading.

The Short Story

The difference between a short story and a novella or novel cannot be judged simply by length. Edith Wharton (1862–1937), an American writer of short stories and novels, wrote that character is the most important element in a novel, while "situation" is more important in the short story. It might be more accurate to say that it is the *interaction of character with situation and the resultant conflict that drives the short story*. Still, many contemporary short stories do not have characters in the traditional sense, while other stories may not even involve a conflict.

Just as writers have extended the length of the short story, making the line between story, novella, and novel difficult to determine—perhaps irrelevant—so the story has been condensed into variants like the *postcard story* or *microfiction*. Are these short stories? Can you identify elements of character, setting, plot, mood, or conflict?

> For sale: baby shoes, never worn.—Ernest Hemingway

> The last man on Earth sat alone in a room. There was a knock at the door.
> —Anonymous

The following creative definitions by students in a fiction-writing workshop draw attention to other elements of a successful short story, expanding the definition so you can see what a short story *does*—not just that it is short and a story or that it involves a conflict between a character and a situation:

Student's Definition	Explanation
It should provide some kind of continuous dream which the reader can enter, commune with, and leave having felt something.	This definition stresses the effect of stories on their readers; stories are a shared experience that evoke feelings.
It is a fully realized world. After passing through this world, the reader sees his or her own world differently.	In this definition, the story takes place in "a fully realized world," despite its brevity; the short story renders a complete picture of something.
It is a narrative wherein a character absorbs an experience.	This definition conveys the importance of character; furthermore, the character undergoes an experience. The reader is offered an opportunity for learning, from either what the character did or didn't do.
It is a slice of life—the thinner the better.	This definition suggests that a story represents universals in as succinct or condensed way as possible by showing us an important example ("slice") of the whole.

The Single Effect

One of the earliest developers of the short story, American Edgar Allan Poe (1809–1849), claimed that, unlike the novel, the successful short story should be of a length to be read at one sitting and should focus on one effect that serves to unify its elements. According to Poe, writers of short fiction should decide what this single effect is to be and select incidents that help bring it about. Such a dictate stresses a necessary *economy* of the story—the judicious use of atmosphere, dialogue, mood, imagery, and so on, that results in a unified effect. In many short stories, the single effect relates to a discovery a character makes about nature, society, other people, or about him- or herself.

The Novel Tradition

A **novel** is an extended fictional prose narrative involving one or more characters undergoing significant experiences over a span of time. The term is from the Italian *novella*, a short, realistic prose work popular in the late medieval period. The word *novel* means "new," and the fictional works of Daniel Defoe brought to English a new prose form, very different from the popular romances of the middle ages that depicted the imaginary exploits of heroes, such as Beowulf and King Arthur and the Knights of the Round Table. The English novels were notable at first for their realism: Defoe's *Journal of the Plague Year*, *Robinson Crusoe*, *Moll Flanders*; and for their efforts at psychological detail: Samuel Richardson's *Pamela* and *Clarissa*, and Henry Fielding's *The History of Tom Jones, a Foundling*. Yet the novel is not always a realistic form.

In France, the *roman* retained its connection to the romance of the middle ages (Voltaire's *Candide*; Alexandre Dumas's *The Three Musketeers*) through anti-heroes of the influential writers of the nineteenth century (Honoré de Balzac's *Père Goriot*, Gustave Flaubert's *Madame Bovary*), evolving towards modern preoccupations with various sorts of ideals and anti-ideals, especially the political and social, and that were approached through irony and satire (Albert Camus's *The Plague*; Jean-Paul Sartre's *Nausea*) and the *nouveau roman* (new novel), which breaks from many of the conventions of the form itself (Alain Robbe-Grillet's *Jealousy*).

The two words *novella* and *roman* suggest two directions for the novel: towards realism and towards romance or idealism. The English novel's early appeal to the rising numbers of middle-class readers was based partly on its depiction of real-life characters with whom readers could identify. The English novel has proven an adaptable form, and many different kinds of novels have flourished in its roughly three centuries of development. A necessarily brief overview of prominent novelistic forms in English follows.

The plot-centred **picaresque novel** (seventeenth and eighteenth centuries) tells a story composed of loosely related, realistic incidents or episodes featuring a low-born, usually male, hero called a *pícaro* (*picaroon* if the hero is female), a merry rogue on a journey who survives by his wits; though often deceptive and dishonest, the hero is not immoral, but his encounters reveal the corruption of others and of society.

The character-centred **epistolary novel (novel of letters)** (eighteenth century) uses letters to advance the plot and reveal depth and variety of characterization; it features a middle- or upper-class, usually female, protagonist in social settings like drawing rooms or salons, and at social assemblies. The epistolary novel flourished for a time but then experienced a decline in readership. Inevitably, though, elements were absorbed into emerging forms, such as the eighteenth-century sentimental novel, which stressed character and feeling over incident.

The **Gothic novel** or **Gothic romance**, an immensely popular form from 1790 to 1820, possessed typical features related to plot, setting, and mood. Making liberal use of the supernatural, the Gothic novel featured entrapped heroines dominated by tyrannical older males who represented the repressions of political, social, or religious authorities. Many of the elements of Gothic novels were absorbed into later novelistic forms—its influence today is felt in popular horror books and films like the *Twilight* series and television shows like *Buffy the Vampire Slayer*.

The **historical romance**, popularized by Sir Walter Scott early in the nineteenth century, exploited conventions of romance, including larger-than-life characters performing heroic deeds of historical significance. Later in the century, such writers as Robert Louis Stevenson and Rudyard Kipling maintained the genre's popularity under the gradually diminishing glow of British imperialism.

The **Victorian novel** (mid- to late-nineteenth century) represented a culmination of the previous styles with its elaborate plot development and profusion of characters. One kind of Victorian novel is the **bildungsroman**, or novel of self-education; Charlotte Brontë's *Jane Eyre* and Charles Dickens's *David Copperfield* and *Great Expectations* are examples. Elizabeth Gaskell, Dickens, and others also wrote **social-problem novels**, which drew the attention of their readers to contemporary social and political issues.

The **modernist novel** of the twentieth century, owing to the influence of psychological theories, is often concerned with exploring psychological and perceptual states; many novelists of the modernist period (1895–1945), such as James Joyce and Virginia Woolf, sought through technical innovation to disrupt the conventions of the Victorian novel. Modernist novels tended to be more experimental, open-ended, and morally ambivalent than their Victorian predecessors.

Novella

Since a novella (or **novelette**) occupies the middle space between a short story and a novel, it's not surprising that it shares some of the characteristics of the short story as well as some of those of the novel. A novella usually is more fully developed in one or more areas of plot, character, and setting than a short story, but is less developed than a novel in all these areas.

How to Approach Fiction

Some tools for analyzing stories, novels, and novellas are discussed below. Many of the terms also are useful in analyzing drama and narrative or dramatic poetry.

Plot

The plot is the arrangement or sequence of actions in a story, novel, or drama.

Plot Structure. You may be familiar with the pyramidal division of plot into *rising action*, *climax* (the high point of the conflict), and *falling action* (*resolution* or *denouement*). In most dramas, novels, and in many stories, the rising action is preceded by the *exposition*, which introduces background information. The *initiating incident* begins the rising action. *In medias res* describes the strategy of beginning a story in the midst of an important action.

Fiction involves one or more kinds of **conflict**, which usually take the form of obstacles the character must overcome to achieve a goal. Conflict—the initiator of and driving force behind the actions or events of a short story, novel, or drama—may arise from the character's motivation or through forces lying outside the character. The conflict is usually introduced early and instigates the rising action.

Many other structural devices lend coherence to a story; for example, authors may use a *framing* technique in which the beginning and the end mirror one another in setting or situation. In some novels, a character narrates the beginning and the end with the story of the main character evolving within this narrative frame. Other forms of *parallelism* can be used to suggest similarities or differences between characters, or to show the development in a character at different points in a novel.

Plots may be closed or open-ended. A traditional way to provide *closure*, especially in novels of social interaction, such as the *novels of manners* of Jane Austen, is through a marriage. The actions or events of the plot may be unified (closely related) or only loosely related, as in the episodic plot of a picaresque novel, in which case, the over-arching structure may take the form of a journey. A *quest* is a journey with a specific goal, usually a valuable object. The quest is completed when the hero/heroine overcomes all the obstacles and has brought the object back to his or her society. However, the *quester* may fail in the quest; invariably, the failed quester undergoes an important learning experience while trying to satisfy the terms of the quest.

The incidents that make up a plot can be ordered in various ways: most simply, they may be arranged chronologically (time order); even in the chronological order, however, other devices or effects can be used—for example, the writer may use *chronological telescoping* as *foreshadowing*, creating suspense through the anticipation of a future action or result, or *flashbacks*, moving back in time to narrate important events, perhaps as a character recollects them.

Character

Henry James (1843–1916) was one of the earliest writers to treat the novel as an art form, one that combined meticulous technique with moral vision. In "The Art of Fiction" (1893), James asks "What is a picture or a novel that is *not* of character?" Through point of view, says James, the author can keep in focus the character's consciousness. Writers' fidelity to the consciousness of the protagonist produced the *psychological realism* of many English novels of the late nineteenth and early twentieth centuries.

Character Type. Novels usually have at least one *round* (fully developed and complex) and several *flat* (one-dimensional, undeveloped) characters. The main character in a work of fiction or drama is called the *protagonist*. One expects the protagonist to be the round character. The novel may also have an *antagonist*, who opposes the protagonist. An antagonist often reveals hidden or submerged aspects of the protagonist. The *doppelgänger*, *double*, or *shadow self* is used by some authors to express a character's alter ego or alternative, usually diametrically opposite, expression of the self, as Hyde is to Jekyll in Robert Louis Stevenson's *The Strange Case of Dr. Jekyll and Mr. Hyde*. A *foil* is a character who *provides contrast to* another character, though the two characters don't necessarily oppose one another.

Character Development. Character may be disclosed through direct narration, in description or exposition, or indirectly through dialogue or action. A character's development may be represented primarily through his or her thoughts or through that character's actions. Character development usually occurs through a learning experience: in an *initiation story*, a young protagonist makes the transition to adulthood, from innocence to experience. The learning experience could be one of suffering, resulting, as it often does in drama, especially tragedy, in an intense moment of recognition or insight. In short fiction, James Joyce introduced the concept of the *epiphany*, a character's sudden recognition in an ordinary event or object of something personally illuminating.

Setting

Setting is the place and time of the work. In contrast to short stories, there is usually more than one main setting in novels, and the time may span several days (occasionally less) to several years or, in the case of some nineteenth-century novels, generations. Setting can be shown through concrete detail conveyed through diction and imagery. Selective use of imagery can also create a specific atmosphere, which may be important in creating a mood. *Regionalism* is the realistic portrayal of the beliefs and behaviours of characters from a distinct area; examples include William Faulkner (Mississippi), Stephen Leacock (Orillia, Ontario), Alice Munro (southwestern Ontario), and Jack Hodgins (Vancouver Island).

Narration

Narrative point of view is the personal perspective or angle of vision from which the narrative is told.

Narrator (field of vision). An *omniscient* ("all knowing") *narrator* sees and tells the whole story in the third-person, moving to different scenes, and in and out of the minds of characters; a *limited omniscient narrator* can move in and out of the minds of one or more characters, but often is limited to the consciousness of the main character; a *first-person narrator* reports from his or her own experiences (using the first-person (*I*) voice).

Narrator (involvement). A first-person narrator does not always reflect the most subjective viewpoint; this voice can be relatively detached, narrating events from the *observer* or uninvolved perspective. This narrator can also, of course, be involved in the action. First-person *involved* narrators may narrate events in which they play a significant role. A writer may use special techniques to represent internal consciousness, such as *inner monologue* or *stream of consciousness* to show the mind in flux or the transient emotions, thoughts, and sensations of a character; both these techniques attempt to represent raw perceptions at the pre-verbal or subconscious levels.

Narrator (reliability). Narrators may be reliable or unreliable. A reliable narrator can be trusted to relay a truthful picture of events and character. Most third-person narrators can be considered reliable.

An *unreliable narrator* may be naïve; that is, he or she may not be in possession of all the facts or may be too inexperienced to see things as they are or to make sound judgements. The *naïve narrator*, then, may be limited in his or her capacity to understand and explain, such as Mark Twain's young narrator, Huckleberry Finn, in *Adventures of Huckleberry Finn* (1885).

On the other hand, a narrator may consciously or unconsciously deceive the reader, in order to avoid confronting unpleasant facts about him- or herself or due to a bias or prejudice. Unreliable narrators can vary greatly in their unreliability. A writer's use of an unreliable narrator produces irony, as there is a discrepancy between the narrator's perceptions and the reality of a situation. Through unreliable narration, writers convey the complexity of perception and the human capacity for (self-)deception.

Orientation to Reality

> My task . . . is, by the power of the written word, to make you hear, to make you feel—it is, before all, to make you see. That—and no more, and it is everything.
> —novelist/short-fiction writer Joseph Conrad (1857–1924)

Realism. The popularity of the novel from its inception has been due in part to its ability to portray ordinary people, places, and circumstances. Realism in the novel has produced many sub-genres, including social realism, psychological realism, and historical realism. Because the term *realism* is so broad, it is difficult to define. In the general sense, it refers to the need of the fictional writer to portray things as they really are, "to make you see," as Conrad says.

Realism also can be considered a distinct literary tradition that began in Europe as a response to *romance* and to contemporary scientific discoveries and theories about the place of humans in the universe—for example, the theory of evolution that gained prominence after Charles Darwin published *On the Origin of Species* in 1859. Such theories looked back to other mechanistic views of humans and their world, such as those of Copernicus and Isaac Newton. Since it seemed less and less truthful for artists to dwell on idealized human traits, writers turned increasingly to the everyday interactions among ordinary people, showing middle-class characters in a recognizable environment and using an accumulation of realistic detail to do so. Editor Wayne Grady has called realism the "most characteristic feature" of the Canadian short story. Some critics see realism primarily as a technique or method, viewing *naturalism*, rather, as the school of realistic writing applicable to fiction and drama.

Naturalism. Naturalism is an outgrowth of realistic writing in the late nineteenth and early twentieth centuries that stressed humanity's helplessness before external forces, such as those of one's society or natural environment, or before internal ones, such as heredity. French novelist Émile Zola (1840–1902) drew an analogy between the naturalistic writer and the laboratory scientist, both of whom examine phenomena dispassionately and draw conclusions based on evidence. Frequently, naturalistic writers portray their protagonists as victims of fate.

Romance. The romance may be distinguished from the novel. Romance deals with imaginary, though usually conventional, heroes and heroines. However, characters may be exalted and their goals idealized. American novelist Nathaniel Hawthorne (1804–1864) called his works romances because they owed an allegiance not to "the probable and ordinary course of man's experience" but to "the truth of the human heart." Like *realism*, *romance* is a term that has been made complex by overuse.

Departures from the realism/romance divide. *Reality* is not an absolute term. A work may be oriented to reality while utilizing a symbolic framework, although on the surface, symbols and realistic detail might seem incompatible. Similarly, *science fiction* and *fantasy* may invert or subvert some of the standards of objective reality and still be considered realistic; in this case, the relevant question would not be "Could it happen in our world?" but "Could it happen *in the world created by the writer*?" **Magic realism** combines the objectively real and the surprise of the unreal or unexpected; in magic realism, the created world is magical and real at the same time. **Metafiction** defines its own boundaries of the real by focusing on the story it-self as the testing ground of the "real"; one of the themes in a work of metafiction is the status of fiction and fiction-making: metafiction uses the work itself to explore this status.

Much critical writing today attempts to examine the many faces of **postmodernism**. Postmodernism is certainly not restricted to fiction; indeed, it incorporates diverse aspects of contemporary culture. Although notoriously difficult to define, postmodernism in literature tends to reject such assumptions as the authority of the author, univocal (one-voice) perspectives, unifying narratives, and other "absolutes"; in their place, it stresses plurality, possibility, and "play."

How to Approach Drama

When you think about drama, you may recall plays you studied in high school, including those by William Shakespeare. Most of Shakespeare's plays are classified as tragedies or comedies, but the general term *drama* (from the Greek *dran*, "to do" or "to perform") refers to a story acted out by actors on a stage or in front of a camera. The creator of drama is called a dramatist or *playwright*. The second syllable, *wright*, means "maker," as in *wainwright*, not "writer," and it is important to remember that, in the truest sense, plays are "wrought," carrying a connotation of construction in their making, because the intention is not just that they be written and read, but that they be mounted as productions and observed. Thus, when you read a play, it is essential to imagine it as performance and spectacle—not just as dialogue on a page.

Aristotle (384–322 BCE) called drama an "imitated human action." He declared that a drama should observe the three *unities* of time, place, and action. By **unity of time** he limits the play's action to approximately one day; by **unity of place** he limits it to one setting; and by **unity of action** he limits it to a single set of incidents that are related as cause and effect and "having a beginning, a middle, and an end." Although the unities are not strictly observed by playwrights (for example, most of Shakespeare's plays depart from this rule), their observance does help create dramatic focus and intensity, necessary elements in theatre where the audience must remain attentive for at least two hours to absorb the full experience of the spectacle.

Drama in Western cultures dates back to Ancient Greek and Roman drama, which had its beginnings in ceremonial rites. Comedy evolved from fertility rites, while tragedy originated from rites connected with the life-death cycle. The three major ancient Greek playwrights, Aeschylus, Sophocles, and Euripides (all circa 525–400 BCE), used Greek myth and legend to fashion tragedies that centred on the downfall of noble figures. Their plays featured heroes or heroines in their struggle against an unavoidable destiny. A group of people forming a **chorus** commented on the action. Aeschylus' main concern was with the cosmic significance of tragic destiny; Sophocles and Euripides focused more on the psychology of the protagonist in his or her struggle with that destiny.

William Shakespeare (1564–1616) exemplifies Elizabethan drama, considered "the golden age" of English drama. Elizabethan dramatists combined elements from ancient drama with newer, native forms to produce a wide variety of dramatic forms, from histories and chronicle plays to comedy, romance, and tragedy. The Puritan government that temporarily replaced the Stuart monarchy disapproved of the theatre and closed London playhouses in 1642. When the theatres re-opened in 1660, comedies of manners and domestic tragedies prevailed and drama became more a form of entertainment exclusive to the educated classes during the Restoration period and into the eighteenth century.

As does the modern novelist, the modern dramatist is likely to locate the principal action of the play within the minds of the characters; psychological interest and the contemporary theme of alienation are reinforced by experimental techniques that made the drama relevant to contemporary audiences. Several modern playwrights sought to revive traditional dramatic practices: in the twentieth century Eugene O'Neill attempted to update the commentator function of the Greek chorus in *Mourning Becomes Electra* (1931); Arthur Miller in *Death of a Salesman* (1949) wrote a modern American tragedy in the classical tradition.

Although certainly not all works of drama can be classified as comedies or tragedies, the divisions between them have traditionally defined, for the playwright, the boundaries of human experience, because comedy and tragedy are concerned with human limits.

Comedy

In viewing human limits as weaknesses, comedy celebrates the lesser—the carnal or physical—self. Comedy uses laughter as a form of displacement, enabling its audience to identify the "other" as debased, silly, pretentious, or unimportant.

Low comedy traditionally draws its characters from low-life figures, that is, socially or morally inferior stereotypes: servants, shopkeepers, prostitutes. Low comedy lacks a serious moral purpose and may be used, as in many of Shakespeare's plays, to divert temporarily the attention of the audience from weightier matters (**comic relief**); low comedy as **farce** depends on the idea of the absurd and draws attention to events that appear meaningless or valueless out of context—the pratfall, for example.

High comedy is more sophisticated and traditionally uses characters from a higher socio-economic class; the humour of high comedy appeals more to the intellect (characterized as **wit**), having such targets as social pretensions and character inconsistencies. It typically has a more complex function than low comedy, dealing with serious issues like human relationships—even dealing with the subjects of tragedy from a perspective of lightness and humour.

Satire can be considered a genre apart from comedy or tragedy, but its use of ironic humour aligns it to high comedy. In addition to humour, satire uses ridicule and irony to undercut, critique, or attack human institutions, ostensibly for the purpose of improving them. Satire may be mild, intended to make society's members more aware (Horatian satire) or harsh, intent on attacking these institutions (Juvenalian satire). Related to satire is **parody**, in which the writer imitates another literary work, poking fun at it and/or revealing its weaknesses.

Comic plot. Fortune, chance, and coincidence are the major external forces that drive the plot of comedy; inner forces that determine comic action include such instincts and motivations as physical desire, greed, envy, ambition, and concern with appearances. In the end, base human desires usually are punished, while continuity is suggested by a marriage between the most worthy and virtuous characters.

Comic theme. One of the most important themes in drama is that of identity, perhaps because in drama the onstage character is isolated in a way that he or she usually is not in a novel—because all drama is character-driven due to limitations of time and space necessitated by the stage. **Asides, monologues,** and **soliloquies**—speeches in which a character reveals his or her own thoughts for the ears of the audience alone—can be used to underscore this sense of isolation. Comedy may revolve around exchange and multiplicity of identity. In most of Shakespeare's comedies, for example, there are frequent changes of identity and/or mistaken identities.

Tragedy

Tragedy celebrates the greater, ennobling self by viewing the limits to human strengths tested against more powerful forces; tragedy involves cataclysmic change from prosperity to intense suffering and, usually, the death of the protagonist (the **denouement** or **catastrophe**). This suffering arouses a complex mix of emotions in its audience in which fear and pity are particularly strong. Traditionally, the characters of tragedy are high-status individuals, royal personages; this, however, is not the case with most tragedies written in the last 200 years. It is essential, though, that we see the tragic protagonist as admirable in some way.

Tragic plot. The exterior forces of fate or destiny are associated with tragedy; the inner force that drives the protagonist in classical tragedy is pride (**hubris**) or some such trait that exists in an extreme or distorted form (**tragic flaw,** or **hamartia**).

Tragic theme. The theme of identity is important in tragedy, also, but from the perspective of the tearing away and negation of identity. In both ancient Greek and Shakespearean tragedy, the protagonist is a king or high-status figure, making the fall from the greatest height as devastating as possible for an individual and in social terms as well, for the loss of the monarch would overturn the entire society. Shakespeare's King Lear falls from king, to an old man divested of kingly power, to a madman in a storm in a wilderness (heath) prior to his death.

The Literary Research Essay

Since information about conducting research and using secondary sources effectively (Chapter 6) and documenting them correctly (Chapter 7,) has already been given, this section focuses on specific strategies for dealing with literary sources.

Primary and Secondary Sources

Primary sources are the literary works (original sources) that you are analyzing; primary sources could also include letters, interviews, or diary entries of the writer. **Secondary sources** are studies (books, articles, and other media) that comment on or analyze one or more aspects of the primary work. Secondary sources include criticism relating to the work itself or to the writer's life (biographical criticism), as well as historical, cultural, linguistic, and other kinds of discourse that incorporate literary works. Using secondary sources in your analysis will broaden your paper; it will show how your observations about a work relate to what others have said. Researching the views of other readers and critics should also serve to strengthen your analysis.

How to Use Secondary Sources

1. Use a source to provide general information or to introduce something you will be discussing:

    Provide general information: Gerald Vizenor, a contemporary critic and Native American spokesperson, writes that "movies have never been the representations of tribal cultures; at best, movies are the deliverance of an unsure civilisation" (179).

    Introduce: Author Miriam Bird once said, "travel is more than the seeing of sights; it is a change that goes on deep and permanent, in the ideas of the living" (11). Similarly, the journeys the two characters undergo leave an indelible effect on them, changing the way they see the world and respond to others.

2. Use a source to support, explain, or expand your point:

    Support: It is not vanity that drives the protagonist, an unproven knight, in Browning's narrative poem "Childe Roland to the Dark Tower Came," and he is far from idealistic as well. As James Stonewall states, "it is a simple desire to finish his quest, to finally put an end to his journey, that motivates Roland" (76).

    Explain: Dick tries to teach Rosemary that the values she has adopted are corrupt, immature, and over-simplified. Post–World War I American prosperity had already promoted the doctrine that youthfulness and wealth could buy one's social position, but, as Stern argues, it was the movies that "midwifed into full birth" this American mythology (115).

    Expand: The wreck itself is a dense image, and through its complexity, Rich is able to illustrate the complexity of myths. The wreck represents "the history of all women submerged in a patriarchal culture; it is that source of myths about male and female sexuality which shape our lives and roles today" (Mcdaniel, par. 7).

3. Use a source to disagree or to qualify:

    Disagree: Donohue's fixation on the "elfin child" Pearl places undue emphasis on the ways we redeem our (innocent) children, rather than on the novel's more important concern with the ways society judges sin.

    Qualify: Herb Wyile asserts that Chance "displays . . . insidious racism. His vision for his epic is grounded in a self-exculpatory, racist triumphalism characteristic of the western" (3). This may be the case, but since it is Chance's perspective, he likely considers it the truth.

Reliability of Sources

As with secondary sources for expository research essays, you must be careful with the kinds of sources you use, especially if you use the Internet for research (see Chapter 6, Reliability of Internet Sources, page 140); university-related websites are the most reliable.

Reliable. Critical studies of the work (books, articles in journals or from essay collections, etc.); other media and online resources affiliated with universities and officially designated agencies or organizations.

Unreliable. Internet sites that feature essays on specific literary works by unnamed authors, or writers who give their name but include no accreditation or biographical data; discussion groups, and other unofficial postings, such as the home pages of enthusiasts or unofficial postings of student essays.

Questionable. The expansion of the Internet has made commercial "study guides" readily accessible. However, remember that these quick-fix guides invariably present mechanical and superficial treatments of generic topics; they are seldom insightful or offer a reading that you wouldn't be more than capable of yourself. You should ask your instructor before using such a source, and, of course, if you do use one, you must cite all such sources in your essay.

Currency of Sources

Unless you are specifically commenting on the reception of the work in the time it was written or the cultural/historical conditions that affected the work, prefer current sources to older ones as you would in other disciplines where older sources often become outdated. Another advantage of beginning with recent criticism is that such sources often refer to useful older criticism. Sometimes just scanning the "Works Cited" section at the end of a recent article will provide you with potentially useful sources.

However, there may be a classic commentary on your subject, such as Aristotle and Plato on poetry and drama, Samuel Johnson on Alexander Pope, Matthew Arnold on William Wordsworth, T.S. Eliot on W.B. Yeats, and other acknowledged authorities; your instructor can steer you towards such secondary sources.

Most post-secondary institutions offer access through their library systems to online versions of scholarly journals. Libraries may provide this through large electronic subscription services such as *Academic Search Complete*, *Project Muse*, or *Literature Online* (LION), enabling students to access full-text articles in a wide variety of literary journals, from general ones to those specializing in the literature of a specific time period (such as *Victorian Studies*, *Journal of Modern Literature*, and *Studies in English Literature 1500–1900*); literature of a particular country or region (such as *Scandinavian Review*, *Canadian Literature*, and *New England Quarterly*); literature categorized by genre (such as *Poetry*, *Studies in Short Fiction*, and *Studies in the Novel*); literature associated with movements (such as *American Transcendental Quarterly*, *Modernism/ Modernity*, and *Feminist Studies*); literature and culture (such as *African American Review*, *Folklore*, and *Journal of Popular Culture*); literature on an individual author (such as *Shakespeare Studies*, *Dickens Quarterly*, and *Emily Dickinson Journal*); and interdisciplinary studies (such as *Biography: an interdisciplinary quarterly*; *Literature and Psychology*; and *Mosaic: a journal for the interdisciplinary study of literature*).

Most library arts and humanities databases allow you to search by author, subject, title, keyword, and journal, as well as to limit your search (see Chapter 6, Online Searches, page 154).

Drafting and Revising the Literary Essay

The works you use as primary and secondary sources are written differently from your own tone and style—they may be stylistically dense with many figures of speech and, perhaps, unfamiliar words. You need to write in a direct and straightforward fashion to manage and integrate these other voices. Dealing with the complexities of literary texts can present challenges to your own writing: remember that convoluted language or sentence structure impedes understanding of complex thought; it also wastes words (see Chapter 12).

Introduction and thesis statement. Like any essay, the literary analysis should include an introduction with an identifiable thesis statement, which should name the topic and primary works (if they have not been named); it should indicate your approach to the topic. Your thesis must be carefully planned and clearly stated (see Chapter 4, The Thesis Statement).

Two sample introductions follow: in the first, student writer Loni Getty develops her introduction logically, beginning with a generalization and narrowing it down to a specific thesis; in the second, from an exam essay, Richard Sexton uses the dramatic method by applying a brief quotation to the topic of freedom before narrowing it to a specific thesis:

> The New World's struggle to forge a distinct identity outside the shadow of Old World Europe is reflected in much of the fiction on nineteenth-century American writers. Two such fiction writers, Herman Melville and Nathaniel Hawthorne, explore and question this evolving American identity by constructing characters who are outsiders forsaking the dominant values of their time. In Hawthorne's *The Scarlett Letter* Hester Prynne rejects the repressive intolerance and rigidity of America's Puritan values, while Melville's Bartleby, in "Bartleby, the Scrivener," withdraws from the materialistic, self-centred individualism of Wall Street, New York, and American business ideals. Each character struggles to function in a world that lacks empathy and basic kindness.

> In George Orwell's novel *1984*, one of Big Brother's infamous slogans is "Freedom is Slavery." American writers such as Mark Twain and Herman Melville also explored this paradox in the previous century. Twain's *Adventures of Huckleberry Finn* and Melville's "Bartleby, The Scrivener" have main characters in situations where they are least free when they have gained physical freedom. Both works embody this central paradox of freedom and enslavement.

Body paragraphs—integration of sources. Take care to integrate direct quotations effectively. The challenge in writing literary essays, because you will probably refer often to the text to support your points, is to weave quotations logically and gracefully into your sentences (see Chapter 6, Methods of Integrating Sources, page 165). The following is not well integrated:

> The moose is seen as a strong, noble figure: "like a scaffolded king, straightened and lifted his horns" (30).

To be grammatical and clear, something must be added:

Revised: The moose is seen as a strong, noble figure: "like a scaffolded king, [he] straightened and lifted his horns" (30).

Remember that much of the support in a literary analysis will come from primary sources: you make a point and follow with a quotation. As a general rule, do not provide a direct quotation and follow it by a comment about it. Doing so will produce a choppy and mechanical analysis:

"His fin, / Like a piece of sheet-iron, / Three-cornered, / And with a knife-edge" (3–6). In these lines, E.J. Pratt uses imagery to reveal the shark's machine-like power.

Revised: In these lines, E.J. Pratt uses imagery to reveal the shark's machine-like power: "His fin, / Like a piece of sheet-iron, / Three-cornered, / And with a knife-edge" (3–6).

Similarly, do not insert a direct quotation into the middle of your sentence if it results in an awkward structure:

In the third line, Stafford uses imagery, "This is the field where grass joined hands," to stress the unity of the scene.

Revised: In the third line, Stafford uses the image of a "field where grass joined hands" to stress the unity of the scene.

When citing from primary texts, check all your references carefully. Poetry citations should refer to line numbers rather than page numbers. Use the solidus (slash) to indicate line divisions in poetry with a space on both sides (/). For three or more lines of poetry, indent and use block format. For prose, use this format when you quote more than four lines of text (see Chapter 6, Direct Quotation, page 166, for block format).

If the poem is divided into sections, precede the line number by the section number, separating the two by a period. Thus, a parenthetical citation for the last four lines of Samuel Taylor Coleridge's "The Rime of the Ancient Mariner" would look like this: (VII.622–25). For short poems, such as Robert Frost's "Stopping by Woods on a Snowy Evening," line numbers usually are optional, but you should check with your instructor. For works of fiction in various editions, you should cite the page numbers in your edition, then follow with a semi-colon, a space, and chapter (ch.) or section (sec.) number. Plays should be referenced by act number, scene number, and line numbers, separated with periods with no spaces in between.

Examples:

In the end, Tess acknowledges her punishment: "'I am ready,' she said quietly" (417; ch. 58).

"The rarer action is / In virtue than in vengeance" (*The Tempest* 5.3.27–28).

For the use of ellipsis points to omit words in direct quotations, see Chapter 6, Omitting Material: Ellipses, page 168.

The follow body paragraph from student Stefan Virtue's essay on Edgar Allan Poe's "The Cask of Amontillado" illustrates the successful integration of a primary and a secondary source. Because Virtue alternates between his sources, he needs to include a complete parenthetical citation each time. He also integrates his quotations grammatically and smoothly, adding information he considers necessary:

> Montresor and Fortunato wend their way through the catacombs replete with the implied juxtaposition of wine, skulls, and skeletons. At this stage in the story, Fortunato has forgotten about Montresor's great and numerous family. He asks about the Montresors' coat of arms and motto. Montresor describes the shield as "[a] foot crush[ing] a serpent rampant whose fangs are embedded in the heel. . . . *Nemo me impune lacessit* [no one insults me without punishment]" (Poe 18). Montresor's mockery of Fortunato, with its ironic foreshadowing, fails to deter Fortunato from his quest for the Amontillado. Symbolically, Fortunato is already bound and helpless by the vice of the grape (Platizky 207). Finally, after arriving at the end of the vaults, Montresor chains Fortunato to the granite wall, and mockingly and sarcastically "implore[s]" (Poe 19) his victim to return, teasing him sadistically until the last brick is in place (Platizky 207).

Conclusion. Like the conclusion of any essay, the conclusion of a literary analysis should remind the reader of the thesis, perhaps by rephrasing it or by summing up one or two of the essay's most important points. Below, student writer Jessica Boyle concisely summarizes the differences between the stories' protagonists while suggesting their universality:

> Women may have various responses in their struggles for power and control in a male-dominated society. Some accept their fate; some fight for their freedom. Some ultimately accept the benefits and comforts in letting another person govern their life, as the sisters in Mansfield's "Daughters of the Late Colonel"; others, like the narrator in Gilman's "The Yellow Wallpaper," are willing to accept the risks of the struggle—even at the cost of their sanity.

Titles. Students sometimes have a harder time coming up with a title for a literary essay than for an expository one. Be especially careful that your title isn't too broad; it should refer directly to the works you analyze:

Too broad: "Humanity's Quest"; "The Desire for Freedom"; "Distortion of Reality in Modern Literature"; "The Theme of Race."

By specifying the titles of the individual work(s), the writers could have made their essay titles more meaningful and useful. On the other hand, a title may be specific but uninformative:

Uninformative: "An Essay on Stephen Crane's 'The Monster'"; "Ted Hughes's 'Hawk Roosting'"

Informative and Interesting:

"A Frankenstein of Society's Making: Stephen Crane's 'The Monster'"

"A Hawk's Guide to Megalomania"

See Chapter 7, pages 195–206 for specifics of MLA documentation.

Sample Student Literary Research Essay—MLA Style

The following essay explores a theme common to a short story and a poem, using the texts and secondary sources for support. The short story, "The Yellow Wallpaper," is summarized, and the poem, "My Papa's Waltz," is reproduced below.

Sample Student Essay

Summary of "The Yellow Wallpaper," by Charlotte Perkins Gilman, first published in 1892

"The Yellow Wallpaper" comprises journal entries of an unnamed woman narrator over a period of three months, during which her husband, John, has leased "a colonial mansion." The couple has a new baby, looked after by a nanny, and the narrator is forbidden any activity, including writing, while she recovers from "nervous depression." Although she believes that work and change would do her good, she complies with her husband's wishes, except for writing in her journal, which she hides from her husband and sister-in-law. Confined to an upper room she believes was once a nursery, she is repelled by its yellow wallpaper, but for lack of anything to do studies it intently, becoming more and more obsessed by it.

Over time, she discovers a pattern beneath the surface pattern; and what begins as "a formless sort of figure" later becomes a woman or several women "creeping behind the pattern." The woman shakes the bars of the outer pattern, which are revealed by moonlight; during the day, the trapped woman, like the narrator, is "subdued." The narrator's physical health improves as her obsession deepens; she suspects John and his sister also take an interest in the wallpaper. In the week before the expiry of the lease, the narrator thinks she sees the woman creeping about the grounds. On the last day, the narrator is determined to free the woman forever and, to do so undisturbed, locks the door and throws the key out a window. Armed with rope to tie up the woman if she tries to get away, the narrator completes the job by ripping off the wallpaper. In the final scene, the narrator is creeping around the room's perimeter as John enters, then faints. Stepping over him, the narrator says, "I've got out at last . . . . And I've pulled off most of the paper, so you can't put me back!"

"My Papa's Waltz"
by Theodore Roethke

The whiskey on your breath
Could make a small boy dizzy;
But I hung on like death:
Such waltzing was not easy.

We romped until the pans
Slid from the kitchen shelf;
My mother's countenance
Could not unfrown itself.

The hand that held my wrist
Was battered on one knuckle;
At every step you missed
My right ear scraped a buckle.

You beat time on my head
With a palm caked hard by dirt,
Then waltzed me off to bed
Still clinging to your shirt.

—Copyright 1942 by Hearst Magazines, Inc., from *The Collected Poems of Theodore Roethke* by Theodore Roethke. Used by permission of Doubleday, a division of Random House.

Reading 22

Gilman's "The Yellow Wallpaper" and Roethke's "My Papa's Waltz":
An Exploration of Ambivalence
by Kiyuri Naicker

[1] We often look at our world in terms of opposites or dualities. Only the bravest writers attempt to explore the grey areas of life where binaries converge and borders are not clearly defined. Some have persevered and created scenarios in which our traditional methods of perception fail us, forcing us to peer into this undefined area. Much can be uncovered about human nature in these instances. Two authors, in particular, have excelled in examining these interstices as they occur in domestic relationships: Charlotte Perkins Gilman and Theodore Roethke. The works analyzed here investigate what lies between the poles of sanity and insanity, abuse and affection. The ambiguous situations they have created draw our attention to societal concerns and ultimately urge us to question how we interpret the world around us.

[2] At the turn of the century, relatively little was understood about the progression of mental disorders. In her story "The Yellow Wallpaper," Gilman takes us on one woman's journey into madness through a first-person perspective. The story describes the transitional period between sanity and insanity, during which reality slips away and disorder slowly takes over. This fictitious account is based on Gilman's own experiences with neurasthenia and depression, which she underwent early in her marriage. A widespread belief during this period was that mental illness in women stemmed from moral deviance, and it was treated accordingly. In Gilman's case, her physician concluded that she needed to live as domestic a life as possible and limit herself to two hours of "intelligent" life a day. "The Yellow Wallpaper" was written to challenge the prevalent "domestic ideology" of the time; it is largely regarded as a feminist work. In this blurry region of conflicting realities, issues concerning the role of women in a patriarchal society, especially in relation to the medical world, began to surface. The narrative Gilman created "chronicles how women have been socially, historically, and medically constructed as not only weak, but sick beings" (Suess 61). The character never overtly accuses her oppressors for the state she finds herself in, but the story places the blame for the narrator's insanity on her situation rather than on herself. Jeannette King and Pam Morris explain that early feminist readings such as this were important because they "rectified the tendency to enclose the heroine's problems within her own abnormal psychological state" (37). This story forces one to look at what has actually transpired in the mind of the narrator, something that was generally avoided at the time in the treatment of mental disorders. As is evident in the narrator's interactions with her physician husband, the capacity of women to assess their own mental health was not taken seriously, and their concerns regarding their conditions were often marginalized. The outcome of this story points to the dangers of inadequate communication between physician and patient. Paula A. Treichler, for instance, reads the story as "an indictment of the complex and unhealthy relationship between women and medical language" (72).

[3] It is also an indictment of the view towards women and creativity at the time. The narrator's writing was seen to be the cause of many of her problems, and any attempts she made to continue with her craft were done in a furtive and guilty manner. Conrad Schumaker believes that it demonstrates "what happens to the imagination when it is defined as feminine (and thus weak) in a patriarchal Victorian society that values only the practical" (591). The original purpose of this piece was therefore to change the view of the prescribed "rest cure" for women with neurasthenia; however, the cure itself had roots in a patriarchal medical realm that came

under the magnifying glass as a result. The imposed confinement that Gilman underwent and the negative effects she consequently suffered are apparent in the story; the physician husband acts lovingly but succeeds in imprisoning his wife and driving her over the brink of sanity. Apart from providing an early feminist perspective, this story also illustrates how easily we can hurt those we love, and how trusting we can be of our aggressors.

Roethke explores this balance between affection and abuse more thoroughly in "My Papa's Waltz." Through his carefully ambivalent description, he has created a piece in which the two coexist in the same energetic scene. Roethke went to considerable lengths in his word choice to create ambiguity. Original poetic manuscripts reveal many revisions, the most drastic occurring in the fourth stanza. The first two lines originally read, "The hand wrapped round my head / Was harsh from weeds and dirt," but were changed to, "You beat time on my head / With a palm caked hard by dirt" in the printed version (McKenna 38). The diction in the revision is much more strongly ominous.   [4]

In contrast, one of the earlier titles was "Dance with Father," but the title was later changed to "My Papa's Waltz"(39). The final title has more affectionate, lighthearted overtones. This has the effect of "plung[ing us] into the comic and tragic tension" of the poem (Janssen 44). Speculation on the tone of this poem has divided many readers. This effectively illustrates the extent to which interpretation depends on an individual's perspective. According to H.R. Swardson,   [5]

> The words of a poem create a series of filters that eliminate possible meanings. In the universe of possible readings, comparatively few precipitate through all the filters. But in a poem like "My Papa's Waltz," several different readings do succeed in making their way through. At that point, the "preferred reading" is not found in the text, but in the interaction of reader and text. (4)   [6]

Those who see the joy in the poem place much emphasis on the rhythm and simple rhyme of the piece, and take the image of the waltz literally. The drunken father is seen as playfully tipsy, lavishing affection on the boy, which readers may have experienced with their own usually reserved fathers after they have had a few drinks. However, those who see the darker side of the poem view the waltz and rhythm ironically. These elements set a dizzying pace for the succession of fearful images remembered by the boy. The whiskey on his father's breath, the shaking room, his frowning mother, and the marred hand of his father (possibly from previous beatings) all flash past him on this terrifying journey around the kitchen. Words like "battered," "scraped," "death," and "beat" are implicated in recounting fear rather than joy. The element of alcohol also enhances the potential for violence and loss of control, according to many. As Bobby Fong observes, "The poem is like a seesaw, where the elements of joy . . . are balanced against the elements of fear . . . . A seesaw tips easily, and 'My Papa's Waltz' is susceptible to the pressure of personal experience" (80).   [7]

Given that both elements are present, it is more pertinent to question why they are there rather than argue for one perspective over the other. The ambivalence of the poem illustrates the extent to which the poles of affection and abuse converge, especially for those in dependent relationships. For example, it is possible that the child knows on some level that a terrifying incident has transpired, but in recalling the incident has "regressed into areas of the psyche where powerful thoughts and feelings—the raw materials and driving power of our later lives—remain under the layers of rationale and of civilized purpose" (Snodgrass 81). According to Snodgrass, he is therefore, out of civility and self-preservation, refraining from mentioning the abuse that has occurred. However, it is more likely that the boy himself does not know   [8] where the rapture ends and the terror begins. He has difficulty in separating the abusive monster from the loving father, and perhaps does not view them as distinct, opposing forces, as we tend to do. When the "waltz" ends, he still clings to his father who carries him up to bed. Roethke seems to be suggesting that the two extremes are perhaps not as distant as we would like to imagine. Blurring the lines in such a volatile situation makes it easy to understand how domestic violence is perpetuated through generations. The boy in this case has not attached solely negative connotations to the event and may find himself interacting with his own future son in this manner. The whole scene lends itself well to the idea of perpetuity, as stated by Ronald Janssen:

[9]
> As an image of still larger patterns, the idea of the waltz raises the image of the dance of death, the dance of life, and we are led to think not only of the succession of daily experiences but also the succession of generations as a kind of pattern as the younger generation moves into the older. (45)

[10] Despite the indefinite tone and imagery of the poem, it still succeeds in conveying the nuances of a very complex scene. The tone manages to avoid being deliberately condemning in addressing a highly sensitive subject, and as a result invites honest interpretation and introspection.

[11] Both the works discussed above provide complex and subtle social commentaries. Gilman and Roethke have explored everyday domestic life that exists between the dualities around which we tend to cluster. Their force lies in what they have left unsaid, leaving room for interpretation and, through it, self-examination. By leading us into areas we would normally never venture, they raise issues in feminism and domestic violence that are still pertinent today. As these authors' works suggest, relationships are seldom simple or polar.

Works Cited

Fong, Bobby. "Roethke's 'My Papa's Waltz.'" *College Literature* 17 (1990): 79–82. Print.

Janssen, Ronald. "Roethke's 'My Papa's Waltz.'" *Explicator* 44.2 (1986): 43–44. Print

King, Jeannette, and Pam Morris. "On Not Reading Between the Lines: Models of Reading in 'The Yellow Wallpaper.'" *Studies in Short Fiction* 26.1 (1989): 23–32. Print.

McKenna, John J. "Roethke's Revisions and the Tone of 'My Papa's Waltz.'" *ANQ* 11.2 (1998): 34–39. Print.

Schumaker, Conrad. "'Too Terribly Good To Be Printed': Charlotte Gilman's 'The Yellow Wallpaper.'" *American Literature* 57.4 (1985): 588–99. Print.

Snodgrass, W. D. "That Anguish of Concreteness—Theodore Roethke's Career." *Theodore Roethke: Essays on the Poetry*. Ed. Arnold Stein. Seattle: U of Washington P, 1965. 81. Print.

Suess, B.A. "The Writing's on the Wall: Symbolic Orders in 'The Yellow Wallpaper.'" *Women's Studies* 32.1 (2003): 79–97. Print.

Swardson, H. R. "The Use of the Word Mistake in the Teaching of Poetry." *ADE Bulletin* 91 (1988): 4–13. Print.

Treichler, Paula. A. "Escaping the Sentence: Diagnosis and Discourse in 'The Yellow Wallpaper.'" *Tulsa Studies in Women's Literature* 3.1–2 (1984): 61–77. Print.

Chapter 10

Sentence Essentials

Grammatical Groundwork

For some, grammar is simply a set of rules to be learned; for others, it is a way to improve their writing and further their understanding of how the English language is put together. What correct grammar will *always* help do is help create a channel of clear communication between writer and reader.

In general, the rules of grammar apply to all writing across the academic disciplines. That means you will need to follow rules that define acceptable academic writing. Academic writing is formal writing, so learning the rules of formal usage and correct grammar is vital. In this chapter and Chapter 11, we approach grammar formally, but without excess terminology.

Although formal grammatical rules are stressed throughout, not all the writing you do at university is formal. For example, when you take notes on a lecture, you may be concerned solely with content, using point form or even just key phrases. You might correspond with classmates by email, in which case you will probably write more informally, using colloquialisms or other "casual," everyday language.

Informal writing may also apply to certain kinds of business, technical, or journalistic writing. Some writing samples in this book, like Reading 1 in Chapter 1, page 20, are designed for a wider reading public than are academic studies and employ more informal language and looser sentence structure. In all your writing assignments, you should consider your instructor the final judge on the level of formality required. For more information on the differences between formal and informal writing, see Chapter 12, page 401.

> Guidelines for usage determine what words are suitable for a typical reader or listener. The typical reader of academic prose is different from the typical reader of a popular book, an office memo, a blog, or an email. Therefore, the level of usage is different.

EXERCISE 10.1

Find one example each of formal and informal prose from a magazine, newspaper, or book. Consider how the formal example could be changed into informal prose, taking into account such factors as vocabulary, sentence length and variety, tone of voice, and audience. Rewrite it as informal prose, keeping it about the same length. Then, rewrite the informal example as formal prose, considering the same factors and keeping it about the same length.

The Grammar of Reading and Writing

As a reader, your comprehension depends on your ability to recognize grammatical and other linguistic "signposts" that are embedded in the English language. The processing of grammar and syntax is, therefore, inherent in the act of reading.

As a writer, you are responsible for ensuring that readers can understand your message, so you need to become familiar with grammatical rules if you are to write effectively. Knowing and applying these rules will help open up the channel of communication from you, the writer, to your reader. Grammatical errors interfere with communication and possibly baffle your reader just as misspellings or faulty usage may.

In addition to ensuring the reader's clear understanding of your message, the proper use of grammar makes a good impression. Just as dressing for the occasion improves your standing in the group you are interacting with, the proper use of language creates a positive image, adding to your credibility as a writer.

The fastest, least complicated way to learn English grammar is to familiarize yourself with the basic *concepts* that underlie the rules of grammar. The pages that follow teach a concept-based grammar, beginning with the smallest word-units in the sentence: the parts of speech. From there, we look at what a simple sentence is, how to recognize phrases and clauses, and how to join clauses to form more complex sentence types.

Introducing . . . the Parts of Speech

Before considering the **sentence**, the basic unit of written communication in English, you need to be able to identify what makes up a sentence. A sentence can be divided into individual words, which, in turn, can be categorized as different parts of speech. Phrases and clauses are larger units than individual words. Being able to identify the forms and functions of the parts of speech will help you understand these larger units, too. The seven major **parts of speech** are nouns, pronouns, adjectives, verbs, adverbs, prepositions, and conjunctions. (*Interjections*, such as *oh!* and *hey*, usually express surprise or other emotion, and are not grammatically related to the rest of the sentence.)

The Parts of Speech at Work

When you are hired by an organization, given a job title, and a detailed job description, the job title is what you will be called; but the full job description explains your responsibilities, duties, or functions within the organization. The parts of speech, too, have specific, assigned roles within their organizational structure, the sentence.

As mentioned, words may have many meanings and may even serve as different parts of speech. *Cause* may be a noun and used as the subject of a sentence, such as "The *cause* was worthy of support." *Cause* may also be a verb and used as the predicate of a sentence, such as "The accident on the highway *caused* me to miss my flight." When one meaning of a part of speech is assigned to a function in a sentence, *that meaning* cannot be applied to a different part of speech in the same clause. For example, when a noun is the subject of the verb in a clause, it cannot also be object of the verb in the same clause. This is clear in the following: "Frasier has gone to see Frasier." Evidently the second *Frasier* must refer to a different person of the same name, or, perhaps, to a television program or a town, or some other thing.

Each part of speech is described below, with examples of its uses. The charts introducing each section give definitions to help you identify that part of speech; they also list its major functions in the sentence. Moving from the ability to identify the categories of the parts of speech to being aware of their functions within the sentence (their job description) will help you apply the rules of grammar.

Nouns and Pronouns

Nouns and pronouns are the *significant* words in a sentence because they name people, places, things, and ideas.

Table 10.1   Nouns and their Functions

Identification	Functions
Noun (*nomen*: "name"): name of a person, place, thing, or idea. • *proper* nouns refer to names and begin with a capital letter • *common* nouns refer to class or a general group and are not capitalized • *concrete* nouns refer to physical objects and things experienced through the senses • *abstract* nouns refer to concepts, ideas, and abstractions • *count* nouns name things that can be counted • *non-count* nouns refer to things that can't be counted • *collective* nouns refer to groups comprising individual members	1. **Subject**: performs the action of the verb (the doer of the action); sometimes called the *simple subject* to distinguish it from the *complete subject* that includes the simple subject plus its modifiers 2. **Object** (also called the *direct object*): receives the action of the verb 3. **Object of a preposition** (also called the *indirect object*): is usually preceded by a preposition (such as *between*, *in*, *with*) 4. **Subjective Complement** (also called the *predicate noun*): follows a linking verb (often a form of *to be* such as *is*, *are*, *was*, *were*) and can be linked to the subject 5. **Appositive**: is grammatically parallel to the previous noun or noun phrase
Pronoun (*pro + nomen*: "in place of the noun"): usually takes the place of a noun in a sentence. See Pronouns below.	Since pronouns generally replace nouns, they share the functions of nouns (see "Noun" above).

1. **Subject.** The subject noun usually performs the action (but see Chapter 12, page 409 for examples of the passive construction, where the subject does not perform the action). In the following examples, the subject is in boldface; the action word, the verb, is italicized:

   Dan *stood* at the front of the line-up.

   She *awoke* before dawn.

   The **rain** in Spain *falls* mainly on the plain.

   The subject usually comes before the verb but sometimes follows it, as, for example, with some questions:

   Was the final **exam** difficult?

2. **Object (of the verb)** is also called the **direct object**. It is the receiver of the action of the verb. Here, the object is in boldface; the verb is italicized:

   James *beat* **Dan** into the movie theatre.

   Erin *let* **him** into the house.

   They *chopped* the **logs** for firewood.

3. **Object of the preposition** (also called **indirect object**). The noun or pronoun is usually preceded by a preposition. Here, the object is in boldface; its preposition is italicized:

She awoke *before* **dawn**.

The rain *in* **Spain** falls mainly *on* the **plain**.

I never heard *of* **it** before.

4. **Subjective Complement (completion).** The noun or pronoun that "completes" the subject after a linking verb. Here, the subjective completion is in boldface; the linking verb is italicized; the subject is underlined:

<u>Rayna</u> *was* the first **person** to get a job after graduation.

5. **Appositive.** A noun, noun phrase, or pronoun that is grammatically parallel to a preceding noun or pronoun and that rephrases or (re)names the preceding noun. Here, the appositive is in boldface; the preceding noun is italicized:

Madeline's *cats*, **Evie and Nanny**, have very different personalities.

The subject of the sentence is "cats"; the names of the cats are **in apposition to the subject** (the names are not part of the simple subject).

Pronouns

Personal pronouns refer to people and things; in the possessive case, they can function as adjectives, as does "her" in this example: Here, the pronouns are in boldface:

He ran all the way to the sea. **She** sat down because **her** feet were blistered.

Relative pronouns (*that*, *which*, *who*) introduce dependent clauses that *relate* the clause to the rest of the sentence; these clauses usually function adjectivally. Here, the relative pronouns are in boldface:

The book, **which** I lost on the bus, was about Greek history. The student **who** found it returned it to me.

Interrogative pronouns (*how*, *what*, *when*, *where*, *which*, *who*, *why*) introduce questions. Here, the interrogative pronouns are in boldface:

Where is the book I lost on the bus? **How** can I thank you enough for returning it?

Demonstrative pronouns (*that*, *these*, *this*, *those*) point to nouns; they can function as adjectives. Here, the demonstrative pronouns are in boldface:

This is the *day* of reckoning.

This *day* will be long remembered.

Indefinite pronouns (such as *any*, *everything*, *some*) refer to unspecified individuals or groups; they do not require an antecedent and may form their possessives in the same way as nouns. Here, the indefinite pronouns are in boldface:

It is **anyone's** guess when the boat will arrive, but **everyone** should wait on the dock.

Reflexive pronouns have the form of personal pronouns with the -*self* suffix; they refer **back** to the subject as the receiver of an action. Here, the subject is italicized and the reflexive pronoun is in boldface.

Ben congratulated **himself** on his successful election.

Table 10.2 Verbs and their Functions

Identification	Functions
Verb (*verbum*: "word"): conveys an action, state, or condition, or precedes another (main) verb. The different kinds of verbs have different functions.	1. **Main verb** may be *transitive* (takes a direct object) or *intransitive* (does not take a direct object) and usually conveys an action, not necessarily physical, in the predicate. 2. **Helping** or **auxiliary verb** precedes main verb to form a complex tense (indications of the time, continuance, or completeness of the action) or to express a *mood* such as obligation, necessity, probability, or possibility; or *voice*, (whether the relation of verb to subject is active or passive). 3. **Linking verb** is followed by a *predicate noun* or *adjective* that refers back to the subject.

Intensive pronouns also have the form of personal pronouns with the *-self* suffix; they serve to reinforce their antecedents. Here, the subject is italicized and the intensive pronoun is in boldface:

The *teacher* **herself** was often late for class.

Reciprocal pronouns refer to the separate parts of a plural antecedent. Here, the reciprocal pronoun is in boldface and the antecedent is italicized:

People need to accept and tolerate **one another**.

Verbs

Verbs convey an action, state, or condition. There are three different kinds of verbs, each having different functions.

The various tenses of English verbs are illustrated in Appendix A.

1. **Main verbs** express action, condition, or a state of being. Some kinds of action are not necessarily visible— *imagine*, *suggest*, and *think* are examples of action verbs in which the "action" is interior or mental. Verbs may be modified by adverbs or adverbial phrases.

   Nicole **helps** her father at the store every Saturday.

2. **Helping verbs** (also called **auxiliary verbs**) combine with main verbs. The two most common helping verbs are *to be* (*am*, *are*, *is*, *was*, *were*, *will be*, etc.) and *to have* (*have*, *has*, *had*, etc.) Forms of *to be* are used in the *progressive* tenses; forms of *to have* are used in the *perfect* tenses (see Appendix A).

   She **has** helped her father at the store for two years.

   Modals are verb forms placed before the main verb to express necessity, obligation, possibility, probability and similar conditions: *can*, *could*, *will*, *would*, *shall*, *should*, *may*, *might*, *must* and *ought to* are modals (see Appendix A).

   She **would** help on Sunday, too, if not for her other weekend job.

3. **Linking verbs** like *to be* are used to connect subject and predicate in one of the six ways shown in the examples below. Here, the linking verbs are in boldface:

Expressing identity: Today **is** Saturday.

Expressing condition: I **am** upset.

Expressing state: These **are** my colleagues.

Expressing opinion: We **are** for freedom of speech.

Expressing total: One and one **are** two.

Expressing cost: The fundraiser **is** $200 a plate.

Other verbs that imply *to be* also may function as linking verbs. Here, the linking verbs are in boldface:

Mildred **becomes** [begins to be] faint as the night **grows** [continues to become] cold.

Compare the use of "acted" in these two examples:

He **acted** the part of Hamlet *splendidly*.

He **acted** *sick* by staying home from school.

In the first sentence, "acted" is a main verb used transitively (takes the object "part"); it is modified by the adverb "splendidly." In the second sentence, "acted" is used as a linking verb—he acted (behaved as one who *is*) sick—the verb implies *to be*—and thus is followed by a subjective complement, the predicate adjective "sick" (see "Subjective Complement" below).

Modifiers: Adjectives and Adverbs

Adjectives and adverbs modify, or give more information about, the major parts of speech—nouns and verbs. *Articles*, such as *a*, *an*, and *the*, and determiners, such as *her* and *this*, may precede nouns and can be considered to function adjectivally.

Adjectives modify nouns and usually precede them. Adjectives follow linking verbs, where they *modify the subject* as *predicate adjectives*. Here, the adjective is in boldface and the modified noun is italicized.

They attended the **delightful** *party*.

Here, the predicate adjective is in bold, the linking verb is italicized, and the subject is underlined.

The <u>party</u> *was* **delightful**.

Adverbs modify verbs, adjectives, and adverbs.

1. Here, the boldface adverb modifies the italicized verb.

Jake *turned* **suddenly**.

2. Here, the boldface adverb modifies the italicized adjective.

That looks like a **very** *contented* cow.

Table 10.3 Adjectives and Adverbs and their Functions

Identification	Functions
Adjective (*ad* + *jectum*: "put near to"): a word that modifies and precedes a noun or follows a linking verb; it answers the question "Which?," "What kind?," or "How many?"	1. **Adjectival modifier** describes or particularizes a noun and precedes it. 2. **Subjective complement** (also called the *predicate adjective*) follows a linking verb (see "Nouns and Pronouns" above) and modifies the subject.
Adverb (*ad* + *verb*: "to the verb"): a word that modifies a verb, adjective, adverb, or even an entire sentence; it often ends in *-ly* and answers the question "When?," "Where?," "Why?," "How?," "To what degree?," or "How much?"	1. **Adverbial modifier** describes or particularizes a verb and may precede or follow it; an adverb may also modify an adjective or another adverb; a *sentence adverb* may be the first word of the sentence and modify the entire sentence. 2. **Conjunctive adverb** belongs to a specific group of adverbs and may be used to connect two independent clauses.

3. In this example, the boldface adverb modifies another adverb (italicized).

> They lived **quite** *happily* together.

Some adverbs can also act as **conjunctions** to connect two independent clauses. Here, the conjunctive adverb is in boldface:

> Richard was hired by the publicity firm on Monday; **however**, he was fired on Tuesday.

Note the semicolon separating the clauses and the comma after "however."

Joiners: Prepositions and Conjunctions

Prepositions and conjunctions are classed together here as they connect different parts of a sentence.

Prepositions join nouns and pronouns to the rest of the sentence and add information to the subject or predicate. Where there is a preposition, you will usually find an object of the preposition (noun or pronoun) following. Prepositions introduce prepositional phrases, which function as *adjectives* or *adverbs*, depending on what part of speech they are modifying. In the following examples, the preposition is in boldface, the object of the preposition is italicized, and the prepositional phrase is underlined:

> You will find the letters **in** the *attic*.

> She worked **during** the summer *vacation*.

> They laughed **at** *him*.

Commonly used prepositions. The noun or pronoun that follows a preposition usually functions as the object of the preposition. Many prepositional phrases, such as *as*

Table 10.4 Prepositions and Conjunctions and their Functions

Preposition (*pre + ponere*: "to put before"): a small word/short phrase that often refers to place or time.	1. **Preposition** joins the following noun or pronoun to the rest of the sentence.
Conjunction (*con + junction*: "join together"): a word/phrase that connects words, phrases, and clauses of equal or unequal weight or importance. For a list of common subordinating conjunctions, see page 328.	1. **Coordinating conjunction** joins *equal* units, including independent clauses; there are seven coordinating conjunctions. 2. **Subordinating conjunction** joins *unequal* units, including independent and dependent clauses. 3. **Correlative conjunction** joins *parallel* units; they join in pairs.

well as, *in spite of*, and *on account of*, are not listed as prepositions (see list below), but can often be recognized as such by the fact that a noun or pronoun follows.

about	between	like	since
above	beside(s)	near	than
across	beyond	next (to)	through
after	by	of	throughout
against	despite	off	to
along	down	on	toward(s)
among	during	onto	under
around	except	opposite	until
as	for	out	up
at	from	outside (of)	upon
before	in	over	with
behind	inside	past	within
below	into	regarding	without

Conjunctions have two main joining functions: they can join equal or unequal units.

1. **Coordinating conjunctions** join *equal* units—words to words, phrases to phrases, clauses to clauses. An important use of coordinating conjunctions is to join *independent clauses* in compound sentences. Here, the coordinating conjunction is in boldface. Note the comma before the conjunction:

   Tanya objected to their new roommate, **but** Mercedes liked her.

   Coordinating conjunctions are often referred to as the FANBOYS (*for, and, nor, but, or, yet, so*).

2. **Subordinating conjunctions** join *unequal* units, usually a *dependent* clause, which it begins and is part of, to an *independent* clause. Here, the subordinating conjunction is in boldface. Note the comma in the second sentence:

   He plans to exercise his option **once** the season is over.

   Once the season is over, he plans to exercise his option.

3. **Correlative conjunctions** occur in pairs and require parallel structure. Here, the correlative conjunctions are in boldface:

Either you will support me, **or** you will not be able to borrow my car.

Both Ali **and** his father work at the community centre on Saturdays.

EXERCISE 10.2

↻ Check answers to select questions

Read the following paragraph and identify the following:

1. 5 nouns
2. 2 pronouns
3. 6 verbs
4. 3 adjectives
5. 2 adverbs
6. 4 prepositions
7. 2 conjunctions

Once we left the main road and turned down a narrow side street, we were in nothing more than an extended slum. The car came to a stop in front of a house that was far better than any of the others around it. Set back a little from the street, it was a well-kept bungalow. The cemented front garden had a garish marble fountain in the middle, with an arrangement of plastic flamingos and penguins around it. The windows had heavy bars across them, and even the front door had an extra door of iron bars in front of it. My grandmother did not get out; instead she had the driver toot his horn imperiously. A woman stepped out of the front door, and when she saw the car, she immediately nodded and smiled and went back inside. (Selvadurai, Shyam. "The Demoness Kali." *Short Fiction & Critical Contexts*. Ed. Eric Henderson and Geoff Hancock. Don Mills: Oxford UP, 2010. 384. Print.)

Introducing . . . the Sentence

Because the sentence is the basic unit of written (though not of spoken) communication, you need to know how to identify incomplete sentences in your writing so you can make them complete in formal writing. In order to know what an incomplete sentence is, you need to first consider the concept of the sentence.

What Is a Sentence?

It's not always easy to identify a complete sentence. Which of the following is a sentence?

Write!

Right!

Now, consider this pair:

Seeing As Believing.

Seeing Is Believing.

Although you may have been able to correctly identify "Write!" and "Seeing Is Believing" as complete sentences, the examples show that just the appearance of a

A Closer Look

Forms of the Verb to be

Although verbs often convey an action, some verbs do not express what a subject is doing, but rather express a condition or state of being. The most common of these verbs are forms of *to be*: *is, are, was, were, has been, have been, will be*, and so on. Because you will use these verbs often, you need to become familiar with them and recognize them as a particular kind of verb (see "Linking verbs," page 319).

word or group of words isn't a reliable guide to identifying a sentence. In commands, the subject *you* is implied (see below, page 324); therefore, "Write!" means *You write!* and is a complete sentence. A **sentence fragment** is the term for a less-than-complete sentence. "Right!" and "Seeing As Believing" are examples of fragments. "Right!" is missing both subject and predicate: *You are right!* is complete. "Seeing As Believing" is a noun phrase; there is no predicate.

Some textbooks define a sentence as a complete thought. Most complete sentences express a completed thought or idea, but if we define a sentence simply as a complete *thought*, we need to know what a thought is. However, this definition is useful in identifying one type of incomplete sentence, a dependent clause fragment—see p. 328.

Which of these word groups is a sentence?

Rules of grammar.

Grammar rules!

If we accept "rules" in the second example as a colloquialism (an informal word or expression), then the second word group would form a sentence with "rules" as the verb. The first, however, is not a sentence because nothing is happening and no comment *about* the rules of grammar is being made. Some groups of words can be recognized as sentences because a word or words suggest something is happening or a relationship is being observed.

The word "rules" in the second sentence tells us something the writer is observing about "Grammar." The first word also is necessary to make the sentence complete; it indicates *what* "rules." So, you can say that complete sentences need two things:

1. A *subject* that answers the reader's question "What or who is this about?"
2. A *predicate* that tells us something the subject is doing or what is being observed about it.

A sentence, then, is *a word or group of words that expresses a complete thought.* More important, it can be defined grammatically: *a sentence is a group of words that contains at least one subject and one predicate and needs nothing else to complete its thought.*

A question that can help determine the subject of a sentence is "Who or what is doing the action in the sentence?" When you ask this question, you are attempting to connect a verb, the main part of the predicate, to a noun or pronoun, the main part of a subject. Consider a very simple sentence:

Dogs bark.

The answer to the question "Who or what is doing the action in the sentence?" is "Dogs." So, "Dogs," a noun, is the subject.

To determine the predicate of a sentence, you can ask the question, "What does the subject do?" The answer is "bark." A predicate will always include a *verb*. The line in this sentence divides the subject from the predicate:

Dogs | bark.

The sentence "Dogs bark" is very brief. How can we make this sentence longer and more interesting? Adding words or phrases to a subject make it more informative, but it doesn't usually change its basic structure. The line between subject and predicate will remain; the difference will be that a reader will know more about the dogs. Similarly, we could add words or phrases to the predicate so we would know more about their barking:

Dirty, dangerous dogs | bark balefully behind the barn.

The reader has been told that the dogs are "dirty" and "dangerous." The predicate also has more information: the reader has been told *how* the dogs barked ("balefully") and *where* they barked ("behind the barn"). The longer sentence illustrates how you can make statements more interesting by adding words or phrases, *modifiers*, to the subject and to the predicate. The subject together with its adjectival modifiers is called the **complete subject**; the main noun or pronoun alone is sometimes called the **simple subject** to distinguish it from the complete subject.

Another way you can give more information in a sentence is to add more subjects and predicates. When you add one or more subject-predicate units, the sentence is no longer simple. While simple sentences convey one complete thought, more complex sentences can convey more than one complete thought.

When you look to see whether the word group has a subject, make sure you don't mistake a noun or pronoun in a prepositional phrase for a subject. (See "Fragment 2—add-on fragment," below.) In this sentence, there are two nouns in the complete subject: "end" and "troubles." The first noun is the true subject; "troubles" is preceded by the preposition "of" and cannot be linked with the verb "is."

The *end* of our troubles | *is* in sight.

The Invisible-Subject Sentence

The need for a subject and a predicate in every complete sentence suggests that the minimum English sentence must contain at least two words. There is one exception: an **imperative sentence**, which is a command, may consist only of a predicate (verb). The subject, which is always implied, is the pronoun *you*, although it is invisible. For example, in the imperative sentence, "Listen!" the subject *you* is understood to be the subject: "[You] listen!" In the command, "Go to the store!" *you* is understood to be the subject: "[You] go to the store." Notice that *you* could be plural, i.e., the command could be to more than one individual; indeed, all readers of the work could be implied.

Which of the following are complete sentences? Draw a line between the subject and the predicate. Mark with an S those that contain only a subject and a P to those that contain only a predicate. Indicate an N if there is neither subject nor predicate.

1. The cat on the window ledge.
2. Wanted to bury his treasure where it would never be found.
3. A door in the wall.
4. Dropped the ball with only ten yards to go.
5. A sweet-smelling fragrance.
6. Opportunity knocks.
7. Is willing to give a presentation.
8. The high levels of stress of today's students.
9. Can schizophrenia be cured?
10. Hundreds of geese in the field.
11. Send in the clowns!
12. An enemy of the people.
13. Pay attention to the number of times that you end a sentence with a preposition.
14. All dressed up with no place to go.
15. This term will be my most successful one ever.

EXERCISE 10.3

Check answers to select questions

Four Errors of Incompletion

The first step to ensure that all your sentences are complete is to check that there is a noun or pronoun subject to connect with a verb in the predicate. However, checking for fragments can be a little more complicated than this. To help you recognize *all* kinds of fragments in your writing, they are divided into four types below.

Fragment 1—lacks subject or predicate. In this type of fragment, discussed above, either a subject or a predicate is missing.

In sentence 10 of Exercise 10.3, "Hundreds of geese in a field," something essential is missing. What about geese in a field? Do they exist? Are the geese doing something? What did they look like? Who saw them? To answer any of these questions is to complete a thought—and the sentence. For example:

Hundreds of geese in a field | were resting before the next stage of their long journey.

Mr. Elford | imagined hundreds of geese in a field.

In the first example, a predicate has been supplied. In the second example, a subject, Mr. Elford, and a verb, "imagined," have been introduced, and the "hundreds of geese in a field" have become part of the predicate, the direct object of the verb "imagined."

The following sentence is also incomplete because it consists only of a subject. In this case, the noun "instructor" is followed by a word group that expands on the subject. The subject is not doing anything:

An instructor who never gives an A.

"Who never gives an A" tells us what kind of instructor he or she is but goes no further. To turn this into a complete sentence, you would need to complete the thought by adding a predicate:

> An instructor who never gives an A *marks too hard*!
>
> An instructor who never gives an A *sets very high standards*.

Come up with two other ways to complete this fragment.

EXERCISE 10.4

 Check answers to select questions

Complete the following fragments, all of which lack a predicate.

1. The cellphone that I lost yesterday.
2. The brilliant idea that came to me in the middle of the night.
3. A leader who is capable of motivating others.
4. The kind of doughnut that doesn't have a hole in the middle.
5. The baseball bat that was put in the museum.

EXERCISE 10.5

Check answers to select questions

To the remaining fragments in Exercise 10.3, add a subject and/or predicate to create grammatically complete sentences.

Fragment 2—add-on fragment. Add-on fragments contain neither complete subject *nor* predicate. Writers can mistake them for complete sentences because in speech a pause is usual between them and the preceding sentence; you may mistakenly associate a pause or drawn breath with a new sentence. The easiest way to fix these kinds of fragments is to make them part of the previous sentence or to supply missing essentials, such as subject and predicate. Punctuation may not be needed; at other times, you can use a comma or a dash.

Add-on fragments may begin with transitional words and phrases: *such as*, *like*, *for example*, *including*, *also*, *as well as*, *except (for)*, *besides*, *especially*, and similar words. They may also begin with prepositions like *on*, *in*, and *to*.

> *Fragment*: Exaggerated images of fitness are everywhere. Especially in teen-oriented magazines.
>
> *Corrections*:
>
> Exaggerated images of fitness are everywhere, *especially* in teen-oriented magazines.
>
> Exaggerated images of fitness are everywhere—*especially* in teen-oriented magazines.
>
> *Fragment*: Sewage contains more than 200 toxic chemicals that are flushed down sinks or toilets. Not to mention the runoff from roads.
>
> *Correction*: Sewage contains more than 200 toxic chemicals that are flushed down sinks or toilets, *not to mention* the runoff from roads.

When you begin a sentence with a word like *in*, *to*, *at* (i.e., a preposition), check to see that the sentence expresses a complete thought and includes both a subject and a predicate.

Fragment: On a mountaintop in the remotest region of the Yukon.

Who or what is there and what is taking place?

Corrections:

A confused goat | *stood* on a mountaintop in the remotest region of the Yukon.

On a mountaintop in the remotest region of the Yukon, *the climbers* | *unfurled a flag*.

Fragment 3— -ing fragment. A third kind of fragment occurs when an incomplete verb form ending in *-ing* or *-ed/en*, or a base verb form, is mistaken for a complete verb. To avoid sentence fragments, always ensure you write a *complete* verb form. Here are some examples of incomplete verb forms:

> *being*, *listening*, *studying*, *thinking* (present participle form of verb)
> *given*, *taken*, *thought*, *written* (past participle form of verb)
> *to be*, *to begin*, *to look*, *to tell* (infinitive form of verb)

While *complete* verb forms can be joined to a subject by adding a helping verb, incomplete verb forms can't be:

Incomplete: She listening, they given . . .

Complete: She *was listening*, they *are given* . . .

A common sentence error is mistaking the *-ing* part of a verb form for a complete verb form. The following are examples of fragments with incomplete verb forms:

Holiday crowds *milling* around shopping malls.

What are the crowds doing? If you said "they are milling," you have changed the fragment into a complete sentence by adding the helping verb *are*:

Holiday crowds | *are milling* around shopping malls.

Fragment:

As a new doctor fascinated by innovative surgery procedures.

Correction:

As a new doctor, he | *was fascinated* by innovative surgery procedures.

A Closer Look

Fixing -ing Fragments

You can recognize an *-ing* form of the verb as incomplete because it is missing the helping verb it would need to make it complete. It is also missing a subject. One way to fix an *-ing* fragment, then, is to complete it by adding a helping verb and a noun or pronoun.

Fragment: Looking ahead to Chapter 8 of the textbook.
Correction: The students were looking ahead to Chapter 8 of the textbook.

It's important to be able to identify these kinds of incomplete verb forms in your sentences and not treat them as if they were complete forms. However, they have legitimate and useful roles to play in your writing—not as verbs but as nouns, adjectives, and even adverbs. "Eating" is the subject of this sentence:

> *Incomplete verb form as noun*: *Eating* sensibly | is the best way to lose weight.
> *Incomplete verb form as adjective*: My *growling* stomach | told me it was time to eat.

"Growling" is an adjective modifying "stomach," the noun subject. Note that there is another incomplete verb form in this sentence, "to eat," which is also acting as an adjective, modifying "time."

There is more than one way to fix the following fragment error:

Fragment: City Hall instigating a new policy despite tough economic times.
Corrections:
City Hall | *was instigating* a new policy despite tough economic times.
Instigating a new policy | is inadvisable in tough economic times.

In the first correction, a complete verb form has been made from the incomplete form. In the second one, "Instigating" has become the noun subject of the sentence.

Fragment 4—dependent clause fragment. A dependent clause fragment is the most common type of fragment. That is because, at first glance, a dependent clause looks a lot like a grammatical sentence.

Independent clauses are equivalent to simple sentences: they have a subject and a predicate and need nothing else to complete them. *Dependent* clauses also contain a subject and a predicate, but they express incomplete thoughts because the information they contain is *dependent on* information in the independent clause. That is one way you can tell a dependent from an independent clause. (Recall that one definition for a complete sentence is that it expresses a *complete* thought.)

Another way that dependent clauses can be identified is by the word they begin with—a subordinating conjunction or a relative pronoun. Here are some of the most common subordinating conjunctions and relative pronouns:

after	ever since	though	whether
although	if	unless	which
as	if only	until	whichever
as if	in case	what	while
as long as	in order that	whatever	who
as soon as	once	when	whoever
as though	rather than	whenever	whom
because	since	where	whose
before	so that	whereas	why
even though	that	wherever	

Dependent clause fragments sound incomplete and leave us wondering about the missing part. Consider this fragment:

> Because his car wouldn't start this morning.

You can think of dependent clauses as searching for an answer to something—in this case, *what happened because his car wouldn't start?* When you provide that information in an independent clause, you will have a complete sentence. You can also test a sentence for completeness by asking whether the word group is true or false. "Because his car wouldn't start this morning" can be neither true nor false due to missing information.

Because his car wouldn't start this morning, he was late for his first day of work.

The subordinating conjunction that introduces the dependent clause indicates the relationship of that clause to the independent clause, such as one of cause–effect (*as*, *because*), time (*before*, *since*, *when*, *while*), or contrast (*although*, *though*, *whereas*). (For more information about subordinating conjunctions as joiners, see page 321.) If you take away the subordinating conjunction, you are left with a subject and a predicate and a sentence that expresses a complete thought. Another way to fix a dependent clause fragment, then, is to take away the subordinating conjunction; you will have a simple sentence expressing one idea. However, it may not be the idea you intended to convey:

His car wouldn't start this morning.

This is a complete sentence, but it does not explain the consequences of his car not starting.

Note that a dependent clause could either precede or follow the independent clause. The placement of the dependent clause often determines whether you use a comma to separate it from the main idea.

Like subordinating conjunctions, relative pronouns (see pages 317 and 328) introduce clauses that sound incomplete by themselves. Dependent clauses introduced by relative pronouns usually follow the word or phrase that they modify ("images" in the sentence below).

Fragment: The media bombards us with images of underweight women. Which give an unrealistic representation of the female body.

Corrected: The media bombards us with images of underweight women, which give an unrealistic representation of the female body.

Does the word group contain a subject (tells who or what), and is there an action performed by the subject?	If NO . . . ⟶	It's a fragment
Does the word group consist of only nouns/pronouns preceded by prepositions?	If YES . . . ⟶	It's a fragment
Is the only identifiable verb form in the word group an infinitive (e.g., *to be, to know, to learn*)?	If YES . . . ⟶	It's a fragment
Does the only identifiable verb form in the word group end in *-ing*, *-ed*, or *-en* and is not preceded by a helping verb (e.g., *is, were, has been*)?	If YES . . . ⟶	It's a fragment
Does the word group begin with a subordinating conjunction (one of the words on page 328) and does not express a completed thought?	If YES . . . ⟶	It's a fragment

Fast-Track

●●●●●

Finding Fragments

EXERCISE 10.6

↻ Check answers to select questions

The following groups of words may or may not be sentences. If they are not, identify what kind of fragment they illustrate (lacks subject or predicate, add-on fragment, *-ing* fragment, dependent clause fragment). If they are fragments, make them into complete sentences with a subject and a predicate.

1. Ensuring that you write in complete sentences.
2. Huge tears rolled down his cheeks.
3. Being that she was insured as the principal driver.
4. Whenever they called her into work.
5. He promised to call on her tomorrow. To see if she was still all right.
6. He must be guilty. Since he's already confessed.
7. I won't vote tomorrow. Unless I hear something that makes me change my mind.
8. Introducing our next prime minister.
9. A row of stately elms interspersed with sprightly cedars.
10. Swimming on her back.
11. Walking beside the tracks, he eventually reached the town.
12. Because spiritual values are more enduring than material ones.
13. Stress can make us victims of illnesses. Including mild to life-threatening ones.
14. The student sauntered into class. After he opened the door and cautiously peeked inside.
15. Which leads to another popular argument for lowering the drinking age.
16. For example, the famous TV show *American Idol*.
17. This is the information age. When ideas are literally at your fingertips.
18. The opposition to vaccinations is a manifestation of fear. That the side effects will be more harmful than the disease itself.
19. Learning about people from different ethnic groups.
20. Stress can have devastating effects on many groups of people. Such as depression in those who fail to meet their own expectations.
21. Golf courses always include obstacles. These being water hazards and sand traps.
22. More than half of depressed adolescents are given antidepressants. Which raises the question of whether they are the best long-term solution.
23. Although there are options in today's schools for Aboriginal students to learn about their culture.
24. Sounds and textures are common features of dreams. While smell and taste are usually absent.
25. On 4 November 2008, millions of viewers tuned in to see one of America's most historic elections. If not the most historic ever.

EXERCISE 10.7

↻ Check answers to select questions

Each of the following passages contains four sentence fragments. Underline them. Then, correct them by joining them to complete sentences or by adding information. Each passage contains three *kinds* of fragment error, as discussed above. Which kind of fragment error is *not* present in each passage?

1. Although it is known that the people who inhabited the island were of Polynesian descent. In 1994, DNA was extracted from 12 skeletons found on the island, and it was proven to be from people of Polynesian descent. Furthermore, it was

suggested that these Polynesians came from Southeast Asia. From the fact that the crops grown by the indigenous people were native to Southeast Asia. For example, bananas, sugarcane, taro, and sweet potato. For more than 30,000 years prior to human settlement of the island, the area was a subtropical forest of trees and woody bushes. Towering over a ground layer of shrubs, herbs, and grasses.

2. International concern has grown in recent years over the proliferation of weapons of mass destruction, but weapons used to exterminate enemy forces are nothing new. In World War I, artillery was used. In addition to gas, machine guns, grenades, and bombs. The 1940s brought more powerful weaponry. As well as the first nuclear weapon. A weapon capable of killing hundreds of thousands of people. After World War II, the Cold War began, as Russia and the US became involved in an arms race. Building hundreds of nuclear weapons more potent than those used in World War II.

Introducing . . . Phrases and Clauses

Phrases and **clauses** are grammatical units within the sentence that are larger than one of the parts of speech by itself but usually smaller than a complete grammatical sentence. (The exception is an independent clause, which is equivalent to a simple sentence.)

Prepositions join nouns and pronouns to the rest of the sentence, while conjunctions handle the other joining functions. **Coordinating** conjunctions join two or more independent clauses while **subordinating** conjunctions and relative pronouns join dependent and independent clauses. By joining clauses, you can form different sentence types.

Phrases

Phrases function as nouns, verbs, adjectives, and adverbs. When they act as these parts of speech, it is important to remember that they do so as a unit, though each word *within* the unit may be made up of a different part of speech and have a function distinct from that of the unit itself.

Phrases | function (*as a unit*) (*within the sentence*).

"As a unit" and "within the sentence" are functioning as adverbs, modifying the verb "function". (Recall that adverbs modify verbs.) The first phrase answers the question "How?" while the second answers the question "Where?" of the verb. But though each phrase is acting adverbially, the individual words within the unit have distinct functions, none of which is adverbial.

as = preposition

within = preposition

a = indefinite article

the = definite article

unit = noun (object of preposition "as")

sentence = noun (object of preposition "within")

> A phrase is a group of two or more grammatical linked words which, lacking a subject and/or predicate, can be thought of as functioning as a single part of speech.

Prepositional Phrases

Prepositional phrase units act as either adverbs or adjectives. As you've seen above, a group of words that includes more than one part of speech can, as a unit, modify a verb. If it does, it is said to be functioning **adverbially** (as an adverb) within the sentence.

> She drove me (*into town*) so I could do my laundry.

The prepositional phrase "into town" begins with the preposition "into" and is followed by the noun "town," the object of the preposition. But if you look at the phrase as a unit, you can see that "into town" is functioning as an adverb modifying the verb *drove* by explaining where the action took place: *Drove where? Into town.*

Similarly, a group of words can modify a noun or pronoun, in which case it is functioning **adjectivally** (as an adjective). Consider the prepositional phrases (indicated by parentheses) in these sentences:

> An obsession (*with* Star Wars) | led to her career (*as an astronomer*).

"With *Star Wars*" is a prepositional phrase that gives us more information about (i.e., modifies) the noun "obsession." It is functioning as an adjective.

> with = preposition
>
> Star Wars = proper noun (object of preposition with)

The second phrase, "as an astronomer," modifies the noun "career," functioning as an adjective.

> as = preposition
>
> astronomer = noun (object of preposition as)

Adjectival phrases usually *follow* the noun or pronoun they modify. This order is different from that of one-word adjectives, which usually *precede* the noun they modify.

Prepositional phrases do not contain the actual subject of a sentence. In the following sentence, "At the beginning of class" does not contain the actual subject even though it begins the sentence:

> *At the beginning of class,* students in Japan bow to their teacher.

The subject here is "students," and "at the beginning of class" is a prepositional phrase telling *when* they bow. Since it answers "When?" of the verb "bow," you know it is acting adverbially in the sentence.

Noun and Verb Phrases

In this example, the indefinite pronoun "Some" combined with its modifier, "of the injured," makes up a **noun phrase**. The entire phrase, "Some of the injured passengers," functions as the subject in this sentence because it tells us *who* "had to be hospitalized":

> *Some of the injured passengers* | had to be hospitalized.

Phrases, then, can function as noun subjects or objects.

Finally, consider the following sentence, in which a **verb phrase** acts as a unit in the sentence, conveying the action of the subject "We":

We *will be looking* carefully for the person with a red flag on her backpack.

Verb phrases are very common since you will often need to use helping verbs with main verbs to create different tenses beyond the one-word simple tenses (verb phrases are italicized):

Simple present: I think, you say, she takes . . .

Simple past: I thought, you said, she took . . .

Present progressive: I *am thinking*, you *are saying*, she *is taking*. . .

Past perfect: I *had thought*, you *had said*, she *had taken*. . .

In addition to forms of *to be* and *to have*, verb phrases occur when modals, a special kind of helping verb, combine with main verbs to convey ability (*can, could*), possibility (*may, might*) necessity (*must, have*), and other meanings.

For more information about the tenses and the modals, see Appendix A, page 439.

First, identify the word groups in parentheses as adverbial, adjectival, noun, or verb phrases. Then, identify the subject of the sentence.

1. Yesterday, (the price of food) was the main item (in the news).
2. (Some of my favourite books) (have gone) out of print.
3. The room (with the two computers) (has been locked) (from the inside).
4. A search (of the abandoned house) (turned up) several cartons (of stolen goods).
5. The best player (on our paintball team) broke his arm and (will be lost) (for the season).

EXERCISE 10.8

 Check answers to select questions

---

Clauses

A word group larger than a phrase that can be broken down into two grammatical units, a subject and a predicate, is called a **clause**. In the following sentence, the subjects are in bold, the verbs are italicized, and the conjunction (joiner) is underlined. Clauses can be combined to create longer or more complex sentences than simple sentences:

Frances never *answers* questions in class <u>unless</u> the **teacher** *calls* on her.

First clause: Frances never answers questions in class

Second clause: unless the teacher calls on her.

A clause is a group of words containing both a subject and a predicate.

The first part of this sentence could stand alone as a sentence, as it has a subject, "Frances," a predicate verb, "answers," and needs nothing else to complete its thought. The second part could not stand alone as a sentence—the word "unless" makes it a dependent clause fragment.

Thus, this sentence illustrates two different kinds of clauses: (1) an **independent clause**, which can stand alone as a sentence, and (2) a **dependent clause**, which cannot stand alone as a sentence. It is especially important to be able to distinguish an independent clause from a dependent clause in order to avoid writing a sentence fragment. As discussed under "Fragment 4—dependent clause fragment" (page 328), a dependent clause contains an idea subordinate to (dependent on) the idea of the main clause.

EXERCISE 10.9

↻ Check answers to select questions

Identify all independent and dependent clauses in the following sentences by underlining independent clauses and placing parentheses around any dependent clauses. For help, you can refer to the list of subordinating conjunctions below, page 335; these kinds of conjunctions introduce dependent clauses. Remember that pronouns, such as *I* or *it*, can act as subjects.

1. While drug testing has become more common, athletes are still taking drugs.
2. Although I think winter is here, the temperature is not cold enough for snow.
3. I became hooked on reality shows when I began watching them with my roommate.
4. In most parts of North America, Daylight Saving Time begins in March.
5. The battle against cancer will continue until a cure is found.
6. While it is important that students volunteer, mandatory volunteerism introduced at many schools does not instill a sense of civic duty.
7. The folk music of the '60s and '70s often encouraged peace; however, the message was not always received.
8. Studying grammar does not guarantee good grades, but it certainly helps.
9. Despite her good intentions, the governor general has not been able to satisfy many Canadian politicians.
10. Plastic water bottles have become the focus of public scorn, though more pressing moral concerns need attention.

Using Conjunctions to Join Clauses

The seven coordinating conjunctions are *for, and, nor, but, or, yet, so*. The coordinating conjunctions spell out the acronym FANBOYS.

An independent clause by itself is equivalent to a *simple sentence*. "Frances never answers questions in class" is a simple sentence consisting of an independent clause. Clauses are used as building blocks to construct more complex sentences. The function of a **coordinating conjunction** is to connect *equal* units, such as two independent clauses. The function of a **subordinating conjunction** is to connect *unequal* units, such as an independent clause and a dependent clause. Different rules for punctuation apply to independent and dependent clauses connected this way.

Sentence Patterns

Compound. Sentences formed by two or more independent clauses joined by a coordinating conjunction are called **compound sentences**. (Conjunctive adverbs, like *however*, can also join independent clauses.) We can see these kinds of conjunctions (italicized) operating as joiners in the following examples:

The woodwinds warbled, *and* the strings sang sweetly.

Our profits in the first quarter showed a ten per cent increase, *but* in the second quarter, they dropped again.

I discovered there was a great deal written on my topic, *so* I knew I would have to narrow my search.

A sentence can have two subjects or two verbs and still be a simple sentence (but not two subjects *and* two verbs). Coordinating conjunctions join equal units, so as well as joining two independent clauses, they can join two nouns that are the subject of one verb or two verbs governed by one subject. Such compound-subject and compound-predicate constructions can occur in simple sentences. However, a compound *sentence* contains two independent clauses, *each* with its own subject and verb.

Here is an example of a simple sentence with a compound predicate:

Jason *awoke* before dawn *and listened* happily to the sounds of the new day.

Note that there is no comma before the conjunction "and" because the two verbs it connects are parts of the same clause. The sentence below contains two subjects and two predicates:

Jason *awoke* before dawn, *and* **he** *listened* happily to the sounds of the new day.

Don't use a coordinating conjunction to begin a sentence. Words like *and*, *but*, and *or* should occur only *within* a sentence where they join two equal units, such as two independent clauses:

Incorrect: The popularity of Facebook is undeniable. And it shows no sign of abating.

Corrected: The popularity of Facebook is undeniable, *and* it shows no sign of abating.

Complex sentences. A sentence formed by one independent clause joined by a subordinating conjunction to a dependent clause is called a **complex sentence**. In a complex sentence, two or more subordinating conjunctions may connect two or more dependent clauses to an independent clause. We can see these kinds of conjunctions operating as joiners in the following examples:

Plagiarism is a problem at many universities *where* much research these days is conducted through the Internet.

Although much work has gone into developing artificial organs, the results, to date, have been disappointing.

In the first sentence, "where" is the subordinating conjunction that begins a dependent clause and joins it to the preceding independent clause. In the second sentence, the dependent clause comes first, but the subordinating conjunction "although" nevertheless joins the dependent to the independent clause.

In the sentence below, an independent clause is followed by two dependent clauses; *after* and *that* are the subordinating conjunctions that join them:

Ena began taking night classes *after* her company announced *that* there would be layoffs in the near future.

You need to carefully distinguish clauses in order to punctuate them correctly. For example, in this sentence, a dependent clause intervenes between the subordinating conjunction "that" and the rest of the dependent clause. The dependent clause that interrupts is italicized:

The students felt it was unfair that, *because the instructor was late*, they weren't given enough time for the test.

Common subordinating conjunctions and relative pronouns:	
after	though
although	unless
as	until
as if	what
as long as	whatever
as soon as	when
as though	whenever
because	where
before	whereas
even though	wherever
ever since	whether
if	which
if only	whichever
in case	while
in order that	who
once	whoever
rather than	whom
since	whose
so that	why
that	

A Closer Look

Dependent Relative Clauses

One kind of dependent clause doesn't begin with a subordinating conjunction but with a **relative pronoun**. Such adjectival clauses "relate" back to the noun they follow, specifying it or giving additional information about it. Relative pronouns include *who*, *whom*, *which*, and *that*. The **relative clause** is underlined and the relative pronoun italicized:

Environmentalist David Suzuki wrote the essay *that* we read last week.

The guest speaker was introduced by the college's vice-president, *who* was clearly unprepared as he repeatedly stumbled over his words.

In the last sentence, *who* is a relative pronoun introducing a dependent (relative) clause that modifies "vice-president." It is followed by a dependent clause beginning with the subordinating conjunction *as*.

Relative pronouns introducing dependent clauses can sometimes be omitted. For example, in the sentence below, "whom" can be omitted, yet it is understood to introduce the dependent (relative) clause "[whom] she admires most," which modifies "actresses":

One of the actresses she admires most is Kate Beckinsale.

For more on relative pronouns, see page 383.

Compound-complex sentence. The last sentence type, a **compound-complex sentence**, combines a compound sentence (independent clause + coordinating conjunction + independent clause) with a complex sentence. It will contain two independent clauses along with one or more dependent clauses. For example:

The woodwinds warbled, the brass bellowed, *and* the strings sang sweetly, *though* the timpani thundered, almost drowning out the other instruments.

EXERCISE 10.10

C̄ Check answers to select questions

Examples of the four sentence types appear below. (a) identify the type of sentence; (b) for compound, complex, and compound-complex sentences, underline independent clauses, circle conjunctions, and put parentheses around dependent clauses. Identify each sentence type.

1. The class average was low in the first semester, but it has gone up this semester.
2. Since the beginning of time, people have worn fur for warmth.
3. The mosquitoes are biting again, and the BBQs are being fired up.
4. She ran the race in record time but collapsed at the finish line.
5. Salmon oil is a supplement that lowers cholesterol.
6. Expository writing explains or informs the reader about something.
7. Snowboarding began in the early '70s, and it has grown in popularity ever since.
8. His library privileges have been suspended until he pays his fines.
9. The committee began its search in September and has not yet found a suitable candidate.
10. She is convinced that she will get an A in the course.
11. Studies show that while smoking is declining nationally, more than 25 per cent of those aged 20–24 continue to smoke.
12. The end of the transatlantic slave trade came in 1807 when importing slaves was finally banned in the US.

13. Music is essential in schools because it gives students a chance to excel in a non-academic subject.

14. The first non-Inuit to reach the North Pole was James Peary, though his claim has often been disputed.

15. After Orri learned Greek cooking, we ate psomi with every meal, but since he switched to Indian cuisine, we seldom have it anymore.

EXERCISE 10.11

C Check answers to select questions

To demonstrate your familiarity with the different kinds of clauses and joiners, construct compound, complex, and compound-complex sentences from the independent clauses (simple sentences) below. After you have joined the clauses in the most logical way, identify the sentence type: compound, complex, or compound-complex. Ensure that you have at least one example of each type of sentence. Small changes can be made so that it is easier to make up complex sentences, and sentence order may be changed.

1. They intended to eat at Benny's Bistro.
    They saw a long line-up outside Benny's.
    They went to Kenny's Kitchen instead.

2. There may be nearly two million kinds of plants in the world.
    There are likely at least as many different kinds of animals.
    No one can know how many species have evolved, flourished, and become extinct.

3. Timothy Findley's story "Stones" takes place in Toronto.
    Norman Levine's "Something Happened Here" takes place in northern France.
    Both stories describe the tragic assault by Canadian troops on Dieppe during the Second World War.

4. We may suspect that earth is not unique as a life-bearing planet.
    We do not as yet have any compelling evidence that life exists anywhere else.
    We must restrict our discussion of the pervasiveness of life to our own planet.

5. Drug-testing procedures for Olympic athletes are becoming more and more elaborate.
    Athletes often feel they have to boost their performance.
    They want to compete at the same level as their competition.

Errors of Combining

A fragment in formal writing suggests the writer does not fully understand what a sentence is. But sometimes writers run one sentence into another, suggesting they don't know where to end the sentence. The two major errors in ending a sentence are the **run-on sentence** (sometimes called "the fused sentence") and the **comma splice**, or the comma fault.

The Run-On Sentence

A writer of a run-on sentence joins two sentences without stopping. Doing this is like running a stop sign without changing speed. The writer charges through the end of the first complete thought and into the second one without separating the statements.

This writer does not place a period at the end of the first sentence and so does not capitalize the first letter of the word that should begin the second sentence.

A sentence may contain one, two, or more subject–predicate units, and these units (independent clauses) must be either separated by a period or joined correctly so the reader can distinguish one main idea from another.

Incorrect:

The cruise to Alaska was full Yumi decided to fly to Jamaica instead.

The Dene peoples live in Northern Canada they speak different languages.

Once you determine where the first clause ends and the second one begins, make them into two simple sentences or use a comma and the appropriate coordinating conjunction to join them.

Corrected:

The cruise to Alaska was full. Yumi decided to fly to Jamaica instead.

The cruise to Alaska was full, *so* Yumi decided to fly to Jamaica instead.

The Dene peoples live in Northern Canada. They speak different languages.

The Dene peoples live in Northern Canada, *and* they speak different languages.

The run-on sentences below contain two complete thoughts, or two main ideas. Lines indicate the division between subject and predicate; double lines show where the first sentence ends and the second begins, and where a period or a comma and coordinating conjunction should be placed.

Incorrect:

Few Koreans | have animals in their homes // pets | are not a large part of Korean culture.

Toxic chemicals and pollutants | do not disappear // they | accumulate in our natural resources.

Corrected:

Few Koreans have animals in their home. Pets are not a large part of Korean culture.

Few Koreans have animals in their homes, *for* pets are not a large part of Korean culture.

Toxic chemicals and pollutants do not disappear. They accumulate in our natural resources.

Toxic chemicals and pollutants do not disappear, *but* they accumulate in our natural resources.

> A run-on sentence isn't just a long sentence: it's a major grammatical error in which two subject–predicate units (two "sentences") are not properly separated.

The Comma Splice

An error more common than the run-on sentence is the comma splice—the joining of two complete sentences by only a comma. This error is like slowing down at a stop sign without coming to a full stop, then charging through. The comma has many uses *within* the sentence, but, by itself, a comma cannot be used to connect two sentences.

The simplest way to avoid a comma splice is to think about where one complete thought (independent clause) ends and the next begins and to place a period there or use a comma and a coordinating conjunction. A comma splice sometimes occurs when two clauses are very closely related or the second clause seems a continuation of the first one. In formal writing, it's important to be able to separate two independent clauses.

Incorrect:

Fights in hockey are more than pointless, they are often dangerous.

Legalizing marijuana is not just the better choice, it is the right choice.

Although the second clauses in these sentences are closely related in meaning to the preceding clauses, they are not part of those clauses and must be separated from them by something stronger than just a comma. As you will see in later sections (pages 354 and 357), a "stop" form of punctuation, such as a semicolon or colon, may be a good choice in these cases:

Corrected:

Fights in hockey are more than pointless. They are often dangerous.

Fights in hockey are more than pointless; they are often dangerous.

Legalizing marijuana is not just the better choice. It is the right choice.

Legalizing marijuana is not just the better choice; it is the right choice.

Remember that a pronoun generally replaces a noun that precedes it in a sentence. Like a noun, a pronoun can act as the subject of a clause. In each of the following sentences, a pronoun is the subject of the second clause. Lines indicate the division between subject and predicate; double lines show where the first sentence ends and the second begins, and where a period or the comma and coordinating conjunction should be placed:

Incorrect:

Working in a busy office environment | was completely new to her, //she | had always worked at home.

Censorship | does not just mean getting rid of swearing and nudity, //it | can also mean blocking an idea or viewpoint.

Corrected:

Working in a busy office environment was completely new to her. She had always worked at home.

Working in a busy office environment was completely new to her, *for* she had always worked at home.

A comma splice isn't just a problem in comma usage; it's a major grammatical error in which a comma alone is used to separate two complete thoughts.

Censorship does not just mean getting rid of swearing and nudity. It can also mean blocking an idea or viewpoint.

Censorship does not just mean getting rid of swearing and nudity, *but* it can also mean blocking an idea or viewpoint.

Remember that if you wish to use a comma to connect two independent clauses, you must also use one of the seven coordinating conjunctions. You cannot use a comma before words like *however*, *therefore*, or *thus* to join two independent clauses. That would also produce a comma splice. When you use these words between independent clauses, choose one of two options: (1) Put a period after the first independent clause and begin the next sentence with the "joiner," such as *however*; or (2) precede the joiner by a semicolon, so that it will now introduce the second independent clause. For more information about using words other than coordinating conjunctions to join two main ideas, see page 430.

Fast-Track

Errors of Combining

Does one independent clause follow another one with no punctuation in between?	If YES . . . ⟶	you may have written a run-on sentence
Have you separated one independent clause from another with only a comma?	If YES . . . ⟶	you may have committed a comma splice
Have you joined two independent clauses with a comma followed by a joining word that is not a coordinating conjunction?	If YES . . . ⟶	you may have committed a comma splice

EXERCISE 10.12

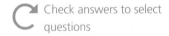
Check answers to select questions

Fix the sentences below by using a period to make two separate sentences (or if you already know the rules for using other forms of punctuation to join independent clauses, you can use them). Also, identify whether the sentence is a run-on or a comma splice.

1. I took two buses to get downtown it was a long way.
2. Our neighbour's dog howled all last night, it was just impossible to get a night's sleep.
3. I was frightened during my first driving lesson the instructor yelled at me.
4. It's easy to punctuate sentences, just put a comma whenever you pause.
5. Janne ate as quickly as he could then he went upstairs to finish his homework.
6. The incidence of breast cancer has increased, it takes the lives of many women today.
7. Homelessness has existed for centuries, literature on the subject dates back to the feudal period in Europe.
8. Humans are imitators, conforming is something they are good at.
9. Mozart composed his first minuet at the age of five he wrote his first symphony before he turned nine.
10. Asthma is a common problem among Canadians, exposure to second-hand smoke in public places can intensify this condition.

Determine what is wrong in the following sentences. It could be a fragment, a run-on sentence, or a comma splice; then, make the correction.

1. He managed to pass the year though he seldom did his homework, what will happen to him next year is anyone's guess.
2. The opening ceremonies were delayed. On account of rain.
3. She went to France for the summer. It being a fine opportunity to learn another language.
4. Though they both liked to read, they usually read different books, she read adventure stories while he liked detective stories.
5. While books are still the main source for acquiring knowledge.
6. The only way a person can learn. To pay attention to what is going on in class.
7. He was too tall and thin to excel at sports. Except basketball, of course.
8. The concept that "bigger is better" is part of our culture, it is promoted by both advertisers and the media these days.
9. Understanding the theory of relativity and its impact on our daily lives.
10. Martin Luther King led protests during the civil rights movement, his enthusiasm and his will to end discrimination made him a leader.
11. The Romans were willing to change their religious beliefs quite easily, the Greeks, however, were less willing to do this.
12. Although TV can corrupt the minds of innocent children if it is not monitored closely.
13. The computer is not the only way to access email today, telephones and palm pads may come equipped with email capability.
14. It seems that the North American mass media prescribes two roles for women, they can be sex objects or passive housewives.
15. Martial arts are attracting more people than ever before. Especially those who want to gain self-control and self-awareness.
16. We can no longer turn our backs to what is happening in the north it is time to take action.
17. Nintendo held a launch party in Times Square, New York, it was hosted by a local VJ.
18. Racism in Canada exceeded just social and personal racism, it was institutional racism.
19. A story of an Indo-Canadian woman who rejected her arranged marriage.
20. Carpal Tunnel Syndrome has many causes, the most common is repetitive wrist movements.
21. The tobacco in cigarettes is not the only problem, they contain many dangerous chemicals as well.
22. One of the most tragic events of the twentieth century. The detonation of the atomic bomb over Hiroshima.
23. Podcasts are current, up-to-date and appear automatically, thus they can be enjoyed anywhere at any time.
24. In the final book of the series, Harry visits his parents' grave and sees two inscriptions on their graves the inscriptions refer to passages from the Bible.
25. Many factors contribute to poverty. Including geographic factors, disease, and lack of education or health care.

EXERCISE 10.13

Check answers to select questions

EXERCISE 10.14

Identify the sentence errors in the following paragraph; they may include fragments, run-on sentences, and comma splices. Then, correct them.

In recent decades, our society has become obsessed with body image through fitness and weight loss this infatuation can be seen in the popularity of fad diets. Such as the Atkins diet and its many variants. Fitness routines popular today include yoga and Pilates, there has also been a marked increase in the number of women having plastic surgery. In general, the obsession with body image is a greater concern for females than for males. Since many women are socialized to equate self-worth with physical appearance. One of the causes of this socialization is the popular media. Which often portrays unrealistic standards of the ideal body type.

Punctuation, Pronouns, Modifiers, and Parallelism

Commas: Do They Matter?

Does the precise placement of those visually challenged marks on paper *really* matter? The short answer is "yes," because readers look for commas in specific places to help them read. When a comma is missing or placed where it shouldn't be, the reader might have to reread the sentence, looking for another cue to its meaning. Furthermore, if you make comma errors, your reliability will be affected.

Missing commas in the short sentences below could confuse a reader:

The day after a deadly tornado ravaged much of the countryside.

Although dating services may ask you for a photo appearance is less important than personality.

Applying one of the comma rules discussed below means placing commas after "after" in sentence 1 and after "photo" in sentence 2.

As a student, you will be writing essays or reports for many of your classes. As a future working professional, you may write letters, email, reports, summaries, memoranda, or other documents that need to be punctuated. Correctly punctuated sentences with commas, as well as with other punctuation marks, will help you communicate your meaning. Correct comma use guides the reader through the sentence, clarifying the relationships among its parts.

Myths about comma use abound, such as the "one breath rule," which states that wherever you naturally stop to pause, you should insert a comma. However, commas assist the silent reader more than the one who reads aloud. If you are coaching yourself to read a speech aloud, you may want to place commas where you plan to pause for breath, but in formal writing, the "one breath rule" is simply too vague to be of use; it can even lead you astray.

The word *comma* comes from the Greek word *komma*, meaning "cut" or "segment." In general, commas separate (segment) the smaller or less important units in a sentence. Working with coordinating conjunctions, however, they are also used to separate large units, independent clauses. In a sentence, commas separate

1. items in a series
2. independent clauses
3. parenthetical (non-essential) information
4. some adjectives; parts of dates, addresses, titles; and the like.

Rule Category 1: Items in a Series

Use a comma after each item in a list or series. This rule category applies to three or more grammatically parallel items whether single words—such as nouns, verbs, or adjectives—phrases, or clauses.

A series of three nouns:

It doesn't matter whether the items in the series are words, phrases, or clauses.

A series of three predicates:

Every Saturday, Davina gets up, drowns herself with coffee, and stumbles to the door before she realizes what day it is.

A series of three clauses:

Come to the Broadmead Art Tour tomorrow: view artworks in a variety of media, add to your collection, and meet with talented artists on their doorstep.

A series or list is *three* or more of something. When you refer to *two* of something with a joiner in between like *and*, you do *not* usually use a comma unless *and* is joining two independent clauses. The grammatical name for a group of words made up of two of something (such as two nouns or two verbs) is a **compound.**

The comma before the last item in a series of three or more items, referred to as the **serial comma,** is often omitted in informal writing:

Informal: My three favourite months are April, June and September.

However, there are places where using the serial comma makes a sentence much easier to follow. It should *not* be omitted if the last element or the one that precedes it is a compound (contains two items). In this example, the last item in the list is a compound, a single thing, "toast and jam," comprising two elements: "toast" and "jam":

She ordered orange juice, an omelette with cheese, and toast and jam.

The serial comma is especially helpful where the second-last or last item is significantly longer than the other items:

The two-year specialization includes 10 half-courses, two full courses that involve internships in health care facilities, and a research paper.

Rule Category 2: Independent Clauses

The rule for independent clauses applies to three related situations: (a) two independent clauses joined by a coordinating conjunction; (b) introductory word, phrase, or clause followed by an independent clause; and (c) an independent clause followed by a concluding word or phrase.

(a) **Compound sentence.** Use a comma before the coordinating conjunction in a compound sentence (two joined independent clauses).

The course was supposed to be offered in the fall, *but* it was cancelled.

The grocery store is two kilometres away, *so* he never walks.

Dyana was the best dancer on the cruise ship, *and* she won an award to prove it.

Remember that the comma goes *before*, not after, the coordinating conjunction.

Short Independent Clauses. The comma between independent clauses may be omitted if the second clause is very short or if the clauses are so closely related that they could be considered compounds (i.e., the ideas are hard to separate). In this example, the comma may be omitted between "dress" and "and" because the clauses are short:

"She wore the dress and I stayed home," sang Danny Kaye in the movie *White Christmas.*

(b) **Introductory word, phrase, or clause.** Use a comma after an introductory word, phrase, or clause followed by an independent clause.

After six years as committee chair, it was time for her to retire.

In order to get the maximum enjoyment from his stereo equipment, Curtis put it in a room where the acoustics were excellent.

In the following example, the introduction is one word, a **sentence adverb**, an adverb that modifies the independent clause that follows it:

Unfortunately, we have run out of mineral water.

When a sentence begins with a dependent clause that is followed by an independent clause, a comma follows the dependent clause (italicized here):

While the drinking age is 19 in most provinces, it is only 18 in Alberta.

When she first encountered the Canadian educational system, she was surprised by the many differences between the North American and Japanese systems.

Compare with rule 2c, below.

(c) **Concluding word or phrase.** In general, use a comma after an independent clause that is followed by a concluding word or phrase.

W.J. Prince wrote to his client Larry Drucker, asking direction in the case.

Rule 2c applies when a statement is followed by a reference to the person or group that made the statement:

"We still think of a powerful man as a born leader and a powerful woman as an anomaly," Margaret Atwood once said.

Students who participate in sports or social activities at school are more likely to consider themselves satisfied with their lives compared to those who do not, according to a recent study.

Concluding dependent clause. Rule 2c does not usually apply when an independent clause is followed by a dependent clause (but see A Closer Look, Essential and Non-essential Dependent Clauses). So, if you begin with a dependent clause and follow with an independent clause, use a comma to separate the clauses, as rule 2a states, but if you *begin with an independent clause and conclude with a dependent clause*, you do *not* generally use a comma.

A Closer Look

Essential and Non-essential Dependent Clauses

1. He seldom visits the zoo, though he lives only one block away.
2. He often visits the zoo when he is in town.

In sentence 1, the dependent clause gives additional information. Although this information may be important, it is not essential to the main idea of the sentence. The main idea is that the man seldom visits the zoo. But in sentence 2, the dependent clause, "when he is in town," completes the thought, giving us essential information. After all, the man has to be in town in order to visit the zoo. If the information in the dependent clause is additional (non-essential) information, you should precede the dependent clause by a comma.

You will be right more often than not if you use the simplified rule that depends on the order of the independent and dependent clauses (see above). However, dependent clauses that begin with *although*, *even though*, *though*, or *whereas* often suggest a contrast with the independent clause and do not "complete" its meaning. In these cases, the dependent clause containing additional information should be preceded by a comma.

The sleek Siamese cat lay on the *sofa where* it was sunny. (essential, completes the thought in the independent clause)
The sleek Siamese cat lay on the *sofa, whereas* the old Labrador retriever curled up by the fire. (additional information)

Rule Category 3: Parenthetical Information

When you place something in parentheses, you signal to the reader that this information is less important than what is outside the parentheses. Commas operate similarly to separate less important from more important information in the sentence. The three rules in this category will help you decide whether the information is non-essential (additional) or essential; then, you can punctuate accordingly.

(a) **Non-restrictive (non-essential) phrase or clause.** Use commas before and after a non-restrictive phrase or clause. A non-restrictive clause often begins with one of the relative pronouns *which*, *who/whom*, or *that*. It follows a noun, which it modifies.

Although the information in **non-restrictive** clauses may be important, it *can* be left out without changing the essence of the sentence:

Non-restrictive: Many students, *who take out loans*, have a heavy debt burden on graduation.

If you take out what is in italics, you are left with a sentence that says simply "Many students have a heavy debt burden on graduation."

By contrast, a **restrictive** clause is *essential* to the meaning of the sentence. If you left it out, the sentence would mean something different or would be ungrammatical. If the information in the clause is essential, omit the commas. This example is a more specific statement about *only* those students who take out loans, so no commas are used:

Restrictive: Many students *who take out loans* have a heavy debt burden on graduation.

Note: Use *who* to refer to people in restrictive and non-restrictive clauses. Use *which* to refer to non-humans in non-restrictive clauses, and *that* to refer to non-humans in restrictive clauses:

The actor who [not *that*] appeared in the movie *Outbreak* also appeared in *Sweet Home Alabama*.

A Closer Look

Punctuating Relative Clauses

It is important to look closely at a clause that begins with *which*, *who*, and *that* in order to punctuate it correctly. When the clause gives additional (non-essential) information, separate the clause from the rest of the sentence by commas. If it gives essential information, do not use a comma. Consider these sentences:

1. Tony, *who often wears a leather jacket*, was identified as one of the rescue team.
2. A man *who wore a leather jacket* was identified as one of the rescue team.

The main idea in sentence 1 is that Tony was identified as part of the rescue team. Tony's leather jacket may be important elsewhere in a larger narrative, but in this sentence, it is not part of the main idea; therefore, the information about his jacket is enclosed by commas. *Note that two commas are required*, just as two parentheses would be required.

You can test whether information in a clause beginning with *who*, *which*, or *that* is essential: if you omit the clause and the sentence says something different, you've proven that the information is essential. In sentence 2, the information about the jacket is essential to the identification of this person on the team. If you were to leave out the clause "who wore a leather jacket," the sentence would say simply that a man, not a woman, was on the rescue team.

(b) **Appositive.** Use commas to set off an **appositive**, which is a noun—word or phrase—that is grammatically parallel to a preceding noun or phrase. It *names, rephrases, specifies, or explains* the noun or noun phrase that comes just before. In these examples, the appositives are underlined, and an arrow points to the noun that each identifies or explains:

Her first work, <u>a short story collection called *Drying the Bones*</u>, was given outstanding reviews.

Seal hunting, <u>a traditional means of livelihood among the Inuit</u>, has been criticized by some environmentalists.

Use commas only for a true appositive. Sometimes the second noun completes the first noun, giving essential information. In such cases, you do not set off the second noun with commas. If in doubt, take the second noun or noun phrase out of the sentence and see if the sentence is complete without it and makes grammatical sense.

Can you explain why commas are placed around "king of the beasts" in the following sentence but not before "Aesop," the name of the Greek writer? Which is the true appositive? Hint: try taking "king of the beasts" and "Aesop" out of the sentence to test for essential versus non-essential (additional) information:

The lion, king of the beasts, is the subject of many fables by the Ancient Greek writer Aesop.

Although it is not strictly an appositive, you can use the appositive rule for a word or phrase that can be considered a subsets of a larger set—like a phrase beginning with *such as* or *including*.

The celebration of certain holidays, such as Christmas and Halloween, has been banned by several local school boards.

Combining Rules

In the following sentence, the appositive rule 3b and independent clause rule 2a are illustrated:

His first purchase, [3b] the painting of the Northern Ontario Landscape by Tom Thompson, [3b] is now worth thousands of dollars, [2a] but he says he will never sell it.

(c) **Adverb or adverbial phrase.** Use commas to set off an adverb or adverbial phrase that interrupts the flow of the sentence from subject to predicate, or from verb to object or subjective completion. Such a word or phrase often emphasizes or qualifies a thought. See page 356 for a list that includes *after all*, *for example*, *however*, *indeed*, *in fact*, *needless to say*, *therefore*, and many more.

Use commas to set off the name of a person being directly addressed. The following sentence has two interrupters, "Frank" and "beyond a doubt":

"I must say, Frank, that your performance on the aptitude test demonstrates, beyond a doubt, that you would make an excellent engineer."

There are times, especially in informal or semi-formal writing, when two commas around a small word that interrupts the sentence may produce clutter. Except in the most formal writing, commas around adverbial interruptions can be omitted if they directly follow a coordinating conjunction, such as *but*, to avoid three commas in close proximity.

Commas can be omitted: Leslie worried about her driver's test, but in fact she aced it.

Not incorrect, but cluttered: Leslie worried about her driver's test, but, in fact, she aced it.

Rule Category 4: Conventional and "Comma Sense" Uses

Stylistic convention more than grammar dictates that you use commas between co-ordinate adjectives before a noun; in dates, addresses, and titles; and before and after direct quotations.

Commas between adjectives. Adjectives modify nouns and usually precede them. When two or more adjectives are *coordinate*, or equal and interchangeable, separate them with a comma. When the adjectives are *non-coordinate*, or unequal and not interchangeable, do not use a comma.

Coordinate adjectives: big, friendly dog; tall, white tower; proud, condescending man

Non-coordinate adjectives: white bull terrier; welcome second opinion; incredible lucky break

One way to determine if adjectives are coordinate is to mentally place the word *and* between the adjectives, as in "big (and) friendly dog." If this makes sense, then the adjectives are coordinate and commas are required. Applying this test to "white (and) bull terrier" produces a meaningless phrase, as it contains non-coordinate adjectives; therefore, commas are not used.

Quotation in a sentence. Use commas to separate a quotation from the rest of the sentence, as in an attribution (i.e., where a source is named):

The sign says, "trespassers will be prosecuted."

"I am not a crook," said Richard Nixon.

Commas should not be used mechanically before all direct quotations. Let the grammar of the sentence determine whether a comma should be used:

Comma incorrect: The computer is often accused of, "promoting superficial and uncritical thinking."

Comma correct: According to the writer, "the computer promotes superficial and uncritical thinking."

Address. Commas separate names and locations in an address:

The Prime Minister of Canada, 24 Sussex Drive, Ottawa, Ontario, Canada

Convention also dictates that you place a comma *after* the name of the province or state if the sentence continues:

I lived in Calgary, Alberta, until I moved back to Ontario.

Date:

October 7, 1951

A comma is not used if you begin with the day and follow with the month and year, nor is it used with the month and year alone:

7 October 1951 and October 1951

Degrees, titles, and similar designations:

Sabrina Yao, M.D., Ph.D., F.R.C.P.S.

Numbers. Under the metric system, there is a space rather than a comma between every three digits in a number of more than four digits (the space is optional with four-digit numbers). You will often see the non-metric format where a comma separates every three digits starting from the right:

The output of chemical wastes was 13 890 457 kilolitres per day for that factory.

In 2006, the population of Nunavut was 29 474, according to Statistics Canada.

The US Defense Department listed 2,356 casualties earlier in the year.

Quotation Marks. The convention in North America is to place commas and periods *inside* quotation marks:

The new topic, "Where Ecological Ends Meet," has been posted.

Other marks of punctuation, such as semicolons, are placed *outside* quotation marks:

We have been told that our meals "are not gratis"; however, the company has paid for our transportation.

If a citation follows a direct quotation, however, the period or comma is put *after the citation*:

Taking one's surroundings for granted has been dubbed "environmental numbness" (Gifford, 1976, p. 17).

In some cases, you will have to apply "comma sense." If a sentence sounds confusing when you read it over, it may be necessary to insert a comma. Commas in the following sentences ensure the sense intended:

In 1971, 773 people were killed in an earthquake in Peru.

He told the student to come now, and again the following week.

Have you written *three* or more items in a series?	If YES . . . ⟶	use commas to separate them
Have you referred to *two* items joined by a coordinating conjunction?	If YES . . . ⟶	do *not* use a comma
Have you written a compound sentence (i.e., two independent clauses joined by a coordinating conjunction)?	If YES . . . ⟶	use a comma before the coordinating conjunction
Have you begun a sentence with a word, phrase, or dependent clause where an independent clause follows?	If YES . . . ⟶	use a comma before the independent clause
Have you ended a sentence with a word or phrase where an independent clause precedes it?	If YES . . . ⟶	use a comma before the concluding word or phrase
Have you ended a sentence with a dependent clause where an independent clause precedes it?	If YES . . . ⟶	do *not* use a comma (but see page 346 for exceptions)
Have you written a dependent clause that begins with *who*, *which*, or *that*?	If YES . . . ⟶	use two commas if the clause gives additional information and can be omitted without changing sentence meaning
Have you written a word group that names or explains the preceding noun?	If YES . . . ⟶	use two commas that enclose the word group
Have you used a word or phrase that interrupts sentence flow (for example, for emphasis)?	If YES . . . ⟶	use two commas that enclose the interrupter
Have you used two coordinate (interchangeable) adjectives before a noun?	If YES . . . ⟶	use a comma between them
Have you used direct quotations, addresses, dates, numbers, or titles in your sentence?	If YES . . . ⟶	use commas as required by convention (see Conventional and Comma Sense Uses, page 349)

Fast-Track

●●●●●

Using Comma Rules

●●●●●

EXERCISE
11.1

⟳ Check answers to select questions

Add commas to the following sentences if required, and name the rule category that applies. There is one comma rule to apply in each sentence.

1. After her inaugural speech several members of the house rose to congratulate her.
2. The optional package includes bucket seats dual speakers and air-conditioning.
3. We have collected more than $20,000 and there is a week remaining in our campaign.
4. Metaphors similes and personification all are examples of figurative language.
5. As one can see the tower is leaning four-and-one-half metres to the south.
6. Hardly daring to breathe Nelson took a quick look at the valley far below him.
7. Although many are called few are chosen.
8. The magnificent country estate is hidden behind a long elegant row of silver birches.
9. "We can't achieve peace in our time if we assume war is inevitable" he said.
10. Her house was a newer one with dark wood trim and large open rooms.
11. As well as the Irish many Africans were forced to leave their families behind during times of famine.
12. Because of the humidity levels it feels hotter than the actual temperature.
13. Joe Clark the former prime minister has a famous wife.
14. Even though most people are aware of global warming and climate change fewer are aware of the term "carbon footprint."
15. James Earl Jones who is the voice of Darth Vader in *Star Wars* is a well-known actor.
16. The *Globe and Mail* is a popular paper across Canada whereas the *Toronto Star* was created for the Toronto and area market.
17. Trust is important in any relationship and it always takes time to develop.
18. The types of RNA required for protein synthesis are messenger RNA transfer RNA and ribosomal RNA.
19. People have immigrated to Canada from countries in Asia Europe the Middle East and Central and South America.
20. The committee studying the proposal is a mixture of health officials journalists and politicians.
21. Caffeine a stimulant is unregulated and completely legal.
22. Since climate change is a global problem it requires global solutions.
23. Diesel-powered cars have long been on the North American market yet they have never been widely accepted by the typical motorist.
24. The aggression effect of a video game depends on the type of game the way it is played and the person playing it.
25. Now a widely accepted theory evolution was discounted when Charles Darwin published *On the Origin of Species* in 1859.

●●●●●

●●●●●

EXERCISE
11.2

⟳ Check answers to select questions

Add commas to the following sentences, if and where required. There is more than one comma rule to apply in most sentences.

1. I had planned to go to Calgary but my bus was delayed for more than four hours so I decided to go back home.
2. Juliet studied medicine at The University of Western Ontario in London Ontario before becoming a doctor near Prince Albert Saskatchewan.

3. Like Jane Austen's character Emma the heroine of *Clueless* Cher is less superficial than she first appears.

4. Nick and Nicole were married on April 20 1995 but they separated two years later.

5. Jessica Julep the mayor of Nowhere Nova Scotia provided inspirational leadership.

6. The simple sentence as we've seen is easily mastered by students but compound sentences necessitate an understanding of various forms of punctuation.

7. The waste of our resources including the most precious resource water is the major environmental problem that Canada is facing today.

8. British general Sir Frederick Morgan established an American-British headquarters which was known as COSSAC.

9. The book with the fine red binding on the highest shelf is the particular one I want.

10. Agnes Campbell Macphail the first woman elected to Canadian Parliament served for 19 years beginning her career in 1921.

11. The first steam-powered motorcycle known as the "bone-shaker" led to the bikes we use today.

12. Following successful completion of the English test another skills test is taken which is in a written format.

13. He combed through directories of professional associations business and trade associations and unions looking for possible contributors to his campaign.

14. Oliver Wendell Holmes an American was known as a master essayist but Canadian Barry Callaghan is also internationally respected as an essayist.

15. After visiting her ancestral homeland China and meeting her sisters from her mother's first marriage Amy Tan wrote the novel *The Joy Luck Club*.

16. The soldier with the red coat in the picture fought on the side of our enemies the Americans.

17. In 1885 the Canadian government introduced a racist bill the Chinese "head tax" which forced every Chinese person entering the country to pay a $50 fee.

18. Currently ranked fourth behind heart disease stroke and respiratory infections AIDS is set to become No. 3 say researchers in a new report.

19. Leslie Hornby known as "Twiggy" became a supermodel overnight and was identified by her skinny 90-pound body.

20. Jeff Deffenbacher Ph.D. a specialist in anger management thinks that some people have a low tolerance for everyday annoyances.

Add commas in the paragraphs below, following the rule categories as discussed above and avoiding comma splices. A few commas have been included to help with comprehension, but they may be incorrect.

1. If you asked people to name the most gruelling and challenging race in the world most of them would probably say that it was an auto race such as the Indianapolis 500, few people would name the Tour de France which is a bicycle race. Thousands of cyclists however vie for an elite position in this annual event. Even with the modern advances in bicycle technology cyclists still find the course very challenging, it offers a variety of climbs including slight inclines hills and steep grades.

EXERCISE 11.3

Check answers to select questions

The Tour de France has a history that dates back about one hundred years, in the years to come the race will continue to challenge inspire and glorify new riders.

2. Autism is a much misunderstood problem, often children with autism are viewed as a "handful" and "hyperactive." Very little is known of its causes and characteristics can vary making a diagnosis difficult. In children it is even harder because normal children can exhibit some of the characteristics associated with autism. Although autism can cause many behavioural difficulties autistic children can still live near-normal lives if they are surrounded by understanding caregivers. Working with autistic children can change a person and make one realize the need for better understanding and education. Treating autism can be difficult because often there is no feedback from the patient. Over the years there have been many ideas of how to treat autism but not all were correct and have at times made treatment problematic.

Other Forms of Punctuation

The careful use of semicolons, colons, dashes, and parentheses gives your writing polish and precision. The colon and semicolon are stronger, more emphatic marks of punctuation than the comparatively mild-mannered comma. For stronger breaks, longer pauses, and to show emphasis, learn where to use these marks in your writing.

Semicolon

As discussed, one of the major functions of commas is to separate independent clauses in a compound sentence. Two rules for semicolon use also involve independent clauses; the third rule is to separate items in a series that contains commas.

1. **To join independent clauses.** You may use a semicolon rather than a comma and a coordinating conjunction to join independent clauses if there is a close relationship between the clauses. Using a semicolon to join two independent clauses, rather than a comma + a coordinating conjunction, signals to the reader the close connection between the ideas in the two clauses. Consider the following examples:

   a) Strong economies usually have strong school systems, and investment in education is inevitably an investment in a country's economic future.

   b) Strong economies usually have strong school systems; weak economies generally have weak school systems.

In sentence (a), the second clause is logically related to the preceding one; however, they have different subjects and are not so closely related that a semicolon would be called for. In sentence (b), however, both clauses are concerned primarily with the relationship between economic strength and school systems. That focus in each clause justifies the use of a semicolon. A semicolon is often used if you want to stress a contrast between two independent clauses as in the examples below:

Scott was impatient to get married; Salome wanted to wait until they were financially secure.

Organically grown food is generally high in nutrients; processed food is not.

Note that the semicolons in both sentences could be replaced by a comma and the coordinating conjunction *but*—they could *not* be replaced by a comma alone.

Here are other examples where a semicolon is a good choice to stress the close relationship between independent clauses:

Gymnastics is not just any sport; it's one of the most challenging and physically taxing of all sports.

Some children may have lost a parent due to illness or divorce; others may have been cared for by grandparents or other relatives.

Do *not* use a semicolon to separate an independent clause from a dependent clause. The rules for separating independent and dependent clauses are given on page 346; they involve commas, not semicolons.

To review, the rules for independent clauses we have looked at so far demonstrate many options for connecting important ideas:

> You can begin a new sentence after you have expressed your first idea. This is particularly useful if you are conveying a lot of information that makes it hard for a reader to follow or if the sentence is just too long.
> You can join the two clauses by using a comma plus a coordinating conjunction.
> You can use a semicolon in place of a period and a new sentence or in place of a comma plus a coordinating conjunction if you want to stress the closeness of the ideas in the independent clauses.
> **To join independent clauses using a conjunctive adverb.** A fourth option is the use of a semicolon with a conjunctive adverb/transitional phrase followed by an independent clause. Conjunctive adverbs and transitional phrases are too numerous to list, but all are used to connect two independent clauses. Note the comma *after* the conjunctive adverb in each example:

My roommate lacks charm, friendliness, and humour; *still*, he is an excellent cook.

A recent study has found a surprising correlation between a rare form of sleeping disorder and those with telephone numbers that include the number six; *however*, the conclusion is being challenged by several researchers.

Here are some of the most common conjunctive adverbs and transitional phrases:

accordingly	in addition	meanwhile	on the other
afterward	in fact	moreover	hand
also	in the meantime	namely	still
as a result	further(more)	nevertheless	subsequently
besides	hence	next	that is
certainly	however	nonetheless	then
consequently	indeed	otherwise	therefore
finally	instead	similarly	thus
for example	later	on the	undoubtedly
if not	likewise	contrary	

Be careful not to confuse the words and phrases discussed above with another large group of joiners, subordinating conjunctions, which join dependent to independent clauses (see page 321). *Although* and *whereas* are sometimes mistaken for conjunctive adverbs, but they are subordinating conjunctions that introduce dependent clauses; they cannot be used to join two independent clauses.

A Closer Look

Using Adverbs to Join Independent Clauses

A common error is to miss the distinction between adverbs like *however* and *therefore* acting as ordinary adverbs (interrupters) and these same words acting as conjunctive adverbs (joiners). The following sentence pair illustrates this distinction. In sentence 1, commas are required because the adverb occurs in the midst of the clause as an interruption between the subject "he" and most of its predicate. In sentence 2, a semicolon is required before the conjunctive adverb because "however" is joining two independent clauses:

1. Dr. Suzuki will not be in his office this week; he will, *however,* be making his rounds at the hospital.
2. Dr. Suzuki will not be in his office this week; *however,* he will be making his rounds at the hospital.

In the following sentences, the word that changes its function from interrupter to joiner is "therefore":

1. The CEO has been called away for an emergency briefing; her secretary, *therefore,* will have to cancel her appointments.
2. The CEO has been called away for an emergency briefing; *therefore,* her secretary will have to cancel her appointments.

Notice that the only apparent difference between these sentences is word order: in Sentence 1, "therefore" is the third word of the clause, whereas in Sentence 2, it begins the second clause. If you look closely, though, you can see that changing the position of a word like *however* or *therefore* can change its function. In Sentence 2, an independent clause precedes and follows "therefore," necessitating the semicolon before and the comma after. (The comma is required since "therefore" also acts as an introduction preceding an independent clause.)

EXERCISE 11.4

The following sentences are punctuated correctly. The italicized word or phrase is either an ordinary adverb acting as an interrupter or a conjunctive adverb (joiner). Rewrite the sentence by moving this word/phrase to another place in the second clause in which its function will be different. Punctuate accordingly.

Check answers to select questions

Example:
The weather this summer was very wet; *however*, it did not make up for the drought we have experienced.

The weather this summer was very wet. It did not, *however*, make up for the drought we have experienced.

Or:

The weather this summer was very wet; it did not, *however*, make up for the drought we have experienced.

1. One of my roommates rode her bicycle to school most of the time; she was more physically fit, *as a result*, than my other roommate, who didn't even own a bicycle.
2. SPCA officers work for but are not paid by the government. It is donations, *in fact*, that provide their salary.
3. If homelessness continues to increase, it will be costly for taxpayers; *moreover*, homelessness affects downtown businesses.
4. Many professional golfers have used the same caddy for years; *for example*, Steve Williams has caddied for Tiger Woods since 1999.
5. Scientists tend to strongly support stem-cell research. Most evangelical Christians, *however*, just as strongly oppose it.

---

2. **To separate items in a series.** Serial semicolons can be used between items in a series if one or more of the elements contain commas. Without semicolons, these sentences would be confusing:

Her company included Alex Duffy, president; Marie Tremble, vice-president; John van der Wart, secretary; and Chris Denfield, treasurer.

Bus number 1614 makes scheduled stops in Kamloops, BC; Valemount, BC; Jasper, Alta.; and Drayton Valley, Alta., before arriving in Edmonton.

You may also use semicolons to separate items in a list where each item is a long phrase or clause, especially if there is internal punctuation. Using semicolons to separate the items makes this sentence easier to read:

The role of the vice-president will be to enhance the school's external relations; strengthen its relationship with alumni, donors, and business and community leaders; implement a fundraising program; and increase the school's involvement in the community.

> Note that the rule for items in a series is the only rule for using semicolons that does not involve independent clauses. You should use semicolons *only* to join independent clauses in one of the two ways discussed above or to separate items in a series where, otherwise, confusion might result.

Colon

It is often said that while a semicolon brings the reader to a brief stop, the colon leads the reader on. The colon has three main uses: (1) to introduce quoted material; (2) to set up or introduce a list or series; and (3) to answer, complete, or expand on what is asked or implied in the preceding independent clause.

1. **To set up a quotation.** When you use direct quotations in your essays, you can set them up formally with a colon:

The *Oxford English Dictionary* defines the word "rhetoric" this way: "The art of using language so as to persuade or influence others."

Health Canada has made the following recommendation for dentists: "Non-mercury filling materials should be considered for restoring the primary teeth of children where the mechanical properties of the material are safe."

Direct quotations can also be set up less formally. In such cases, a comma, or perhaps no punctuation at all, may be required. To determine which is needed, look at the sentence as if it contained no quotation marks and see if one of the rules for using commas applies:

According to the American Academy of Dermatology, "a tan is the skin's response to an injury, and every time you tan, you accumulate damage to the skin."

The most general definition of evolution is "any non-miraculous process by which new forms of life are produced" (Bowler 2).

In the first sentence, a comma rule dictates the use of a comma before the quotation; in the second sentence, there is no rule that would necessitate a comma before the quotation. A comma after "is" would be incorrect.

2. **To set up or introduce a list or series.** The most formal way to set up a list or series is to write an independent clause and follow with a colon and the list of items:

In 1998, the CBC outlined three challenges for the future: to attract more viewers to Canadian programming, to increase the availability of "under-represented" categories, and to direct its resources towards this kind of programming.

Avoid the temptation to insert a colon just before you start the list unless it immediately follows an independent clause. Normally, you would *not* use a colon after *including* or *such as*, or right after a linking verb like *is* or *are*, though these words are often used to set up a list or series.

Incorrect colon: Caffeine withdrawal can have many negative effects, such as: severe headaches, drowsiness, irritability, and poor concentration. (A comma is also incorrect after *such as*.)

Unnecessary colon: One of the questions the committee will attempt to answer is: Does our current public health system work?

3. **After an independent clause followed by a word, phrase, or clause that answers or completes it.** What follows a colon may answer, complete, or expand on what is asked or implied in the preceding independent clause. The answer or explanation could range from a word to an independent clause. Like the comma and semicolon, then, the colon can be used after an independent clause; however, what follows the colon must answer a question asked in the previous clause:

In your reading, you may sometimes see a colon used unnecessarily to set up a list or a quotation (especially before a block quotation). In such cases, the writer has made a stylistic choice. However, bear in mind that unnecessary colons, like unnecessary commas, can impede more than assist understanding.

There is only one quality you omitted from the list of my most endearing characteristics: my modesty. (answers WHAT quality)

David's driving test was a memorable experience: he backed over a curb, sailed through two stop signs, and forgot to signal a left turn. (answers WHY the test was memorable)

The New Testament of the Holy Bible gives the ultimate rule for Christians: to treat others the way you want them to treat you. (answers WHAT rule)

If what follows the colon is at least the equivalent of an independent clause, you may begin it with a capital letter. It is perfectly acceptable to begin with a small letter, however, as in the examples above.

> Remember that unless you are using semicolons to separate items in a series, both what *precedes* and what *follows* a semicolon should be an independent clause.
>
> What *precedes* a colon should be an independent clause.

Dashes and Parentheses

Although some writers use dashes and parentheses interchangeably, their functions are different. Imagining this scenario might help: you are in a crowded room where everyone is talking. Somebody takes you aside and begins speaking in an unnaturally loud voice about the latest rumour. You look around. People are listening, which is the design of the person talking. A couple of minutes later, somebody else approaches and very discreetly begins whispering the same information in your ear.

Using dashes is like giving information that is meant to be overheard, to be stressed. But information in parentheses is more like an aside. It conveys additional information which is not important enough to be included in the main part of the sentence.

Dashes, then, set something off and can convey a break in thought. You can use dashes sparingly to emphasize a word or phrase; two dashes (one dash if the material comes at the end of a sentence) draw the reader's attention to what is between the dashes.

You can type two hyphens to indicate a dash (--); if you don't leave a space after the second hyphen, your computer may automatically convert the hyphens to an em-dash like this: —.

Don't use one hyphen if you want to set off a word or phrase. Hyphens are a mark of spelling—not of punctuation.

Use parentheses sparingly to include a word or phrase, even occasionally a sentence, that isn't important enough to be included as part of the main text; where dashes emphasize, parentheses de-emphasize:

"Crayolas plus imagination (the ability to create images) make for happiness if you are a child" (Fulghum 10).

You may also use parentheses to refer to a source in a research essay. This parenthetical use is illustrated in the example above to refer to the source of the quotation about Crayolas. For information about parenthetical documentation methods, see Chapter 7.

Punctuating parenthetical insertions depends on whether the statement in parentheses is (1) a complete sentence in itself or (2) part of the larger sentence. If the parentheses enclose a complete sentence, the period should be placed *inside* the second parenthesis, as the period ends only what is between parentheses. The following sentence illustrates this rule:

(The period in this sentence goes inside the second parenthesis.)

If parentheses do not enclose a complete sentence, punctuate the sentence just as you would if the parenthetical insertion were not there. The sentence below shows a comma that has nothing to do with the parenthetical insertion but that is required to separate independent clauses; note that this comma follows the closing parenthesis. Notice also that "both" begins with a lower case letter:

Cassandra wanted to be an actor (both her parents were actors), but she always trembled violently as soon as she stepped on a stage.

Fast-Track

●●●●●

Rules for Semicolons, Colons, Dashes, and Parentheses

Have you written two independent clauses that are closely related in meaning or that strongly contrast?	If YES . . . ⟶	use a semicolon between clauses
Have you used a word/phrase like *however* to join two independent clauses?	If YES . . . ⟶	use a semicolon before the joiner and a comma after it
Have you written a list or series in which one or more items contain commas or are very long?	If YES . . . ⟶	use semicolons between items
Have you used a direct quotation?	If YES . . . ⟶	you may use a colon before the direct quotation if the statement before the quotation is an independent clause
Have you written a list or series?	If YES . . . ⟶	you may use a colon before the series if the statement before the series is an independent clause
Does a word, phrase, or clause answer or complete a preceding independent clause?	If YES . . . ⟶	use a colon between the independent clause and the word, phrase, or clause that follows
Do you want to stress or set off a word, phrase, or clause from the rest of the sentence?	If YES . . . ⟶	you may use dashes for emphasis
Do you want to include less important information in your sentence?	If YES . . . ⟶	you may use parentheses to show that this information is less important

EXERCISE 11.5

↻ Check answers to select questions

Replace commas in the sentences below with the most appropriate form of punctuation (semicolon, colon, dashes, parentheses). In some cases, the commas are correct and should not be replaced.

1. April showers bring May flowers, May flowers bring on my asthma.
2. A developing salmon goes through four stages, the alevin, the fry, the smolt, and the adult.
3. Every essay needs three parts, an introduction, a body, and a conclusion.
4. He paused to admire the splendid sight before his eyes, the ruins of Montgomery Castle.
5. Mayumi tended to look on the good side of things, Glenn usually saw the bad side.
6. The following is not a rule for comma use, put a comma wherever you pause.
7. It is probable, though not certain, that she will be promoted to the rank of corporal next year.
8. It was the best of times, it was the worst of times.
9. Marselina has a fine ear for music, unfortunately she can't sing a note.
10. In my health sciences class, we studied the four main food groups, dairy products, meats, carbohydrates, and fruits and vegetables.
11. The Online Dictionary defines animal cruelty this way, "treatment or standards of care that cause unwarranted or unnecessary suffering or harm to animals."
12. Whenever I order designer clothing for my boutique, I shop in Toronto, Canada, Buffalo, New York, and London, England.
13. The tuition increase has affected many lower income families, therefore, there is an even greater demand for student loans.
14. Brian never tired of misquoting Shakespeare, "the quality of mercy is not stained."
15. Virginia Woolf had this to say about the essay, "Of all forms of literature it is the one which least calls for the use of long words."
16. First advice to those about to write a novel is the same as Punch's to those about to wed, don't (Victor Jones).
17. Each kind of stem cell has potential advantages and disadvantages, however, the least successful today are those harvested from human embryos.
18. In a compound sentence, use a comma to join independent clauses where there is a coordinating conjunction, use a semi-colon where two such clauses are not joined by a coordinating conjunction.
19. His plans for the new development included the following, an apartment complex, single-family residences, a 60-store mall, and a multi-use recreation centre.
20. Oil, electricity, and solar power are popular sources for heating homes in Ontario, however, the most popular is natural gas.
21. The tour includes visits to the following museums, the Prado in Madrid, Spain, the Louvre in Paris, France, and the Rijksmuseum in Amsterdam, the Netherlands.
22. It was the ideal summer job, you were outdoors in lovely weather, you were active, and the pay was more than reasonable.
23. School cafeterias often offer unhealthy options, such as hot dogs, which have virtually no nutritional value, hamburgers, which have a high fat content, and poutine, known as "heart attack in a bowl."
24. The zero emissions of a battery-electric vehicle come with a drawback, the emissions are only as clean as the means used to generate the power.
25. This year's conference on the environment is intended to focus concern on three main areas, global warming, pollution, and the destruction of natural habitat.

26. The art of writing the news lead is to answer as many of the following five questions as possible, Who?, What?, Where?, When?, and How?

27. The current figures of mercury absorption have been announced by the ADA, however, the group's review has been criticized as misleading.

28. A lack of essential nutrients can result in deficiencies, for example, a vegetarian may have iron deficiency.

29. As rainwater travels downwards through the soil, it may collect a number of pollutants, furthermore, an extended period of time may elapse before this pollution is discovered.

30. Freewriting can be a useful means of overcoming blocks, it can help you write when you're not in the mood, it can generate ideas, even if you are the kind of writer who has a hard time coming up with main points, and it can energize your writing.

EXERCISE 11.6

Below is Edward Lear's nonsense poem "The New Vestments." Write it in paragraph form, making sense out of nonsense by punctuating it for correctness and effectiveness. Most of the original end-of-line punctuation has been taken out, and some internal punctuation also has been omitted; some of the nineteenth-century spellings have been changed.

There lived an old man in the kingdom of Tess
Who invented a purely original dress
And when it was perfectly made and complete
He opened the door and walked into the street
By way of a hat he'd a loaf of Brown Bread
In the middle of which he inserted his head
His Shirt was made up of no end of dead Mice
The warmth of whose skins was quite fluffy and nice
His Drawers were of Rabbit-skins but it is not known whose
His Waistcoat and Trousers were made of Pork Chops
His Buttons were Jujubes and Chocolate Drops
His Coat was all Pancakes with Jam for a border
And a girdle of Biscuits to keep it in order
And he wore over all as a screen from bad weather
A Cloak of green Cabbage leaves stitched all together.
He had walked a short way when he heard a great noise
Of all sorts of Beasticles Birdlings and Boys
And from every long street and dark lane in the town
Beasts Birdles and Boys in a tumult rushed down
Two Cows and a half ate his Cabbage-leaf Cloak
Four Apes seized his Girdle which vanished like smoke
Three Kids ate up half of his Pancaky Coat
And the tails were devoured by an ancient He Goat
An army of Dogs in a twinkling tore up his

Pork Waistcoat and Trousers to give to their Puppies
And while they were growling and mumbling the Chops
Ten boys prigged the Jujubes and Chocolate Drops
He tried to run back to his house but in vain
Four Scores of fat Pigs came again and again
They rushed out of stables and hovels and doors
They tore off his stockings his shoes and his drawers
And now from the housetops with screechings descend
Striped spotted white black and gray Cats without end
They jumped on his shoulders and knocked off his hat
When Crows Ducks and Hens mad e a mincemeat of that
They speedily flew at his sleeves in trice
And utterly tore up his Shirt of dead Mice
They swallowed the last of his Shirt with a squall
Whereon he ran home with no clothes on at all
And he said to himself as he bolted the door
"I will not wear a similar dress any more
"Any more any more any more never more!"

Correct or add commas in the following passages. Among your changes and additions, include *at least* one semicolon and one colon. Some commas have been included to help with reading; however, they may not be correct.

1. Cocaine an alkaloid obtained from coco leaves is a stimulant to the nervous system, unfortunately it is one of the most addictive drugs and it is possible to overdose and die on first use. Among the 3 million users today 500,000 are highly addicted. Cocaine users describe the high as a euphoric feeling, they feel energetic and mentally alert, however this feeling wears off in as little as 20 minutes. Users responses to the drug vary but may include the following, hyperactivity elevated blood pressure and heart rate and increased sexual interest. Large amounts of cocaine such as more than 100 milligrams can cause bizarre erratic and violent behaviours.

2. Labour shortages during the late nineteenth century in Canada became an impediment to progress and something had to be done to fix this problem. For white politicians and business owners the solution seemed obvious, exploit cheap labour. Chinese immigrants provided exactly what was needed to boost the labour scene, they were male unskilled and cheap. Between 1881 and 1885 approximately 17,000 Chinese immigrants arrived in Canada, Chinese men were employed in masses, their jobs included those in mining forestry canning and above all railroad construction. Sir Matthew Begbie the Chief Justice of BC said "Chinese labourers do well what white women cannot do and what white men will not do."

EXERCISE 11.7

↻ Check answers to select questions

A Closer Look

Punctuation Prohibitions

Several common errors in punctuation are summarized below. Learning the rules for punctuation and being aware of these common errors will greatly enhance your writing skills.

No-Comma Rules

Do *not* use a comma to separate simple compounds (two of something with a word like *and* between). Writers sometimes generalize this non-rule from the "items in a series" rule: recall that a series comprises *three or more* items. A separate rule applies to compound sentences where a comma is required before the coordinating conjunction.

Incorrect:

Some of the heaviest damage from steroid use occurs to the heart, and the liver. (two nouns)

Logging reduces the number of old-growth forests, and destroys these habitats. (two predicates: "reduces" and "destroys")

Do *not* use a comma to separate the subject and the predicate. This non-rule is probably the result of writers mistakenly applying the "pause" non-rule.

Incorrect:

The only way our society is going to be fixed, is if we change our laws.

One advantage in using helicopters to fight fires, is the accuracy of their drops over the scene of the fire.

It is easy to be distracted by parentheses and mistakenly insert a comma between a subject and a predicate. The example below could be corrected by adding a comma after "Medicine" and removing the parentheses:

Incorrect:

The American College of Sports Medicine (a body that advances research into exercise and sports), considers all physically active females at risk for developing eating disorders.

Do *not* use a comma alone to join independent clauses or with a word other than a coordinating conjunction. This produces a comma splice, a serious grammatical error.

Incorrect:

Football is one of the most popular sports in North America, it is also one of the most brutal of all sports.

You must use the buttons provided at the bottom of the pages to navigate through the application, otherwise, you could lose your connection. [from an online application form]

No-Semicolon Rules

Do *not* use a semicolon before a fragment. In the first two incorrect examples, below, what follows the semicolon is an incomplete verb form (an *-ing*). In the third incorrect sentence, what follows is a prepositional phrase: "such as" and two nouns. In all the sentences below, a comma should replace the incorrect semicolon to separate the independent clause from the concluding fragment.

An independent clause should follow a semicolon unless semicolons are being used to separate items in a series.

Incorrect:

When the media portrays minorities, it often stereotypes them; leading audiences to reinforce the stereotype through their behaviour.

Valuable land is destroyed when it is cleared for grazing; reducing habitats for other animals.

For many years, Canada has been a leader in multiculturalism, along with a few other countries; such as the United States and England.

Do *not* use a semicolon to introduce a list or series; a colon is correct.

Incorrect:

Shakespeare's last plays are sometimes called romances and include the following; *Cymbeline, A Winter's Tale, and The Tempest.*

Apostrophe

Technically, the apostrophe isn't a mark of punctuation; it is a mark used within a word that has two main uses: (1) to indicate the possessive case of a noun or indefinite pronoun; and (2) to show where one or more letters have been omitted, as in a contraction.

1. Apostrophe for Possessive Case

The possessive case in nouns and pronouns indicates ownership and similar relationships, such as association, authorship, duration, description, and source of origin, between two nouns. The possessive is a short form indicating that the second noun belongs to or is associated with the first noun. When a noun has an apostrophe to show the possessive, it is functioning adjectivally and can be replaced by the corresponding possessive pronoun. Most pronouns, however, do not show the possessive through an apostrophe.

> the hard drive of the computer = the computer's hard drive (*its* hard drive)
>
> the landlady's apartment (ownership) (*her* apartment)
>
> the tenants' rights (association) (*their* rights)
>
> Dvorak's *New World Symphony* (authorship) (*his* symphony)

Singular noun. The usual rule for a *singular* noun, including proper nouns (nouns that begin with a capital letter) ending in *s*, *ss*, or the *s* sound, is to add "'s" to make it possessive.

> the attorney's portfolio; Mr. Price's car; the week's lesson

Indefinite pronoun. Like nouns, but unlike other kinds of pronouns, many indefinite pronouns add an apostrophe + *s* to show the possessive:

> In times of stress, it is not in *one's* best interest to act quickly or reflexively. (the best interest of one)

Plural noun. To make a plural noun possessive, add an apostrophe after the *s*:

> the islands' inhabitants; the Hansons' children; the Gibbses' marriage certificate; two weeks' lessons; the readers' perceptions

Make sure you carefully distinguish between singular and plural when applying the rules for possessives:

> company (singular) + 's ⟶ the company's profits (one company)
>
> companies (plural) + ' ⟶ the companies' profits (more than one company)
>
> society (singular) + 's ⟶ our society's attitude toward war (one society)
>
> societies (plural) + ' ⟶ past societies' attitudes toward war (many societies)

A few plural nouns do not end in *s*: *children, women, men, people.* Because they have irregular endings, they are treated as singular nouns:

> the popular children's book; the women's group

Proper noun ending in *s*. Because it may look and sound awkward to add an apostrophe + *s* to a proper noun ending in *s*, some authorities would write "Tracy Jarvis' book," meaning "the book of Tracy Jarvis." Others would follow the rule for singular nouns by adding an apostrophe + *s*: Tracy Jarvis's book. Whichever rule you follow, it's important to be consistent in applying it.

Joint ownership. In the case of joint ownership, where two nouns share or are equal parties in something, only the last noun should show the possessive. Ensure from the context that both nouns reflect a truly equal, shared relationship. In the following sentences, the assumption is that Salem and Sheena shared duties as hosts at one party but that the general manager and the district manager are paid separate wages:

> I attended Salem and Sheena's party.
>
> Morana raised the general manager's and the district manager's wages.

In the example below, the two educators do *not* share the same belief or theory:

> *Incorrect*: Piaget and Montessori's beliefs about how children learn were similar in many ways.
>
> *Correct*: Piaget's and Montessori's beliefs . . . .

An apostrophe is not used with a simple plural unless it is needed for clarity with numbers, letters, or symbols. Example: Adrian got two A's and three B's on his transcript.

2. Apostrophe to Show Contraction

The second main use of the apostrophe is to show missing letters within a word. Contractions are not generally used in formal writing. You should check with your instructor to see if they are acceptable in your assignment.

People often confuse the contraction *it's* (*it is*) with the possessive form of the pronoun *its* (as in *I gave the dog its bone*). The contraction *who's* (*who is*) is sometimes confused with the possessive form of *who* (*the man whose house I'm renting*).

EXERCISE 11.8

↻ Check answers to select questions

Decide which nouns in the following sentences require the possessive; then add apostrophes and make any other necessary changes.

1. In South Africa, the current crime rate is using up much of the countrys GDP.
2. Parents and teachers often complain about televisions influence in todays society.
3. The Crosses house is up for sale, and its list price is $179,000. [The last name is Cross.]
4. Ones education should not depend on the financial resources of ones parents.
5. The schools biggest draw for new students was the brand new recreation complex.
6. The course I took required two hours homework a day.
7. The mayors biggest asset is her commitment to the citys future growth.
8. In anorexia nervosa, a patients fingernails and teeth may be damaged due to a lack of calcium.
9. Apples, oranges, mangoes, and tomatoes are the stores specials today.
10. Work songs and street vendors cries are examples of traditional African-American music styles.
11. This weeks classifieds had several jobs for legal secretaries, all requiring three years experience in solicitors work.
12. The topic of the term paper is a comparison between George Grants and John Ralston Sauls theories of Canadian identity. [The last names are Grant and Saul.]
13. To avoid rejection, narcissists often attempt to control others behaviours towards them.
14. As a child whose parents were relatively well off, I thought all my relatives lives were as easy as mine.
15. Our societys fascination with celebrities lives is a product of the medias daily obsession.
16. Books, music, and DVDs can be found on Amazon.com, one of the Internets most popular sites.
17. The young man stated his churchs mission is to spread Jesus message to people throughout the world.

18. Drugs called immunosuppressants can interfere with the bodys ability to fight infection.

19. Nowadays, rap is used to express a persons experiences, feelings, and opinions.

20. Climate change is caused by harmful chemicals that trap the suns energy in the earths atmosphere.

21. The Smiths and the O'Neils won the trip to see the Seattle Mariners play the Blue Jays in the Mariners home town. [The teams' names are Mariners and Blue Jays.]

22. Video game players do not want to have total control over the main characters and those characters actions; the games unpredictability is part of its attraction.

23. The introductory paragraph should capture the readers interest while developing the writers credibility.

24. The desire of Pip in Charles Dickens Great Expectations to find his place in the world illustrates the works main theme.

25. James Joyces, Amy Tans, and Alistair MacLeods short stories will be analyzed to explore the development of their child protagonists. [The last names are Joyce, Tan, and MacLeod.]

EXERCISE 11.9

Punctuate the following passage for correctness and effectiveness, using commas and other forms of punctuation as appropriate. Minimal punctuation has been provided in places to aid in understanding; however, some punctuation may be incorrect. Correct all errors in apostrophe use. The passage concerns the response to an investigative article entitled "Spin Doctors," posted on the Canadian news and information website Canoe.

Reader reaction was swift and impassioned. The sites traffic which averages 65 to 70 million views each month experienced an additional 50,000 page views within the first 10 days of the posting. The investigation drew more than 400 letters to the editor hundred's of emails to the message boards and more than 16,000 responses to an online poll.

The intensity of the response surprised veteran investigative journalist Wayne MacPhail the articles author. Although the sheer volume of letters was unexpected it proved to him that there was an audience for online journalism in Canada. MacPhail has experimented with hypertext reporting since the late 1980s but outside of "Spin Doctors" he believes that by and large newspapers have done a "woeful job" of building an audience for Web-based investigative reporting . . . .

Unlike it's media rivals Canoe has never made journalism it's only or even its most important focus. A headline announcing the top story of the day appears underneath the Canoe banner but there are so many other things to do, shopping email contests Web utilities and lifestyle tips all compete with the news.

The CNEWS section isnt necessarily the first place people are expected to go on the network though it is usually at the top of the highlighted sections. It is also part of the site that changes the most during daylight hours. In other words when cnews changes the entire home page changes. A "This Just In" feature was recently added but theres no set schedule for posting stories. Despite this expansion of the news section Canoes promotional material drives home the message that the site is about much more than current events. One recent ad reads, "shop chat email read, in that order."

—adapted from Tara Stevens, "Paddling into Cyberspace."

Agreement

A verb must agree in number with its subject; similarly, a pronoun must agree in number, person, and gender with its antecedent. These forms of agreement underscore the close connection between a subject and the verb it governs, along with the close connection between a noun and the pronoun that replaces it.

Subject–Verb Agreement

You will not usually have to stop and think about whether a verb agrees in number with its subject, especially if English is your first language. However, determining whether a subject is singular or plural is not always straightforward. In the specific instances explained below, the rules help the writer apply the important principle of subject–verb agreement.

Finding the Subject

Usually, the subject of a sentence or clause is the noun or pronoun that performs the action of the verb (or that exists in the state or condition expressed by the subjective complement). In most cases, the subject precedes the verb and is easy to find (italicized in this example):

> *Kevin and Nigel* are happy that they passed the exam.

Sometimes the subject is harder to spot for one of the following reasons:

1. The sentence begins with *Here is/are*, *There is/are*, *There has/have been*, etc. The subject follows the verb, rather than precedes it; you have to look ahead in the sentence to the first noun/pronoun to determine whether the subject is singular or plural.

   > There *are* many *reasons* for supporting the legalizing of marijuana.

   > Here *is* one *person* who supports raising the drinking age.

2. The sentence is phrased as a question. You may need to look ahead to determine the number of the subject:

   > What *is* the main *reason* for legalizing marijuana?

   > Where *are* all of the *people* who are in favour of raising the drinking age?

3. The subject is delayed. Because the sentence begins with a prepositional phrase, the noun in the phrase may *seem* to form the subject, but the true subject is found later in the sentence. You can rearrange this kind of sentence to confirm that you have, in fact, used a delayed subject construction:

   > With the dependence on caffeine *come withdrawal symptoms*.

   > *Sentence rearranged with subject first*: *Withdrawal symptoms come* with the dependence on caffeine.

   > Among Graham's favourites *was the recent album* by Green Day.

   > *Sentence rearranged*: *The recent album by Green Day was* among Graham's favourites.

4. The subject is governed by a linking verb that has a plural complement. Don't be distracted by what follows the verb; the subject alone determines plurality of the verb:

> The *topic* for discussion tomorrow *is* the pros and cons of indoor tanning.

5. The subject is followed by one or more prepositional phrases that contain nouns and/or pronouns that are *not* the subject. Writers sometimes forget that the common word *of* is a preposition and that the following noun or pronoun is the object of the preposition, not the subject. If there are several nouns before the verb, backtrack carefully to find the noun or pronoun that governs the verb. In the examples below, the prepositional phrases are crossed out so that the subject and verb (italicized) stand out:

> A long *list* ~~of items, including vegetables, fruits, meats, and several kinds of bread,~~ *was* handed to Tao.

> The *roots* ~~of his dissatisfaction with the course~~ *go* very deep.

Mistaking the Subject

In the examples in 3, above, one of the nouns "dependence" or "caffeine" in the first sentence, and "favourites" in the second sentence, could be mistaken for the subjects of "come" and "was," respectively; however, these nouns are preceded by prepositions. A noun or pronoun that directly follows a preposition cannot act as a subject; it is the object of the preposition. (See Chapter 10, page 316.)

A related problem occurs when a writer mistakes a prepositional phrase or even a dependent clause for a subject. The sentences below can be fixed by omitting the preposition and beginning the sentence with the noun subject. In the incorrect sentence below, "By choosing" has been mistaken for the subject:

> *Incorrect*: By choosing to take a few correspondence courses may afford a student athlete greater flexibility in meeting academic requirements.

> *Correct*: Choosing to take a few correspondence courses may afford a student athlete greater flexibility.

In this example, "With the development of the computer" has been mistaken for the subject:

> *Incorrect*: With the development of the computer led to automated robots on the production line.

> *Correct*: The development of the computer led to automated robots on the production line.

In the example below, "Although Edna thinks of her children at the last moment before her death," a dependent clause, has been mistaken for the subject (dependent clauses contain their own subjects):

> *Incorrect*: Although Edna thinks of her children at the last moment before her death does not change the fact she is still willing to leave them.

Correct:

Although Edna thinks of her children at the last moment before her death, she is still willing to leave them.

Edna thinks of her children at the last moment before her death, though this does not change the fact she is willing to leave them.

See also Precision and Logic in Chapter 12 for information about faulty predication (page 419), in which subject and predicate are not logically aligned.

Rules for Subject–Verb Agreement

1. **Compound subject joined by *and*.** Two subjects joined by the conjunction *and* require a plural verb form.

   Thanh *and* his friend *are* visiting Ottawa.

   Occasionally, a compound subject expresses a single idea. In both examples below, the compound subject can be treated as a singular subject, since the elements are so closely connected that they can't be separated without changing the meaning:

   Rhythm and blues was always popular with younger audiences.

   To compare and contrast the roles of setting in the novels *is* sure to be a question on the exam.

2. **Compound subject joined by *or*.** When the compound subjects are linked by the conjunction *or*, or with the correlative (or paired) conjunctions *either . . . or* or *neither . . . nor*, the verb form is determined by the noun or pronoun nearest the verb. These conjunctions suggest a choice between one thing or the other much more than *and*, which clearly suggests two or more of something, requiring the plural verb.

   The chairs *or the table is* going to auction.

   Neither famine nor *floods are* going to force the people to leave their homes.

   If you changed the order of the nouns making up the compound subject in the above sentences, you would need also to change the number of the verb.

3. **Compound subject joined by prepositional phrase.** A prepositional phrase can also be used to join two nouns in a compound subject. *Along with, as well as, combined with, in addition to,* and *together with* are examples of such phrases. These phrases do not have the strength of the conjunction *and*. When you use one of these joiners, you stress the first element more than the second one. Logically, then, the verb is *singular* if the first element of the compound is *singular*:

   The *instructor, as well as* her students, *is* going to be attending the symposium on the environment.

   The Australian *prime minister, along with* his ministers for education and foreign affairs, *is* set to arrive tomorrow.

If the writer of the first sentence above wanted to stress equality, the sentence should read: "The instructor *and* her students *are* . . . ."

4. **Collective noun as subject.** A collective noun refers to a group. It is singular in form but may be either singular or plural in meaning, depending on the context. Examples of collective nouns include *audience, band, class, committee, congregation, family, gang, group, jury, staff,* and *team.*

   Whenever the context suggests the members of the group are to be thought of as *one unit,* all doing the same thing or acting together, the verb form is *singular*; when the members are considered as *individuals,* the corresponding verb form is *plural*:

   Singular (jury acts as unit): The jury *is* out to consider the evidence before it.

   Plural (class will ask questions individually): After the lecture, the class *are* going to ask questions of the guest speaker.

   Most often, collective nouns are considered singular, so, if in doubt, choose the singular form. If a plural verb with a collective noun sounds odd, you can rephrase the subject so that the collective noun functions adjectivally before a clearly plural noun:

   After the lecture, *class members are* going to ask questions of the guest speaker.

5. **Singular subject followed by plural noun.** With the following phrases, the verb form is singular, even though the noun or pronoun that follows is usually plural: *each of, either/neither of, every one of, one of,* and *which one of.* The verb form following *the only one who* also will be singular.

   One of our 115 students *has* written an A+ essay.

   Alec is *the only one of* those attending who *has* difficulty speaking before a large group.

6. **Indefinite pronoun.** An indefinite pronoun refers to a nonspecific individual or object. Most indefinite pronouns are considered singular and take a singular form in agreement. *Anybody, anyone, anything, each, either, everybody, everyone, everything, neither, nobody, no one, nothing, one, someone,* and *somebody* are singular indefinite pronouns.

   Some authorities believe that when context clearly warrants the use of plural agreement with the antecedents *everyone* and *everybody,* as in the second sentence below, you may use the plural pronoun:

   Everyone is going to stand when the opening ceremonies begin.

   When the pepper was spilled, *everyone* rubbed *their* noses.

7. **Portions and fractions.** There is a separate rule for a phrase expressing a portion or a fraction followed by *of,* such as *all, a lot, a number, any, a variety, (one-) half, more, most, much, none, part, plenty, some,* and *the majority/minority.*

When using a compound subject, look at the word(s) doing the joining to determine whether the subject is singular or plural.

The form of the verb depends on whether the noun or pronoun following *of* is singular or plural.

None of the missing **pieces** *have* been found yet.

Some of the **losses** incurred with the companies' merger *are* being absorbed by the shareholders.

Half of the **pie** *is* gone.

One-third of the **employees** *are* out on strike.

8. **Collective quantity**. Subjects expressing collective distance, time, money, weight, or mass are singular:.

    Twelve miles is not a great distance to an experienced hiker.

    When the subject is *the number of*, the verb is singular (in contrast with rule 7):

    The number of people attending the courses *has dropped* in the last two years.

9. **Singular noun ending in *s***. Some nouns end in *s*, but because they usually refer to a singular concept or subject, they require the singular form of the verb. Examples include *athletics, billiards, darts, economics, gymnastics, politics, physics, mathematics, measles, mumps, news*, and *statistics*.

    Statistics is an inexact science; no *news is* good news

    Depending on their context, many of these nouns can be considered plural and should then take a plural verb form. For example, *statistics* could refer to a set of facts, rather than to one subject:

    The *statistics* on global warming *are* alerting politicians to the need for world-wide action.

10. Whether the titles of artistic works or the names of companies are singular or plural in form will not affect the verb. A singular verb will be needed to agree with the subject.

    Montreal Stories is a collection of Mavis Gallant's fiction; McClelland & Stewart *is* the publisher.

11. **Gerunds** (noun verbals) can act as subjects; you can recognize them by their *-ing* ending. They are singular so will be followed by a singular verb form, though what follows them may be plural.

    Understanding quantum physics, though difficult, *is* essential for today's theoretical physicist.

12. **Plural indefinite pronouns**. Logically, the following are plural and require the plural form of the verb: *both, few, many, parts of, several*:

    A well-educated *few seem* to care about correct grammar and punctuation these days, but *both are* essential parts of the writing process.

> Most errors in subject–verb agreement are due to one of these three situations: use of a compound subject; use of an indefinite pronoun as the subject; intervening words between the subject and the verb.

Pronoun–Antecedent Agreement

Most problems in pronoun–antecedent agreement apply to **personal pronouns**, such as *she, he, they*, and *them*, as well as the possessive pronoun forms, *its* and *their*. The **antecedent** of a pronoun is the noun it replaces, and a pronoun must agree with its antecedent noun in number. If you have difficulty finding the antecedent, see if it, or an equivalent form, can be substituted for the pronoun in the sentence, as in the examples below:

The first thing that usually strikes us about *a person* is his or her [*a person's*] physical appearance.

The dieter should realize that diets will only work when he or she [*the dieter*] restricts his or her [*the dieter's*] caloric intake.

Most of the rules for subject–verb agreement also apply to pronoun–antecedent agreement. For example, a compound antecedent requires the plural form of the pronoun and of an adjective formed from a pronoun (possessive pronoun):

Connie *and* Steve *have* invited me to *their* cottage.

If the compound subject includes the words *each* or *every*, the singular form should be used:

Each book and magazine in the library *has its* own entry.

When two antecedents are joined by *or* or *nor*, the pronoun agrees with the closest antecedent (see rule 2 of subject–verb agreement on page 370):

Neither the prime minister *nor his advisors were* certain how to implement *their* proposal.

As with subject–verb agreement, a collective noun antecedent requires the singular pronoun form if it is thought of in the collective sense, as a unit; if the context suggests that individuals are being referred to, the pronoun takes a plural form (see rule 4 of subject–verb agreement on page 371):

Our hockey team will play *its* final game against *its* archrivals. (The team will be playing as a unit.)

The team will be receiving *their* new jerseys Friday. (Individual team members each will be given a jersey.)

With a pronoun referring to a portion or fraction, agreement depends on whether the noun following *of* is singular or plural (see rule 7 of subject–verb agreement, page 371):

Studies show that a large *number of college and university students are* cheating on *their* exams and essays; however, a much larger number are not.

If the pronoun has an indefinite pronoun antecedent such as *one*, *anybody*, or *someone*, the singular form applies, as it does with subject–verb agreement (see rule 6 of subject–verb agreement on page 371):

One should be careful about pronoun agreement, or *one's* teacher will certainly point out the error to *one*.

Personal pronouns refer to persons. The *first person* refers to the one *doing* the speaking or writing; *second person* refers to the one *spoken to*; *third person* refers to the one *spoken about*. See page 382 for the forms of personal pronouns.

Although grammatically correct, the sentence above could be improved by using a personal pronoun to replace the indefinite pronoun "one." However, you must be careful to use a *singular* pronoun to replace an indefinite pronoun like "one" as the writer of this sentence has failed to do:

> *Incorrect*: *One* should be careful about pronoun agreement, or *their* teacher will certainly point out the error to *them*.

In the sentence below, a singular pronoun replaces the singular antecedent "one"—; however, the sentence is incorrect because the possessive adjective "his" and the personal pronoun "him" refer to only one gender:

> *Also Incorrect*: *One* should be careful about pronoun agreement, or *his* teacher will certainly point out the error to *him*.

In the next section, we discuss problems that can arise when you want to replace an indefinite pronoun or a generic singular noun by a singular pronoun.

Pronouns at Work

Problematic Pronouns: Inclusive Language

In recent years, the efforts of many writers to avoid gender bias have driven them to a gender-neutral, but grammatically incorrect, use of *they*, *them*, or *their* with the singular indefinite pronoun. The inclusion of both correct pronouns in the form *him or her* or *his or her* is awkward compared to the inclusive *him*, but is preferable to an incorrect *their* and better than a form that may appear sexist. In the sentence below, the writer has used both singular forms to replace the antecedent "student":

> *Correct*: A student must footnote *his or her* references, or the teacher will expect *him or her* to correct the oversight.

The problem of pronoun–antecedent agreement is especially common among student writers when the antecedent noun is either an indefinite pronoun or a singular noun referring to a person where gender is unspecified—a generic noun such as *reader*, *writer*, *student*, *teacher*, *individual*, *character*, or *person*. Here are three options to consider when you have used an indefinite pronoun or a generic singular noun and want to follow with a pronoun.

Option 1. Replace the plural pronoun with both singular personal pronouns (or possessive adjectives). This option is nearly always acceptable in academic writing, but can be seen as awkward and repetitive in journalistic and workplace writing.

> *Ungrammatical*: Anybody not willing to put in long hours for little pay should give up *their* idea of becoming a writer.
>
> *Not gender–neutral*: Anybody not willing to put in long hours for little pay should give up *his* idea of becoming a writer.
>
> *Correct*: Anybody not willing to put in long hours for little pay should give up *his or her* idea of becoming a writer.

Option 2. Change the singular antecedent into the equivalent plural form and use the plural pronoun.

> *Those* not willing to put in long hours should give up *their* ideas of becoming writers. (Note the plural "ideas" to agree with "those" and "their.")

Option 3. Revise the sentence so that you don't need a pronoun to replace the noun. This option is not always possible and may occasionally sound too informal for academic writing.

> If you are not willing to put in long hours for little pay, you should give up the idea of becoming a writer.

In the short paragraph below, fix pronoun–antecedent agreement errors, using at least one of each of the three inclusive language options discussed above.

> If a child begins to perform poorly at school nowadays, they will likely be sent to a school counsellor to deal with the situation. Everyone assumes that attention deficit disorder is the culprit, and they just as automatically assume that drugs are the answer. On the other hand, perhaps the child is just not interested in a particular subject, or they do not understand the material. Parents, in turn, treat the child as if he is the problem instead of listening to him to find out how he can be helped.

EXERCISE 11.10

↻ Check answers to select questions

Chose the correct form of the verb and/or pronoun in the sentences and make any other necessary changes in agreement. Rewrite the sentence if that will produce a better result.

1. Everybody who supported the motion raised (his/her/their) hand.
2. Neither the film's director nor its producers (was/were) on hand to receive (his/her/their) prestigious award.
3. The instructor as well as the students (thinks/think) the room is too small.
4. It is unfortunate when a person no longer cares what others think about (him/her/them).
5. One should never expect to succeed unless (one/they) (is/are) willing to persist—even against the odds.
6. It is the tried and true that (provides/provide) the ultimate refuge in mediocrity.
7. Everyone who works during the year (is/are) obliged to file (his/her/their) income tax return.
8. Her set of baby teeth (was/were) complete when she was only eighteen months old.
9. He was one of those few candidates who (was/were) able to win re-election.
10. None of the company's products (requires/require) testing on animals.
11. Lining the side of the highway (is/are) a lot of billboards advertising fast food restaurants.
12. Every specimen of the horned grebe (has/have) a distinctive tuft on each side of (its/their) head.
13. Media and information technology training (provides/provide) students today with important communication skills.
14. Neither team members nor their coach (expects/expect) the season to last another game.
15. The maximum number of people allowed on this elevator (is/are) 30.

EXERCISE 11.11

↻ Check answers to select questions

EXERCISE 11.12

↺ Check answers to select questions

Most of the following sentences contain one or more subject–verb agreement and/or pronoun–antecedent agreement errors. Correct the sentences as needed.

1. Every person in the community should have the right to attend a university and create new opportunities for themselves.
2. Especially unique to adolescent depression are physical symptoms, such as headaches.
3. The tonal quality of Amati's violins are excellent, but not perfect.
4. Over the past week, there has been some unexplained occurrences on the girls' floor of the residence.
5. Small class sizes and a low student population means few opportunities to meet new people.
6. A typical poem by Emily Dickinson leaves the reader searching for another line or even another stanza to satisfy their craving for closure.
7. Use of the leaves of the coca plant for its stimulant effects dates back thousands of years.
8. A coalition of neighbourhood organizations, students, and unions are currently forming to oppose the university's proposed plan.
9. Everyone who has purchased tickets is eligible for the grand prize, but they must be residents of Canada to claim their prize.
10. If a child is denied the opportunity to play, how can they develop emotionally and physically?
11. Participation and public education is necessary in a true democracy.
12. When a person contracts jaundice, their skin as well as the white part of their eyes turn yellow.
13. Another round of intense labour negotiations have not produced a settlement, so each union member has been told to do his duty on the strike line.
14. Before rendering its unanimous verdict, the jury was polled individually.
15. Almost nothing shapes a person's true character as much as their home.
16. The nature and role of human resources in organizations have undergone tremendous change in the last two decades.
17. In P.K. Page's poem, it is apparent that the landlady's prying nature and lonely life has made her forget her place.
18. Stereotyping and the use of degrading language in the book serves to reinforce its theme.
19. His overriding concern with rules and regulations, together with his excessive neatness and demand for order, suggests a mild obsessive-compulsive complex.
20. A person who continually disregards others' feelings will pay for their neglect sooner or later.
21. The encouragement of curiosity, questioning, and discussion is vital to the success of today's school environment.
22. In Japanese culture, a person's reputation along with their social standing depend on the concept of "saving face."
23. Medieval universities established a system of education and academic credentials that continue to function in today's universities.
24. The give and take in any relationship is the most important factor in sustaining it.
25. Although the Canadian Forces is still one of the best-trained military in the world, the training standards and morale of the forces is declining, according to some people.

Other Problems with Pronouns

In addition to agreement problems, there are other potential pronoun pitfalls: errors in *pronoun reference*, *pronoun case*, and *pronoun consistency*.

Pronoun Reference

For a moment, consider life without pronouns.

A Lost Loonie Leads to a Lesson Learned

Alex and Alex's lawyer, Alan, left in Alex's limousine for Loonies Unlimited to buy Alex's landlady, Alice, a litre of light lemonade. Alice told Alex and Alan to also buy a litre of light lemonade for Alice's long-time lodger, Alison. When Alex and Alan alighted at Loonies Unlimited, Alex and Alan were alarmed that Alex had left Alex's loonie in Alex's loft. So Alphonse, of Loonies Unlimited, allowed Alex and Alan only one litre of lemonade, along with a length of limp licorice, and Alphonse loudly lamented Alex's and Alan's laxness.

Newsflash: The pronoun has just been invented! Rewrite the "Lost Loonie" paragraph, replacing as many nouns as possible with pronouns, ensuring that it is clear what noun (antecedent) the pronoun is referring to. If in doubt about the clarity of antecedents, refer to the section that follows.

EXERCISE 11.13

Check answers to select questions

As discussed, most pronouns take the place of nouns, and the noun that the pronoun replaces is called the **antecedent**—literally, the one that "goes before" the pronoun. *Each pronoun you use in your writing should refer clearly to its antecedent.* Formal writing requires your adherence to this principle; more informal writing often permits its looser application (especially with Broad Reference, below). Pronouns replace specific nouns; *the relationship between pronoun and antecedent must always be clear.*

You can test for pronoun reference errors in your writing by seeing whether you can replace a pronoun by a specific noun that precedes the pronoun in the sentence (i.e., its antecedent):

Pronoun replaced by specific noun:

As reality shows become more popular, they [*reality shows*] have become more and more bizarre.

Unclear which noun acts as antecedent:

Reality shows have become more popular while their participants have become more and more bizarre; consequently, they [*reality shows? participants?*] can no longer be believed.

There are four kinds of pronoun reference errors, which can be repaired in different ways.

1. **No reference (missing antecedent).** This error occurs where the pronoun has no apparent noun antecedent. Consider this sentence:

Following the prime minister's speech, *he* took several questions from reporters.

The personal pronoun "he" apparently replaces "prime minister's," which is a possessive adjective. Pronouns replace nouns, not adjectives.

In the following sentence, the noun antecedent is implied but not actually stated; grammatically, the reference, "Canada," is missing:

One thing that Canadians are especially proud of is *its* national health-care system.

Where there is no antecedent, one must be provided or the pronoun changed into an appropriate noun:

After the *prime minister* spoke, *he* took several questions from reporters.

Or:

After speaking, *the prime minister* took several questions from reporters.

One thing that *Canadians* are especially proud of is *their* national health-care system.

A tendency in speaking, and sometimes in informal writing, is the use of the impersonal third-person pronoun *it* or *they* to refer vaguely to some unmentioned authority. In formal writing, you should avoid this habit:

They say there's nothing like a nice car to make you popular.

Don't begin a sentence with a preposition, such as *at*, *by*, *for*, *in*, *on*, or *with*, and then follow it with a pronoun whose antecedent is the object of the preposition. The sentence should be revised to include an antecedent/subject of the clause. The examples below illustrate this problem (and its solutions), which sometimes occurs in a rough draft when a writer is trying to get ideas down quickly:

Incorrect: With the new Formula One scoring system, *it* keeps fans excited throughout the season.

Correct: The new Formula One scoring system keeps fans excited throughout the season.

Or:

With the new Formula One scoring system, fans remain excited throughout the season.

2. **Remote reference**. A reader should not have to hunt for a noun antecedent if it is too far from the pronoun that replaces it:

In George Orwell's prophetic book *1984*, people's lives were watched over by television screens. These screens, along with brainwashing techniques, enabled people to be kept under firm control. *It* is an example of dystopian fiction.

The personal pronoun "It," in the third sentence, takes up the thread too late, and many nouns have intervened. Repetition of the noun is often the best solution where the antecedent is far away from the pronoun.

3. **Ambiguous (squinting) reference.** This error occurs when the pronoun seems to refer to two or more nouns, either of which could be the antecedent:

When *Peter* gave *Paul his* driver's licence, *he* was very surprised to see that it had expired.

Who was surprised in this sentence? The pronoun "he" could refer to either Peter or Paul.

Other examples:

The problem for readers aspiring to look like the models in women's magazines is that *their* photos have been airbrushed. ("Their" has two possible grammatical antecedents: "readers" and "models.")

In 1916, a member of the Russian parliament denounced Rasputin before *his* colleagues. (Does "his" refer to the member's colleagues or to Rasputin's?)

While it is sometimes possible to correct ambiguous reference by repeating the noun intended to act as the antecedent, the result is not always pleasing:

When *Peter* gave *Paul* his driver's license, *Peter* was surprised to see that it had expired.

Rewriting may be the better solution:

On giving his driver's license to Paul, Peter was surprised to see that it had expired.

The problem for readers aspiring to look like the models in women's magazines is that the models' photographs have been airbrushed.

In 1916, a member of the Russian parliament denounced Rasputin before the house.

4. **Broad reference (vague reference).** This error occurs when the pronoun (often *that*, *this*, or *which*) refers to a group of words, an idea, or concept, rather than one specific noun:

Children these days are too prone to lazy habits, such as watching television. *This* shows we have become too permissive.

"This" replaces too much—in effect, the whole preceding clause. By contrast, the meaning of the sentence below is unambiguous, even though the pronoun "which" doesn't replace a specific noun here, but rather the fact that she "received top marks":

She received top marks for her final dive, *which* gave her the gold medal in that competition.

In the following sentence, the pronoun "this" appears to refer to an idea, rather than a noun antecedent; as a result, the precise meaning of the second independent clause is unclear:

Many older drivers are retested if they have had medical problems, but *this* needs to go further.

Broad reference often requires that a sentence be rewritten. Sometimes, the easiest way is to provide a noun and change the demonstrative pronoun into a demonstrative adjective. (Demonstrative adjectives have the same form as demonstrative pronouns—*that*, *these*, *this*, *those*—but, as adjectives, they precede nouns as modifiers, rather than take their place.)

Children these days are too prone to lazy habits, such as watching television. *This tendency* shows that we have become too permissive.

Many older drivers are re-tested if they have had medical problems, but *this re-testing* needs to go further.

You could also omit "this" in the second sentence.

While there is perhaps a "broad" allowance for broad reference error, depending on the level of formality required, *it* is a personal pronoun, and, like all personal pronouns, should always have a clear noun referent.

Poor: We try not to mention specific businesses by name in our article; however, it can't be avoided in some situations.

Better: We try not to mention specific businesses by name in our article; however, we can't avoid names in all situations.

EXERCISE 11.14

Broad pronoun reference errors are particularly distracting when they occur repeatedly as a writer tries to develop a point. After reading the following paragraph, revise it to fix the errors in broad pronoun reference:

> Genetically modified foods have been engineered to flourish in harsh environments. *This* will help alleviate the need for usable farmland as *it* will enable farming to occur on lands once considered unsuitable for growing crops. *This* will be a major benefit to many nations in Africa, Asia, and South America where there is a shortage of food and available land.

EXERCISE 11.15

↻ Check answers to select questions

Identify the kind of pronoun reference errors in the following sentences; then, correct the errors by making necessary revisions. In the first five sentences, the pronoun that needs to be changed is italicized.

1. *It* says in my textbook that pronouns should always have a clear referent.
2. Whenever a staff meeting is called, *they* are required to attend.
3. Racism is a disease that will continue to plague society until *it* is non-existent.
4. Sixty per cent of our pesticides are used on cotton, and *this* is our major groundwater pollutant.
5. During Roosevelt's Pearl Harbor speech, *he* identified the US as a peaceful and tolerant nation.
6. I know it said No Parking, but I went ahead and parked there anyway. They gave me a $20 fine.
7. Her second novel was far different from her first. It was set in the remote Hebrides.
8. Previous Afghan successes were significant victories; for example, they last waged war against the powerful Soviet Union.

9. Some psychologists and researchers believe in the "innate" theory of prejudice. According to this theory, ingrained prejudice is cross-cultural and awareness of race is one of the earliest social characteristics to develop in children. These findings may help account for its popularity.

10. During the dinosaur age, they lived in a rapidly changing environment.

11. It is the right of everybody to have access to knowledge, and this means access to the education of choice.

12. In Chapter 21 of my textbook, it analyzes the success of the Liberal Party in Canada.

13. Supervisors may discourage workers from reporting injuries since they receive annual bonuses for low injury rates.

14. Children often hide their compulsive behaviours from friends and family due to feelings of shame, causing them to remain undiagnosed.

15. To experienced "gamers," the quality of the video card is crucial; this is because the latest games require a high standard of video card.

16. The Catholic kings of Spain rallied the country to fight their enemies, the Moors. This became known as the "Reconquista."

17. Huck Finn was the physically abused son of Pap, who harasses Judge Thatcher when he is drunk. This creates sympathy in the reader, which makes him more likeable.

18. By teaching today's youth safe and healthy approaches to sexuality, it will elevate their self-esteem.

19. Part of the appeal of driving an SUV is that they are big and look impressive beside the "merely mortal" car.

20. Japanese smokers consume more than twice the number of cigarettes as American smokers do, and it continues to increase steadily.

Pronoun Case

Some personal, relative, and interrogative pronouns change their form to reflect their function in the sentence. The grammatical term for this form is *case*. You need to be aware of those situations and look at the pronoun's function in order to use the correct form.

Personal Pronoun

A **personal pronoun** refers to a person. The *first person* refers to the one *doing* the speaking or writing; *second person* refers to the one *spoken to*; *third person* refers to the one *spoken about*. Most nouns can be considered third person and can be replaced by third-person pronouns.

Table 11.1 can help you distinguish between one group of pronouns and another. It's important to be able to distinguish between them, because the role that a personal pronoun plays in a sentence will determine whether you use the pronoun form from the first group (subjective) or from the second one (objective). Notice that the second-person pronoun *you* doesn't change its form.

In the table, consider the pronoun forms under Subjective Singular and Subjective Plural:

He was swimming in the pool.

Table 11.1   Personal Pronouns

	Subjective Singular	Subjective Plural	Objective Singular	Objective Plural
First person	I	we	me	us
Second person	you	you	you	you
Third person	he, she, it	they	him, her, it	them

"He" is subject of the sentence, the third-person singular masculine form of the pronoun.

"He" is the correct form because it is the subject of the clause/sentence, so it is said to be in the **subjective case**. The following sentence illustrates what happens when the pronoun plays a different grammatical role from that of subject:

I was swimming in the pool with *her*.

The subject "I" is first-person singular, but the other pronoun in the sentence is acting as object of the preposition "with." When it acts as the object of a verb or of a preposition, it is in the **objective case**.

If you are in doubt about the correct form of a personal pronoun, determine the grammatical role it plays in the sentence and then use the corresponding case form:

She spoke so softly to the teacher that it was difficult for *him* to understand *her*.

"She" is the *subject* of the verb "spoke"; "him" is the *object* of the preposition "for"; "her" is the *object* of the infinitive "to understand."

Notice the different pronouns in these two sentences:

Anna, the King, and *I* are going out for Chinese food tonight. ("I" is part of the subject.)

Anna arrived late for her dinner with the King and *me*. ("Me" is part of a prepositional phrase; it is object of the preposition "with.")

To decide which form to use:

1. determine the grammatical relationship involved: Is the pronoun subject of a clause/sentence, or the object of a verb, preposition, or infinitive? Then,
2. choose the appropriate form (subjective or objective). Until the forms become familiar, you can refer to the pronoun chart above.

Although the principle of pronoun case with personal pronouns is quite straightforward, it can be tricky to apply in compounds:

Tina and (*I*/*me*) plan to attend Mavis's wedding on May 15.

Strategy: Isolate the pronoun from the noun to determine the correct form:

~~Tina and~~ I plan to attend Mavis's wedding on May 15.

Mavis's wedding will be a joyous occasion for ~~Tina and~~ me.

Table 11.2 Possessive Personal Pronouns with Complements

	Adjectival Singular	Adjectival Plural	Subjective Complements Singular	Subjective Complements Plural
First person	my	our	mine	ours
Second person	your	your	yours	yours
Third person	his, her, its	their	his, hers, its	theirs

We s̶t̶u̶d̶e̶n̶t̶s̶ believe firmly that our rights should be given back to us.

Our rights should be given back to us s̶t̶u̶d̶e̶n̶t̶s̶.

Possessive pronoun. A pronoun also changes its form in the possessive (adjectival) form (e.g., "my *uncle's* pet alligator"; "*his* pet alligator").

The book doesn't belong to Anthony but to Kristy; it is *hers*.

"Hers" is the noun form of the possessive pronoun replacing the antecedent "Kristy." The adjectival form is seen in the following sentence:

The book doesn't belong to Anthony but to Kristy; it is *her* book.

Table 11.2 completes Table 11.1 by including the possessive forms of pronouns.

> Never use an apostrophe when you use a form like *hers* ("belongs to her") or *theirs* ("belongs to them.")

Relative Pronoun

A relative pronoun *relates* the dependent clause it introduces to the noun that it follows (see page 317). A relative clause, then, usually functions as an adjective, modifying the preceding noun. Of the major relative pronouns (*that, which, whichever, who, whoever*), only *who* and *whoever* change their form depending on whether they are being used as the subject of the clause or as object of either the verb or a preposition in the clause.

To determine the case of a relative pronoun, look at the role the relative pronoun plays within the clause; in other words, the answer to whether you use *who* or *whom* will be found in the clause that the relative pronoun introduces.

If either of the pronouns *who* or *whoever* is subject of the clause or is the subjective completion, use the subjective form. If the pronoun is acting as an object of the verb or of a preposition in the clause, use the objective form: *whom* or *whomever*. Consider these two sentences; italics indicate the dependent (relative) clause:

1. The old man shouted at *whoever happened to be within listening distance*.

2. The old man should be free to shout at *whomever he chooses*.

In sentence 1, "whoever" is the subject of the clause it introduces ("whoever happened to be within listening distance"). In sentence 2, "he" is subject of the clause, and the relative pronoun is in the objective case. If you see that the relative clause has a subject, you can be certain that the relative pronoun will *not* be the subject of the clause. In sentence 2, "he" does the choosing and is the subject of the verb; "whomever" is the object of the verb.

One test for case is to substitute the third-person form of the personal pronoun for the relative pronoun in the relative clause. "Whoever [relative pronoun] happened to be within listening distance" would become "he/she [personal pronoun] happened to be within listening distance." In sentence 2, the relative clause would read, "he chooses he," which sounds, and is, incorrect.

Determining pronoun case with relative pronouns always involves determining the function of the relative pronoun that begins the clause. Which of the sentences below is correct?

1. Jeong-Gyu is someone who, we firmly believe, will go far.
2. Jeong-Gyu is someone whom, we firmly believe, will go far.

Sentence 1 is correct. "Who" is the subject of the relative clause "who will go far." "[W]e firmly believe" is not part of the relative clause but part of another clause (with another subject) that interrupts the relative clause.

Jeong-Gyu is someone who, we firmly believe, will go far.

Interrogative Pronoun

The **interrogative pronouns** (*what, which, whichever, who, whoever*) are always asking questions. Once you know how to determine the case of the relative pronouns, *who/whom*, the interrogatives shouldn't give you too much trouble. Again, you need to determine their function to determine pronoun case. Of the three interrogatives, it is *who* and *whoever* that change, depending on their function in the sentence:

With whom did you go out on Saturday night? (object of the preposition)

Who says you should never reveal your feelings? (subject of the verb)

Whom would you recommend for the new opening? (object of the verb)

If a pronoun is part of a prepositional phrase, it normally follows the preposition. However, it's possible to structure the sentence so the pronoun precedes the preposition (e.g., "Whom is the note for?"). If you end a sentence with a preposition, you can rearrange the sentence so the preposition comes before the pronoun. It is then clearer to see that the *objective case* should be used for the pronoun:

Whom did Professor LeGuin direct the question *to*?

The more formal usage makes it easier to determine case:

Rearranged sentence: To whom did Professor LeGuin direct the question?

It is now clear that "whom" is the object of the preposition "to."

EXERCISE 11.16

↻ Check answers to select questions

Choose the correct form of the pronoun.

1. Management often forgets about the needs of (we/us) wage-earners.
2. (Who/whom) should run for office this election?
3. I have no intention of speaking to (they/them).
4. The person (who/whom) finishes first will be rewarded.
5. You recommend (who/whom) for the position?

6. As she entered the room, a mysterious feeling came over (she/her).
7. Margaret Laurence was a novelist (who/whom) entertained her readers with well-developed plots and realistic characters.
8. People (who/whom) use memory aids tend to be better spellers.
9. The instructor explained the different cases of pronouns to Gail and (I/me).
10. "Hey, buddy, (who/whom) did you mean to refer to when you used that insulting term?"
11. (Whoever/whomever) fails to address the most important issue—unemployment—will find themselves among the unemployed.
12. The last person (who/whom) she wanted to see at the track meet was her former coach.
13. My fifth grade teacher always let her favourite students—Mallory, Cindy, and (I/me)—help her with clean-up.
14. I wanted to ask her (who/whom) the note should be addressed to.
15. The young narrator's goal is to bring back a present for his friend's sister (who/whom) he admires from afar.
16. Chris's rival, Mike, lasted longer in the ring than (he/him).
17. We were allowed to invite (whoever/whomever) we wanted to the party.
18. I proposed that Geordie and (I/me) would stack chairs after the meeting.
19. "Only certain areas will be affected," said Marc Bierkens, (who/whom), along with two other researchers, conducted the study.
20. The newly renovated house is a very pleasant place for my brother and (I/me) to live.
21. During his career, Jackie Robinson was subjected to racial hatred from many people (who/whom) he came in contact with.
22. Prejudices decrease when children observe non-prejudiced behaviour by peers (who/whom) children associate with during their pre-teen years.
23. Christy so drastically changes his personality that his own father can barely believe it is (he/him).
24. "[I]n these fits I leave them, while I visit / young Ferdinand, (who/whom) they suppose is drowned." —Shakespeare
25. Choose the grammatical poem:

    (a) Roses are red,
    Butterflies are free;
    You must choose
    Between him and me.

    (b) Roses are red,
    Birds can fly;
    You must choose
    Between he and I.

Pronoun Consistency

A pronoun must agree in number, gender, and person with its antecedent. In many instances, you will refer to different persons in the same sentence, and it's acceptable to do so, as long as the change isn't arbitrary. On the other hand, if you want simply to replace a preceding noun with a pronoun, the pronoun should be the same *person* as its antecedent. Remember that nouns are usually treated as third-person and are replaced by third-person pronouns.

Incorrect: During final exams, if *students* must go to the washroom, raise *your* hand so *you* can be escorted there. ("Students" is third-person; "your" and "you" are second-person.)

Correct:

During final exams, if *students* need to go to the washroom, *they* should raise their hands . . . .

Or, more informally:

During final exams, if *you* need to go to the washroom, raise *your* hand . . . .

Further examples:

Incorrect: It is possible that *our* desire to make life easier for *ourselves* will, in fact, make *humans* redundant. ("Our" and "ourselves" are first-person; "humans" is third-person.)

Correct:

It is possible that *our* desire to make life easier for *ourselves* will, in fact, make *us* redundant.

It is possible that the desire to make life easier for *humans* will, in fact, make *them* redundant.

Incorrect: Educators today should teach *students* learning skills, such as how to manage *your* money.

Correct: Educators today should teach *students* learning skills, such as how to manage *their* money.

EXERCISE 11.17

↻ Check answers to select questions

The following paragraph contains errors in pronoun consistency, along with some awkward use of third-person pronouns. When you rewrite the paragraph, strive for correctness and effectiveness. First decide which person you want to refer to consistently. This decision might be based on the level of formality you want to use (first- and second-person pronouns, such as *I/me* and *you*, are considered more informal than third-person pronouns, such as *he/she* and *him/her*).

You can definitely learn a lot from educational TV; we can learn things that we cannot learn from written texts. If one is a major in Commerce, for example, and if he or she watches the business news, he or she can understand the commerce textbook better by applying what he or she learns from the news. Similarly, I think that watching sports programs can provide people with excitement. Watching sports can also give us a better understanding of the game. On the other hand, if one chooses to watch comedy all the time, people are not going to gain any real benefits. I feel comedies are generally meaningless.

Sentence Construction Errors

Writing in complete sentences and using the appropriate conjunctions to join clauses will help you form grammatical sentences. However, there are other potential problems in constructing sentences. Major sentence construction errors are discussed below under four categories: (1) misplaced modifiers, (2) dangling modifiers, (3) faulty parallelism, and (4) faulty comparisons.

Sentence construction errors result from forgetting two basic principles in English grammar: (1) Modifiers should have a word to modify in the sentence, and they should be placed as close as possible to these words; (2) Coordinate (equal) elements in a sentence must be grammatically parallel and complete. Misplaced modifiers and dangling modifiers are examples of errors that can result when the first principle is not adhered to. Faulty parallelism and faulty comparisons result when the second principle is not followed.

Misplaced Modifiers

The main function of adjectives is to modify nouns, while the main function of adverbs is to modify verbs. Prepositional phrases can also function as adjectives or adverbs. Misplaced modifiers, then, can be either adjectives or adjectival phrases, or adverbs or adverbial phrases. They are misplaced when mistakenly placed next to a part of speech they are not intended to modify.

The meaning of a sentence in English heavily depends on word order, or *syntax*; it is partly through syntax that writers communicate their meaning and that the reader understands the message.

Adjectival Modifiers

The usual position for a one-word adjective is immediately before the noun it is intended to modify, but adjectival phrases and clauses usually *follow* the noun they modify. Most misplaced adjectival modifiers are phrases or clauses. Consider the following examples of misplaced modifiers:

Incorrect: They headed for a child in the front row *with a long overcoat*.

It is the child, not the front row, wearing the long overcoat. The adjectival phrase should follow the noun "child":

They headed for a child with a long overcoat in the front row.

The furnace thermostat is located upstairs, *which displays the temperature settings*.

In this sentence, the adjectival (relative) clause, "which displays the temperature settings," is placed next to the adverb "upstairs" instead of closest to the noun "thermostat."

The furnace thermostat, which displays the temperature settings, is located upstairs.

Adverbial Modifiers

Misplaced adverbs and adverbial phrases are more common than misplaced adjectives and adjectival phrases because adverbs can often be moved in a sentence without affecting meaning. However, moving them does sometimes affect meaning, and it is safest to place them right before or after the word or phrase they are supposed to modify.

The meaning of the following sentence could be misconstrued:

Students should buy this book because it will give them all the information they need to know about writing *in a convenient form*.

Presumably, the writer did not want to highlight "convenience in writing," but that the book "will give them . . . information . . . in a convenient form."

> *Correct*: Students should buy this book because it will give them, *in a convenient form*, all the information they will need to know about writing.

Because of the misplaced prepositional phrase in the sentence below, the writer seems to be saying that on being convicted, the criminal will have to "do time" in two provinces:

> *Incorrect*: The conviction carries a penalty of eight to ten years *in two provinces*.
>
> *Correct*:
>
> *In two provinces*, the conviction carries a penalty of eight to ten years.
>
> *Or*:
>
> The conviction *in two provinces* carries a penalty of eight to ten years.

Fixing Misplaced Modifiers

When the misplaced modifier "in two provinces" in the previous example is placed before or after the verb it should modify, "carries," the problem is fixed. The solution to misplaced modifiers, whether an entire clause, a phrase, or a single word, is simple: move them.

The following misplaced modifier makes the sentence awkward or misleading:

> *Incorrect*: The instructor marked the essay I wrote *unfairly*.
>
> *Correct*:
>
> The instructor *unfairly marked* the essay I wrote.
>
> *Or*:
>
> I thought the instructor *marked my essay unfairly*.

When you are writing quickly, trying to get your ideas down, misplaced modifiers can occur anywhere in a sentence; however, they often occur at the end, almost as an afterthought. That is the place to begin checking:

> *Incorrect*: Cars today produce large amounts of toxic chemicals that can damage human cells *if inhaled*.
>
> *Correct*: Cars today produce large amounts of toxic chemicals that, *if inhaled*, can damage human cells.

One-Word Modifiers

You need to be careful in placing one-word modifiers in the sentence, especially with limiting adverbs like *almost*, *barely*, *even*, *just*, *only*, *merely*, *nearly*, and the like.

Does one little word out of place *really* affect the meaning of the sentence? Consider how the meaning of the following statement changes, depending on where the "little" word *only* is put:

> Jared didn't do his homework yesterday.

Seven Answers to the Question, "Is Jared a Lazy Student or a Conscientious One?"

1. *Only Jared* didn't do his homework yesterday.

Everyone but Jared did his or her homework; "only" is an adjective modifying "Jared."

2. Jared *only didn't do* his homework.

The meaning of this sentence is ambiguous. It could mean the same as sentence 1 or that Jared did other things—but not his homework. It could also mean that the fact Jared didn't do his homework wasn't important.

3. Jared didn't *only do* his homework yesterday.

Now "only" is an adverb modifying the verb "do" and suggests that Jared did do his homework and other things as well.

4. Jared didn't do *only his homework* yesterday.

Placing "only" before "his homework" means that Jared definitely did his homework and other things as well. It might also mean that Jared was involved in doing someone else's homework in addition to his own.

5. Jared didn't do his *only homework* yesterday.

Placing "only" between "his" and "homework" implies that Jared might under other circumstances have had much more homework, but yesterday had only a lesser amount, which he nevertheless did not do.

6. Jared didn't do his homework *only yesterday*.

Jared normally does his homework but only yesterday did not.

7. Jared didn't do his homework *yesterday only*.

Perhaps Jared is not such a lazy student after all: the only day he didn't do his homework was yesterday!

Dangling Modifiers

Dangling modifiers appear to modify nouns they are not intended to modify. Dangling modifiers can be the grammatical equivalent of life's most embarrassing moments: a modifier that is dangling can give the communication a quite different, sometimes humorous, meaning from the intended one. The sentence below seems to refer to precocious parents:

When only seven years old, my parents decided to enroll me in a Highland dancing course.

Now, consider the following sentence from a résumé, which never mentions the applicant at all:

When not working or attending classes, my hobbies are gardening, doing macramé, and bungee-jumping.

As dangling modifiers are often *-ing* participle (adjectival) phrases, they are sometimes called **dangling participles**. Grammatically, they modify the closest noun. These adjectival phrases, then, are dangling because the intended noun or noun phrase is not in the sentence. That's why it doesn't help to move the modifier.

The way to correct dangling modifiers is (1) to provide the noun or noun phrase in the independent clause to give the modifier something to modify, or (2) to turn the dangling phrase into a dependent clause with a subject:

> When only seven years old, I was enrolled by my parents in a Highland dancing course. (1)
>
> When I was only seven years old, my parents decided to enroll me in a Highland dancing course. (2)
>
> When not working or attending classes, I enjoy several hobbies, including gardening, doing macramé, and bungee-jumping. (1)
>
> When I am not working or attending classes, my hobbies include gardening, doing macramé, and bungee-jumping. (2)

While misplaced modifiers frequently appear at the end of a sentence, dangling modifiers usually are found at the beginning—somewhat less often at the end—of a sentence, and even occasionally in the middle. With misplaced modifiers, the needed information is in the sentence, and the modifier needs to be moved as close as possible to the word or phrase it is intended to modify. With dangling modifiers, the essential information *is not in the sentence*. The examples below will show you how to identify dangling modifiers by asking the appropriate questions.

In this example, poetic description is undercut by the statement that the clouds are arriving in Calgary, when more likely the writer is describing his or her arrival:

> When arriving in Calgary, the clouds had scattered, and the sky was aglow with bands of pink and red.

In the next example, the book seems to have written itself:

> Though a well-known writer, his latest book failed to make the best-seller's list.

The question to ask in the first example is, "Who is arriving in Calgary?" In the second, we must ask, "Who is the well-known writer?" Since the answers are not in the sentences, the modifiers must be dangling. In both cases, (1) the missing information needs to be provided in the independent clause, or (2) the dangling phrase needs to be turned into a dependent clause that can modify the independent clause that follows:

> *Corrected*:
>
> When arriving in Calgary, I saw that the clouds had scattered, and the sky was aglow with bands of pink and red. (1—information has been provided in the independent clause)
>
> When I arrived in Calgary, the clouds had scattered, and the sky was aglow with bands of pink and red. (2—dangling phrase has been changed to a dependent clause)

Corrected:

Though a well-known writer, he failed to make the bestseller's list with his latest book. (1)

Though he was a well-known writer, his latest book failed to make the bestseller's list. (2)

In the following example, the dangling modifier is at the end of the sentence:

Incorrect: Verbal and non-verbal skills are greatly enhanced when living in a foreign country.

Who is living in a foreign country? This information is missing, so the participial phrase "when living" is dangling. To correct it, add information:

Corrected:

When living in a foreign country, you are able to enhance your verbal and non-verbal skills. (1)

Or: Verbal and non-verbal skills are greatly enhanced when you live in a foreign country. (2)

The intended meanings of the following sentences are obscured or distorted due to modifier problems. Working in groups, identify the particular problem (misplaced or dangling modifier) and determine the grammatical (incorrect or ambiguous) meanings of the sentences. Then, fix the sentences using one of the methods above. The sentences are either headlines or leads to actual news stories.

1. Elderly Alberta woman fends off purse snatcher with walker.
2. Jellyfish injures swimmers from beyond the grave.
3. Deriving inspiration from the novel *Uncle Tom's Cabin*, Walker's characters embody the racial tropes that reinforce stereotypical representations of African-Americans.
4. Gunmen mow down partiers with machine guns in Bolivia.
5. The oilsands giant was recently found guilty of failing to take appropriate steps to prevent the deaths of more than 1,600 birds in a St. Albert courtroom.
6. Explorer who first reached North Pole indisputably dies at 80.
7. Scientists have been trying to determine why people need sleep for more than 100 years.
8. Cougar attacks five-year-old boy, expected to survive.
9. Officer fired for waitress photo on cop car with rifle.
10. The googly-eyed Puss-in-Boots looks nothing like the cat fans used to love in the new movie.

EXERCISE 11.18

↻ Check answers to select questions

Correct the following sentences, each of which contains a modifier error. In some instances, it will be necessary to reword the sentence for clarity and correctness.

1. In our city, shady characters lurk on quiet corners that offer a variety of drugs.
2. Over the years, several world-class cyclists have had spectacular careers, such as Eddie Merckx and Greg LeMond.

EXERCISE 11.19

↻ Check answers to select questions

3. Running down the street without a care in the world, two pedestrians had to quickly move out of his way.
4. Being a member of the Sikh community, my paper will be given a strong personal focus.
5. Built in mere minutes, you will have a fully interactive website for your business or for your personal use.
6. Benefits will only result from a smoke-free environment.
7. Germany has built an extensive network of highways through its countryside, known as the Autobahn.
8. Trying to find a job today, employers are stressing verbal and written communication skills more than ever before.
9. People's rights to privacy should be forfeited when caught in criminal behaviour.
10. This species of snake will eat frogs, mice, and small pieces of meat in captivity.
11. Walking through the streets of Srinigar, devastation and fear are immediately evident.
12. As a beginner, my instructor taught me about the respect one karate student must show to another.
13. Tylenol and Aspirin effectively reduce pain when experiencing a fever.
14. Speaking from experience, tans that dye the top layer of the skin last for about one week.
15. Moving to Nebraska at the age of 10, Jim Burden's narrative reveals the reflections of one his age.
16. Being an Elizabethan playwright, I am certain that Shakespeare would have been a major influence on Marlowe.
17. Opening the door unexpectedly, his eyes fell upon two of his employees sleeping in front of their computers.
18. As a serious snowboarder, it is exciting to observe the growth of this sport.
19. In John Donne's "Death, Be Not Proud," Death has a personality that is usually only given to a human being.
20. The boy in "Araby" returns home empty-handed without the highly valued object, in this case, a gift for Mangan's sister that most quests require.
21. Darwin's theory of evolution may be contested on the grounds that species may cease to appear abruptly.
22. Another example of imagery of light and dark in *Heart of Darkness* occurs when Marlow encounters an African dying in a clearing with a white scarf.
23. Based primarily on the work of Karl Marx, socialists see the creation of profit as a complex process.
24. Having an emotional personality, Beethoven's music identified him as a nineteenth-century Romantic.
25. A mother and her daughter were recently reunited after 18 years in a checkout line.

The Parallelism Principle

Elements in a sentence exist in relationships that could be pictured geometrically. Balanced constructions give a sentence grace and strength, while unbalanced constructions make a sentence weak and unstable, as a misaligned wall in a building undermines a building's stability. A sentence must be constructed so that words and phrases parallel in the logic of the sentence are parallel in the grammatical structure of the sentence.

Coordinate elements are *equal* elements. Checking for parallelism is checking to ensure that the elements in a sentence that have the *same grammatical function* are expressed in parallel structures.

When studying paragraph coherence (Chapter 4), you looked at using repetition and balanced structures. Learning the fundamentals of parallelism in this section will help ensure that your writing is both grammatically correct and easy to read. Apply the principle of parallelism carefully to ensure grammatical correctness, and work to ensure that the grammatically parallel structures you use lend clarity and smoothness to your writing.

Experienced writers have mastered the principles of parallel structures and use them routinely in their writing; balanced structures are rhetorically effective structures. Consider, for example, the following excerpt from Francis Bacon's essay "Of Youth and Age" (1601), which is made up almost entirely of parallel words, phrases, and clauses. Without parallel elements, shown by italics, this paragraph would be very hard to follow:

> A man that is *young in years*, may be *old in hours*, if he have lost no time. But that happeneth rarely. Generally, youth is like the *first cogitations*, not so wise as *the second*. For there is a youth *in thoughts*, as well as *in ages* . . . . Young men, in the conduct and manage of actions, *embrace* more than they can hold; *stir* more than they can quiet; *fly* to the end, without consideration of the means and degrees; *pursue* some few principles, which they have chanced upon absurdly; *care not* to innovate, which draws unknown inconveniences; *use* extreme remedies at first; and, that which doubleth all errors, *will not acknowledge or retract* them; like an unready horse, that will neither *stop* nor *turn*. Men of age *object* too much, *consult* too long, *adventure* too little, *repent* too soon, and seldom *drive* business home to the full period, but *content* themselves with a mediocrity of success.

Student writer Allison McClymont was able to utilize parallel structures to create a dramatic opening for her essay on school uniforms:

> In the hallways of today's high school, students congregate in various cliques, using their dress as an indicator of their conformity: there are the "jocks" in their letterman jackets, the "nerds" in their high pants and suspenders, the "cheerleaders" in their short skirts and sweaters, and the "arties" in their paint-covered hippie clothes. Other easily identifiable cliques include the "gangsters," the "preppies," the "moods," the "punks," the "weirdos," and "the band geeks."

Read the following sentences. Although their meanings are clear, they don't *sound* balanced. In fact, they're not balanced because the important words in the compound or list aren't all the same part of speech: each sentence contains an error in parallel structure. The words you need to pay attention to are italicized:

1. Ian would rather *snack* on some chips than *eating* a regular dinner.
2. The basic human needs are *food, clothes, shelter*, and *having a good job*.

3.   After her 10-kilometre run, she felt *weak*, *tired*, and *she badly needed water*.

4.   Our cat enjoys *watching* TV, *looking* out the window, and *to sleep* at the foot of our bed.

5.   Neither a *borrower* be, nor *lend* to others.

Identifying and Fixing Parallelism Problems

Use a two-stage approach to identify and fix parallel structures in your writing:

First, identify structures where there should be parallelism: *lists, compounds, correlative conjunctions,* and *comparisons*. For example, in the following sentence there is a compound object of the verb "prefer":

1.   Ian would prefer *to snack* on some chips rather than *eating* a regular dinner.

Second, when you have identified which part(s) are not grammatically parallel, make them so. The two objects of the verb "prefer" in the sentence 1 above are not expressed in parallel fashion: "to snack" and "eating." Either the verbal noun (infinitive form of the verb acting as a noun) or the gerund (-*ing* verb form acting as a noun) can function as objects, so either of these changes is correct:

Ian would prefer *to snack* on some chips than *to eat* a regular dinner.

Or:

Ian would prefer *snacking* on chips to *eating* a regular dinner.

Identify in the following sentences the parts of speech that have the same functions, and use four nouns in a list to make it grammatically parallel:

2.   The basic human needs are *food*, *clothes*, *shelter*, and *having* a good job.

Using three predicate adjectives, make this list in the sentence below parallel. You could also fix the sentence by using three independent clauses: "she felt weak," etc.:

3.   After her 10-kilometre run, she felt *weak*, *tired*, and *she badly needed water*.

Use three gerunds to make the list in the sentence below parallel. Next, correct the sentence using three infinitives:

4.   Our cat enjoys *watching* TV, *looking* out the window, and *to sleep* at the foot of our bed.

Use two verbs after the correlative (paired) conjunctions *neither* and *nor* to make the following sentence parallel:

5.   Neither a *borrower* be, nor *lend* to others.

You could also follow Shakespeare's example in his play *Hamlet* and use two nouns after the conjunctions: Neither a *borrower* nor a *lender* be.

When checking for parallel structure, consider first the structurally essential words like nouns and verbs (not their modifiers). But if adjectives or adverbs appear in a list *by themselves* without words to modify, ensure they are in parallel form. Look at any larger grammatical units, such as prepositional phrases, which also should appear in parallel relationships with other prepositional phrases. Similarly, dependent clauses should be parallel with dependent clauses, and independent clauses with independent clauses.

The examples below apply the two-step method to lists, compounds, correlative conjunctions, and comparisons.

A List or Series

A list or series comprises three or more items. Whenever you list something, you need to check for parallel structure. For example, if you use an expanded thesis statement that lists your essay's main points, you need to ensure that all the items in the list are grammatically parallel:

> *Incorrect*: Research into cloning should be encouraged as it could lead to cures for diseases, successful organ transplants, and put an end to infertility problems.

> *Correct*: Research into cloning should be legalized as it could lead to | *cures* for diseases, | successful organ *transplants*, | and *solutions* to infertility problems.

The elements are now parallel. Notice that to avoid repeating the word "cures," a word with a similar meaning has replaced it.

Note: Length is not necessarily a factor in parallelism: for example, a simple noun would normally be considered parallel with a noun phrase (but not with a prepositional phrase) because both have the same grammatical function.

The following sentence contains two nouns preceded by adjectives and a noun followed by an adjectival (prepositional) phrase. The important words here are the nouns:

> Discipline in single-sex schools has been shown to directly affect | regular *attendance*, good *grades*, and *standards* for dress and behaviour.

The following thesis statements include lists where the items are not parallel:

> *Incorrect*: The major forms of eating disorders involve the compulsion to count calories, to constantly exercise, and the need to alter one's appearance.

> *Correct*: The major forms of eating disorders involve the compulsion | *to count* calories, *to* constantly *exercise*, and *to alter* one's appearance.

> *Incorrect*: Buddhism teaches that one's karma can be affected by many things: your generosity to those less fortunate, your behaviour to strangers, and if you treat even your enemies with respect.

The list of noun, noun, clause needs to be changed to noun, noun, noun:

> Buddhism teaches that one's karma can be affect by many things: your *generosity* to those less fortunate, your *behaviour* to strangers, and *respect* even for your enemies.

You also need to be careful that items in a list are *logically*, as well as grammatically, parallel. The following list contains five nouns/noun phrases, but not all of the items are logically parallel. Which item does not belong in the list? Why?

> Common injuries in the meat-packing industry include chemical burns, broken bones, lacerations, amputations, and even death.

Compounds

You need to apply the principle of parallel structure to **compounds**. A coordinating conjunction, such as *and*, *or*, or *but*, can signal a compound, as can a prepositional phrase joiner such as *as well as*; in a comparison, *than* or *as* may join the two elements being compared.

Once you've identified a compound, look at the important word or phrase in the first element of the compound and ensure that the second element that follows the joiner uses the parallel grammatical structure. Several examples of compounds follow:

> *Incorrect*: It is actually cheaper | *to convert* a used vehicle into an electric vehicle than | *buying* a new gas-powered model.

> *Correct*: It is actually cheaper | *to convert* a used vehicle into an electric vehicle than | *to buy* a new gas-powered model.

Some compounds that cause trouble are those with helping verbs. In these cases, it may be helpful to draw a line where the first element begins and another where the second begins (after the conjunction). Then, see if both parts line up with the main verb that follows; you can draw a line there too. The main verb in the sentence below is "worked":

> *Incorrect*: The prohibition of marijuana and the laws in place for it | *do not* and | *have never* | worked.

> *Test*: The prohibition of marijuana and the laws in place for it | *do not* . . . worked and *have never* worked.

> *Correct*: The prohibition of marijuana and the laws in place for it *do not work* and *have never worked.*

Sometimes a compound phrase ending in a preposition doesn't line up with what follows. Here is an example of a compound in which the words that follow the verbs don't line up with the object. Again, the presence of a coordinating conjunction can alert you to these tricky kinds of compounds:

> *Incorrect*: Most people under 30 *are familiar or have heard of* the rapper Snoop Dogg.

> *Correct*: Most people under 30 | *are familiar with or* | *have heard of* | the rapper Snoop Dogg.

> *Incorrect*: "We have to change our production methods to make sure the products we sell are *as good* or *better as* any in the world," said the Minister of Agriculture.

Correct: "We have to change our production methods to make sure the products we sell are | *as good as* | or *better as than* | any in the world," said the Minister of Agriculture.

Correlative Conjunctions

A specific kind of compound involves correlative conjunctions. These are joiners that work in pairs (*both . . . and*, *either . . . or*, *neither . . . nor*, *not . . . but*, *not only . . . but also*). Logically, the part of speech that follows the first half of the compound should also follow the second half. It might be helpful to draw a line after each conjunction:

Incorrect: A college diploma today is an investment *not only* | in students' financial resources *but also* | their time.

What follows "not only" is a prepositional phrase that begins with "in"; therefore, a prepositional phrase, not just a noun ("time"), must follow the second member of the pair:

A college diploma today is an investment *not only* | *in* students' financial resources *but also* | *in* their time.

Incorrect: The lack of classroom availability means *either* constructing new buildings *or* lower the number of students accepted into programs.

Correct: The lack of classroom availability means *either constructing* new buildings *or lowering* the number of students accepted into programs.

Comparisons

Under Compounds, above, we looked at comparisons as compound structures requiring parallelism. However, sometimes faulty comparisons have less to do with grammar than with logic.

Because comparisons are always made between one thing and another thing, both these elements must be fully expressed for the comparison to be complete. Often either the comparison is left incomplete or the terms being compared are incompatible; that is, they cannot be compared because there is no basis for comparison.

Note: *Than* is the word for comparisons, not the adverb related to time, *then*. Other words and phrases can also signal comparisons: *as*, *compared to*, *different (from)*, *like*, *similar (to)*, etc.

Writers need to ask if the two parts of a comparison are grammatically parallel, if both parts of the comparison are fully expressed, and if the two objects of the comparison can logically be compared. In this sentence, the reader is left to assume whom males are being compared to:

Incomplete: An unfortunate stereotype is that males are more scientific and less intuitive.

Complete: An unfortunate stereotype is that males are more scientific and less intuitive *than females*.

Incompatible: I have found that students are less judgmental in university compared to high school.

You can ask what precisely is being compared to what and if the comparison is logical; in this case, the writer is comparing a perceived trait of students at university to high school itself. People must be compared to people:

Compatible: I have found that people are less judgmental in university than they are in high school.

The two sides of the comparison are now complete and compatible.

What is being compared in the sentences below? Are the terms comparable? The writer is comparing running times (for men) to women:

Incompatible: In the study, men's running times were recorded for 30 more years than women.

Compatible: In the study, men's running times were recorded for 30 more years than women's times.

EXERCISE 11.20

↻ Check answers to select questions

In the word groups that follow, there are three or four main points related to a topic. Build parallel structures in thesis statements for each topic. Make whatever changes are necessary to achieve parallelism and use whatever order of points seems natural.

Topic 1: Why I like toe socks:
- warm and comfortable
- they are the latest fashion in socks
- come in many colours and designs

Topic 2: The advantages of yoga:
- to relax and reduce stress
- to exercise
- also can meet people in yoga classes

Topic 3: The importance of computers to students:
- they provide entertainment
- cutting down on homework time is important
- you can obtain a wealth of information quickly

Topic 4: Living with roommates:
- they can create a lot of mess
- invade your personal space
- you can talk to them about your problems

Topic 5: The benefits of coffee:
- coffee helps you wake up
- its rich, satisfying flavour
- it improves your concentration

Topic 6: The comparison of two recreational drugs:
- their possible dangerous side effects
- who uses them
- the effects they produce in the user

Topic 7:   The facts about organically grown food:
- the way organically grown food is farmed
- the cost of these kinds of foods
- their nutritional value

Topic 8:   The advantages of home birthing:
- allows the parents to maintain control over their surroundings
- a positive and friendly place for the child to be born
- is as safe as a hospital birth if common sense is used

Topic 9:   School uniforms are beneficial:
- promote school identity and school pride
- they save parents money and hassle
- reduce the pressure of students to conform to the latest fashions
- to make it easier for school authorities to enforce discipline

Topic 10: The legalization of marijuana:
- it is less addictive than some other illegal drugs
- the Canadian government has already made it legal under certain circumstances
- governments could increase their revenue by selling it
- making it legal would reduce crime since people wouldn't have to obtain it illegally

The sentences below contain parallelism errors. Identify each kind of error (series, compound, correlative conjunction, or comparison) and fix the errors.

1.   A good journalist is inquisitive, persistent, and must be a good listener.
2.   Music can directly affect your thoughts, emotions, and how you feel.
3.   In this essay, I will be looking and writing about the role of women in the military.
4.   Tiddlywinks is not only a game of considerable skill but also strategy.
5.   Television can affect children in a variety of negative ways since children often lack judgment, are naturally curious, and easily influenced.
6.   There are three main qualities that a leader must possess: a leader must be enthusiastic, organized, and have creativity.
7.   Aman never has and never will be good at golf.
8.   She was not only the best teacher I have ever had, but also I was impressed by her wardrobe.
9.   Tremors may occur on either or both sides of the body.
10. There are many reasons why people choose to or enjoy watching television.
11. A recent study has found that Caucasian children acquire self-awareness at an earlier age than other ethnic groups.
12. Being imprisoned for a long time can result in a dependency on the institutional environment, a lack of meaningful relationships, and there can be a loss of personal identity.
13. We can help combat global warming by using renewable energy sources, researching carbon sequestration, starting carbon taxes, and all the little things we can do as individuals.

EXERCISE 11.21

 Check answers to select questions

14. I want to emphasize that my work as MP in this riding has not, and will not, be affected by political developments.
15. When Jim has the choice of either jumping or to stay on the doomed ship, he chooses to jump.
16. Physical education teaches children not only to work well together but also patience and discipline.
17. Smoking should be banned because it raises health-care costs, physically harms both smokers and non-smokers, and because cigarette production damages the environment.
18. Allowing prostitution in controlled environments will reduce the risk of violence, decrease drug abuse, and even combats disease through regular testing.
19. What made Beethoven's music different from other composers was his expressive style.
20. Recent studies suggest that wellness depends on three main factors: feeling good about yourself, your everyday eating habits, and being comfortably active.
21. Although two very different American writers, Nathaniel Hawthorne and Mark Twain's works are nevertheless similar in many ways.
22. Differing viewpoints in a work of fiction not only add conflict, but they can also reveal differences in characters' ages, genders, and upbringings.
23. Those who exercise regularly show a decrease in anxiety, depression, fatigue, and elevated vigour.
24. In Sonnet 130, Shakespeare stresses the reality of his mistress rather than portraying her as something she is not.
25. According to a recent poll, the premier has more support among college students than the general public.

Chapter 12

Achieving Clarity and Depth in Your Writing

Effective Style: Clarity

What is style? If you have written a research essay, you will know that the word *style* is applied to documentation formats, such as the rules for citing sources using MLA or APA guidelines. Style is also a term applied to individual writers—say, a dense, descriptive writing style versus a spare, terse style. Although every writer has a unique style, when you are writing factually with a specific purpose for a specific audience, you need to put *clarity* above your distinctive writing style. More than a half-century ago, Wendell Johnson stressed the importance of clarity:

> For writing to be effective . . . it may or may not be grammatically correct, but it must be both clear and valid. It can be clear without having validity, but if it is unclear its validity cannot well be determined. . . . We ask of the writer, "What do you mean?" before we ask, "How do you know?" Until we reach agreement as to precisely what he is writing about, we cannot possibly reach agreement as to whether, or in what degree, his statements are true.
> —Wendell Johnson, "You Can't Write Writing"

Clarity depends on various factors. If you were writing for a general audience on a specialized topic and used words that were unfamiliar to most readers, you would not be writing clearly, though a specialist might understand you. Word choice and level of language, then, are important factors in clear and effective writing. But they are not the only factors discussed in this chapter.

The "art" of writing clearly is really not an art or talent at all: it is the result of hard work and attention to detail. Few writers—experienced or inexperienced—write clearly without making several revisions. Much of the revising process, in fact, consists in making the language reflect the thought behind it.

One of the differences between experienced and inexperienced writers is that the former expect to spend much of their time revising their prose; they ask not just, "Is this clear?" but also, "Can this be put more clearly?" Student writers should ask themselves the second question, too. If the answer is "yes" or "maybe," try paraphrasing it (rephrasing it). Can you do this easily? Does your paraphrase express the point more clearly? When you paraphrase something you've written, you often find that the second version is closer to what you intended to say.

What, then, is clear writing? Writing is clear when it is grammatical, concise, direct, precise, and specific. When you revise, you can ask yourself not just "Is the writing clear?" but also the following questions:

> › *Is it grammatical?* Chapters 10 and 11 have provided most of the information you need to write understandable, grammatically correct sentences.
>
> › *Is it concise?* Do you use as many words as you need and no more than you have to? Have you used basic words and simple constructions that reflect what you want to say?
>
> › *Is it direct?* Have you used straightforward language and avoided **circumlocutions**? Is the structure of your sentences as simple as possible given the complexity of the point you are trying to express?
>
> › *Is it precise?* Does it say exactly what you want it to say? When you are writing for a reader, *almost* or *close enough* is *not* enough. Would another word or phrase more accurately reflect your thought?

When you are writing for an audience, it is not enough that *you* understand your ideas. *Your readers* need to understand what is being written. Revise your work with this thought in mind.

Circumlocution, meaning "speak around," refers to using more words than necessary to express an idea, or not coming to the point.

> 〉 *Is it specific?* Is it as detailed as it needs to be? Is it concrete—not vague or abstract?

Writers who carefully work to make their writing more grammatical, concise, direct, precise, and specific will likely produce an essay that is clear. However, experienced writers aim also for forceful writing. To this end, they may introduce variety and emphasis in their writing.

EXERCISE 12.1

The following paragraphs are from student essays. The first is from an argumentative essay; the second is from a literary analysis. Try to find examples that illustrate stylistic problems summarized above. How could the writer be more concise, direct, precise, and specific? Do stylistic problems impair understanding? Where?

1. There is an idea in society today that suggests that all embryonic stem cells are the result of destroyed embryos. This comes from the fact that this branch of science is still in its developing stages, and the overall public is largely unaware of the real situation when it comes to stem cells. There is an idea circulating that suggests that innocent human embryos would be killed to cure someone who doesn't take care of his or her physical being. However, the fact is that there are other resources for embryos, such as leftover or discarded embryos from in-vitro fertilization. What is more recent is the idea that one could turn typical adult cells that are produced throughout the body into powerful stem cells . . . .

2. In the second work discussed in this paper, "Borders," by the aboriginal writer Thomas King, a young boy travels with his mother to the border where they run into multiple problems relating to identity. The lack of communication between characters, namely, the mother of the narrator and the border guards, is very evident in the entirety of the story and creates a symbolic connection to real-life issues that pertain to aboriginal peoples in North America today. These issues have to do with acceptance and, arguably, the ability to impose your standards on people whose standards are very different from your own.

Revising for Style

Why should so much effort be devoted to concise and direct writing? For one thing, such writing is easy to follow and keeps the reader's interest. Unnecessary repetition and other kinds of clutter may cause a point to lose its sharpness. Furthermore, just as concise and direct writing makes you seem reliable, wordy, indirect writing may give the impression that you lack confidence in what you're saying, that you are just trying to impress the reader, or that you are trying to use more words to reach a word limit. Finally, when you use more words than you have to or express yourself in a roundabout way, you greatly increase the odds of making grammatical and mechanical errors.

Where directness and concision are discussed, it is not just a question of *more versus less.* Thus, it would be absurd to generalize that less is *always* best. However, wordy structures are usually weak as they shift the emphasis from strong words to weaker ones, for example, from an active subject or strong verb—substantial words— onto a passive subject or a weak verb.

Familiarizing yourself with common practices that stress less important elements in a sentence will enable you to decide whether to use the more concise phrasing or, occasionally, use a variant if it conveys a better rhythm or stresses a particular meaning. Reflecting on stylistic choices during revision gives you more control over the ideas you want to communicate, just as other features of the writing process do, as discussed in earlier chapters.

Consider the two sentences below and why you might choose to use one or the other if you wanted to advise someone about a choice of university to attend or job to apply for. The two sentences say much the same thing, but their stress is subtly different:

> It is important that you make the right decision as your future will depend on it!

> Decide carefully, for your future is at stake!

Clearly, the second sentence is more concise, but is it the better sentence? Perhaps it is—if you wanted to stress the decision-making process more than the decision. The first sentence is longer and begins weakly with the expletive structure "It is . . . ." It also contains a weak verb, "make." But the sentence might be preferable if you wanted to stress the decision itself. Its tone is also gentler: it is insistent but not threatening. When you revise for style, consider your purpose and audience, just as you do when planning your essay, drafting your introduction, and focusing on other stages.

Cutting for Concision

To achieve concision, cut what is inessential. How do you determine what is unnecessary? The simple test is whether you can omit words without changing the meaning and whether your statement is effective.

Many common stylistic patterns that student writers adopt, especially in their early drafts, are described below under specific categories. Your instructor may indicate problems with concision by putting parentheses around unneeded words or by writing "wordy" or "verbose" in the margin. You should not think of this as criticism so much as advice directing you to more readable writing.

Student writers may also unconsciously shift the stress away from where it should lie—the main nouns and verbs. Certainly it is not always wrong to use two of the same parts of speech consecutively, and to banish all passive constructions would unreasonably limit writers. The strategies that follow can guide you as you revise your essay. (See the reading starting on page 428 for an example of revisions that one student made as she moved from rough to final draft.)

Doubling Up: The Noah's Ark Syndrome

Writers sometimes suffer from double vision. When they write, two words automatically pop up: two verbs, two nouns, two adjectives, or two adverbs. Experienced editors offer this formula: one + one = one-half. In other words, if you use two words when one is enough, you are halving the impact of that one word. When you do choose to use two of the same parts of speech, ensure that the two words don't convey the same thing:

> The administrative officer came up with an ~~original,~~ innovative suggestion for cost-cutting. (Anything innovative is bound to be original.)

> The event will be held at ~~various~~ different venues.

Ensure that one of the words doesn't incorporate the meaning of the other, as does "different" with "various" in the second example. This also applies to phrases containing words that are unnecessary because the meaning of the phrase can be understood without them. Be especially wary of verb–adverb combinations; ensure that the adverb is necessary:

> The airport was ~~intentionally~~ designed for larger aircraft. (Can a design be unintentional?)

> She ~~successfully~~ accomplished what she had set out to do. (The word "accomplished" implies success.)

Needless nouns steal the thunder from other parts of speech, including other nouns and verbs. In the following example, we are not really talking about a world, but about politics:

> *The world of* politics demands that you kowtow to the ineptitude of others.

In this sentence, the phrase "the fields of" is redundant because "ecology" and "biodiversity" are fields of study:

> The efforts of conservationists in *the fields of* ecology and biodiversity are leading to renewed efforts to save old-growth forests.

Below, the phrase containing *author* and *name* is redundant because these nouns are implied in the context:

> *An author by the name of* Seth Grahame-Smith wrote a best-seller lampooning Jane Austen's *Pride and Prejudice.*

Redundant Verb–Adverb Pairings

Here are some common verb–adverb pairings and other combinations that usually are redundant:

(clearly) articulate	estimate/approximate (roughly)	ponder (thoughtfully)
climb (up)		praise (in favour of)
combine/join (together)	(eventually) evolve (over time)	progress (forward/ onwards)
(harshly) condemn	examine (closely)	protest (against)
(carefully) consider	(anxiously) fear	(successfully) prove
descend (down)	fill (completely)	refer/return/revert (back) to
dominate (over)	finish (entirely)	rely/depend (heavily) on,
drawl (lazily)	(strictly) forbid	(symbolically) represent
dwindle (down)	gather/assemble (together)	sob (uncontrollably)
emphasize/stress (strongly)	gaze (steadily)	(completely) surround
(better/further) enhance	hurry (quickly)	unite (as one)
(totally) eradicate/ devastate	(suddenly) interrupt	vanish (without a trace)
	plan (ahead)	

Repetitive Adjective–Noun Pairings

Be wary, too, of such repetitive adjective–noun pairings as the following:

advance warning	knowledgeable specialist	powerful blast
brief encapsulation	mutual agreement	sharp needle
dead carcass	new beginning	terrible tragedy
fiery blaze	past memory	timeless classic
future plan	positive benefits	total abstinence

Redundant Phrases

Redundancies are evident in such familiar phrases as these:

consensus of opinion	in actual fact	time frame/period/span
end result/product	this point in time	years of age

Phony Phrases and Clumsy Clauses

Phrases you can do without. Many prepositional phrases are more economical as one-word modifiers. Look for redundant prepositional phrases after verbs and nouns:

> *Unnecessary*: For now, the patient's kidneys are functioning *at a normal level*.

The prepositional phrase "at a normal level" can be replaced by the adverb "normally":

> *Better*: For now, the patient's kidneys are functioning *normally*.

Here the phony phrase is introduced by the preposition "for":

> *Unnecessary*: The bill was legislated in 1995 *for a brief period of time*.

> *Better*: The bill was *briefly* legislated in 1995.

Non-specific nouns may be connected to phony phrases beginning with *on*, *to*, or other prepositions. Watch for prepositional phrases that include non-specific nouns like *basis*, *degree*, *extent*, *level*, *manner*, and *scale*:

> on/at the international level; on a larger scale; on a regular basis; to a great/considerable degree/extent

Such phrases can usually be replaced by appropriate adverbs:

> *Unnecessary*: Jindra checks her answering machine *on a regular basis*.

> *Better*: Jindra checks her answering machine *regularly*.

Clauses you can do without. Relative clauses are adjectival and may sometimes be replaced by a corresponding adjective preceding the noun. In this example, "that is high in protein" is a relative (adjectival) clause modifying "diet":

> *Unnecessary*: Most body-builders follow a strict diet *that is high in protein*.

> *Better*: Most body-builders follow a strict, *high-protein* diet.

The Small but Not-So-Beautiful

Even small words, such as prepositions and articles, may be omitted. A writer may think these words make an ordinary phrase sound just a little more impressive. In the examples below, parentheses indicate words that can be omitted:

He was (the) last out (of) the door.

(The) taking (of) life can never be condoned.

Look at the following passage and consider what can be deleted—big words and small—without changing the meaning of the sentence:

The city of Toronto has one of the most ethnically diverse of cultures in all of North America. The city has a population of 2.5 million people and is also the home of a variety of sports teams that play in professional leagues.

The word *that* can be used as a pronoun (demonstrative and relative), an adjective, and a subordinating conjunction. It can often be omitted if the subject of the second clause introduced by *that* is different from the subject of the preceding clause. By methodically checking your first draft for unnecessary *that*s, you can improve sentence flow. Look back at the first paragraph in Exercise 12.1. How many *that*s can you take out of the paragraph?

Taking "that" out of the sentence below does not affect the structure of the sentence—even though it makes the sentence more readable. In both cases, "that" introduces a dependent clause; the independent clause in the sentence is "I thought":

I thought (that) Silas was going to go to the same school (that) his brother went to.

Now unravel the meaning of the following statement:

It's certain that that "that" that that person used is ungrammatical.

Rabbit Words

An *intensive* is an example of a "rabbit word," one that reproduces quickly and may overrun the landscape of your prose. An intensive adds emphasis to the word or expression it modifies but has little meaning on its own. However, due to overuse, it often does not emphasize at all. In all levels of formal writing, intensives should be rooted out whenever they do not truly add emphasis, such as in the simple sentence below:

She is ~~certainly~~ a(n) ~~very~~ impressive speaker.

Words like *certainly* and *very* are overused. Many intensives are adverbs modifying verbs or adjectives. In some instances, you can simply use a stronger verb in place of a weak verb and an intensive, or a stronger adjective in place of the intensive plus a weak adjective; or, you can just eliminate the intensive, as in:

It was a ~~very~~ unique idea.

Unnecessary: He was very grateful for his warm reception.

Better:

He was gratified by his warm reception.

Or:

He appreciated his warm reception.

The words and phrases in the two lists below can be used in your writing if you truly want to stress or qualify a point. Most often, though, they can be omitted.

Overused Intensives

absolutely	extremely	markedly
actually	fundamentally	naturally
assuredly	highly	of course
certainly	in	particularly
clearly	fact	significantly
completely	incredibly	surely
considerably	inevitably	totally
definitely	indeed	utterly
effectively	interestingly	very

Overused Qualifiers

apparently	in effect	rather
arguably	in general	relatively
basically	kind of	seemingly
essentially	overall	somewhat
generally	perhaps	sort of
hopefully	quite	virtually

Examples:

Overall. In most cases, the word *overall* can be omitted. For example, in the sentence below, it can be added as a modifier almost anywhere—yet, wherever it is, it contributes nothing to the sentence's meaning:

> *Overall* in the poem "Easter 1916," Yeats uses imagery to convey a theme of sadness.

> In the poem "Easter 1916," Yeats uses imagery *overall* to convey a theme of sadness.

> In the poem "Easter 1916," Yeats uses imagery to convey an *overall* theme of sadness.

Arguably. Using this adverb is too often a way of saying something and not saying it at the same time:

> Maurya's fate at the end of the play "Riders to the Sea" is arguably worse than that of her husband and sons.

If her fate is worse than her sons, just say it! If the point is "arguable," then argue it!
    More words and prepositional phrases that may clutter:

aforementioned	consequent to	in reference to
amidst	despite the fact that	in regard to
amongst	due to the fact that	in terms of
analogous to	each and every	in the final analysis
as a result of	in accordance with	in view of the
as to	in comparison to	fact that
at this point in time	in conjunction with	inasmuch as
cognizant of	in connection with	irregardless

notwithstanding the fact that	so as to	whether or not
oftentimes	subsequent to	whilst
pertaining to	the majority of	with regard to
	thusly	with respect to

Go to your school's database and find some corporate annual reports. See if you can find any examples of unnecessary words or redundant constructions. Choose two or three examples and rewrite them in more concise prose.

EXERCISE 12.2

Writing Directly

Writing should get straight to the point, but indirect writing stresses the less important parts of the sentence. Passive constructions are indirect because they displace the subject, although they may be acceptable or even preferable when you do not want to stress the subject or if the exact subject is unknown.

Passive Constructions: The Lazy Subject

Effective, direct English is geared towards the *active*, not the *passive*, voice. In a passive construction, the subject of the sentence is *not* doing the action. Ordinarily, the subject *is* acting, as in the following:

Ezra placed the book on the table.

Changing the sentence so that the object becomes the (non-active) subject requires changing the word order and adding words:

The book was placed on the table by Ezra.

Note the differences between these two sentences. In the second sentence, the direct object, "book," has become the subject and the original subject, "Ezra," is now at the end of the sentence, the object of the preposition "by." The verb form has changed too. The sentence now has a subject that is acted on rather than acting itself. The passive subject sentence requires more words to provide the same information.

The passive voice uses a form of the verb *to be* followed by a past participle. If the actor is named, it will be the object of a prepositional phrase that begins with *by*. Although you can identify the passive by the verb forms that compose it—the past, present, or future form of *to be* plus a past participle—don't confuse the identifying verb forms of the passive with a construction in which a form of the verb *to be* is used along with the past participle as a predicate adjective. For example, in the following sentence, the subjects are clearly the actors; you can't add the preposition *by* after "determined" or "pleased." This sentence uses an active construction:

Dana was determined to succeed at any cost; I am pleased to see him succeed.

In the following sentence, there are three indicators of a passive construction:

The door was opened by a tall, sinister man.

1. The subject ("door") is not doing the action expressed by the verb "open"
2. The preposition "by" precedes the actor ("man")
3. The simple past of *to be* combines with the past participle of the main verb to form the passive voice of the verb.

To change a passive to an active construction:

1. Move the subject so that it follows the verb as the direct object.
2. Move the object of the preposition *by*, the actor, to the beginning of the clause to replace the passive subject.
3. Get rid of the identifying passive forms of the verb and the preposition *by*.

A tall, sinister man ~~was~~ opened the door ~~by~~.

Below is a slightly more complicated example. In its active form, the sentence contains fewer words and the thought is expressed more directly:

Passive: The special commission was informed of its mandate by a superior court judge last Monday.

Active: A superior court judge informed the special commission of its mandate last Monday.

As a general rule, *don't use the passive voice if the active will serve*. However, the passive is acceptable or is even the better choice when:

(a) the subject isn't known, or is so well known it doesn't need stating. In the following example, it is unnecessary to mention that *the voters* elected the prime minister:

Pierre Trudeau was first elected prime minister in 1968.

(b) passivity is implied, or the context makes it seem natural to stress the receiver of the action. In this sentence, the massages are more important than the person giving them:

When a cyclist completes a hard workout, massages are usually performed on the affected muscles.

In the first sentence below, the woman obviously is the passive recipient of the action of the thugs; in the second sentence, she is doing the action:

Acceptable passive: The woman was kidnapped and held hostage by a band of thugs.

Questionable passive: Several of the thugs were picked out of a line-up by the woman.

Therefore, in the second sentence, the active is preferred:

Active: The woman picked several of the thugs out of a line-up.

Occasionally, you may choose the passive voice because the rhythm of the sentence requires it, or because it is rhetorically effective. In this sentence, the librarian's near-sightedness is important; the adjective's position near the end of the sentence gives it emphasis:

The books obviously had been arranged by a near-sighted librarian.

A Closer Look

Academic Writing and the Passive

There are cases in academic writing, especially in the sciences, in which the passive may be used to stress the object of the study or the method of research, as below, where the method, *comparison*, is the subject:

Through case studies, a comparison of two common methods for treating depression will be made [*by the writer*].

In the following examples from academic writing, the passive is preferred either because the actor doesn't matter or because the writer wants to stress the receiver of the action:

The emergence of second-hand smoke SHS [as a cancer hazard] has been offered as a viable explanation for the increased enactment of local smoking restrictions (Asbridge, 2003, p. 13).

In 1891 the science of embryology was shaken by the work of the cosmopolitan German biologist and vitalist philosopher Hans Driesch (Bowring, 2004, p. 401).

The following sentences use passive constructions. Determine which are appropriately in passive voice and which inappropriately. Change unnecessary uses of the passive voice to form active constructions. In some sentences, the actor or "active" subject is not part of the sentence, so you may have to add it to the sentence (see example sentence below). Be prepared to justify your decisions to leave some sentences as passive constructions.

EXERCISE 12.3

↻ Check answers to select questions

Example:
Passive: The suspect's behaviour had been watched for more than one month.
The suspect's behaviour had been watched (by the police) for more than one month.
Active: The police had watched the suspect's behaviour for more than one month.
Decision: Leave as passive because "suspect's behaviour" is more important to the meaning than "the police."

1. I was given two choices by my landlord: pay up or get out.
2. It was reported that more than 1,000 people were left homeless by recent flooding.
3. Theo's protest was heard by the fairness committee.
4. At Wednesday's committee meeting, the problem of parking in the downtown core was discussed.
5. Beethoven's Third Symphony, the *Eroica*, originally was dedicated to Napoleon, but the dedication was erased after Napoleon proclaimed himself emperor.
6. Education needs to be seen by the government as the number one priority.
7. Many acts of self-deception were committed by Bertha, the protagonist of "Bliss."
8. The belief in a powerful and infallible Creator is commonly held today.
9. Poverty in First Nations communities must be addressed by the federal, provincial, and First Nations' governments.
10. There are two ways of looking at rights-based ethics that were put forward by Immanuel Kant.

Black Hole Constructions

Inappropriately passive constructions not only use too many words but also place the stress where it doesn't belong, weakening the entire sentence. Other indirect constructions can also weaken a sentence. You can consider them the black holes of writing: they swallow up the substance of the sentence.

> *It was . . .*

It was Mary Shelley who wrote *Frankenstein* in 1816.

As simple as this sentence is, it begins weakly by displacing the logical subject, "Mary Shelley," and substituting the bland and unnecessary "It was." The sentence is stronger and more direct when the most important noun is made the subject:

Mary Shelley wrote *Frankenstein* in 1816.

If a relative pronoun (*who*, *which*, or *that*) follows the displaced subject, consider getting rid of the "empty" subject (*It was*, *There is*, *Here is*) and the relative pronoun to make the statement more direct and concise:

Unnecessary: There are a variety of different strategies that you can use to reduce excess verbiage in your writing.

Better: You can use various strategies to reduce verbiage in your writing.

Occasionally, you may want to use *It was* or a similar construction for rhetorical effect. In such a case, emphasis, rather than directness, may determine your choice.

> *One of*—a redundancy to be avoided:

Poor: The path you have chosen is one of danger and uncertainty.

Better: The path you have chosen is dangerous and uncertain.

You have chosen a dangerous, uncertain path.

> *The reason . . . is because*, which is both illogical and redundant:

Incorrect: The reason Jessica is lucky is because she has a horseshoe on her door.

Correct: Jessica is lucky because she has a horseshoe on her door.

Weak Verb + Noun

Writers often fall into the habit of using a weak verb and a corresponding noun rather than a verb that directly expresses the meaning. Often the noun that follows the verb can be changed into a strong verb; at other times, a one-word verb can sum up the verb phrase. In these examples, a weak verb phrase supplants the more direct alternative:

Weak constructions:

1. I *had a meeting* with my staff, and I am now asking you to *provide a list* of all your clients.

2. Inexperienced writers *have a tendency* to be wordy.

3. She *made changes* to the document, *making clear* what was ambiguous.

Stronger constructions:

1. I *met* with my staff, and now ask you *to list* all your clients.
2. Inexperienced writers *tend* to be wordy.
3. She *changed* the document, *clarifying* ambiguities.

Do not needlessly use the present progressive tense where the simple present will suffice (see Appendix A, Tense Encounters with Verbs):

Although both authors *are discussing* [*discuss*] multiculturalism, only Iyer *is understanding of* [*understands*] the uniqueness of Canada's version.

> Note: in the weak phrase *has an effect on*, where *has* is the verb and effect is the noun, remember that the corresponding verb form is *affect*.
>
> Global warming *affects* shifting major weather patterns. Its *effects* are being widely felt throughout the globe.

EXERCISE 12.4

↻ Check answers to select questions

Make the following sentences more concise and direct.

1. Historians agree that Canada made a significant contribution to the war effort in France and Belgium.
2. To determine whether video games are addictive, researchers have had many interviews with gamers and designers.
3. It is important for schools to take into consideration the ways that the school environment has an effect on behaviour.
4. Several devices in the story bring to prominence the theme of revenge.
5. The first-person point of view in Raymond Carver's "Feathers" provides the reader with a connection to the simple, working-class narrator.

Numbing Nouns

Nouns that pile up in a sentence can create a numbing effect. This is especially true with *nominals*, nouns formed from verbs. There is nothing wrong with using a polysyllabic noun formed from a verb—unless a more concise and direct alternative exists. Table 12.1 shows how nominals can be turned back into verbs.

Clear expression in literary essays is sometimes a challenge to students due to their unfamiliarity with terminology or to the temptation to make a point sound complex and, thereby, significant:

The conflict between Billy and Claggart ultimately serves as a device in the interruption of the reader's attempts at a coherent interpretation of the novel as an ideological message. In addition to problematizing definitive interpretations, this technique effectively secures a lasting relevance for the novel.

Table 12.1 Nominals

Nominal	Verb	Sentence with Nominal	Sentence without Nominal
accumulation	accumulate	The accumulation of evidence is overwhelming.	The evidence is overwhelming.
classification	classify	We will now proceed with the classification of Vertebrata.	We will now classify Vertebrata.
intention installation	intend install	Our intention is to complete the installation of the new system this month.	We plan to finish installing the new system this month.

The thought in these sentences can be expressed more directly and clearly by omitting words and reducing the number of nominals:

> The conflict between Billy and Claggart challenges a coherent ideological reading of the novel, making definitive readings difficult and ensuring the novel's relevance.

Euphemism

A **euphemism** is an indirect expression considered to be less harsh or offensive than the term it replaces. Many ancient cultures used euphemisms to avoid naming their enemies directly. They believed that naming gave power to those they feared, so they invented ways around saying their names; the word *euphemism* comes from the Greek word that means "to use words for good omen." We sometimes do the same today out of consideration and kindness to those who may be suffering, as a way of speaking about taboo subjects and objects, or as a form of satire or irony. For example, the euphemisms for *die* are numerous, with *pass away* or *pass on* being the most common.

Although euphemisms can be used to protect us from the unpleasant, they can be used also to falsely reassure. For example, *urban renewal* avoids the implications of *slum clearance*, *revenue enhancement* has a more positive ring than *tax increase*, and *collateral losses* attempts to sidestep the fact that civilians have been killed during military action.

We also sometimes use euphemisms to try to give more dignity and a sense of importance to special objects, actions, or vocations: *pre-owned automobile* for *used car* and *job action* for *strike*. The Plain English Campaign recently awarded a Golden Bull Award to the writers of a document that described the act of laying a brick in a wall as "install[ing] a component into the structural fabric."

The following classified ad uses some verbose and euphemistic language:

> We are seeking an individual who possesses demonstrated skills and abilities, a sound knowledge base coupled with the experience to provide service to mentally challenged teenagers with "unique" and significant challenging behaviours.

The requirements of the position could have been written in half the words:

> Applicants need proven skills, knowledge, and experience to serve mentally challenged teenagers with challenging behaviours.

A special category of "acceptable euphemisms" are those that we, as a society, agree should be substituted for expressions that have acquired inappropriate connotations. For example, to refer to someone in a wheelchair as a "cripple" inappropriately stresses the disability and its limiting attributes. More sensitively and more accurately, this person is *physically disabled* or *physically challenged*.

EXERCISE 12.5

In groups, think of 10 euphemisms, either ones you've heard of or made-up ones. Then, read them to the rest of the class, who will guess what they are meant to describe.

Prepackaged Goods: Clichés

Clichés are overworked and unoriginal phrases. Inexperienced writers may reach for them in a vain attempt to "spice up" their writing. Clichés may be *dead metaphors*: expressions drained of their novelty through overuse. Although they may appear in some informal writing, they are poor substitutes for informative, imaginative words.

If commentary on the cliché were to be made in clichés, you would find the prose wordy and confusing:

> Expressions considered clichés today were in their prime a veritable breath of fresh air. However, with the passage of time (more years than you can shake a stick at), they became the stuff of idle minds until after time immemorial they assumed the mantle of respectability and were accepted verbatim as par for the course. Writers worth their salt should avoid clichés like the plague or they will stop all readers with a good head on their shoulders dead in their tracks (to call a spade a spade and to give the devil his due).

EXERCISE 12.6

In this short passage adapted from a travel feature, find evidence of tired and predictable writing, citing particular words and phrases that could be made more effective or accurate. Although newspaper features use informal writing, it should be descriptive and concrete. How could you make this passage more interesting?

> We're up and about at the crack of dawn, and from outside our cabin we can see the peak of a small mountain looming in the distance. Our ship glides effortlessly over the fathomless blue sea, and soon the mountain's craggy features come into view.
>
> "It's breakfast, honey," my wife, Jen, sings from inside the cabin, and soon our impeccably dressed waiter knocks softly on our door. As we sit down to partake of the delectable repast, I feel as though I could pinch myself. Yes, here we are, aboard a luxurious liner, about to drop anchor off the coast of one of the world's most fabled isles.

EXERCISE 12.7

↻ Check answers to select questions

The following sentences can be revised for greater concision and directness. Make whatever changes you believe are necessary and be prepared to justify these changes.

1. Tanya has been invited to provide us with a summary of the significant main points of her findings.
2. The unexpected eruption of the volcano changed the Western Samoan island into a fiery, blazing inferno.
3. At first the wallpaper is completely detested by the narrator, but she later comes to believe that it is the path leading her to the freedom that she so much desires.
4. The protagonist of *Life of Pi* was confronted with the necessity of making the decision about whether he wanted to continue on living or not.
5. It was in 1964 that the Beatles first made their inaugural tour of the North American continent.
6. The disappearance of even one single species at the lower end of the food chain can have dire adverse effects in many instances on the survival of various other species.

7. Although Copernicus's radical idea that the earth made revolutions around the sun was once considered an extreme heresy and was ridiculed mercilessly by his peers, the idea eventually gained gradual acceptance.

8. The fact is that for a great many years now antibiotics have been utilized on a regular basis by many people as a cure for each and every symptom that they develop over the course of their entire lifetimes.

9. Perhaps in the heat of emotion the act of capital punishment would seem to be a feasible idea, but when you come to think of it rationally, this act would accomplish virtually next to nothing at all.

10. In protest of their salary freeze, all of the teachers who teach at the high school in Oak Bay have made the unanimous decision not to undertake any tasks of a supervisory nature until the school board has conducted a fair and impartial salary review.

11. Vehicles that have the four-way drive feature option are an extremely practical and pragmatic form of transportation for the majority of the Canadian population in this day and age.

12. There are many people in our society today who have serious drug addictions that take complete and utter control over their lives.

13. From the beginning of its conception, Canada has been a country concerned with promoting an active multicultural society, although the reality of unity within the country is still a large, unanswered question in the minds of most of the people of Canada.

14. A French scientist by the name of Louis Pasteur was the first individual to make the discovery that microbes were harmful menaces to the well-being and healthy functioning of the human body.

15. The reason yoga allows us to live a healthy lifestyle is due to the fact that it provides a strong basis for the efficient functioning of the body's endocrine system.

EXERCISE 12.8

↻ Check answers to select questions

Rewrite the following passage, aiming for concise, direct writing.

In medieval English universities, such as Oxford and Cambridge universities, chest loans were made available to students who were able to demonstrate their financial neediness. Students would make use of an item, usually a book, as a form of collateral against an interest-free loan that was taken from a chest of money that had been put in place by a benefactor. Nowadays, the only thing that resembles the concept of the benefactor is the branch of government that disburses loans and grants for students who are lacking in sufficient funding resources.

Recent studies have conclusively demonstrated that the vast majority of Canadian students over 26 years of age have an average debt of in excess of $20,000 relating to their overall education. The bulk of these costs relates to the expenses incurred by tuition fees and ordinary, everyday cost of living expenses. These expenses do not generally take into account the very high cost of student textbooks, which are required purchases for most of a student's courses at university. In regards to textbooks, students may have the option of buying brand new textbooks or purchasing less expensive used texts, and in some instances they are able to borrow required readings from a library.

Working toward Precision: Wise Word Choices

Informal writing. For most university writing assignments, you will need to use formal writing. Because you may be used to writing informally when using the Internet or when text messaging—even, perhaps, from your high school English courses—you may puzzle over the ways that informal writing differs from formal writing. In informal writing

> › language may be close to speech or chatty with colloquialisms, idiom, or even slang
> › contractions are acceptable (e.g., *don't, can't, shouldn't, it's*)
> › the first-person (*I, me*) and second-person (*you*) voice may be used
> › sentence fragments may be used occasionally for dramatic effect
> › short paragraphs are the rule rather than the exception
> › citations for research sources are not given.

In your essays, you should avoid contractions, unless your instructor tells you otherwise. Certainly, unless you are quoting someone, you should always avoid slang, colloquialisms, and jargon. For example, you would not use any of the following in a formal essay: *mindset, price tag, quick fix, downside, upfront, stressed* (*out*), *okay, do drugs, give the green light, grab the reader's attention, put* (*someone*) *down, fall for, obsess* (*about something*), *pan out, put on hold, put a positive spin* (*on something*), *opt for, tune out, no way, the way to go, go to great lengths, go overboard, way more* (*of something*), *a lot.*

In addition, avoid merely quantitative words and phrases, such as *great, incredible, beautiful, terrible,* and the like; they are non-specific. Of course, you also should refrain from using words and expressions that might suggest to some readers a gender, sexual, racial, cultural, or other bias.

Your word choices involve much more than thinking about the level of formality. Effective writers choose their words and phrases carefully. In the following three examples from student essays, the writers did not choose carefully:

> The mass production of plastics and ready-to-use products is growing at a *stagnating* [sic *staggering*] rate.

Note: *staggering* is informal; the writer could have used *rapid, rapidly increasing,* or *exponential,* or a specific number, such as *doubling every year.*

> The Shakespearean sonnet is an *oppressed* [sic *compressed*] form of poetry.

> After successfully completing police officer training camp, the applicant can finally *swear* [sic *be sworn in*] and become a police officer.

Rather than making extreme blunders, more often a writer chooses a word that is not quite precise for the purpose. These kinds of "near misses" can distract or confuse the reader. You should not let the search for the exact word prevent you from fully expressing your ideas in a first draft. But when revising, you should look up the meanings of all words you're in doubt about—even if you're only a little unsure about its meaning. Don't rely on a spell-checker, which wouldn't have caught these errors.

You can use a thesaurus to look for words similar in meaning to avoid repeating a word too often. But a thesaurus should always be used along with a reliable dictionary.

Colloquialisms are words and expressions acceptable in conversation but not in formal writing.

An *idiom* is a phrase whose meaning is understood only within the context of the phrase itself. For example, "his bark is worse than his bite" cannot be understood by the meanings of the individual words but only by its customary usage.

Avoid using informal verbs such as *saw, has seen,* etc., when you mean *resulted in* or *occurred*:

The policy that was implemented two years ago *has seen* a 40 per cent drop in violent crime.

Revised: The policy that was implemented two years ago *has resulted in* a 40 per cent drop in violent crime.

Most thesauruses, such as the ones that come with word-processing programs, simply list words similar in meaning; they do not provide connotations for the words. A word's connotation includes its possible meanings in its given context, and since contexts can vary, so can the meanings of the same word.

Some dictionaries help you to be precise not only by defining the main entry but also by providing distinctions among similar words. In addition to illustrating the way a word is used by providing examples, many mid-sized dictionaries distinguish the main entry from other words with similar meanings. For example, the *Gage Canadian Dictionary*, which lists more than six meanings for the adjective *effective*, also defines two words similar to *effective* in meaning but different in connotation:

> *Syn. adj.* 1. **Effective, effectual, efficient** = producing an effect. **Effective**, usually describing things, emphasizes producing a wanted or expected effect: *several new drugs are effective in treating serious diseases*. **Effectual**, describing people or things, emphasizes having produced or having the power to produce the exact effect or result intended: *his efforts are more energetic than effectual*. **Efficient**, often describing people, emphasizes being able to produce the effect wanted or intended without wasting energy, time, etc.: *A skilled surgeon is highly efficient*.

Similarly, the *Student's Oxford Canadian Dictionary*, which lists seven meanings for the adjective *nice*, offers the following examples of words that may be more appropriate or more forceful than *nice* in certain contexts:

> we had a **delightful/splendid/enjoyable** time
>
> a **satisfying/delicious/exquisite** meal
>
> a **fashionable/stylish/elegant/chic** outfit
>
> this is a **cozy/comfortable/attractive** room
>
> she is **kind/friendly/likeable/amiable**
>
> our adviser is **compassionate/understanding/sympathetic**
>
> a **thoughtful/considerate/caring** gesture

For more about determining a word's meaning from its context, see Chapter 1, Using Context Clues, page 24.

Sound should also play a role in word choice. You should avoid placing words with similar sounds in close proximity (the "echo effect"):

> Endorphins enable the body to heal itself and *gain pain* relief.

You should also be wary of unintentional puns in a work of scholarship:

> The first experiments in music therapy were *noted* during World War I.

Also, do not write ironically or sarcastically unless you are certain that your reader shares your attitude:

> It is well-known that college students under stress need to exercise their livers on the occasional Friday night.

Remember that the hallmark of academic writing is an objective voice, one that is unbiased.

Precision and Logic

Choosing your words carefully will help make your writing precise. But sometimes, imprecision may result from illogical thinking or from writing down an idea quickly. To determine if something you've written really makes sense, you need to look carefully at the relationship among the parts of the sentence, especially at the *relationship between the subject and predicate*. **Faulty predication** exists if a verb cannot be logically connected to its subject. In general, avoid the phrases *is when* and *is where* after a subject in sentences that *define* something. For example, in the following sentence *faulty predication*, which is a thing, is illogically referred to as a time or a place:

> *Incorrect*: Faulty predication is when/where a verb cannot be logically connected to its subject.

> *Correct*:

> Faulty predication *occurs where* [i.e., in a sentence] a verb is not logically connected to its subject.

> Faulty predication *is* an illogical juxtaposing of a subject and a verb.

Consider this comment on the setting of Joseph Conrad's *Heart of Darkness*:

> The Congo represents an inward journey for the character Marlow.

The Congo is a country and a river. How can a country or a river represent a journey? Of course, a *trip* through a country or on a river could represent an inner journey.

In another kind of faulty predication, an inanimate object is falsely linked to a human action:

> Some opponents claim that PE *programs are unwilling* to accommodate the needs of all students.

The programs aren't "unwilling," since this implies a will, though teachers or administrators may be "unwilling":

> Some opponents claim that the *administrators* of PE programs *are unwilling* to accommodate the needs of all students.

Be careful that a linking verb (e.g., *be* and its various forms, such as *is*, *are*, *were*) does not illogically connect a subject to a predicate noun or adjective (See Linking verbs, in Chapter 10, page 319):

> The *twenty-first century* may well *be a step* in a new direction for the human race as we gradually come to embrace alternative energy sources.

A time period cannot logically *be* a step, so the sentence should be revised:

> In the 21st century, the human race may gradually embrace alternative energy sources, taking a step in a new direction.

When checking for faulty predication, identify the subject and verb; then, ensure that the subject can perform the action that the verb describes.

EXERCISE 12.9

Identify the subject and verb in the sentences below, revising to avoid faulty predication and/or other illogical statements.

1. The science of physiognomy believed that a person's facial features could reveal one's character and moral disposition.
2. Previous research studying motorists using hand-held devices while on the road claimed that 20 per cent of all accidents were directly related to these devices.
3. The use of social networking sites can be used to talk to someone who is hard to contact through other means.
4. The theme of the poem is the fact that she hates her father for leaving her when she was only eight years old.
5. The crucial line in Margaret Avison's poem claims that everyone will eventually encounter his or her life's whirlpool.

EXERCISE 12.10

Circle every example of informal diction in the following paragraph; then, rewrite it using formal diction. There may be one or two places where the word or phrase is colloquial but necessary due to context or the fact it can't be rephrased easily.

Having the winter Olympic Games held in Vancouver was a once-in-a-lifetime opportunity, and it seemed like a great idea. It helped create world recognition for this world-class city, helping to really put it on the map. On top of that, it was a fun and exciting time for our people. However, after sober second thought, it is clear that while the Games might pay for themselves, who will end up paying for the upgrades necessary to get Vancouver in good shape for the Games? Even with both the provincial and federal governments chipping in for a fair amount of the costs, because we are dealing in billions of dollars, even a small chunk of that cost is a lot of money. These small chunks will come from the pockets of the taxpayer, some of whom were not big fans of the Games at all and did not take in a single event. But although these direct costs are bound to be steep, it is the hidden costs of the Games that will be the real killer.

Verbs with Vitality

Verbs are the action words in a sentence. Look at the verbs in your sentences. Could you replace them with stronger, more descriptive verbs? Could you replace verbs like *be* and *have*, which convey a state or condition, with verbs of action? Common verbs, such as *do*, *make*, *go*, and *get*, are not specific. Could you replace them with more precise or emphatic verbs?

EXERCISE 12.11

↺ Check answers to select questions

Read the following paragraph and underline places where you would revise verbs to make them more expressive and descriptive.

By the 1800s, inventions were beginning to put people out of work. One of the first inventions that resulted in rebellion was in the craft guild. In 1801, Joseph Jacquard became known as the inventor of the Jacquard loom. This loom was capable of being programmed by pre-punched cards, which made it possible to create clothing design patterns. This invention led to the creation of the Luddites, who were a group made up from the craft guild. These people were against any type of manufacturing technology and went about burning down several factories that were using this new technology. The Luddites were around only for a couple of years, but the name Luddite is still used to describe people who are resistant to new technologies. The Jacquard loom was, in effect, an invention that replaced people. It could do great designs quickly and without making any errors. The replacement of people by machines was beginning.

The most common verb in English, *to be*, takes many different forms as an irregular verb: *am*, *is*, *are*, *was*, *were*, *will be*, etc. and appears frequently as a helping verb. Your writing will be more concise if you omit the forms *being* or *to be* whenever they are unnecessary.

The results of the study can be interpreted as ~~being~~ credible.

Hypnosis has been proven ~~to be~~ an effective therapy for some people.

If you can easily omit a form of *to be*, do so.

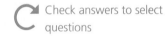

EXERCISE 12.12

Decide whether the form of the verb *to be* is needed in the sentences below and revise accordingly.

1. She dreamed of a carriage being pulled by two fine horses.
2. In 313 BCE, Constantine I declared Christianity to be the official religion of Rome.
3. One source on the website is about the research today being done on twins.
4. Being able to perceive life from varying angles is one of the key elements to being a good writer.
5. Helga Dittmar considers the mass media to be the most "potent and pervasive influence" on young women today, being the strongest contributor to negative body image.

↻ Check answers to select questions

As people put on the spot by journalists and the public, politicians have sometimes chosen vague language to avoid committing themselves to statements they may regret later. A more cynical view suggests that taking refuge in abstract, indefinite language enables them to say little while appearing informed and in control. Notice the lack of specificity in the following comment by former American politician Colin Powell, reported by the Associated Press:

"We knew that the ICRC had concerns, and in accordance with the matter in which the ICRC does its work, it presented those concerns directly to the command in Baghdad. And I know that some corrective action was taken with respect to those concerns."

EXERCISE 12.13

Suggest how the following passage could be improved by using more specific language and by omitting unnecessary words and phrases.

The time period between 1985 and 1989 was a difficult one for graffiti artists in New York City. This was a time when graffiti barely stayed alive because of the harsh laws and efforts of the Metropolitan Transit Authority, which is known as the

MTA. This period was called the period of the "Die Hards" because of the small number of die-hard artists who were able to keep graffiti from dying out completely. As a result of the measures of the MTA against graffiti art and artists, there was a lack of paint available for use and the level of enforcement was extremely high. The only important thing that was happening during these years was the use of markers for tagging. These tags were usually small, of poor artistic quality, and were finished quickly by the artists. These tags can be seen today at some bus stops and in some washrooms throughout the city.

Common Words That Confuse

English has many word pairs that are confusing either because the two words look similar (for example, *affect* and *effect*) or because they have similar, but not identical, uses (for example, *amount* and *number*)—or both. In most cases, the dictionary is the best resource for unravelling difficulties that pertain solely to meaning, but usage can be more complicated. The words below are the "Top Twenty-five" that continue to give student writers the most trouble. Hints and examples are provided to help you distinguish them.

For a guide to spelling, there is no better resource than the dictionary; if you have the slightest doubt about the spelling of a word, consult a dictionary—don't rely on a spell-checker.

> **accept, except. Accept** is a verb meaning "to receive, to take what is offered." **Except** is a preposition meaning "other than" or "leaving out."
>
> **Hint:** Think of the "crossing out" connotation of *x* in *except* to remind you that *except* means "leaving out."
>
> The bargaining committee accepted all the terms except the last one.

> **affect, effect. Affect** is a verb meaning "to influence or have an effect on." **Effect**, a noun, means "a result." As a verb, effect is less often used; it means "to bring about" or "to cause"—not "to have an effect on."
>
> **Hint:** Try substituting *influence* in the sentence; if it fits your intended meaning, *affect* is the word you want.
>
> The news of Michael Jordan's return to basketball greatly affected his fans. The effect was also felt at the box office; an immediate hike in ticket prices was effected.

> **allot, a lot. Allot**, a verb, means "to portion out"; **a lot** can be an adverb (*I sleep a lot*) or a noun (*I need a lot of sleep*) meaning "a great deal." *A lot* is too informal for most academic writing; you should use the more formal *a great deal*, *many*, *much*, or similar substitutes. The one-word spelling, *alot*, is incorrect.
>
> My parents allotted me $500 spending money for the term, which was not a lot considering my shopping habit. (informal)

> **all right, alright. All right** is all right, just as *a lot* is a lot better than *alot*; *alright* and *alot* are not words.

> **allude, elude.** Both are verbs, but they mean different things. **Allude** (to) means "to refer to something briefly or indirectly"; **elude** means "to avoid or escape, usually through a clever manoeuvre or strategy." *Allude* should be followed by *to*: e.g., "In the poem, Hardy alluded to the end of the century."

Hint: *Allude* is the verb from which the noun *allusion* (a kind of reference, see **Allusion**) is formed; you can associate the *e* in *elude* with the *e* in *escape*.

In his prison memoirs, the bank robber alluded to the time in the desert when he eluded capture by disguising himself as a cactus.

> **allusion, illusion.** You may have come across the literary use of **allusion**, meaning an historical, religious, mythic, literary, or other kind of outside reference used thematically or to reveal character in a work. An **illusion** is something apparently seen that is not real or is something that gives a false impression.

Hint: Since the most common mistake is misspelling *allusion* as *illusion* in literary essays, you could remember that *allusion*, meaning an outside reference, *al*ways begins with *al*.

The title of Nathanael West's novel *The Day of the Locust* is an allusion to the Book of Exodus in the Bible.

Optical illusions often use graphics to fool our senses.

> **among, between.** The simple distinction is that **between** refers to two persons or things and **among** to more than two.

The senator found himself between a rock and a hard place.

Ms. O'Grady stood among her adoring students for the school picture.

Between may be the obvious choice even if more than two things are involved. For example, "Interlibrary loans are permitted between campuses." Even though a number of campuses may be part of the interlibrary loan system, any one exchange takes place between two campuses.

> **amount, number.** Use **amount** to refer to things that can't be counted; **number** refers to countable objects.

Hint: Think of using numbers when you count.

The number of errors in this essay reveals the amount of care you took in writing it.

> **beside, besides.** **Beside** is a preposition meaning "next to," "adjoining"; **besides** has several meanings as a preposition; as an adverb **besides** means "in addition (to)."

Hint: Think of the extra *s* in besides as an additional letter to remind you of "in addition to."

Beside the telephone was the telephone book, besides which she had an address book.

> **bias, biased. Bias** is a noun that refers to a "tendency to judge unfairly"; **biased** is an adjective that means "having or showing a preferential attitude." A person can have a bias (a thing); be a biased person (adjective modifying *person*); or can be biased (predicate adjective after a linking verb). A person cannot be bias. Also, a person is biased or has a bias *against* (not *to*, *towards*, or *for*) something or someone.

His bias against the Rastafarian lifestyle caused him to overlook some of its ideals.

> **cite, sight, site. To cite**, a verb, is "to refer to an outside source." (The complete naming of the source itself is a citation.) **Sight** (noun or verb) refers to seeing, one of the five senses. **Site**, when used as a noun, is a location or place (usually of some importance). The most common error in essays is the use of *site* when *cite* is meant.

Hint: Remember that *cite* is a verb referring to "the act of giving a citation"; *site* is "where something is situated or sits."

She said the ruins were excavated in 1926, citing as proof the historic plaque that commemorated the site.

> **e.g., i.e. E.g.** is an abbreviation for the Latin *exempli gratia*, meaning "for the sake of example"; **i.e.** is an abbreviation for the Latin *id est* meaning "that is." Use "e.g." before one or more examples; use "i.e." if you want to elaborate on or clarify a preceding statement. In both cases, use a period after each letter and a comma after the abbreviation. Because they are abbreviations, they should be avoided in formal writing.

Hint: The first letter in *example* tells you that examples should follow "e.g.".

J.K. Rowling defied the common formula for success in the children's book market by writing long novels, e.g., *Harry Potter and the Goblet of Fire, Harry Potter and the Order of the Phoenix*. Some of Rowling's novels have episodic plots that contain many well-developed characters; i.e., they tend to be long.

> **fewer, less. Fewer** is the quantitative adjective of comparison and refers to things that can be counted; **less** is the qualitative adjective of comparison, referring to amount and things that can be measured.

Don't believe the notice on the mayonnaise jar: "Contains 40% less calories." Calories can be counted.

There were fewer than a dozen people at the nomination meeting.

The less said about his defection, the better.

> **good, well. Good,** an adjective, should clearly modify a noun (e.g., "a good story") or be used as a subjective complement (predicate adjective, e.g., "the child was good until bedtime"). It cannot be used as a predicate adjective after verbs that express an action, although it is frequently heard in speech,

especially in sports ("I was hitting the ball good"). "I feel good" may refer to feeling healthy; "That watch looks good" may refer to its satisfactory or attractive appearance.

Incorrect: She beat the batter good.

Correct: She is a good cook and beat the batter well.

As an adjective, **well** means "in good health" or "satisfactory." As an adverb, it has several meanings, including "thoroughly" and "satisfactorily."

Hint: Do not use *good* as a predicate adjective after an action verb; you may use it before a noun or right after an intransitive (linking) verb.

Making a good donation to the Children's Hospital made the corporation look good (i.e., "appear altruistic" *not* "appear good-looking").

Although just having come out of the hospital, she looked well and continued to feel well during her recovery. (i.e., *well* is used as an adjective after linking verbs and means "healthy.")

> **its, it's.** **Its** is a possessive adjective meaning "belonging to it." Remember that a pronoun possessive form (except some indefinite pronouns) does not include an apostrophe. **It's** is the contraction for *it is*, the apostrophe indicating that the letter *i* is left out.

> **Hint**: Try substituting *it is* if you're having problems identifying the correct form; if it fits, then use *it's*; if it doesn't, use *its*. (*Its* is usually followed by a noun.)

It's foolish to judge a book by its cover.

> **lay, lie.** Both are verbs. **Lay** is a transitive verb, which must always be followed by a direct object (either a noun or a pronoun). Although it appears archaically in poetry and in song, it is *incorrect* to say, "I'm going to lay down to rest." **Lie** is an intransitive verb; it is not followed by an object.

> **Hint**: You always *lay* something down, as a hen does an egg. Then it *lies* there.

He lay the baby in the crib before going to lie down.

Contrast:

He had *lain* on the ground for twenty minutes before someone noticed him. (*lain* is the past participle of *lie*)

Kim Campbell *laid* to rest the notion that a woman couldn't be prime minister. (*laid* is the past participle of *lay*)

> **led, lead.** **Led** and **lead** are forms of the irregular verb **to lead** (long ē); the present tense is also **lead**. However, the past tense and the past participle are **led** (short ĕ). Writers may become confused by the noun *lead*, the metal, which looks like "to lead," but is pronounced like *led*. Therefore, when they

come to write the past tense *led*, they may wrongly substitute the noun *lead*, rather than the verb.

Hint: Don't be led astray by thinking there is an *a* in *led*"

Although she led in the polls by a 2:1 margin three months ago, today she leads by only a slight margin.

> **loose, lose. Loose** is the adjective meaning "not tight"; **lose** is a verb meaning "not to be able to find," or "to be defeated."

Hint: When you lose something, it is lost. *Lost* is spelled with one *o*.

If you don't tighten that loose button, you're going to lose it.

> **onset, outset.** Both are nouns that mean a "beginning." **Outset** means "setting out," for example, on a journey or to do something; you can also use the phrase "at the outset" to refer to the early events of a narrative or play. **Onset** refers to a force or condition that comes upon one.

At the outset of my fourth decade, I experienced the onset of mild osteo-arthritis.

> **than, then. Than** is a conjunction used in comparisons ("He's happier than he knows"). **Then** is an adverb with temporal connotations meaning "consequently," "at that time," "after that," etc.

Hint: If you're comparing one thing to an*other*, use "th*an*." "Th*en* 'tells when'."

Warren said he was better at darts than Mark, and then he challenged him to a game to prove it.

> **their, there, they're. Their** is a possessive adjective meaning "belonging to them"; **there** is an adverb meaning "in that place"; **they're** is the contraction of *they are*, the apostrophe indicating that the letter *a* is left out.

Hint: If you're uncertain about *they're*, substitute *they are*; *there* (meaning "in that place") is spelled the same as here ("in this place") with the letter *t* added.

There is no excuse for the rowdy behaviour in there; they're supposed to be in their rooms.

> **to, too. To** is a preposition indicating "direction towards"; **too** is an adverb meaning "also."

Hint: *To* will usually be followed by a noun or pronoun as part of a prepositional phrase; substitute *also* for *too*.

The next time you go to the store, may I come along, too?

> **usage, use.** Many writers overuse **usage**, which refers to "a customary or habitual pattern or practise." It applies to conventions of groups of people, such as "language usage of the English." Usage shouldn't be used simply to characterize a repeated action.

Incorrect: The usage of fax machines and e-mail has allowed businesses to increase their efficiency.

Example: I have no use for people who are always correcting my usage of "whom."

> **who's, whose. Who's** is the contraction of *who is*, the apostrophe indicating the omission of the letter *i*. **Whose** is the possessive adjective meaning "belonging to whom?"

Hint: Try substituting *who is*. If it fits, then *who's* is the correct form.

Whose turn is it to do the dishes?

Who's going to do the dishes tonight?

> **you're, your. You're** is the contraction of *you are*; **your** is a possessive adjective that means "belonging to you."

Hint: Try substituting *you are*. If it fits, then *you're* is the correct form.

You're going to be sorry if you don't take your turn and do the dishes tonight.

Here is a list of 50 additional words that often give students trouble. Although students may confuse them, more often they use the term in the first column when that in the second column is intended.

Don't Say . . .	When You Mean
adolescents	adolescence (the *time* one is an adolescent)
around	about (in reference to numbers)
associated to	associated with
attribute to	contribute to
compliment	complement
conscience	conscious
continuous	continual
could of/would of	could have/would have
council	counsel
demise	death
different than	different from
downfall	disadvantage
downside	disadvantage
farther	further (*farther* applies to physical distance)
first off	first
half to	have to
imply	infer
insure	ensure
issues	problems
lifestyle	life
like (a preposition)	as (a conjunction)
locality/location	place
majority of	most
man	human/humanity

manpower	resources
mindset	belief
misfortunate	unfortunate
multiple	many
none the less	nonetheless
obsess about	to be obsessed about
obtain	attain
passed	past
popular	common
principal	principle
references	refers to ("references" is a plural *noun*)
reoccur	recur
seize	cease
so	very
thanks to	due to
that	who/whom
thru	through
till	until
to transition	to change
uninterested	disinterested
upon	on
weather	whether
were	where
which	who/whom

As you progress through your course, you may find other groupings of words that you have problems with. Add them, along with definitions and correct usage, to the list above.

EXERCISE 12.14

Choose 10 of the words from the list above that you know give you trouble. Find the definitions of these words and then write sentences using the words correctly.

Revising for Concision, Directness, and Diction: A Sample Student Draft

Using the editing form on page 450, peer editor Dawn-Lee Ricard suggested changes to her classmate Adrienne Poirier's essay on aggression. She also commented in the text and margins of the draft itself, providing helpful suggestions for direct and concise prose. Most of the introduction and the first body paragraph with editing by Ricard and Poirier herself appear below.

First Draft

It has long been debated whether aggression and violence are inherent or

learned; to this day ∧ there are ~~still many~~ varying opinions. ~~In~~ ∧ the beginning of the
,   *At*

1900s, it was widely accepted that the way humans behaved ~~had every thing to do~~ **depended on** ~~with~~ their ~~biological makeup~~ **biology** (Macionis, Jansson, & Benoit, 2008, p. 169). Sigmund Freud, creator of ~~the psychoanalysis~~ **psychoanalytic** theory, believed ~~that~~ each person had an aggressive drive ~~within them.~~ **, which he called** ~~He called this drive~~ "the death instinct**,**" ~~and held~~ **believing** that it was impossible to rid ~~completely~~ yourself of it (p. 166). However, ~~more~~

2nd person is not used in formal academic work

recent studies ~~have begun to~~ show that aggressive and violent behaviour have less

Check agreement? "behaviour" is singular

to do with natural instinct and more to do with how people learn to deal with situations that may lead to such behaviour. Research states that ~~the majority of~~ **most** violent behaviour is ~~in fact~~ learned behaviour (Elliott, 1994, p. 3). Studies have

"Researchers state" or "studies demonstrate"

shown that when someone participates in aggressive acts, that person becomes more aggressive, backing up the opinion that aggression and violence are learned . . . .

Supporting the view?

Early childhood is ~~a very~~ **an** important stage for demonstrating non-aggressive behaviour, as children can begin to show aggressive behaviour as early as

Modelling? Adrienne, do you mean that parents need to model this kind of behaviour?

two and a half years ~~of age~~ **old** (Murray-Close & Ostrov, 2009, p. 830). Once a child has established an aggressive personality**,** it can be ~~very~~ difficult to restore positive behaviour in them. Farrington (as cited by Pepler & Rubin,

Consider "constructive"

1991) observed that aggression in childhood could worsen and turn into "delinquency and hostility" in ~~the teenage years~~ **adolescence** and remain throughout the child's life (p. xiii). ~~What~~ parents often don't realize ~~is~~ they ~~are teaching~~ **teach** their children aggressive behaviour when trying to do the ~~exact~~ opposite.

No contractions in formal writing

For example, reprimanding ~~a child's aggression~~ **a child for aggressive behaviour** by shouting, grabbing, or threats is almost

This citation can be deleted

worse than not reprimanding the child at all (Fraser, 1996, p. 349). Witnessing

this ~~kind of behaviour~~ causes the child to revert ~~back to it~~ as soon as he or
　　　　　　　type of reprimand

she is upset (Fraser, 1996, p. 349). Even worse is ~~the direct witnessing of~~ physical
　　　　　　　　　　　　　　　　　　directly experiencing

or emotional abuse (Elliott, 1994, p. 3). Such negative reinforcement does

not have to come from a parent but can ~~be as simple as~~ watching a violent TV
　　　　　　　　　　　　　　　　occur when simply

program.

Final Draft

In her final draft, Poirier used most of Ricard's suggestions for concision, directness, and diction, rewording some passages herself.

It has long been debated whether aggression and violence are inherent or learned; to this day, there are varying opinions. At the beginning of the 1900s, it was widely accepted that the way humans behaved depended on their biology (Macionis, Jansson, & Benoit, 2008, p. 169). Sigmund Freud, creator of psychoanalytic theory, believed each person had an aggressive drive, which he called "the death instinct," holding that it was impossible to rid oneself of it (p. 166). However, recent studies show that aggressive and violent behaviour has less to do with natural instinct and more to do with how people learn to deal with situations that may lead to such behaviour. Researchers believe that most violent behaviour is learned behaviour (Elliott, 1994, p. 3). Studies have shown that when someone participates in aggressive acts, that person becomes more aggressive, which supports the idea that aggression and violence are learned . . . .

Early childhood is an important stage for demonstrating non-aggressive behaviour to children, as they can begin to show aggressive behaviour as early as two and a half years old (Murray-Close & Ostrov, 2009, p. 830). Once a child has established an aggressive personality, it can be difficult to restore constructive behaviour in them. Farrington (as cited by Pepler & Rubin, 1991) observed that aggression in childhood could worsen and turn into "delinquency and hostility" in adolescence and remain throughout the child's life (p. xiii). Parents often do not realize that they teach their children aggressive behaviour when trying to do the opposite. For example, reprimanding a child for aggressive behaviour by shouting, grabbing, or threats is almost worse than not reprimanding the child at all. Witnessing this type of reprimand causes the child to revert to it as soon as he or she is upset (Fraser, 1996, p. 349). Even worse is directly experiencing physical or emotional abuse (Elliott, 1994, p. 3). Such negative reinforcement does not have to come from a parent but can occur when simply watching a violent TV program.

Providing Depth: Variety and Emphasis

When you revise an early draft to improve clarity, you will likely find opportunities to make your prose more interesting. Variety and emphasis in your writing will make what is competent also *compelling*. Variety and emphasis are worthwhile goals in all forms of essays: literary, argumentative, and expository.

Sentence Variety

Length

You can vary the lengths of sentences for rhetorical effect. Just as short paragraphs suggest underdeveloped points, short, choppy sentences could suggest a lack of content. On the other hand, several long sentences in a row could confuse a reader.

That doesn't mean you should write only sentences that are between 15 and 20 words long. Although sentence length alone is no measure of readability, consider revision if you find you have written more than two very short or very long sentences in a row.

To connect short sentences you can use appropriate conjunctions. Simple sentences can be joined by one of the seven coordinating conjunctions. If the idea in one sentence is less important than the idea in the sentence before or after it, use the subordinate conjunction that best expresses the relationship between the sentences. You can join independent clauses with a semicolon or a colon.

You can also join independent clauses with a conjunctive adverb or transitional phrase, ensuring that a semicolon precedes the connecting word or phrase). You may be able to grammatically connect phrases or clauses through a parallel relationship, such as apposition. The second phrase or clause could also modify the preceding word, phrase, or clause—for example, a relative (adjectival) clause could give information about a preceding noun clause. See Chapter 11 to review punctuation rules.

Generally speaking, you waste space when you begin a new sentence by repeating part of the previous sentence, or by beginning a new paragraph by recapitulating part of the previous one. Although repetition can be used to build coherence, it should not create redundancy:

> In 1970, Gordon O. Gallup created the mirror test ~~This test was~~, designed to determine whether ~~or not~~ animals are self-aware.

●●●●●

EXERCISE 12.15

The following paragraph consists of too many short sentences. Using the strategies mentioned above, revise the paragraph to make it more effective.

(1) During the earth's long history, there have been various periods of glaciation. (2) This fact is well known. (3) There is also evidence of one great glacial event. (4) It is possible that the earth was once completely covered by ice and snow. (5) Skeptics argue this is impossible. (6) They say that the earth could never have become this cold. (7) The idea of the tropics being frozen over is unlikely, they believe.

When checking your work for overly long sentences, consider breaking up sentences with more than two independent clauses or one independent clause and more than two dependent clauses. See if the relationships between the clauses are clear. If they are not, divide the sentences where clauses are joined by conjunctions, by transitional words and phrases, or by relative pronouns.

EXERCISE 12.16

↻ Check answers to select questions

The following paragraph consists of sentences that are too long. Using the strategies mentioned above, revise the paragraph to make it more effective.

(1) Finding a definition for "the homeless" is difficult, but the most common definition, which is used both in the media and in current research, defines the homeless as those who lack visible shelter or use public shelters. (2) Literature about homelessness is sparse, and it was not until the 1980s that the incidence of homelessness began to be reported in the media, but homelessness has existed for centuries, and literature on the subject dates back to the feudal period in Europe.

Structural Variety

You can experiment with phrasal openings to sentences. Consider beginning the occasional sentence with a prepositional phrase, a verbal phrase, or an absolute phrase instead of the subject of the sentence.

Prepositional phrases begin with a preposition followed by a noun or pronoun (see page 320); they are adjectival or adverbial and modify the closest noun (adjectival) or verb (adverbial). A **participial phrase**, which ends in *-ing*, *-ed*, or *-en*, is a verbal phrase acting as an adjective. An **infinitive phrase**, which is preceded by *to*, can act adjectivally or adverbially as a sentence opener. An **absolute phrase**, consisting of a noun/pronoun and a partial verb form, modifies the entire sentence.

In this short excerpt from an essay about the death of a moth, Virginia Woolf uses a prepositional phrase opening, an absolute phrase that introduces an independent clause, and two verbal phrase openings:

> *After a time*, <u>tired by his dancing</u> apparently, he settled on the window ledge in the sun, and **the queer spectacle being at an end**, I forgot about him. Then, <u>looking up</u>, my eye was caught by him. He was trying to resume his dancing, but seemed either so stiff or so awkward that he could only flutter to the bottom of the window-pane; and when he tried to fly across it, he failed.

Note the types of modifiers:

After a time: prepositional phrase

<u>tired by his dancing</u>; <u>looking up</u>: verbal phrases

the queer spectacle being at an end: absolute phrase

Creating Emphasis

Writers may create emphasis by presenting main points or details in a particular order. Two kinds of sentences vary in the order in which they present the main idea: **periodic** and **cumulative** sentences.

> Make sure that when you use a participial phrase at the beginning of a sentence that you include the word it is intended to modify so that it does not dangle. (See Dangling Modifiers, page 389.

A **periodic sentence** begins with a modifier—word, phrase, or clause—before the independent clause. A cumulative sentence works the other way: it begins with an independent clause, followed by a modifying or parallel word, phrase, or clause. While a periodic sentence delays the main idea, creating anticipation, a cumulative sentence develops the main idea by drawing it out. Many sentences are slightly or moderately periodic or cumulative, depending on whether the writer has begun or ended with modifiers. However, a writer can employ either periodic or cumulative sentences to create a specific effect. Independent clauses are shown by italics below.

Periodic:

Unlike novelists and playwrights, who lurk behind the scenes while distracting our attention with the puppet show of imaginary characters—and unlike the scholars and journalists, who quote the opinions of others and take cover behind the hedges of neutrality—*the essayist has nowhere to hide* (Scott Russell Sanders, "The Singular First Person").

Cumulative:

The root of all evil is that we all want this spiritual gratification, this flow, this apparent heightening of life, this knowledge, this valley of many-colored grass, even grass and light prismatically decomposed, giving ecstasy (D.H. Lawrence, *Studies in Classic American Literature*).

A writer can delay the main idea, generating tension by beginning with a prepositional phrase:

Behind the deconstructionists' dazzling cloud of language lie certain more or less indisputable facts (John Gardner, *The Art of Fiction*).

Other ways to achieve emphasis include parallel structures and repetition—techniques that also help in paragraph coherence—and rhythms that call the reader's attention to important ideas. The end of a sentence in itself provides emphasis, since a reader naturally slows down when approaching the last part of a sentence and pauses slightly between sentences.

The two paragraphs below employ parallel structures, repetition, and rhythm for emphasis.

A.   My professors, many of whom were to become very famous, did not tend to be philosophic and did not dig back into the sources of the new language and categories they were using. They thought that these were scientific discoveries like any others, which were to be used in order to make further discoveries. They were very much addicted to abstractions and generalizations, as Tocqueville predicted they would be. They believed in scientific progress and appeared (there may have been an element of boasting and self-irony in this) to be convinced that they were on the verge of a historic breakthrough in the social sciences, equivalent to that scored in the sixteenth and seventeenth centuries in the natural sciences . . . . These teachers were literally inebriated by the unconscious and values. And they were also sure that scientific progress would be related to social and political progress. (Allan Bloom, *The Closing of the American Mind* New York: Simon & Schuster, 1987)

Analysis: Bloom employs the most common structural pattern of subject-verb-object in all his sentences, establishing a predictable rhetorical pattern that complements the predictability and uniformity of his professors that he wants to stress. Thus, "My professors," the subject in the first sentence, is replaced by the pronoun "they" in the following three sentences; in the fourth sentence, "they" is the subject of two clauses. To avoid too many identical openings, Bloom continues with the same rhythm but varies the subject slightly: the last two sentences begin with "These teachers" and "And they," respectively.

B. Tales about Pythagoras flew to him and stuck like iron filings to a magnet. He was said, for example, to have appeared in several places at once and to have been reincarnated many times. Taken literally, this idea can be consigned to the same overflowing bin which contains the story that he had a golden thigh; but taken figuratively, it is an understatement. Pythagoras—or at least Pythagoreanism—was everywhere and still is (Anthony Gottlieb, *The Dream of Reason.* New York: W.W. Norton, 2000, 21).

Analysis: The most obvious technique in paragraph B is the use of figurative language: Gottlieb uses a simile in the first sentence ("like iron filings to a magnet") and a metaphor in the third sentence ("overflowing bin"). However, he effectively uses sentence length and rhythm to make the paragraph more appealing still. The paragraph is framed by short simple sentences that stress Pythagoras's importance. The middle sentences develop the main idea through examples. Gottlieb's final sentence, though the shortest, contains strong stresses: the use of dashes allows the writer to repeat the name Pythagoras without seeming redundant, while heavy accents fall on the final two words.

EXERCISE 12.17

In one or two well-developed paragraphs, analyze the following student introductions for their rhetorical effectiveness, including sentence structure/variety, repetition, or other techniques to create variety, emphasis, and readability. (You may want to reread The Introduction in Chapter 4, page 84.)

1. Russia has always had a certain "Russianness" about it. Its experiences have not been especially different from those of most other nations, yet Russia succeeds in maintaining a curious "otherness." There is something alien about that land, about the largest nation in the world, about a country situated at the midpoint of east and west, about the land of revolution: there is something alien about Russia. It functions, in a sense, by being dysfunctional, a concept the West has never understood and the East has never cared to examine. For thousands of years, Russia has maintained this "otherness," and the rest of the world has

hailed it as Russia's true identity. However, an exploration of its culture, history, ideologies, and media reveals that Russia's identity cannot be reduced to an ill-defined "otherness": Undoubtedly, Russia is much more than the *other* country.

—Student writer Angela Kruger

2. Right now, television screens around the world are filled with images of South Africans celebrating together and hooting loudly on vuvuzelas, loud plastic horns, as the country hosts the 2010 Soccer World Cup. Sport, in particular soccer and rugby, has become an important unifier in South Africa, a country that had, and still has, sharp racial divisions. The international success of South Africa's sports teams usually sparks celebrations across racial lines. For example, the achievements of the national teams in the 1995 Rugby World Cup and 2010 Soccer World Cup caused universal jubilation. However, sport is still often divided along ethnic lines. The World Cup winning rugby team of 1995 included only one black player, while the soccer team at this year's World Cup has one white player (who never left the bench). South African rugby, with the support and resources of the economically dominant whites, has excelled on the international stage, winning its second World Cup in 2007; by contrast, South African soccer, with the support and limited resources of the non-whites, has not excelled. Recognizing the potential of sport to reconcile historically hostile racial groups, the new multi-racial governments have declared public support for all national teams and have tried a number of initiatives to make sport more representative of the country's racial make-up. These initiatives include introducing development programs for deprived communities and imposing colour quotas on rugby teams. Slowly, despite persistent racial divisions, sport is becoming a national unifier in South Africa.

    —Student writer Yvonne du Plessis

Proofreading: Perfection *Is* Possible

In publishing, *editing* refers to the revising of a work before it is formatted, whether for a book, a newspaper, a magazine or journal, or other medium. *Proofreading* refers to the final check of the formatted material—either done on screen or in the form of paper "proofs" printed from the formatter's electronic files.

While someone who edits and suggests revisions to a document is mainly concerned with improving it, the proofreader is looking for errors. The proofreader is the document's last line of defence before it falls under the public eye. Ironically, poor proofreading may be the first thing noticed in the published document.

In spite of its importance, proofreading is usually one of the neglected stages for student writers working under deadline to submit an essay. Exhausted from the final efforts of putting the essay together, students may think that tiny errors are unimportant compared to other parts of the process stressed throughout the term. However, distracting errors may strike your instructor in a completely different light: they could be seen as careless, a sign of a lack of effort or respect for the reader.

Whether or not proofreading is seen as tedious, it is best performed as a mechanical process. By taking a systematic approach to the essay at this stage, you can be more confident that the work of many hours, days, or even weeks will be more readable to the person marking it.

Proofreading Methods

Documents may be read **in teams** with one person reading aloud while the other follows the printed copy silently. When it is your work being proofread, it is best if you read aloud since you may more easily catch errors you've missed as a writer. This method works on the principle that two readers are twice as likely to spot errors as one person. It may also be more enjoyable than working alone. Clearly, it works only if a second reader is available and both readers are knowledgeable about writing and committed to the task.

Reading forward is the method of reading the paper aloud or to yourself but more slowly and carefully than you would usually do, paying attention both to the words and to the punctuation. Because it can be hard to concentrate solely on the words apart from the meaning, it's best to read through the essay at least once for meaning and then at least once again for spelling and other errors.

Reading backward is the method by which you start at the end and read to the beginning word by word or sentence by sentence. This technique forces your attention on the writing; it works well for catching spelling errors. However, it is time-consuming, and you may miss some punctuation and other "between the words" errors, as well as words that are dependent on their context.

Reading syllabically, you read from the beginning, breaking every word into syllables. This is faster than reading backward, works well for catching internal misspellings, and is quite effective for catching missing and extra words and for correcting word endings (which may be overlooked when you read forward). However, it is a slower method than reading forward word by word, requires some discipline to master, and can be hard on the eyes if done for a long time.

Guidelines for Proofreading

> Probably the main reason for essays with careless errors is that not enough time was allotted for proofing. The half hour not set aside for proofreading can undo the work of several hours.

> Plan to let at least a few hours pass before you look at the essay for the final time (overnight is recommended).

> Having someone else go over the essay can be helpful but is no substitute for your own systematic proofing. Instructors are not likely to be sympathetic to the cry of baffled frustration, "But I had my roommate read it over!"

> Use a spell-checker but don't rely on it. Remember the poem that made the rounds on the Internet a few years ago: *Eye halve a spelling chequer / It came with my pea sea / It plainly marques for my revue / miss steaks eye kin knot sea . . . .* A spell-checker will not see any difference between *there house is over their two* and *their house is over there too.*

> Experiment with the different proofreading methods discussed above and use the ones you feel most comfortable with and that work best for you. When you start proofreading using one particular method, though, you should use it until you finish reading.

Common Errors

Categories of typical errors to watch for and correct in your writing:

> All areas where consistency is required—spelling, capitalization, abbreviations, hyphenation, numbers, internal punctuation, and other places where choices pertaining to the mechanics of writing may be involved

> Proper nouns (especially unfamiliar names), acronyms, etc. Are all references to authors and titles spelled correctly?

> Middles and endings of words, for spelling and for agreement

> Small words, such as articles and prepositions (*a, an, and, as, at, if, in, it, of, or, the, to,* etc.)

> Words that have different spellings but the same pronunciation (homophones)—e.g., *to/too, their/there/they're, role/roll, cite/site, led/lead, manor/manner*

> Font style (italic, bold, Roman: applied correctly and consistently? Applied to *all* necessary words?) Have you used italics for complete works, such as books and films, and placed works within larger works, such as essays, articles, short stories, and poems, within quotation marks?

> End punctuation (periods and question marks)

> Quotation marks applied appropriately? Both opening and closing quotation marks present? Have double and single quotation marks been alternated correctly? Periods and commas inside; colons and semicolons outside? Similar checks can be made for parentheses.

> All citations, both in-text and on the final page of the essay. Check both for accuracy (author, title, journal name, date, and page numbers) and for consistency. Are all citations documented according to the style of your discipline—including capitalization, punctuation, and other conventions?

Essay Presentation

Your audience and purpose are relevant to how you present your essay; for example, a scientific or engineering report probably would look quite different from an essay for English class—for one thing, it might have headings, whereas the English essay would probably not. A research essay, too, must conform to the documentation style of your discipline; on the other hand, if you are writing a personal essay and not using references, presenting your essay may mostly be a matter of following directions for title, typeface, margins, spacing, indentation, page numbering, and identifying information.

Although document design can vary, you can be sure of one thing: if your instructor asks you to format your essay a certain way, he or she will look to see that you followed these instructions. Therefore, if you are unsure about essay presentation, ask for help.

Unless you are told otherwise, you can refer to the following (based on MLA guidelines):

> Most instructors require essays to be typed. Use good-quality white paper, printing on one side. If you wish to conserve paper by printing on both sides, check with your instructor first.

> Leave 2.5 centimetre (1-inch) margins on all sides. The first page should include identification information positioned flush left (i.e., starting at the

left margin). List information in the following order: your name and student ID, if applicable; instructor's name (use the title that your instructor prefers—e.g., Professor Robert Mills, Dr. M. Sonik, Ms. J. Winestock, etc.); course number and section, if applicable; submission date. Double space, then insert the essay's title, centred.

> Double space the text of your essay; this makes it much easier for the instructor to correct errors and add comments. *Also double space* any "Notes," the "Works Cited" page, and block quotations.

> Indent each paragraph 1.25 centimetres (one-half inch)—do *not* use additional spaces to separate paragraphs, and leave a single space (not two spaces) after each period before beginning the next sentence.

> Number pages using Arabic numerals in the upper right-hand corner preceded by your last name; place about 1.25 centimetres (one-half inch) from top and flush right; your word-processing program can probably create this kind of header automatically. If you need to include prefatory pages (such as a Contents page or a formal outline), use lower-case Roman numerals (i, ii, iii) for those pages.

> Title pages are usually optional, though some instructors require them. Position the essay's title down one-third of the page with your name about halfway down; near the bottom of the page include course number, instructor's name, and submission date. All items should be centred. Begin your essay on the second page (numbered 1) under the centred title.

> No illustrations or colours, other than black and white, should be on any pages unless you use graphics directly relevant to your essay—for example, charts or diagrams for a scientific study. Use a paper clip to attach the pages (some instructors ask for stapled pages)—especially, don't dog-ear them. Don't use folders, clear or coloured, unless asked for. (If you do use a folder, the left-hand margin should be slightly wider than the other margins to enhance readability.)

> Prefer common fonts, such as Times New Roman, Arial, or Garamond (not Courier New or cursive ones). Use 10- to 12-point type size. *Do not* justify lines to the margins in academic papers or reports (i.e., set the paragraphing for flush left and use a *ragged* right line at the margin). Finally, ensure that the text of your essay is easy to read. An essay printed in draft mode or from a cartridge that is almost out of ink will not be easy to read.

Tense Encounters with Verbs: A Summary

Tense refers to time when the action or condition expressed by the verb takes place. Each tense can take one of four *forms*: **simple, progressive, perfect,** and **perfect progressive.** These forms further describe the aspect of the verb, as to when its action began, and its duration or completion.

The auxiliary (helping) verb for most forms determines the complete form of the verb. The auxiliary verb for the progressive tenses is *to be* (*is*, *was*, *will be*); for the perfect tenses, it is *to have* (*has*, *had*, *will have*).

Present Tenses

Simple present (action or situation exists now or exists on a regular basis):

I call	We call
You call	You call
He/she/it calls	They call

I usually call for the pizza; you call for it this time.

Present progressive (action is in progress):

I am sending	We are sending
You are sending	You are sending
He/she/it is sending	They are sending

Mr. Kahn is sending the package to you by courier.

Present perfect (action began in the past and is completed in the present):

I have eaten	We have eaten
You have eaten	You have eaten
He/she/it has eaten	They have eaten

I have eaten the apple you gave me.

Present perfect progressive (action began in the past, continues in the present, and may continue into the future):

I have been hoping	We have been hoping
You have been hoping	You have been hoping
He/she/it has been hoping	They have been hoping

We have been hoping to receive news from the Philippines.

Past Tenses

Simple past (action or situation was completed in the past):

I saw	We saw
You saw	You saw
He/she/it saw	They saw

Garfield saw the moon rise last night over his burrow.

Past progressive (action was in progress in the past):

I was talking	We were talking
You were talking	You were talking
He/she/it was talking	They were talking

> James and Beth were talking about storms when the hurricane warning flashed onto their computer screen.

Past perfect (action was completed in the past prior to another action in the past):

I had finished	We had finished
You had finished	You had finished
He/she/it had finished	They had finished

> Alex had finished the second assignment when the storm knocked out power to his computer.

Past perfect progressive (action in progress in the past):

I had been practising	We had been practising
You had been practising	You had been practising
He/she/it had been practising	They had been practising

> The golf team sophomores had been practising for the tournament all summer, but when school started their coach announced his resignation.

Future Tenses

Simple future (action will occur in the future):

I will see	We will see
You will see	You will see
He/she/it will see	They will see

> I will see the Rocky Mountains on my way to Vancouver.

Future progressive (action will be continuous in the future).

I will be walking	We will be walking
You will be walking	You will be walking
He/she/it will be walking	They will be walking

> Norm and Martee will be walking in the Marathon of Hope next Saturday morning.

Future perfect (action in the future will be completed):

I will have gone	We will have gone
You will have gone	You will have gone
He/she/it will have gone	They will have gone

> Sally will have gone around the moon several times before the ship leaves its lunar orbit.

Future perfect progressive (actions are ongoing up to a specific future time):

I will have been studying · · · · · · · · · We will have been studying

You will have been studying · · · · · · · · You will have been studying

He/she/it will have been studying · · · · · They will have been studying

> With the completion of this assignment they will have been studying verbs for 13 years.

Remember that verbs can reflect mood (conditional, subjunctive) and voice (active, passive), and auxiliary verbs can be used to indicate **conditions**, such as necessity (I should go), obligation (you must go), and possibility (he may go).

Modal Auxiliaries

Modals can be considered a special category of helping verb that make the meaning of a main verb more precise. They are usually followed by the bare infinitive, which does not include *to*. Some common uses of modals are listed below.

> *Can* expresses capability:

Clothing *can* really say a lot about a person.

Compare the following sentences and note their different meanings. Here, the simple present tense is used to show a repeated action (see above):

In the summer, Nina *swims* every day.

Here, the modal *can* is used with the bare infinitive to show ability or capability; *is able to* can be substituted for *can*:

In the summer, Nina *can swim* every day.

> *Could* expresses capability in the past tense:

When she lived near a lake, Nina *could* swim every day.

> *Should* expresses necessity or obligation. Compare the following sentences and note their different meanings:

Incorrect statement (i.e., not factually true):

There *are* gun laws in all states in the US that prevent people from killing each other.

Correct but weak:

There *have to be* gun laws in all states in the US.

Correct and effective:

There *should be* [or *must be*] gun laws in all states in the US.

> *May* and *might* express possibility. *May* often conveys a stronger possibility than *might*:

Since she has the prerequisites, Bianca *may* enroll in the second-year course.

Although she worked late, she *might* decide to go to the party.

❯   *May* also expresses permission:

Students *may* bring beverages into the study area but not food items.

❯   *Will* expresses probability:

Since she has the prerequisites, Bianca *will* enroll in the second-year anthropology course.

❯   *Would* expresses a repeated action in the past:

When she lived near a lake, Nina *would* swim every day. (Compare with *Could*, above.)

A Special Case: Online Learning and Writing

Increasingly, students and teachers alike are discovering the advantages of using computers for more than word-processing. A few years ago, only the most adventurous teachers were creating Web pages; now, students can take full courses online and many courses include online components. Although *online* is equated with *innovative*, it is becoming more likely that you will encounter some kind of Internet classroom during your post-secondary education.

The Pros and Cons

Many students are hesitant to take Web-based courses, thinking that sophisticated computer skills might be required. However, if you can use a word-processing program to create text documents and if you can manage email, you already possess the basic skills for any online learning situation. Although systems of course delivery vary, they are designed to be used by people who are not computer specialists, and they all include support networks for those who encounter difficulties. In addition to the "help" links that every system includes, however, is another resource: most institutions have online "help desks" that students can access via the Internet or by telephone. If your keyboard freezes or your system crashes, someone is nearby to talk you through each step of the recovery process. Each encounter with such resources has an additional benefit: one learns a bit more about using servers and/or software, which increases self-confidence.

Online curriculum delivery offers considerable flexibility and independence, but places more responsibility on the student than classroom learning does. You need disciplined work habits and awareness of your own writing strengths, for example. No one will remind you to complete your readings or your assignments, and computer-related problems are considered poor excuses for late essays. If you have questions about course materials, you need to take the initiative and contact your instructor directly. For students who tend to let more talkative peers speak up in class, this setting will not help you to change your habits and you may find yourself disadvantaged.

On the other hand, many introverted students find it much easier to communicate with their teachers via email, enjoying the freedom of anonymity. Many students are attracted to online learning because of its unusual freedom and adaptability: like more traditional forms of distance education, students frequently have the option of creating their own work schedules, by deciding on when they "attend" class, for instance. However, unlike traditional distance education courses, online courses usually offer greater student–teacher and student–student interaction.

Most online courses feature some kind of "discussion" forum in which students and their teachers communicate by posting messages (like email messages) organized into specific topic areas. Such "message boards" allow you to "speak" publicly—in much the same way that you would in a classroom—and receive comments or feedback from others in the course. These discussion forums allow private communication, too: instead of emailing a classmate or your teacher through your regular server, course email/discussions are restricted to people registered in your course.

The amount and frequency of contact within a class can vary widely, as do the kinds of assignments. Many students prefer to post their thoughts at least weekly; they feel less isolated, and the familiarity allows them to ask questions with less self-consciousness. In online writing courses, regular participation is extremely helpful, because you are writing constantly. Most student writers in such courses discover that their writing skills improve even more dramatically than in more conventional settings, because the more they write, the easier it becomes.

The kinds of assignments you will encounter in an online writing course will be roughly equivalent to those you would find in any university writing course. There may be group projects and presentations, "timed" essays and quizzes, as well as chat rooms for "real time" discussions. Usually, the syllabus for the course will look like any you would receive in person, although course descriptions may include more detail. The same is true of the course notes: teachers generally try to anticipate questions or difficulties more overtly than they would in the classroom and the amount of work will be about the same.

A Sample Online Discussion

What follows is an excerpt from an online discussion of the short story "The Demon Lover," by Anglo-Irish writer Elizabeth Bowen. The story is set during the London Blitz of 1941, the most infamous of the World War II bombings of England. As the protagonist, Mrs. Drover, searches in her London house for items to take back to her temporary home in the country, she finds a mysterious letter apparently written by her lover, a soldier to whom she had made a rash vow 25 years before. Gradually, she becomes convinced that the lover, presumed dead, is in the house with her and expects her to meet him at the "prearranged hour." The discussion topic below addresses the nature of the story as either a supernatural tale or a story of psychological breakdown.

Author: AMANDA CAMPBELL

Date: Monday, February 22, 2010 11:55am
Could it be that Mrs. Drover herself might be dead? Could it be that she is coming back to this house which seems to be rundown and where the caretaker no longer works? As Mrs. Drover passed, "no human eye watched her." This might imply that she does not exist and therefore no one can see her. She is a supernatural body that has come back to the place where she once lived. Maybe she does not know herself that she is dead and that she believes that she is alive. Words used early in the story, such as "dead," "shuttered," "dark," and "dead air," led me to believe that there was some supernatural element. The letter from her lost love might have been sitting on the table for years waiting for her to come home to. But maybe it could all be just a dream. The screams that come from Mrs. Drover at the end of the story may indicate her waking up from a horrible dream.

Author: ERIKA JOHNSON

Date: Monday, February 22, 2010 1:05pm
My initial thoughts were aligned with Amanda's in that it appears as though Mrs. Drover has died. In the first few paragraphs, Bowen describes a scene that is dark and gloomy, and repeatedly uses "dead" to affirm the lifeless, cold atmosphere of the house. Also, if Mrs. Drover had a caretaker for the house and he was off that particular week, there is no way a house could accumulate so much dirt, dust, and film in such a short time. After reading the story over again, it would be my guess that Mrs. Drover is in fact having a sort of mental breakdown where all her past thoughts and emotions are rushing up, possibly because of the letter. Although she may be dreaming, the letter is a sort of catalyst to confront and deal with her past experiences

(involving her presumably dead fiancé). Through her dream she is able to walk through the vacant house and experience the life that she once had. The letter symbolizes lost love and gives her a chance to remember and reflect on a life that could have been.

Author: ALSTON ACHARYA

Date: Monday, February 22, 2010 2:40pm
One of the reasons I feel the story is psychological is the strict focus on the main character. If there were other characters, someone to witness a ghost or something of that sort, then it could be more easily considered supernatural. But since there is only one major character, all focus is on her and her perception. If it's a psychological story of how she loses her mind and is dealing with her own guilt, then no witness is necessary.

Author: MARIE PERRY

Date: Monday, February 22, 2010 2:59pm
I think "The Demon Lover" is a supernatural tale showing the horrors of war. The setting focuses on bombs and bombing, and Mrs. Drover thinks of the bombs. Mrs. Drover is haunted by this sinister lover who seems to be war itself. Women's lovers left for war, and they made promises to wait for each other, just as Mrs. Drover did to the faceless man. When he dies she is upset and eventually tries to start life anew. The letter from the lover brings back memories of this horrid war and inspires panic and anxiety from her. When she meets him in the taxi, it is as though she has come face to face with one of the most terrifying things in the world, something that shouldn't have a face. Mrs. Drover meets a supernatural devil who takes her to hell, and that devil is war. What person in his or her right mind wouldn't scream?

Author: OLIVER LECLAIR

Date: Monday, February 22, 2010 8:26pm
Before reading Amanda's response, the possibility of Mrs. Drover being dead did not register. Having reread the story with the idea of her being dead, I can see that the letter itself supports it. The letter was delivered to a "shuttered" house, and only the absent caretaker had access to the house. The letter was not addressed and lay on undisturbed dust, which implies that a person did not place it there. The possibility of Mrs. Drover's death is implied within the letter itself when the writer "K" states that "nothing has changed." Death is perpetual. Finally, the "arranged" hour that Mrs. Drover so desperately tries to avoid and the fact that the letter applies to whatever day she reads it convey the sense of her trying to escape either a death that has already arrived or that she knows is inevitable and near.

Author: LIAM BRIDGER

Date: Monday, February 22, 2010 11:51pm
I see this story as being a dream or, I suppose, a nightmare. The idea of Mrs. Drover not being watched by any human eye can be thought of as no one else around, simply because no one needs to be around in a dream. The feelings of paranoia are consistent with the common dream of being chased where you sense something is after you but have no clue where it may be. Certainly the ending where the victim meets the horrible face mere inches apart strikes me as supernatural, almost a cliché movie ending. However, it could also lean towards the psychological, as the dreams and nightmares of people, though perhaps including supernatural entities, are still conjured up by disturbed minds.

Peer Edit Forms

Peer Edit Form: Formal Outline

The essay outline provides the structure on which the essay itself will be built. Therefore, as an editor, you should pay special attention to the relation among the parts (introduction, body paragraphs, conclusion), to the order of points (least important to most important? Most to least? Some other logical order?), as well as to the strength and effectiveness of each main point. Is each one adequately developed? Is the claim supported/question answered/hypothesis proved?

Instructions

Use the check boxes below to record the fact that you have considered and evaluated the criteria. Use the space following to add suggestions, comments, questions, and advice.

Introduction

- ☐ Does it attract your interest?
- ☐ Does it announce the topic?
- ☐ Does it contain a two-part direct thesis statement announcing the topic and showing the reader what the writer contends about the topic?
- ☐ Is the claim one of fact, value, or policy?
- ☐ Is the thesis statement interesting, specific, and manageable?
  - ☐ Interesting?
  - ☐ Specific?
  - ☐ Manageable?
  - ☐ Clear?
- ☐ Does the essay appear expository? Argumentative? What shows you this?

Body Paragraphs

- ☐ Does each paragraph contain at least one main idea that can be easily identified as such? If not, which paragraphs don't do this?
- ☐ Does each paragraph contain at least two sub-points that help develop the main point? If not, which paragraphs don't?
  - ☐ Formal *topic* outline used?
  - ☐ Formal *sentence* outline used?
  - ☐ Other kind of outline?
- ☐ Has the writer been able to provide support for his/her argument? If not, suggest ways that he/she could use kinds of evidence to do this (e.g., examples, facts/statistics, personal experience, outside sources, etc.).
- ☐ Do the paragraphs appear to be organized using any of the rhetorical patterns discussed in Chapter 5 (e.g., definition, cause/effect, problem–solution, compare and contrast?) If not, can you suggest methods for any of the paragraphs?
- ☐ Are the main points ordered in a logical and persuasive way? If not, what could you suggest as an alternate arrangement?
- ☐ Are there at least two levels represented in the outline (main points and sub-points)? Are the elements of coordination and subordination applied correctly? Is parallel structure applied to main points and the levels of sub-points?

Conclusion

- ☐ Does it successfully summarize or restate the argument without sounding repetitious?
- ☐ Does it go beyond the introduction by enlarging on the implications of the thesis, by urging a change in thought or call to action, or by making an ethical or emotional appeal?

Final comments or suggestions?

Writer's Name: _____

Editor's Name: _____

Peer Edit Form: Research Essay First Draft

Your first draft is the stage at which you make the transition from large-scale structural concerns to those focusing on integrating your research with your own ideas to create a synthesis—in your final draft, you will work further on these areas, along with the attempt to achieve conciseness, clear expression, grammatically sound prose, etc.

Instructions

Use the check boxes below to record the fact that you have considered and evaluated the criteria. Use the space following to add suggestions, comments, questions, and advice. In addition, underline places in the essay where you would like to draw the writer's attention to possible grammatical problems (such as fragments, comma splices, apostrophes, lack of parallelism, misplaced or dangling modifiers, pronoun agreement and/or consistency), or stylistic problems (such as passive constructions or other instances where the writing could be made more concise, direct, or forceful— you should also note possible spelling errors along with errors in mechanics and presentation).

Introduction

- ☐ Is the introduction successful?
    - ☐ Interesting?
    - ☐ Announces subject and contains thesis statement with a claim of fact, a hypothesis to be tested, or a question to be answered?
    - ☐ Suggests the main way the argument will be organized?
- ☐ Does the writer establish him- or herself as credible and trustworthy? How?

Body Paragraphs

- ☐ Does the essay seem complete, and does the order of the paragraphs appear logical?
- ☐ Look at paragraphs individually. Are any too short? Too long?
- ☐ Is each paragraph unified (relates to one main idea)? If not, which ones aren't?
- ☐ Is each paragraph coherent? If not, which ones aren't?
- ☐ Do paragraphs contain topic sentences?
- ☐ Is the order of the sentences natural?
- ☐ Are there appropriate transitions between sentences, enabling you to see the relationship between consecutive sentences?
- ☐ Does the writer successfully use repetition, rephrasing, synonyms, or other devices to achieve coherence?
- ☐ Does each paragraph seem developed adequately?
- ☐ Has the writer used secondary sources effectively? Note any exceptions.
- ☐ Do all the sources seem reliable?
- ☐ Does the writer use a sufficient number of sources? Is there an over-reliance on one source? Which one?
- ☐ Does the writer show familiarity with the sources used?

- [ ] Do the secondary sources appear to be relevant to the points discussed?
- [ ] Is each reference integrated smoothly into the essay?
  - [ ] Stylistically?
  - [ ] Grammatically?
- [ ] Has the context been made sufficiently clear in each instance?
- [ ] Are brackets and ellipses used correctly?
- [ ] Are any other kinds of evidence produced in addition to secondary sources (for example, analogies, personal experience, illustrations, examples, or field research—e.g., interviews)?
- [ ] Does the essay appear to be fundamentally focused on exposition (explaining) rather than argumentation (persuasion)?

Conclusion

- [ ] Does the conclusion function as a satisfying ending? Does it summarize and/or generalize?

Other Criteria

- [ ] Has the writer presented him- or herself credibly?
  - [ ] Conveyed knowledge?
  - [ ] Seems trustworthy and reliable?
  - [ ] Appears to be fair?
- [ ] Is the writer's voice impartial and objective?
- [ ] Has the writer used any elements of style to assist in the argument (e.g., imagery, analogies—figurative language, distinctive voice or tone, particular choice of words, sentence variety, etc.)? Can you suggest any additional stylistic features that might help?
- [ ] Are there any places in the draft where the language seemed unclear or an incorrect word was used?

Final comments or suggestions?

Writer's Name: _____

Editor's Name: _____

Peer Edit Form: Argumentative Essay
First Draft

Your first draft is the stage at which you make the transition from large-scale structural concerns to those focusing on your developing argument—in your final draft, you will work further on these areas, along with clear expression, grammatically sound prose, etc., responding to editorial suggestions as well as your clearer conception of your argument as a result of having written the draft.

Instructions

Use the check boxes below to record the fact that you have considered and evaluated the criteria. Use the space following to add suggestions, comments, questions, and advice. In addition, underline places in the essay where you would like to draw the writer's attention to possible grammatical problems (such as fragments, comma splices, apostrophe problems, lack of parallelism, misplaced or dangling modifiers, pronoun agreement, case, and/or consistency errors), or stylistic problems (such as passive constructions or other instances where the writing could be made more concise, direct, or forceful—you should also note possible spelling errors along with errors in mechanics and presentation).

Introduction

- ☐ Does the introduction function successfully?
  - ☐ Interesting?
  - ☐ Announces subject and contains thesis statement; is the claim arguable? Is the claim one of value or policy?
  - ☐ Suggests the main way the argument will be organized (e.g., definition, cause/effect, time order, division, compare and contrast, question/answer, etc.)?
- ☐ Does the writer establish him/herself as credible and trustworthy? How?
- ☐ Is the argumentative purpose clear?

Body Paragraphs

- ☐ Does the argument seem complete, and does the order of the paragraphs appear logical?
- ☐ Look at paragraphs individually. Are any too short? Too long?
- ☐ Is each paragraph unified (relates to one main idea)? If not, which ones aren't?
- ☐ Is each paragraph coherent? If not, which ones aren't?
- ☐ Do paragraphs contain topic sentences?
- ☐ Is the order of the sentences natural?
- ☐ Are there appropriate transitions between sentences, enabling you to see the relationship between consecutive sentences?
- ☐ Does the writer successfully use repetition, rephrasing, synonyms, or other devices to achieve coherence?
- ☐ Does each paragraph seem developed adequately? If not, which ones aren't?

- ☐ What kinds of evidence are produced? Are they used effectively?
  - ☐ Examples, illustrations?
  - ☐ Personal experience?
  - ☐ Analogies?
  - ☐ Precedents?
  - ☐ Outside authorities/secondary sources?
  - ☐ Other?
- ☐ Are there points where the argument seems strained, weak, incomplete, and/ or illogical? Are there any fallacies (e.g., cause/effect fallacies, fallacies of irrelevance, emotional/ethical fallacies)?

Conclusion

- ☐ Does the conclusion function as a satisfying ending? Does it summarize and/ or generalize?

Other Criteria

- ☐ Has the arguer presented him- or herself credibly?
  - ☐ Conveyed knowledge?
  - ☐ Seems trustworthy and reliable?
  - ☐ Appears to be fair?
- ☐ Is the opposing view acknowledged?
- ☐ Is the writer's voice impartial and objective?
- ☐ Are there any examples of slanted language?
- ☐ Is the opposing view successfully refuted (as in the point-by-point method)?
- ☐ Has the writer used any elements of style to assist in the argument (e.g., imagery, analogies—figurative language, distinctive voice or tone, particular choice of words, sentence variety, etc.)? Can you suggest any additional stylistic features that might help?
- ☐ Are there any places in the draft where the language seems unclear or an incorrect word is used?
- ☐ If the writer used sources, are they integrated smoothly and grammatically? Are all direct quotations, summaries, paraphrases, and ideas acknowledged?

Final comments or suggestions?

Writer's Name: _____

Editor's Name: _____

Peer Edit Form: Literary Essay First Draft

Your first draft is the stage at which you make the transition from large-scale structural concerns to those focusing on your developing analysis—in your final draft, you will work further on these areas, along with clear expression, grammatically sound prose, etc., responding to editorial suggestions as well as your clearer conception of your analysis as a result of having written the draft.

Instructions

Use the check boxes below to record the fact that you have considered and evaluated the criteria. Use the space following to add suggestions, comments, questions, and advice. In addition, underline places in the essay where you would like to draw the writer's attention to possible grammatical problems (such as fragments, comma splices, apostrophe problems, lack of parallelism, misplaced or dangling modifiers, pronoun agreement, case, and/or consistency errors), or stylistic problems (such as passive constructions or other instances where the writing could be made more concise, direct, or forceful—you should also note possible spelling errors along with errors in mechanics and presentation).

Introduction

- ☐ Is the introduction successful?
    - ☐ Interesting?
    - ☐ Announces subject and contains thesis statement with a claim of interpretation? Suggests the writer's purpose: Review? Text-centred analysis? Context-centred analysis?
    - ☐ States the work(s) being discussed and the organizational method, if appropriate (e.g., compare and contrast)?
    - ☐ Suggests most important focus (character, point of view, setting, mood, tone, analysis of technique)?
    - ☐ Gives appropriate background, if needed?
- ☐ Does the writer establish him- or herself as credible and trustworthy? How?

Body Paragraphs

- ☐ Does the reading/analysis seem complete, and does the order of the paragraphs appear logical?
- ☐ Look at paragraphs individually. Are any too short? Too long?
- ☐ Is each paragraph unified (relates to one main idea)? If not, which ones aren't?
- ☐ Is each paragraph coherent? If not, which ones aren't?
- ☐ Do paragraphs contain topic sentences?
- ☐ Is the order of the sentences natural?
- ☐ Are there appropriate transitions between sentences, enabling you to see the relationship between consecutive sentences?
- ☐ Does the writer successfully use repetition, rephrasing, synonyms, or other devices to achieve coherence?
- ☐ Does each paragraph seem developed adequately?

- □ What kinds of evidence are produced?
  - □ Examples from the text(s)?
    - □ Representative and relevant?
    - □ Are there a sufficient number?
  - □ Textual references cited appropriately (according to the conventions for citing poetry, fiction, and drama)?
  - □ Has the context been made sufficiently clear in each instance?
  - □ Are brackets and ellipses used correctly?
- □ If secondary sources have been used, are they integrated smoothly and grammatically? Are all direct quotations, summaries, paraphrases, and ideas acknowledged?
  - □ Secondary sources used effectively (to introduce or provide general information; support, explain, or expand; disagree or qualify)?
  - □ Other kinds of evidence used?
- □ Are there points where the reading seems strained, weak, incomplete, and/or illogical?

Conclusion

- □ Does the conclusion function as a satisfying ending? Does it summarize and/or generalize?

Other Criteria

- □ Has the writer presented him- or herself credibly?
  - □ Conveyed knowledge?
  - □ Seems trustworthy and reliable?
  - □ Appears to be fair?
- □ Has the writer used any elements of style to assist in the argument (e.g., imagery, analogies—figurative language, distinctive voice or tone, particular choice of words, sentence variety, etc.). Can you suggest any additional stylistic features that might help?
- □ Are there any places in the draft where the language seemed unclear or where an incorrect word was used?

Final comments or suggestions?

Writer's Name: _____

Editor's Name: _____

Answers to Exercises

Note that your responses may vary from those given here.

Chapter 1

Exercise 1.4

1. b. The instructor announced class cancellation yesterday.
2. b. Todd is sarcastically voicing his displeasure (c. is a possible inference).
3. c. The school has been designed for students with behavioural problems.
4. a. Meghan will likely face many challenges at the university,
5. d. No inference is possible about the author's beliefs.

Chapter 2

Exercise 2.5

1. high school history teachers: neutral?
   phys-ed teachers: positive
   high school students: mixed
2. NHL hockey fans: mixed?
   referees' union: positive
   NHL team owners: negative
3. pet owners: mixed?
   city council: positive
   pet breeders: negative
4. a citizen's rights group: negative
   RCMP officers: positive
   dentists: neutral
5. students who own laptops: positive
   students who do not own laptops: negative? neutral?
   instructors who have taught for 20 years or more: negative

Exercise 2.8

2. Borderline Personality Disorder is a controversial condition.
   It is a topic (it is not complete enough to serve as a thesis).
   Possible subject: personality disorders
4. More hybrid cars are on the market than ever before.
   It is a topic.
   Possible subjects: cars; alternative energy sources; consumerism
6. "Managed trade" involves government intervention, such as the imposition of tariffs.
   It is a topic (it simply says what managed trade is).
   Possible subjects: economic theories; international commerce
8. Studying the classical languages in school is unnecessary today.
   It is a thesis.
   Topic: classical languages
   Possible subjects: university subjects; languages; Greek and Roman history

10. Enrolling in a dance class can help people with disabilities.
    It is a thesis.
    Topics: teaching/learning dance; coping with disabilities
    Possible subjects: dance; disabilities

Chapter 3

Exercise 3.1

What is life? According to the most ancient traditions, life pervades nature and the universe. For Western culture, this view changed with the Greek philosophers who distinguished between the animate and the inanimate. Seventeenth- and eighteenth-century philosophers and scientists saw animals simply as machines, but biologists didn't agree, and now the line between the living and non-living is unclear. Today, scientists are building artificial systems with properties previously associated with life, creating a new era of research called "a-life." The "logical properties of life" are taken from natural organisms and applied to "non-living systems." Such investigations will challenge our place in nature. (102 words)

Chapter 4

Exercise 4.1

2. c.   Cellphones dominate the lives of many people in society today.

Exercise 4.2

2. In addition, exercise is a solution to the ever-growing problem of obesity.

Exercise 4.4 I: Coherence through word choice

2. The *amount* of competition and training that goes into golf requires a high level of physical fitness.
4. The narrow *structure (shape)* of glacial fjords protects them from the effects of high waves and storm damage.
6. Sports today have become more competitive, and parents may *enroll* their children in competitive sports at too young an age.
8. Adopting a vegetarian lifestyle would no doubt have a major *impact in* ending world hunger.
10. To *ensure* that teenagers do not drive drunk, the drinking age should be raised to 19, when teens are mature enough to deal *responsibly* with alcohol.

Exercise 4.4 IV: Coherence through transitions

b.   Massive energy consumption is having a negative impact on the planet. *For example*, in the summer of 2006, western Europe experienced some of the hottest weather on record. <u>*Moreover*</u>, this temperature increase is not an isolated occurrence. *In fact*, almost every credible scientist today believes that the earth is experiencing climate change due to the emissions of greenhouse gases from cars and coal-burning power plants. Ninety per cent of the energy used in the US comes from fossil fuels such as oil, coal, and natural gas (Borowitz 43), *but* problems arise from other sources, too. *For example*, nuclear power plants leave radioactive by-products, making storage difficult. *Unfortunately*, dams are not much better as nearby populations must be relocated, and the surrounding habitat is destroyed.

Exercise 4.4 V: Coherence through use of repetition, parallel structures, and transitions

2.

The topic sentence is the first sentence.

But, *Instead* (transitions of contrast or qualification)

As a result (transition of cause and effect)

in effect (transition of emphasis—or, summary)

Since this paragraph ends by defining "the trivialization effect," it is logical to expect that the following paragraph will expand on this definition in some way, perhaps by discussing one or more effects that trivializing the news has on its audience.

Exercise 4.6

2. Although email is a modern communications miracle, it is also the biggest nuisance ever invented. (abrupt)
4. I guess we would all like to look like Angelina Jolie if we could. (irrelevant)
6. Leprosy is, without doubt, the most brutal disease known to humanity. (overstated)
8. The movement of people away from the Catholic Church today is mostly due to its teachings on issues like abortion, women's equality, and homosexuality. (abrupt)
10. In all American literature, no character ever gave more thought to moral decisions than Huckleberry Finn does. (overstated)
12. Desperate times call for desperate measures. (abrupt)
14. It is said that ignorance is bliss. (obvious)
16. Health and academic success have long been considered interrelated. (acceptable)
18. Imagine that you are a woman standing before a mirror. (Irrelevant)
20. High school students should have the chance to participate in a wide variety of non-competitive activities in their physical education classes. (abrupt)

Exercise 4.7

C

2. Simple. *Expanded*: As consumers, we must keep ourselves informed about the activities of the industries we support in order to be knowledgeable consumers, which will ultimately make us better citizens of today's world.
4. Simple. *Expanded*: Education is viewed as a benefit to individuals, but too much education can have negative results by narrowing one's vision and separating one from others who are less educated.

Exercise 4.9

2. a. dramatic
    b. captures reader's imagination and familiar stereotype seen in movies
    c. ". . . one must understand how mobsters operate—not what they appear to be on the surface, but the structure, conduct, and economic realities that created their power and enable them to maintain it." Expanded
    d. credible: reveals that he has the unique perspective required for this topic
    e. essay: cause–effect; compare and contrast used in this paragraph
4. a. logical
    b. effective; develops logically
    c. "Anabolic steroid abuse plays a large role in bodybuilding, often resulting in adverse health effects." Simple
    d. credible: reveals knowledge of bodybuilding and IFBB
    e. cost-benefit, focusing on costs

Chapter 5

Exercise 5.1

The classification and example rhetorical patterns are used. The final sentence (thesis statement) suggests that the essay itself will be organized according to the cost-benefit method (arguing the benefits of vegetarianism).

Exercise 5.5

2. A (policy)
4. E (fact)
6. E (fact)
8. A (policy)
10. E (fact)

Exercise 5.6

In these answers, the original claim is identified below.
2. value
4. fact (could be used as a value claim)
6. policy
8. value
10. policy
12. policy
14. policy

Chapter 6

Exercise 6.4

2. *words changed, but sentence structure same: better paraphrase*: In an attempt to find ways to fix damage, create harmony, and build confidence, restorative justice brings together community, victim, and victimizer (Zher 5).

4. *sentence structure changed, but words identical: better paraphrase*: To reduce the odds of depression and increase feelings of self-worth in athletes, a supportive coach or other role model is beneficial.

Chapter 7

Exercise 7.1

1. b. Paul Olsen said it has now been proven that the shift from Triassic to Jurassic forms of life "occurred in a geological blink of an eye" (Mayel, par. 4).

2. b. Our most urgent challenge today is recognizing the need to act to prevent the destruction of our environment. Biologically speaking, the world is "experiencing an eco-holocaust," as the world is becoming polluted with society's wastes, and more than 50,000 life forms disappear each year (Suzuki, 1999, p. 45).

4. *The following are suggested answers. There may be purposes for which other kinds of integration are better suited.*

   b. no paraphrase: memorably phrased; authoritative source

   d. factual information; can be paraphrased:
   Over the long term, the sexual orientation of a family's parents is not as important as harmonious relationships among family members, and same-sex parents produce children who are as well-adjusted as those of heterosexual parents, according to research.

   f. factual information; can be paraphrased:
   The health of people in inner cities, particularly those under 13 years old, is threatened by excessive carbon dioxide in the air.

   h. statistical information; can be paraphrased:
   Doctors in the US do not need special qualifications to perform aesthetic plastic surgery; approximately 11 million such surgeries by specialists and non-specialists were recorded in 2006.

   j. no paraphrase: wording of important legal document

Chapter 8

Exercise 8.3

2. Not specific; phrases like "a major problem" and "make sense" lack precision

4. Not interesting; it's an obvious claim. A more controversial, but arguable, claim might be that the costs of using email outweigh its well-known benefits.

6. Not interesting; a general audience would likely not be interested in this specific benefit of no-fault insurance (though an audience of auto insurers probably would be)

8. Not arguable; would make a better thesis statement for a personal essay in which the writer could make full use of personal experience and, perhaps, narration

10. Not manageable. Writers need to show that policy claims are viable and can realistically be instituted.

Exercise 8.4

2. Inductive reasoning is flawed as the means for gathering the evidence was faulty; hence, a conclusion could not be drawn.

Exercise 8.7

A.
2. Doubtful causes
4. Either/or
6. It does not follow (Desk-thumping also implied)
8. It does not follow
10. Two wrongs make a right

B.

Tina rebutted, "But nobody actually drives 30 on those streets!" (bandwagon or two wrongs make a right)

Steve replied, "But we could get stuck behind a little old lady, and everybody knows how slowly they drive." (common knowledge)

"Besides, we can speed on the main street; there are never any cops on that street, so we won't get a ticket." (fortune-telling)

Tina said, "No, let's take the side streets: we always go that way." (tradition)

"And there have been two accidents recently on the main street, so the side streets are safer." (hasty generalization)

Exercise 8.8

2.
- The legalization of marijuana would destroy society as we know it today (desk-thumping)
- sentences 2–6 (slippery slope)
- "sink to a despicable level" (slanted language)

Chapter 10

Exercise 10.2

nouns: road, street, slum, car, stop, house, bungalow, garden, fountain, middle, arrangement, flamingos, penguins, windows, bars, door, grandmother, driver, horn, woman

pronouns: we, that, any, it, them, she

verbs: left, turned, were, came, was, had, did, toot, stepped, saw, nodded, smiled, went

adjectives: main, narrow, extended, better, well-kept, cemented, garish, marble, plastic, heavy, iron, front

adverbs: far, out, imperiously, immediately, back, inside

prepositions: in, in front of, from, around, across, with, of

conjunctions: once, and, when

Exercise 10.3

2. Wanted to bury his treasure where it would never be found. (P)
4. Dropped the ball with only ten yards to go. (P)
6. Opportunity | knocks. (complete sentence)
8. The high levels of stress of today's students. (S)
10. Hundreds of geese in the field. (S)
12. An enemy of the people. (S)
14. All dressed up with no place to go. (N)

Exercise 10.4

2. The brilliant idea that came to me in the middle of the night seemed ordinary by the light of day.
4. I have a strange craving for the kind of doughnut that doesn't have a hole in the middle.

Exercise 10.5

2. The imaginative child wanted to bury his treasure where it would never be found.
4. The wide receiver dropped the ball with only ten yards to go.
8. The high levels of stress of today's students can lead to illnesses.
10. Hundreds of geese in the field create a big mess!
12. An enemy of the people should never be alone in a dark alley.
14. It is sad to be all dressed up with no place to go.

Exercise 10.6

2. Huge tears rolled down his cheeks.
4. Whenever they called her into work, *she was about to leave town for a holiday.* (dependent clause fragment)
6. He must be guilty *since* he's already confessed. (dependent clause)
8. *The party president is* introducing our next prime minister. (-*ing*)
10. Swimming on her back, *she eventually reached the shore.* (-*ing*)
12. Because spiritual values are more enduring than material ones, *most of my memories of Christmas are of joyous occasions, not of expensive gifts.* (dependent clause)
14. The student sauntered into class *after* he opened the door and cautiously peeked inside. (dependent clause)
16. Much successful American entertainment is a spinoff of a British original—for example, the famous TV show *American Idol.* (add-on)
18. The opposition to vaccinations is a manifestation of fear that the side effects will be more harmful than the disease itself. (lacks predicate in original)
20. Stress can have devastating effects on many groups of people, such as depression in those who fail to meet their own expectations. (add-on)
22. More than half of depressed adolescents are given antidepressants, which raises the question of whether they are the best long-term solution. (dependent clause)
24. Sounds and textures are common features of dreams while smell and taste are usually absent. (dependent clause)

Exercise 10.7

2. International concern has grown in recent years over the proliferation of weapons of mass destruction, but weapons used to exterminate enemy forces are nothing new. In World War I, artillery was used. <u>In addition to gas, machine guns, grenades, and bombs</u>. The 1940s brought more powerful weaponry. <u>As well as the first nuclear weapon</u>. <u>A weapon capable of killing hundreds of thousands of people</u>. After World War II, the Cold War began, as Russia and the US became involved in an arms race. <u>Building hundreds of nuclear weapons more potent than those used in World War II</u>.
—no dependent clause fragment is present

Corrected:
International concern has grown in recent years over the proliferation of weapons of mass destruction, but weapons used to exterminate enemy forces are nothing new. In World War I, artillery was used, in addition to gas, machine guns, grenades, and bombs. The 1940s brought more powerful weaponry, as well as the first nuclear weapon, a weapon capable of killing hundreds of thousands of people. After World War II, the Cold War began, as Russia and the US became involved in an arms race, building hundreds of nuclear weapons more potent than those used in World War II.

Exercise 10.8

2. (Some of my favourite books) (have gone) out of print.
           noun   verb
             S

4. A search (of the abandoned house) (turned up) several cartons (of stolen goods).
    noun   adjectival   verb   adjectival
      S

Exercise 10.9

2. (Although I think winter is here), <u>the temperature is not cold enough for snow</u>.
4. In most parts of North America, <u>Daylight Saving Time begins in March</u>. ("In most parts of North America" is a phrase modifying the verb in the independent clause.)
6. (While it is important that students volunteer), <u>mandatory volunteerism introduced at many schools does not instill a sense of civic duty</u>.
8. <u>Studying grammar does not guarantee good grades</u>, but <u>it certainly helps</u>.
10. <u>Plastic water bottles have become the focus of public scorn</u>, (though more pressing moral concerns need attention).

Exercise 10.10

2. Since the beginning of time, <u>people have worn fur for warmth</u>. (simple—"Since" is a preposition in this sentence, not a subordinating conjunction)
4. <u>She ran the race in record time ⬭but⬭ collapsed at the finish line</u>. (simple—"but" is joining "ran" and "collapsed," two verbs. You can see that it is not joining two independent clauses as "collapsed" has no separate subject from "ran.")
6. <u>Expository writing explains ⬭or⬭ informs the reader about something</u>. (simple—see number 4)

8. <u>His library privileges have been suspended</u> ((until) he pays his fines). (complex)
10. <u>She is convinced</u> ((that) she will get an A in the course). (complex)
12. <u>The end of the transatlantic slave trade came in 1807</u> ((when) importing slaves was finally banned in the US). (complex)
14. <u>The first non-Inuit to reach the North Pole was James Peary,</u> ((though) his claim has often been disputed). (complex)

Exercise 10.11

2.
Although there may be nearly two million kinds of plants in the world, and there are likely at least as many different kinds of animals, no one can know how many species have evolved, flourished, and become extinct. (compound-complex)
4.
We may suspect that Earth is not unique as a life-bearing planet, but since we do not as yet have any compelling evidence that life exists anywhere else, we must restrict our discussion of the pervasiveness of life to our own planet. (compound-complex)

Exercise 10.12

2. Our neighbour's dog howled all last night. It was just impossible to get a night's sleep. (comma splice)
4. It's easy to punctuate sentences: just put a comma whenever you pause. (comma splice)
6. The incidence of breast cancer has increased. It takes the lives of many women today. (comma splice)
8. Humans are imitators. Conforming is something they are good at. (comma splice)
10. Asthma is a common problem among Canadians. Exposure to second-hand smoke in public places can intensify this condition. (comma splice)

Exercise 10.13

2. The opening ceremonies were delayed on account of rain. (fragment)
4. Though they both liked to read, they usually read different books: she read adventure stories while he liked detective stories. (comma splice)
6. The only way a person can learn is to pay attention to what is going on in class. (fragment)
8. The concept that "bigger is better" is part of our culture. It is promoted by both advertisers and the media these days. (comma splice)
10. Martin Luther King led protests during the civil rights movement. His enthusiasm and his will to end discrimination made him a leader. (comma splice)
12. Although TV can corrupt the minds of innocent children if it is not monitored closely, in moderation and under supervision, children more than three can benefit from many of its programs. (fragment)
14. It seems that the North American mass media prescribes two roles for women: they can be sex objects or passive housewives. (comma splice)
16. We can no longer turn our backs to what is happening in the north; it is time to take action. (run-on)

18. Racism in Canada exceeded just social and personal racism; it was institutional racism. (comma splice)
20. Carpal Tunnel Syndrome has many causes; the most common is repetitive wrist movements. (comma splice)
22. One of the most tragic events of the twentieth century was the detonation of the atomic bomb over Hiroshima. (two fragments)
24. In the final book of the series, Harry visits his parents' grave and sees two inscriptions on their graves; the inscriptions refer to passages from the Bible. (comma splice)

Chapter 11

Exercise 11.1

2. The optional package includes bucket seats, dual speakers, and air-conditioning. (items in a series)
4. Metaphors, similes, and personification all are examples of figurative language. (series)
6. Hardly daring to breathe, Nelson took a quick look at the valley far below him. (independent clause: introductory phrase)
8. The magnificent country estate is hidden behind a long, elegant row of silver birches. (miscellaneous: coordinate adjectives)
10. Her house was a newer one with dark wood trim and large, open rooms. (miscellaneous: coordinate adjectives)
12. Because of the humidity levels, it feels hotter than the actual temperature. (independent clause: introductory phrase)
14. Even though most people are aware of global warming and climate change, fewer are aware of the term "carbon footprint." (independent clause: introductory dependent clause)
16. *The Globe and Mail* is a popular paper across Canada, whereas the *Toronto Star* was created for the Toronto and area market. (independent clause: dependent clause conclusion)
18. The types of RNA required for protein synthesis are messenger RNA, transfer RNA, and ribosomal RNA. (series)
20. The committee studying the proposal is a mixture of health officials, journalists, and politicians. (series)
22. Since climate change is a global problem, it requires global solutions. (independent clause: introductory dependent clause)
24. The aggression effect of a video game depends on the type of game, the way it is played, and the person playing it. (series)

Exercise 11.2

2. Juliet studied medicine at The University of Western Ontario in London, Ontario, before becoming a doctor near Prince Albert, Saskatchewan.
4. Nick and Nicole were married on April 20, 1995, but they separated two years later.
6. The simple sentence, as we've seen, is easily mastered by students, but compound sentences necessitate an understanding of various forms of punctuation.

8. British general Sir Frederick Morgan established an American-British headquarters, which was known as COSSAC.

10. Agnes Campbell Macphail, the first woman elected to Canadian Parliament, served for 19 years, beginning her career in 1921.

12. Following successful completion of the English test, another skills test is taken, which is in a written format.

14. Oliver Wendell Holmes, an American, was known as a master essayist, but Canadian Barry Callaghan is also internationally respected as an essayist.

16. The soldier with the red coat in the picture fought on the side of our enemies, the Americans.

18. Currently ranked fourth behind heart disease stroke and respiratory infections, AIDS is set to become No. 3, say researchers in a new report.

20. Jeff Deffenbacher, Ph.D., a specialist in anger management, thinks that some people have a low tolerance for everyday annoyances.

Exercise 11.3

2. Autism is a much misunderstood problem. Often children with autism are viewed as a "handful" and "hyperactive." Very little is known of its causes, and characteristics can vary, making a diagnosis difficult. In children, it is even harder because normal children can exhibit some of the characteristics associated with autism. Although autism can cause many behavioural difficulties, autistic children can still live near-normal lives if they are surrounded by understanding caregivers. Working with autistic children can change a person and make one realize the need for better understanding and education. Treating autism can be difficult because often there is no feedback from the patient. Over the years, there have been many ideas of how to treat autism, but not all were correct and have, at times, made treatment problematic.

Exercise 11.4

2. SPCA officers work for but are not paid by the government; **in fact,** it is donations that provide their salary.

4. Many professional golfers have used the same caddy for years; Steve Williams, **for example,** has caddied for Tiger Woods since 1999.

Exercise 11.5

2. A developing salmon goes through four stages: the alevin, the fry, the smolt, and the adult.

4. He paused to admire the splendid sight before his eyes: the ruins of Montgomery Castle.

6. The following is not a rule for comma use: put a comma wherever you pause.

8. It was the best of times; it was the worst of times.

10. In my health sciences class, we studied the four main food groups: dairy products, meats, carbohydrates, and fruits and vegetables.

12. Whenever I order designer clothing for my boutique, I shop in Toronto, Canada; Buffalo, New York; and London, England.

14. Brian never tired of misquoting Shakespeare: "the quality of mercy is not stained."

16. First advice to those about to write a novel is the same as Punch's to those about to wed: don't (Victor Jones).

18. In a compound sentence, use a comma to join independent clauses where there is a coordinating conjunction; use a semi-colon where two such clauses are not joined by a coordinating conjunction.

20. Oil, electricity, and solar power are popular sources for heating homes in Ontario; however, the most popular is natural gas.

22. It was the ideal summer job: you were outdoors in lovely weather, you were active, and the pay was more than reasonable.

24. The zero emissions of a battery-electric vehicle come with a drawback: the emissions are only as clean as the means used to generate the power.

26. The art of writing the news lead is to answer as many of the following five questions as possible: Who?, What?, Where?, When?, and How?

28. A lack of essential nutrients can result in deficiencies; for example, a vegetarian may have iron deficiency.

30. Freewriting can be a useful means of overcoming blocks; it can help you write when you're not in the mood; it can generate ideas, even if you are the kind of writer who has a hard time coming up with main points; and it can energize your writing.

Exercise 11.6

The first fifteen lines are shown below. Of course, there are punctuation options for these and the rest of the poem.

There lived an old man in the kingdom of Tess, who invented a purely original dress, and when it was perfectly made and complete, he opened the door and walked into the street. By way of a hat, he'd a loaf of brown bread, in the middle of which he inserted his head. His shirt was made up of no end of dead mice, the warmth of whose skins was quite fluffy and nice. His drawers were of rabbit-skins (but it is not known whose). His waistcoat and trousers were made of pork chops; his buttons were jujubes and chocolate drops. His coat was all pancakes with jam for a border and a girdle of biscuits to keep it in order. And he wore over all, as a screen from bad weather, a cloak of green cabbage leaves stitched all together.

Exercise 11.7

2. Labour shortages during the late nineteenth century in Canada became an impediment to progress, and something had to be done to fix this problem. For white politicians and business owners, the solution seemed obvious: exploit cheap labour. Chinese immigrants provided exactly what was needed to boost the labour scene: they were male, unskilled, and cheap. Between 1881 and 1885, approximately 17,000 Chinese immigrants arrived in Canada. Chinese men were employed in masses; their jobs included those in mining, forestry, canning, and, above all, railroad construction. Sir Matthew Begbie, the Chief Justice of BC, said, "Chinese labourers do well what white women cannot do and what white men will not do."

Exercise 11.8

2. Parents and teachers often complain about **television's** influence in **today's** society.

4. **One's** education should not depend on the financial resources of **one's** parents.

6. The course I took required two **hours'** homework a day.

8. In anorexia nervosa, a **patient's** fingernails and teeth may be damaged due to a lack of calcium.

10. Work songs and street **vendors'** cries are examples of traditional African-American music styles.

12. The topic of the term paper is a comparison between George **Grant's** and John Ralston **Saul's** theories of Canadian identity.

14. As a child whose parents were relatively well off, I thought all my **relatives'** lives were as easy as mine.

16. Books, music, and DVDs can be found on Amazon.com, one of the **Internet's** most popular sites.

18. Drugs called immunosuppressants can interfere with the **body's** ability to fight infection.

20. Climate change is caused by harmful chemicals that trap the **sun's** energy in the **earth's** atmosphere.

22. Video game players do not want to have total control over the main characters and those **characters'** actions; the **game's** unpredictability is part of its attraction.

24. The desire of Pip in Charles **Dickens's** *Great Expectations* to find his place in the world illustrates the **work's** main theme.

Exercise 11.10

If a child begins to perform poorly at school nowadays, **he or she** will likely be sent to a school counsellor to deal with the situation. ~~Everyone~~ **Parents (People) assume** ~~assumes~~ that attention deficit disorder is the culprit, and they just as automatically assume that drugs are the answer. On the other hand, perhaps the child is just not interested in a particular subject or ~~they do~~ **does** not understand the material. Parents, in turn, treat the child as if he **or she** is the problem instead of listening ~~to him~~ to find out how he **or she** can be helped.

Exercise 11.11

2. Neither the film's director nor its producers were on hand to receive their prestigious award.

4. It is unfortunate when a person no longer cares what others think about him or her.

6. It is the tried and true that provides the ultimate refuge in mediocrity.

8. Her set of baby teeth was complete when she was only eighteen months old.

10. None of the company's products require testing on animals.

12. Every specimen of the horned grebe has a distinctive tuft on each side of its head.

14. Neither team members nor their coach expects the season to last another game.

Exercise 11.12

Alternatives are given in some cases, and other alternatives may be possible.

2. Especially unique to adolescent depression are physical symptoms, such as headaches. (correct)

4. Over the past week, there have been some unexplained occurrences on the girls' floor of the residence.

6. A typical poem by Emily Dickinson leaves the reader searching for another line or even another stanza to satisfy his or her craving for closure.

Alternative: A typical poem by Emily Dickinson leaves readers searching for another line or even another stanza to satisfy their craving for closure.

8. A coalition of neighbourhood organizations, students, and unions is currently forming to oppose the University's proposed plan.

10. If a child is denied the opportunity to play, how can he or she develop emotionally and physically?

Alternative: If children are denied the opportunity to play, how can they develop emotionally and physically?

12. When a person contracts jaundice, his or her skin as well as the white part of his or her eyes turns yellow.

Alternatives:

When people contract jaundice, their skin as well as the white part of their eyes turns yellow.

When a person contracts jaundice, the skin as well as the white part of the eyes turns yellow.

14. Before rendering its unanimous verdict, the jury was polled individually. (correct)

16. The nature and role of human resources in organizations have undergone tremendous change in the last two decades. (correct)

18. Stereotyping and the use of degrading language in the book serve to reinforce its theme.

20. A person who continually disregards others' feelings will pay for the neglect sooner or later.

Alternative: People who continually disregard others' feelings will pay for their neglect sooner or later.

22. In Japanese culture, a person's reputation along with his or her social standing depends on the concept of "saving face."

24. The give and take in any relationship is the most important factor in sustaining it. (correct)

Exercise 11.13

Alex and his lawyer, Alan, left in Alex's limousine for Loonies Unlimited to buy Alex's landlady, Alice, a litre of light lemonade. She told them to also buy a litre of light lemonade for her long-time lodger, Alison. When they alighted at Loonies Unlimited, they were alarmed that Alex had left his loonie in his loft. So Alphonse, of Loonies Unlimited, allowed them only one litre of lemonade, along with a length of limp licorice, and he loudly lamented their laxness.

Exercise 11.15

2. Whenever a staff meeting is called, employees are required to attend. (no reference)

4. Sixty per cent of our pesticides, our major ground water pollutant, are used on cotton. (ambiguous reference)

6. I know the sign indicated *No Parking*, but I went ahead and parked there anyway. An officer gave me a $20 fine. (no reference in both sentences)

8. Previous Afghan successes were significant victories; for example, the country last waged war against the powerful Soviet Union. (no reference)
10. During the dinosaur age, dinosaurs lived in a rapidly changing environment. (no reference)
12. In Chapter 21 of my textbook, the author analyzes the success of the Liberal Party in Canada. (no reference)
14. Children often hide their compulsive behaviours from friends and family due to feelings of shame, causing these behaviours to remain undiagnosed. (ambiguous reference)
16. The Catholic kings of Spain rallied the country to fight their enemies, the Moors. This movement became known as the "Reconquista." (broad reference)
18. Teaching today's youth safe and healthy approaches to sexuality will elevate their self-esteem. (no reference)
20. Japanese smokers consume more than twice the number of cigarettes as American smokers do, and this trend continues to increase steadily. (broad reference)

Exercise 11.16

2. Who should run for office this election?
4. The person who finishes first will be rewarded.
6. As she entered the room, a mysterious feeling came over her.
8. People who use memory aids tend to be better spellers.
10. "Hey, buddy, whom did you mean to refer to when you used that insulting term?"
12. The last person whom she wanted to see at the track meet was her former coach.
14. I wanted to ask her whom the note should be addressed to.
16. Canada has long been a haven for Americans who have rejected their country's politics.
18. I proposed that Geordie and I would stack chairs after the meeting.
20. The newly renovated house is a very pleasant place for my brother and me to live.
22. Prejudices decrease when children observe non-prejudiced behaviour by peers whom children associate with during their pre-teen years.
24. "[I]n these fits I leave them, while I visit / young Ferdinand, who they suppose is drowned." —Shakespeare

Exercise 11.17

Informal: You can definitely learn a lot from educational TV; you can learn things that cannot be learned from written texts. If you are a major in Commerce, for example, and if you watch the business news, you can understand the commerce textbook better by applying what you learn from the news. Similarly, watching sports programs can be exciting and can also give you a better understanding of the game. On the other hand, if you choose to watch comedy all the time, you are not going to gain any real benefits. In general, I think that comedies are meaningless.

Formal: Educational TV has many benefits and can teach people things they cannot learn from written texts. If a person is a major in Commerce, for example, and watches the business news, he or she can understand the commerce textbook better by applying what is learned from the news. Similarly, watching sports programs can provide people with excitement and also give them a better understanding of the game. On the other hand, if people choose to watch comedy all the time, they will not gain any real benefits as comedies, generally, are meaningless.

Exercise 11.18

2. Jellyfish from beyond the grave injures swimmers.
4. Gunmen with machine guns mow down partiers in Bolivia.
6. Explorer who indisputably first reached North Pole dies at 80.
8. Cougar attacks five-year-old boy, who is expected to survive.
10. The googly-eyed Puss-in-Boots in the new movie looks nothing like the cat fans used to love.

Exercise 11.19

2. Over the years, several world-class cyclists, such as Eddie Merckx and Greg LeMond, have had spectacular careers.
4. As I am a member of the Sikh community, my paper will be given a strong personal focus.
6. Benefits will result only from a smoke-free environment.
8. When they look for employees today, employers are stressing verbal and written communication skills more than ever before.
10. In captivity, this species of snake will eat frogs, mice, and small pieces of meat.
12. When I was a beginner, my instructor taught me about the respect one karate student must show to another.
14. Speaking from experience, I can say that tans dyeing the top layer of the skin last for about one week.
16. I am certain that Shakespeare, being an Elizabethan playwright, would have been a major influence on Marlowe.
18. As a serious snowboarder, I find it exciting to observe the growth of this sport.
20. The boy in "Araby" returns home empty-handed without the highly valued object that most quests require, in this case, a gift for Mangan's sister.
22. Another example of imagery of light and dark in *Heart of Darkness* occurs when Marlow encounters an African with a white scarf dying in a clearing.
24. Having an emotional personality, Beethoven wrote music that identified him as a nineteenth-century Romantic.

Or: Beethoven, who had an emotional personality, wrote music that identified him as a nineteenth-century Romantic.

Exercise 11.20

Topic 2: Yoga offers many benefits: it enables you to relax and reduce stress, to exercise regularly, and, through yoga classes, to meet people with similar interests.

Topic 4: One disadvantage of having roommates is that they can create a lot of mess and invade your personal space, but having a roommate gives you someone to talk to about your problems.

Topic 6: I will be comparing two recreational drugs by exploring their users, their general effects, and the dangerous side effects they can produce.

Topic 8: There are several advantages in home birthing: it is a positive and friendly place for the child to be born, it enables the parents to maintain control over their surroundings, and it is as safe as a hospital birth if common sense is used.

Topic 10: Marijuana should be legalized as it is less addictive than some other illegal drugs, governments could increase their revenue by selling it, and its legalization would reduce crime since people wouldn't have to obtain it illegally. Moreover, the Canadian government has already made it legal under certain circumstances.

Exercise 11.21

2. Music can directly affect your thoughts, emotions, and feelings. (series)
4. Tiddlywinks is a game not only of considerable skill but also of strategy. (correlative conjunctions)
6. There are three main qualities that a leader must possess: a leader must be enthusiastic, organized, and creative. (series)
8. She not only was the best teacher I have ever had, but also had an impressive wardrobe. (correlative conjunctions)
10. There are many reasons why people choose to watch or enjoy watching television. (compounds)
12. Being imprisoned for a long time can result in a dependency on the institutional environment, a lack of meaningful relationships, and a loss of personal identity. (series)
14. I want to emphasize that my work as MP in this riding has not been, and will not be, affected by political developments. (compounds)
16. Physical education teaches children not only to work well together but also to have patience and discipline. (correlative conjunctions)
18. Allowing prostitution in controlled environments will reduce the risk of violence, decrease drug abuse, and even combat disease through regular testing. (series)
20. Recent studies suggest that wellness depends on three main factors: feeling good about yourself, eating well every day, and being comfortably active. (series)
22. Differing viewpoints in a work of fiction not only add conflict but also can reveal differences in characters' ages, genders, and upbringings. (correlative conjunctions)
24. In Sonnet 130, Shakespeare stresses the reality of his mistress rather than portrays her as something she is not. (compounds—comparisons)

Chapter 12

Exercise 12.3

2. Acceptable passive. (The grammatical subject does not need to be specified.)
4. Acceptable passive if the matter was discussed by members of the committee. (The grammatical subject does not need to be specified.)
6. Change to active: The government needs to see education as the number one priority. (Making "government" the active subject gives more force to the statement.)

8. Change to active: Many people today believe in a powerful and infallible Creator. (It is important to know *who* believes this.)
10. Change to active: Immanuel Kant proposed two ways of looking at rights-based ethics. (The sentence is wordy and indirect without an active subject.)

Exercise 12.4

Your sentences might be different from the examples below.
2. To determine video game addiction, researchers interviewed many gamers and designers.
4. Several devices in the story stress the revenge theme.

Exercise 12.7

Your sentences might be different from the examples below.
2. The volcano's eruption changed the Western Samoan island into an inferno.
4. The protagonist of *Life of Pi* had to choose between life and death.
6. The disappearance of even one species near the bottom of the food chain often adversely affects other species' survival.
8. For many years, people regularly have used antibiotics to cure a variety of diseases in their lives. (Indirect writing increases the likelihood of errors in usage— indeed, errors of all kinds: symptoms may be "relieved," but not "cured.")
10. To protest their salary freeze, all Oak Bay high school teachers have decided not to undertake supervisory tasks until the school board conducts an impartial salary review.
12. Many people in society today have drug addictions that control their lives.
14. The French scientist Louis Pasteur was the first to discover that microbes were menaces to the human body.

Exercise 12.8

1. In medieval English universities, such as Oxford and Cambridge, chest loans were available to students in financial need. They would use an item, usually a book, as a form of collateral against an interest-free loan taken from a chest of money donated by a benefactor. Today, the only thing resembling the concept of the benefactor is the branch of government that disburses loans and grants for students with inadequate funds.

   Recent studies have proven that most Canadian students over 26 years old have a debt of more than $20,000 relating to their education. Most of these costs are incurred by tuition and everyday living expenses and do not include the high cost of textbooks required for most university courses. Students may choose between new textbooks and cheaper used texts, or sometimes can borrow required readings from a library.

Exercise 12.9

2. Previous research studying motorists using hand-held devices while on the road found that 20 per cent of all accidents were directly related to hand-held devices.

Or: Previous researchers studying motorists using hand-held devices while on the road claimed that 20 per cent of all accidents were directly related to hand-held devices.

4. The theme of the poem is that she hates her father for leaving her when she was only eight years old. (A poem's theme cannot be a "fact.")

Exercise 12.11

By the 1800s, inventions <u>were beginning</u> (had begun?) to put people out of work. One of the first inventions that <u>resulted in</u> (triggered? provoked?) rebellion <u>was</u> (affected those?) in the craft guild. In 1801, Joseph Jacquard <u>became known as the inventor of</u> (invented?) the Jacquard loom. This loom <u>was capable of being</u> (could be/ was?) programmed by pre-punched cards, which made it possible to create clothing design patterns. This invention <u>led to the creation of</u> (gave rise/birth to? spawned?) the Luddites, a group made from the craft guild. These people <u>were against</u> (opposed?) any type of manufacturing technology and <u>went about burning down</u> (set fire to?) several factories that <u>were using</u> (used?) this new technology. The Luddites <u>were around only</u> (existed?) for a couple of years, but the name Luddite is still used to describe people who <u>are resistant to</u> (resist?) new technologies. The Jacquard loom, in effect, replaced people. It could <u>do great designs</u> (create complex patterns?) quickly and <u>without making any errors</u> (flawlessly?). The replacement of people by machines <u>was beginning</u> (had begun?).

Exercise 12.12

2. In 313 BCE, Constantine I declared Christianity the official religion of Rome.
4. Perceiving life from varying angles is a key element of a good writer.
Or: Perceiving life from varying angles is a sign of a good writer.

Exercise 12.16

Revision suggestions:
Defining "the homeless" is difficult. However, both the media and current research commonly refer to the homeless as those who lack visible shelter or who use public shelters. Literature about homelessness is sparse, as the media did not report on the incidence of homelessness until the 1980s. Nevertheless, it has existed for centuries with literature on the subject dating from the feudal period in Europe.

INDEX

CREDITS

Grateful acknowledgement is made for permission to reprint the following:

Pages 20–2: Reading 1 from Daniel Wood, "Embrace the Mediocrity Principle", published in The Tyee, December 24, 2008.

Pages 61–2: Reading 3 from with permission of Stephen Henighan.

Pages 67–8: Reading 6 from the Society of Authors as agent of the Estate of Virginia Woolf.

Pages 69–70: Reading 7 from Reprinted with permission from 1993 Yearbook of Science and the Future, © 1992 by Encyclopaedia Britannica, Inc.

Pages 118–20: Reading 9 from Meredith M. Kimball Copyright 1999, Canadian Psychological Association. Permission granted for use of material.

Pages 184–91: Reading 16 from Valkenburg, Patti M., and Jochen Peter, 'Social Consequences of the Internet for Adolescents: A Decade of Research', in Current Directions in Psychological Science, Volume 18, Number 1, February 2009, pp. 1–5(5) [Blackwell Publishing].

Pages 257–71: Reading 19 from 'No Olympics on stolen native land': contesting Olympic narratives and asserting indigenous rights within the discourse of the 2010 Vancouver Games, by Christine M. O'Bonsawin, in Sport in Society, Vol. 13, No. 1, January 2010, 143–156.

Page 281: Poem from 'Stopping by Woods on a Snowy Evening', 1922, by Robert Frost. Reprinted with permission of Henry Holt and Company.

Page 292: Poem from 'Metamorphosis', by Leona Gom, in The Collected Poems, by Leona Gom, 1991, Sono Nis Press.

Page 309: Poem from "My Papa's Waltz", copyright 1942 by Hearst Magazines, Inc., from COLLECTED POEMS OF THEODORE ROETHKE. Used by permission of Doubleday, a division of Random House, Inc.

Pages 362–3: Poem from 'The New Vestments', by Edward Lear